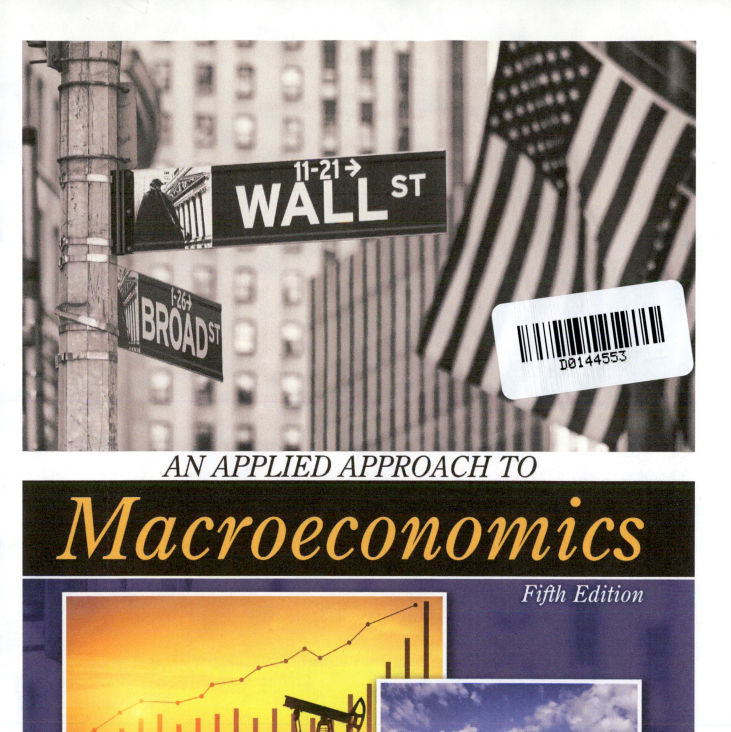

AN APPLIED APPROACH TO

Macroeconomics

Fifth Edition

Jack A. Chambless

Kendall Hunt
publishing company

Cover images © Shutterstock, Inc.

www.kendallhunt.com
Send all inquiries to:
4050 Westmark Drive
Dubuque, IA 52004-1840

Copyright © 2007, 2009, 2011, 2014, 2017 by Kendall Hunt Publishing Company

ISBN: 978-1-5249-2270-2

Published in the United States of America

Contents

Preface

A Message to the Student

The problem with economics is that economists teach it. Like all economists, I must endure endless diatribes from people who feel compelled to tell me that they would rather perform root canal surgery on a rabid wolverine than sit through a discussion of President Trump's views on international trade, Federal Reserve policies, the history of income taxes, the multiplier effect, or pretty much any other economics topic. This is unfortunate, because in reality economics need not be boring, difficult, or abstract. In fact, this social science can be among the most enlightening – and possibly, entertaining classes a student could ever take – when it is presented in a manner that is relevant to the lives of the people in the classroom.

It is my goal to help prepare you to become an economically-literate human being, by presenting real world issues to you in a controversial, timely, and (hopefully) humorous manner. It is a statistical impossibility that you will find every page of this book to be engaging and enjoyable. I can only hope that by the end of the semester, you will know a great deal more – and perhaps care a lot more – about the world around you than you did when you started the class.

As a first-time economics student in the spring of 1986, I was bewildered by how boring and mundane the author of my book made this valuable subject. It seemed that he went out of his way to write a book that would impress his colleagues but totally forgot that his audience was made up largely of novices in the field.

I have tried to give every sentence of this text careful consideration to help you gain the most from your reading. I have no desire to waste your time or talk over your head. Every part of this book was written with the understanding that students of today are more likely to insist on real–world application, rather than theoretical examples. In a world of immediate access to information, any author better be prepared to offer up something that is of instant value to the reader. Of course, to get the most out of this book, you need to actually read each chapter – more than once – and ask your professor questions about anything that is unclear. Use the concept checks, classroom debates, and chapter reviews to facilitate your learning.

Concept Checks

Each concept check is designed for you to stop your reading and think about a subject that has just been covered or will be covered in the next few pages. The questions were created to make you think critically about issues that are central to the study of economics. You can find answers to these questions by emailing me at jchambless@valenciacollege.edu or by logging on to the book's website – www.jackchambless.com – where many of the answers can be found in various websites, essays, and newspaper editorials. The course website also provides my email address, physical mailing address, and phone number if you want to discuss any part of this book.

Suggested Classroom Debates

What would a college classroom be like if no one ever argued? I realize it is hard to have debates in algebra or meteorology classes, but economics is a subject filled with thousands of debated issues. Economists disagree often on economic policy proposals and do so in a very spirited manner. This text will therefore give you the chance (assuming your professor is willing to go along) to debate controversial issues of our time.

Make sure you rely on the geniuses who gave us the Internet to help with your answers. It will also serve you well to suspend your emotional reactions in order to respond to some of these controversial questions in an enlightened, mature manner.

You will notice that virtually every chapter of this book has one or more topics devoted to current events like the post-Recession economic sluggishness, immigration issues, global warming, the controversial health care legislation, the 2016 election, oil prices, and the economic policies of the Obama Administration. Please use these topics to add to your list of classroom discussions. I hope you enjoy this added feature and will take the opportunity to use it to enhance your analytical tools.

You should also feel free to follow my blog at http://jackchambless.blogspot.com/. I welcome your opinion in any of my postings.

CHAPTER REVIEWS

One thing you will notice about this book, is that it takes sort of an "old-school" approach to things. I have decided not to add PowerPoint slides, interactive software, and so forth. I seem to recall when I was a student we had a book, a professor, and some chalk. That was it. We did not need all of the "bells and whistles" in order to get a great economics education. My comparative advantage does not lie within the realm of technology. Therefore, at the end of every chapter you will have a few questions that will allow you to apply what you have learned to some hypothetical or real-world issue. The pages can be removed so that you can submit your work to your professor.

RECOMMENDED BOOKS

As much as I would like to believe that the only economics book a student ever needs to read is this one, I must acknowledge that there are some other books out there you might find incredibly helpful. I highly recommend the following:

The Law by Frederic Bastiat
The Road to Serfdom by F.A. Hayek
The Wealth of Nations by Adam Smith
The Forgotten Man by Amity Shlaes
The FairTax Book by Neal Boortz and John Linder
The Making of Modern Economics by Mark Skousen
Vindicating the Founders by Thomas G. West
Give Me a Break by John Stossel
Myths, Lies and Downright Stupidity by John Stossel
The Commanding Heights by Daniel Yergin and Joseph Stanislaw
Your Money or Your Life by Sheldon Richman
The Triumph of Liberty by Jim Powell
FDR's Folly by Jim Powell
The Libertarian Reader by David Boaz
Free to Choose by Milton and Rose Friedman
Locke, Jefferson and the Justices by George M. Stephens
Empire Builders by Burton Fulsom
The Myth of the Robber Barons by Burton Fulsom
Eat the Rich by P.J. O'Rourke
The Farm Fiasco by James Bovard

Freakonomics by Steven D. Levitt and Stephen J. Dubner
Lost Rights by James Bovard
Terrorism and Tyranny by James Bovard
An American Life by Ronald Reagan
Reagan's War by Peter Schweizer
The Vision of the Anointed by Thomas Sowell
The City on a Hill by Michael Reagan
The Ten Things You Can't Say in America by Larry Elder
More Liberty Means Less Government, Our Founders Knew This Well by Walter E. Williams
Up from Slavery by Booker T. Washington
Education and Capitalism by Herbert J. Walberg and Joseph L. Bast
Eco-nomics by Richard L. Stroup
Atlas Shrugged by Ayn Rand
The End of Prosperity by Arthur Laffer
Hamilton's Curse by Thomas DiLorenzo
New Deal or Raw Deal? by Burton Folsom
How Capitalism Saved America by Thomas DiLorenzo
After the Welfare State by Tom G. Palmer
Freedom's Forge by Arthur Herman
The Big Three in Economics by Mark Skousen
Secrets of the Temple: How the Federal Reserve Runs the Country by William Greider
A Republic—If We Can Keep It by Lawrence W. Reed and Burton Folsom
1776 by David McCullough
John Adams by David McCullough
Please stop helping us by Jason L. Riley
The Revolution by Ron Paul
JFK and the Reagan Revolution: A Secret History of American Prosperity by Lawrence Kudlow & Brian Domitrovic

A MESSAGE TO THE PROFESSOR

The phenomenon of economic ignorance is so widespread, and its consequences so frightening, that the objective of reducing that ignorance becomes a goal invested with independent moral worth.

Israel Kirzner

A great deal of thought was put into this book from the standpoint of what the professor needs to make economics enjoyable, without compromising the depth and structure that our discipline requires of us in the classroom.

I must first caution the professor by openly acknowledging that this textbook tries to fill a niche in the economics textbook market by openly promoting the concept of free markets, economic liberty, and limited government. If you are inclined to disagree with these notions, this book is not for you. There are several books on the market that dance around these concepts in fear of seeming unbalanced.

I submit that world economic history has vindicated the concept that economic liberty and limited government involvement in economic systems is the most efficient model. It is for that reason that the book comes from a free market approach to economic reasoning. This does not mean that the book fails to point out the shortcomings and costs of free markets. Far from it. You will find ample material that examines the risks associated with economic liberty. I hope you will find this approach to be a welcome and refreshing departure from standard economics textbooks.

This book also relies far less on mathematics and graphs than some other books do. In my more than 26 years in the college classroom, I have come to realize that many students hate economics because we don't make it relevant enough. I contend that students will love our classes if we focus on making them lifetime users of economic concepts. One way we can do this is to get them excited about the applications of our wonderful discipline without "graphing them to death."

I hope you will join me in my attempt to make our valuable discipline one that is no longer viewed as one of the worst subjects a student can take. With any success, we can make economics rank at or near the top of everyone's list of the best classes they could ever take.

RECOMMENDED VIEWING

I have found that video aids are very useful for learning about the science of economics.

One series stands out in particular as an outstanding supplement to the material you will read in this text. It is the "Stossel in the Classroom" series.

John Stossel is a television correspondent who has gained worldwide acclaim for his pro-liberty, pro-free-market approach to economic issues. According to Mr. Stossel, "I started out by viewing the marketplace as a cruel place, where you need intervention by government and lawyers to protect people. But after watching the regulators work, I have come to believe that markets are magical and the best protectors of the consumer. It is my job to explain the beauties of the free market." (*Oregonian*, 10/26/94)

Stossel has put together several segments, averaging 45 minutes in length, that educators around the nation have found to be very valuable. In particular, I recommend the following segments to coincide with the reading material.

Is America Number One?
Greed
John Stossel Goes to Washington
The War on Drugs: A War on Ourselves?
The Blame Game
Freeloaders
Stupid in America
Sick in America
Illegal Everything

I also recommend the PBS series, *The Commanding Heights,* for an in-depth examination of 20th Century economic history and the economics of globalization.

On the course website you can also find many movies that have direct economic applications that your students might enjoy. On the SPEECHES link of the course website, you can find several audio and video links that may be of some use to you. I welcome any recommendations you might have with respect to videos, websites, books, or other materials that you believe would add to the quality of our efforts.

About the Author

Jack A. Chambless is a professor of economics and professional speaker. He has received numerous teaching awards from Valencia College, The University of Texas, and North Carolina State University. In addition to teaching Principles of Microeconomics and Macroeconomics, he has also taught honors courses in economics, two online courses, and special topics courses entitled "Applied Microeconomics" and "Oil, Economics and Terrorism." He has also worked as a professional sports agent and as an energy economist for the Sarkeys Energy Center at The University of Oklahoma and the Research Triangle Institute in Raleigh, North Carolina.

A graduate of The University of Oklahoma and North Carolina State University, his fields of specialization include the political economy, labor economics, energy economics, and industrial organization.

He has a monthly column in *The Orlando Sentinel* and has had his work published in *The Wall Street Journal, The University of Miami Law Review, The Public Utilities Fortnightly, The Dallas Morning News, The Chicago Tribune, The Boston Herald,* and many other domestic publications. His work has been cited in *The Wall Street Journal, USA Today, U.S. News & World Report, Reason Magazine, The Foreign Press Review, The Atlanta Journal & Constitution, The Detroit News, The British Caledonian Press,* and many other foreign and domestic publications.

In addition to teaching, Professor Chambless speaks frequently around the United States on the Economics of Liberty. He has lectured at the Foundation for Economic Education in New York, Florida and South Carolina, The Young America's Foundation Freedom Fest in Las Vegas, The Florida Libertarian Convention, Penn State University, Rollins College, Georgia State University, and many home-schooled conventions. He has appeared on national television and radio broadcasts including *CNBC's Inside Opinion, FoxNews Europe* and *Your World with Neal Cavuto (FoxNews), The Neal Boortz Show, the BBC, National Public Radio,* and *The Jim Hightower Show.*

Photo by Sarah Chambless

He is also currently serving as a policy advisor for The Heartland Institute – a think tank in Chicago, Illinois and is a Senior Fellow for the James Madison Institute in Tallahassee, Florida.

Professor Chambless enjoys hiking and canoeing in the Northwestern United States, Minnesota, and Canada, photography, and coaching high school baseball in Central Florida.

Acknowledgements

I would like to extend my sincerest thanks to Walter Williams, Armen Alchian, Paul White, Randall K. Russell, Tarteashia Harris, Mark Skousen, and Stephen Margolis for their forthright and constructive comments regarding past editions of this book. I also want to thank Adam Gifford and Joseph Brignone for providing valuable ideas for this edition. I am also indebted (and the thanks are long overdue) to Jack F. Williams, J. W. Ashmore, and William Clark. Dr. Williams was instrumental in giving me the confidence I needed to select economics as my major at The University of Oklahoma back in 1986. My late-night debates and discussions with him served me well going forward. Mr. Ashmore, my first economics professor at Paris Junior College in Paris, Texas, taught economics in a way that made it come to life and seem exciting. I still copy his style today as best I can. Finally, Dr. William Clark – a professor at The University of Oklahoma – gave me my first teaching job as his assistant in the Spring of 1987. Watching his brilliant work inspired me to press towards the career I have now enjoyed for over two decades. I would also like to thank Leah Schneider and Rachel Guhin for overseeing the completion of this edition. Their steadfast work and professionalism made my life much easier.

Any final errors – in writing or judgment – omissions or sarcastic remarks are the sole responsibility of the author.

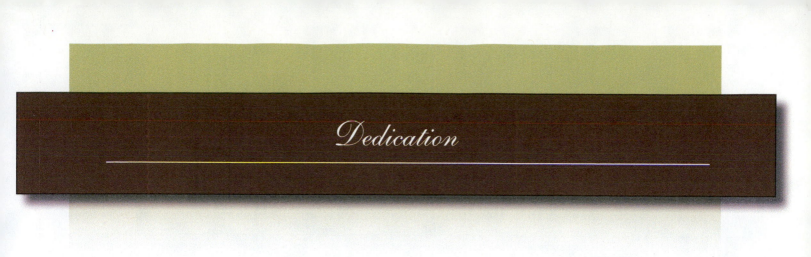

Dedication

For my wife, Sarah – a true believer in the cause of liberty – and the most wonderful person on Earth.

INTRODUCTION *to* ECONOMICS

© Cryber/Shutterstock.com

*W*hoever loves money never has money enough; whoever loves

wealth is never satisfied with his income. This too is meaningless.

As goods increase, so do those who consume them. And what

benefit are they to the owner except to feast his eyes upon them?

ECCLESIASTES 5:10–11, NEW INTERNATIONAL VERSION

YOU ARE IN THE RIGHT PLACE AT THE RIGHT - AND WRONG - TIME...

I sometimes joke with my students that they picked a good time to take an economics class and a bad time to be born.

In 1987 I walked into a college classroom for the first time as an educator, rather than a student. Teaching economics was hard, but teaching in 1987 was easy. The United States was in the midst of one of the greatest economic booms of the 20th century. Illustrating the causes of this unprecedented run of prosperity was a lot of fun. My students could not wait to get out into the "real world" and participate in an economy that seemed to promise a good job to anyone with ambition.

As you begin to read this book it is somewhere between August 2017 and the summer of 2019. If you are a typical college student you were somewhere around the second grade when the United States plunged into what became known as "The Great Recession." From 2007-2009 the unemployment rate rose, median incomes in the United States declined dramatically and countless Americans faced foreclosure.

The years since this recession have not been kind. The economic recovery that began in the summer of 2009 crawled along at the slowest pace of any recovery since World War II. Millions of people stopped looking for work and businesses faced rising costs associated with heightened regulations, taxes and uncertainty.

To some, the previous paragraph is perfect evidence as to why economics is called the "dismal science."

After all, economics, as you will discover, is an examination of the perpetually dissatisfied human being. History reveals a fundamental truth about our species. No matter how much we have, we always want more. The problem is that more is not always available – and sometimes, as our recent times have shown, less and less is all that is available.

What will follow is a lengthy examination of how the science of economics can give all of us a better under-standing of the forces that shape our daily lives and an appreciation (hopefully) for how economics can increase our chances of achieving a greater measure of happiness.

IT'S NOT ABOUT THE MONEY

Many years ago, I was having dinner with some of my relatives in North Carolina. When the check arrived, my cousin (a really smart psychologist) handed me the check and said, "Here, Jack. You're an economist. You figure out the tip."

This is a pretty typical way people talk to economists.

Sometimes while at social gatherings, I have people walk up to me and ask for my predictions on what will happen in the real estate/gold/oil/stock/bond (you get the idea) markets.

I tell them that if I knew the answers to their questions, I would be in a large cabin up in the North Woods near my private lake in the middle of my 1,000 acres of land rather than at the gathering we are at.

The point is that economics is not all about money – and what to do with money. Sure, economists are pretty good at talking about money and even get some predictions correct from time to time, but ostensibly, economics is about much more than our day-to-day finances.

WHAT ECONOMICS IS ALL ABOUT

A few years ago, I was in Oklahoma spending Christmas with my family when I observed a wonderful example of economics in action. My niece – about three years old at the time – excitedly opened her gift from us which contained a Minnie Mouse blanket and toy. Being a huge fan of Minnie Mouse she squealed with delight as this gift emerged from the box. Around one-tenth of one second later she looked up and said, "More??"

Beautiful.

© Sergey Novikov/Shutterstock.com

Were you like her?

Her desire to have "more" than one gift was not a function of poor parenting. Nor was it derived from being related to an economist.

No, she was simply expressing a behavior we are born with – the expression of the problem of scarcity.

> ➤ **Scarcity is the ongoing imbalance between our wants and needs and the resources available to meet those wants and needs.**

Think about it.

From the time we are born we want or need more than we have. We use our lungs to express our desires when we are one-minute old. We use cash to chase what we want or need now. This omnipresent desire for more continues throughout the course of our lives. The study of economics can help us deal with this dilemma.

> ➤ **Economics is the scientific study of how people make decisions in a world where wants and needs are unlimited but resources to meet our wants and needs are scarce.**

The word "economics" is based on Greek roots, but the Greeks didn't have a field of study anything like eco-

nomics. The two Greek roots of the word "economics" are *oikos* – meaning the household or family estate – and *nomos*, which can mean rules, natural laws, or laws made by the government. In essence, the meaning of this word hangs on the concept of people choosing how they will manage their homes and businesses with the available resources at their disposal.

Economics is called a *decision science* because we all have to decide, each and every day, how we will utilize the resources at our disposal to meet our wants and needs.

What are resources? For economists, resources are typically divided up into four categories: Land, labor, capital, and entrepreneurship.

> ➤ **Land** encompasses all *naturally occurring resources* like water, timber, minerals, plant and animal life, and so forth.
> ➤ **Labor** is the *human effort* in the process of producing goods and services.
> ➤ **Capital** takes two forms. The first type of capital is *physical* capital. This is made up of the equipment and tools used to produce goods and services. The other type of capital is *human* capital – the knowledge, education, training, and skills we bring to the process of production.
> ➤ **Entrepreneurship** – based on the French word for *one who assumes risk* – is made up of the men and women who use their resources to invent new products and start new business ventures.

What imbalances are you dealing with at this time? Let's see. First, there is an imbalance between the number of credit hours you have and the number of credit hours you need to complete your degree. There is the imbalance between the amount of money you are currently making and the amount of money you would like to make. So, what are you doing about those two (out of the list of thousands you might be dealing with) imbalances?

You are making decisions with the resources you have. By using physical capital (computers, automobiles, calculators, and so forth) as well as your human capital, you are attempting to close the credit hour imbalance. This will occur when you get your degree. Once that imbalance is closed, you will be in a better position to close, or more likely, narrow the financial imbalances in your life.

So, how much money will close that imbalance? $70,000? $127,000? $4.32 million?

I have some bad news for many of you. If you believe, at this time, that $127,000 would satisfy you, just wait until you get there. Chances are, once you make $127,000 you will start thinking that $200,000 would be better. Then you will allocate your resources toward that goal. Mark Zuckerberg (the founder of Facebook) probably never dreamed of being a billionaire, but a funny thing happened once his net worth hit $1 billion. He kept going to work.

Recessions, of course, make the problem of scarcity even worse as people lose their jobs or face reduction in their work hours or take-home pay. We know how much money we need to eat and pay our other bills but when the economy falters, we must face up to the fact that scarcity will be a more pressing issue than when jobs are plentiful. The 2007-2009 Recession was the longest experienced by the United States since the 1930s. During that recent downturn, incomes fell by an average of 4.2% and the number of Americans living in poverty rose to 14.3% of the population.[1] The subsequent economic recovery did not improve America's economic condition much. By 2014—almost five years after the Great Recession ended—unemployment rates of over 7% and declining incomes persisted. Three years after the recession had officially ended median household incomes had fallen by $2,544, or nearly 5%.[2] Moreover, the cumulative economic growth rate during that time was 6.3%—the slowest rate of economic recovery since World War II.[3] By 2015 median incomes had risen to $56,516 – the first increase since the recession ended in June of 2009, while the unemployment rate in 2016 dropped below 5%.[4]

HOW ECONOMISTS DEAL WITH SCARCITY

Contrary to the belief of many, economists are humans and we feel pain. So when the most recent economic calamity swept the planet, economists felt the impact, too. It's just that we did not feel it as much, on average, as the average person.

This is not because all economists make so much money that we do not have to worry about downturns in the economy. It is because most economists are colossal skinflints (translation: really, really cheap) when it comes to the use of our scarce dollars. Consider this excerpt from *The Wall Street Journal*:

> Academic economists gather in Atlanta this weekend for their annual meetings, always held the first weekend after New Year's Day. That's not only because it coincides with holidays at most universities. A post-holiday lull in business travel also puts hotel rates near the lowest point of the year. Economists are often cheapskates.
>
> The economists make cities bid against each other to hold their convention, and don't care so much about beaches, golf courses or other frills. It's like buying a car, explains the American Economic Association's secretary-treasurer, John Siegfried, an economist at Vanderbilt University.

"When my wife buys a car, she seems to care what color it is," he says. "I always tell her, don't care about the color." He initially wanted a gray 2007 Mercury Grand Marquis, but a black one cost about $100 less. He got black.

Some of the world's most famous economists were famously frugal. After a dinner thrown by the British economic giant John Maynard Keynes, writer Virginia Woolf complained that the guests had to pick "the bones of Maynard's grouse of which there were three to eleven people." Milton Friedman, the late Nobel laureate, routinely returned reporters' calls collect.

Children of economists recall how tightfisted their parents were. Lauren Weber, author of a recent book titled, "In Cheap We Trust," says her economist father kept the thermostat so low that her mother threatened at one point to take the family to a motel. "My father gave in because it would have been more expensive," she says.

"Where do I begin?" says Marisa Kasriel when asked about the lengths to which her father, Northern Trust Co. economist Paul Kasriel, will go to save a buck: private-label groceries, off-brand tennis shoes and his 1995 Subaru, with a piece of electrical tape covering the "check engine" light. Mr. Kasriel says he buys off-brand shoes "so that my lovely children could have Nikes."

David Colander, an economist at Middlebury College in Vermont, says his wife – his first one, that is – was miffed when he went shopping for the cheapest diamond. Economist Robert Gordon, of Northwestern University, says he drives out of his way to go to a grocery store where prices are cheaper than at the nearby Whole Foods, even though it takes him an extra half hour to save no more than $5.

Mr. Gordon, however, is no ascetic. He, his wife and their two dogs live in a 11,000-square-foot, 21-room 1889 mansion on the largest residential lot in Evanston, Ill., outside Chicago.

"The house is full, every room is furnished, there are 72 oriental rugs and vast collections of oriental art, 1930s art deco Czech perfume bottles and other nice stuff," he says.

Some economists may be cheap, at least by the standards of other people, because of their training or a fascination with money and choices that drives them to the field.

Wharton School professor Justin Wolfers and a colleague gave a friend $150 to hire movers instead of helping him to move themselves.

In recent research, University of Washington economists Yoram Bauman and Elaina Rose found that economics majors were less likely to donate money to charity than students who majored in other fields. After majors in other fields took an introductory economics course, their propensity to give also fell.

"The economics students seem to be born guilty, and the other students seem to lose their innocence when they take an economics class," says Mr. Bauman, who has a stand-up comedy act he'll be doing at the economists' Atlanta conference Sunday night. Among his one-liners: "You might be an economist if you refuse to sell your children because they might be worth more later."[5]

Republished with permission of Dow Jones, Inc., from "Secrets of the Economists' Trade: First, Purchase a Piggy Bank," by Justin Lahart, *The Wall Street Journal*, January 20, 2010; permission conveyed through Copyright Clearance Center, Inc.

If you find yourself thinking that economists are a bit odd, consider this…

I once cut down a Christmas tree in a field next to my parent's house in Oklahoma, borrowed rope from my Dad, tied the tree to the roof of my vehicle, and drove 1,178 miles back to Florida with my almost free tree – in October. Okay, the tree turned brown by Thanksgiving and people laughed at me and took pictures the entire trip, but I cannot bear the thought of having to buy a tree that will only be in my house for a few weeks.

I buy almost all of my clothes at thrift stores and garage sales; only drive used cars; cut my own firewood so that I can avoid turning on the heat in the winter; purchase gifts for family members at the same garage sales I buy my clothes; use eBay to sell their gifts once they have stopped using them and never, ever pay interest to a credit card provider.

I should also mention that almost all of our family vacations involve sleeping in the woods in a tent. I just think anything more than $19 is too much to pay for sleeping.

The point that this is designed to make is simple. Economists are often bewildered by the spending patterns of people. We all face monetary scarcity, but using credit cards to purchase brand-new items, all of the time, even when our debts pile up before our eyes, is a recipe for magnifying the financial scarcity that is already there. We simply think it makes sense to spend as little as possible in many areas of our lives, so that we have the ability to allocate the savings to other areas of our lives where we are not that frugal (I like nice restaurants) or where we believe the payoff will be greater (investing in a business or retirement fund, for example).

TERRORISM AND THE PROBLEM OF SCARCITY

Between 1795 and 1800 the United States paid nearly $1 million in tribute to Barbary pirates off the coast of Africa in order to keep American ships from incurring even greater losses. In 1801 Thomas Jefferson refused to make the payment, stating, "We mean to rest the safety of our commerce on the resources of our own strength and bravery."

"I concentrate on the importance of continuing holy war actions against America, militarily and economically. This economic hemorrhaging continues until today, but requires more blows. And the youth should try to find the joints of the American economy and hit the enemy in these joints, with God's permission."

Osama bin Laden
December 27, 2001

Once considered the world's foremost terrorist, Osama bin Laden shocked millions with the glee he expressed on worldwide television broadcasts following the terrorist strikes against the United States. With his

CONCEPT CHECK

In 2016 President Trump called for the deportation of nearly 11 million people who were living in the United States illegally. In considering the imbalance between the price of goods and services we want to pay and the price we have to pay, would deportation on this scale increase, or decrease this imbalance? Why?

© Joseph Sohm/Shutterstock.com

account of how his plan was carried out with far greater success than even he could have imagined, Mr. bin Laden illustrated to the entire world that terrorism is not a random act of violence, but rather an exercise in economics.

Born in Saudi Arabia around 1957, Osama was not raised in a life of poverty. His father, Mohammed bin Laden founded a construction company, and with royal patronage, became a billionaire. However, as the seventeenth son, born in a society where family status is highly important, Osama would have been deemed "less important" than his older brothers.

As a student at King Abdul Aziz University in Jedda, Saudi Arabia, Osama studied management and *economics*, coming under the influence of religious teachers who introduced him to the wider world of Islamic politics. Perhaps the first major instance where scarcity entered his adult life was during the Soviet invasion of Afghanistan in 1979. Osama supported the Afghan resistance (as did the United States), which became a jihad, or holy war. In this instance, Osama worked toward closing the imbalance between the number of Soviet troops he wanted in Afghanistan (zero) and the number that actually existed at this time.

By the mid-1980s, bin Laden had moved to Afghanistan, where he established an organization, Maktab al-Khidimat (MAK), to recruit Islamic soldiers from around the world who later formed the basis of an international network. The MAK maintained recruiting offices in Detroit and Brooklyn in the 1980s.[6]

The Taliban arose from the religious schools set up during the war against the Soviet invasion. After the Soviet Army withdrew in 1989, fighting erupted among various factions who sought control over the Afghan government. In response to the chaos, the fundamentalist Taliban was formed and within two years had captured most of the country.

After the Soviet withdrawal, bin Laden returned to Saudi Arabia and worked in his family's construction business. In 1990, in response to the Iraqi invasion of Kuwait, the Saudi government allowed American troops to be stationed in Saudi Arabia. Bin Laden was incensed that non-believers (American soldiers) were stationed in the birthplace of Islam. He also charged the Saudi regime with deviating from true Islam.

Bin Laden was expelled from Saudi Arabia in 1991 because of his anti-government activities. He eventually wound up in Sudan, where he worked with Egyptian radical groups in exile. When the United States set up military operations in Saudi Arabia to remove Iraq from Kuwait, bin Laden protested to the Saudi royal family, arguing that the U.S. was only in Saudi Arabia to secure oil supplies and, if allowed to, would never leave.

In 1992 bin Laden claimed responsibility for attempting to bomb U.S. soldiers in Yemen and for attacking U.S. troops in Somalia the following year. In 1994 pressure from the U.S. and Saudi Arabia prompted Sudan to expel bin Laden, and he returned to Afghanistan.

In 1998, bin Laden called for all Americans and Jews, including children, to be killed. He had since been connected to terrorist bombings at the U.S. embassies in Kenya and Tanzania, the attack against the USS Cole and the September 11, 2001 attacks in New York City, Pennsylvania and Washington, D.C. and others around the globe in 2003 and 2004.

The problem of scarcity, for Osama bin Laden, was straightforward. There was an imbalance between the number of Americans and Jews who were dead and the number he wanted dead. There was an imbalance between the number of weapons he needed to accomplish this goal and the number of weapons he had. Even with a fortune estimated at $250 million, there was an imbalance between the amount of money he needed to carry out his goal and the amount of money he had.

With the United States actively bombing his al-Qaeda network and arresting key leaders, there was a growing imbalance between the amount of resources and people he had to work with (now that he is dead) and the resources and people he needed to work with. Over the past few years we have witnessed a transition from Al-Qaeda-based terrorism to terrorism carried about by ISIS and ISIS-sympathizers all over the globe. Despite bombing campaigns and heightened security measures in Europe and the United States, ISIS was able to carry out carnage on a mass scale.

The astute economics student should be aware of the fact that the United States faces the problem of scarcity in this ongoing war on terrorism. Imagine the resources we need as a nation in order to eliminate every terrorist cell in the world. How much money would that cost? If we have enough money, do we have enough technology, and surveillance, and people, to pull off this task?

Since September 11th, there has also been a marked decline in the overall liberty enjoyed by Americans. The federal government has increased its presence in our mail, email, phone conversations, Internet searches and travel plans.[7] Many wonder how much more civil liberty can be given up in order to impose scarcity on the global terrorist network.

If we get rid of every terrorist by 2019, are there children who will grow up to become terrorists by 2038? Can we stop every person who enters the U.S. and accurately gauge his or her intentions? Do we have the patience that a prolonged war requires? Could we prevent a nuclear or biological attack for the remaining years of this republic?

As you can see, the probability of eliminating the imbalance between the amount of safety and security we want and the amount we have is very, very low. We may never eliminate the imbalance. In economics, you learn that sometimes the best we can do is to narrow the imbalances in our lives.

MAKING "GOOD" DECISIONS

Have you known someone who makes really bad decisions almost all the time? On the flipside, do you know anyone that seems to have their life together when it comes to dating, money, school, and just about everything else? It could be that luck floats around and lands on some people while it misses others. Or, it could be that some people make better decisions than others with their scarce resources. In this section, you will learn how economists evaluate human behavior and how to be one of those people who seem to get things right more often than not.

Take, for example, the decision to get married. This important decision is replete with examples of the problem of scarcity – both before and after you are wed.

For many people, marriage is a way to narrow the imbalances in their lives that have to do with children, love, companionship, security and income. Of course, getting married often creates other imbalances related to free time, debt, work hours and more. With a divorce rate that historically hovers around 50 percent, one might ask, "Is marriage a rational choice?" Good question. Here is how to answer it.

If someone proposes – or even hints that they might propose – marriage someday, before you answer you should get out a sheet of paper and a pen, create three columns, and label the columns with the words BENEFITS; DIRECT COSTS; OPPORTUNITY COSTS.

What do these columns mean? It means that you are attempting to engage in *rational behavior*.

> ➤ **Rational behavior is said to exist when human beings engage in a decision-making process where, at the time the decision is made, the expected direct benefits of the decision equal, or exceed, the expected direct cost, plus the opportunity cost of their decision.**
> ➤ **Benefits are the monetary and/or nonmonetary gain expected from any decision.**
> ➤ **Direct costs are the known, or expected out of pocket costs and the probability of something negative occurring as a result of the decision.**
> ➤ **Opportunity cost is the cost of choosing to use resources for one purpose, measured by the value of the next best alternative for using those resources.**

In considering the rationality of marriage, let's look at the way you go about buying a new cell phone.

First, you realize that your life is being ruined, or slowed down, by your phone that was produced just 18 months ago.

With this unacceptable problem of increased communication scarcity, you go out looking for the latest and greatest phone. You find one that costs say, $650. The first question you must answer is, "Will I get $650 in benefits from this phone?" Then, you consider the $650 price plus the other direct costs associated with data plans, etc. Then, you must evaluate what else you could spend the $650 on. As we will see, that second best choice (food) is also part of the cost of any decision.

One could argue (as economists who study marriage do) that the *benefits* of marriage could be measured by gains in companionship, financial security, children and any other positive elements you believe might be attainable.

The *direct cost* of marriage could be measured by the financial costs of a shared household, higher income taxes (the IRS is not going to let you get away with this decision free of charge), less personal freedom, the sharing of resources and other observable costs.

Finally, the *opportunity* cost of marriage might be the foregone opportunity to remain single – and any value that would have been generated – or perhaps the lost chance to marry someone else whom might have been a respectable choice. The important part to remember here is that once you make a decision, there is always a second best, foregone opportunity you have to incur.

So, how do you know if you are making a rational cell phone or marriage choice?

It is pretty simple. If you believe, at the time you are making the decision, that the benefits equal or exceed the sum of the direct and opportunity costs you are making a *rational* choice.

If, on the other hand, you calculate that the direct plus opportunity costs are greater than the benefits you would be *irrational* to make that choice.

SUMMARY

IF Benefits $\geq$ Direct Cost + Opportunity Cost = Rational Behavior

IF Benefits $<$ Direct Cost + Opportunity Cost = Irrational Behavior

MORE ON RATIONAL BEHAVIOR

Before we delve into examples of when human beings engage in irrational behavior, some final thoughts to keep in mind.

First, *your benefits and costs are unique to you* – as are the benefits and costs to some other person. If you decide that buying a brand new car for $27,000 will confer greater benefits than the sum total of all of the monetary costs *plus* the opportunity cost of the next best thing you could have done with $27,000 (a used car; a lot of nice clothes and your rent payment for six months, for example) then you have made a rational choice – even if everyone you know tells you that you are an economic moron.

Of course, this concept presupposes that if you see someone smoking crack behind a dumpster, you cannot assume they are irrational. You would need to ask them to explain the benefits of crack smoking, along with how much the crack cost and what else they could be doing with their time. It could be that there are many rational crack smokers out there behind the dumpsters.

Second, it is important to understand that *economists assume that people are inherently rational*. That means that we are born with an internal drive to do things that benefit us more than it costs us. Many students have trouble with this assumption, which is understandable. After all, given the average age of the person reading this book, one could assume that most students have seen their friends do so many outrageous things that it would be a safer bet to argue that we are inherently irrational and simply get lucky with good decisions from time to time.

This is not the case. Consider this: When your friend – whom you think is irrational – is driving their modified Honda Civic 112 miles per hour, on the shoulder, while listening to their music so loud that the windows shake, what do they do when they come over the top of a hill and see a highway patrol officer? How long does it take for them to slow down?

If your answer is "somewhere around .001 seconds," then you have confirmed that biologically we all have a desire for self-preservation. We eat, sleep, avoid death as much as we can and make other decisions that get most of us into old age.

Sometimes, as we will see later on, people do make arguably irrational choices, but it is not as often as you might think.

Finally, *economists tend not to evaluate the rationality of a decision ex post facto, or "after the fact."* We are most interested in the cost-benefit calculation leading up to the decision that is being made, in order to accurately assess the rationality of the choices people make.

ARE PEOPLE EVER IRRATIONAL?

> ➤ **Irrational behavior is where an individual makes a decision knowing that the costs exceed the benefits.**

Once upon a time, economics was pretty easy for economists. We simply told our students that inherently people are rational, and that was that. After all, you recall the scenario where your friend is speeding and then instinctively slows down, right?

But what about people who speed up when they see a police officer turn on the blinking lights? What about people who know they are in big trouble but proceed to engage in a high-speed chase where they run other drivers off the road, plow over an unsuspecting armadillo or two, and then pull out a gun and start shooting at the pursuing officer? Is that kind of behavior rational? It seems that cable television is filled with programs dedicated to the irrational man.

Traditional economics would suggest that the person who is in the high-speed chase simply decided that the benefits of the chase, measured by some probability of escape, were greater than the potential costs of death or incarceration. Vernon L. Smith and Daniel Kahneman might vigorously disagree. These guys — one an economist from George Mason University, the other a professor of psychology from Princeton — won the 2002 Nobel Prize in Economics by essentially "proving" that people act in an irrational manner more than we think.

Mr. Kahneman is the first psychologist to share in the Nobel Prize. He and Professor Smith took economics into the laboratory and, through repeated tests — using students as guinea pigs — the researchers found that the assumption that self-interested individuals will consider the benefits and costs of their actions in a systematic manner that yields rational outcomes is not always true.[8]

Instead, they found that people repeatedly make errors in judgment that can be predicted and categorized. One important discovery was that people are averse to recognizing their losses. This is another way of saying that we irrationally tend to live in denial.

For example, suppose you were holding on to a brief case with an unknown amount of cash in it. In front of you is another brief case, also containing an unknown amount of cash. You are told that one of the brief cases has $1,000 in it, while the other one has $1 million in it. You are given the choice of opening the brief case on the table — and keeping whatever is in it — or you can take $600,000 to not open either one. If this sounds familiar, it should because it was the basis for a game show called *Deal or No Deal*.

© Sergei Bachlakov/Shutterstock.com

In the preceding example, you have a fifty percent chance of getting $1 million. .50 × $1 million = $500,000. That means you *should* take the guaranteed $600,000, right? Yes, if you are *rational*. No, if you are like many of the contestants, who, facing even lower odds of getting the million bucks routinely kept playing rather than taking the offers of guaranteed money.[9]

One of the dilemmas for traditional economic theory is that it can't explain why people do generous things with their money, such as leaving large tips for servers in restaurants they'll never visit again. Behavioral economists reason that it's because people have an emotional preference for fairness that competes with the desire to maximize wealth.

This new field of study could help us understand why some Latin American and European cultures are prone to accept high taxes and burdensome government rules – yet don't always seem to mind,[10] while others seem to revolt at the very mention of greater government intrusion. We could also learn more about why people refuse to leave their homes as hurricanes approach,[11] how people can overcome racism[12] and much more by considering the role that *emotions* play in the decision making process.[13]

WAS JESUS IRRATIONAL?

On February 25, 2004, Mel Gibson's movie – *The Passion of the Christ* debuted in over 4,000 theaters across the country. This extremely controversial and violent movie depicted Mr. Gibson's view – and the view of others – of what the last 12 hours of Jesus' life may have been like. Christians and non-Christians alike had widely divergent opinions on the degree to which Gibson's portrayal of these historical events was accurate. However, what seems to be almost universally agreed upon is that Jesus was a real being who lived and was crucified approximately 2,000 years ago. It is also considered a universal truth that crucifixion was one of the most horrific forms of punishment human beings have ever used.

A question that might be an interesting one for economists to tackle is whether or not Jesus was a rational man. Specifically, if history is accurate in that Jesus spent approximately three years of his life as the self-proclaimed son of God, knowing the penalty for such a claim, what possible benefits could he have received from going through with his crucifixion?

To an economist, we would want to know what Jesus believed to be the benefits of being crucified. What were the direct costs of his crucifixion – for him? What was the opportunity cost of being crucified?

History records that Jesus argued that only by his crucifixion could the world be saved from sin. That seems to suggest that he believed the benefits of his death to be

great and was willing to give up his life (the direct cost) as well as the value of the next best choice, which to Jesus seemed to be the lost salvation of mankind.

So, was he rational, or irrational?

APPLICATIONS OF COST-BENEFIT ANALYSIS

WELCOME TO THE 29-HOUR WORKWEEK

When you were young your parents may have used incentives to get you to do things that they wanted you to do. Sometimes those incentives might have come in the form of an award and sometimes in the form of a threat.

> ➤ **Incentives are anything that changes the costs and benefits of a decision.**

Some of you might have had some trouble ending the habit of having "accidents" in your diaper while you were playing with your friends outside. Perhaps while you were playing the benefits of interrupting your fun to run to the bathroom were too low, while your diaper seemed to work well and the opportunity cost of missing play time made the costs of going inside too high.

If your parents offered you candy, or money, or extra time playing video games for every time you successfully used the bathroom then this was their way of raising the benefits of going to the bathroom to a level they hoped would exceed your costs. This is an example of a *positive incentive*.

Some of you might have had parents that told you that for every time you did not go to the bathroom you would have to spend 30 more minutes cleaning your room. This *negative incentive* was designed to increase the costs of having accidents to the point where it would be more rational to run inside.

Sometimes the government acts like parents in order to change behavior that is deemed unacceptable.

One recent example that comes to mind is a provision in the Patient Protection and Affordable Care Act (signed by President Obama on March 23, 2010).

The chapter on health care later in the text will examine many of the features of this law. For our purposes in this section on cost-benefit analysis we will focus on one particularly controversial mandate that forces businesses with fifty or more workers to provide health insurance coverage – or pay a monetary fine of $2,000 per worker – for all workers employed 30 or more hours per week.

It does not take an economist to deduce what this provision of the law – a form of negative incentive - has done for thousands of American businesses with rational men and women running them in order to earn a profit.

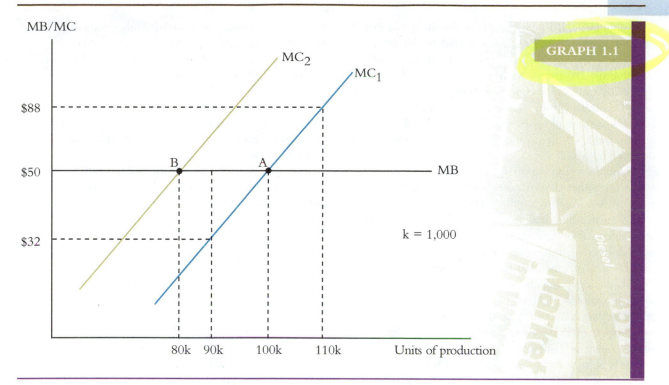

GRAPH 1.1

Think of it this way. Suppose you ran a business with 100 workers – all of which were full-time employees working 40 or more hours per week.

When your workers were hired you clearly told them that their compensation and benefits would not include any health insurance coverage. Of course it is easy to see where many prospective workers would turn down a job offer from you, but 100 accepted, voluntarily and proceeded to work.

One day you are told that even though your employees were never forced to work for you and you had a mutual agreement with them over hours, compensation and benefits, this would not be sufficient and it would no longer be legal.

You are told that for all 100 workers you will provide health coverage, which could amount to hundreds of thousands of dollars, or more, per year – or pay a fine when you file your tax returns.

Graph 1.1 and the use of *marginal analysis* illustrates what might happen next.

> **Marginal analysis is the examination of incremental changes in the benefits and costs of any decision.**

Every hour you are open for business you incur costs associated with labor, fuel, materials, electricity, repairs, maintenance and more. Therefore your *marginal cost* of operating your business has a positive slope (MC1), showing rising costs per hour of work.

> **Marginal cost – the additional cost of any repeated decision.**

Suppose every hour your employees are working you derive a marginal benefit (in this case, money) of $50.

> **Marginal benefit – the additional benefit of any repeated decision.**

Since, in this case the marginal benefit of production is constant, the marginal benefit curve is flat – no matter what you produce you can sell your production for $50 per unit.

Left alone (translation – no forced provision of health care), what level of production would you choose?

If you answered, "100,000 units," you are correct. That is because every level of production up to 100,000 carries with it a higher marginal benefit than marginal cost. Simply put, if you are doing something over and over again where the extra benefits exceed the extra costs, keep doing it!

Once you get to 100,000 units of production the marginal benefit ($50) equals the marginal cost ($50) and therefore you should not produce one more unit. Doing so would mean the marginal cost would not surpass the marginal benefit and economic losses from this irrational choice would emerge.

Now let's add a negative incentive telling you that all of your workers will now be provided health insurance – by you – or else you will send more of your profit to Washington, D.C. in the form of a fine.

With this major new cost added to your business, what would happen to your marginal costs of production? It is straightforward to see that your costs would rise.

In graph 1.1 we can see the new marginal cost curve depicted by MC2.

Now how many units would you produce?

Notice that if your costs increase it would be irrational to continue to produce 100,000 units. Doing so would mean a marginal cost of more than $50 but a constant marginal benefit of $50. This means that the economically rational thing to do – assuming you care about profit – is to *cut production* to 80,000 units.

Reducing production would mean you now need fewer hours of work to be performed.

The law tells you that if you have more than 50 workers all of those working more than 30 hours per week must have insurance.

It is pretty easy to see what would happen next.

By cutting your work force back to 29 hours per week, or reducing your labor force to 49 employees you could save money on health insurance and avoid a fine. The 29-hour workweek would, of course, mean lower production levels (80,000 in this case), lower profits (from offering less to the market) and lower total earnings for your workers (who used to get paid for 40 or more hours per week), but at least you are still existing as a business – until a better option, perhaps in another country, emerges.

This is precisely what has occurred since the passage of the Affordable Care Act.[14] Even though the provision requiring employers to provide care was postponed to 2015, in 2013 and 2014 businesses all over America were already acting on the new law by adjusting full-time to part-time employment patterns. The Bureau of Labor Statistics found that during the January-July 2013 time frame one of the largest surges in part-time hiring had taken place.[15] Moreover, the number of hourly employees working 30-34 hours per week (more than 10 million Americans) dropped by an average of 146,500 per month in 2013 while the number working 25-29 hours per week rose by 119,000 per month.[16] Meanwhile, 97,000 full-time jobs were lost during that same period.

As a side note to all of this, one day I was in a meeting at my college when we were given the news that keeping our adjunct professors at 30 or more hours per week would cost our college millions of dollars in new health insurance costs.

Of course that would have meant higher tuition and fees and reduced services.

To all of this, one of my colleagues asked, "Why can't we just give all of our adjuncts a pay raise so they can afford health insurance?"

What my colleague failed to see is a pay raise sufficient to cover health insurance would also have to be recovered by our college in the form of higher tuition and fees and/or reduced services.

In economics you will learn that everything we do comes with a cost. Formerly full-time employees are already finding this out the hard way.

IS OFFSHORE OIL DRILLING A TERRIBLE IDEA?

According to the journal *Science*, during the summer of 2010 a total of 4.4 million barrels (185 million gallons) of crude oil spilled into the Gulf of Mexico when BP's offshore oil rig exploded.

During much of that summer, the price of crude oil hovered around $80 per barrel. That means that BP lost $352 million – before any government fines, lawsuit settlements, or cleanup costs – when the rig failed.

Do you suppose BP executives, when overseeing the construction of the Horizon rig, sat in a meeting and said, "Gee, let's see if we can have a rig that will someday leak $352 million of our product into the ocean, cause everyone to hate us, get the government crawling into our lives, lawyers salivating with glee over all of the money they will make from us – AND have the television networks showing dead birds and fish with our product all over them!" "That would be a great business idea!!"

A bad idea?

Pardon the sarcasm, but one necessary condition for learning economics is to be able to suspend emotion when analyzing economic events, so that you can clearly assess the cost-benefit calculations that led to an event and therefore rationally respond to that event.

The BP oil spill was simply the predictable result of a series of rational decisions made by politicians, oil company executives, consumers, and engineers. Let's look at it.

Ever since the creation of the internal combustion engine, human beings have traveled from point A to point B via the burning of dead dinosaurs. The petroleum derived from organic matter has always been sold at a price, rather than given away to the nicest drivers free of charge.

Rational drivers have always thought that they would rather pay low prices than high prices for fuel, so rational oil companies have spent decades trying to locate the lowest cost petroleum so that consumers would see an acceptable price and use more of the product over time.

From east Texas in the 1920s to the Middle East after that, to Alaska in the 1970s and eventually into the ocean, the quest for large quantities of oil to meet the demands of a growing world economy has always led to new exploration.

When the Organization of Petroleum Exporting Countries (OPEC to you and I) was formed in 1960, the world was suddenly faced with the prospect of buying oil from a region that controlled the largest reserves of petroleum – and large reserves of anger toward the United States.

A series of political events (to be covered in later chapters) led to dramatic reductions in the supply of oil flowing from the Middle East to the U.S. during the 1970s. The result was skyrocketing prices and a political push from voters to find oil in places that were not located in countries that did not like us much.

In 1989, Shell Oil announced that it had discovered the Auger oil field nearly 3,000 feet below the surface of the Gulf of Mexico. This set off a mad rush by other oil companies to explore for oil in this region.[17] This was a rational move. The cost of dealing with hostile nations as our primary supplier had grown too high. The prospect of extracting oil from U.S. waters was too good to pass up and the cost of drilling for oil in the ocean was falling as technology continued to improve.

On November 28, 1995, President Bill Clinton signed the Deepwater Royalty Relief Act – an act that dramatically lowered the royalties that oil companies had to pay the federal government for oil pumped out of the ocean floor. Mr. Clinton felt that the benefits of this act would be twofold – first, it would lower the cost of U.S. oil production, leading to greater supplies and lower consumer prices, and second, low consumer prices would keep the economy strong which tends to help politicians stay in office.

Of course, the cost of this act, one could argue, was a higher chance of something going wrong as more and more rigs would ultimately be constructed.

Any rational business, when constructing a new facility, is going to seek to keep costs down in order to enhance the chances of earning profit. An investigation by the U.S. Minerals Management Service found that the Deepwater Horizon rig was a "risky" and less expensive design that was used by BP in 42% of its rigs – far more than was used by other oil companies.[18] Economically, this may have seemed like an appropriate risk to take. After all, before 2010 exactly zero oil rigs had exploded with this design. This could have led BP officials to assume that the probability of a major spill was extremely low, justifying the use of a less expensive system for pumping oil.

Compounding matters was the fact that BP relied on federal government models that simulated what would occur if an oil spill ever became a reality. According to the U.S. government models, an oil spill would have a very low likelihood of reaching U.S. soil and would rapidly evaporate or be dissipated by waves in the ocean. The models used by the government had not been updated since 2004.[19] Four months after he took office, President Obama was warned by a federal court in Washington, D.C. that the government was unprepared for a major spill at sea and was too reliant on "irrational" environmental analysis of the risks of offshore drilling. Facing losses in federal royalties of over $10 billion, the Obama Administration supported greater offshore drilling activity.[20]

One can easily see where BP – and the federal government – thought the Deepwater Horizon rig was an economically rational rig to employ in this region. The perceived cost of something going wrong was low. The probability of an oil spill creating an environmental disaster appeared to be low as well. The desire to make profit from oil was – and is – a huge reason to build a rig that is effective, so that the oil can be claimed and sold off to those who refine it into gasoline and other products.

Now that the "low probability event" has taken place, students in an economics class should ask, "What is the most rational response to the BP oil spill?" The answer to that question really depends on how you define benefits and costs in this case. Some of you might argue that the costs associated with the damage done to the environment, the jobs destroyed in fishing and tourism-related industries, and the risks of another spill happening in the future is greater than any benefits associated with oil from the Gulf of Mexico.

Others could argue that too many jobs would be lost in the oil industry and too many people would be hurt by rising gasoline prices, to justify any curtailment of oil production in the Gulf. They might also add that many scientists have been astonished by how quickly the oil seems to have dissipated and how wildlife in this area has rebounded at a faster rate than predicted.[21]

In 2013 a garment factory in Bangladesh collapsed, killing more than 1,100 workers. A teenaged girl named Mahinur Akhter was pulled from the building alive and planned to return to the garment district where she earned $90 to $100 per month making clothing for some of the world's leading suppliers. Read more about her and others by logging on to http://online.wsj.com/news/articles/SB10001424127887324049504578543391644877374

Are these women rational to work under these conditions and for this type of pay? Why, or why not?

© gazmandhu/Shutterstock.com

For your purposes in this class, what is most important is to understand how the use of cost-benefit analysis can help all of us assess any situation in a practical, rather than emotional, manner. This can lead to better decision making for you, our businesses, and our government officials.

THE ECONOMICS OF TEXTING WHILE DRIVING – USING PROBABILITY THEORY

Do you text message people while you are driving? If you answered, "yes," is there something wrong with you? Individuals involved in the practice of texting while driving are 23% more likely to meet with an accident compared to their counterparts who follow the norms of safe driving. A truck driver who indulges in texting while driving is 23.2 times more likely to meet with an accident.[22]

By 2016, texting while driving had become the leading cause of death among teenagers, according to the Cohen Children's Medical Center, with more than 3,000 killed each year.

Studies also reveal that the dangers of texting while driving are more than those associated with drunk driving. Texting while driving increases your chances of getting involved in a car crash by six times compared to driving under the influence of alcohol.

On the surface, the decision to text while operating 2,000 lbs. of machinery in the near proximity of innocent people, might have no obvious economic properties. When we dig below the surface, though, we will see that economics can explain this problem.

The expected benefit to the text messenger is the *probability* (the chance, between zero and one-hundred percent) that they will safely send and/or receive the desired information. The self-interested text messenger is not sending a text message in order to help his or her fellow man, they are doing it to help themselves.

The *direct cost* of texting while driving is measured by the probability of having an accident; the probability of getting injured, dying, or injuring/killing someone else, as well as (in states where this is illegal) the probability of getting caught, the probability of getting punished, and the expected or known penalty if you are charged.

Suppose the probability of getting into an accident is .023 (this means that 2.3% of text messengers, under similar circumstances, crash their vehicle).

Suppose if you are in an accident you have a 47% chance of being injured. Finally, suppose the average injury costs $3,250 in medical bills. Mathematically, you then have a 1.08% chance of getting an injury from texting while driving (.023 × .47 = .0108). So, is escaping injury 99% of the time worth a 1.08% chance of an injury?

If you have a 1.08% chance of an injury and the average injury costs $3,250, then each time you text while driving costs you $35.13 (.0108 × $3,250). Remember, if you don't have a wreck with injuries 99% of the time you are texting, then 99% of the time your medical bill is zero dollars. The ONE TIME you have a wreck and get hurt you pay $3,250, so the average cost per texting incident is only $35.13.

The second cost associated with texting or any other behavior for that matter, is the *opportunity cost*.

If you decide to text while driving, you forgo whatever good would have come out of driving with two hands on the wheel.

As absurd as it may seem, texting while driving, while more dangerous than being drunk and arguably more selfish than many other activities, is not necessarily an irrational act. That is why people keep doing it. It is also why economists know that asking people to be courteous is laughable. You don't change behavior by asking people to care about other humans. You change behavior by changing the benefit-cost calculation.

Suppose every state had the negative incentive of $10,000 tickets for texting while driving and the positive incentive where police officers got a 10% cut from every ticket issued where texting while driving could be proven. *Then* you would see a huge change in behavior.

No economist I know has suggested such a drastic measure — yet. However, all economists know that texting while driving is not going to go away under the current laws and national begging campaign.

THE ECONOMICS OF GLOBAL WARMING — IS THERE A RATIONAL SOLUTION?

"We're the first generation to feel the impact of climate change, and we're the last generation that can do something about it. We only get one planet. There's no Plan B."

President Obama

Unless you have been living under a rock the last few years, you are well aware of the raging debate that goes on day after day, concerning the degree to which human beings have put our planet in danger of dying.

On one side of the argument you will find those who believe that they have concrete data that the planet is warming at a rate that cannot be due to normal cyclical changes in temperature patterns, but rather due to the fact that human beings create horrific levels of pollution from the burning of oil, coal, wood, and many other resources. According to the Intergovernmental Panel on Climate Change (IPCC), an agency of the United Nations, during the 1980s and 1990s global warming appeared to be occurring at a rate of between 0.15 and 0.17 degrees Celsius per decade, for a possible increase over the next century of 1.5 to 1.7 degrees C.[23]

For people like former Vice President, Albert Gore, the Earth cannot sustain our current pace that sees 94 million barrels of oil burned *every day*. If we continue,

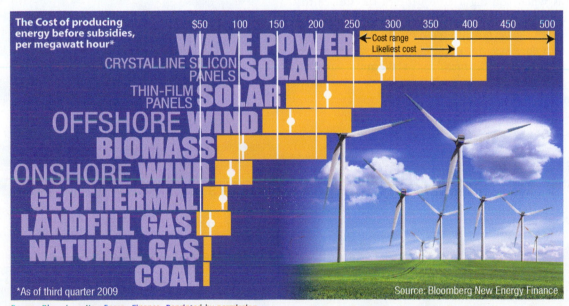

Source: Bloomberg New Energy Finance. Reprinted by permission.

Gore and others charge, the planet will warm to the point where critical ice formations will melt, sea levels will rise and hundreds of millions of people – and other living creatures – will be dead, or impoverished or crowded into smaller and smaller places.

On the other side we have people – scientists and non-scientists alike – who cast a very skeptical eye toward the notion that humans are the main cause of global warming and whether global warming is occurring at all. Critics point out that it is impossible to tell how much of the recent warming trend is natural or manmade. According to NASA's Goddard Institute, six of the ten warmest years on record were in the 1930s and 1940s – well before carbon dioxide emissions began to accelerate to present day levels.[24]

It is also worth noting that in November of 2009, a file appeared on the Internet that contained thousands of emails and other documents from the Climatic Research Unit at the University of East Anglia in Great Britain. The emails and documents, which became known as "Climategate," showed that scientists from all over the world had suppressed and even falsified climate data in order to magnify the threat of global warming.[25]

Of course, any of you reading this section of the book could go online and find thousands of articles that side with one group or the other. The point of this part of the chapter is not to prove who is right. The point is to bring some economic clarity into this debate so that we can be poised to tell our elected representatives how much, if any, of our scarce tax dollars should be devoted to the goal of cooling off the Earth.

On the surface, you would be hard-pressed to find many Americans who would not be thrilled to see new jobs and greater use of renewable energy systems like solar, wind, and ocean-generated electricity.

It is when you dig a little beneath the surface that some very questionable economics appear.

First, the government's track record in creating reliable, clean energy is not impressive. Part of the problem is associated with the first law of thermodynamics – "Energy is neither created, nor destroyed." That means that in order to create energy, you must use energy and

that energy does not come with zero pollution. Second, the last time the country got serious about moving away from dirty energy like coal and petroleum was in the late 1970s and early 1980s – and the government failed miserably.

From 1973 until the early 1980s the U.S. faced an "energy crisis" that led to dramatic increases in government-funded projects to reduce our reliance on foreign oil (sound familiar) and create less air pollution.

Repeatedly, tens of billions of dollars in expenditures for everything from synthetic fuels from shale to coal gasification, biomass, wind, solar, and other projects, failed to deliver energy at anywhere near the cost of oil and coal.[26] The inherent problem that government planners could not overcome was the fact that petroleum (especially low-cost Middle East petroleum), even at historically high prices, was much cheaper to use than other forms of energy to power our cars.

From 2009-2013 $8.4 billion in taxpayer money was given to companies to build wind farms – large windmills designed to generate electric power. Given this free money companies were much less careful in where the wind

Photo courtesy Jack Chambless

SUGGESTED CLASSROOM DEBATE

If a warming planet threatens the food supply for wolves – that thrive on very cold weather – how much would you be willing to pay in gasoline taxes, per gallon of gasoline, in order to increase the probability that wolves and other species do not become extinct over time?

farms were built. In fact, the Department of Energy found that the subsidies had led to farms being built in places with wind conditions 16% *worse* than the average unsubsidized wind farm from a decade earlier.[27] Meanwhile, the price of power generated by wind increased from $37 per megawatt-hour to $54 during this time.

For many economists, spending of the taxpayers' money to continue to look for energy sources that are *more expensive* and often less efficient than what we currently have, is a waste of money.[28] After all, if we are going to fight global warming, the consumers will ultimately be the ones who will have to be willing and able to purchase the new alternative energy technologies – assuming those technologies even appear. As the previous table clearly illustrates, "cleaner sources" of energy would quickly clean out the wallets of even the most well-intentioned consumer.

Surveys do show that a large majority of Americans (the world's largest energy consumer) have a desire to "go green" as long as the cost is not too great.[29]

Therein lays a major dilemma. If the government spends hundreds of billions of dollars and does not deliver a cheap alternative to oil, how will we ever get enough alternative energy usage to fight global warming – assuming global warming can and should be fought?

Furthermore, if elected officials pass legislation that is inefficient (meaning it does not pass the cost-benefit test) we could not only fail to achieve major reductions in the temperature of the planet, but we would see major economic disruptions that could, at the minimum, inconvenience people, and at the maximum, harm more people than rising temperatures have. Consider this…

In 2009 the U.S. House of Representatives passed climate legislation that would impose an 80% reduction in carbon emissions by the year 2050. This legislation would reduce the level of overall emissions to the same amount the U.S. produced in the year 1875, when we had no cars and only 40 million people.[30] How many jobs would be destroyed – and how many families would thus be negatively impacted – by such a law? Since the legislation calls for massive taxes on coal and oil, we would have to face far higher prices for electricity, gasoline, and all products that rely on fuel and electricity.

You may also recall the government's "Cash for Clunkers" program, which took taxpayer dollars and doled out payments up to $4,500 to anyone willing to turn in a gas-guzzling used vehicle for one that got marginally better gas mileage. We were told that this program would contribute to less pollution and help the economy grow. Yet this $2.85 billion initiative had the unexpected effect of dramatically lowering the supply of functioning used cars, which led to higher car prices in the middle of a recession.[31]

It also hurt new car sales in the months following the end of the program, since many people simply bought the car they were going to buy anyway a few months ahead of schedule – lowering the demand later on.

Do you remember when the federal government told us that our gasoline would now have corn-based ethanol added to it? We were told that burning a key ingredient in popcorn would reduce fossil fuel usage and thus help save polar bears from having to stand on floating ice cubes.

Well, it hasn't worked out that way. In fact, even Albert Gore, the Nobel Prize winner who has spent his political career warning all of us about the dangers of global warming, recently acknowledged what scientists have been saying the past few years. Biofuels made from corn actually *increase* carbon emissions at a faster rate than simply burning fossil fuels.[32] Billions of dollars of taxpayer money has been artificially reallocated to corn-growing states and corn-supporting politicians only to see a net increase in the very pollution we were supposed to be fighting.

In 2011, crop prices – led by corn – increased dramatically, leading to higher rates of food scarcity for hundreds of millions of poor people around the globe.[33] By forcing up the demand for corn used to make ethanol, the amount of corn left for human consumption has fallen. This has naturally led to higher prices for corn, and products with corn and corn byproducts. Ranchers feed their cattle with products that contain corn. With higher prices for feed, they must raise prices for beef and other meat products. This leads to a reduction in the ability of financially-challenged families to buy as much food as they otherwise would. Higher corn prices have also led more and more farmers to grow corn rather than wheat, soybeans, and other crops. This trend has caused a decrease in the supply of wheat and soybeans, and higher prices for those crops, too.

In 2015, President Obama pledged to reduce carbon-dioxide emissions by 80% by 2050. Hillary Clinton and Bernie Sanders also supported this plan.[34] To achieve this goal would mean reducing CO2 emissions from 16.15 tons (2012 emissions) to 3.23 tons, which is the equivalent of what Mexico produces.

President Obama did face an obstacle to this goal when the Supreme Court blocked his Clean Power Plan in 2016, arguing that the Environmental Protection Agency was wrong to argue that taking into account the costs imposed on the states was not a relevant factor.[35]

President Obama and Mrs. Clinton might be surprised by a recent study of 74 million human deaths in 384 locations across 13 areas that found that 0.5% of all deaths were associated with heat, while 7% of deaths are related to cold. In the U.S. alone, about 9,000 people die every year from heat, while 144,000 die from cold.[36]

THE QUESTIONS EVERY ECONOMY MUST ANSWER

Now that we have looked at how economics applies to personal choices and public policy we turn our attention to broader issues of how a basic economy functions. An *economy* is the mechanism through which resources are organized to meet the wants and needs of those who live in society. An economy can be as small as an individual – after all, you are attempting to use resources to meet your own needs – or it can mean the economy of a neighborhood, city, county, state, region of a state, region of a country, country, continent, or planet!

Typically, the mechanism (more on this in chapters 2 & 3) for "organizing" resources is one that combines profit-seeking businesses and individuals with government agencies. Rarely do we see only the government making all of the choices and rarer yet do we see anarchy – only individuals making the decisions.

No matter what mechanism that is selected, there is no guarantee that poverty will disappear or that everyone will have the same access to goods and services. The economy of any area is a dynamic force made up of one, or perhaps billions of people, all striving to survive and prosper. The degree to which the people will achieve this goal depends on how participants choose to manage resources and allocate goods and services. In essence, every economy must answer three questions:

- What to produce?
- How to produce it?
- For whom to produce?

A big part of the answer to the first two questions entails an examination of the resources that an economy has to work with. The state of Utah has a large number of highly educated individuals and wonderful natural tourist attractions. Combined with an entrepreneur-friendly busi-

ness environment, Utah enjoys the designation as one of the best states to seek a job in.[37] West Virginia, on the other hand, while rich in coal resources, is poor in terms of its policies toward new businesses and poor in terms of human capital. Thus, West Virginia continually ranks near, or at the bottom of the United States in terms of wealth creation.[38]

One of the reasons the United States is relatively rich is because of our abundant natural resources. After all, when compared to most nations, the U.S. has much more farming land, fresh water, timber, minerals, and natural gas. However, bountiful natural resources are not the ticket to prosperity. In Congo, a nation rich in diamonds, tyrannical rulers have kept the Congolese people from participating in free trade.[39] On the other hand, Hong Kong is extremely poor in natural resources but extremely rich in terms of per capita income (income per man, woman and child) because – as we will see in the next chapter – the government there largely leaves people alone.

Having a lot of labor is also a nice thing to have. China's economy is growing rapidly because China has hundreds of millions of adults who are available for work. The same is true for India. Yet, having a lot of people is also not sufficient to satisfy the needs of an economy. India and China are still poor countries compared with much of Europe and America.

What about capital? Is that the magic solution to the problem of scarcity? While it is true that having tremendous technology, large amounts of equipment and other physical tools helps, one only needs to look at the former Soviet Union to find out how useless capital is as a primary creator of wealth. Not only did the Soviet Union rank near the top of the world in military and space technology, but in terms of human capital, this country had some of the brightest engineers and scientists on the planet. Yet, it was not enough to take care of the average Soviet citizen.

As it turns out, in answering the first two questions of "What?" and "How?", the key resource seems to be the number of entrepreneurs an economy has. That's right. Those nations that tell people to take risks creating new products and services – and then allow the risk takers to

CONCEPT CHECK

Log onto www.jackchambless.com. Find the MISC. link and scroll down until you find the Heritage Foundation findings on global economic freedom by country. You should take a detailed look at a variety of nations and the factors used to evaluate their level of entrepreneurship to gain a clearer picture of why some resource-rich countries are relatively poor, while other resource-poor countries are rich.

© kavalenkava/Shutterstock.com

reap, and keep, the rewards stemming from those risks, tend to be the richest countries in the world.

ANSWERING THE QUESTION OF "FOR WHOM?"

Perhaps the most difficult question facing the participants in any economic system is the question of who will get the goods and services that are produced. The answer to this question has contributed to revolutions, wars, and wide-ranging government intrusions into people's lives. In many respects, this seems to be a fairly simple question. In the United States, this question is answered largely by the concept of *ability to pay*.

Ability to pay means that if you want a ticket to see the Boston Red Sox play baseball or a new iPod or three pounds of Alaskan king crab, all you have to do is look at the price of each of these items. Then look at how much money you possess. If you have enough money and you agree with the price that is required, congratulations! You will have your ticket, your iPod, and your crab.

There are some goods and services, however, where the concept of ability to pay creates a dilemma for our country. Should police and fire protection be based on the ability to pay? Can you imagine calling 911 one night to report a serial killer walking around in your house only to have the operator ask you if you have the requisite $49.95 to capture killers, plus a $500 surcharge for serial killers? What about fire protection? You can see the problems there.

The fire department announces that from now on you have to pay $15 per month for fire department insurance. If you pay and your apartment catches on fire, you are covered. What if you pay but your neighbor decides to use his $15 to buy crack? You wake up one night with your hair on fire because your neighbor's crack pipe fell off his bed and set the entire complex ablaze.

What about higher education? Should college tuition be based on the ability to pay? In 2016 Hillary Clinton and Bernie Sanders campaigned on the promise to provide "free" tuition at public universities and community colleges. Given the rising level of student debt, both Mr. Sanders and Mrs. Clinton clearly understand the problem of financial scarcity and the cost/benefit calculation many American families must make each year with respect to college. They also seem to understand the relationship between an educated society and a healthy economy. However, not everyone would agree that every family in America should be able to afford college.

Frederic Bastiat, a renowned economist of the nineteenth century, once argued that public education is a form of *plunder*, where government steals from the taxpayers (some of whom are childless) to provide for education.[40] To Bastiat, education is best left to the private sector (i.e. pay for your own kid to go to school) if society desires a high-quality education for our children and minimal plunder of the taxpayer.

Who's right? It depends on whether you are prone to use normative or positive analysis.

> ➤ **Normative analysis is a way of looking at economic policies that rely on our value judgments about "what ought to be."**

If you believe that education is fundamentally a right of our existence, you would probably argue that every person, regardless of ability to pay, should be entitled to higher education.

> ➤ **Positive analysis is a way of looking at economic policies without the use of one's value judgments. With positive analysis, statements such as "If, then" are common.**

If you are in the camp that argues that "if" we provide education for all, "then" we must be willing to face higher taxes, overcrowded classrooms, a huge surplus of college graduates flooding labor markets, more unemployment for many with college degrees and so forth,[41] you are making a statement based on fact rather than feelings. The "then" part of the equation is often referred to as the *law of unintended consequences*.

> ➤ **The law of unintended consequences is the principle that for every law, or policy that is implemented with one set of objectives or goals in mind, there is always one or more unintended consequences that will stem from that law or policy.[42]**

If you tend to view the world from a more normative standpoint, it should be pointed out that a very real danger of that way of thinking is that you lose sight of the economic costs and unintended consequences of your value judgments. Saying education should be a right begs the question as to what cost we should incur to guarantee this right. Imagine what higher education would look like if every American family could afford it. First, to make it affordable to the poorest of the poor, it would have to be provided at virtually no cost to millions of Americans. Yet, it would still cost money to pay for all of the classes, facilities, and support services. If millions could get higher education at no personal cost, who would pay the balance due?

You cannot say, "Other families with kids in college" because raising the tuition and fees on middle-income and

CONCEPT CHECK

Where does normative and positive analysis come in to the debate on the issue of how best to reduce police shootings of black Americans? Does the Law of Unintended Consequences impact your answer? Why, or why not? Would it be rational for police departments to reduce their presence in urban areas in the wake of these shootings? Why, or why not?

© a katz/Shutterstock.com

wealthier families would then make it more unaffordable for many of them.

Could we keep all of the fees low to no cost at all and simply force professors and administrators to work for dramatically lower, subsistence-level pay? Ask your economics professor what she or he would do if their pay was slashed to help make education affordable for every American.

Could we simply tell the taxpayers they have to foot the bill to keep the costs low? The problem there is that the taxpayers with no children would have a terrific complaint and those with children in college – who are now paying higher taxes – would be worse off as well.

As you can see, when good intentions bump up against economic reality we start to see very quickly why, in economics, there is no such thing as a "free lunch."

ENDNOTES

1 See "Slump Over, Pain Persists" by Sara Murray, *The Wall Street Journal*, September 21, 2010; and "Lost Decade for Family Income" by Conor Dougherty & Sara Murray, *The Wall Street Journal*, September 17, 2010.

2 See "Negative $4,019," *The Wall Street Journal*, August 25-26, 2012 page A12.

3 See "The Great Recession has been Followed by the Grand Illusion," by Mortimer Zuckerman, *The Wall Street Journal*, March 26, 2013 page A13.

4 See "America Gets a Raise, Finally" *The Wall Street Journal,* September 14, 2016.

5 See "Secrets of the Economist's Trade: First, Purchase a Piggy Bank" by Justin Lahart, *The Wall Street Journal*, January 2-3, 2010. *The Wall Street Journal* by Dow Jones & Co. Copyright © 2010. Reproduced with permission of Dow Jones & Company, Inc. in the format Textbook via Copyright Clearance Center.

6 See http://www.infoplease.com/spot/osamabinladen.html

7 See "Repeal the Patriot Act" by Andrew P. Napolitano, *The Wall Street Journal*, March 5, 2004.

8 See "Nobel Winners for Economics are a New Breed" by Jon E. Hilsenrath, *The Wall Street Journal*, October 10, 2002, pg. B1.

9 See "Why Game Shows Have Economists Glued to Their TVs" by Charles Forelle, *The Wall Street Journal,* January 12, 2006.

10 See "Inequality and Happiness: Are Europeans and Americans Different?" by Alberto Alesina, Rafael Di Tella and Robert MacCulloch, Unpublished paper, June 2002; and "Anger over free-market reforms fuels leftward swing in Latin America" by David J. Lynch, *The USA Today*, February 9, 2006.

11 See "Riding it Out" by Linda Shrieves, *The Orlando Sentinel*, September 1, 2005; and "Excuses for braving Katrina are fatal" by Joshua Norman, *The Orlando Sentinel*, February 19, 2006.

12 See "Racism Studies Find Rational Part of Brain Can Override Prejudice" by Sharon Begley, *The Wall Street Journal*, November 19, 2004, page B1.

13 Economist Ulrike Malmendier has found that buyers on eBay – an online auction site – are given the chance of bidding on an item or using a feature called Buy it Now, where the shopper can buy immediately, 43% of the time, buyers ended up bidding up the item to a higher price than the original Buy it Now price. For some buyers, the research found a greater desire to win the auction than to save money using the Buy it Now feature.

14 See "ObamaCare and the '29ers', *The Wall Street Journal*, February 23-24, 2013.

15 See "ObamaCare and the Part-Time Economy" by Andrew Puzder, *The Wall Street Journal,* October 11, 2013 page A15.

16 See "Here Comes the Unaffordable Careless Act" by Karl Rove, *The Wall Street Journal*, August 29, 2013 page A13 and "The Coming ObamaCare Shock" by Daniel P. Kessler, *The Wall Street Journal,* April 30, 2013 page A17.

17 See "An Oil Thirsty America Barreled into 'Dead Sea'" by Neil King Jr. & Keith Johnson, *The Wall Street Journal*, October 9-10, 2010.

18 See "BP relied on Cheaper Wells" by Russell Gold & Tom McGinty, *The Wall Street Journal*, June 19-20, 2010.

19 See "BP Relied on Faulty U.S. Data" by Neil King Jr. & Keith Johnson, *The Wall Street Journal*, June 24, 2010; and "Drilling for Better Information" by L. Gordon Croviz, *The Wall Street Journal*, June 28, 2010.

20 See "Obama Decried, Then Used Some Bush Drilling Policies" by Neil King Jr. and Keith Johnson, *The Wall Street Journal*, July 6, 2010.

21 See "Global-warming predictions hurt cause" by Mike Thomas, *The Orlando Sentinel*, January 13, 2011.

22 http://www.buzzle.com/articles/dangers-of-texting-while-driving.html

23 See "Ten Principles of Energy Policy" by Joseph Bast, The Heartland Institute, 2008, pg. 9.

24 See "Not So Hot" *The Wall Street Journal*, August 29, 2007.

25 See "Climate Science in Denial" by Richard S. Lindzen, *The Wall Street Journal*, April 22, 2010, p. A23.

26 See *Energy Economics and Policy* by James M. Griffin and Henry B. Steele, Academic Press Inc., 1986.

27 See "Wind-Power Subsidies? No Thanks." by Patrick Jenevein, *The Wall Street Journal*, April 2, 2013 page A13.

28 See "The Mystery of Energy Independence" by Joseph Bast, *The Heartlander*, June-July 2008.

29 See "What Price Green?" by Anjali Athavaley, *The Wall Street Journal*, October 29, 2007, pg. R6.

30 See "The Carbon Recession" *The Wall Street Journal*, May 12, 2010.

31 See "Ou Est Le 'Cash for Clunkers'?" By Victor Dial, *The Wall Street Journal*, January 7, 2011.

32 See "Al Gore's Ethanol Epiphany" *The Wall Street Journal*, November 27-28, 2010.

33 See "Prices Soar on Crop Woes" by Scott Kilman & Liam Pleven, *The Wall Street Journal*, January 13, 2011.

34 See "How to Lower U.S. Living Standards" by Robert Bryce, *The Wall Street Journal*, September 22, 2015, page A15.

35 See Supreme Court Blocks Obama Administration's Clean Power Plan, by H. Sterling Burnett, *Environment & Climate News*, February 2016.

36 See "An Overheated Climate Alarm" by Bjorn Lomborg, *The Wall Street Journal*, April 7, 2016.

37 See "Incentives Spur Utah's Growth" by Jim Carlton, *The Wall Street Journal*, November 27-28, 2010.

38 See "Robert Byrd's Highways to Nowhere" by Brian Bolduc, *The Wall Street Journal*, July 10, 2010.

39 See "Piles of Diamonds Fail to Enrich Congo" *The Orlando Sentinel*, May 20, 2001.

40 See *The Law*, by Frederic Bastiat, pg. 18.

41 See "Clinton's Free-College nonsense would plunder taxpayers and dupe students" by Jack A. Chambless, *The Dallas Morning News*, August 15, 2016 and "Clinton's Bailout for the College-Industrial Complex, by Charles J. Sykes, *The Wall Street Journal*, August 23, 2016.

42 For example, laws passed to force car manufacturers to increase the fuel efficiency of automobiles has led to more people dying in traffic accidents. Congress wanted to help people save gas and money, but the car companies, to comply with the law, used lighter materials that do not offer a much protection. See "CAFÉ is Bad for Your Health" by Sam Kazman, *The Wall Street Journal*, November 14, 2005, pg. A23; and "Burn, Baby, Burn" by John Tierney, *The New York Times*, February 7, 2006, pg. A25.

CHAPTER REVIEW

1. Does the issue of scarcity enter into a person's decision to become an illegal immigrant? Why, or why not?

2. What is the opportunity cost of marriage? How does the opportunity cost differ from the direct cost?

3. A study published in *The Wall Street Journal* found that football players are more likely to get a concussion as helmet technology improves. Does this mean football players are irrational? Why?

4. Compare and contrast normative and positive analysis in the issue of providing health care benefits to people who live in poverty.

THE ECONOMICS *of* LIBERTY

© pathdoc/Shutterstock.com

*H*istory demonstrates that time and again, in place after place, economic growth and human progress make the greatest strides in countries that encourage economic freedom. Government has an important role in helping to develop a country's economic foundation. But the critical test is whether government is genuinely working to liberate individuals by creating incentives to work, save, invest, and succeed.

RONALD REAGAN

MUCH ADO ABOUT SOMETHING

> All people, however fanatical they may be in their zeal to disparage and to fight capitalism, implicitly pay homage to it by passionately clamoring for the products it turns out.
>
> Ludwig von Mises

Several years ago, Mark Skousen – a world-renowned economist – visited Mongolia to present a series of lectures on economic history. While he was there, he was treated like a rock star. His lectures on the merits of capitalism were met with standing-room-only crowds of people who hung on his every word as he regaled the audience with the story of how capitalism triumphed over communism.

When Professor Skousen shared his experience with me upon his return, I must admit I was pretty jealous. Maybe I felt that way because he is just better at what he does than I am. On the other hand, my jealousy may have come from hearing that his audience received the concept of economic liberty with such attentiveness and appreciation. I actually found myself daydreaming of having students standing on their chairs in wild applause as I lectured on self-interest and private property rights. Then I woke up. What a shame.

Back in the reality of the American college classroom, economists are generally greeted with a heightened sense of apathy and indifference when we lecture on economic freedom. Maybe it is because American college students don't care about such things. Or, could it be that those of us born in a free and prosperous nation simply take liberty as a given? That might be it.

By the end of this chapter you might never take economic liberty for granted again.

WHEN LIBERTY DID NOT EXIST

It is probably hard for you to imagine a world where your chances of being a slave or servant to some king are higher than your chances of being free. However, not so long ago this was precisely the fate that the majority of the world faced, from birth. Today, most people in the world who are wealthy, accumulated their wealth by serving their fellow man. A thousand years ago, most of the world's richest people got rich by plundering and enslaving their fellow man.

In the year 1000, the richest man in Moorish Spain, one of the richest countries in that year, took the name Al-Mansur (Arabic for "The Conqueror"). His name was appropriate, inasmuch as he successfully accumulated more than six million pieces of gold from the raids against Christian Spain.

Bill Gates is rich, but Mr. Gates would be embarrassed to discuss his bank account with Machmud of Ghazni. The ruler of a kingdom of central Asia at the beginning of the second millennium, Machmud resided in an opulent palace with more than 400 poets hired to entertain him.

Machmud maintained his lifestyle by invading India annually for more than 25 years, looting temples for gold and jewels. In 1019, it is recorded, he took so many captives that the price of slaves plummeted for several years. Of course, before Machmud and Al-Mansur, the world had the Egyptian empire that enslaved Jewish people.

After Machmud and Al-Mansur, Britain ruled over much of the world – which did not make the various kings of England many friends in much of Europe, Asia, and Africa. In each instance, ransom, murder, theft, plunder, and slavery were common practices in the process of wealth accumulation.[1]

FROM JOHN LOCKE TO THE "GREAT EXPERIMENT"

John Locke (1632-1704) was an Englishman who lived under the rule of Charles II. He became famous with the publication of two treatises on government in 1690.

From the time the first governments existed until 1690, the world's inhabitants believed (or had accepted the fact) that men derived their rights from government and that any expansion in human, civil, religious, political, or economic rights must therefore come from the hand of government.

Locke's treatises challenged this view. According to Locke, the state of nature was one in which "all men are by nature free, equal and independent" and all enjoy "the rights of life, liberty and property."[2]

Locke argued that people "consent" to enter into social contract – such as offering their labor services to an employer – and "accept the bonds of government" in order to better protect their rights. He argued that government is based on the consent of the people and that an "absolute monarch" is "inconsistent with civil society."

It was Locke's contention that, in its natural state, property is not owned by anyone and that people come to own property by combining their labor with it. In other words, you and I use our skills, education, and training to earn money, and with that money we buy homes, cars, DVD players, and other things. Locke's historically unique position was that government did not own property. He felt that people owned property and that the primary function of government was to protect property rights.

This "natural law" theory of the relationship between government and the people was quite unsettling for the British monarchy – and for good reason. After all, what ruler wants to wake up one morning to realize that a revolutionary groundswell is taking place, and that the basis for the revolt is the idea that government is too big, too oppressive, and too limiting, and that the desired government for the future would be one where the people, rather than some king, would rule?

Government gains power by subjecting people to rules and regulations that limit freedom. The monarchy saw Locke – and his contention that the people have the right to "resume their original liberty" by dissolving their bonds with government – as a direct threat to the king's power.

Locke's work was the basis for the call to revolution within the colonies in the 1700s. Thomas Jefferson ranked Locke as one of the most important thinkers on liberty. In fact, a quick reading of the Declaration of Independence illustrates how heavily Jefferson borrowed from Locke in his defense of the American Revolution[3]:

Source: John Locke, 1632 to 1704. Photograph. Retrieved from the Library of Congress, https://www.loc.gov/item/2004672071/. (Accessed March 10, 2017.)

We hold these Truths to be self-evident, that all men are created equal, that they are endowed by their Creator with certain unalienable Rights, that among these are Life, Liberty, and the Pursuit of Happiness—That to secure these Rights, Governments are instituted among Men, deriving their just Powers from the Consent of the Governed, and whenever any Form of Government becomes destructive of these Ends, it is the Right of the People to alter or abolish it, when a long Train of Abuses and Usurpations, pursuing invariably the same Object, evinces a Design to reduce them under absolute Despotism, it is their Right, it is their Duty, to throw off such Government.

The birth of the United States was the world's first major experiment with government based on the protection of life, liberty and property. Nowhere else on Earth was liberty celebrated as it was in the United States, and yet even our own nation has not enjoyed a history devoid of the zero-sum exploitation of human beings. The institution of slavery lasted until 1865. Even after slavery ended, segregation and discrimination remained.

The taking of the lands that American Indians had lived on for generations, along with the forced movement of these indigenous people and even the slaughter of those who resisted, is a testament to the fact that any government – even one with liberty as the basis of its creation – can selectively ignore the "natural rights" of mankind,

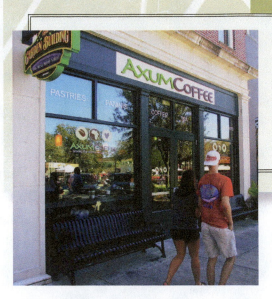

A few years ago, Pastor Renaut van der Riet of Mosaic Church in Oakland, Florida started a coffee shop called Axum. Unlike other coffee shops, Axum donates 100 percent of all profits to the city of Axum, Ethiopia for the express purpose of bringing fresh water and other services to this impoverished area.[11] Does this encourage more, or less profit-seeking behavior by Pastor van der Riet and Axum employees? Why?

Photo courtesy of Jack Chambless

when government's goals are blocked by the liberty of the individual.

Today, more and more nations are experimenting with the concepts born out of the writings of John Locke. Dictators and despotic governments are becoming increasingly rare – and the people of the world happier[4] – as more nations discover the merits of free markets and free people.

LIBERTY AND CAPITALISM

In the last chapter we examined the types of resources every economy uses to determine what goods and services to produce and how to produce them. You may recall that the first three resources – land, labor, and capital – are important, but woefully insufficient in explaining the vast differences that exist in the level of wealth enjoyed by the nations of the world.

World history has shown that those nations that pursue capitalism to the greatest extent possible are the nations that generate the highest standards of living for people up and down the economic spectrum. Capitalism, in its purest form, has delivered more people from starvation and homelessness than any other economic system ever experimented with.[5] In order to better understand how this could be so, we should begin with a definition of capitalism.

> ➤ **Capitalism is an economic system that is based on free exchange, contracts, and self-interested activities that do not violate the right to life, liberty, and private property.**

How many of you have heard that capitalism is an economic system based on greed, lies, stealing, corruption, fraud, exploitation, environmental degradation, and other forms of mean behavior? If this is what you have heard, you are not alone. The media is filled with examples of how much people hate capitalists. How many movies have you seen where some profit-seeking businessperson is the villain? The list is endless.[6]

If you turn on the television, or read the newspaper, you will find many articles on the "absurd" profit being earned by oil executives,[7] or corporate scandals or "heartless" companies charging "outrageous" prices for medicine, homes, or food.

Politicians and religious leaders often jump on the anti-capitalism bandwagon as well. While he was president, Barack Obama once said, "The basic idea is that if we put our blind faith in the market and let corporations do whatever they want and we leave everybody else to fend for themselves, then America somehow automatically is going to grow and prosper."[8] Not to be outdone, Pope Francis argued, "Today everything comes under the laws of competition and survival of the fittest, where the powerful feed upon the powerless. As a consequence, masses of people find themselves excluded and marginalized: without work, without possibilities, without any means of escape."[9]

By contrast, books like *Atlas Shrugged* (by Ayn Rand) celebrate the capitalist as a hero of society – an uncommon sentiment these days.[10]

Looking at the definition of capitalism, it might seem a bit odd that people would find this economic system offensive. After all, don't we all pursue our self-interest to make more money? Don't we all have some – and seek more – private property? Isn't trade and voluntary exchange something we naturally pursue?

HOW THINGS GET DONE

On July 16, 2012 President Obama famously told supporters during a speech, "If you've got a business, you didn't build that. Somebody else made that happen." Now consider these words from Frederic Bastiat 160 years earlier.

> Here are a million human beings who would all die in a few days if supplies of all sorts did not flow into Paris. It staggers the imagination to try to comprehend the vast multiplicity of objects that must pass through its gates tomorrow, if its inhabitants are to be preserved from the horrors of famine, insurrection, and pillage. And yet, all are sleeping peacefully at this moment, without being disturbed for a single instant by the idea of so frightful a prospect. What then, is the resourceful secret power that governs the amazing regularity of such complicated movements, a regularity in which everyone has such implicit faith, although his prosperity and his very life depend upon it? The power is an absolute principle, the principle of free exchange. We put our faith in that inner light which Providence has placed in the hearts of all men, and to which has been entrusted the preservation and the unlimited improvement of our species, a light we term self-interest, which is so illuminating, so constant, and so penetrating, which it is left free of every hindrance.

Think back for a moment to when you were a child. How did you learn to share your toys with other children? Did it come naturally, or was it more comfortable being selfish? Now think about your reason for being in this class. Did you decide to take economics because you wanted to make sure your professor had a full class? Perhaps you are in college because you read somewhere that college graduates are less likely to become criminals, and out of your desire to reduce your neighbor's chances of being robbed you began your college career?

If you have a job, why do you work? Is it so the customers of your company will be happy? Is it so your company will make profit? You know darn well what the answer to every one of these questions is. In every instance, your *self-interest* is the driving force.

Should you feel guilty? After all, shouldn't human beings do things for one another because we love one another and have risen above the Darwinian pursuit of self-preservation? Maybe you do feel guilty, but perhaps you shouldn't.

It is important to acknowledge that there are a lot of things we do out of *benevolence* and *love* for our fellow man. Opening a door for an elderly person or helping a child who has fallen down qualify as examples. Giving our time or money to charity and being faithful to our loved ones is also a good thing to do.

While doing things in a selfless manner is laudable, when we consider most human acts we reach one immutable conclusion: that, inherently, people do things out of self-love.

HOW THIS BOOK REACHED YOUR HANDS

I would like to be able to say that I spent long hours researching and writing this book because I care so much about America's economics students, that I felt compelled to educate them with my words of wisdom. I would like to say that, but it would be a lie. In reality, I wrote this book because I care very deeply about my wife, my children, and myself. I am guilty of being self-interested.

As it turns out, the lumberjack who cut down the tree to make the paper that is in this book is also self-interested. So is the engineer who designed his saw. So is the factory worker who built the saw. The truck driver who hauled the lumber to the paper plant is self-interested. The oil company that made the diesel fuel for the trucker is self-interested, as is the tire maker, the truck manufacturer, and the people who put asphalt on the road from the forests of Oregon to the paper mill in Idaho. Come to think of it, so are the people who made the road signs in Idaho.

Why isn't love of our fellow man enough to provide us with paper?

I am pretty sure the person who created the software I used to word-process this book probably does not care too much about the economic necessities of some college professor in Florida. I'll bet Bill Gates cares about Bill Gates. I think Fred Smith is self-interested, too. He's the guy who runs Federal Express – the company I used to ship book materials to my publisher in Dubuque, Iowa.

Speaking of the publishing company, I know the folks who work there and they are very nice. But there's something funny: They did not offer to publish my book without earning any money from it. How stingy. Kendall Hunt has a motivation known as self-love that leads its employees to desire food, vacations, clothing, and other things that my book helps create. This keeps the company from publishing this book for nothing. After the copy editor put the finishing touches on the book, she sent it to a printing company. Those greedy people actually charged Kendall Hunt money to print the book! The nerve!

Then the book was shipped (free of charge?) to your bookstore that gave you the book for free because you have a nice face, right? No. The bookstore, depending on the level of competition it faced in the textbook market, decided what price to charge you. After all, if they gave books away for free, where would their wages and salaries come from – the tooth fairy?

Then you showed up at the store. Where did you get your money? If you are like most college students, you had to work very hard at a job to earn the money for this book. Did you go to work out of love for your fellow man? Well, did you? You probably went to work out of a love for yourself. The company hired you because they love to make money and you were needed to help them do that.

Once you had your hard-earned money in your hand, you handed it over to the bookstore that sold you the book. Of course, we haven't even touched on the cash register company that helped create your receipt, the corrugated box company that made the boxes your book was shipped in, or the shoe company that made the shoes you wore to walk into the bookstore.

It is quite possible that thousands of people, all working to provide for their own lives, worked together to bring this book to you. Out of the spontaneous behavior of self-loving individuals came the orderly production and distribution of this product.

This idea of "spontaneous order" was championed by the economist, Friedrich Hayek.[12] According to Hayek, the idea that a harmonious, evolving order arises from the interaction of a decentralized, heterogeneous group of self-seeking individuals with limited knowledge. This order, he claimed, was not "designed" nor could be "designed" by a social planner, even a very wise one, but merely "emerged" or evolved spontaneously from a seemingly complex network of interaction among people with limited knowledge.[13] This means that no one person really knows how to create a book. It takes many self-interested people to work together to create this book. As we all act on our self-love, we inevitably serve one another. Therefore, the money we earn could be called "certificates of performance."[14]

With these certificates of performance we earn the right to file a claim on goods and services our fellow man produces. I did not have to care about you to write the book. I only had to care about myself. But out of this self-love, you got your book, I get my royalty checks, and my local grocer, the cable television provider, and many, many others get to acquire my certificates as I patronize their establishments. Adam Smith would be proud of all of us.

THE FATHER OF ECONOMIC THOUGHT

1776 was a watershed year for the United States. In that year our forefathers informed the King of England that they were tired of paying high taxes with little or no say in how their lives would be run. With the signing of the Declaration of Independence came an era in which individuals would be allowed to experiment with newfound freedom to chart the course of their lives.

Across the ocean another document was published that did not create as much controversy as the nasty letter the colonies sent to England, but it would eventually be almost as significant in shaping the lives of people in the United States and around the world.

CONCEPT CHECK

In the winter of 1775 George Washington complained about the "lack of patriotism" that farmers in New England were showing in the wake of a series of price increases that farmers put in place for food sold to American troops preparing to fight the British.[15] Go online to read Leonard Read's classic essay, "I, Pencil" then explain how this essay clearly illustrates the argument that capitalism, not patriotism gave the troops the best odds of being fed that winter.

© Everett-Historical/Shutterstock.com

Adam Smith was a Scottish professor of logic and moral philosophy who, in 1776, published a landmark book titled *An Inquiry into the Nature and Causes of the Wealth of Nations.* The book, originally delivered in lecture form at Glasgow University, was the most comprehensive treatment of economics, and its ramifications for politics, that had ever been attempted. It was in this book that Smith beautifully articulated the proposition that man, by his very nature is driven to make decisions based on the overriding feeling of self-interest. Specifically, Smith said:

> In almost every other race of animals, each individual, when it is grown up to maturity is entirely independent, and in its natural state has occasion for the assistance of no other living creature. But man has almost constant occasion for the help of his brethren, and it is in vain for him to expect it from their benevolence only. He will be more likely to prevail if he can interest their self-love in his favor, and show him that it is for their own advantage to do for him what he requires of them.[16]

Let's ponder the enormity of Smith's statement for a moment and consider its implications. Many of you might be under the impression that Smith is prescribing a recipe for a greedy society, where people care only about their own well-being and do nothing to help their fellow man. In reality Smith is arguing that enlightened self-interest — the type of behavior where both parties end up better off than before, is what gets things done in our world — even when it comes to miracles....

Photo by Hulton Deutsch/Contributer/Getty Images

HOW ADAM SMITH HELPED WITH THE "MIRACLE ON ICE"

On February 22, 1980, I was sitting in the living room of my best friend when, at 13 years of age, I witnessed one of the great moments in the history of the United States – and in the history of self-interested pursuits.

While I did not think of it that way at the time, the victory by the United States Olympic hockey team over the Soviet Union was indeed the triumph of capitalism. In fact, for the 20 men and the coach that led them to the greatest moment in U.S. sports history, the name Adam Smith could have been evoked during the aftermath of this stunning win and it would not have been too far-fetched to do so.

The American economy – and America itself – was in deep trouble in 1980. Prices were rising rapidly, unemployment was over 10% and a terrible sense of hopelessness had gripped the American people. It was also dur-ing that time that the Soviet Union was expanding its doctrine of tyranny in Asia, Africa, and Latin America. In many ways it seemed America's best days were behind us, while the Soviet Union was on the way to the terrible Cold War victory its government had predicted.

That is when 20 college age men and a hockey coach from The University of Minnesota proceeded to save our country from the pits of economic despair.

Most of you reading this book do not recall when the Olympics relied on amateur athletes. That means you also don't recall that the Olympics used to have a whole lot more to do with geopolitics than it does today.

During the Cold War (1947-1991) the United States and the Soviet Union never fired a missile or a bullet at one another. The Olympics turned out to be a political battlefield, where athletes from both nations competed for the implicit right to claim superiority over one another.

In 1980, the U.S. faced a daunting task. The USSR had won the gold medal in hockey in 1964, 1968, 1972, and 1976 and was considered by far, the best team in the world – including the National Hockey League. In fact, the Soviets humiliated a team of NHL All-Stars by a score of 6-0 before the winter games began.

Most of the Soviet players like Vladislav Trediak, Sergei Makarov, and Valery Kharlamov had played together for a decade or more. Many Soviet players, while not allowed to play for money, were handsomely subsidized by their government and were afforded luxuries that the average Soviet citizen could only dream about. In essence, while the

Olympic rules stated that no professionals could compete, the Soviet Union had its own professional players.

On the other hand, the United States could only use players that had never earned money as real professionals. This meant that the team was totally comprised of players that were either in college, or had recently finished college. Most of the players had never played together only seven months before the Lake Placid games. Many of the players despised one another, as a result of heated rivalries between Minnesota and Boston-area athletes.[17]

It was this hand that was dealt to Herb Brooks, the man in charge of putting a team together.

The day before the 26th anniversary of the "Miracle on Ice," I spoke with Jack O' Callahan, one of the more famous players from this team. I asked Mr. O' Callahan to look back on this team and assess the extent to which self-interest played a role in its success. What follows are the questions I asked and Mr. O' Callahan's answers. This should help you see that Adam Smith was never far off from the events that unfolded.

To what extent did self-interest play a role in your willingness to make the sacrifices Coach Brooks demanded of you?

Answer: I can't really look at it as pure self-interest as that implies that all I cared about was myself. However, there was an element of self-interest. I was definitely interested in furthering my development as a hockey player and learning more about myself as an athlete and competitor. I was excited to play for a new coach with new ideas and philosophies and I was determined to play on that team.

My view at the time was that I would not have much of a professional hockey career after the Olympics and I was very excited about being at the Olympic Games, representing my country, sharing that experience with my family and teammates, etc. I totally understood the beauty of being an Olympic athlete, win or lose. I viewed myself as a total team player, but if I try to boil down how much of my efforts were selfish or individual based, it all disconnects. I was interested in challenging myself on whatever level necessary to be a better player and to help make my team a better team so we could reach our potential and compete at the highest level during the games. Is that self-centered? Maybe, but also, maybe not; perhaps, without realizing it, a little of both.

Did the fact that you were an amateur in 1980 make a difference in the effort you put forth?

Answer: Not really, we viewed ourselves as the U.S. Olympic Hockey team and as much as that implied amateurism, we didn't really dwell on that aspect. In a more clear sense, there were no NHL players in those Olympics and therefore everyone was "amateur." We didn't really think about it, that was just what the Olympics were at that time. We were just playing hockey. I don't think any hockey player in an Olympic event or in any important competition would give anything less than their absolute best effort.

The Olympics, the nationalism aspect, the environment, and the code of competitive athletes all demands that. The difference for us is that we spent seven months together growing as a team, learning about one another in a team environment. That aspect made us much, much stronger than had we been 20 quality players thrown together and given 2 days to prepare. Given our preparation experiences, our team was much stronger than 20 individuals taken separately.

Did you and your teammates consider the goal of winning a gold medal to be something that would help your personal careers or were you more interested in the accomplishment of the team as a whole?

Answer: I can only speak to my feelings, but I can probably speak for the team when I say that my thoughts of winning the gold (when I allowed myself to think about it) was only that it would be fun and tremendously rewarding on a team accomplishment level. The part about how this could benefit us as individuals only may have entered our thoughts when the agents started talking to us after we had won.

Also, winning gold did not exactly create a greased skid into the NHL. I spent the next two years playing for the Blackhawks farm team in Moncton, New Brunswick and many guys ended up in the minors for at least a little while, some guys forever. We mostly viewed our Olympic experience as something separate and special, rather than a means to an end. It was all about setting a goal and through a lot of sweat and personal challenges, having an opportunity to reach that goal. The most fun is always in the pursuit, not necessarily the result.

Do you believe that professional hockey players should be used in the Winter Olympics? Why, or why not?

Answer: I like seeing the best players in the Olympics, at every level. If they are professionals, fine, if not, fine also. When there were amateurs, everyone was always saying that the eastern bloc countries were getting paid and there was all this grousing about that. People whine about anything, and if we went back to the way it used to be, they would complain and if we stay the way we are, they'll complain. At least with the only rule being that the best players make the team, the playing field is level. It's the same in the other sports, how do you legislate out athletes that are compensated to compete?[18]

How do you hold other nations accountable to what the US considers professional? Why do we get to make the rules? What we have to accept is that there are great athletes in the world and not all of them are from the US. We need to cherish great athletic feats and accomplishments even when those athletes are not Americans. We also need to look at the positives, not the negatives.

Could part of the reason the Soviet Union lost in 1980 be due to the fact that their players grew up in a Communist system that denied them the opportunity to seek out their self-interest?

Answer: I really don't think any of that mattered. They were just hockey players, like us. In those times of the Soviet Union, their self interest was all about the safety of their families and extended families. Believe me, they were plenty self-motivated. It is all relative. There were many reasons why they lost and one of the main reasons is that the U.S. hockey team in 1980 was highly talented and tremendously prepared. You have to add to that, the fact that the USSR may have been a little over-confident given that they had just beaten us 10-3 and basically were beating everyone else pretty handily.

The confluence of these facts leads me to believe that the reason we had a chance to win was, for that one game, we were better prepared than our opponents who, typically, were the most prepared team in the world. They may have let their guard down. We were definitely better prepared mentally but also, we were much better prepared physically and emotionally than our opponents realized. During those Olympics, we surprised a lot of good teams with our physicality, our raw emotional intensity, our passion, our talents, our abilities, and our overall commitment to one another. It was very special and that is why people continue to talk about it, [37] years later.

In the years following the 1980 games two interesting things have occurred. First, if you watch the Disney movie, *Miracle*, you will notice at the end of the movie, an update on where all of the players from the American team are now. You will undoubtedly notice that the vast majority

of them are capitalists. Many, like Jack O' Callahan, are involved in financial markets. Others are real estate developers, NHL coaches, doctors and public speakers.

The second fact is that since the United States began using professional athletes in the winter games, we have never won another gold medal.

Does this mean that the professional athletes are not self-interested? No. It most likely means that since they are already making hundreds of thousands, if not millions of dollars per year, their individual self-interest has already been attained, making it much more difficult to get excited about playing for free. It also makes it unrealistic that the professionals would give up seven months of pay to train with one another for the Olympics. When combined with the fact that the Cold War is over, it is unlikely we will ever see 20 young men pull off something of this magnitude again – even if it is in our self-interest to see another 'miracle' on ice.

PROFIT VS. NOT-FOR-PROFIT: WHICH MOTIVATION SAVES MORE PEOPLE?

"Our logistics capability in Katrina was woefully inadequate. I was astonished to see we didn't have the capability most 21st-century corporations have to track the flow of goods and services."

Michael Chertoff, Secretary,
Department of Homeland Security

While we are undertaking this thorough investigation of enlightened self-interest, it might be a good time to compare self-interested businesses and individuals to government agencies in order to see why people tend to

© Evan Meyer/Shutterstock.com

SUGGESTED CLASSROOM DEBATE

Senator John McCain once said that America's greatest moral shortcoming is its failure to "devote ourselves to causes greater than our self-interests."[19] Do you agree or disagree with this statement? Why? What do you suppose Adam Smith would say? Do you believe that causes that are "greater than our self-interests" are actually rooted in our self-interests? Why, or why not?

be more frustrated with one than with the other. Can you guess which one? If you yelled, "Government!!" then you are not alone.

Do you remember hurricane Katrina? Do you remember what happened before and after Katrina? If you are not sure, let's refresh your memory.

On March 1, 2006 the Associated Press released video footage of a meeting of federal officials that took place days before Katrina devastated the Gulf Coast. In the video,[20] federal disaster officials warned President Bush that Katrina could breech the levees and flood New Orleans and overwhelm rescuers.[21]

Critics of the Bush Administration point out that Mr. Bush did not ask the federal officials a single question during this meeting. In fairness to Mr. Bush, it really wouldn't have mattered how many questions he asked. The chances of the federal government effectively managing the preparation before the hurricane hit, the response after it hit, the rebuilding years after it hit, or the next time a hurricane hits was – and is still – very small.

This reality is not because storms are unpredictable in their path, size and damage. No, the reason government failed then – and will fail again – is because government does not have the same motivation for doing things as the private sector. The private sector is motivated by profit. When you buy food, do you rely on some government office to supply it, or do you go to the for-profit grocery store? Did the Bureau of Nice Garments make your clothes? Was your car built by the Department of Transportation? You get the idea.

Government agencies, by their very nature, are more likely to be unproductive at solving problems because those agencies are *not-for-profit*. Since profit is not a motive – or even allowed – in the public or government sector, the incentive to find the most economical solution to any given problem is generally lacking without the forced help from taxpayers.[22] The lack of *consequences* also hurts the chances that government will serve us well. When a business operates with a high level of inefficiency and/or incompetence, people can refuse to give their money to that business. Government is the only institution allowed to use force to make you pay for its services. Therefore, if lousy service is offered, you cannot refuse to send your taxes to the agency you are upset with.

Think about Federal Express and the post office. With whom would you trust a life-

critical package? What about government (public) schools versus private schools? Why do private school kids perform better, on average? Why do we see so many reports about the number of foster children whom various state governments have lost?[23] What if a private day care facility lost kids or let them die? How long would it take for bankruptcy proceedings to begin?

In 2016, banking giant Wells Fargo got caught creating thousands of fake accounts for customers who never asked for them. This ruined the credit ratings of many Americans and led to a firestorm of congressional interrogations of Wells Fargo's CEO. That same year, the company that produces the Epipen – a device that saves the live of allergy sufferers – was grilled by Congress for astounding increases in prices.

To many Americans, these are just two examples of companies that "got caught" doing bad things and are symptomatic of a larger problem of corporate greed and corruption. However, when mounting evidence shows up that various government agencies like the Bureau of Indian Affairs or the Bureau of Land Management have either lost billions of taxpayer dollars,[24] or have helped burn down forests and homes through careless oversight,[25] do we get to bankrupt that ineffective government agency, or do they simply get more money to try to fix their mistakes?

Consider how often you do business with a person or company that really does not care much about you. That may seem harsh, but do you believe that strangers who serve you and produce the goods you buy love you? Do you need them to love you?

In reality, they do not. Yet, out of the last 100 times you bought something from one of these strangers, how many times did the good or service satisfy you? If the answer is close to 100, why is that? Well, it is because they

Can capitalism clean up this mess?

SUGGESTED CLASSROOM DEBATE

The Cruisers and Convoys Act of 1708 established a prize court that awarded British naval crews with cash from the sale of enemy ships they seized.[26] What would happen if the U.S. government established a prize court that awarded military personnel and law enforcement officials with cash for capturing terrorists?

love themselves and know that unless you come away happy you will no longer give them your money. This ability to deny strangers a livelihood keeps them motivated to serve you well.

By contrast, think about your interactions with government agencies. What would happen if your local coffee shop decided to operate like the driver's license office? What if private schools mimicked the efforts of your local public school? How long would your favorite restaurant be open if it served you as fast and efficiently as the TSA agents at the airport or the Internal Revenue Service when you have a tax question? What if your doctor modeled his office after the Department of Veteran's Affairs? What if the toll roads worked like the "free" government roads? You get the idea.

So, what if we privatized FEMA and turned over its operations to Wal-Mart? Why Wal-Mart? Well, for starters it could be argued, rather easily, that Wal-Mart did a far better job before and after Katrina than FEMA did. Before the storm hit, Wal-Mart began stocking the shelves of stores in the Gulf region with goods that would be in great demand before and after the storm. Trucks were lined up in the outlying areas of the devastated areas waiting with even more water, food, and other necessities.

Even though Katrina damaged 89 Wal-Mart stores, the company moved quickly to reopen most of them and provided over $4 million in housing aid for its workers. In total, 2,500 trailer-loads of water and emergency supplies arrived to assist the Red Cross and other charities while FEMA officials were still arguing about how bad the hurricane really was.[27]

Meanwhile, by every measurable account, FEMA, along with local politicians in New Orleans and Louisiana, blew it.

Not only was there the colossally slow response to the disaster before and after it struck,[28] but as it turns out, FEMA used our hard-earned tax dollars in a way that would get every executive at Wal-Mart arrested and sent to prison.

Six months after the storm, records indicated that many residents of the Gulf Coast had taken advantage of FEMA's lax oversight to bilk taxpayers out of tens of millions of dollars. Residents impacted by the storm were supposed to get $2,000 per household. They were told to provide a name, social security number, and address.

Some people were able to get payments of $2,000 up to *18 times* by using fake names, fake social security numbers, social security numbers of dead people, and addresses that often were nothing more than vacant lots.[29] In addition, you may recall hearing about all of the blue tarps that the government bought with our money at prices far greater than what we would pay at Home Depot. You might also remember all of the trailers you bought for victims of Katrina that were never delivered or the hotel rooms and cruise ship cabins people stayed in for months with no regard to the cost. In fact, when hurricane Gustav hit in September of 2008, people had to be evacuated from trailers that the taxpayers were still subsidizing three years after Katrina.

This is not new for FEMA. In the past, FEMA has used your money to pay for floods in areas that did not flood, hurricane damage in areas where hurricanes did not strike, and fires in areas that did not burn.[30]

What if Wal-Mart, or Lowes, or Home Depot did that? Can you imagine how far the stock price of each company would fall? Profits would decline, the corporate bond rating would fall and the stockholders would demand a government investigation of the fraud and mismanagement of their resources.

Fortunately, we don't see corporations engaging in consistently stupid and wasteful behavior. The free market has a way of finding companies — and punishing them — for behaving wastefully. It is called losses, bankruptcy, and unemployment.

Of course, this does not mean that capitalists never do bad things. We sometimes see that people who call themselves capitalists really don't know Adam Smith at all.

When "Capitalists" give Capitalism a Bad Name

Because of capitalism, we have endless varieties of toothpaste, bread, clothes, cars, music, and more. Because of capitalism, we have almost immediate responses to consumer demand for faster computers, picture-taking cell phones[31] and portable Blu-Ray players. Capitalists like Bill Gates have given away billions of dollars in profits to help with vaccines around the world and other causes.[32] Yet, the men and women who have created all of these incredible goods and services have simultaneously proven that they often suffer from *socio-political myopia* – a short-sighted view of how society and political systems shape our desires within the economic system.

What did Bernie Sanders mean when he called for an end to Crony Capitalism?

In effect, businesses and individuals often succumb to the age-old temptation to be greedy. It can also cause people who claim to be supporters of capitalism to lobby for special rules and regulations designed to favor their companies and harm their competitors. The lobbying leads to a great deal of money flowing to the politicians willing to assist in this game of "crony-capitalism."[33] Television journalist, John Stossel, has championed the cause of enlightening people of the dangers of subsidies, bailouts, and special favors for businesses.[34]

The recession of 2007-2009 helped shed a great deal of light on how far away we are from the ideas of Adam Smith. Under Adam Smith's view of capitalism, our government would not have taken trillions of dollars away from current and future taxpayers to rescue General Motors, the banking and insurance industries, or home-owners who bought houses that they ultimately could not afford.

A key function of capitalism is that people are allowed to pursue whatever peaceful exchanges they desire, as long as they understand that they will bear the responsibility for their choices. Under capitalism, we see rappers, dancers, software engineers, chefs, musicians, and mechanics all seeking ways to make more money by doing something better, faster, or cheaper. When capitalism works well, we end up with folks like Tom Hanks and Taylor Swift – millionaires who gave us what we wanted. Capitalism does not pass judgment on how wealthy we should be allowed to be or whether what we offer to society is really important. The system simply tells us to proceed to take risks but not to expect the forced taking of our fellow man's money if we do not succeed.[35]

Corporate leaders often complain that union workers make too much money and that government bosses them around with respect to the pay of lower-level workers. Yet, it was corporate leaders who failed to notice that disgruntled individual workers might someday become disgruntled *groups* of workers. Now many labor unions have pushed wages to levels that are arguably not commensurate with productivity gains (see the airlines), and profits have suffered.

In addition, minimum wage laws also impact businesses in a negative way. Owners and managers contend that they should be allowed to freely contract with labor for a wage that equals the prevailing equilibrium pay rate. The right to freely enter into contracts with one another over pay is a major part of what makes capitalism work. Without contracts – and the enforcement of them – we see nations collapse into poverty as people become increasingly mistrustful of one another.

However, pragmatic capitalists must understand that human beings do not always like the wage that is created in a contractual agreement. If people believe they "deserve" more money, they will use the arm of government to alter contracts where they can. This was the case in the 1930s when people – increasingly distrustful of businesses – pushed for the establishment of the minimum wage.[36] We will see in chapter 8 the minimum wage laws have been a disaster for poor and unskilled Americans. Yet, people at the bottom of the economic ladder continue to support the forced increases in compensation under the guise of "fairness" and "justice." This explains why, in 2014, President Obama proposed an increase in the minimum wage to $10.10 per hour in his push for greater income equality in the United States.[37] It also explains why Bernie Sanders and Hillary Clinton campaigned for a $15 per hour minimum wage in 2016.

Lawsuits concerning employee discrimination, sexual harassment, and product liability are increasing in number every year. One wonders how litigious our nation would be if fast-food restaurants – seeing the lawsuit trend – would have rushed in with healthier foods or nutrition facts *before* the lawyers smelled money. One wonders if corporations would face as many discrimination suits if they would have seen the growing social intolerance for economic injustice toward minorities and women. How could any rational business not see the demonstrations of the 1960s leading to new laws for the disabled, the elderly, and women? Yet, we still have businesses losing millions because of the myopic way they see societal evolution.

The elections of Barack Obama was a culmination of a series of events that mirrored the election of Franklin D. Roosevelt in 1932. Voters in 1932 and 2008 were convinced that capitalism had failed and that something had to be done to rein in greedy businesses. Fear has a way of causing human beings to vote for drastic changes. Roosevelt convinced voters that Wall Street had ruined their lives and that government had to step in and pass massive new regulations and taxes in order to restore the economy. Mr. Obama repeatedly argued that the economy had been driven into a ditch by the failed practice of unfettered capitalism.

President Obama, echoing the sentiments of millions of Americans, embarked on a campaign to re-regulate capitalism. In the next chapter, we will take an extensive

© wavebreakmedia/Shutterstock.com

look at the new laws and regulations passed during his first term in office.

It is important to note that economists are frequently asked, "Was the housing crisis and subsequent recession proof that capitalism failed?"

Economics students must understand that recessions and financial crises are a natural part of capitalism. No economy ever grows uninterrupted. Whether it is from floods, drought, wars, disease, sudden drops in consumer spending, changes in government policies, or any number of other events, we always experience economic downturns. We will see throughout the rest of the book that the housing crisis was a predictable event – as was the recession that followed. Capitalism provides no guarantees of constant wealth, just the guarantee that you will be allowed to pursue wealth.

CAPITALISM AND TOLERANCE

One of the primary reasons why there are no nations practicing pure capitalism is due to the fact that under capitalism, there are many areas where we would all have to restrain our own moral convictions in order to preserve the freedoms of our fellow citizens.

If you have ever thought that you are an Adam Smith capitalist, consider these questions:

Would you be willing to live in a country where gambling, drugs, and consensual prostitution between adults is legal? What are your views on social security, Medicare, unemployment compensation, farm support payments, foreclosure relief, and Aid to Families with Dependent Children?

What about income and property taxes? What should the law be in those areas?

Capitalism – in its purest form – requires a great deal of tolerance on your part and on the part of your fellow man. In a capitalistic society, the aforementioned markets where drugs are bought and sold, gambling occurs, and adults agree to exchange money for sexual favors, would all be legal. If someone uses the money that they peacefully earned to engage in any of these activities, liberty demands that we not interfere so long as our rights are not infringed upon. In capitalism, there would be exactly zero pennies allocated to fix the troubles of your fellow man, courtesy of taking the tax dollars (private property) away from some other party. Doing so would constitute theft (more on this in the next chapter). In capitalism, income and property taxes would not exist – these constitute a confiscation of property. The entire country, your state, county, and city would be run on voluntary (sales) taxes.

So, are you a capitalist?

Would anything be illegal under capitalism? Of course. Arson, child pornography, slavery, murder-for-hire, and any other market where someone's life, liberty, or property is threatened or taken away, would be against the law. Capitalism does not mean "anything goes." It means that you have the liberty to pursue your self-interest in a peaceful manner.

It also means your private property is protected.

Capitalism and Your Rights

After such an extensive look at the importance of self-interest, you might be inclined to think that all an economy needs to be healthy is a bunch of money-pursuing individuals running around inventing new things and showing

© kaprik/Shutterstock.com

up for work on time. While that helps, it is only half the root structure of a healthy economic system. The other half of the equation is what happens to your money and your property once you have worked so hard to earn it.

The 1776 Virginia Declaration of Rights reads:

> That all men are by nature free and independent, and have certain inherent rights, of which when they enter into a state of society, they cannot by any compact, deprive or divest their posterity; namely, the enjoyment of life and liberty, with the means of acquiring and possessing property, and pursuing and obtaining happiness and safety.

In 1795 the Supreme Court declared:

> The right of acquiring and possessing property, and having it protected, is one of the natural, inherent, and unalienable rights of man. No man would become a member of a community, in which he could not enjoy the fruits of his honest labor and industry. The preservation of property then is the primary object of the social compact.[38]

Finally, in Thomas Jefferson's First Inaugural Address, he stated:

> A wise and frugal government shall restrain men from injuring one another, shall leave them otherwise free to regulate their own pursuits of industry and improvement, and shall not take from the mouth of labor the bread it has earned. This is the sum of good government.[39]

When the Founding Fathers declared that we all have a right to *life* that means that government has an obligation to protect us from people who try to end our lives. No one should be allowed – they argued – to take your life if you are not trying to violate the rights of that person.

Liberty, to the Founders, meant your right to do *anything that is peaceful*. Thomas Jefferson would have never had a Constitutional problem with your selection of belly rings, tattoos, cigarettes, or rap music. He and the other Founders supported your right to independent thoughts and even offensive words – so long as your words do not take away the life, liberty, or property of others.

SUGGESTED CLASSROOM DEBATE

In 2010, a judge in Minnesota ordered a woman to pay $1.5 million in fines for sharing 24 digital songs. Do you believe that sharing music, books, movies, and other files over the Internet constitutes a violation of someone's private property rights[40]? Why or why not?

Finally, the Founders believed that if you pursue your self-interest in a peaceful manner, you should be allowed to keep the money you earn and peacefully spend it as you wish, again, as long as you are not violating the rights of others. Your *property rights* are thus the right to pursue, and keep, the money and goods you acquire.

YOUR INTERESTS

> "Capitalism has become more responsive to what we want as individual purchasers of goods, but democracy has grown less responsive to what we want together as citizens."[41]
>
> Robert Reich

Under our Constitution, the government has a legal obligation to secure our rights. We don't have to prove we deserve our rights; they are part of the contract we have with our elected officials. What can be confusing for some people is the distinction between rights and interests. Simply put, you have an interest in anything that is not a right. Confused? Consider this example:

A man walks into a store hoping to get change for a dollar. He asks the shop owner for change so he can make a phone call. The shop owner tells him that he will give change only if the man buys something.

The man brings a canned soft drink back to the counter. The shop owner tells him the drink costs 85 cents. The potential customer claims that if he pays 85 cents, he will not have enough money left to make the phone call.

Does the customer have a right to change? Does he have a right to a soft drink for less than 85 cents? For that matter, does he have a right to be in the store at all?

Clearly, the customer has the right to not be killed for peacefully entering the store. The law is also pretty clear

Should people with 12 children have a right to this?

that if a store is "open to the public," the public can shop around without fearing that forced transactions will take place. If the man buys the drink for 85 cents, he has the right to the remaining 15 cents of his private property. He also has the right to 12 ounces of soft drink if that is what the soft drink company indicates is in the can.

However, he has no right to the price he desires or to be in the store under any circumstances he deems correct. The key here is that people must *consent* to exchange private property. Until the terms of exchange are agreed upon, he simply has interests he wants met.

With that in mind, what if we simply expanded the list of rights, to include a house?

WHY WE HAVE ONLY THREE RIGHTS

Several years ago Representative Charles Rangell (D) from New York stood before the U.S. Congress and proposed an amendment to the United States Constitution that read:

> Constitutional Amendment—States that all U.S. citizens shall have a right to a home, which shall not be denied or abridged by the United States or any State.

Representative Rangell was joined by co-sponsors, Donna Christensen, Carolyn Kilpatrick, Dennis Kucinich, and Barbara Lee. Not joining Mr. Rangell were Thomas Jefferson, James Madison, Ben Franklin, George Washington, and the other Founding Fathers who were spinning in their graves that day.

Using normative analysis, it is easy to see why one might argue that such an amendment is a kind and decent thing to do. After all, who among us derives any joy from seeing a homeless person? No one I know.

However, if we apply positive analysis we would ask, "If housing is a right, then how would government secure this right?"

Think about it for a minute. Does the government have to steal from your neighbor to secure your property? Does the government have to kill someone to secure your right to life? Does the government have to tell people who like rap music not to listen to it so you can enjoy jazz? The answer is pretty obvious. To secure our rights the government has to use force only if someone is violating our rights.

If the government says we have the right to life, liberty, property, and a home; that means you no longer have to do anything to have a home. It is automatically yours. But how do we give you a home if you do not currently have one? If you guessed that the government would have to take away the homes and/or money of other people, then congratulations! You are on your way to becoming an economically literate member of the human race.

Maybe the government would have to go around and find out how many people have more than one home and force them to give away all but one. Maybe the government could force people to work for Habitat for Humanity, to build homes for everyone who does not have one. Maybe the government could ask for donations to the IRS for the "Right to a Home Fund." Oh, for a minute there I forgot that the government rarely asks for donations. Instead, the government would most likely raise taxes to pay for all the new homes that would have to be built.

I wonder: If we would have the right to a home, would we have the right to say what kind of home? Could really nice people who have no home get a mansion? Could people with big families and no home get a four-car garage? Would the disabled be guaranteed the right to a home that accommodates their disabilities? Would the elderly be guaranteed the right to a home with free heating? Would the lazy get free elevators to help them get upstairs?

As you can see, when we evaluate the economic effects of adding to the list of rights we find many hidden costs that would have dire consequences. This is precisely

© Maria Dryfhout/Shutterstock.com

what is occurring in Zimbabwe, where President Robert Mugabe has unilaterally taken property away from farmers who have owned land for years and has transferred it, by force, to people who had an interest in having the land. As a result, widespread famine and disease has broken out as the new owners, ill-equipped to farm the land, have been unable to feed Zimbabwe's people.[42]

Perhaps that is why the Founders realized that life, liberty, and property were all that could be guaranteed as rights. The rest of the list – our interests – would have to be earned.

CAN CAPITALISM SAVE THE MANATEE?

"If your culture is based on free enterprise, anything-goes capitalism, then everything's going [extinct] sooner or later."

James Lloyd, professor, University of Florida[44]

When the Pilgrims arrived in America they learned a powerful and almost fatal lesson during their first years in our country. Initially, they intended to establish a system of common ownership of property with everyone working for the common good and taking from the general storehouse what they needed. They nearly starved to death.[45]

The next harvest, however, was plentiful.[46] It was during the third winter that Governor Bradford told the remaining colonists that, in the spring, people would be allowed to grow food on their own property and trade with one another. No longer would *common property* – property owned by all, and therefore owned by no one – be utilized.

At the dawn of the 21st century, the West Indian Manatee is severely endangered, with approximately 4,800 manatees left in the world. What do the pilgrims and

SUGGESTED CLASSROOM DEBATE

In 1823 Edward Smith – a Canadian official based in Fort Chipewyan – noted that the arrival of white fur traders had decimated the animal population that Canadian Indians had relied upon for their survival for centuries. Smith noted, "….their country exhausted of beaver and large animals and by whom? – By the wild ambitious policy of the whites who study their own interest first and then that of the natives."[43] In your opinion, did the Canadian (and for that matter, the American) Indians have an *interest* in large animal populations, or a *right* to large animal populations? Why?

endangered animals have in common? They each teach a valuable lesson of the problem of *common property* and the role of private property, self-interest, and entrepreneurship.

Whenever something is common property it tends not to be taken care of very effectively. All you have to do to prove this statement is look out your window the next time you are at a stop sign. On the ground you will see enough cigarette butts to cover half of North Carolina. Since no one owns the street, no one has an explicit interest in making sure the street is taken care of. How many smokers do you suppose throw cigarette butts on their driveway? A driveway is private property, which means ruining it would exact an economic price on the person who owns it. This is the *Tragedy of the Commons*. Common property is not treated in an efficient manner because no one individual has an incentive to preserve the good.

Manatees are an example of the common property problem. No one owns the waterways where they travel. No one owns the manatees. Therefore boaters have little express interest, beyond avoiding fines, to take care of manatees. You can see several examples of this fact by the number of boat motor scars that are pervasive on the manatees in Florida.

However, since many people have a desire to see, and interact with manatees, some entrepreneurs near Crystal River, Florida have opened businesses that take people out in wetsuits to swim with the manatees.

The manatee tour operators that have joined this market have a vested interest in making sure that people proceed through these waters at a safe speed. The vested interest is the potential for lost profit if manatees continue to be killed and eventually become extinct. By selling the rights to swim with manatees, they make sure that their boats are not intrusive to this animal and that customers obey the very strict regulations on approaching them.

If we simply asked people to be careful and left it at that, how many people – with no financial stake at all in the manatee population – would make sure they preserved this species? Asking our fellow man to be careful near the manatees might persuade some to heed the rules or do the morally right thing. However, our chances of seeing the manatees survive increase with private property rights being established in these waterways. With private property comes the right to put a price on that property. The moment that happens people are much more judi-

Photo courtesy Jack Chambless

cious in their use of the resource and measurable positive externalities are created.

> ➤ **A positive externality exists when a transaction between two parties leads to spillover benefits to individuals who were not part of the original transaction.**

Economists argue that when a transaction between two parties leads to each party being made better off and third parties benefiting as well, the most prudent thing the government can do is encourage this activity so that we will all be better off.

The manatee tour business is not alone in injecting capitalism into environmental protection. In South Africa, more than 10,000 private hunting reserves help fuel a $620 million per year hunting industry. Here, safari hunting enables wealthy individuals to shoot lions, leopards, elephants, buffalo and rhinoceros. Some 16 million animals roam these preserves, compared to less than four million in the national parks. On the preserves, breeders and private security teams have helped increase the population of these animals while on government-run land, poachers are decimating them.[47]

In Mongolia, wild goat herders are given training on alternative ways to earn income in the global economy in exchange for not killing the endangered snow leopard that often threatens their goats. This program has helped move people out of a relatively low paying occupation into a higher paying one, all while helping save the remaining 1,000 or so leopards.[48] In China, tiger farms are being

CONCEPT CHECK

In 2013, a massive typhoon devastated the Phillipines. Why is it far more likely that recovery will be slower in the Phillipines than it will be for the victims of flooding in North Carolina in 2016? Visit http://www.heritage.org/index/ to assist your answer.

used to raise tigers for sale to people who believe in the medicinal value of these animals. This has helped ease pressure brought by poaching wild tigers.[49]

Finally, environmental groups are learning about Adam Smith as they try to protect pristine lands. One San Francisco-based group recently purchased 600,000 acres from a timber company in order to keep northern Idaho's St. Joe River from being developed by home and hotel-building companies.

Increasingly, environmental protection groups are learning that a very effective way of preserving land, plants and animals is to rely more on the exchange of private property through conservation banks, private property trades, and purchases of vital ecosystems rather than through waiting on government or mass pleas for people to "work together for the common good."[50] In places where common property rights abound, fishing grounds become depleted and rare species face extinction.[51]

These examples – and many more that can be found with research on your part – illustrate the powerful role that incentives play in an economy where private property rights and self-interest are combined. When used properly, self-interested behavior can accomplish both economically desirable outcomes as well as morally, or socially-desirable outcomes.

WHY CAPITALISM AND EMINENT DOMAIN LAWS ARE NOT COMPATIBLE

"You look at it and think, Gosh almighty, we've got to get this stuff out of here. I mean, it's so bad looking. Those houses are in horrible condition."

Boone Pickens

Who is Boone Pickens and what is he talking about? Well, he is a billionaire oilman and graduate of Oklahoma State University. Not long ago, he donated $165 million to his alma mater to build a sports complex. The problem

is that many people in the neighborhood where OSU wanted to build the complex did not want to accept OSU's offer of 70% of the value of their homes to move.[52] In the opinion of Mr. Pickens and OSU, it was time for the government to kick the homeowners out so OSU athletes can have enough room to stretch…

We close this chapter with a recent development that every man, woman and child in the United States should be aware of. While it has been years in the making – and was addressed by the Founders – the issue of what *eminent domain* really means has only recently been settled in the United States Supreme Court. The ramifications of this decision continue to reverberate around the U.S. and cast a long shadow over the future of liberty-based capitalism.

If you take a quick look at the fifth amendment to the Constitution you will see that the Founding Fathers gave the government the power to take your home or business away from you, as long as it was for the purpose of serving the public (military bases, highways, bridges and so forth) and as long as the government provided you with a just price for your property. Thus, the phrase "eminent domain" means "superior ownership."[53]

For the bulk of the life of the United States, eminent domain cases revolved around projects that largely served the common good of the citizens of the U.S. In 1795, Supreme Court justice William Paterson said, "The despotic power, as it is aptly called by some writers, taking private property when state necessity requires, exists in every government. It is, however, difficult to form a case, in which the necessity of a state can be of such a nature, as to authorize or excuse the seizing of landed property belonging to one citizen, and giving it to another citizen." However, in the past couple of decades, more and more cases have cropped up where the government has taken away private property from one person only to ostensibly hand it over to another *private* entity.[54] Clearly, you did not read anything in the Constitution that provides for any person or company taking away your property, so what gives?

Suppose you live in a city that has a professional sports team. One day the owner of the team decides that he would like to build a new stadium – in your neighborhood, and the ones next to your neighborhood. He shows up at a

SUGGESTED CLASSROOM DEBATE

Did the Founding Fathers make a mistake by ever allowing the taking of private property for any reason? Is it possible to achieve the greater good without ever having to resort to forced confiscation of private property? Why, or why not? Does pure capitalism have room for eminent domain? What is President Trump's background on this issue? Conduct YouTube research to find out.

meeting of all the homeowners and offers to pay all of you 10% more than the assessed value of your homes; 80% of the residents agree, 20% – including you, disagree.

He buys out most of your neighbors and then offers you and the remaining holdouts 30% more than the market value. More people agree to sell, but you and many others refuse to sell at that, or any price.

The owner then goes to the city council and tells them of his dilemma. After all, he can't have your house in the middle of the field, can he?

The city council tells him that he will just have to find another spot. Since a football stadium is a private business (does he give away tickets and food for free?), there is no Constitutional provision for taking your home.

Then he tells the city council that you and your neighbors collectively pay $147,331.09 per year in property taxes and, if he is allowed to move in, he will pay over $2 million in property and sales taxes to the city.

"So what," says the city council.

Then he leans forward and asks them, "What do you use taxes for?"

"Well, taxes are put toward public use projects," replies the council.

"Precisely," says the owner. "If you kick these people out, I will pay more than them in taxes and thus, you will have more money to put toward expanding projects that benefit the public!"

The next thing you see is a bulldozer crushing your house.

KELO V. NEW LONDON, CONNECTICUT

"The beneficiaries are likely to be those citizens with disproportionate influence and power in the political process, including large corporations and development firms. As for the victims, the government now has license to transfer property from those with fewer resources to those with more. The Founders cannot have intended this perverse result."

Sandra Day O' Conner, former Supreme Court Justice in her dissenting opinion in *Kelo v. New London, Connecticut*

On June 24, 2005 I was standing in a bait shop in Tyler, Texas preparing for a day of fishing with one of my old friends from high school. I had promised my wife that while we were on vacation I would avoid reading newspapers, inasmuch as the stories in them make me even more pessimistic than I naturally am.

I happened to glance over at the newspaper rack when I noticed that the *Dallas Morning News* had a headline about eminent domain.

As much as I wanted to resist, I couldn't. I picked up the paper and there in front of me was the news that private property rights – and capitalism itself – had been dealt a significant blow.

Would President Trump agree that is a proper use of eminent domain?

Susette Kelo and her friends put up an incredibly laudable fight. When the city of New London told her to get out so developers could put up something "superior" to her home, she took her government to court. The case worked its way through the system where it was inevitably decided – by one vote – that she, and the rest of us, were simply occupying a space rather than enjoying the rights we were intended to have.

Writing for the majority in this 5-4 decision, Justice John Paul Stevens argued that, "promoting economic development is a traditional and long accepted function of government" and that local officials are better positioned than federal judges to decide what's best for a community.[55] Immediately following the ruling, the mayor of Arlington, Texas declared, "This is the final decision, the final appeal. I don't think there is anything out there that is a danger to us now."[56]

What was the mayor talking about? If you guessed a new football stadium for the Dallas Cowboys, congratulations.

The Cowboy's owner, Jerry Jones wanted a new stadium. Standing in his way were 15 homes, or lots, and 4 apartment complexes. Not any more. The new stadium opened in 2009.[57]

As a side note to this discussion, the planned development in New London, Connecticut was for a new campus for the Pfizer Corporation. It was never built and today, where Susette Kelo's house once stood there is a giant pile of dirt.[58]

CAPITALISM AND CHARITY

One of the most pressing questions for proponents of capitalism is, "who will take care of the poor, the elderly and the infirmed?"

If you answer, "no one," not so fast.

In 2014 alone, private citizens in the United States gave $358.38 billion to charity – the highest figure in 60 years. This figure occurred at the same time the U.S. was experiencing the slowest economic recovery in more than 70 years. It is worth noting that this figure represents an amount of money that is greater than the entire economic output of most nations in the world.

Why would a nation whose economy is largely rooted in capitalistic principles give anything to help the world's poor? After all, as we will see in the next chapter, hard-working Americans are already paying hundreds of billions of dollars in taxes every year to support social welfare spending for the poor, the disabled and the elderly. Why give on top of what we are forced to pay?

Because we can.

In most nations around the world, citizens are either relatively poor or heavily taxed to the point where giving to others in need is not a viable option. America's nearly $18 trillion economic output puts us in the position to voluntarily part with our income and profits to do even more than we are compelled to do.

The Founding Fathers – the authors of American capitalism – supported this model.

According to Thomas G. West in his book, *Vindicating the Founders:*

> From the earliest colonial days, local governments took responsibility for their poor. However, able-bodied men and women were generally not supported by the taxpayers unless they worked. They would sometimes be placed in group homes that provided them food and shelter in exchange for labor. Only those too young, old, weak or sick, and who had no friends or family to help, were taken care of in idleness.

While it may come as a surprise to you that a combination of local government welfare and private charity dates back to the early days of our nation, it should not. After all, capitalism celebrates the concept of voluntary cooperation. Many human beings in capitalistic nations choose to voluntarily cooperate with other people who are in need of food, clothing and shelter. It is because of our great wealth that we can afford to do this. Oppressed

SUGGESTED CLASSROOM DEBATE

Many of the poorest nations in the world are in Africa – a continent that is rich in natural resources. Many economists who study Africa have found that higher levels of foreign aid have actually caused poverty to increase in Africa.[61] Yet, Bill Gates has argued that Africa needs more – and better aid.[62] Use the footnotes provided to research poverty in Africa, then discuss with your classmates whether or not capitalism would work better than aid.

nations – like many we will examine in the next chapter – do not have the means to do this.

ENDNOTES

1 This is still the case for many nations today. North Korea's Kim Jong il, Burma's Than Shwe and Sudan's Omar al-Bashir are but a few of the tyrants that ruin the lives of their people with the denial of liberty.

2 For more on Locke, see http://plato.stanford.edu/entries/locke/ as well as *Locke, Jefferson and the Justices: Foundations and Failures of the U.S. Government* by George M. Stephens, Algora Publishing, New York, 2002.

3 It is also important to note that the founders borrowed from the Iroquois Indians in creating a nation based on liberty and property rights. See "The Founding Sachems" by Charles C. Mann, *The New York Times,* July 4, 2005.

4 See "Survey Says: People are Happier" by Matt Mabe, *Business Week,* August 20, 2008.

5 See *The Making of Modern Economics* by Mark Skousen, M.E. Sharpe, 2002; *How Capitalism Saved America* by Thomas J. DiLorenzo, Crown Forum, 2004; *The Triumph of Liberty*, by Jim Powell, The Free Press, 2000; *The Commanding Heights* by Daniel Yergin and Joseph Stanislaw, Simon & Schuster, 1998; and *Give me a Break* by John Stossel, Harper Collins, 2004.

6 See "Hollywood has a New Villain," by Deborah Hornblow, *The Orlando Sentinel,* August 13, 2004.

7 See "Backlash Spreads as Profit Surges at Oil Companies" by Jeffrey Ball, John J. Fialka and Russell Gold, *The Wall Street Journal,* October 28, 2005. See *The Triumph of Liberty*, by Jim Powell, The Free Press, 2000, p. 19.

8 See "Capitalism Saved the Miners," by Daniel Henninger, *The Wall Street Journal,* October 14, 2010.

9 See "Pope Francis, Unfettered" by William McGurn, *The Wall Street Journal,* September 22, 2015.

10 See "Capitalist Heroes" by David Kelley, *The Wall Street Journal,* October 10, 2007.

11 See "Church hopes coffee house will change lives of Ethiopians" by Jeff Kunerth, *The Orlando Sentinel,* January 14, 2014.

12 For more on Hayek see *Friedrich Hayek: A Biography* by Alan Evenstein, Palgrave Publishers Ltd., New York 2001.

13 See the essay entitled, "I, Pencil" by Leonard Read at http://www.econlib.org/LIBRARY/Essays/rdPncl1.html and http://cepa.newschool.edu/het/profiles/hayek.htm for more on Hayek.

14 See "Giving Back" by Walter Williams at www.jewishworldreview.com.

15 See *1776* by David McCullough, Simon & Schuster, New York, 2005, page 57.

16 See *An Inquiry into the Nature and Causes of the Wealth of Nations*, Adam Smith, the Modern Library, New York, p. 15.

17 See *The Boys of Winter*, by Wayne Coffey, Crown Publishers, 2005.

18 Mr. O'Callahan has hit on an interesting idea here. While many people believe that Olympians were amateurs up until the last couple of decades, in reality there were many professional athletes centuries ago that competed in the Olympics. See "UF Scholar Shakes Up History of Olympics" by Jack Stripling, *The Gainesville Sun,* February 18, 2006.

19 See "Candidates Join to Tout Their Faith" by Charles Babington and Beth Fouhy (AP), *The Orlando Sentinel,* August 17, 2008.

20 Log onto OrlandoSentinel.com/news then click on Nation/World for the video.

21 See "In Tape, Bush Warned on Katrina" by Margaret Ebrahim and John Soloman, *The Orlando Sentinel,* March 2, 2006.

22 See "Clean Energy Sources: Sun, Wind and Subsidies" by Jeffrey Ball, *The Wall Street Journal,* January 8, 2010, p. A13.

23 See "Foster-care Abuse Rises Sharply" by Rene Stutzman, *The Orlando Sentinel,* June 22, 2002.

24 See www.earthportals.com/Portal_Messenger/bia.html

25 See www.naiaonline.org/body/articles/archives/forest_burn.htm

26 See "Incentives vs. Government Waste" by John Steele Gordon, *The Wall Street Journal,* May 14, 2010, p. A19.

27 See "How Wal-Mart Responded to Katrina" by Beth Hoffman, *The Freeman,* October 2005, pg. 10.

28 See "Officials Standoff Stymied Response" *The Orlando Sentinel,* September 11, 2005; "Behind Poor Katrina Response, A Long Chain of Weak Links" by Robert Black, Amy Schatz, Gary Fields and Christopher Cooper, *The Wall Street Journal,* September 6, 2005.

29 See "Audit Finds FEMA Bilked of Millions" by Megan O'Matz, *The Orlando Sentinel,* February 14, 2006.

30 See "FEMA Says it Overpaid" by Megan O'Matz and Sally Kestin, *The Orlando Sentinel,* January 11, 2006; "Wildfires Sparked Furry of Claims" by Sally Kestin, *The Orlando Sentinel,* September 18, 2005; and "Cheaters Get 'Easy Money' from FEMA" by Sally Kestin, Megan O'Matz, John Maines and Jon Burstein, *South Florida Sun-Sentinel,* September 18, 2005.

31 For example, in Africa, capitalism has led to millions of people being connected to family members for the first time in years as cell phone makers continue to lower prices and offer more towers. See "Cell Phones Catapult Rural Africa to 21st Century" by Sharon LaFraniere, *The New York Times,* August 25, 2005.

32 See "Yes, Bill Gates really does think he can cure the world," *The Economist,* January 25-February 4, 2005.

33 See "An Economy of Liars" by Gerald P. O'Driscoll Jr., *The Wall Street Journal,* April 20, 2010, p. A21.

34 For an extensive look at this issue see http://stossel.blogs.foxbusiness.com/2010/01/14/crony-capitalism-v/

35 One company, Southwest Airlines, was the only airline to refuse a taxpayer-financed bailout after the attacks of September 11th. Now, Southwest is routinely the only airline turning a profit. See "Southwest's Earnings Soar" *The Orlando Sentinel,* April 15, 2005; and "Orlando's New No. 1" by Beth Kassab, *The Orlando Sentinel,* January 19, 2006.

36 See "Paul Remarks Have Deep Roots" by Jonathan Weisman, *The Wall Street Journal,* May 22-23, 2010, p. A3.

37 See "$10.10 minimum-wage plan spurs debate" *The Orlando Sentinel,* January 14, 2014.

38 See the Virginia Declaration of Rights (1776), in Founders Constitution, ed. Kurland and Lerner, 1:6.

39 See Vindicating the Founders: Race, Sex, Class and Justice in the Origins of America, by Thomas G. West, Rowman & Littlefield Publishers, Inc., 1997, p. 38; and Thomas Jefferson, First Inaugural Address (1801) in Writings, 494.

40 For more on this issue, see "Don't Stop Believing in Risk of Song Sharing" by Joe Barrett, *The Wall Street Journal,* November 5, 2010.

41 See "Supercapitalism is good for consumer, bad for the citizen" by Robyn Blumner, *St. Petersburg Times,* September 23, 2007, pg. 5P.

42 See "Zimbabwe's economic fall unprecedented 'in peacetime'," by Lesley Wroughton, *The Globe and Mail,* July 27, 2005.

43 Source: The Royal Alberta Museum; Edmonton, Alberta, Canada.

44 See "Lovable But Not Flashy" by Linda Shrieves, *The Orlando Sentinel,* September 28, 2005.

45 See "The Tragedy of the Commons" at http://www.srmason-sj.org/council/journal/oct99/gcmesoct.html and www.americanheritage.com/98/oct/022.htm. "Property Rights: Basis of Prosperity" by Carol Saviak, *The Orlando Sentinel,* November 22, 2007.

46 See "The Essence of Americanism" by Leonard Read, from a 1961 lecture at the Foundation for Economic Education.

47 See "A Bull Market of a Different Kind" by Patrick McGroarty, *WSJ. Money,* Spring 2014.

48 See "In Mongolia, Incentives to Keep Leopards Alive" by Leslie Chang, *The Wall Street Journal,* June 17, 2002, pg. A17.

49 See "China's Tiger Farms Spark a Standoff" by Shai Oster, *The Wall Street Journal,* February 13-14, 2010.

50 See "Saving the Environment: Money Talks" by Malcolm G. Scully, *The Chronicle of Higher Education,* November 23, 2001; "Green Groups See Potent Tool in Economics" by Jessica E. Vascellaro, *The Wall Street Journal,* August 23, 2005; "A Fish Story" *The Wall Street Journal,* November 6, 2003; and "Conservation Banks Catch On, Aiding Wildlife and Builders" by John J. Fialka, *The Wall Street Journal,* February 22, 2006.

51 See "Global Fishing Trade Depletes African Waters" by John W. Miller, *The Wall Street Journal*, July 18, 2007; and "Sad Truth About Tigers in India" by Mehul P. Dixit, *The Orlando Sentinel*, August 9, 2007.

52 See "Boone Picken's Gift to Oklahoma State Sparks Local Rivalry" by Ryan Chittum, *The Wall Street Journal*, March 30, 2006.

53 See http://www.fff.org/freedom/fd0412a.asp for more on the history of eminent domain.

54 There are thousands of such cases. See, for example, "Eminent Domain Takes Center Stage in Redevelopment Debates" by Samuel R. Staley, *Budget & Tax News* (The Heartland Institute), April 2005; "Daytona wins right to force Boardwalk sale" by Ludmilla Lelis, *The Orlando Sentinel*, August 20, 2005; Eminent Domain: Is It Only Hope for Inner Cities?" by Ryan Chittum, *The Wall Street Journal*, October 5, 2005; "Chicago May Seize Homes, Businesses for Airport" by Steve Stanek, *Budget & Tax News* (The Heartland Institute), December 2005.

55 See "Eminent Domain Upheld" by Hope Yen, *The Dallas Morning News*, June 24, 2005; and "Court Says Public Purpose Trumps Private Property Rights" by Steve Sanek, *Budget & Tax News* (The Heartland Institute), August 2005.

56 See "In light of stadium, ruling pleases Arlington" by Jeff Mosier and Jim Getz, *The Dallas Morning News*, June 24, 2005.

57 There is some good news. After this ruling, many states began enacting legislation that would make it more difficult for private property owners to lose their homes. One bank (BB&T) even adopted a policy of refusing to loan money to any business that was seeking to use eminent domain over another private party. See "Utah Bans Eminent Domain Use by Redevelopment Agencies" by Henry Lamb, *Environment & Climate News* (The Heartland Institute), June 2005; "States move to protect property" By Emily Bazar, *USA Today*, August 3, 2005; "Bill puts a rein on controversial view of eminent domain" by Kenneth R. Harney, *The Orlando Sentinel*, November 6, 2005; and "Financial giant takes a stand on eminent domain" by Brooke A. Masters, *The Orlando Sentinel*, January 26, 2006.

58 See http://video.foxbusiness.com/v/3952136/stossel-on-eminent-domain/#sp=show-clips

59 See https://givingusa.org/giving-usa-2015-press-release-giving-usa-americans-donated-an-estimated-358-38-billion-to-charity-in-2014-highest-total-in-reports-60-year-history/

60 See *Vindicating the Founders* by Thomas G. West, 1997 pp. 132-133.

61 See "Why Foreign Aid is Hurting Africa" by Dambisa Moyo, *The Wall Street Journal*, March 21-22, 2009; "Africa Needs Growth, Not Pity and Big Plans" by Matt Ridley, *The Wall Street Journal*, November 27-28, 2010; and "A Continent of New Consumers Beckons" by Peter Wonacott, *The Wall Street Journal*, January 13, 2011.

62 See "Africa Needs Aid, Not Flawed Theories" by Bill Gates, *The Wall Street Journal*, November 27-28, 2010.

CHAPTER REVIEW

1. What would capitalism, in its purest form, say about the institution of slavery?

2. From the perspective of Adam Smith, would it be legal for gas stations to raise prices during a hurricane? Why, or why not?

3. Where do hockey sticks come from? Be specific and don't forget about "I, Pencil."

4. Why are food stamps and income taxes inconsistent with the principles of capitalism?

THE ECONOMICS *of* SECURITY

© larry1235/Shutterstock.com

We all declare for liberty; but in using the same word we do not all mean the same thing. With some the word liberty may mean for each man to do as he pleases with himself, and the product of his labor; while with others, the same word may mean for some men to do as they please with other men, and the product of other men's labor. Here are two, not only different, but incompatible things, called by the same name – liberty. And it follows that each of these things is, by the respective parties, called by two different and incompatible names – liberty and tyranny.

ABRAHAM LINCOLN

THE OPPOSITE OF LIBERTY

"Denying families that security {in the form of unemployment benefits} is just plain cruel. We're a better country than that. We don't abandon our fellow Americans when times get tough – we keep the faith with them until they start a new job."[1]

President Obama

As the proud father of three children, I know all too well how important it is for them to feel safe and secure. When they were little they would ask me to lie next to them when a late-night thunderstorm rolled through our town. They used to ask me to go upstairs before them, to turn on the lights because the darkness was a little unsettling. By providing them with the security they desire, I made them feel comfortable at those particular moments. What they did not realize is that there is a trade-off between security and freedom. Every time I went upstairs ahead of them to secure them, they lost the freedom to be upstairs alone to play and/or get into mischief without Daddy bothering them.

The same is true with respect to the relationship between government and our economic system. For many people capitalism is undesirable because this system inherently requires *personal responsibility*. In our natural state, we seek to avoid pain. As a result, we humans will seek to have someone else shoulder the responsibility for our choices if we can. The moment we ask government to bear responsibility for our shortcomings we invite government into our lives to guide our behavior and restrain our liberty.

As we saw in chapter two, individuals often reject the choice of maximum liberty and personal responsibility, as they call themselves capitalists! The examples are endless. After September 11th, the airline "capitalists" ran to Washington, D.C., to beg Congress for a $15 billion bailout to help cover the inevitable losses that were going to accrue from fewer people flying. The steel industry recently asked for – and got – higher taxes placed on foreign makers of steel. The steel "capitalists" did not want to face the competition that comes from Russia and other countries. Farm "capitalists" get billions of dollars every year in tax money to keep them in farming. Artists get more than $100 million of your money each year because they feel they could not make enough money on their own in the capitalistic art market. And so on and so on.

Of course, private citizens also often desire protection from the normal pitfalls of life. More than 70 percent of all taxes you pay is now transferred to another human being. This could be in the form of food stamps, where in 2017 over 43 million Americans were recipients.[2] It is also Social Security and Supplemental Security Income recipients, which exceed 65 million Americans.[3] It even includes millionaires who now receive your money to cover their health expenses. Under the new health care legislation the *Wall Street Journal* found that:

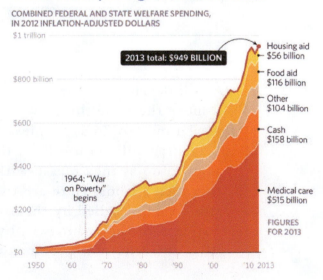

Total Welfare Spending Reaches $949 Billion

COMBINED FEDERAL AND STATE WELFARE SPENDING, IN 2012 INFLATION-ADJUSTED DOLLARS

2013 total: $949 BILLION

- Housing aid $56 billion
- Food aid $116 billion
- Other $104 billion
- Cash $158 billion
- Medical care $515 billion

FIGURES FOR 2013

1964: "War on Poverty" begins

Source: Heritage Foundation research using data from U.S. Office of Personnel Management and other official government sources.

In many states, an elderly person may own a home valued at $802,000, plus home furnishings, jewelry and an automobile of uncapped value while receiving long-term Medicaid support. In addition, they are allowed to have various life-insurance policies, retirement accounts with unlimited assets, $115,920 in assets for a spouse, income from Social Security, and a defined-benefit pension plan.[4]

THE FANNIE MAE & FREDDIE MAC STORY...

When home values began to collapse and foreclosures accelerated in 2007-2010, many Americans – who would have been furious if the government limited how much profit they could earn on their home – begged the government to provide assistance when prices moved the other direction.[5]

The monumental downturn in this market culminated with the U.S. Treasury Department announcing the government takeover of the mortgage companies Fannie Mae and Freddie Mac in September 2008.

Each of these companies were chartered by the government but operated as private firms with shareholders and private sector relationships with businesses and individuals.

For years when a person would take out a mortgage on a home, the bank that processed and provided the initial loan would sell the note on the house to one of these two giant firms. But the bank would not simply sell one loan at a time. Banks all over America would bundle together thousands and thousands of loans and sell the package as "pooled mortgages," that allowed investors in Freddie Mac and Fannie Mae to earn profits from the loans that were bought from the banks.[6]

The problem was that those profits turned into enormous losses when the housing market began to see a collapse in prices. One of the principle causes (but not the only cause) of this downturn can be traced back to 2002.[7]

On June 18, 2002, President Bush gave a speech on, among other things, the state of home ownership in America. Mr. Bush said,

The goal is, everybody who wants to own a home has got a shot at doing so. The problem is we have what we call a homeownership gap in America. Three-quarters of Anglos own their homes, and yet less than 50% of African Americans and Hispanics own homes. That ownership gap signals that something might be wrong in the land of plenty. And we need to do something about it.

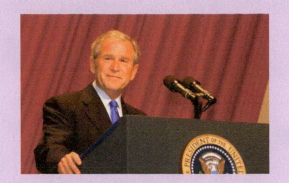

We are here in Washington, D.C. to address problems. So I've set this goal for the country. We want 5.5 million more homeowners by 2010 – million more minority homeowners by 2010. Five-and-a-half million families by 2010 will own a home. That is our goal. It is a realistic goal. But it's going to mean we're going to have to work hard to achieve the goal, all of us. And by all of us, I mean not only the federal government, but the private sector, as well.

I'm going to do my part by setting the goal, by reminding people of the goal, by heralding the goal, and by calling people into action, both the federal level, state level, local level, and in the private sector.

And so what are the barriers that we can deal with here in Washington? Well, probably the single barrier to first-time homeownership is high down payments. People take a look at the down payment, they say, 'that's too high, I'm not buying.' They may have the desire to buy, but they don't have the wherewithal to handle the down payment. We can deal with that. And so I've asked Congress to fully fund an American Dream down payment fund which will help a low-income family to qualify to buy.

We believe when this fund is fully funded and properly administered, which it will be under the Bush administration, that over 40,000 families a year – 40,000 families a year – will be able to realize the dream we want them to be able to realize, and that's owning their own home.

The second barrier to ownership is the lack of affordable housing. There are neighborhoods in America where you just can't find a house that's affordable to purchase, and we need to deal with that problem. The best way to do so, I think, is to set up a single family affordable housing tax credit to the tune of $2.4 billion over the next five years to encourage affordable single family housing in inner-city America.

The third problem is the fact that the rules are too complex. People get discouraged by the fine print on the contracts. They take a look and say, 'well, I'm not so sure I want to sign this. There's too many words. There's too many pitfalls.' So one of the things that the Secretary is going to do is he's going to simplify the closing documents and all the documents that have to deal with homeownership. It is essential that we make it easier for people to buy a home, not harder. And in order to do so, we've got to educate folks. Some of us take homeownership for granted, but there are people – obviously, the home purchase is a significant, significant decision by our fellow Americans. We've got people who have newly arrived to our country, don't know the customs. We've got people in certain neighborhoods that just aren't really sure what it means to buy a home. And it seems like to us that it makes sense to have a outreach program, an education program that explains the whys and wherefores of buying a house, to make it easier for people to not only understand the legal implications and ramifications, but to make it easier to understand how to get a good loan.

There's some people out there that can fall prey to unscrupulous lenders, and we have an obligation to educate and to use our resource base to help people understand how to purchase a home and what – where the good opportunities might exist for home purchasing.

Finally, we want to make sure the Section 8 home-ownership program is fully implemented. This is a program that provides vouchers for first-time homebuyers which they can use for down payments and/or mortgage payments.

So this is an ambitious start here at the federal level. And, again, I repeat, you all need to help us every way you can. But the private sector needs to help, too. They need to help, too. Of course, it's in their interest. If you're a realtor, it's in your interest that somebody be interested in buying a home. If you're a homebuilder, it's in your interest that somebody be interested in buying a home.

And so, therefore, I've called – yesterday, I called upon the private sector to help us and help the homebuyers. We need more capital in the private markets for first-time, low-income buyers. And I'm proud to report that Fannie Mae has heard the call and, as I understand, it's about $440 billion over a period of time. They've used their influence to create that much capital available for the type of homebuyer we're talking about here. It's in their charter; it now needs to be implemented. Freddie Mac is interested in helping. I appreciate both of those agencies providing the underpinnings of good capital.[8]

If we look at the long history of home ownership in America, it was a simple reality of life that if you wanted a home you had to have good credit, stable employment, and normally a down payment of 20% of the value of the home or banks would turn you away.

Mr. Bush – and the federal government – put pressure on the banking sector to loosen those rules in order to provide more security to prospective homebuyers.

From 2002 through much of 2006 millions of Americans with shaky credit, an unstable employment picture and little or often no money down, were able to qualify for loans as a result of this pressure to extend capital to more people.

As we will see in chapter seven, the demand for homes was artificially inflated to the point where prices skyrocketed and people began pouring money into new subdivisions and investment properties that could be easily "flipped" for a profit.

In Florida, Nevada, Texas, California and other pockets of the country, there seemed to be no end to the increase in home values.

When the end came – and it always does – the very same banks, investors and homeowners who so jubilantly jumped into the housing market – even when it was not financially sound to do so – were then left with rapidly declining values and an inability to make payments, whether it was to investors or to other banks.

Rather than allow the market to punish those who were financially reckless – and therefore set the stage for a more efficient and economically sound housing and banking market in the future – the federal government opted to takeover Fannie Mae and Freddie Mac and infuse $200 billion of the taxpayers' money into these newly nationalized entities.[9]

The mortgage bailout is not the end of the story. It would take a thousand pages to cover the vast array of security-based programs that have evolved over the last several decades. In this chapter, we will look at how the economic systems of communism, socialism, and the mixed economy seek to create – or impose – security in order to battle the problem of scarcity. The results range from horrific human suffering to mere inconvenience and annoyance.

COMMUNISM – THE ULTIMATE SECURITY BLANKET?

Several years ago, I had the opportunity to debate a Marxist economist at one of America's foremost private universities (to watch the debate go to https://www.youtube.com/watch?v=Wdjz2zCCXU0).

After our nearly two-hour dialogue I drove to an Irish restaurant with the professor I debated, along with a few of his colleagues who also professed to be followers of Karl Marx. Over some for-profit beer and some for-profit food, we began to discuss the nature of our work. When one of them asked me how many classes I teach in a typical semester, I said, "Seven."

"Seven!?!" He shrieked. "You're exploited!"

I tried to explain to him that it was my choice to teach seven classes, but he insisted that I only thought I wanted to teach seven classes. In reality, he argued, my employer was simply taking advantage of me instead of paying me a decent enough salary to teach only two or three classes. I am not sure what the word "decent" means, but I do know that Karl Marx would have been proud of my fellow economist for recognizing my "suffering."

Karl Marx was a German philosopher who, after 18 years of reflection, angst, and deliberation, produced one of the most influential books in the history of economic thought. *Das Capital* (German for the Capital) was a 2,500 page, four-volume treatise on markets, capitalism, and the perceived exploitation of human beings. In this breath-takingly complex document was a recurring theme: that enlightened self-interest, contrary to the writings of Adam Smith, is a destructive, exploitative force, rather than the force of good. Marx went so far as to argue that:

> Capital is dead labour, that vampire-like, only lives by sucking living labour.

Marx was not oblivious to the inner workings of free markets. His fundamental understanding of labor as an input in the production process was sound. He even bought and sold American and English stocks, earning enough money to write his colleague, Friedrick Engels in 1864 and brag, "The time has now come when with wit and very little money one can really make a killing in London."[10]

Where Marx severely departed from Adam Smith was in his argument that the nature of capitalism is to monop-olize labor resources and, in turn, exploit workers by earning profit on the surplus value that they generated.[11] By surplus value, Marx meant the difference between the wages labor is paid and the price charged for a good or service. For Marx, labor was the sole determinant of value therefore there should be no profit for any business – only returns to labor for their efforts.

Along with Frederick Engels, Marx went on to publish *Manifesto of the Communist Party* that provided a detailed prescription for saving the world from the clutches of capitalism. Among the items included in their recommendations were:

1. Abolition of property in land and application of all rents of land for public purposes

© Dariush M/Shutterstock.com

2. A heavy progressive or graduated income tax
3. Abolition of all right to inheritance
4. Confiscation of all the property of all emigrants and rebels
5. Centralization of credit, the means of communi-cation and transport in the hands of the state.[12]
6. Centralization of the means of communication and transport in the hands of the State.
7. Extension of factories and instruments of production owned by the State; the bringing into cultivation of wastelands, and the improvement of the soil generally in accordance with a common plan.
8. Equal liability of all to labour. Establishment of indus-trial armies, especially for agriculture.
9. Combination of agriculture with manufactur-ing industries; gradual abolition of the distinction between town and country, by a more equitable dis-tribution of the population over the country.
10. Free education for all children in public schools. Abolition of children's factory labour in its present form. Combination of education with industrial pro-duction.

As it is easy to see, Marx reviled the concept of eco-nomic liberty and believed that the government should take away money and property to provide for the equality and security of the masses.

Marxian ideology got its day in the sun on November 7, 1917, when Russia fell under the weight of revolution to Vladimir Lenin and the Council of People's Commissars. On December 30, 1922, the Union of Socialist Soviet Republics (USSR) came into being. Immediately the leaders of the Soviet Union made trade, private property and the participa-tion in free markets a criminal act and replaced market-based exchange with government planning in an attempt to answer the questions of "What," "How," and "For whom."

Applying the Theory of Communism

> Sixteen men in Moscow today are attempting one of the most audacious economic experiments in history…they are laying down the industrial future of 146 million people and one-sixth of the land of the area of the world for fifteen years. These sixteen men salt down the whole economic life of 146 million people for a year in advance as calmly as a Gloucester man salts down his fish.
>
> Stuart Chase

Lenin faced an immediate economic crisis in the Soviet Union. Industrial production had fallen to levels not seen since 1913, and internal dissent was mounting. With his attempts at nationalizing the economy and regulating production faltering, Lenin created his New Economic Policy (NEP) that allowed peasants to sell their surpluses at free-market prices, and some small-scale industries were returned to private ownership. As a result, by 1926, production levels and the overall health of the economy began to improve, but Lenin, who died in 1924, did not live to see this change.

> One death is a tragedy. A million deaths is a statistic.
>
> Josef Stalin

His successor, Josef Stalin, had a very different perspective on managing the economy of the Soviet Union. Stalin believed that his country would be best served by a massive campaign to build up Russian industry by making the country more self-reliant and more centrally planned.

In 1929, he began his first "Gos-Plan" – a series of five-year plans designed to control output, employment, and prices. Under central planning the Soviet Union assigned production quotas to all state-run factories, farms, and other production facilities.

In a capitalist system, there is no central planning of markets. Markets are dynamic and ever-changing. Imagine trying to plan exactly what the output level of Internet services needs to be in five years or even five weeks from now. It would be a daunting task to say the least. However, you must bear in mind that Stalin perceived a day when planning would satisfy all of the wants and needs of his people. By assigning production quotas, he hoped to meet those needs without allowing profit to occur. Ironically, millions of Soviet citizens died of starvation or were executed during this attempt to meet what were often unrealistic quotas.

> Stalin was personally responsible for the murder of more people than any other human being in the 20th century—and probably any other century. Stalin took Lenin's system of slave labor camps and turned it into a vast secret empire in the depths of Siberia. Lenin chose to let millions starve to death in order to sustain his war effort, but Stalin went further by deliberately engineering famines on an even greater scale. Finally, Stalin crossed the one line that Lenin would not, by ordering the executions of fellow Communists on a massive scale.[13]

Under communism, the government helps "secure" people from the "exploitative" prices of the free market by making it illegal to charge prices above the government-set level. Rampant shortages persisted in Russia and other Eastern European nations as a result of this policy. In many cases, getting a new apartment, car, or television set took years of waiting. Shortages of food, electric power, and medicine were also severe. In some years, the average Soviet citizen spent an average of four out of every five working days standing in lines, hoping that a stick of butter or loaf of bread would be available.

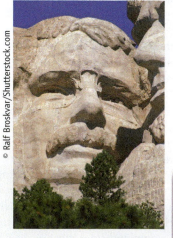

© Ralf Broskvar/Shutterstock.com

CONCEPT CHECK

In the early 1900s President Theodore Roosevelt said, "The man who wrongly holds that every human right is secondary to his profit must now give way to the advocate of human welfare, who rightly maintains that every man holds his property subject to the general right of the community to regulate its use to whatever degree the public welfare may require it."[14] Was President Roosevelt's statement a reflection of the values of Karl Marx? Why, or why not?

Marx did not call for leaders to use the type of brute force that Stalin, Kim Jong-il or Fidel Castro have used in the name of communism. In fact, just like we have never seen a purely capitalistic economy, we have also never witnessed pure communism. What we see in Cuba and North Korea – and what was used in the former Soviet Union – was a 'command and control' system, rather than the voluntary pursuit of profits and the resulting betterment of mankind. Then again, Marx should have been able to recognize that it is biologically unnatural for people to deny their self interest or avoid the pursuit of profits and the resulting betterment of mankind. Indirectly, Marx helped cause the rise of Stalin by advocating naïve economic policies.[15]

IS SOCIALISM ANY BETTER?

> The inherent vice of capitalism is the unequal sharing of the blessings. The inherent vice of socialism is the equal sharing of misery.
>
> Winston Churchill

During the 2016 Presidential primaries, Vermont Senator Bernie Sanders found himself in the enviable position of being adored by millions of college-age voters. In state after state, Mr. Sanders trounced Hillary Clinton among millennials.

Part of the attraction to Mr. Sanders – a self-proclaimed "democratic-Socialist" was his constant comparisons of America to Scandinavian nations that practice, according to Mr. Sanders, a much better form of economic policy rooted in socialism. A good place to start in looking at this claim would be to first define the word.

> ➤ **Socialism is an economic system that combines markets with a generous social welfare state; government ownership of selected industries, along with greater government regulations of businesses, paid for by income taxes on private citizens and business owners that often exceed 50 percent of earnings.**

The structural foundation of socialism is an inherent mistrust in Adam Smith's advocacy of self-interested activities. The communists wanted no one to be allowed to pursue Smith's vision and no provision for ownership of private property.

The socialist allows for the pursuit of self-interested behavior and private property ownership, but invites significant government control over the degree to which self-interested pursuits can occur and the amount of property that can be owned.

Residents of Scandinavia know this all too well.

IS SWEDEN PARADISE?

If concern for the quality of human life were part of the Winter Olympics, Sweden—along with strong performances in skiing, the biathlon and hockey—would rout the rest of the world on the way to a gold-medal performance. Located in northern Europe, Sweden is home to over nine million people.

Most of us are very familiar with at least one company that comes from this picturesque nation: IKEA furniture. Let's consider how different our lives would be if we left the U.S. to go to work for this popular company.

As a new employee you might first want to know what benefits you would be entitled to.

For starters, to deal with the possibility that you might be overworked, the government passed the Working Hours Act of 1982 that provides for a statutory maximum of 40 hours on average, per week, over a period of four weeks. The law also prohibits night work

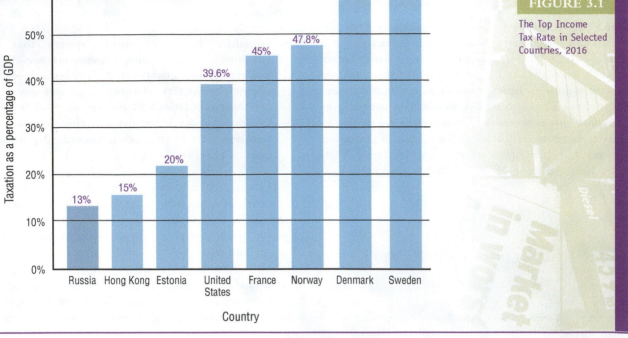

FIGURE 3.1

The Top Income Tax Rate in Selected Countries, 2016

and stipulates that the employee must have, per week, at least 36 hours of continuous time off.

Should you ever ask to work overtime to make some extra money for cross-country skiing lessons, you will be informed that you may not work more than 48 hours in four weeks or 50 hours over a calendar month.[16] The Working Hours Act also prohibits putting in more than 200 hours per year in overtime.

Suppose you are hired as a part-time worker at IKEA, but you really want to work full-time. In Sweden, part-timers qualify for a subsidy – paid for by the taxpayers, where, "in case of involuntary part-time the wage earner can be compensated for the difference between full-time and part time through the unemployment insurance system if the qualification rules are fulfilled."[17]

Should you happen to get married and end up with a little Swedish-American bundle of joy a year later, do not worry about day care, or health care costs. Child care and health care benefits are ostensibly "free" (i.e. the tab is picked up by taxpayers) in Sweden. Should you choose to stay home with your child, you are covered by the Child Care Leave Act of 1978 that allows you *and your companion* to take up to ten months of leave from your job, at 80% of your previous pay rate! In addition, one of you will be given the right to stay away from the job for an additional month, at 90% of your prior pay.

If you think ten months is not enough bonding time between you and little Bjorn, you can opt for the plan that allows for 15 months, at 60% of your pay, to stay at home. It gets even better.

One parent maintains the right to reduce his or her work hours until the child is eight years old, while leave for temporary care of a child totals 60 days per year. All of this comes at a guarantee that your job will be there for you when you return, with the mere requirement that you and/or your companion have been employed for at least six months consecutively or 12 months during the last two years, prior to the child's birth.

Suppose when you come back to work, you lose your job because of a new global financial crisis. Don't fret, because in Sweden, workers who have worked for at least five months during the 12 months prior to unemployment, qualify for 300 days of unemployment insurance at 80% of previous income if they are under 55 years of age and 450 days if they are over 55.

By now, many of you may have your bags packed and are on hold with a major airline trying to find out ticket prices to Stockholm. Before you go, perhaps a couple of minor details should be provided.

First, in order to pay for all of these "free" programs, the top tax rate on the most successful Swedish workers is 57%. This tax rate does not include property, sales, and other taxes Swedish citizens have to pay. By contrast, the top tax rate in the U.S. was 39.6% at the time of this writing.[18] In Hong Kong it is 15%. Not surprisingly, many times the free services end up costing the most.

A recent study found that the average Swedish household has a median income that is lower than the median income of African-Americans. If Sweden was a U.S. state, its income would make it the poorest of all the states.[19] This might be why more and more Swedish voters have begun to push for less taxation and social services. After all, when accounting for the people who do not have jobs, plus those who are taking advantage of

CONCEPT CHECK

In 2016, Canada ranked 6th in the world in overall economic freedom, which was not only far higher than the United States but represented the third largest gain in economic freedom among all developed nations. Canadian household wealth exceeded $363,000 (compared to just over $319,000 in America).[24] Log on to http://www.heritage.org/index/country/canada to read how this happened and fully explain what you learned.

© Filipe Frazao/Shutterstock.com

Sweden's generous sick leave policies, the effective unemployment rate was between 20% and 25% for much of the last decade.[20]

Recognizing that a large tax burden, aging population and exploding welfare state is a long-run recipe for economic calamity, Sweden has recently undertaken some reforms that has moved this Scandinavian nation slowly away from entrenched socialism towards a slightly more capitalistic one. For starters, the corporate income tax rate was slashed to 22 percent in 2012.[21] Perhaps more significantly, the Swedish government has reformed its version of Social Security. The change involved partial privatization, a gradual increase in the retirement age, and automatic reductions in the guaranteed state pension, adjusted annually to reflect increases in longevity.[22] Not surprisingly, in 2014 Sweden's economic freedom ranking increased from "moderately free" to "mostly free."[23]

THE PROBLEM WITH FRANCE AND GREECE AND VENEZUELA AND....

> Government is a broker in pillage and every election is an advanced auction on stolen goods.
>
> H.L. Mencken

Sweden is not alone in its security-induced economic struggles. In France, restaurant owners face labor laws that limit workers to 43 hours per week – unless the restaurant owner pays overtime of up to 150% of the basic wage rate plus money for "compensatory time off." That probably doesn't matter much because France's 19.6% tax on all restaurant meals helps hold down the number of customers.[25]

Moreover, if an employee takes maternity leave in France, the employer must keep the job open for the worker for three years. France even pays couples $850 and $1,215 per month if the parents of two kids will agree to have a third.[26] After all, with so many retirees and other people to support, the French government is going to need plenty of tax payers in the future.

French labor law keeps most stores closed all day Sunday and they can only be open for 10 hours on other days because French workers are not permitted to work more than 35 hours per week.[27] French courts recently ruled that after an employee has been with a company for at least "two paychecks," it will cost the company 3 to 12 months of pay to get rid of that worker, should they want to dismiss him or her.

Not surprisingly, France has a struggling economy that produces very few new products or jobs. The tension that high unemployment and poverty brings is the primary cause for the recent wave of riots that France's immigrants participated in.[28]

On the other hand, even when the French government attempts to interject the free market into its system, riots break out. In March of 2006, the government

CONCEPT CHECK

In the year 274 A.D., Roman emperor Aurelian declared the right to relief (welfare benefits) be hereditary. Aurelian gave welfare recipients government-baked bread, and added free salt, pork and olive oil. Read "The Fall of Rome and Modern Parallels" online at http://www.fee.org/the_freeman/detail/the-fall-of-rome-and-modern-parallels#axzz2qadZPOkD then email the author with your thoughts on the degree to which the United States is on a similar path.

proposed rules that would make it easier for French employers to fire younger workers. Demonstrators took to the streets protesting this change to a more competitive economy.

Such a result is not surprising. According to a recent poll, out of 20 countries surveyed, French citizens expressed the lowest level of faith in the free market. Only 36% of French citizens agreed that the free market is the "best system on which to base the future of the world." – This is compared to 71% in the U.S., 66% in Great Britain, and 74% in *China*.[29]

This did not prevent former French president, Nicolas Sarkozy from unveiling an ambitious plan to reduce taxes and welfare spending in France. Calling the social welfare system "unjust" and "financially untenable," Mr. Sarkozy pushed for legislation that would end France's 35-hour work week; a reduction in wealth and income taxes and the abolishment of inheritance taxes.[30]

Yet France's new president, Francois Hollande was granted authority by French courts to proceed with a plan to raise the top income tax rate from 45 percent to 75 percent in 2014.[31] Meanwhile, Denmark and other western European nations are going through capitalistic reforms, largely in response to the rapid rise of Estonia, Poland and other eastern European nations.[32] As these former Communist countries continue to push for free market

reforms, the rising standard of living has led to more jobs and opportunities for eastern and western Europeans alike. As more companies flee the high-tax, heavy welfare states of the West, more pressure has been put on France and other nations to pursue reforms that will keep jobs and tax revenue from fleeing entirely.

This was one of the reasons for the election of Angela Merkel as Chancellor of Germany. Ms. Merkel was elected largely on a platform that reminded people of Margaret Thatcher.[33] Ms. Thatcher cut taxes and subsidies to businesses and fought Britain's powerful labor unions in a successful push to move England away from socialism. Now German voters seem to have warmed to the idea of becoming more competitive on the world stage.[34]

Recently, Germany relaxed regulations that used to force businesses to close at 6 p.m. each evening. Led by Finance Minister Wolfgang Schauble, and former Chancellor, Gerhard Schroder - who cut income taxes and eased hiring and firing laws[35] - Germany has also managed to lower taxes and cut government spending over the past few years. The result has been a sharp increase in Germany's level of production, income, and exports, and one of the strongest economic recoveries in the world.[36] Ironically, this long-time supporter of generous government payouts in the name of economic security, has now begun a campaign to encourage the United

Don't worry, live happy

The fourth World Happiness Report was released recently in time for World Happiness Day (March 20). South Africa is listed in the bottom half and ranked 116th from 157 countries.

The main analysis of happiness among and within nations continues to be based on individual life evaluations, roughly 1,000 per year in each of more than 150 countries.

South Africa's average score of 4.459 out of 10 is less than the world average (5.353), but more than the average for Sub-Saharan Africa (4.370).

Seven of the top 10 countries are in Europe, while eight of the bottom 10 are in sub-Saharan Africa.

The results partially implement the Aristotelian presumption that sustained positive emotions are important for a good life.

Key for segments

- **GDP per capita**
- **Social support**
- **Healthy life expectancy**
- **Freedom to make life choices**
- **Generosity**
- **Perceptions of corruption**
- **Dystopia** (Hypothetical country, so named because it has values equal to the world's lowest national averages for each of the six key variables)

Happiest countries

	Country	SCORE
1	Denmark	7.526
2	Switzerland	7.509
3	Iceland	7.501
4	Norway	7.498
5	Finland	7.413
6	Canada	7.404
7	Netherlands	7.339
8	New Zealand	7.334
9	Australia	7.313
10	Sweden	7.291
11	Israel	7.267
12	Austria	7.119
13	United States	7.104
14	Costa Rica	7.087
15	Puerto Rico	7.039
16	Germany	6.994
17	Brazil	6.952
18	Belgium	6.929
19	Ireland	6.907
20	Luxembourg	6.871

Least happiest countries

	Country	SCORE
116	South Africa	4.459
139	Ivory Coast	3.916
140	Cambodia	3.907
141	Angola	3.866
142	Niger	3.856
143	South Sudan	3.832
144	Chad	3.763
145	Burkina Faso	3.739
146	Uganda	3.739
147	Yemen	3.724
148	Madagascar	3.695
149	Tanzania	3.666
150	Liberia	3.622
151	Guinea	3.607
152	Rwanda	3.515
153	Benin	3.484
154	Afghanistan	3.360
155	Togo	3.303
156	Syria	3.069
157	Burundi	2.905

States to reduce our level of deficit spending in order to avoid runaway debt and higher taxes in the future.[37]

In Spain, Portugal, Sudan, Venezuela, Bolivia, Greece, and other parts of the world, governments continue to expand their power – all in the name of fairness and the social good – only to see hundreds of thousands of bright, highly motivated people leave these nations for places like Hong Kong, Ireland, Brazil, and Australia.[38] Greece, in particular, has fallen on hard times. According to the World Bank, Greece ranks 109th out of 183 nations in the ease of doing business; 140th in the amount of time it takes to start a business; 154th in protecting investors and equally low in everything from enforcing contracts to flexibility in labor relations.[39]

Not surprisingly, Greece suffers from high levels of tax evasion,[40] heavy debt, rising unemployment, riots, and a condition of near bankruptcy that required a bailout by the European Union in 2010.[41]

This trend is all because increased taxes and excessive regulations have drastically reduced the incentives that entrepreneurs need to serve their fellow man.

Then there is the current catastrophe in Venezuela. Fifteen years after revolution turned the government over to Hugo Chavez and his successor, Nicolas Maduro, Venezuela is in chaos. In 2016 fully 87 percent of citizens in this oil-rich nation did not have enough income for food. Inflation rates (annual prices increases) reached 700 percent that same year and the murder rate of 90 per 100,000 residents was second highest in the world.[42] The confiscation of private property and rapid move towards socialism has failed to deliver on the promises of greater standards of living for poorer Venezuelans.

CAN SOCIALISM MAKE YOU HAPPY?

Not all people are unhappy with socialism. It is critical to your understanding of socialism that you consider the fact that people in Europe and Latin American have freely elected socialist leaders. The leaders – while campaigning for office – told them that they would receive certain taxpayer-financed benefits. The politicians also told them that the benefits would come at the cost of much higher tax rates than capitalistic nations have. Venezuelan voters – who saw Hugo Chavez seize more than 2.5 million acres of private property – were well aware that he was not going to push for Venezuela to become the next Hong Kong.

As Bernie Sanders supporters routinely pointed out, nations like Denmark, Norway and Finland see socialistic politicians winning elections and we *do not see* a massive migration of people away from Europe to America. This means that socialism can be, for many people, the system that delivers the most happiness – even if half their money leaves them by force. In fact, many studies show that some of the most socialistic nations in the world have some of the happiest people.[43]

Economists who have investigated this paradox have found that one of the primary differences between nations that embrace socialism and those that pursue capitalism is the divergent *cultural influences* that are found around the world. Simply put, what makes some people happy – more money and more stuff – does not make others happy.[44] It has been empirically shown that Europeans tend to be much happier when they perceive that their government is actively correcting for inequality in earnings.[45]

There is some evidence that certain places in the United States also desire European-style socialism. Many organizations rank states by economic freedom. Some states tend to embrace lawmakers that advocate zero state income and sales taxes and limited regulations. Other states like New York, California, Minnesota, Illinois,[46] and Michigan have much higher tax and regulatory burdens, and actively assist the poor with generous social welfare programs.[47]

Over the past twenty years, the state of California has lost over 3.4 million residents. Companies like Facebook, eBay, LegalZoom, PayPal and Yelp have opened offices in Texas and Arizona in the wake of significant tax increases that now has Californians facing state income tax rates as high as 13.3 percent.[48] New York – another highly taxed and regulated state – has lost the same 3.4 million people over the last *ten* years. Here again, Texas, with no state income tax and minimal government services, has been the beneficiary, leading many economists to speculate that Texas might become the dominant economic model for states who desire greater wealth, revenue and political representation.[49]

Texas is not alone. Alaska, Florida, Nevada, New Hampshire, South Dakota, Tennessee, Washington and Wyoming also have no state income tax and Louisiana, North Carolina, Oklahoma and Kansas are rapidly moving in that direction.[50] New Hampshire, with the state motto of 'Live Free or Die' has even become home to the 'Free State Project' with a campaign featuring 101 reasons to move to this small New England State.[51]

Yet, for many people, the quality of life in New York, Minnesota, and California is still far greater than it is in states where people are expected to be more self-reliant.[52]

HOW UNHAPPY EUROPEANS – AND AMERICANS – COULD USE FREDERIC BASTIAT

In 1849, French economist Frederic Bastiat penned a short book entitled, *The Law*. It was in this book that he prescribed a recipe for any society that wishes to support justice, economic progress, and happiness for the largest part of society. The problem with socialism, according to Bastiat, is that the socialist sees human beings as mounds of clay to be molded in the manner the government official deems necessary to bring about the "greater good" of society. This compels government to use force and coercion to carry out the grand vision of greater security for mankind.

The great flaw with the current European model, Bastiat argued, is that the socialists are so eager to do good that they are willing to resort to theft to accomplish their benevolent goals. He argued that, in a civilized society, none of us has the right to use force to plunder the property of our fellow man.

Even if we intend to charitably give our neighbors' property to the poor, we would be arrested if we rob him to do so. By what right then, Bastiat asked, do we have to use our votes to take away the money (through taxation) of our fellow man in order to give it to someone who has no legal claim to it? Isn't this simply *legalized plunder*?

Socialists believe that people aren't charitable and that businesses are corrupt. As Warren Sapp – a millionaire former football player – once argued, "We've designed a system for people to cheat and steal and pillage, so that the rich get richer and the poor don't get a damn thing."

People with socialist leanings see government as a sort of savior, a healer of all that ails us. This means that in much of Europe and America, voters eagerly support increasing taxes on the most successful citizens. This in turn, is called things like "justice," "fairness," or "equitable."

You will recall from the last chapter that Americans donated more than $300 billion per year to private chari-ties in 2014. This amount is consistent with previous years where data is available. This figure was more than the entire Gross Domestic Product of 157 countries – including Norway, the Czech Republic, Portugal, Denmark and Finland.[54] Adjusting for inflation and population changes, GDP per person in America has risen over the past 50 years by about 150%, while charitable giving per person has risen by about 190%.[55]

In summary, socialism does not confer the type of evil and oppression we see in the command and control economies. Nor does socialism create the rampant poverty we see where communism is experimented with. Yet, as Bastiat so accurately pointed out, there is still an element of force that all socialistic nations must use in order to create the "fair" society they desire. That is perhaps why people in China and India are moving from socialism to capitalism.[56]

THE 33% DILEMMA

In 2005, prime ministers of India and China agreed to an economic "strategic partnership" that represented an important and natural step in the continued globalization of the world economy, and one that could have a dramatic effect on Americans in the 21st century.

With about one-third of the world's people, the agreement between China's Wen Jiabao and India's Manmohan Singh could, in the estimation of many economists, spell significant and far-reaching problems for the United States.

It is important for Americans to understand that this warming of relations between Asia's growing economic powers is rooted in their perception of shared self-interests in selling their goods and service to the West, most importantly, the United States and European Union countries.

Their emergence as key players in the international economy, stems from a rejection of the centrally planned economies of the previous half-century that had led them further down the road to poverty.

© Scanail1/Shutterstock.com

CONCEPT CHECK

Log on to the Heritage Foundation rankings of economic freedom for the year you are reading this chapter. Look up the nation of Estonia, which ranks higher than the United States in economic freedom. This has happened for many reasons.[53] Where do you see Adam Smith's influence in the policies pursued by Estonia's government?

It also stems from the growing premium on the value of human capital in the world economy – both in the global-technology sector where India has excelled and in manufacturing where China has been taking market share from western companies.[57]

In 1947, India gained its independence from Great Britain and immediately charted a course born out of a belief in the power of technically planned socialism. Prime Minister Jawaharlal Nehru nationalized the coal, steel and machine-tool industries and launched a massive government campaign to create the technological infrastructure that would be necessary to bring Indians out of poverty.

Led by the economist P.C. Mahalanobis, the Indian Statistical Institute created a mathematical model designed to plan every facet of the economy.

Two years later, the communist takeover of China created the experiment known as the Great Leap Forward. The Maoist plan to modernize the Chinese economy by abolishing private-property rights and forcibly organizing farmers into industrial production led to the starvation of millions of Chinese citizens and decades of unprecedented poverty.

Today, an economic miracle is under way in both countries as they have turned their backs on socialism and discovered capitalism with a vengeance.

From 2007-2010, India's economy grew at an astounding rate of 7.4-9.2%,[58] surpassing China for the first time as the country with the fastest rate of economic growth.[59] China has also averaged nearly double-digit increases in its gross domestic product during the past several years.

Literacy rates in both China and India have risen sharply. China now produces four times more engineers than the United States. Moreover, fully 30% of the world's computer-software engineers are now from India.

Another telltale sign of economic growth is the fact that in both nations the population is rising at a decreasing rate – an indication the economy has entered a sustained period of rising wealth and opportunity.

At the current rate of economic growth, China will produce a GDP larger than the United States within the next two decades, while India will have a per-capita income equal to the United States' by 2066 or earlier.[60]

Precisely how India and China reversed decades of poverty and despair is fairly straightforward.

In 1991, the Indian government took a momentous decision when it began dismantling state control over the economy. Under the leadership of Rajiv Gandhi and Narasimha Rao, the government lowered tariffs and taxes, did away with public-sector monopolies and liberalized rules and regulations for willing entrepreneurs.[61]

The result was 170 million fewer Indians living in poverty than in 1980.[62] In 2004, the Indian government pushed through further reductions in tariffs on machinery items, computers, cellular phones, and power-transmission equipment.

China began its economic reforms during the 1980s with liberalization of profit-seeking in the agricultural sector. The 1990s and this decade have brought an acceleration of the free-market rejection of Marxian economics.

The Clinton administration bolstered China's attempts to trade internationally when it relaxed the human-rights test that China had been forced to pass to gain most-favored nation status.

As a result, artificial and inflationary barriers to Chinese goods fell sharply. Consequently, the high productivity in Chinese factories carried over into much lower prices for Americans shopping at Wal-Mart and other retail stores and created China's 2012 purchasing power of over $12.6 trillion – second only to that of the United States.[63]

In 2004, China, borrowing heavily from the supply-side policies of Ronald Reagan, reduced the marginal tax rate on businesses from 28% to 24%.[64] In addition, the value-added tax was cut and, for the first time since 1949, China amended its constitution to guarantee all citizens the right to own private property.

In the past, students from India and China would come to America to study engineering and then stay here – most of the jobs in Silicon Valley were created by immigrant entrepreneurs. Today, a reverse brain drain is occurring in which Indian and Chinese students, buoyed by rising standards of living in their homeland, are leaving the United States to start businesses in their native land.[65] U.S. companies like Starbucks, Ford, and General Electric have also noticed that India, in particular, has become a very productive

nation to invest in[66] – whether the investment is in human or physical capital.

On November 16, 2010, *The Wall Street Journal* published a long article entitled, "China's 'State Capitalism' Sparks a Global Backlash." I would like to strongly suggest that at this time you put down the book, go online to find this article and read every ominous word of it….

China, with a projected 2054 GDP of $70 trillion (U.S. projected GDP is less than $40 trillion for that year) has recently undergone yet another economic transformation that is taking this nation from a net copier of technology to a net creator of technology, with a fascinating blend of free market capitalism and government planning.[67] This form of "state capitalism" is being watched very carefully by economists all over the world in an attempt to ascertain the degree to which other nations might find it tempting to move in this relatively unique direction.

In a nutshell, China's government has fostered an environment from which entrepreneurs in key selected industries such as alternative energy technology and rare earth minerals, can freely pursue profits with government support in everything from currency markets to access to financial capital. As this article clearly illustrates, this is not a command and control type of economy. Nor is it capitalism or socialism.

It remains to be seen whether China can maintain the type of state capitalism that it has fostered. We could end up seeing China fall victim to the same political pressure that other nations do when planning is a key feature of an economy. Eventually, the pressures of capitalism and planning collide and either the nation moves toward freer markets or reverts back to state control.

One thing is certain however. The United States – and the rest of the world – had better not take China lightly. As world history has repeatedly shown, nations don't stay on the top of the economic heap forever – or for very long. This century may well be the one where the United States answers to one, or more nations, rather than being the dominant country that we have been for more than one hundred years.[68]

IS THE MIXED ECONOMY THE PERFECT MIX?

So far it is unlikely that many of you have decided to move to North Korea or France. Still, you might find yourself disinclined to argue that capitalism is the ideal system. After all, shouldn't there be at least some minimal economic security provided by government? Wouldn't an economic system that allows us a great deal of freedom, while restraining greed and securing us from random unfortunate events, be ideal? Let's look at what that system would do. To see it, just open your eyes, because the United States is a good example of a mixed economy.

> ➤ **A mixed economy is one that combines free markets with social welfare spending, government regulations and restrictions on private property ownership. In a mixed economy, government interference in the economy is not as significant as in socialism but markets are not as free as in capitalism.**

In America, you are allowed to pick your major; open a business; move to another state; keep most of your money (most people get to anyway); buy the house, cars, and foods you can afford; and run your life largely in a manner that you see fit. Our economy produces over $18 trillion in output each year, which is equal to every nation in Europe *combined* and higher than Japan, China, Brazil and every other nation on Earth.

This man makes money by advertising large airline seats on the sidewalks of New York City. Would pure capitalism ever create jobs like this – at a wage that helps this man take care of his family – or do we have to have government regulate what American Airlines pays him to make sure he is treated fairly?

Photo courtesy Jack Chambless

CONCEPT CHECK

Over the past few years the Brazilian economy has struggled with recessions and rising poverty after years of growing prosperity. Find the article, "Brazil's Giant Problem" from the April 23-24, 2016 *Wall Street Journal* to learn more about what has happened in this country. What have been the leading causes of Brazil's recent economic troubles?

© Charles Harker/Shutterstock.com

When we look around the stores and malls of the United States, we see billions of goods and services that fit both our wants and needs. Poor people in America are some of the richest poor people in the world. Research by The Heritage Foundation[69] shows that:

- 80 percent of poor households have air conditioning. In 1970, only 36 percent of the entire U.S. population enjoyed air conditioning.
- 92 percent of poor households have a microwave.
- Nearly three-fourths have a car or truck, and 31 percent have two or more cars or trucks.
- Nearly two-thirds have cable or satellite TV.
- Two-thirds have at least one DVD player, and 70 percent have a VCR.
- Half have a personal computer, and one in seven have two or more computers.
- More than half of poor families with children have a video game system, such as an Xbox or PlayStation.
- 43 percent have Internet access.
- One-third have a wide-screen plasma or LCD TV.
- One-fourth have a digital video recorder system, such as a TiVo.

Clearly, the United States is not – nor has ever been – a capitalist nation. Nor are we a socialist nation as some would have you believe. There is a distinct difference in the degree to which self-interested activities are encouraged here compared to Hong Kong (the most capitalist place) and Western Europe. Our taxes are lower and the welfare state not as generous as many nations that rank as "mostly free" or "moderately free." As a result, the average American earned, on average, $130 per day compared to China's $20 per day and India's $10 per day.[70]

Yet, as you are reading this chapter, the mixed economy the United States has evolved towards is showing some signs of inching (sprinting?) towards the more socialistic policies of much of the rest of the world.

IS AMERICA BECOMING A SOCIALIST COUNTRY?

Experience should teach us to be most on our guard to protect liberty when the government's purposes are beneficial. Men born to freedom are naturally alert to repel invasion of their liberty by evil-minded rulers. The greater dangers to liberty lurk in insidious encroachment by men of zeal, well-meaning but without understanding.

Justice Louis Brandeis, *Olmstead v. United States*
277 U.S. 479 (1928)

At first glance, the question of America becoming less free seems absurd. However, decades ago, in a landmark book entitled, *The Road to Serfdom*, Friedrich Hayek, an Austrian economist sounded a warning to the United States and other nations. The warning is now getting a fresh look, and Hayek, once dismissed by the intellectual elite, has come to the forefront of the battle over economic liberty.[71] Hayek's message is simple: Over time, countries that pursue a mixed economy allow government to increase its power to tax, spend, and regulate. The result is an incremental slide from the good intentions of government security to the oppressive hand of government force.

It would seem, by most objective standards that America – recessions notwithstanding – is still a great place to live today. After all, economists point out that geographic mobility is a good indicator of which economies are working well. Have you noticed how many people from around the world want to move here?

However, there is a growing body of evidence to suggest that America is indeed moving further and further away from the ideas of Adam Smith and John Locke. In 2017, the United States fell to seventeenth place in the rankings of global economic freedom.[72] The 2017 ranking was the lowest in modern times for America. Moreover, for the first time in the history of these rankings, America fell out of the rankings of "free" and into the list of "mostly free" nations while falling behind previously socialistic Chile and Lithuania and the formerly communist nation of Estonia.[73]

THE EVIDENCE

> The inevitable progression of things is for government to gain ground and for liberty to yield.
>
> Thomas Jefferson

In evaluating where the United States is moving on the economic freedom scale, economists look at changes in taxes, government spending, regulations and civil liberties for a guide. In the pages that follow we will examine each of these four to ascertain the degree to which America is moving away from – or towards – the principles of Adam Smith and our Founding Fathers.

THE HISTORY OF INCOME TAXES IN AMERICA

> We must make our election between economy and liberty or profusion and servitude. If we run into such debts as that we must be taxed in our meat and in our drink, in our necessities and our comforts, in our labors and our amusements, for our callings and our creeds, as the people of England are, our people, like them must come to labor 16 hours in the 24, and give the earnings of 15 of these to the government for their debts and daily expenses; and the 16th being insufficient to afford us bread, we must live as they now do, on oatmeal and potatoes; have no time to think, no means of calling the mismanagers to account; but be glad to obtain the subsistence by hiring ourselves to rivet their chains on the necks of our fellow sufferers.
>
> Thomas Jefferson

As you can see, Mr. Jefferson had very definitive ideas on the consequences of taxes on liberty. For that reason, from the ratification of the U.S. Constitution in 1787 until 1913, there was no such thing as the federal income tax. Now that you have fallen off your chair, it is time to get back up and read on.

From 1791 through 1802, the U.S. government was supported by internal taxes on distilled spirits, carriages, refined sugar, tobacco and snuff, property sold at auction, corporate bonds, and slaves. The War of 1812 brought about the nation's first sales taxes on gold, silverware, jewelry, and watches. In 1817, however, Congress did away with all internal taxes, relying on tariffs on imported goods to provide funds for running the government.

In 1862, in order to support the Civil War effort, Congress enacted the nation's first income tax law. During the Civil War, a citizen from a northern state earning $600–$1,000 per year paid at the rate of 3%. This was also the year that inheritance taxes debuted. By 1866 the Internal Revenue Service was collecting more than $310 million, the highest amount in the 90-year history of the U.S. The Act of 1862 established the office of the Commissioner of Internal Revenue.

The Commissioner was given power to assess, levy, and collect taxes and the right to enforce the tax laws through seizure of property and income and through prosecution. This mechanism is still with us today.

In 1872, the income tax was eliminated in favor of taxes on tobacco and distilled spirits (booze) but had a short revival in 1894–1895. In 1895, the U.S. Supreme Court decided that the income tax was unconstitutional because it was not apportioned among the states in conformity with the Constitution.[74]

1913

For the first 45,438 days of America's life, the people did not have "the fruits of their labor" touched with a comprehensive federal income tax. That all changed on February 3, 1913 when Congress ratified the Sixteenth Amendment to the U.S. Constitution which reads:

> The Congress shall have power to lay and collect taxes on incomes, from whatever source derived, without apportionment among the several States, and without regard to any census or enumeration.

As the table following illustrates, the first income tax was applied to the highest incomes in America ($20,000 in 1914 translates to well over $250,000 in today's money) and was relatively modest in terms of the percentage of income taken.[75]

INCOME RANGE	MARGINAL TAX RATE[76]
$20,000–$50,000	1%
$50,001–75,000	2%
$75,001–$100,000	3%
$100,001–$250,000	4%
$250,001–$500,000	5%
$500,001 and above	7%

By the end of World War I, the top income tax rate had risen from 7% to 77%. In fiscal year 1918, annual internal revenue collections passed the billion-dollar mark for the first time, rising to $5.4 billion by 1920. By World War II, tax collections had increased to $7.3 billion. Yet it was a little-publicized change in the way taxes are collected that caused the explosion of revenue to $43 billion by 1943.

In 1942, Congress raised income taxes dramatically – ostensibly to pay for the mounting war effort and Franklin Roosevelt's "New Deal" social programs. For the first time, income taxes were to be collected from tens of millions of people who previously had been exempt from income taxation. The "class tax (tax on the rich)" became known as the "mass tax." In those days, people had to pay their taxes all at once – in the spring. As the spring of 1943 rolled around, Congress feared that even with a war raging, the voting public would not stand for this massive tax increase. Enter Mr. Beardsley Ruml.

Mr. Ruml was, at that time, chairman of the board of directors of the New York Federal Reserve Bank and treasurer at R.H. Macy & Co. When approached by Henry Morgenthau, the Treasury Secretary at the time, Mr. Ruml heard Mr. Morgenthau lament, "Suppose we have to go out and arrest five million people?" Fearing mass tax evasion, Mr. Ruml suggested that the government change the way we pay our taxes. Mr. Ruml suggested that the government get businesses to collect taxes for it.

The idea was simple. Have businesses deduct a percentage of a worker's gross pay every week and send the money to Washington, D.C. This "pay as you go" plan was argued to be much simpler and kinder, since workers would no longer be asked to worry about one tax bill once a year. The government would simply take a little from each paycheck, and the problem would be solved. This was the birth of the federal income tax withholding that is still with us to this day.

You can imagine what happened to federal income taxes after that point. The top tax rate hit 88.9% during the war.[77] This was not the highest proposed tax rate, however. In a message to Congress on April 27, 1942, FDR stated:

> Discrepancies between low personal incomes and very high personal incomes should be lessened; and I therefore believe that in time of this grave national danger, when all excess income should go to win the war, no American citizen ought to have a net income, after he has paid his taxes, of more than $25,000 a year.[78]

The Treasury then advised Congress:

> To implement the President's proposal, the Treasury now recommends the enactment of a 100 percent war supertax on that part of income after regular income tax which exceeds a personal exemption of $25,000.[79]

With the war supertax in place for the 1943 taxable year, Congress soon discovered that even in a time of war people care about incentives.

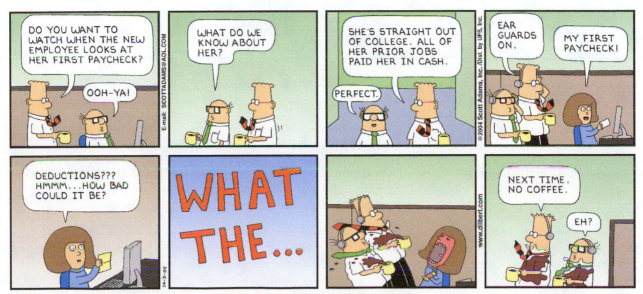

For that year, the IRS reported that a grand total of zero Americans had filed returns showing earnings of more than $25,000! The 100% tax had led to 100% tax evasion, and soon President Roosevelt rescinded the executive order.[80]

THE KENNEDY-REAGAN ERA

In 1962, the federal budget deficit stood at $7.1 billion – the third largest shortfall since World War II. The U.S. was on the precipice of even greater funding shortfalls as the combined effects of the space race, Cold War outlays and the Vietnam conflict loomed.

Moreover, from 1948 to 1960 the United States had endured a total of four recessions. The prevailing economic viewpoint from Franklin D. Roosevelt through Dwight Eisenhower had been for the government to maintain high levels of spending to (hopefully) boost economic growth and job creation but leave income tax rates high in case the economy grew too fast and threatened the country with price increases. This mindset had the unintended effect of causing more frequent recessions and rising unemployment rates.[81]

Thus, with sluggish economic growth and an ambitious goal of creating 5 percent economic growth having led to his election in 1960, John F. Kennedy stood before the Economic Club in New York in December of 1962 and said, "It is increasingly clear that … an economy hampered by restrictive tax rates will never produce enough revenues to balance our budget just as it will never produce enough jobs or enough profits. In short, it is a paradoxical truth that tax rates are too high and tax revenues are too low and the soundest way to raise the revenues in the long run is to cut the rates now."

The following year, President Kennedy was successful in producing legislation that would lower the top income tax rate from a staggering 91% to 70%.

This was the top rate until 1981. In that year, the number of tax brackets was 14, to go along with the rate of 70%, on the most successful Americans. By 1986, the number of income tax brackets was down to two, and the top rate was 28%. What happened?

Photo courtesy Jack W. Chambless

Photo courtesy Chuck Bigger

"At the peak of my career at Warner Bros., I was in the ninety-four percent tax bracket; that meant that after a certain point, I received only six cents of each dollar I earned and the government got the rest. The IRS took such a big chunk of my earnings that after a while I began asking myself whether it was worth it to keep on taking work. Something was wrong with a system like that. When you have to give up such a large percentage of your income in taxes incentive to work goes down.

When government confiscates half or more of a corporation's profit, the motivation to maximize profits goes down, and owners and managers make decisions based disproportionately on a desire to avoid taxes, they begin looking for tax shelters and

SUGGESTED CLASSROOM DEBATE

Log on to the course website – www.jackchambless.com, click on SPEECHES and scroll down to find the short speeches by John F. Kennedy and Ronald Reagan on the subject of income taxes. Would their proposals be good for the United States in the coming years? Why or why not?

loopholes that contribute nothing to the growth of our economy. Their companies don't grow as fast, they invest less in new plants and equipment, and they hire fewer people.

Any system that penalizes success and accomplishment is wrong. Any system that discourages work, discourages productivity, discourages economic progress is wrong. If on the other hand, you reduce taxes and allow people to spend or save more of what they earn, they'll be more industrious; they'll have more incentive to work hard, and money they earn will add fuel to the great economic machine that energizes our national progress. The result is more prosperity for all—and more revenue for government. A few economists call this principle supply-side economics. I just call it common sense."

Ronald Reagan

In 1981, Reagan signed into law the largest tax cut in the history of the United States – a $750 billion reduction over six years. The Tax Reform Act of 1986 lowered individual income tax rates over a five-year period and helped create an estimated 43 million jobs.[82]

GEORGE H. W. BUSH & BILL CLINTON'S TAX RECORD

On April 10, 1980 George H. W. Bush was embroiled in a battle with Ronald Reagan for the Republican nomination for President. In a speech on Reagan's tax plan, Mr. Bush became the first person to refer to his tax cut pro-

posals as "Voodoo economics" (see https://www.youtube.com/watch?v=o8hnM6xNjeU) for more on this.

Even though Mr. Bush was able to witness the effect of Reagan's tax cuts – and the greater revenue that followed – from his position as President Reagan's vice-president, he apparently was not paying attention.

In 1990, President Bush passed the Revenue Collection Act, which added the 31% bracket to income taxes as well as higher gas taxes. Later, taxes were increased for boats, planes, jewelry, and expensive cars.

It should come as no surprise that Mr. Bush's tax increases helped push the U.S. economy into a recession in 1990-91 after enjoying the longest peacetime recovery in American history.

This recession helped get Bill Clinton elected in 1992 but did not stop the trend towards higher taxes. President Clinton topped the Bush tax hike with the 1993 Revenue Reconciliation Act, which raised taxes by the largest amount ($250 billion) in the history of any nation on Earth. The Clinton tax hike added the 36% and 39.6% brackets to the federal income tax code that was with us until 2001.

Fortunately for Mr. Clinton, the combination of low interest rates and a surging technology sector eased the burden of his tax increase, and the economy continued to grow, although studies show that the economy did not grow as much as it could have had his tax hike not been enacted.[83]

The slowdown in economic growth that followed Bill Clinton's tax increase was enough to propel the Reagan Republicans back to power in the 1994 Congressional midterm elections. In that year, led by Reagan supporters like Newt Gingrich, the Republicans swept to power in both the House of Representatives and the U.S. Senate.

From 1994 through 2000 Bill Clinton turned into one of the biggest supporters of tax cuts in Washington, D.C.

For starters, he lowered the capital gains tax from 28 to 20 percent, which lead to greater revenue for the federal government and rising levels of job-creating investments. The tax on the profit from the sale of a home fell from 28 to zero percent and Mr. Clinton signed legislation that saved millions of Americans from paying taxes on their retirement savings when he helped create the Roth IRA.

By the time he left office the American economy was experiencing record economic growth, falling unemployment and the first federal budget surpluses in decades.

In 2016, the average American worked until April 24 just to meet his or her $4.99 trillion state and federal tax obligation. This means that for the average American, the first 113 days of that year were spent working just to pay for the 16th amendment.

© Joseph Sohm/Shutterstock.com

Did their differences cost her the election?

THE GEORGE W. BUSH AND BARACK OBAMA YEARS

"Probably the least efficient way of giving the economy a boost, is to give large tax cuts to millionaires and billionaires."

Barack Obama

"Anyone who thinks we can move this economy forward with a few doing well at the top, hoping it'll trickle down to working folks running faster and faster just to keep up – they just haven't studied our history."

Barack Obama

The election of George W. Bush in 2000 saw a continuation of the policies pursued by President Clinton. Apparently Mr. Bush learned from his father's mistakes because the capital gains tax rate fell to a decades low of only 15 percent.

In 2001 and 2003, President Bush signed legislation that lowered income taxes. These tax cuts included a reduction in marginal tax rates and a variety of other cuts to assist married couples, families with children, single mothers, and seniors. Some hailed the tax cuts – to be phased in over 10 years – as the beginning of a long battle to reduce the tax burden of working Americans. Economists who liked the idea of the cuts were concerned that they were too small and would take too long to implement to be fully effective.

Whatever the opinion of economists, the Bush tax cuts were given an expiration date of January 1, 2011.

In December 2010, President Obama signed legislation that extended the tax rates created in the Bush years through 2012. In addition, Mr. Obama agreed to lower the employee's portion of the payroll (FICA) tax from 6.2% to 4.2% for 2011 only.[84] His decision to extend, and even slightly reduce our tax burdens stemmed from the 2010 midterm elections that saw a huge increase in the number of tax-cutting candidates who won their elections.

In 2012 President Obama signed The American Taxpayer Relief Act that *raised* the top income tax rate from 35 to 39.6% beginning in 2013 and ended the payroll tax cut he had allowed the previous year. The tax on investment income was increased from 15 to 20 percent. His 2014 budget called for even more tax increases by changing the amount of money Americans could make within each tax bracket.

FEDERAL INCOME TAX BRACKETS, 2015–2016

Rate		Single	Joint
25%	2015	$37,450–90,750	$74,900–$151,200
	2016	$37,650–$91,150	$75,300–151,900
28%	2015	$90,750–$189,300	$151,200–$230,450
	2016	$91,150–190,150	$151,900–$231,450
33%	2015	$189,300–$411,500	$230,450–$411,500
	2016	$190,150–$413,350	$231,450–$413,350
35%	2015	$411,500–$413,200	$411,500–$464,850
	2016	$413,350–$415,050	$413,350–$466,950
39.6%	2015	$413,201+	$464,850+
	2016	$415,050+	$466,950+

Source: IRS.GOV

In addition, President Obama created a surtax of 3.8% on investment income for individuals who earned at least $200,000 ($250,000 for households); raised the dividends tax from 15 to 43.4%; imposed an excise tax

SUGGESTED CLASSROOM DEBATE

There is currently legislation in the U.S. Congress that seeks to abolish the IRS, eliminate income taxes, and replace the current tax system with a national sales tax.[85] Should the United States pursue this course of action? Why, or why not? Many nations, including Iraq, Romania, Russia, and Estonia have adopted a flat income tax.[86] Would this make more sense? To learn more about the "Fair Tax" proposal log onto www.fairtax.org.

on Americans who choose not to buy insurance as well as an excise tax on Americans who purchase premium or "Cadillac" health care plans; a new tax on drug and medical device manufacturers; a tax on indoor tanning services and more.[87]

As President Obama prepared to leave office in the fall of 2016, Donald Trump and Hillary Clinton offered their vision for the taxes they felt should be paid.

Mrs. Clinton proposed raising the top income tax rate to 43.6 percent (the highest rate since 1985) and pushed for a new way of taxing capital gains (profit from investments) which would replace the 23.8% rate under Mr. Obama with rates from 27.8 to 47.4% depending on how long a person held an investment.[88] She also called for a new "exit tax" on American companies that relocate to foreign countries.[89]

Donald Trump arrived at Election Day promising to lower the number of tax brackets to three, with rates of 12, 25 and 33 percent. The capital gains tax he promised would also have three brackets of zero, 15 and 20 percent.

President Trump's case for lower tax rates was sidetracked a bit with the disclosure that he may have managed to avoid paying any income taxes (as a billionaire) for several years.[90] Critics charged that rich people like Mr. Trump need to pay their "fair share" of taxes. Some rich Americans even openly called for higher, rather than lower rates, on top-earners.

WHY SOME RICH PEOPLE DESIRE HIGHER TAXES

While he was running for president, Mr. Obama was asked by Charles Gibson (you can watch this exchange on YouTube) why he supported raising capital gains taxes when there was ample evidence that when Bill Clinton lowered capital gains taxes, the government earned more revenue. In response, Mr. Obama said, "Well Charlie, what I've said is that I would look at raising the capital gains tax for purposes of fairness."

While some of you would recoil at such an answer, you need to understand that there are many rich Americans who actually support the idea of higher taxes on themselves and their wealthy brethren. Bill Gates Sr. once said, "I am a fan of progressive taxation. I would say our country has prospered from using such a system — even at 70% rates to say nothing of 90%."[91]

You will not be hard-pressed to find many actors, actresses, athletes, academics, and even business owners who

vote for politicians who argue that rich folks should pay more.

Part of the reason for this seemingly odd desire is because of a theory that beyond a certain level of income, rich people do not get as much use from each dollar earned than a poor person would from obtaining an extra dollar. This makes intuitive sense. After all, if you make $10 million per year, how will your life be transformed if you suddenly make an extra $100? On the other hand, if you make $8,000 per year, that $100 is a much bigger percentage boost to your standard of living.

Thus, often politicians — and voters — ignore the deleterious effects that higher taxes have on economic progress, job creation, and wealth — and line up behind the "fairness" argument to support a more socialistic transformation of the income tax code. This has led to changes in the income tax code over time that now has only 53% of all Americans who actually pay taxes. 47% of us — through the proper deductions, the Earned Income Tax Credit and other means — have managed to no longer owe the federal government a dime.[92] For many economists, this creates an important question:

If the United States ever gets to the point where 51% of the people no longer pay taxes, what tax rate will those people vote for the other 49% to pay?

GOVERNMENT SPENDING

> I do not believe that Washington should do for the people what they can do for themselves through local and private effort.
>
> John F. Kennedy

High taxes are not the only measure of socialism. The amount of and type of government spending is also part of the equation. In this regard there is either good news or bad news depending on your personal beliefs about the role and size of government. If you are in favor of increased government spending in the name of making our country more "secure," then you should be very, very pleased with the following information. As the next few pages clearly illustrate, the federal government feels your pain and is all too happy to use your money to help ease it.

If we add up total federal spending during the entire eight years of the Reagan administration and the first two years of the first Bush administration, we see that total federal outlays amounted to $9.486 trillion.

This period covers the massive military buildup to end the Cold War and the cost of Operation Desert Shield in 1990. Federal spending during the last two years of the Bush administration and the entire eight years of the Clinton administration totaled $15.400 trillion. This was in spite of the fact that military spending either grew slowly or was cut (the only area of spending that ever fell) during this time.

COMPASSIONATE CONSERVATISM (AND LIBERALISM) AT WORK

"We will insist on a budget that limits and tames the spending appetite of the federal government. A taxpayer dollar ought to be spent wisely, or not spent at all."

George W. Bush

When George Bush ran for president in 2000, he campaigned as a "compassionate conservative."

When President Bush unveiled his first budget in 2001, it called for $28 trillion in new spending over 10 years.[93] To get a visual idea of that figure, imagine 28,000,000,000,000 one-dollar bills placed end-to-end. They would circle the orbit of the Earth around the sun approximately 30 times. By the time Mr. Bush unveiled his budget for fiscal year 2009, government spending under his watch had grown by 57% – and this does not include spending for the war on terror or the invasion of Iraq.[94] This figure is compared to a decrease in government spending (after adjusting for inflation) by 0.7% during Bill Clinton's first term in office.[95]

In 2012 federal spending totaled $3.457 trillion. Of that figure, $773 billion was allocated to Social Security; $472 billion for Medicare; $541 billion for social welfare payments and $251 billion for Medicaid. These figures mean that $2.037 trillion or 58.9% of the entire federal budget was a transfer of income from one citizen to another – in just these four categories.[96]

This does not include other transfer programs, subsidies to farms and businesses, foreign aid and more.

When President Obama took office the federal national debt stood at $10.6 trillion. By October 2016 the national debt was $19.6 trillion – the largest increase of any U.S. President.[97]

You may recall that 47% of Americans no longer pay income taxes. With over 49% of our population of over 323 million people receiving assistance from the forced taking of their fellow man's money, it is readily apparent that the United States is extremely close to what economists call the tax and entitlement "tipping point" – the point at which more Americans are net recipients of taxpayer aid rather than net contributors to the economy.

THE FOUNDERS' VIEW OF GOVERNMENT SPENDING

Article 1, Section 8 of the Constitution, gives Congress the authority to spend our tax money on national defense, federal debt, and items that promote the general welfare of U.S. citizens.

Perhaps it would help if we could explain what the Founders meant by the term, *general welfare*.

The powers of the federal government are enumerated; it can only operate in certain cases; it has legislative powers on defined and limited objects, beyond which it cannot extend its jurisdiction.

James Madison 1788

They are not to do anything they please to provide for the general welfare, but only to lay taxes for that purpose. To consider [Otherwise], would render all the preceding and subsequent enumerations of power completely useless. It would reduce the whole instrument to a single phrase, that of instituting a Congress with power do to whatever would be for the good of the United States; and, as they would be the sole judges of the good or evil, it would be also a power to do whatever evil they please. Certainly no such universal power was meant to be given them. It was intended to lace them up straightly within the enumerated powers and those without which, as means, these powers could not be carried into effect.

Thomas Jefferson 1791

If Congress can do whatever in their discretion can be done by money, and will promote the General Welfare, the Government is no longer a limited one, possessing enumerated powers, but an indefinite one, subject to particular exceptions.

Thomas Jefferson 1791

I hope our courts will never countenance the sweeping pretensions which have been set up under the words 'general defense and public welfare.' These words only express the motives which induced the Convention to give to the ordinary legislature certain specified powers which they enumerate, and which they thought might be trusted to the ordinary legislature, and not to give them the unspecified also; or why any specifications? They could not be so awkward in language as to mean, as we say, 'all and some.' And should this construction prevail, all limits to the federal government are done away.

Thomas Jefferson 1815

Table 1.1—SUMMARY OF RECEIPTS, OUTLAYS, AND SURPLUSES OR DEFICITS (–): 1789–2018

(in millions of dollars)

Year	Total			On-Budget			Off-Budget		
	Receipts	Outlays	Surplus or Deficit (–)	Receipts	Outlays	Surplus or Deficit (–)	Receipts	Outlays	Surplus or Deficit (–)
1789–1849	1,160	1,090	70	1,160	1,090	70	....	....	....
1850–1900	14,462	15,453	-991	14,462	15,453	-991	....	....	....
1901	588	525	63	588	525	63	....	....	....
1902	562	485	77	562	485	77	....	....	....
1903	562	517	45	562	517	45	....	....	....
1904	541	584	-43	541	584	-43	....	....	....
1905	544	567	-23	544	567	-23	....	....	....
1906	595	570	25	595	570	25	....	....	....
1907	666	579	87	666	579	87	....	....	....
1908	602	659	-57	602	659	-57	....	....	....
1909	604	694	-89	604	694	-89	....	....	....
1910	676	694	-18	676	694	-18	....	....	....
1911	702	691	11	702	691	11	....	....	....
1912	693	690	3	693	690	3	....	....	....
1913	714	715	-*	714	715	-*	....	....	....
1914	725	726	-*	725	726	-*	....	....	....
1915	683	746	-63	683	746	-63	....	....	....
1916	761	713	48	761	713	48	....	....	....
1917	1,101	1,954	-853	1,101	1,954	-853	....	....	....
1918	3,645	12,677	-9,032	3,645	12,677	-9,032	....	....	....
1919	5,130	18,493	-13,363	5,130	18,493	-13,363	....	....	....
1920	6,649	6,358	291	6,649	6,358	291	....	....	....
1921	5,571	5,062	509	5,571	5,062	509	....	....	....
1922	4,026	3,289	736	4,026	3,289	736	....	....	....
1923	3,853	3,140	713	3,853	3,140	713	....	....	....
1924	3,871	2,908	963	3,871	2,908	963	....	....	....
1925	3,641	2,924	717	3,641	2,924	717	....	....	....
1926	3,795	2,930	865	3,795	2,930	865	....	....	....
1927	4,013	2,857	1,155	4,013	2,857	1,155	....	....	....
1928	3,900	2,961	939	3,900	2,961	939	....	....	....
1929	3,862	3,127	734	3,862	3,127	734	....	....	....
1930	4,058	3,320	738	4,058	3,320	738	....	....	....
1931	3,116	3,577	-462	3,116	3,577	-462	....	....	....
1932	1,924	4,659	-2,735	1,924	4,659	-2,735	....	....	....
1933	1,997	4,598	-2,602	1,997	4,598	-2,602	....	....	....
1934	2,955	6,541	-3,586	2,955	6,541	-3,586	....	....	....
1935	3,609	6,412	-2,803	3,609	6,412	-2,803	....	....	....
1936	3,923	8,228	-4,304	3,923	8,228	-4,304	....	....	....
1937	5,387	7,580	-2,193	5,122	7,582	-2,460	265	-2	267
1938	6,751	6,840	-89	6,364	6,850	-486	387	-10	397
1939	6,295	9,141	-2,846	5,792	9,154	-3,362	503	-13	516
1940	6,548	9,468	-2,920	5,998	9,482	-3,484	550	-14	564
1941	8,712	13,653	-4,941	8,024	13,618	-5,594	688	35	653
1942	14,634	35,137	-20,503	13,738	35,071	-21,333	896	66	830
1943	24,001	78,555	-54,554	22,871	78,466	-55,595	1,130	89	1,041
1944	43,747	91,304	-47,557	42,455	91,190	-48,735	1,292	114	1,178
1945	45,159	92,712	-47,553	43,849	92,569	-48,720	1,310	143	1,167
1946	39,296	55,232	-15,936	38,057	55,022	-16,964	1,238	210	1,028
1947	38,514	34,496	4,018	37,055	34,193	2,861	1,459	303	1,157
1948	41,560	29,764	11,796	39,944	29,396	10,548	1,616	368	1,248
1949	39,415	38,835	580	37,724	38,408	-684	1,690	427	1,263
1950	39,443	42,562	-3,119	37,336	42,038	-4,702	2,106	524	1,583
1951	51,616	45,514	6,102	48,496	44,237	4,259	3,120	1,277	1,843
1952	66,167	67,686	-1,519	62,573	65,956	-3,383	3,594	1,730	1,864
1953	69,608	76,101	-6,493	65,511	73,771	-8,259	4,097	2,330	1,766
1954	69,701	70,855	-1,154	65,112	67,943	-2,831	4,589	2,912	1,677

See footnote at end of table.

Table 1.1—SUMMARY OF RECEIPTS, OUTLAYS, AND SURPLUSES OR DEFICITS (–): 1789–2018—Continued

(in millions of dollars)

Year	Total			On-Budget			Off-Budget		
	Receipts	Outlays	Surplus or Deficit (–)	Receipts	Outlays	Surplus or Deficit (–)	Receipts	Outlays	Surplus or Deficit (–)
1955	65,451	68,444	-2,993	60,370	64,461	-4,091	5,081	3,983	1,098
1956	74,587	70,640	3,947	68,162	65,668	2,494	6,425	4,972	1,452
1957	79,990	76,578	3,412	73,201	70,562	2,639	6,789	6,016	773
1958	79,636	82,405	-2,769	71,587	74,902	-3,315	8,049	7,503	546
1959	79,249	92,098	-12,849	70,953	83,102	-12,149	8,296	8,996	-700
1960	92,492	92,191	301	81,851	81,341	510	10,641	10,850	-209
1961	94,388	97,723	-3,335	82,279	86,046	-3,766	12,109	11,677	431
1962	99,676	106,821	-7,146	87,405	93,286	-5,881	12,271	13,535	-1,265
1963	106,560	111,316	-4,756	92,385	96,352	-3,966	14,175	14,964	-789
1964	112,613	118,528	-5,915	96,248	102,794	-6,546	16,366	15,734	632
1965	116,817	118,228	-1,411	100,094	101,699	-1,605	16,723	16,529	194
1966	130,835	134,532	-3,698	111,749	114,817	-3,068	19,085	19,715	-630
1967	148,822	157,464	-8,643	124,420	137,040	-12,620	24,401	20,424	3,978
1968	152,973	178,134	-25,161	128,056	155,798	-27,742	24,917	22,336	2,581
1969	186,882	183,640	3,242	157,928	158,436	-507	28,953	25,204	3,749
1970	192,807	195,649	-2,842	159,348	168,042	-8,694	33,459	27,607	5,852
1971	187,139	210,172	-23,033	151,294	177,346	-26,052	35,845	32,826	3,019
1972	207,309	230,681	-23,373	167,402	193,470	-26,068	39,907	37,212	2,695
1973	230,799	245,707	-14,908	184,715	199,961	-15,246	46,084	45,746	338
1974	263,224	269,359	-6,135	209,299	216,496	-7,198	53,925	52,862	1,063
1975	279,090	332,332	-53,242	216,633	270,780	-54,148	62,458	61,552	906
1976	298,060	371,792	-73,732	231,671	301,098	-69,427	66,389	70,695	-4,306
TQ	81,232	95,975	-14,744	63,216	77,281	-14,065	18,016	18,695	-679
1977	355,559	409,218	-53,659	278,741	328,675	-49,933	76,817	80,543	-3,726
1978	399,561	458,746	-59,185	314,169	369,585	-55,416	85,391	89,161	-3,770
1979	463,302	504,028	-40,726	365,309	404,941	-39,633	97,994	99,087	-1,093
1980	517,112	590,941	-73,830	403,903	477,044	-73,141	113,209	113,898	-689
1981	599,272	678,241	-78,968	469,097	542,956	-73,859	130,176	135,285	-5,109
1982	617,766	745,743	-127,977	474,299	594,892	-120,593	143,467	150,851	-7,384
1983	600,562	808,364	-207,802	453,242	660,934	-207,692	147,320	147,430	-110
1984	666,438	851,805	-185,367	500,363	685,632	-185,269	166,075	166,174	-98
1985	734,037	946,344	-212,308	547,866	769,396	-221,529	186,171	176,949	9,222
1986	769,155	990,382	-221,227	568,927	806,842	-237,915	200,228	183,540	16,688
1987	854,288	1,004,017	-149,730	640,886	809,243	-168,357	213,402	194,775	18,627
1988	909,238	1,064,416	-155,178	667,747	860,012	-192,265	241,491	204,404	37,087
1989	991,105	1,143,744	-152,639	727,439	932,832	-205,393	263,666	210,911	52,754
1990	1,031,958	1,252,994	-221,036	750,302	1,027,928	-277,626	281,656	225,065	56,590
1991	1,054,988	1,324,226	-269,238	761,103	1,082,539	-321,435	293,885	241,687	52,198
1992	1,091,208	1,381,529	-290,321	788,783	1,129,191	-340,408	302,426	252,339	50,087
1993	1,154,335	1,409,386	-255,051	842,401	1,142,799	-300,398	311,934	266,587	45,347
1994	1,258,566	1,461,753	-203,186	923,541	1,182,380	-258,840	335,026	279,372	55,654
1995	1,351,790	1,515,742	-163,952	1,000,711	1,227,078	-226,367	351,079	288,664	62,415
1996	1,453,053	1,560,484	-107,431	1,085,561	1,259,580	-174,019	367,492	300,904	66,588
1997	1,579,232	1,601,116	-21,884	1,187,242	1,290,490	-103,248	391,990	310,626	81,364
1998	1,721,728	1,652,458	69,270	1,305,929	1,335,854	-29,925	415,799	316,604	99,195
1999	1,827,452	1,701,842	125,610	1,382,984	1,381,064	1,920	444,468	320,778	123,690
2000	2,025,191	1,788,950	236,241	1,544,607	1,458,185	86,422	480,584	330,765	149,819
2001	1,991,082	1,862,846	128,236	1,483,563	1,516,008	-32,445	507,519	346,838	160,681
2002	1,853,136	2,010,894	-157,758	1,337,815	1,655,232	-317,417	515,321	355,662	159,659
2003	1,782,314	2,159,899	-377,585	1,258,472	1,796,890	-538,418	523,842	363,009	160,833
2004	1,880,114	2,292,841	-412,727	1,345,369	1,913,330	-567,961	534,745	379,511	155,234
2005	2,153,611	2,471,957	-318,346	1,576,135	2,069,746	-493,611	577,476	402,211	175,265
2006	2,406,869	2,655,050	-248,181	1,798,487	2,232,981	-434,494	608,382	422,069	186,313
2007	2,567,985	2,728,686	-160,701	1,932,896	2,275,049	-342,153	635,089	453,637	181,452
2008	2,523,991	2,982,544	-458,553	1,865,945	2,507,793	-641,848	658,046	474,751	183,295
2009	2,104,989	3,517,677	-1,412,688	1,450,980	3,000,661	-1,549,681	654,009	517,016	136,993

See footnote at end of table.

Table 1.1—SUMMARY OF RECEIPTS, OUTLAYS, AND SURPLUSES OR DEFICITS (–): 1789–2021—Continued

(in millions of dollars)

Year	Total			On-Budget			Off-Budget		
	Receipts	Outlays	Surplus or Deficit (–)	Receipts	Outlays	Surplus or Deficit (–)	Receipts	Outlays	Surplus or Deficit (–)
2010	2,162,706	3,457,079	-1,294,373	1,531,019	2,902,397	-1,371,378	631,687	554,682	77,005
2011	2,303,466	3,603,056	-1,299,590	1,737,678	3,104,450	-1,366,772	565,788	498,606	67,182
2012	2,449,988	3,536,951	-1,086,963	1,880,487	3,029,363	-1,148,876	569,501	507,588	61,913
2013	2,775,103	3,454,647	-679,544	2,101,829	2,820,836	-719,007	673,274	633,811	39,463
2014	3,021,487	3,506,114	-484,627	2,285,922	2,800,061	-514,139	735,565	706,053	29,512
2015	3,249,886	3,688,292	-438,406	2,479,514	2,945,215	-465,701	770,372	743,077	27,295
2016 estimate	3,335,502	3,951,307	-615,805	2,537,845	3,161,649	-623,804	797,657	789,658	7,999
2017 estimate	3,643,742	4,147,224	-503,482	2,816,874	3,318,636	-501,762	826,868	828,588	-1,720
2018 estimate	3,898,625	4,352,222	-453,597	3,035,354	3,467,898	-432,544	863,271	884,324	-21,053
2019 estimate	4,095,054	4,644,309	-549,255	3,196,845	3,702,365	-505,520	898,209	941,944	-43,735
2020 estimate	4,345,701	4,879,818	-534,117	3,413,847	3,871,656	-457,809	931,854	1,008,162	-76,308
2021 estimate	4,571,990	5,124,248	-552,258	3,591,774	4,052,084	-460,310	980,216	1,072,164	-91,948

* $500 thousand or less.

Note: Budget figures prior to 1933 are based on the "Administrative Budget" concepts rather than the "Unified Budget" concepts.

Source: IRS.gov.

Our tenet ever was that Congress had not unlimited powers to provide for the general welfare, but were restrained to those specifically enumerated, and that, as it was never meant that they should provide for that welfare but by the exercise of the enumerated powers, so it could not have been meant they should raise money for purposes which the enumeration did not place under their action; consequently, that the specification of powers is a limitation of the purposes for which they may raise money.

Thomas Jefferson 1817

The federal government is acknowledged by all to be one of enumerated powers. The principle, that it can exercise only the powers granted to it....is now universally admitted.

Chief Justice John Marshall 1819

With respect to the words 'general welfare,' I have always regarded them as qualified by the detail of powers connected with them. To take them in a literal and unlimited sense would be a metamorphosis of the Constitution into a character which there is a host of proofs was not contemplated by its creators.

James Madison 1831

I cannot undertake to lay my finger on that article of the Constitution which granted a right to Congress of expending, on objects of benevolence, the money of their constituents.

James Madison 1794

THE LEGACY OF ALEXANDER HAMILTON

From the preceding quotes it should be relatively clear that the Founding Fathers believed that general welfare meant spending money only to protect our rights and spending on only those categories specifically enumerated in Article 1, Section 8. (For the complete list, see the back of the book where the entire U.S. Constitution can be found.)

If the Founders had their way, the federal budget for this fiscal year would be hundreds of billions of dollars, lower than it is. How did we get to the point where out of every $100 you pay in taxes, over $70.50 is simply given to someone else? The blame, or credit, depending on your perspective, falls largely on Alexander Hamilton.

© M Shcherbyna/Shutterstock.com

You may recall from your history studies that Alexander Hamilton was a brilliant man. At 18 years of age he was writing editorials. George Washington thought enough of him to make him an aide. Hamilton went on to become the country's first Treasury Secretary and is largely responsible for helping to establish the good credit of the United States' early government.[98] Yet it was his work during the Constitutional Convention that has helped lead America down the road toward socialism.

During the convention, Hamilton – who once told Washington that he "long since learned to hold public opinion of no value" – delivered a five-hour speech. During his speech he proposed election of a president and senators for life by electors with property. Hamilton argued for the abolishment of state governments. The president was to have the veto and be able to enforce – or ignore – any law.[99]

Moreover, and perhaps most damagingly, Hamilton argued that the general welfare clause of the Constitution should not be confined to the enumerated powers of Congress, but rather Congress should be able to apply government spending in a more liberal manner so long as Congress could argue that the spending was for the "general welfare." Hamilton went on to argue that, "The power to raise money is plenary and indefinite [in the Constitution]…The terms general Welfare were doubtless intended to signify more than was expressed. It is therefore of necessity left to the discretion of the National Legislature, to pronounce upon the objects, which concern the general Welfare, and for which…an appropriation of money is requisite and proper. [Otherwise] numerous exigencies incident to the affairs of a nation would have been left without a proper provision."[100] Hamilton's proposals were rejected flatly. In fact, not one member of the convention seconded any of his ideas. Yet in 1936, Hamilton's views on government spending became the law of the land.

THE UNITED STATES V. BUTLER

When Franklin D. Roosevelt was elected president in 1932, he came into office promising America a "New Deal." The "old deal" was that government had limited powers to tax and spend and Americans had to rely on their own creative energies for their well-being. Roosevelt immediately began changing the relationship between government and the people. It was under his direction that a whole host of welfare and public works projects were created. The only problem was that the Supreme Court kept ruling his new programs unconstitutional – that is, until 1936.

Frustrated with the Supreme Court, Roosevelt began discussing the idea of adding one new Supreme Court justice for every sitting justice over the age of 70.[101] That would have pushed the total number of justices from 9 to 15. Surely anyone can see the political windfall that would have been bestowed upon FDR. With six extra justices – all appointed by FDR – the Supreme Court would have been packed with people more sensitive to his political agenda.

As part of the 1933 Agricultural Adjustment Act, Congress implemented a processing tax on agricultural commodities, from which funds would be redistributed to farmers who promised to reduce their acreage. The Act intended to solve the crisis in agricultural commodity prices that was causing many farmers to go under.

The Court found the Act unconstitutional because it attempted to regulate and control agricultural production, an arena reserved to the states. Even though Congress does have the power to tax and appropriate funds, argued Justice Roberts, in this case those activities were "but means to an unconstitutional end," and violated the Tenth Amendment.

However, the court unwittingly sowed the seeds of a socialist forest by going on to say:

> …the grant is that public funds my be appropriated to provide for the General Welfare of the United States….Since the foundation of the Nation, sharp differences of opinion have persisted as to the true interpretation of that phrase. Madison asserted that it amounted to no more than a reference to the other powers enumerated in the subsequent clauses of the same section; that, as the United States is a government of limited and enumerated powers, the grant of power to tax and spend for the general

welfare must be confined to the enumerated legislative fields committed to the Congress. Hamilton, on the other hand, maintained the clause confers a power separate and distinct from those later enumerated, is not restricted in meaning by the grant of them and Congress consequently has a substantive power to tax and to appropriate, limited only by the requirement that it shall be exercised to provide for the General Welfare of the United States. Each contention has had the support of those whose views are entitled to weight. Study of all these leads us to conclude that the reading by Mr. Justice Story (the Hamiltonian position) is the correct one. It results that the power of Congress to authorize expenditure of public moneys for public purposes is not limited by the direct grants of legislative power found in the Constitution.[102]

Since January 6, 1936, the United States Congress has had the authority to spend your money as it sees fit. Republicans and Democrats alike now use your money to fund everything from rainforest museums in Iowa to bailouts for banks, insurance companies and automobile manufacturers to "victims" of natural disasters who built houses six feet under the ocean.....

HOW TO GET PEOPLE TO HATE YOU

We have the right, as individuals, to give away as much of our own money as we please to charity; but as members of Congress we have no right so to appropriate a dollar of the public money.[103]

David Crockett

I sure wish Mr. Crockett would have been around to come to my aid in September of 2005. I needed him because it was during that time that I was invited to appear on *Your World with Cavuto* — a *Fox News* program devoted to economics and politics.

I had appeared on Neal Cavutos' show a couple of times in 2004 to talk about the economics and constitutionality of rebuilding homes in Florida in the wake of the hurricanes that came through that summer. So, when *Fox News* called me to talk about the same topic as it applied to residents of New Orleans, I thought it might be a good idea to help educate taxpayers about Article 1, Section 8 of our rulebook. Apparently, the people of Louisiana — and seemingly millions of others around the country — did not really like hearing about James Madison's view of plunder. As one person put it:

"I just saw your disgraceful interview as was rotating from *Fox News* to CNN. Do you truly believe that taxpayers' money should not be used to help New Orleans and surrounding areas? If so, WHAT IS TAX MONEY FOR???

"You are borderline evil for even suggesting that our government, which ideally should function primarily to protect us, do NOTHING to aide a state which is not capable of covering the totality of this natural disaster.

"I am from New Orleans, but currently live in Los Angeles. You are in effect, suggesting that I, my family, friends and everyone from New Orleans suffer because of something we had no control over.

"No amount of logic could justify your ridiculous comments in front of the nation tonight. You're abandoning fellow human beings because you are too selfish to let your tax dollars go to a human cause.

"You made yourself seem like a callous, heartless beast in front of many, many people — despite any good intentions you may have thought you had."

This email was one of the more polite ones I received. The death threats over the phone were even less fun.

The question of what to do about the Gulf Coast in the wake of Hurricane Katrina was an interesting one. The type of normative analysis that is so often connected with socialism would call for taxpayer dollars — of whatever amount necessary — to be used to rebuild New Orleans. This is certainly the Hamiltonian approach the Bush Administration took and one that both Barack Obama and George Bush supported.

But did the rebuilding of New Orleans, with taxpayer dollars, satisfy the "general welfare" test?[104] Did it line up with capitalism?

It is inarguable that the people of New Orleans have every right to go home and rebuild their lives. They can use their money, their insurance, the charity of their neighbor and whatever other resource they can peacefully procure.

However, if we say that a person in New Orleans should be able to get the tax dollars of a person in Maine, are we not calling for the legal plunder that Bastiat talked about?[105] Moreover, if we allow people to rebuild with taxpayer dollars, are we not artificially lowering the cost of living in an area that will get hit again someday?[106]

Photo courtesy Jack Chambless

Is this type of charity enough?

By doing that, are we not going to end up causing the death of even more people who would not have come back, if not for the taxpayer aid? Two years after Katrina hit, there were still 87,000 households living in travel trailers within the same path that the storm took.[107]

If rebuilding New Orleans does pass the general welfare test — after all, it is a major port — wouldn't the corporations who stand to profit from having this city intact rebuild it on their own, in order to keep making profit from jazz, good food and access to the Gulf of Mexico? Wouldn't homeowners who prefer to live in New Orleans do the same thing? Does taxpayer-financed "charity" lead to the problem of moral hazard?[108]

> **Moral hazard - The prospect that a person, or institution insulated from risk may behave differently from the way it would behave if it were fully exposed to the risk. Moral hazard arises because an individual or institution does not bear the full consequences of its actions, and therefore has a tendency to act less carefully than it otherwise would, leaving another party to bear some responsibility for the consequences of those actions.**

SOCIAL INSECURITY?

The following is a direct quote from a friend who works for the Social Security Administration. The quote is in response to my question as to whether we as individuals should have the right to keep even some of our social security taxes to make private investment decisions:

As an SSA employee, and as a private Joe Citizen, I think it's a huge mistake to allow anyone to take any money from their SSA taxes to invest themselves. A huge mistake! If it were not for the social security system, we would have countless elderly people living on the street, in the back room of their kids' houses, etc. Most people need every penny they can get their hands on just to survive.

If the system allows them to keep any of it or invest themselves, they won't invest it. They'll spend it on kid's clothes, rent, food, utilities, G.I. Joe with the Kung Fu grip, etc. Then, when they're 62 or whatever, they'll come up to one of the SSA offices and we'll tell them, Sorry, we gave you yours. You are due no more from this agency. Then what? Homeless, back room of their kids' houses, or worse. There probably are quite a few people who could make their money work for them lots better than the government can. But how do you determine who those people are? Do you let some have their taxes back, and some not? And what happens when those so-called smart people invest in some no-account company and lose their a-----? They'll be back at the SSA office, and we'll say, Sorry, we gave you yours. You are due no more.

From 1776 to 1935 the government's relationship to the citizenry — as it applied to retirement — was pretty straightforward. "Save money if you want to quit working some day," was the message.

During the Great Depression, with hardship hitting elderly Americans in a particularly harsh way, the Roosevelt Administration created our nation's first *forced* retirement plan.[109]

The plan was quite simple. Workers would have part of their paychecks taken (matched by their employers) in the form of a payroll tax. This tax would finance the Social Security Trust Fund — a fund made up of government securities (Treasury bonds, for example) that retirees could draw upon once they met the legal age requirements.

© Joseph Sohm/Shutterstock.com

CONCEPT CHECK

In 2010, President Obama announced a $1.5 billion program designed to assist homeowners facing foreclosure. Mr. Obama, in defense of this plan said, "The money will go to homeowners who have lost their jobs, owe more than their houses are worth, and cannot afford to make monthly payments."[110] Give some specific ways in which this program could lead to the problem of moral hazard for banks, taxpayers, and homeowners who are not facing foreclosure.

In 2016 the first $118,500 of income was taxed at a rate of 12.4% - 6.2% paid by the employee, and, in theory, 6.2% paid by the employer.[111] We use the phrase "in theory" because empirical analysis suggests that much of the payroll tax paid by employers shows up in the form of lower earnings for the worker, higher prices for consumers and less profit for shareholders.

Of course, all of the money you pay in payroll taxes is set aside in a fund, under your name, earning interest – just for you – until you let the Social Security Administration know that you have retired, right?

Yes, if you believe in Santa Claus and the Easter Bunny.

Starting somewhere around .01 seconds after FDR signed the legislation, Social Security became an intergenerational transfer of money from taxpayers to retirees. For example, Ida Fuller, a legal secretary in Vermont, paid a total of $24.75 into social security from 1937 to 1940, when she retired at the age of 65. Her first monthly social security check of $22.54 almost equaled her total paid in taxes. By the time she died in 1975, she had received $22,888.92 in social security checks – or approximately $1,000 for every $1 she paid in.[112]

In 1950 – when there was a lower population and people did not live very long – there were 16 people paying into Social Security for every person receiving benefits. Today, for every 3.3 workers there is a retired person getting their money. By 2050, it will be 2 workers for every retiree. Who knows, with medical breakthroughs and a slowdown in population growth, there might come a day where every retiree in America has their own personal taxpayer!

As this paragraph is being written, the U.S. is less than two years away from the point where more money will be paid out in benefits than is available in the trust fund. Thus, the government will have to use revenues from income taxes to help support Social Security. This is part of the reason why many economists believe that several things will have to happen to "save" Social Security. Among the possibilities include raising the payroll tax and/or payroll tax threshold, raising the retirement age, lowering the benefits paid, or seeking some private sector remedy.

In 2003, former President Bush proposed letting taxpayers keep a portion (less than 3%) of their payroll taxes to invest in funds other than the Social Security Trust Fund. Mr. Bush said, "We must offer younger workers a chance to invest in retirement accounts that they will control and they will own."

David Crockett, James Madison, and Frederic Bastiat may have been applauding Mr. Bush somewhere, but back in America where senior citizens vote and young people do not, his proposal was wiped out by lobbyists representing the interests of older Americans who have the most to lose if taxpayers are ever allowed to invest their own income in accounts that they freely choose.

WHERE WE ARE TODAY

In September 2012 Presidential contender Mitt Romney created a national debate when a video emerged of him saying, "There are 47 percent of the people who will vote for the President no matter what. All right, there are 47 percent who are with him, who are dependent on government, who believe they are victims, who believe the government has a responsibility to care for them, who believe that they are entitled to health care, to food, to housing, to you name it."

Four months later, when Mr. Obama took the oath of office for his second term, he stated, "The commitments we make each other through Medicare and Medicaid and Social Security – these things do not sap our initiative; they strengthen us. They do not make us a nation of takers; they free us to take the risks that make this country great."

Clearly, these two gentlemen – and the voters who were split in 2012 (and are split today) – could not be more different in their views of the value of our social

© Spotmatik Ltd/Shutterstock.com

SUGGESTED CLASSROOM DEBATE

Should Social Security be abolished in favor of total privatization of our retirement plans? Why, or why not? Log on to http://www.nationalaffairs.com/publications/detail/the-future-of-social-security before you answer.

welfare system. Normative analysis being what it is, the reader of this chapter needs to counterbalance the opinions of politicians with some hard data.

First, in 1964 President Lyndon Johnson declared "unconditional war on poverty" in the United States. From 1964 to 2014, the United States government spent $20.3 trillion on anti-poverty programs. Roughly 15 percent of Americans lived in poverty then. That figure is the same today.[113]

In 2016 more than 80 programs existed that used taxpayer dollars to assist poor people in housing, health care, education, food and more. We saw earlier that over 49% of Americans rely on their fellowman for some form of forced income transfer.

When one considers the fact that more and more Americans – especially younger men – have stopped looking for work[114] while the percentages filing for Supplemental Security Income, food stamps, housing and medical assistance and other programs has increased dramatically, it begs the question, "If we have used over $20 trillion in tax dollars to win a war, but the war is still raging, should we spend even more, or change the battle tactic?"

GOVERNMENT REGULATION

> "Businesses should live up to their responsibilities to create American jobs, look out for American workers, and play by the rules of the road."
>
> Barack Obama

I am almost ashamed to admit this, but on the day I sat down to write this section, I found myself staring blankly at the computer screen for what seemed like hours. I kept asking myself, "Where do I begin?" Writing about the monumental growth of government regulations is a lot like trying to write about the universe. You can see the universe is out there, but since you don't see where it ends, how do you explain it?

Since most of you do not currently run a business, it might be wise to start out with a definition of the word, *regulation*.

To the Founding Fathers, the word "regulate" – literally meant "to make normal." If you read Article 1, Section 8 Clause 3 of the U.S. Constitution you can see what is called the 'Commerce Clause' which gives Congress the right to regulate commerce among the states and with the various American-Indian tribes. This clause was inserted in order to eliminate tariffs and other barriers to trade within the states.

Today, if you were to ask one hundred Americans what the word "regulate" means, it is a good bet that a majority of them would answer with words like "slow down," "stop," "prevent," "control" or "manage." Congress agrees. Today, a functional economic definition of the word *regulation* would be:

> ➤ **A regulation is a rule or law imposed by government on business firms.**

None of us want to see seven-year-old children working in sweat shops any more than we want to eat poisoned meat, breathe black air, or fly in planes with a 50/50 chance of crashing into the side of a mountain. A large majority of Americans are in agreement that government is needed to regulate business and industry to keep us safe from "greedy" business people. As a consequence, the government's reach into our lives has expanded every year.

Depending on where you live, you may or may not be allowed to smoke in a bar. You might not be allowed to have your body pierced or lie down in a tanning bed.[115] You might not be allowed to drive without wearing a seat belt. You might not be able to hire whomever you want at the price you and the other person agree to. You might not be able to buy light beer on Sunday. These are some of, as Mr. Obama might say, "rules of the road." One might ask, "How many rules does the road need?" When do the rules of the road do more harm to businesses and individuals than good?

Ironically, these are precisely the questions President Obama sought to address in a surprising editorial in the January 18, 2011 edition of *The Wall Street Journal*.

In his editorial, Mr. Obama explained his rationale for issuing an executive order requiring all federal agencies to "ensure that regulations protect our safety, health, and environment while promoting economic growth."[116] President Obama argued that the federal government needed to examine all regulations with an eye toward throwing out any rules that had become outdated or were stifling job creation.

What is interesting about his editorial, is that it came on the heels of two straight years of massive increases in the number of regulations businesses were forced to adhere to under Mr. Obama's watch. Consider this:

In May 2016 the Competitive Enterprise Institute estimated that the total cost of government regulation was over $1.885 trillion which amounted to a "hidden tax" of nearly $15,000 per family, per year – which is more than the average family's tax burden and more than the entire Gross Domestic Product of Canada in 2016.[117] Regulations on small businesses (those with fewer than 20 employees) cost 36% more than larger firms.

These regulations lead to higher operating costs for businesses, and as John Stossel illustrated in his program entitled "Illegal Everything," the costs show up for all of us in the form of higher prices, fewer job opportunities and growing income inequality as less wealthy Americans struggle to pay the regulatory burden that larger corporations have an easier time managing.[118] After all, what would you do if you ran a business that was saddled with close to $15,000 in costs, per worker? Would you just say, "Oh well, that's fine, I will just earn a lot less profit?"

The Code of Federal Regulations, which compiles all federal regulations, grew by more than 17,500 pages while Mr. Obama was president. This regulatory "guide" for businesses totaled 175,496 pages in 2016, spread over 238 volumes. The index alone took up 1,170 pages.

Ronald Reagan managed to cut the number of pages by 31% - and the economy grew by 30% during his presidency. Yet from 1993 to 2012, 81,883 new rules were added and in the last ten years alone the number of new regulations issued by 63 different federal departments has outnumbered the laws written by Congress 223 to 1.[119]

These regulations often impact small businesses more than larger ones. Researchers at Lafayette University found that the per employee cost of regulatory compliance was $10,585 per worker for firms with 19 or fewer employees compared with $7,755 for companies with more than 500 workers.[120]

In fairness to the Obama Administration, the Bush years were not lacking in government intrusion into the lives of those men and women who produce the goods and services we all enjoy. Under Mr. Bush, the federal government added almost $30 billion in new costs while the number of new federal workers employed to enforce those rules rose by 41%.[121]

It would be a huge oversight to leave out some of the examples of the types of rules businesses face these days. There are not enough trees in the Pacific Northwest that could be turned into the amount of paper needed to cover all of the rules, so I have selected some of the more recent highlights.

The government desires many things for our health. Among them is the safety of the clothes our children wear and the toys they play with. Toward that end, the regulators have really clamped down on the amount of lead our kids are allowed to be near. Of course, everyone knows that exposure to large quantities of lead can impede the cognitive development of little folks, but the rules that are now in place ban products with more than three one-hundredths of 1% lead.

This means that items like zippers, buttons, belts, hinges on a child's dresser, certain bicycles parts, and more, are banned. Even though laboratory tests run by scientists show that lead in these items is not "bioavailable" (cannot be absorbed in the blood no matter how much a toddler chews on it) and is of too small a quantity to do any damage even if swallowed, the regulators have still said, "No."

In the toy industry alone, this irrational regulation led to $2 billion in losses in 2008. The motorcycle industry lost $1 billion in sales from the ban, and major charities like Goodwill and The Salvation Army had to throw away between $100 million and $170 million in used clothes that did not meet the federal government's safety tests.[122]

The Environmental Protection Agency worries about us, too. Businesses that work on older construction sites are required to invest in lead-testing kits, plastic sheeting, respirators, protective clothing, and worker certification programs to deal with the possibility of lead exposure. For a typical mold-removal business, the lead rules add $160,000-$300,000 per year in costs – even though many of the homes they work in were built after 1978 – when no lead paint was sold.[123]

The EPA recently proposed a reduction in the "acceptable ozone level in the air" from .075 parts per million to between .06-.07 parts per million. This might seem like a fairly benign proposal. The EPA estimated that the new rules, which would force every business in America that uses energy (translation: 100% of businesses) to comply, would cost between $19 billion and $90 billion annually. The benefits, according to the EPA would be $13 billion in lower health care costs associated with respiratory illnesses.[124]

When have you ever bought a shirt that was worth $13 to you but cost you between $19 and $90?

CONCEPT CHECK

In many cities around the United States what these girls are doing would be illegal. Their crime? An unlicensed lemonade, coffee and snack stand that also has not received government permits to exist. How do such regulations impact the price of lemonade and the number of stands that exist?

Do you drive a car? Do you use tooth whiteners? Do you have a bank account? If you answered "Yes" to any of these questions, government protectors are looking out for your well-being, too.

In 2009, President Obama ordered car manufacturers to increase the average fuel economy from 27.5 miles per gallon to 39 miles per gallon before this decade ends.

It would be really nice if General Motors and all the rest could achieve this goal as quickly as politicians can order it to happen, but two things stand in the way: consumers, overall, still prefer larger vehicles and the cost of meeting the new regulation would not be low.

On average, the price of new cars would rise by $1,300 after the carmakers folded in the costs of the new technologies needed to meet this requirement.[125]

Moreover, many economists have pointed out that in the past when fuel efficiency standards are forced up, the level of pollution-reduction achieved is far lower than government officials predict. This is because higher car prices encourage millions to hang on to their older, less-efficient cars for a longer period of time. Furthermore, every time we are forced to buy cars that are lighter and more environmentally friendly, the number of traffic fatalities increases.[126]

Another proposed regulation called the Rear-View Camera Rule would require that all cars and trucks be equipped with a rear-view camera and video display on the dashboard. The total cost of this mandate would be $2.7 billion.[127]

If you find yourself gritting your teeth in frustration over this section of the book, you might need to ask yourself if your nice, white teeth are legal or not? What?

If you got your pearly whites from an over-the-counter supplier you are fine. If you prefer to rely on a salon or other business, look out.

Over the past several years dentists from many states have successfully lobbied state governments to force suppliers to teeth-whitening services to have a special license. Over 30 states now prohibit those who are good at whitening teeth the right to do so unless you are a dentist.[128] In many states, dentists charge up to six times what the now closed salons used to charge.

The same situation has happened to barbers. In 2010, 35 people were arrested and put in jail in a part of Orlando, Florida known as Pine Hills. This area is one marked with higher rates of poverty than other parts of Central Florida so businesses are vital to maintaining economic progress here. The 35 jailed "offenders" were dragged away in two separate raids for not having a Florida license to cut hair.[129]

A July 2015 White House study found that no fewer than 60 occupations are regulated in all 50 states, with 1,110 jobs regulated in at least one state. In 1950, 5% of

Is this child in danger?

workers required a state license to serve their fellowman. Today it is 30% with Ohio (33.3% of jobs requiring a license) and Florida (28.7%) leading the way.

For economists, the overriding inefficiency of such licensing rules is quite clear. First, the high costs, hours of testing and ongoing compliance with the law keeps many lower to moderate income Americans from being allowed to compete – at any level – with larger, established businesses.

Second, valuable tax dollars are used in spurious cases where police are called in to raid and arrest people giving other consenting adults a haircut when a rapist they have been looking for might be walking down the sidewalk watching the barbers get hauled away.

Finally, we often say to politicians that rather than have government rules on who can whiten teeth or cut hair, it makes more economic sense to let consumers – both the satisfied and unsatisfied – determine which businesses rise and fall. After all, the refusal to go back to a bad barber – and posting your ruined head on Facebook – is a powerful weapon that consumers have at their disposal.

In the wake of the financial panic that gripped the country in 2008-2009, the Obama Administration moved at lightning speed to change the rules of the banking road.

Among the new regulations passed in 2010 were restrictions on investments banks could make (to prevent the type of hyper-investing in complicated home-mortgage portfolios), requirements that banks hold more cash in reserve, shareholder rights to set executive compensation, and government authority to seize and dismantle financially struggling firms that would pose a danger to the economy.[130]

All together, the 2,300 page law created 243 new rules for the financial industry – including investment and accounting firms[131] – prompting some banking executives to contend that all of the new rules would lead to an end to small community banks.[132]

Over the past few years new companies like Uber, AirBnB and Lyft have transformed the way Americans travel, sleep and do business.[133] Yet, in cities like Austin, Texas (where Uber is banned), these companies are facing governmental challenges to their drive for profit. Should these companies – and their customers – be free to interact without government regulation? Why, or why not? What type of government regulations might make sense? Why?

You will notice that the preceding analysis has not even delved into the laws that make it illegal to summarily fire drug addicts working at your company, or the laws that end secret ballots in union elections, or the laws that do not allow you to shop for health insurance across state lines, or the FDA rules that have led to upwards of 4.7 *million* people who have died prematurely from 1963-1999 while waiting for government permission to use certain medicines.[134]

In its report entitled, "Doing Business 2016" the World Bank ranked the United States at number 7 – behind China (ranked 5th) in the area of regulatory efficiency. This represented a decline from fourth place in 2011.[135]

We have also not mentioned new over-time laws that require businesses to pay salaried workers overtime,[136] President Obama's Clean Power plan, Dodd-Frank financial regulations, mandatory health care coverage that led the founder of Home Depot to argue that his company could have never gotten off the ground under today's regulatory climate,[137] food safety regulations (where regulators keep failing to keep food safe), airport security, state and local rules, or most of the other regulations that the average family pays $10,000 per year for.[138]

What is clear is that Mr. Obama's call for an examination of government regulations was warranted. To the casual reader of this chapter, economists seem to want no rules for the suppliers of goods and services. That is not the case at all. Economists simply call for a cost-benefit test applied to all rules. We also want the cost-benefit test to rely on measurable data so as to make the most rational determination over what the rules should be. In 1981, President Reagan issued an executive order that called for a measure of benefits and costs behind new regulations. President Obama expanded this order by allowing agencies to consider "equity, human dignity, fairness, and distributive impacts."[139]

The inherent difficulty with this amendment to the Reagan order is the difficulty in measuring equity, fairness, or possible violations of human dignity.

Therefore, when Mr. Obama said, "America's free market has not only been the source of dazzling ideas and path-breaking products, it has also been the greatest force for prosperity the world has ever known," America's business leaders were probably appreciative for the change in his tone,[140] but remained skeptical that the right calculations would be used to determine the laws that would govern business going forward.

THE ECONOMICS OF CIVIL LIBERTIES

On September 11, 2001 nearly 3,000 Americans lost their lives during the terrorist attack on our nation. From that day until September 11, 2016 a total of 95 Americans (including the 49 from the Orlando nightclub massacre) had died on U.S. soil from terrorism. Over that time frame, and especially in recent years with the rise of ISIS, more and more Americans have advocated greater government surveillance to hopefully reduce the chances of future attacks. Others have argued that privacy concerns (see the Apple, Inc. vs. the FBI case) outweigh the need to snoop into our phones and emails. Both arguments center on the changes that have taken place with respect to civil liberties in the United States.

You might wonder, "What does the right to free speech and privacy have to do with capitalism, socialism or any other economic system?"

Well, as it turns out, quite a lot. Imagine what our economy would look like if people – and businesses – constantly worried about the degree to which our interactions were being monitored or our speech regulated. Would we feel as free to create, communicate and take risks? Perhaps not.

That is one reason why economists have been concerned about laws that have passed since 9/11.[141]

THE PATRIOT ACT

Shortly after the World Trade Center was reduced to rubble, the U.S. Congress passed a sweeping anti-terrorism law called the Patriot Act. This Act, critics charge, has ostensibly altered, if not severely damaged, the Fourth Amendment to the U.S. Constitution (see the back of the book).

Under the Patriot Act, a secret court can order you to turn over documents, records and other tangible items to the FBI and force you to remain silent about both the seizure and the court order. You cannot challenge the order by appearing before the court prior to the order being issued. And after the order is issued, your attorney – if you have one – will not be successful in stopping it.[142]

The Patriot Act expands the definition of terrorism to include any "acts dangerous to human life that are a violation of the criminal laws of the United States or of any State" or acts that "appear to be intended to intimidate or coerce a civilian population or to influence the policy of a government...."

Under this definition, any demonstrators or protesters involved in a march that turns violent could be classified as terrorists. A Rutherford Institute study points out that "diverse domestic political groups which have been accused of acts of intimidation or property damage, such as Act Up, PETA, and Operation Rescue, could be targeted as terrorist organizations."

The definition of terrorism as "acts that appear to be intended to...coerce a civilian population or influence the policy of a government" could certainly include writing a book, making speeches, teaching, or even buying or reading a book with the intent to spread its ideas to the public.

The Act also gives the government the authority to, without you knowing it, read your mail before you open it and prosecute you on the basis of what it reads; find out where you travel, what you confide to your lawyer and what periodicals you read.[143]

The Bush Administration was also successful in compelling Internet search providers to give the government samples of searches that Americans had gone through on the Internet. Google executives refused to turn over the documents, citing the rights to privacy that their customers have (had, depending on when you might be reading this...).[144]

Supporters of President Obama cheered when he was running for office in 2008 as he sharply criticized the Bush Administration for the aforementioned policies.

However, under Mr. Obama, by many accounts surveillance of ordinary Americans has increased dramatically.

In 2013, President Obama came to the defense of the National Security Administration after it was revealed that the NSA had engaged in massive monitoring of the phone calls, emails and Internet searches of millions of Americans. Mr. Obama called the searches "modest encroachments" on personal privacy, adding, "You know, we're going to have to make some choices as a society."[145]

Part of those choices in recent times has been the increase in the use of drones – unmanned aircraft that can be used by police to monitor activities by residents in America. The federal government has predicted that by 2019 30,000 drones will be in the sky over our homes and property for the stated purpose of protecting us from one another.[146]

GOVERNMENT AT THE AIRPORT

On September 27, 2001, Netscape ran a poll over the Internet that asked, "Are you willing to trade some civil liberties for heightened security?" Of the 137,499 people who answered, 67% said "yes." This answer must have been just what Congress wanted to hear, because later that year the House of Representatives and Senate voted to turn over all airport security to the federal government. In fact, the vote in the Senate was 100-0 in favor of having the same group that runs our public schools and post offices provide safety in the skies. "If you don't have federalism, it doesn't work," said Sen. John D. Rockefeller, D-West Virginia. "You can't professionalize, unless you federalize," agreed Senate Majority Leader Tom Daschle, D-South Dakota.

On February 19, 2002, the federal government took over the supervisory role for the 28,000 screeners who work for private contractors.

In April of 2002, The Transportation Security Administration announced that 60,000 screeners were needed to meet the needs of the nation's airports. The screeners, who will make between $23,600 and $35,400 annually, must have a high-school diploma, GED or equivalent, or at least one year of full-time experience in security work, aviation screener work, or X-ray technician work – and must be a U.S. citizen.

The government's contention has been that if it had been in charge of supervising airport screeners on September 11th, the probability of an attack would have been much lower. Let's look at it. The government runs the United States Customs Department and the Immigration and Naturalization Services. These are the agencies that let the hijackers into the country even though three had expired visas and six had no records at all.

In March of 2002, the INS sent out approved student visas for hijackers Mohamed Atta and Marwan Al-Shehhi, six months after they were already dead from blowing up the World Trade Center! When asked about such a horrific oversight, the head of the INS, James Ziglar, said that INS rules are so complicated that he wasn't sure whether it was illegal for Atta to come back into the country with an expired tourist visa and an application for a student visa.

Atta applied for a student visa on September 19, 2000, and was notified he was approved ten months later. Ziglar said the INS system was so low-tech that forms were tossed into a box and mailed when the box was full.

When asked about his personal qualifications to head the INS, Mr. Ziglar replied, "Well, I have some friends who are immigrants."[147] Yes, that is exactly what he told Congress. Now you can sleep well.

Economist Walter Williams recently joined a legion of critics who would agree with his assessment of airport security.

"Americans have been bamboozled into believing that with federalization of airport security, we'd be safer. After all, according to media reports, Europeans who have a much longer history of dealing with terrorists have government-controlled airport security. Nothing can be further from the truth."

According to Robert Poole, a Reason Foundation air transportation expert (reason.org), 33 out of 35 European airports use private companies for passenger and baggage screening, and that includes high-risk airports such as: Amsterdam, Belfast, Copenhagen, Frankfurt, Hamburg, Paris, and even Tel Aviv's Ben Gurion Airport. At these airports, the government sets security standards. A private for-profit contractor performs the security screening. There are strong oversight and penalties exacted for not meeting the standards.

So what has the new Transportation Security Act (TSA) mandated, and even if the mandates made complete sense, will they be achieved? TSA mandated 100% baggage screening by January 18, 2002. That was not achieved. TSA mandated federal takeover of existing security contracts by February 17, 2002. Again, failure. TSA mandated that 30,000-plus passenger and baggage screeners be federalized and trained by November 19, 2002.[148]

That deadline wasn't met either.

Speaking of deadlines not being met, during the summer of 2015 and 2016 millions of Americans found themselves missing business meetings, vacation schedules, weddings, funerals and more as TSA security lines in airports took on record proportions. Increasingly frustrated airline passengers – along with airlines who lost money due to the missed flights – began asking whether it made sense to continue to have government-led security agents in charge of our nation's busy schedule.

FINAL THOUGHTS

Over the last two chapters you have become an expert in the costs and benefits of every major economic system available to you today. As an economics student, it is up to you to decide which one is the most rational one for you. Somewhere between the mixed economy and capitalism might prompt you to move to New Zealand or New Hampshire. Maybe you would be happier in Norway, or Northern California, where a more socialistic system is in place.

The most important thing to remember is that every choice comes with a cost. If you trust government to take care of you, there will be the cost of reduced economic and civil liberty. If you trust yourself and free markets, there will be the cost of greater personal responsibility. Perhaps it would serve us all well to remember the words of Ronald Reagan, who once said:

"We who live in free market societies believe that growth, prosperity and ultimately human fulfillment, are created from the bottom up, not the government down. Only when the human spirit is allowed to invent and create, only when individuals are given a personal stake in deciding economic policies and benefiting from their success – only then can societies remain economically alive, dynamic, progressive and free. Trust the people."

ENDNOTES

1 See "Vacation's over for president" by Philip Rucker & Scott Wilson, *The Orlando Sentinel*, January 6, 2014.

2 See http://www.fns.usda.gov/pd/29snapcurrpp.htm

3 See http://www.ssa.gov/policy/docs/quickfacts/stat_snapshot/

4 See "Millionaires on Medicaid" by Mark Warshawsky, *The Wall Street Journal*, January 6, 2014.

5 See "No Bailouts for Borrowers" by Andy Laperriere, *The Wall Street Journal*, December 4, 2007, pg. A21.

6 See "How Fed's Bailout Can Affect You" by Kevin G. Hall, *The Orlando Sentinel*, September 8, 2008.

7 It is important to point out that there are many causes – artificial and natural – that contributed to the collapse in housing prices. In 1977, the Community Reinvestment Act forced banks to extend credit to people with less than desirable credit and employment histories. In 1995, President Clinton signed the Gramm–Leach–Bliley Act which allowed commercial banks, investment banks, securities firms, and insurance companies to consolidate. This legislation contributed to the massive bundling of home mortgages into complicated investment packages. Each of these acts led to an artificial increase in home prices and eventually the meltdown in housing prices.

8 For the complete text of the speech, go online to http://www.hud.gov/news/speeches/presrmarks.cfm.

9 See "U.S. Seizes Mortgage Giants" by James R. Hagerty, Ruth Simon and Damian Paletta, *The Wall Street Journal*, September 8, 2008; and "Mortgage Bailout is Greeted with Relief, Fresh Questions" by Deborah Soloman, Michael Corkery and Liz Rappaport, *The Wall Street Journal*, September 9, 2008.

10 For a detailed examination of Marx, see *The Making of Modern Economics* by Mark Skousen, M.E. Sharpe, publisher, 2001, pp. 131–164; See *The Worldly Philosophers*, by Robert Heilbroner, Simon & Schuster, 1968.

11 For the rest of the list, see www.anu.edu.au/polsci/marx/classics/manifesto.html.

12 See *A Concise History of the World*, by Rondo Cameron, Oxford University Press, 1997.

13 See www.gmu.edu/departments/economics/bcaplan/museum/musframe.htm.

14 See *A Republic—If We Can Keep It* by Lawrence W. Reed and Burton W. Folsom, Jr. The Foundation for Economic Education, Irvington, New York, 2001 page 51.

15 See "The Wealth of Nations" by Leszek Balcerowicz, *The Wall Street Journal*, October 6, 2005.

16 See "Working Time Transitions in Sweden" by Dominique Anxo and Donald Storrie of The Centre for European Labour Market Studies, Goteborg, Sweden.

17 Fulfillment requires that the worker puts in 1–34 hours of work per week.

18 As this book went to print, the 2012 Presidential election had not been conducted. The 35% rate was extended for 2011-2012 but was scheduled to rise to 39.6% in 2013.

19 See "Swedes less well off than African-Americans," *Reuters*, May 6, 2002.

20 See "Sweden's Moderates Now Look Electable" by Terence Roth and Louise Nordstrom, *The Wall Street Journal*, September 14, 2005.

21 See "Sweden to Cut Corporate Taxes, Increase Jobs" by Johan Carlstrom, *Business Week*, September 13, 2012.

22 See "To Cut Entitlements, U.S. can look to one of Europe's Welfare States" by Harold L. Sirkin, *The Christian Science Monitor*, July 24, 2013.

23 See http://www.heritage.org/index/country/sweden

24 See "The best of all worlds in Canada" by Stephen Marche, *The Star Tribune*, July 17, 2012 pg. A11.

25 See "France Fails in Bid to Cut Restaurant Tax," *The Wall Street Journal*, February 11, 2004.

26 See "Have more children, France urges citizens" by John Leicester, *The Orlando Sentinel*, September 22, 2005.

27 See "Behind Slow Growth in Europe: Citizen's Tight Grip on Wallets" by Marcus Walker, *The Wall Street Journal*, December 10, 2004; and "In France, Working Long Hours Becomes a Crime" by David Woodruff, *The Wall Street Journal*, June 15, 1999.

28 See "Bonfire of the Vanities" by Theodore Dalrymple, *The Wall Street Journal*, November 7, 2005; "Our Immigrants, Their Immigrants" by Joel Kotkin, *The Wall Street Journal*, November 8, 2005; Les Miserables, *The Wall Street Journal*, November 5-6, 2005; "France needs freedom, not welfare" by Jack A. Chambless, *The USA Today*, November 10, 2005.

29 See "Liberte', Precarite: Labor Law Ignites Anxiety in France" by Andrew Higgins, *The Wall Street Journal*, March 29, 2006.

30 See "French Revolution," *The Wall Street Journal*, September 20, 2007.

31 See http://www.bloomberg.com/news/2013-12-29/france-s-hollande-gets-court-approval-for-75-millionaire-tax.html

32 See "Lazy Europe?" by Daniel Schwammenthal, *The Wall Street Journal*, April 25, 2007.

33 For more on Lady Thatcher, see http://www.youtube.com/watch?v=40NVkfbaMo4

34 See "Europeans discover the value of work" by Peter Brown, *The Orlando Sentinel*, August 27, 2004.

35 See "The Man Who Rescued the German Economy" by Raymond Zhong, *The Wall Street Journal*, July 7-8, 2012 pg. A11.

36 See "The Wirtschaftswunder: Another Look" by Lawrence H. White, *The Wall Street Journal*, September 8, 2010; and "German Economy Steams Ahead" by Brian Blackstone, *The Wall Street Journal*, January 13, 2011.

37 See "Germany Criticizes Fed Move" by Patrick McGroarty, *The Wall Street Journal*, November 8, 2010.

38 See "Is America Number One" ABC News Special with John Stossel, September 19, 1999; "Something's cushy in Denmark" by Mark Landler, *The Orlando Sentinel*, November 20, 2005; "Thousands back land reform in Venezuela" by Christopher Toothaker, *The Orlando Sentinel*, October 9, 2005; "Bolivia sets sights on 10 companies" by Fiona Smith, *The Orlando Sentinel*, March 7, 2006, pg. A5; "Betrayal: Why Socialism Failed in Africa" speech by George B.N. Ayittey at The Foundation for Economic Education, April 2005; "Latin America is skeptical" by Andres Oppenheimer, *The Orlando Sentinel*, February 20, 2006; and "More U.S. Job-Hunters Try Australia" by Geoffrey Rogow, *The Wall Street Journal*, December 27, 2010, p. A11.

39 See "The Greek Economy Explained," *The Wall Street Journal*, May 7, 2010.

40 See "Tax Evasion Dogs Greece" by Sebastian Moffett & Alkman Granitsas, *The Wall Street Journal*, February 10, 2010, p. A13.

41 See "Europe Bankrolls Greece" by Charles Forelle & Marcus Walker, *The Wall Street Journal*, April 12, 2010; "Greek Red Tape Hamstrings Growth, Entrepreneurs Say" by Sebastion Moffett & Alkman Granitsas, *The Wall Street Journal*, May 20, 2010; and "Privatization Can Help Greece" by Allan H. Meltzer, *The Wall Street Journal*, May 21, 2010.

42 See "Venezuela's Hunger is No Game" by Mary Anastasia O'Grady, *The Wall Street Journal*, May 9, 2016 and "Venezuela's 'Savage Suffering'" by Anatoly Kurmanaev and Maolis Castro, *The Wall Street Journal*, February 13–14, 2016.

43 See "Survey Says: People are Happier" by Matt Mabe, *BusinessWeek*, August 20, 2008.

44 See "Whether People Define Themselves as Happy Depends on the Era" by Cynthia Crossen, *The Wall Street Journal*, March 6, 2006.

45 See "Culture matters the most, some say" by Alexander Stille, *The New York Times*, February 18, 2001 (date published in *The Orlando Sentinel*).

46 In 2011 Illinois dramatically increased personal and corporate income taxes. See "Tax Hikes in Illinois; Wisconsin 'Open for Business'" by Daniel Halper, *The Weekly Standard*, January 18, 2011.

47 See "Economic Freedom Greatest in Middle America, Study Says" by Lawrence J. McQuillan, Robert E. McCormick and Ying Huang, *Budget & Tax News* (The Heartland Institute) January 2005, pg. 9.

48 See "The Reverse-Joads of California" by Allysia Finley, *The Wall Street Journal*, May 4, 2013.

49 See "Why Texas is our Future" by Tyler Cowen, *Time Magazine*, October 28, 2013 pp. 30-37.

50 See "The Red-State Path to Prosperity" by Arthur B. Laffer and Stephen Moore, *The Wall Street Journal*, March 28, 2013 page A15.

51 See http://freestateproject.org/about/101-reasons-move-new-hampshire.

52 Minnesota's generous welfare benefits are one reason why immigrants are now pouring into the state, costing taxpayers upwards of $188 million per year in benefits. See "Far from Mexico, immigration an issue" by Martiga Lohn, *The Orlando Sentinel*, February 4, 2006.

53 See "Estonia Creates an Economic Miracle" by Steve Sanek, *Budget & Tax News*, July 2006 pg. 9.

54 Source: CIA World Fact Book.

55 See "A Nation of Givers" by Arthur C. Brooks, *The American*, March/April 2008.

56 See "India's Surging Economy Lifts Hopes and Ambitions" by Paul Beckett, Krishna Pokharel & Eric Bellman, *The Wall Street Journal*, November 28, 2007.

57 See "They're Rounding the First Turn! And the Favorite Is....." by Nicholas D. Kristof, *The New York Times*, January 17, 2006.

58 See http://www.indexmundi.com/india/gdp_real_growth_rate.html

59 See http://timesofindia.indiatimes.com/articleshow/2090174.cms

60 See "Sizzling Economy Revitalizes India" by Amy Waldman, *The New York Times*, October 20, 2003; and "India Everywhere in the Alps" by Mark Landler, *The New York Times*, January 26, 2006.

61 See "There's More to Growth than China…" by Martin Feldstein, *The Wall Street Journal*, February 16, 2006; and "A Passage to Prosperity" by Arvind Panagariya, *The Wall Street Journal*, July 14, 2005.

62 Yet, millions of Indians who live in poverty still have little chance of gaining wealth within India due the Hindu caste system that labels many Indians as ostensibly inferior, from birth. For more, see "Untouchable" by Tom O'Neill, *National Geographic*, June 2003, pp. 2-31.

63 Source: CIA World Fact Book.

64 See "Beijing Sets Tax Plan to Aid Growth" by Matt Pottinger, Kathy Chen and Karen Elliot House, *The Wall Street Journal*, February 6, 2004.

65 See "Global Playing Field: More Level, but it Still Has Bumps" by Joseph Stiglitz, *The New York Times*, April 30, 2005; "Revolutionary China, Complacent America" by Charlene Barshefsky and Edward Gresser, *The Wall Street Journal*, September 15, 2005; and "U.S. Dozes as China Roars" by Peter Morici, *The Orlando Sentinel*, November 13, 2005.

66 See "Starbucks Brews Coffee Plan for India" by Paul Beckett, Vibhuti Agarwal & Julie Jargon, *The Wall Street Journal*, January 14, 2011; "A New Detroit Rises in India's South" by Eric Bellman, *The Wall Street Journal*, July 9, 2010; and "A Glimpse at India, Minus the Red Tape" by Geeta Anand & Amol Sharma, *The Wall Street Journal*, January 14, 2011, p. A16.

67 See "In China's Orbit" *The Wall Street Journal*, November 20-21, 2010, p. C1.

68 See "The Global Jobs Competition Heats Up" by Martin Neil Baily, Matthew J. Slaughter & Laura D'Andrea Tyson, *The Wall Street Journal*, July 1, 2010.

69 See "Understanding Poverty in the United States: Surprising Facts about America's Poor" by Robert Rector and Rachael Sheffield, *The Heritage Foundation*, September 13, 2011.

70 See "How the West (and the rest) Got Rich" by Deidre N. McCloskey, *The Wall Street Journal*, May 21-22, 2016 p. C1.

71 See "Why Friedrich Hayek is Making a Comeback" by Russ Roberts, *The Wall Street Journal*, June 28, 2010.

72 See "The U.S. Loses Ground on Economic Freedom" by Terry Miller, *The Wall Street Journal*, January 12, 2011.

73 See http://www.heritage.org/index/ranking

74 For more on the complex history of the income tax please see "Many Happy Returns—Millions of Them" by Jay Starkman, *The Wall Street Journal*, February 2-3, 2013.

75 Source: National Constitution Center, Philadelphia, PA. See www.constitutioncenter.org.

76 IBID.

77 See "Uncle Sam—50 years in withdrawal" by John Leyden, *The Orlando Sentinel*, July 4, 1993.

78 See The Public Papers and Addresses of Franklin D. Roosevelt, 12 (New York: Harper & Brothers, 1950), p. 90.

79 IBID.

80 See *The Limits of Symbolic Reform: The New Deal and Taxation* by Mark Leff (London and New York: Cambridge University Press, 1984) pp. 290–291.

81 See *JFK and the Reagan Revolution: A Secret History of American Prosperity* by Lawrence Kudlow & Brian Domitrovic, Penguin Random House, 2016.

82 See "Still Morning in America" *The Wall Street Journal*, January 20, 2006; *The Seven Fat Years* by Robert L. Bartley, The Free Press, 1995; and *Reaganomics* by William A. Niskanen, Oxford University Press, 1988.

83 See "Higher Retroactive Tax on Wealthy Is Blamed, in Part, for Slowing Growth" by Fred R. Bleakley, *The Wall Street Journal*, July 6, 1994.

84 See "White House Sees Template in Tax Deal" by Laura Meckler & Jonathan Weisman, *The Wall Street Journal*, December 18-19, 2010, p. A5.

85 See *The Fair Tax Book* by Neal Boortz and John Linder, Regan Books, 2005; "Economists Back 'Fair Tax' Proposal" by Merrill Bender, *Budget & Tax News* (The Heartland Institute), June 2005; and "How to Tax Fairly" by Jack A. Chambless, *The Orlando Sentinel*, April 10, 2005.

86 See "Flat Tax Club," *The Wall Street Journal*, January 6, 2005; and "Do We Want a Free Market in Iraq?" *Forbes*, February 16, 2004, p. 37.

87 For the complete list see http://jeffduncan.house.gov/full-list-obamacare-tax-hikes.

88 See http://taxfoundation.org/sites/default/files/docs/TaxFoundation-FF496.pdf

89 See http://www.wsj.com/articles/clintons-punitive-exit-tax-1471818426

90 See "Trump's Taxes Pose New Setback" by Richard Rubin, *The Wall Street Journal*, October 3, 2016

91 See "The Bill Gates Income Tax" by Arthur Laffer, *The Wall Street Journal*, October 5, 2010, p. A23.

92 See "Nearly half in U.S. escape income tax" by Stephen Ohlemacher, *The Orlando Sentinel*, April 8, 2010.

93 See "A Budget for Taxpayers, Not Tax Consumers" by Stephen Moore, *The Wall Street Journal*, April 12, 2001.

94 See "The Spending Explosion" *The Wall Street Journal*, September 10, 2008, pg. A14.

95 See "Federal Spending soars in Bush's White House" by Ron Hutcheson, *Knight Ridder Newspapers* (appearing in *The Orlando Sentinel*), December 7, 2003, p. A13; "Conservative Republicans Push for Slowdown in U.S. Spending" by Richard W. Stevenson, *The New York Times*, January 22, 2004; "Riding the Omnibus," *The Wall Street Journal*, January 26, 2004; "Promises, Promises But Who's Minding the Budget?" by George Melloan, *The Wall Street Journal*, January 20, 2004; and "President Signs Budget Busting Medicare Reform" by John Skorburg, *Budget & Tax News* (The Heartland Institute), January 2004.

96 See http://www.whitehouse.gov/omb/budget/Historicals.

97 See "Obama's National Debt rate on track to double" by Dave Boyer, *The Washington Times*, October 9, 2013.

98 For a detailed account of his life and influence on the economy, see *Alexander Hamilton* by Ron Chernow, The Penguin Press, 2004.

99 See *Locke, Jefferson and the Justices: Foundations and Failure of the U.S. Government*, by George M. Stephens, Algora Publishing, 2002.

100 See *Hamilton's Curse* by Thomas J. Dilorenzo, Three Rivers Press, New York, 2008 page 30.

101 See "Congress Rediscovers the Constitution" by Roger Pilon, *The Wall Street Journal*, January 4, 2011.

102 United States v. Butler, 297 U.S. 1 (1936).

103 See "Not Yours to Give" from *The Life of Colonel David Crockett*, compiled by Edward S. Ellis (Philadelphia; Porter & Coates, 1884).

104 See "Taxpayers May Face Hurricane Tab" by Elizabeth Williamson, *The Wall Street Journal*, May 31-June 1, 2008.

105 Recent reports do indicate that rich people usually get more money from FEMA than poor people do. See "FEMA refunds assist higher earners most" by Sally Kestin, Megan O'Matz and John Maines, *The Orlando Sentinel*, December 11, 2005.

106 See "Building on the Edge" by Joe Newman, *The Orlando Sentinel*, December 14, 2005.

107 See "Storm victims' housing aid, set to end in August, extended into '09" by Cain Burdeau, *The Orlando Sentinel*, April 27, 2007, pg. A9.

108 For more analysis of moral hazard, see "The gospel according to moral hazard" by Ellen Goodman, *The Orlando Sentinel*, March 24, 2008, pg. A21.

109 The initial tax for this plan was 2% - equally divided between employer and employee. See "Meaning of freedom – a process or a result?" by David Moreland, *The Orlando Sentinel*, February 27, 2010.

110 See "$1.5B foreclosure help" by Peter Nicholas & Ashley Powers, *The Orlando Sentinel*, February 20, 2010.

111 The employee rate fell to 4.2% for 2011 only.

112 See *New Deal or Raw Deal* by Burton Folsom, Jr. Threshold Editions, New York, 2008 page 117.

113 See "How the War on Poverty was Lost" by Robert Rector, *The Wall Street Journal*, January 7, 2014.

114 See "Yes, Mr. President, We Are a Nation of Takers" by Nicholas Eberstadt, *The Wall Street Journal*, January 25, 2013, page A13.

115 See "Van drives around Daytona's ban on body piercing" by Ludmilla Lelis, *The Orlando Sentinel*; and "States Crack Down on Indoor Tanning" by Jennifer Saranow, *The Wall Street Journal*, January 26, 2005.

116 See "Toward a 21st Century Regulatory System" by Barack Obama, *The Wall Street Journal*, January 18, 2011, p. A17.

117 See "The Regulated States of America" by Niall Ferguson, *The Wall Street Journal*, June 19, 2013 page A15.

118 See http://www.youtube.com/watch?v=nBiJB8YuDBQ.

119 See "The Regulated States of America" by Niall Ferguson, *The Wall Street Journal*, June 19, 2013, page A15.

120 See "What's Killing Jobs and Stalling the Recovery" by Marie-Josee' Kravis, *The Wall Street Journal*, June 4-5, 2016 pg. A9.

121 See "Red Tape Rising: Regulatory Trends in the Bush Years" by James L. Gattuso, *Backgrounder* (The Heritage Foundation), March 25, 2008.

122 See "There is No Joy in Toyland" by Anne M. Northup, *The Wall Street Journal*, December 24, 2009.

123 See "New Lead-Paint Law Heavy on Budgets" by Sarah E. Needleman, *The Wall Street Journal*, May 18, 2010.

124 See "EPA Proposes Tighter, Costlier Smog Limits" by Mark W. Peters and Stephen Power, *The Wall Street Journal*, January 8, 2010.

125 See "Light Cars are Dangerous Cars" by Robert E. Grady, *The Wall Street Journal,* May 22, 2009.

126 IBID.

127 See "The Regulatory Cliff is Nearly as Steep as the Fiscal One" by Rob Portman, *The Wall Street Journal,* August 17, 2012.

128 See "Teeth-Whitening Rules Take a Bite Out of Business" by Angela C. Erickson & Paul Sherman, *The Wall Street Journal,* April 30, 2013.

129 See http://articles.orlandosentinel.com/2010-11-12/news/os-sheriff-demings-illegal-barbering-20101112_1_hills-area-barbers-deputies.

130 See "Senate OKs financial overhaul measure" by Janet Hook and Jim Puzzanghera, *The Orlando Sentinel,* May 21, 2010.

131 See "The Uncertainty Principle" *The Wall Street Journal,* July 14, 2010, p. A18.

132 See "The End of Community Banking" by Sarah Wallace, *The Wall Street Journal,* June 29, 2010.

133 See "The Share Economy" by Tomio Geron, *Forbes Magazine,* February 11, 2013 and "Baby, You can Drive my Car" by Joel Stein, *Time Magazine,* February 9, 2015.

134 See "Drug Regulations Cause Millions of Deaths Each Year, Study Finds" by Susan Konig, *Health Care News* (The Heartland Institute), January 2005.

135 See "The Red Tape Conundrum" by Brian O'Keefe, *Fortune,* November 1, 2016.

136 See "Firms fret over impact of overtime pay proposal" by Joyce M. Rosenberg, *The Minneapolis Star-Tribune,* July 20, 2015

137 See "Stop Bashing Business, Mr. President" by Ken Langone, *The Wall Street Journal,* October 15, 2010.

138 See "Principles for Economic Revival" by George P. Shultz, Michael J. Boskin, John F. Cogan, Allan Meltzer, and John B. Taylor, *The Wall Street Journal,* September 16, 2010, p. A23.

139 See "Move Reflects Shift in President's Tone" by David Wessel, *The Wall Street Journal,* January 19, 2011.

140 For more on businesses perspective of Mr. Obama's relationship with them, see "Business Groups Slams 'Hostile' Policies on Jobs" by Elizabeth Williamson and Darrell A. Hughes, *The Wall Street Journal,* June 23, 2010; and "Revisiting the Regulations Affecting Business" by Elizabeth Williamson, *The Wall Street Journal,* July 12, 2010, p. A4.

141 See "The Spying on Americans Never Ended" by Elizabeth Goitein, *The Wall Street Journal,* June 7, 2013 pg. A15.

142 See "Here's a U.S. Secret Revealed: The Fourth Amendment is Dead" by Charles Levendosky, Editorial page editor, *Casper (Wyoming) Star-Tribune,* April 28, 2002.

143 See "Repeal the Patriot Act" by Andrew P. Napolitano, *The Wall Street Journal,* March 5, 2004; and *Terrorism and Tyranny* by James Bovard, Palgrave MacMillan, 2003.

144 See "In Google case, activists see privacy eroding" by Douglas Birch, *The Orlando Sentinel,* January 22, 2006; "Internet Users Thinking Twice Before a Search" by Katie Hafner, *The New York Times,* January 25, 2006.

145 See "U.S. Collects Vast Data Trove" by Siobhan Gorman, Evan Perez & Janet Hook, *The Wall Street Journal,* June 7, 2013 & "Obama Defends Surveillance" by Peter Nicholas & Siobhan Gorman, *The Wall Street Journal,* June 8-9, 2013.

146 Brunswick, *The Star Tribune,* July 22, 2012.

147 See "Congress lambastes INS Chief" by Tamara Lytle, *The Orlando Sentinel,* March 20, 2002.

148 www.jewishworldreview.com/cols/williams.html

CHAPTER REVIEW

1. What are some of the major differences between socialism and the mixed economy? Give specific examples.

2. What would Frederic Bastiat, Alexander Hamilton, and James Madison say about government spending to rebuild homes destroyed in Florida during the October 2016 arrival of hurricane Matthew? Fully explain.

3. What were the major differences between Franklin D. Roosevelt and John F. Kennedy with respect to the role of government in the life of American workers?

4. How do regulations impact the overall level of poverty and employment?

5. Why are civil liberties economically important?

ECONOMICS *as a* SCIENCE

*F*acts are stubborn things.

JOHN ADAMS

THE SCIENCE OF ECONOMICS

Facts do not cease to exist because they are ignored.

Aldous Huxley

We spent the first three chapters laying out the argument that economics can explain the sources of wealth and happiness all over the world. But how do you know whether economists simply think we are right, or whether we can prove we are right?

One of the most significant obstacles economics professors have to overcome each semester is the perception by students that economics is steeped in intellectual guesswork. After all, who among us has not seen economists on CNN, or some other network, debating issues, disagreeing with other scholars, and generally using terminology that the majority of human beings do not understand or even remotely comprehend? In this chapter, we will uncover the scientific processes that form the foundation of economics as a social science. It is here that you will discover that there is virtually no type of human behavior that cannot be explained – to an extent – with the use of logic, economic theory, and mathematics.

This does not mean economists know everything about the causes of human behavior. After all, if we (economists) are so smart, why did we fail to accurately predict the biggest recession to hit the United States in over 70 years? Increasingly, economists are recognizing that the mathematical models we use to explain human decisions, cannot possibly capture all of the variables behind our decisions.[1] As one famous economics professor once said, "Economics is a powerful tool, a lens for organizing one's thinking about the complexity of the world around us. That should be enough. We should be honest about what we know, and what we don't know, and what we may never know. Admitting that publicly is the first step toward respectability."[2]

THE SCIENTIFIC PROCESS

How often has a professor told you that skipping class or working too many hours is bad for your grade? What makes them say this? Isn't it simply common sense that not attending classes you've signed up for raises the probability of working at a terrible job someday? Common sense is nice to have, but wouldn't it be nicer if you knew exactly how many classes you could miss before you end up hurting your grade? How could we help students make definitive judgments about what type of behavior they should pursue while in college? As it turns out, the use of statistics, algebra, and calculus is a good start.

Before you run for the admissions office to drop this class, please be aware that your professor does not expect you to be an expert in matrix algebra or to know the difference between a first order and second order derivative. In this course it is generally assumed that students have limited mathematical expertise, so this chapter will walk you through the basic mathematical process that economists use to explain the causes and consequences of human decisions. To do that, we rely on the concept of an economic model.

> ➤ **An economic model is a way of explaining how some sector of the economy functions.**

The behavior of students in a classroom can be modeled. That means we can show you the mathematical link between certain behaviors and the outcomes you will attain in your classes. To do so involves four distinct steps that makes up the scientific process:

1. The selection of the dependent and independent variables
2. Making assumptions concerning the relationship between the independent and dependent variables
3. Assessing the implications of our assumptions
4. Testing our hypothesis

STEP ONE — VARIABLE SELECTION

In virtually every economics class, there will be a wide range of test scores on any given test. This is interesting, because each student has the same book, the same access to the professor, the same lecture material, and so forth. How can a range of grades from 11–97 be explained? If an economist were asked to provide this explanation, she would first assign a dependent variable to the question at hand.

> ➤ **A dependent variable is a variable whose value depends on some other variable.**

In this case, the dependent variable would be test scores. That is what we are trying to explain, and of course, test scores depend on several independent variables.

> ➤ **An independent variable is a variable whose value is independent of other variables.**

Before we begin picking our independent variables, we should note some rules that apply to model building. First, any variable we pick *must be measurable*. That means we must be able to assign a quantity or dollar amount to that variable. For example, the attitude of a student toward the professor might have an impact on the test grade, but attitude is not measurable; therefore, we would not include it in our list of independent variables. An exception to this rule is when we have situations where there is an "either-or" situation that needs to be addressed.

Suppose a professor wanted to find out if there is a gender-based explanation for test scores. The economist in charge of this model could create a "dummy variable" – a variable that has no numerical value but is still measurable – to incorporate gender. We will see later on how the dummy variable issue is handled.

The second rule is that the variables selected *must make some intuitive sense*. While it is logical to include the number of hours students work each week in this model, it does not make sense to include as a variable the number of times they visited their grandparents when they were six years old. While it is readily apparent that the latter variable is ridiculous, there may be variables that you think should be included but in reality should not be, because they occur with such infrequency, or are so hard to get data for, that the variable is best left out of the model. Keep in mind that usually someone is paying the economist to model some problem. The accountants are going to want the economist to be able to justify why each variable should be picked. The more variables that are selected, the more money the research will cost, and we all know how picky accountants can be about what things cost.

Now that we have some basic understanding of where to begin, let's look at five different variables we might want to consider in a model explaining test scores:

1. Number of classes attended
2. Number of hours spent at work each week
3. Number of study hours per week
4. Gender
5. Number of times the student cheated

Notice that each variable is measurable (survey data would help greatly here) and makes intuitive sense. There are many other variables that could be picked, but for our purposes, these five will be sufficient in understanding the second step in the scientific process.

STEP TWO — MAKING ASSUMPTIONS

Assumptions are made to establish the *cause-and-effect relationship* between our independent variables and our dependent variable. We should stop here for a moment to look at the term "cause and effect." In the world around us, there are three ways to look at the interconnectedness of events. We can say that two events have taken place through coincidence, because they are correlated, or because one event caused the other.

As you might imagine, *coincidence* is the weakest form of connection between two events. For example, suppose the night before your first economics test, your roommate prepares your favorite meal. The next day you score a 96 on the exam. You reach the conclusion that as long as you get your favorite meal the night before a test, you will make a 96, so you stop going to class or studying and simply wait for this lucky meal. The two events happened around the same time, but there is no scientific relationship between the two events.

It has been observed that in most years that a team from the American Football Conference of the National Football League wins the Super Bowl, the U.S. economy is fairly weak. In years a team from the National Football Conference wins, the economy has been strong. Does this mean that if the San Diego Chargers (an AFC team) win the Super Bowl in 2021 that the stock market will fall and unemployment will rise?

Correlation is stronger than coincidence. When two events are correlated, it means that one event has been shown to have some relationship to another event. But that relationship is not strong enough for the scientist to say that the one event will repeatedly cause the second event. For example, there appears to be a correlation between the height of the person running for president and the likelihood of their election. There could also be a correlation between facial symmetry and the odds of winning. This means that if a person is considered homely

The National Hockey League's Minnesota Wild is made up of an almost entirely white roster, while the National Basketball Association's Minnesota Timberwolves has mostly black players. Is this a coincidence? Are there variables that could accurately explain the racial composition of professional sports?

Photo courtesy Jack Chambless

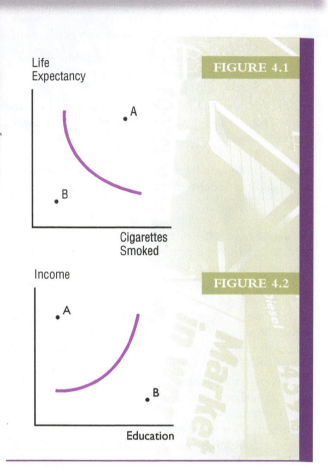

FIGURE 4.1

FIGURE 4.2

or is short, his or her odds of winning are lower, but being homely or short does not guarantee losing. Correlation simply means that it is not a coincidence that people opt for taller, better-looking politicians, but it is not a scientific fact that only those people with those characteristics will be elected.

Causation is the strongest form of connection between an independent variable and a dependent variable. When economists discover a causal relationship between two variables, it means that over and over again the occurrence of one event will cause the occurrence of another event. For example, there is a causal negative relationship between the number of cigarettes smoked and the number of years a person will live. There is a proven positive relationship between the number of years of education a person receives and that person's lifetime income. Figures 4.1 and 4.2 illustrate the concept of causal relationships. What does point A and B on each diagram mean?

In 4.1 we see that, as the number of cigarettes smoked increases over an average person's lifetime, the fewer years that person can expect to live. Point A on 4.1 shows a person who smoked a great deal but lived a long time. Point B shows a person who never smoked and died very young. These are called *statistical outliers*.

SUGGESTED CLASSROOM DEBATE

Does Wal-Mart *cause* towns like Paris, Texas to lose small businesses? Why or why not?

Photo courtesy Jack Chambless

Outliers are observed points that are several deviations away from the normal observed data points. When economists see outliers, we largely ignore them. We ignore them because for every person who lives to be 104 while smoking like a chimney, there are far more people who end up dead from this behavior.

Now that we have a basic idea of what the term, *causation* means, let's go back to our model of your behavior and test scores to look at the assumptions we should make concerning the relationship between the independent and dependent variables. There are five possible assumptions we can make.

THE POSITIVE RELATIONSHIP

Of the five variables we selected, the only one that should have a clear positive causal relationship with test scores is the number of classes attended. As Figure 4.3 illustrates, as the number of classes attended increases, the student can expect his grades to increase. This assumption is made *ceteris paribus,* meaning "everything else being equal."

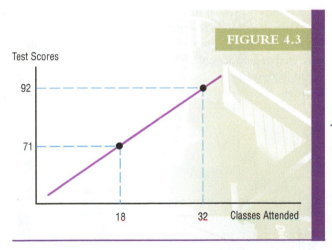

FIGURE 4.3

In other words, assuming normal behavior with respect to studying, alcohol consumption, sleep, and so forth, the typical student can expect to be helped from attending all classes. However, there are many instances where students miss class frequently and still survive, just as there are students who never miss and do poorly. The number of times you go to class is just one variable in

this model. It would be wise to assume that other things matter as well.

THE NEGATIVE RELATIONSHIP

If you are like other college students, you have mastered the art of living in denial when it comes to the relationship between your work hours and your grades. Professors realize many of you are working to support your life, but some of you are working to support your *lifestyle*. You have rationally decided that the benefits of working — a nice car, stylish clothes, etc. — outweigh the opportunity cost of studying and making better grades. Figure 4.4 calls into question whether your priorities are in order.

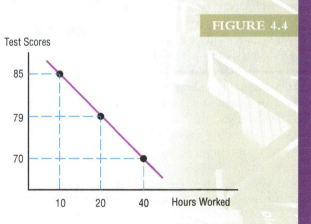

FIGURE 4.4

Notice that if you worked ten hours per week, ceteris paribus, you might average an 85 on your exams. Twenty hours per week might lead to an average of 79. Working 40 hours might mean a 70 average. All students are different, of course, and some can overcome huge workloads,

© HelleM/ Shutterstock.com

CONCEPT CHECK

Recent studies show that college-age Americans spend an average of 53 hours per week on entertainment-related activities like social networking, video games, music, sending text messages, and more.[3] What is the most likely relationship between the hours spent on these activities and a student's grade point average? If students in China and India spend far less time on these activities, what are the implications for wages and salaries for Americans over time?

but for the average student there is a negative relationship between work hours and test scores, whether you want to admit it or not.

ZERO RELATIONSHIP

Why would a scientist load into any model an independent variable that is assumed to have no impact on the dependent variable? In some cases we would not do this. For example, including a variable measuring the impact of the average winnings of an *American Idol* contestant on test scores would not be a wise use of our resources. However, including gender or race might be interesting.

When is enough, enough?

If a professor was concerned that his or her classes were gender or racially biased, including a dummy variable to account for this possibility would be appropriate. The social scientist could simply assign a one to every male in the class and a zero to every woman. In the section on hypothesis testing, we will show how this would help uncover any statistically significant relationship between gender and test scores. Figure 4.5 illustrates the assumption that there is no relationship between the two.

4.6 shows that, as your study hours increase from 5 to 35, your grade will rise from a 60 to 98.[4]

However, notice that with every hour after 35, your grade begins to fall. How could this happen? It is possible that studying more than the optimal number of hours could lead to fatigue, stress over minute details, significant ideas becoming blurred, and other problems arise.

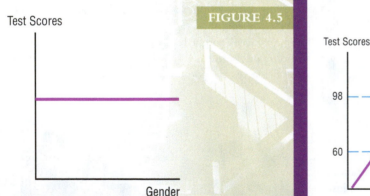

FIGURE 4.5

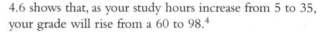

FIGURE 4.6

THE CONVEX RELATIONSHIP

Have you ever over-studied for a test? Most students don't suffer from having a hyperactive work ethic, but, if you do, it could come back to bite you. Consider this scenario:

You have attended all classes, taken perfect notes, sought out advice and answers to your questions, and generally conducted yourself as the model college student. Then it comes time to prepare for your first test. Figure

This means that there are diminishing returns from studying – i.e., studying can be too much of a good thing. When should you stop? It depends on many variables beyond the scope of this chapter, but a good rule of thumb would be to pay close attention to the incremental gains you are making in retention from each hour you study. When those gains come at a slower and slower rate, you are getting close to the best you can do.

THE CONCAVE RELATIONSHIP

Like anything else, the first time a person cheats on a test, they are probably not very good at it. However, with practice, you, too, could become a good cheater! Figure 4.7 illustrates this idea.

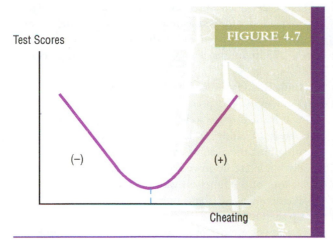

FIGURE 4.7

Test Scores

(−)   (+)

Cheating

Notice that the first several times the student is cheating, there is a negative relationship between cheating and the test score. Perhaps the student is trying to figure out the most efficient way to go about stealing answers and initially gets caught with great enough frequency, or is cheating off the wrong people and test scores suffer. However, beyond the global minimum (the low point on the function), as students continue to improve their cheating skills, their test grades — and chances of becoming a politician — increase.

STEP THREE — THE IMPLICATIONS

In this step we use logic to analyze the implications of the assumptions concerning the relationship among the economic variables. This is an important step to help those who might be paying for, or affected by the research, to understand what we might expect to see occur in the real world if our assumptions are proven right.

Suppose we find that for every increase in work hours by ten hours per week, a student can expect to lose one full letter grade in any given class. The implications of losing one full letter grade could be fewer scholarships, internships, and eventually fewer job opportunities.

With fewer job opportunities would come lower lifetime earnings, more stress, a smaller home, less choices in who the student would be able to marry, a lower retirement income, and so forth. You might find yourself doubting that working too many hours could lead to so many bad things, or you could ask yourself why it is that the students with the best grades in the most difficult majors seem to enjoy a higher probability of lifetime success.

STEP FOUR — TESTING THE HYPOTHESIS

In the first and second steps of our model, we hypothesized that there was a relationship between several different variables and test scores for the typical college student. Step four is where we find out if we were right.

In this step we mathematically verify the interconnectedness between each independent variable and the dependent variable. To do this, the economist first gathers data on each variable in the following equation:

Test scores = b0 + b1 classes attended + b2 work hours + b3 gender + b4 study hours + b5 study hours2 + b6 number of times cheated + b7 number of times cheated2

If you recall basic algebra, test scores are our 'Y' variable, b0 is our intercept term, and the other "bs" represent our *coefficients* on the independent variables. Squaring the study hours variable and number of times cheated variable allows us to find out if there is a convex or concave relationship between those variables and test scores.

Photo courtesy Jack Chambless

CONCEPT CHECK

In a survey of teenage drivers, Allstate Insurance Co. found that girls are reportedly driving more aggressively than boys, with 16% of girls reporting that they drive aggressively (up from 9% in 2005).[5] If this is a new trend for America's roads, what are the implications for insurance rates and consumer prices? Why?

> ➤ **A coefficient is the mathematical connection between the independent and dependent variable that is discovered in the algebraic process known as multiple regression analysis.**

At this time, none of you would be expected to know what multiple regression analysis (sometimes called matrix algebra) is. This will be discovered later on in your college careers if you take more statistics and econometrics classes. The reason it is even mentioned here is because it is important to show that all of the lines you encounter on all of those diagrams are not just lines, but rather actual relationships that have been empirically proven over time. If you can have at least some surface understanding of where the lines come from, you will gain a deeper appreciation for the concepts of supply and demand and many other economic principles.

Economists studying test scores would load all of the data they uncovered into a statistical software package on their computer and set test scores equal to all of the data uncovered. The computer would then be instructed to compute the coefficients for each variable and do a test to determine if each variable is "statistically significant" in explaining test scores.

HOW TO INTERPRET DATA

Suppose the computer spits out the following data for each of the variables selected:

$B0 = 29$
$B1 = 3.11$
$B2 = -4.05$
$B3 = 2.77$
$B4 = 4.53$
$B5 = -1.37$
$B6 = -7.31$
$B7 = 2.08$

What do these numbers mean? Very simply, the results indicate that, if every other variable equaled zero, the average student could expect to earn at least a 29 on any given exam. For every class attended, their test grade increased by 3.11 points.

Every hour of work (measured in increments of ten hours per week, for example) led to a drop in test scores by 4.05 points.

For the dummy variable on gender, since we assigned a one to every male and a zero for every female, the algebraic equation dropped women from the model when it came to this variable. Since the coefficient on gender equals 2.77, it means that being male helped test scores by 2.77 points.

Initially, every hour a student studied raised that student's grades by 4.53 points. After some point (in calculus you will learn how to solve for this "global maximum"), each hour of studying led to a drop of 1.37 points. Cheating hurt the average student by 7.31 points per test initially, but led to improved test scores of 2.08 points after the bottom of the function was reached.

Remember that these numbers were simply created to help shed light on how to interpret the data. The numbers are not as important as the relationships the numbers suggest and the implications that can be drawn from them. Assume for a moment that each coefficient has been proven to be statistically significant – in other words, we can say with 95% certainty that each independent variable has the mathematical relationship to the dependent variable that the coefficients indicate.[6] What would the implications be?

For the professor and the student, the data would provide some empirical support of the assumptions that were made and would help each of them to determine the proper course of action. Students might decide to work less, manage their study hours more effectively, and not miss class. Professors might try to learn ways to account for different learning styles between males and females and how to catch the cheaters! On the other hand, students and professors can ignore the data and run the risk of repeating destructive behavior.

CONCEPT CHECK

Extensive research seems to suggest that beer, in moderation, is good for us.[7] Does this mean that keg parties can help you live a longer life?

Photo courtesy Jack Chambless

APPLYING MODELS TO THE "REAL WORLD"

What fun would the study of economics be if we couldn't apply economic models to everyday life? Most of us are going to spend 80 or more years as living beings on Earth. While we are here, it seems the least we could do is to understand how the world around us works. In this section of the chapter, we will use economic models to more fully understand what Alfred Marshall once called "the ordinary business of life."

CASE STUDY #1 — SHOULD THE ELDERLY BE ALLOWED TO DRIVE? SHOULD YOU?

I know that this is a terrible question to ask. Maybe it is because I only had one grandparent – and I only saw her for a week of my life – that I am not ashamed to ask it. Another reason the question might occur is the number of personal experiences I have had with senior citizens driving 37 miles per hour in the left-hand lane of the interstate. Then again, there is data showing that the relationship between driver age and the fatal crash rate is concave.

As the table below clearly illustrates, your grandparents might be hazardous to our health. Notice that for Florida drivers who are 85 and older, the fatal crash rate is 2.92 per 10,000 licensed drivers. That figure is higher than for drivers 75–84 as well as drivers who are 65–74.

It appears that drivers in the 65–74 age group are at the lowest risk for being in a fatal car crash. People in this group have been driving, on average, for more than 40 years. That experience behind the wheel, combined with the fact that more mature drivers have not yet begun experiencing deterioration of visual acuity, reflexes, and muscle coordination, makes them better drivers than very old senior citizens, on average.

Before we get too worried about seeing a centenarian on the highway, perhaps we should look at the other part of this concave function. You might not be too happy to see that you are in the age group of the people most likely to get wiped out on the roads. If you are 15–24 years of age, the data show a higher fatality rate for you than for your great-grandparents! This makes intuitive sense. Younger drivers are not only less experienced, but are more inclined to drink and drive, speed, send text messages and drive recklessly.[8]

The data seems to suggest that the very young and very old should be of paramount concern.

CASE STUDY #2 — DOES EDUCATION SPENDING MATTER?

If I had one dollar for every time I have heard someone say that the answer to America's education problems is to spend more money, I would have enough money to buy every failing public school in the country. There is just one sticking point: It appears that spending money on underperforming government schools has no impact on the reading scores of our kids.

How could this be true? Don't we all know that we have to spend money to educate children? Of course, we do. Books cost money. So do teachers and buildings.

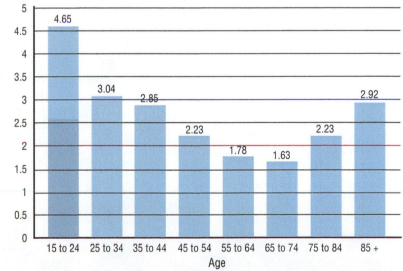

Source: Florida Highway Patrol, 2002 statistics; Florida Department of Highway Safety and Motor Vehicles

SUGGESTED CLASSROOM DEBATE

Should the U.S. model itself after Germany and require people to be 18 years old to drive? Why or why not?

The data suggests that reading scores (as the dependent variable) are impacted by multiple independent variables, but that education spending is not one of them. The variables that might matter include the amount of time parents spend reading to their children, the amount of time teachers spend teaching children to read, and the overall productivity of the school a child attends. However, simply throwing money at a school is no more likely to impact reading scores than throwing lottery money around will reduce the rate of homelessness.

This should be of paramount concern to taxpayers, parents, and politicians. In 2003, President Bush signed the No Child Left Behind Act. This Act provided for a record increase in federal education spending. In 2001, the federal government spent $35 billion on education. In 2006, federal spending hit $84 billion – a 137% increase in five years. For 2009, the total was $91 billion. When we add in state and local expenditures, over $500 billion was spent on education by 2016 and in later years yet, the results (as we will see in the next chapter) are unchanged. Children are still struggling.

In January 2017 the Department of Education released a study which illustrated this fact in a profound manner. The department issued a report showing that the $7 billion spent between 2010 and 2015 on the School Improvement Grants program had yielded no statistically significant change in educational outcomes for American students.[9] Test scores, graduation rates and college enrollment were no different in schools that received grant money than in schools that did not.

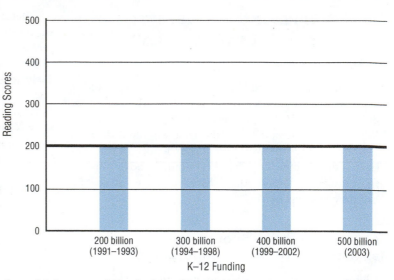

Source: U.S. Department of Education Budget Service and NEAP

CASE STUDY # 3 — LOWER TAXES = MORE REVENUE

When my sons were little, I paid them for picking up oranges and acorns in our yard and on our deck. They got $.05 for every orange they picked up off the ground before I mowed and $.01 for every acorn they picked up off the deck in the winter. (Note: This may sound like I am cheap, but you should see how many oranges and acorns they could pick up…)

To teach them about taxation, I told them that on the first dollar they earn, I planned to take away $.10 and give it away to some other child. For the second dollar, I would take away $.25 and for every dollar over $2, I would make them give me $.40.

After staring at me for a moment, they both told me that they did not want to pick up oranges and acorns anymore.

You might think that they reacted this way because they are the sons of a liberty-loving economist. While I am flattered that you might think that, the real reason they will react negatively to my plan is because they are normal human beings.

Speaking before the Economic Club in New York in December 1962, John F. Kennedy said:

> In the early stages of the state, taxes are light in their incidence, but fetch in a large revenue…As time passes and kings succeed each other, they lose their tribal habits in favor of more civilized ones. Their needs and exigencies grow…owing to the luxury in which they have been brought up. Hence they impose fresh taxes on their subjects…[and] sharply raise the rate of old taxes to increase their yield… But the effects on business of this rise in taxation make themselves felt. For business men are soon discouraged by the comparison of their profits with the burden of their taxes…Consequently production falls off, and with it the yield of taxation.
>
> Ibn Khaldun

> Our true choice is not between tax reduction, on the one hand, and the avoidance of large federal deficits on the other. It is increasingly clear that an economy hampered by restrictive tax rates will never produce enough revenues to balance our budget just as it will never produce enough jobs or enough profits. Surely the lesson of the last decade is that budget deficits are not caused by wild-eyed spenders but by slow economic growth and periodic recessions and any new recession would break all deficit records. In short, it is a paradoxical truth that tax rates are too high today and tax revenues are too low and the soundest way to raise the revenues in the long run is to cut the rates now.

These turned out to be very prophetic words of wisdom. In 1963, the top tax rate was 91%. It was cut to 70% by 1965 – two years after JFK was assassinated. Tax revenues increased by 33% as the economy expanded by 42%. This was not an atypical result.

During the 1920s, Secretary of Treasury Andrew Mellon persuaded Congress to implement tax cuts on income and investments. From 1921 to 1929 the federal government pushed through six separate tax cuts. In particular, the top income tax rate fell from 73% to 24%. During that time period, tax revenues increased from $719 million to over $1 billion.

In 1981 Ronald Reagan came into office promising to cut income taxes. You may recall from chapter two that President Reagan suggested that government would get more revenue from lower tax rates. From 1981 to 1986 tax rates fell dramatically and total federal revenues increased. The federal government collected just over $599 billion from taxpayers in 1981. By 1989 the amount was over $990 billion.[10]

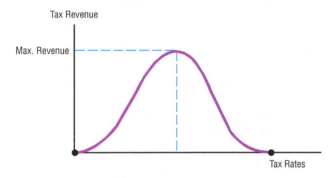

Economist Arthur Laffer became famous for the graph above that shows what Mellon, Kennedy, and Reagan proved to be true.

Notice that if the tax rate equaled 0%, the government would collect no revenue. As taxes increase, revenue begins to increase since few, if any, of us would reduce our work hours, quit our jobs, or alter our behavior in some way that hides income from the IRS.

However, there is a tax rate that will yield maximum revenue for government. What that tax rate is has been debated and empirically studied for more than two decades. Most estimates suggest a rate between 17–23%.[11]

Once the top rate is surpassed, businesses and individuals alike begin to have disincentives to work, create new products, and jobs, and they begin to hide their money by working "off the books" or sheltering their money in untaxed accounts. The result is that the economy suffers from the lack of entrepreneurial undertakings, and the government loses money.

This fact did not keep Barack Obama from campaigning for an increase in income taxes on individuals who earn more than $250,000 per year as well as capital gains taxes.[12] His plan called for using the added revenue from this tax hike to help pay for, among other things, health care for people who do not have insurance and deficit reduction.

The Tax Policy Center estimated that over ten years, Mr. Obama's tax package would *reduce* federal revenues by $2.8 *trillion*.[13] In 2016, Hillary Clinton pressed for even larger tax hikes. Her call for top marginal tax rates of over 45%, along with higher capital gains taxes would fail to produce the revenue she desires if we are currently taxed on the right-hand side of the Laffer Curve. On the other hand, if President Trump's tax reduction plan pushes the United States to the left-side of the peak of this curve, total revenue would fall then too.

CASE STUDY #4 – HAS FOREIGN AID HELPED AFRICA?

All of us have seen the terrible photos and video from various African nations showing the incredible suffering and depravation that is endured on this continent on a daily basis. For many Americans, Africa represents a largely primitive land with little prospects for economic success. Hence, foreign aid is the only logical way to keep people alive. Right?

As it turns out, foreign aid may be one of the important independent variables in explaining why income levels remain so low on this continent.

Multiple studies have shown that over the past fifty-plus years as the U.S. has sent over $500 billion dollars (four times the amount spent rebuilding Germany and Japan after World War II), the level of poverty in Africa has actually increased![14]

This negative relationship between taxpayer aid and income stems from the fact that the African people face two ongoing issues. First, most of the aid is stolen by corrupt African leaders who, as the studies show, are able to use the cash and resources sent by the United States to build enormous mansions and buy luxury cars rather than disseminating the assistance to the people of Africa. The second, and even more significant obstacle, is the fact that most nations in Africa rank very low on the economic freedom index. Rampant corruption, extremely limited, to nonexistent property rights and burdensome regulations place most Africans at the mercy of their governments. As we saw in chapters 2 & 3, without economic freedom, income levels will remain low.

For the people of Africa, growing wealth for their leaders (courtesy of American taxpayers) has afforded the rulers more power to control the people. That type of control has predictably created more poverty for millions of people.

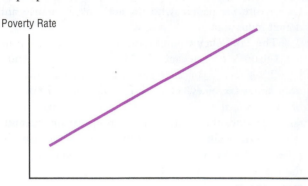

Poverty Rate

Foreign Aid ($)

Photo Courtesy Jack Chambless

CASE STUDY #5 – WILL THE NATIONAL FOOTBALL LEAGUE EXIST 100 YEARS FROM NOW?

One of the more interesting debates that has taken place over the past few years is the relationship between football and a disease known as Chronic Traumatic Encephalopathy (CTE) – a degenerative brain disease that many doctors believe causes erratic behavior, suicidal thoughts and early death.[15]

In 2013, the National Football League settled a lawsuit with former players for $765 million. The suit claimed that the NFL had covered up information about the relationship between concussions and CTE.

In the wake of suicides by former NFL players like future Hall of Famer Junior Seau, more and more atten-

tion is now being given to everything from helmet designs to the basic rules of tackling.

The overriding economic question for this century might cost the NFL even more than $765 billion.[16] That is, what if mothers and fathers of youth players like the ones depicted in this photo decide that the benefits of youth football no longer outweigh the costs, in terms of the probability of a young player suffering from CTE as a grown man? If mothers and fathers become convinced that football is too dangerous, what will be the relationship between the number of youth football players and the long-run profitability of the NFL? How might the NBA and MLS benefit from this issue?

ENDNOTES

1   See "Economists' Grail: A Post-Crash Model" by Mark Whitehouse, *The Wall Street Journal*, November 30, 2010.

2   See "Is the Dismal Science Really a Science?" by Russ Roberts, *The Wall Street Journal*, February 27-28, 2010.

3   See "Kids cram more media hours into a full day" by Bonnie Miller Rubin, *The Orlando Sentinel*, January 21, 2010, p. A8.

4   You will notice on graph 4.6, that it appears that studying zero hours will create a grade of zero. Obviously, this is not so. The graph is drawn this way for exposition purposes. In reality, the intercept term will be greater than zero, meaning that if study hours equaled zero, there would be some grade above zero that would still be earned in most cases.

5   See "Do Girls Speed More Than Boys?" by Joseph B. White and Anjali Athavaley, *The Wall Street Journal*, May 5, 2010.

6   The concept of statistical significance can be reviewed in any basic statistics book.

7   See "Healthy Brew: Beer, It Seems, Is Good for You" by Ken Wells, *The Wall Street Journal*, August 13, 2002.

8   See "100 mph drivers often get just a slap on the wrist" by Scott Powers, *The Orlando Sentinel*, May 15, 2005; and "Driven to Distraction" *The Orlando Sentinel*, February 6, 2005.

9 See "Report: Obama's schools initiative failed" by Emma Brown, *The Washington Post*, January 22, 2017.

10 See "Supply Side 'Alchemy' at Work," by Daniel J. Mitchell, *The Wall Street Journal*.

11 *The Flat Tax* by Robert E. Hall and Alvin Rabushka, Hoover Press, 1985 and www.fairtax.org/.

12 See "Cap Gains Taxation: Less Means More" by Allen Sinai, *The Wall Street Journal*, September 21, 2010.

13 See "Would you care for a spending decrease with that tax cut?" by Debra J. Saunders, *The Star Tribune*, August 6, 2008, pg. A13.

14 See "African Perspectives on Aid: Foreign Assistance will not pull Africa out of Poverty" by Thompson Ayodele, Franklin Cudjoe, Temba A. Nolutshungu & Charles K. Sunwabe, Economic Development Bulletin #2, The Cato Institute, September 14, 2005; "Why Foreign Aid is hurting Africa" by Dambisa Moyo, *The Wall Street Journal*, March 21, 2009 & http://www.youtube.com/watch?v=5VgfE0QYhF0.

15 To learn more about this debate log on to http://www.pbs.org/wgbh/pages/frontline/league-of-denial/ and watch the PBS *Frontline* documentary on the subject.

16 See "Football is on its deathbed" by John Kass, *The Savannah Morning News*, April 27, 2013 page 9A.

CHAPTER REVIEW

1. During the 2016 presidential campaign, Donald Trump repeatedly argued that there was a positive relationship between illegal immigration and crime. To test his theory, what other independent variables could be selected? Justify each.

2. Draw the most likely relationship between the price of gasoline and the sale of large SUVs.

3. What is the relationship between income tax rates and income tax revenue? Why?

4. Why is there a positive relationship between facial symmetry and income?

Chapter Five

THE ECONOMICS *of* CRIME, POVERTY, *and* EDUCATION

A truly moral nation enacts policies that encourage personal responsibility and discourage self-destructive behavior by not subsidizing people who live irresponsibly and make poor choices.

DR. BEN CARSON

THE ECONOMICS OF CRIME

When it comes to the issue of crime, most people would believe that the role of the economist is to explain the cost of crime in terms of the impact on health care costs, productivity, public expenditures, and so forth. For example, a study, by David Anderson of Centre College in the *Journal of Law & Economics*, placed the total annual cost of crime at $1.7 trillion, which is $4,118 per person.[1] While some economists, like Mr. Anderson focus on the direct economic consequence of crime, there are a good number of economists who have also tried to explain the causes of crime.

The decision to commit a criminal act is filled with economic properties. First there is the issue of scarcity. *The Wall Street Journal* once reported that, as bowling shoes became fashionable among teenagers, more young people are stealing bowling shoes from bowling alleys.[2]

The problem of scarcity can help explain this peculiar behavior. Obviously, there is an imbalance between the number of bowling shoes available through legal means and the number of bowling shoes these teenagers have. Stealing them is a way of closing this imbalance. The teen-aged thieves are also self-interested. They are not stealing the shoes for the betterment of mankind, but rather the betterment of their wardrobe.

There is also an opportunity cost associated with this act. Instead of stealing the shoes, the teenagers could offer to buy them or wear some other type of shoe. Are the teenagers rational? If the benefits of stealing the shoes are greater than the opportunity cost, plus the direct cost, then stealing is rational. This is where the discussion of crime, as an economic act, becomes interesting.

The landmark examination of the economics of crime is set forth in a paper by Nobel laureate Gary Becker.[3] Becker argued that, for the criminal, the cost of crime could be broken up into two parts.

We have already mentioned opportunity cost as one of the costs incurred. Upon closer examination, we find that one of the major reasons why people engage in criminal activity is because the opportunity cost of doing so is very small.

Notice that you rarely read about a successful accountant who robs grocery stores on her way home from the office. For people with high levels of education and training, the opportunity cost of crime is quite large. To be criminals, they would have to be willing to run the risk of forgoing their next-best choice. If the next-best choice is accounting or engineering, it makes little sense to don a gorilla mask and start knocking off the local supermarkets.

On the other hand, the evidence indicates that the second-best choice for criminals is one that usually does not pay as well. Most criminals are unskilled and uneducated. Legal means do not pay as well or offer much of a career. To a high school drop-out with no vocational training, becoming an armed robber might seem like the most logical occupation.

CRIME AND PROBABILITY THEORY

To Becker, the second, and far larger, cost is the direct cost of criminal activity. The direct cost includes not only the cost of bullets, ski masks, and gas for the getaway car, but the probability of capture and conviction, the probability of spending time in jail, the length of the sentence, and the probability of parole.[4] Notice the world *probability*. You should recall from chapter one that when a person commits a criminal act, there is a probability between zero and 100% that he or she will end up in prison.[5] Let's look at burglary as an example of how probability theory works.

Edward Rubenstein found that, "Only 7% of U.S. burglaries result in an arrest. Of those arrested, 87% are prosecuted. Of those prosecuted, 79% are convicted. Of those convicted, a mere 25% are sent to prison (most are paroled)."[6] If we multiply all of these probabilities, we find that the potential burglar faces only a *1.2%* chance of going to prison each time he or she creeps into a house looking for a new laptop computer.

Once in prison, the average unlucky burglar will stay there about 13 months, but since the burglar will stay out of jail *over 98% of the time*, the expected cost of each act of burglary — to the burglar — is only 4.8 days.

You can see the dilemma for law enforcement officials. Incarceration for 4.8 days is a very small price to pay for the chance to pilfer thousands of dollars in goodies. One has to wonder what would happen if the average burglar was also good at probability theory. It also makes one wonder why more professional statisticians are not out looking for houses to burgle! With all this in mind, we can see how the discipline of economics can begin to explain the economic process of opting for crime as a vocation. By using economic models, we can move from observing criminal behavior to explaining the *cause* of criminal behavior.

IS AMERICA EXPERIENCING A NEW CRIME WAVE?

After years of falling crime rates in the United States, 2015 & 2016 seemed to return our nation to the 1970s when crime was rampant. From 1973 through 2014 the overall rate of violent crime fell. In 2015, violent crime rates rose by 3.9%. However, when looking at the murder rate in America the numbers were startling.

According to the FBI the murder rate rose 10.8% in 2015.[7] Crime researcher Heather MacDonald found that in the largest 56 cities in the United States, homicides were up 17% - the largest one-year increase in two decades. Washington, D.C. saw murders rise by 56%; in Milwaukee, 73%; in Cleveland, 90. In 2016 726 people were murdered in Chicago.

Social scientists of all disciplines were perplexed by this trend and offered varying theories to explain it. On one side of the fence we saw an increasing number of researchers arguing that there was the 'Ferguson Effect' at work. The theory here is that in the wake of police shootings of black Americans in Ferguson, Missouri and other cities, the backlash against the police had led many officers to resist being overly aggressive in policing economically-challenged areas. Thus, facing a lower direct cost of engaging in crime (stemming from a lower police presence), more people chose to engage in violent acts.[8]

Others argued that legislation dating back to when Bill Clinton was president, along with over-zealous police actions, had created the unintended consequence of more crime. In 1994 President Clinton signed legislation that allocated $8.8 billion to hire 100,000 more police officers and $10 billion for new prisons, along with mandatory prison sentences – including life in prison for three drug offenses.

Meanwhile, in 2015, police killed 1,207 Americans, or 134 Americans per 100,000 officers, a rate that is 30 times the homicide rate overall. One out of 12 killings in the United States that year were by police officers.[9]

Numerous studies by economists, criminologists, sociologists, and other social scientists have been done with no one definitive independent variable having been discovered as the most statistically significant predictor of criminal behavior. However, many factors have been discovered to have played a causal role in the crime rate. The research indicates that drug and alcohol abuse, having been the victim of child abuse, or residing in a decaying community and a weak economy can lead to higher incidence of crime.[10]

On the other hand, active community policing programs, and high levels of educational achievement are significant predictors of lower levels of criminal activity. Surprisingly, the research does not yet support any causal link between the crime rate and violence in the movies or on television.[11] Nor does current research support the notion that economic growth brings down the crime rate.

During the 2007-2009 Recession, many people were afraid that a rising unemployment rate would lead to a surge in property and violent crime. It did not happen. Instead, the trend toward lower crime continued unabated. According to the FBI's Uniform Crime Reports, homicide dropped 10% nationwide in the first six months of 2009; violent crime was down 4.4%, and car thefts fell by 19%.[12]

While none of the aforementioned variables – or the relationship between the variables and crime – should come as a surprise to anyone, there are some that have recently been investigated by economists that yield some interesting results.

THE ECONOMIC IMPORTANCE OF FATHERS

For years the rate of divorce and out-of-wedlock births has been a source of concern to social scientists, but only recently have we had any data to articulate why all of America should be worried about the lack of fathers in the lives of many of our children.

The lack of a father presence in their daughter's lives has been linked to a increased risk for those teenagers of pregnancy. The U.S. Department of Justice, Bureau of Justice Statistics has reported, and Louis Sullivan, former cabinet member of former President Bush, has confirmed, that 70% of the juveniles in state reform institutions grew up in single- or no-parent situations; additionally,

72% of adolescent murderers, 60% of rapists and 70% of the long term prisoners in America grew up without a father in the home. According to a recent report of the U.S. Department of Health and Human Services, children in father-absent families have a much higher risk of drug and alcohol abuse, mental illness, suicide, poor educational performance, teen pregnancy, and criminality.[13]

© Flashon Studio/Shutterstock.com

These numbers – and others like them – have helped spawn a new movement in America to make fathers and mothers more aware of the critical role dads play in the development of children.[14] Thanks to statistical evidence, the role of men has risen above sperm donor to one of paramount importance in reducing America's crime rate.

DO MORE GUNS EQUAL LESS CRIME?

The most foolish mistake we could possibly make would be to allow the subject races to possess arms. History shows that all conquerors who have allowed their subject races to carry arms have prepared their own downfall by so doing.

Adolf Hitler

Rosie O'Donnell would not like John R. Lott much. Ms. O'Donnell, a vocal anti-gun advocate, has, on many occasions, called for a ban on guns. She is not alone. Many Americans view the existence of guns as the major cause of crime in our nation. The problem is that the research does not support this opinion.

John Lott is a professor of economics at The University of Chicago and the author of a controversial book, *More Guns, Less Crime: Understanding Crime and Gun Control Laws.*[15] Professor Lott's work amounts to the most thorough criminological study ever performed on the relationship between concealed weapons laws and the crime rate.

Throughout the nineteenth century, "the right to keep and bear arms" meant exactly what it said: The right to carry a gun was protected just as firmly as the right to own a gun. Some states, particularly in the South, enforced laws against carrying handguns concealed, but the right to openly carry was almost universally respected.

By the 1970s, however, the right to carry had been restricted in most jurisdictions. America was well on the way to treating guns like cigarettes: permissible in private, but completely banned from public spaces.

In 1988, however, Florida initiated a national trend by enacting a "shall issue" handgun permit law, allowing any adult who has a clean record and has taken safety training to obtain a permit to carry a concealed handgun for protection. Now over half the states have similar laws.

Lott collected data from every one of the 3,054 counties in the United States over an 18-year period and examined changes in the rates of nine different types of crime. He also accounted for the effects of dozens of other variables, including variations in arrest rates, in the age and racial composition of a county's population, in national crime rates, and in changes made to gun-control laws, including the adoption of waiting periods. Lott's findings show that

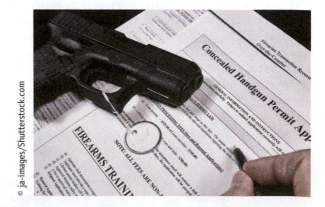

© ja-images/Shutterstock.com

SUGGESTED CLASSROOM DEBATE

Would it make sense to allow students and professors to carry concealed weapons at colleges and universities? Would this reduce the number of Virginia Tech-type incidents?

SUGGESTED CLASSROOM DEBATE

In 2005, Florida enacted a new law called "The Castle Doctrine". In public places the law removes the obligation of a person to flee, allowing people to legally kill attackers if they feel threatened. In person's home they are allowed to legally kill an intruder.[16] Is this new law an appropriate extension of Lott's work, or does it take his findings too far? Where, in your opinion, does the shooting death of Trayvon Martin fit into this analysis?

concealed weapons laws significantly reduce violent crime. On average, the murder rate falls by 10%, that of rape by 3%, and aggravated assault by 6%.

While crime begins to fall off immediately, the benefits of concealed handgun laws take about three years to be fully felt. This is not surprising: In most states, a flood of applications occurs in the first few weeks the law is on the books, followed by a gradual rise in the percentage of the population that has acquired permits. The larger the percentage of the population with permits, the greater the drop in crime, with the percentage ranging from 1-5%.

Apparently, while concealed handgun laws do not reduce the appetite criminals have for other people's property; they do encourage the more rational subset to acquire it in ways that do not put their own lives at risk. And everyone, not just gun carriers, benefits from the reduced crime rate, since aggressors cannot know which potential victims might have a concealed weapon.[17]

In 2010, the United States Supreme Court appeared to agree with Lott's findings, in a ruling where the Court said that the Second Amendment to the Constitution extended nationwide and that federal judges could strike down state laws that prohibit the carrying of firearms.[18]

THE ABORTED CRIME WAVE?

Steven Levitt, an economics professor at the University of Chicago, and John Donohue, a Stanford University law professor, recently completed one of the most controversial studies on crime that has come along in years. Messrs. Levitt and Donohue argue that the legalization of abortion in the early 1970s played a key role – perhaps explaining as much as 50% – in the declining crime rate of the 1990s.[19]

Between 1992 and 1999, murders in the U.S. fell by 35%, robberies fell 39%, and violent crimes fell 26%. Many people speculated that the booming economy might have caused the decline. Others argued that a new "zero tolerance" approach in places like New York City was the primary cause of the lower crime rates. According to Levitt:

The theoretical justification for our argument rests on two simple assumptions: 1) Legalized abortion leads to fewer "unwanted" babies being born, and 2) unwanted babies are more likely to suffer abuse and neglect and are, therefore, at an increased risk for criminal involvement later in life.

The first assumption, that abortion reduces the number of unwanted children, is true virtually by definition.

The second assumption, that unwanted children are at increased risk for criminal involvement, is supported by three decades of academic research.

If one accepts these two assumptions, then a direct mechanism, by which the legalization of abortion can reduce crime, has been established. At that point, the question merely becomes: Is the magnitude of the impact large or small?

Our preliminary research suggests that the effect of abortion legalization is large. According to our estimates, as much as one-half of the remarkable decline in crime in the 1990s may be attributable to the legalization of abortion. We base our conclusions on four separate data analyses. First, we demonstrate that crime rates began to fall 18 years after the landmark Supreme Court decision Roe vs. Wade legalized abortion across the nation, just the point at which babies born under legalized abortion would be reaching the peak adolescent crime years. Second, we show that the five states that legalized abortion in 1970 — three years before Roe vs. Wade — saw crime begin to decrease roughly three years earlier than the rest of the nation. This is a bit more convincing to me but still far from conclusive.

Third, we demonstrate that states with high abortion rates in the mid-1970s have had much greater crime decreases in the 1990s than states that had low abortion rates in the 1970s. This relationship holds true even when we take into account changes in the size of prison populations, number of police, poverty rates, measures of the economy, changes in welfare generosity, and other changes in fertility.

This is the evidence that really starts to be convincing, in my opinion. Fourth, we show that the abortion related drop in crime is occurring only for those who today are under the age of 25. This is exactly the age group we would expect to be affected by the legalization of abortion in the early 1970s. That is where our paper stops. Our paper is a descriptive exercise attempting to explain why crime fell.

The implications of this research cannot be understated. One look at the Internet on this subject will reveal dozens of hysterical, emotional, and biblical responses to the work of Levitt and Donohue. For public policymakers the possibility that aborting unborn children can dramatically lower crime rates presents an interesting subset of questions. Should the government offer to fund all abortions on demand? Should the government target high-crime areas and offer to pay for abortions? Should the private sector – hard hit by property crimes, shoplifting and high health care costs – offer to subsidize abortions?

From a pure cost-benefit approach, paying for abortions would make sense. After all, an abortion costs a few hundred dollars, but criminals inflict far more damage on the nation than that. On the other hand, some would argue that abortion itself is a crime and therefore the cost-benefit analysis might miss some important calculations. If we measure cost in pure dollar terms and do not include the social or moral cost (however we wish to define that), does the cost-benefit approach fall short? That is left for you and other citizens to decide.

THE ECONOMICS OF POVERTY

In chapter one, we saw that every economy must answer questions about what will be produced, how the good and services will be produced, and for whom the goods and services will be produced. The "for whom" part of the equation can present a tremendous set of difficulties for a nation, because in every country there are some people who have access to a tremendous array of goods and services while others find themselves going to bed hungry and cold on any given night. In this section, we will utilize economic models to explain what causes poverty and what society can do about the problem of poverty.

WHO ARE THE POOR?

Before we can start a discussion of the causes of poverty, it is important that we first examine data pertaining to who is poor in America. The U.S. Census Bureau is largely responsible for providing data on poverty rates on an annual basis. The following table summarizes a recent threshold for poverty. A person or family is considered to be poor if he, she, or it falls below these thresholds. The thresholds are considered to reflect the minimum amount a person or family would have to earn each year to meet the most basic needs with respect to food, clothing, shelter, medical attention, and so forth.

For a family of four, the poverty threshold was $24,300 in 2016. It should be noted that when the Census Bureau counts income, it does not include capital gains and non-cash benefits such as public housing, Medicaid, and food stamps.[20]

The Census Bureau is not the only agency that measures poverty. The following table illustrates the "official" poverty level according to the Department of Health and Human Services.

As one might imagine if we have multiple agencies coming up with divergent poverty thresholds – and if those agencies do not count non-income wealth like private property, one can end up with a skewed view of what actually constitutes poverty in America.

In 2016 the Census Bureau concluded that 14.5% of the American population lived below the poverty line. Twenty-one percent of children lived in poverty that year.

TRENDS IN THE POVERTY DATA

There is some good news on the poverty front. People who are born poor do not have to stay poor if economic conditions are favorable to upward mobility. For much of the 1980s and 1990s, the rate of poverty fell in America. The pro-economic growth policies of Ronald Reagan and Bill Clinton helped create this trend, which saw more and more Americans climb the economic ladder.

One 17-year study of lifetime earnings by the Federal Reserve Bank of Dallas found that a mere 5% of people who started out in the lowest 20% of income-earners stayed there over that time period.[21] In the United States there is a great deal of positive movement in total income levels for poorer Americans.[22] This is due in large part to the economic and geographic mobility of our society and the incentives created by the quasi free-market system. When people see that with education, training, and hard work, it is possible to move out of poverty, many people

2016 FEDERAL POVERTY GUIDELINES

FIGURE 5.1

Family size	Gross Annual Income	Gross Monthly Income	Approximate Hourly Wage
1	$11,880	$990	$5.71
2	$16,020	$1,335	$7.70
3	$20,160	$1,680	$9.69
4	$24,300	$2,025	$11.68
5	$28,440	$2,370	$13.67
6	$32,580	$2,715	$15.66
7	$36,730	$3,061	$17.66
8	$40,890	$3,408	$19.66
Over 8: add per person:	$4,160	$347	$2.00

Source: Federal Register vol. 81. no. 15, January 25, 2016, pp. 4036–7. Monthly and hourly income calculated by OCPP and rounded to the nearest dollar and cent, respectively. The hourly rate is based on 40 hours of work per week for a full year (2080 hours). These guidelines are for the 48 contiguous states and the District of Columbia.

will undertake the necessary steps to attempt to strive for success. Some might move into the lower middle class. Others might become firmly middle class, while others can emerge from poverty to become rich.[23]

It is important to note that such economic mobility is fairly exclusive to the United States. In most nations around the world, poverty rates dwarf what we consider poverty in America. In Mexico, an estimated 40 million people live on less than $2 per day, while globally over 2.8 billion of the planet's more than seven billion people live on less than $2 per day. In countries like Haiti, Benin, Liberia, Ethiopia, and Somalia, military dictatorships, the institution of slavery, and the lack of economic freedom have combined to create annual incomes of a few hundred dollars per year and life expectancy rates that would be appalling to the average poor American who has access to subsidized housing, and charities that provide food, Christmas gifts, and medical care.[24]

THE CAUSES OF POVERTY IN AMERICA

If we use the concept of economic modeling to explain poverty in America, we would select annual income as our dependent variable. What independent variables should we

PEARLS BEFORE SWINE © 2006 Stephan Pastis. Reprinted by permission of ANDREWS MCMEEL SYNDICATION. All rights reserved.

Watch the movie entitled, *The Pursuit of Happyness*. How realistic do you think it is for someone to achieve what Chris Gardner achieved, starting from where he did? Why?

© Tinseltown/Shutterstock.com

select? This is where a tremendous debate has entered into the picture. While some variables make perfect sense – educational achievement, years of work experience, age, resource endowments, family size, labor market conditions, and immigration trends come to mind – other variables have recently been suggested that have traditionally been overlooked by economists. Some of the less obvious variables include private vs. public school education, government policies to help the poor, marriage, and the existence of slavery.

For years (centuries?) economists have known that *education* and poverty are inextricably linked. Simply put, a high school drop-out should not expect to earn a six-figure salary over his or her lifetime. Some might, but it would not be a wise use of probability theory to bank on becoming rich after leaving the ninth grade. In reality, one of the biggest components of the income gap is explained by differences in human capital acquisition.

Unfortunately for the poorest and least educated Americans, this trend is accelerating as our "new economy" continues to pick up steam. As technology and the ability to work with technology continues to be a pervasive force in our economy, those individuals – from auto mechanics to aeronautical engineers – who are best suited to utilize technology will be the individuals who earn the highest incomes.[25]

Age and work experience also play a role in explaining income differences and thus poverty rates. People who are impoverished tend to be younger and less experienced individuals. Over time, greater work experience – especially if work experience is not frequently interrupted or truncated by prolonged periods of unemployment – is a key to rising income.[26] Poorer people tend to have longer periods between jobs, minimal work experience, and thus a lower lifetime earnings profile.

Resource endowments and *labor market conditions* in which a person operates also contribute to differences in earnings. Stephen Currey's children will probably not

end up poor. The daughter of a single mother on welfare, on an American-Indian reservation in Montana, probably will be poor as an adult. This is due to differences in initial resource endowments (land, capital, and so forth) and differences in access to resources (schooling) over time. Yet, there are exceptions to this more common outcome.

A good friend of mine grew up desperately poor in our hometown of Hugo, Oklahoma. Through an incredible work ethic, he went on to graduate with a degree in economics from the University of Oklahoma in only three years and eventually Columbia Law School. Today he is a highly successful and affluent attorney in Chicago. He had virtually no resources to speak of as a youngster except a strong desire to emerge from poverty. While he is a statistical outlier, he is also an example that lack of resources need not be an unalterable ticket to poverty.

With respect to *labor market conditions*, the type of employment opportunities a person works toward or finds most available can also explain why some people are so poor. In the Great Plains, rural Americans face much higher rates of poverty because of unfavorable supply and demand conditions. The same is true for inner cities in America. With much higher crime rates, lower quality schools and fewer businesses, the overall hiring patterns in inner cities tends to gravitate towards low-wage, low-skill jobs in fast-food and other industries that do not require higher levels of education and skill.

This is where *geographic mobility* and personal choices can play a role. Where labor market conditions are creating very low annual earnings, you will see higher poverty levels. If a person cannot, or will not, seek chances to move out of a poorer area – or seek the proper education and training to move out of poverty within that region – chronic poverty can persist from one generation to the next. A child born near Silicon Valley has a better chance to see the actual gains from becoming educated than a child in the inner city of Philadelphia.

Speaking of geographic mobility and choices, for years economists and non-economists alike have wondered whether immigration plays a role in explaining

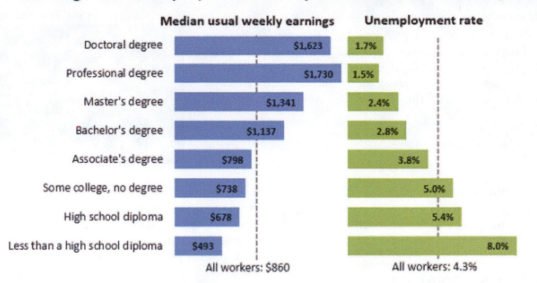

Earnings and unemployment rates by educational attainment, 2015

	Median usual weekly earnings	Unemployment rate
Doctoral degree	$1,623	1.7%
Professional degree	$1,730	1.5%
Master's degree	$1,341	2.4%
Bachelor's degree	$1,137	2.8%
Associate's degree	$798	3.8%
Some college, no degree	$738	5.0%
High school diploma	$678	5.4%
Less than a high school diploma	$493	8.0%
	All workers: $860	All workers: 4.3%

Note: Data are for persons age 25 and over. Earnings are for full-time wage and salary workers.
Source: U.S. Bureau of Labor Statistics, Current Population Survey

poverty in America. The theory is that the more immigrants we have, the larger will be the supply of labor and the lower wage rates will be. To an extent the research bears this theory out. Recent evidence suggests that the most recent wave of undocumented immigrants did cause downward pressure on wage rates for the most unskilled and uneducated Americans.[27]

However, the overwhelming evidence indicates that most unskilled immigrants take jobs that many Americans simply won't take. These jobs include, but are not limited to, migrant work in agricultural fields, clothing production, landscaping, home construction and meat processing plants. Moreover, immigration studies have repeatedly shown that immigrants actually help reduce poverty not only by creating jobs in America but by stimulating the demand for U.S. goods. Immigrants tend to have higher savings rates, better educational achievement, and an entrepreneurial spirit that has led to more jobs and income for America rather than less.

Researchers have also begun to point to the role of *marriage* in predicting poverty. In 1970, 95% of white women and 92% of black women had been married at least once. By this decade that figure was 88 and 63% respectively. 29% of white children are born to unmarried women while 71% of black children are. Economists have found that when we look at lifetime patterns on income generation, marital status is a statistically significant variable in predicting who will be poor – especially for boys. Boys born into single-mother households are likely to struggle with truancy, disciplinary issues and criminal behavior than boys who have both parents in the home.[28] These factors contribute greatly to income prospects over time.

PUBLIC SCHOOLS AND POVERTY

> Today, I can't recommend in good conscience, that an African-American family send their children to the Minneapolis public schools. The facts are irrefutable: These schools are not preparing our children to compete in the world.
>
> Louis King,
> former member of the Minneapolis School Board

Over the past several years, economists have begun to cast a larger net out into the ocean of variables that might explain persistent poverty in America. In particular, we have wondered why, despite the large gains made by black Americans[29] the poverty rate among black people remains higher than any other demographic group.[30] Of course, high rates of poverty are not exclusive to black people in our country. American Indians, whites in the rural south and Appalachia and Hispanics also find economic hardship at higher rates than most Americans.

CONCEPT CHECK

During the 1990's Hillary Clinton said, "The President believes, as I do, that charter schools are a way of bringing teachers and parents and communities together."[31] In 2016 she opposed charter schools while running for president. What are charter schools and how do they impact the quality of education in America?

Economists have now begun to look at educational choices, government policies to reduce poverty, and the institution of slavery as potential explanatory variables.

EDUCATIONAL QUALITY

Common sense – and economic analysis – suggests that there is a relationship between the quality of education a person receives and their lifetime annual earnings. After all, there is a reason the top universities in America publish starting salary data for their graduates.

Over the years, several independent variables have been examined by economists to ascertain the major driving forces in explaining why some states like Minnesota seem to provide a high quality educational environment while others (Florida, for example) do not.

Among the variables that we have studied are: teacher pay; teacher qualifications; total education spending; the role of school choice; union rules and the impact of tenure.

Let's look at each.

ARE AMERICAN TEACHERS UNDERPAID?

According to the Bureau of Labor Statistics in 2011 the average *hourly* wage & benefits of an American K-12 teacher equaled $56.59. This figure was based on total monetary compensation plus pension, health care and other benefits divided by the average yearly work hours of 1,405 hours per year – compared to an average of 2,000 hours per year worked, on average, by private sector employees.[32] By contrast, the average hourly wages and benefits of private sector workers equaled $28.24 that year.

Internationally, American K-12 teachers, depending on the year being evaluated, rank at or near the top of the hourly compensation scale despite frequent claims – held

to be economic facts by many Americans – that "teachers are underpaid." In city after city, more often than not, there is a surplus of teachers available when jobs become available.[33] In chapter six you will learn how a surplus means that the price in a market is actually "too high." When we examine claims that teachers do not make enough money to foster high-quality teaching we have found that in other nations around the world where teachers make less than their American counterparts, the overall test scores – especially in math and science – are much higher. Moreover, private schools in America – as well as charter and home-schooling options – are often far less costly that what taxpayers shell out to support public school teachers. Yet, private, charter and home-schooled Americans routinely beat K-12 public school students in SAT, ACT and other aptitude tests.[34]

Since teacher pay in America ranks among the highest in the world, public school students should be producing near the highest results in the world – if there is in fact a statistically significant relationship between teacher pay and student results – which the results suggest does not exist.

TEACHER QUALIFICATIONS

The U.S. also ranks at the top of the world in total annual spending, per student, on education, with more than $15,171[35] per student, per year in expenditures. In 2011 the U.S. spent $809 billion on public education compared to $130 billion in Germany; $65 billion in Canada; $161 billion in Japan; $123 billion in England and $10 billion in top-performing Finland.[36] Despite all of the money poured into public schools, the results are not statistically impressive.

National Geographic recently conducted a poll that uncovered the fact that half of the 18-24-year-old Americans surveyed could not find New York on a map. Eleven percent *could not find the United States* on a map.[37] In recent international tests given to 15-year-old kids from the 30 countries that make up the Organization for Economic Development and Cooperation, American kids finished 25th in math and 21st in science, prompting President Obama to say, "Incompetent teachers must be identified and weeded out."[38]

Microsoft founder, Bill Gates has gone so far as to argue that America's high schools are "ruining the lives of millions of Americans every year."[39]

Perhaps Mr. Gates will take comfort in knowing that in one school in California, *7–10-year-old students* were recently given a test where they were asked to rate the following activities according to how often they experienced the thought or emotion[40]:

"Touching my private parts too much."
"Thinking about sex when I don't want to."
"Not trusting people because they might want sex."
"Having sex feelings in my body."

Then again, maybe this type of test is not what Mr. Gates needs kids to take to make them better suited to be computer software designers some day.

Mr. Gates would also most likely find it somewhat disturbing that in the last decade approximately 2,750 teachers nationwide had their credentials revoked, denied, surrendered or sanctioned for engaging in sexual misconduct as SAT scores reached their lowest level of the decade in 2008.[41]

Another fact concerning America's government school system is that the overall quality of teachers is lower than in most other developed nations.[42] When economists look at requirements associated with receiving a degree in education; a teaching certificate and a bachelor's degree

in education,[43] the U.S. pales in comparison to the much more rigorous standards expected of teachers in places like Finland, Korea, and other industrialized nations.[44] In the United States, 23% of new teachers come from the top third of their graduating class in college. Only 14% of new teachers in high-poverty schools come from the top third of their class. In Singapore, South Korea, and Finland 100% of new teachers come from the top third of their class.[45] Guess where Singapore, South Korea, and Finland rank in terms of educational quality?

When you combine the entrenched power of the *teachers unions* with rigid rules that make it almost impossible to fire tenured teachers – and the bureaucracy that comes from the growth in administrative jobs – it is much more likely that you will see a higher degree of failure coming from government schools than you would from private schools that do not face such obstacles to effective teaching.[46]

This is not to say that some teachers in some schools aren't doing an incredibly productive job under difficult circumstances. It also does not absolve parents of the responsibility for their child's education. There are numerous outlets on the internet and in the private sector for helping children learn. Garage sales and thrift stores have books that are inexpensive – and libraries are abundant. Studies show that a parent's education achievement and involvement plays a significant role in determining the educational outcomes of children.[47]

However, in state after state "consumers" of government education are not getting the value they expect from their tax dollars – even when they participate in pre-school programs designed to give children a head start on their education.[48]

Students Lag Behind International Peers

In tests of reading, math, and science, U.S. 15-year-olds were out performed by many of their counterparts in Asia and Europe—in some cases placing below the international average.

READING—Average 496			MATH—Average 494			SCIENCE—Average 501		
1.	Shanghai (China)	570	1.	Shanghai (China)	613	1.	Shanghai (China)	580
2.	Hong Kong (China)	545	2.	Singapore	573	2.	Hong Kong (China)	555
3.	Singapore	542	3.	Hong Kong (China)	561	3.	Singapore	551
4.	Japan	538	4.	Taiwan	560	4.	Japan	547
5.	S. Korea	536	5.	S. Korea	554	5.	Finland	545
6.	Finland	524	6.	Macao (China)	538	6.	Estonia	541
7.	Ireland	523	7.	Japan	536	7.	S. Korea	538
8.	Taiwan	523	8.	Liechtenstein	535	8.	Vietnam	528
9.	Canada	523	9.	Switzerland	531	9.	Poland	526
10.	Poland	518	10.	Netherlands	523	10.	Canada	525
24.	U.S.	498	36.	U.S.	481	28.	U.S.	497

Scores were based on a 1,000 point scale. Data from Organization for Economic Cooperation and Development.

SCHOOL CHOICE

So, why don't parents – especially poorer parents whose children are more likely to be in bad schools – simply send their kids somewhere else? After all, 2,000 of America's high schools – less than 15% of the total – are responsible for producing 81% of all Native American dropouts, 73% of all African-American dropouts, and 66% of all Hispanic dropouts.[49]

Suppose you are an American living in Birmingham with a school-age child whom you want to see get the best education possible. In Birmingham, like all other large cities in America, you have three predominant choices – private school, home school, or public school. If you are poor, the chances of your being able to afford a private school education is extraordinarily low, if not equal to zero.

Private school and home schooling – which studies show creates the highest SAT scores[50] and overall academic achievement[51] – is also probably not a viable option. As a poor person in Birmingham – or just about anywhere else, you would not only be hard-pressed to afford time away from work to educate your child, but you might also be relatively uneducated, which means you might not be qualified to teach your child.

That leaves most poor Americans with one real choice – the public, or government-run, school system. If your school system ranks at or near the bottom in test scores, reading and math achievement, college placement, or graduation rates, it might lead you to consider sending your child to a public school in the suburbs where you have heard that the schools are much better. The problem is, in much of America *you do not have the right to send your child to the public school of your choice*.[52] Instead, you must send your child to the public school that is in your district – even if you don't want to. There are a few exceptions for magnet or charter schools, but by and large the public school system in your district has a functional monopoly over your child.

What if, by law, there was only one cell phone company in America? Would the company provide the best product at the best prices, or would you get declining quality and higher prices over time?

In Detroit, over $11,000 in taxpayer money is spent per child each year – and the city sees only 25% of its students graduate from high school.[53] Just over half of Washington D.C.'s students graduate even though spending per pupil is highest in America at over $19,600 per year. Meanwhile Catholic and other private schools spend far less in each city and often have graduation rates above 90%.[54]

Which group of people has the fewest educational choices? If you say poor people, you are correct. Now let us ask which race of people has the highest poverty rates? If you say African-Americans, you are right again.

If we now ask if there is a connection between the lack of school choice for a majority of African-Americans and the poverty rate of African-Americans, we find one immutable conclusion: Many black people in America today are largely trapped by a school system that has few incentives to innovate and even fewer competitors.[55]

Without fear that parents will pull their children out of horrible schools, why should teachers or administrators in these schools seek to improve the quality of education in Birmingham?

In Florida, among the 68 schools to which the state recently gave failing grades, the vast majority were in predominantly poor neighborhoods with mostly black residents. Is it any wonder that black families from Miami, Milwaukee and Washington, D.C., recently fought to gain *vouchers* so that children in the some of the most expensive – and worst – school districts in America could leave for better schools in the private sector?[56] Is it at all surprising that minorities now make up 15% of the more than 2 million home-schooled children, or that home-schooling has increased from 850,000 students in 1999 to an estimated nearly 6 million by 2017?[57]

It is worth noting that in states like Minnesota where students are allowed to attend any school they choose, average SAT and other test scores far exceed states like Alabama where students are confined to a particular school district. Also, in states that have a larger percentage of charter schools, teachers do not enjoy the benefits of *tenure* (life-time contracts) or union protection. Therefore, if a teacher is not working productively they can be let go much faster than in the traditional public school setting.

CAN VOUCHERS REDUCE POVERTY?

In 2002, Florida governor Jeb Bush signed into law the first state-wide school voucher program in the United States.

A voucher is the assignment of a specified amount of tax dollars to a parent to use to send a child to the private school of their choice. In addition to the voucher program, Florida instituted a grading system for all government schools that assigned schools a grade of 'A' through 'F' based on the results of an annual test given to all students. Up to $3,500 of private-school tuition, plus books and transportation costs, were paid by the Florida Corporate Income Tax Credit Scholarship Program, which let businesses divert a portion of their state taxes to these school-choice vouchers.

If a school got an 'F' grade two years in a row, parents could either apply for a voucher, or send their child to another government school of their choice.

About 55,000 people applied for the scholarships, which were available to children who qualify for free or reduced-price lunches in public schools.

In 2006 the Supreme Court of Florida ruled the voucher program unconstitutional, ending, for the time being, part of Florida's experiment with greater competition in the market for education.[58] However, in 2010 the state of Florida expanded the Tax Credit Scholarship Program – a program that allows businesses to donate money to low-income families who seek private schooling.[59]

The voucher movement has gained significant momentum over the past several years. In Arizona, Utah, Georgia, Ohio and other states, parents have taken to the streets and to the voting booth to demand their right to shop around for good teachers.[60]

While this struggle has met with mixed results, economists like Harvard's Caroline Hoxby have helped lend scientific support to school choice by uncovering the statistical impact of choice on public schools.

Dr. Hoxby, and others, have found that there is a statistically significant positive relationship between school choice and the overall test scores of public school kids that *do not change schools*. This means that as more and more kids opt to use vouchers in places like Milwaukee, Wisconsin, the government schools – faced with the Darwinian choice of adapt or die off – have opted to improve the overall quality of instruction in order to keep kids from fleeing.[61] By 2008, Milwaukee Public Schools had lost almost 10,000 students whose parents opted for educational freedom.[62]

© Joana Lopes/Shutterstock.com

This makes intuitive sense. After all, it is the prospect of losing customers to places like Crispers and Panera Bread that prompted McDonalds to roll out healthier foods.

Not surprisingly, teachers unions all over the country have put up vehement opposition to school choice. And why not? What inferior competitor ever welcomes competition? It would be economically irrational for teachers in government schools to embrace competition unless they know they would be picked over the private schools. The current waiting list in America for enrollment in charter schools is over 1 million (up from 350,000 in 2011) as these schools continue to dramatically outperform traditional public schools.[63]

The fact that the unions fight against competition is all economists need to know about what government school teachers think about the quality of the product they put out. When Michelle Rhee was appointed chancellor of Washington, D.C.'s notoriously horrible public schools, she fired 241 teachers and put 737 more on notice for being rated "minimally effective." The result? Test scores began to improve by double-digits and the teachers in the District of Columbia lobbied for Ms. Rhee's resignation.[64]

What remains to be seen is whether poorer Americans – and in particular, black and Hispanic Americans – will continue to gain the freedom they have in all other markets. So far, African-American and Hispanic parents have been the most vocal supporters of vouchers.[65] That is because one of the ways their kids will be able to get out of poverty is if they can get the same educational choices that richer Americans have always enjoyed.[66]

On this issue of choice, President Trump is on record of saying, "Competition is why I'm very much in favor of school choice. Let schools compete for kids. I guarantee that if you forced schools to get better or close because parents didn't want to enroll their kids there, they would get better. Those schools that weren't good enough to attract students would close, and that's a good thing."[67] It remains to be seen if he is able to foster this change on behalf of American parents.

SUGGESTED CLASSROOM DEBATE

The average American home-school family spends $600 per child, per year on educational resources.[68] Should there be laws that force home-school families to spend more – and provide proof that the parents are experts in education? Why, or why not?

The War on Poverty

> To be dependent is to be degraded. Men may pity us, but they cannot respect us.
>
> Proclamation at a convention for black Americans, New York, 1848

One hundred years after Abraham Lincoln signed the Emancipation Proclamation – freeing most of the slaves in the United States, the United States Congress passed the Civil Rights Act. It was around the same time that President Lyndon Johnson accelerated the battle against poverty that began with the administration of Franklin D. Roosevelt.[69]

Roosevelt was responsible for passing legislation that created a taxpayer-funded social welfare network that included, but was not limited to, welfare checks paid to widowed mothers. Roosevelt meant for such welfare to be temporary. He was afraid that welfare would "become the subtle destroyer of the human spirit."

What he did not know is that there is nothing as permanent as a temporary government program. Since 1964 the federal government has spent 20.7 trillion dollars attempting to rid our nation of poverty.[70]

By 2016 there were more than 80 different welfare programs costing taxpayers over $900 billion per year and roughly 100 million Americans (one in three people) received benefits from at least one of them at an average cost of $9,000 per recipient.[71]

While no one can argue that no poor person – of any race – has benefited from social welfare spending, the question for economists centers on the role of government in creating higher poverty rates by damaging the incentives people have to work and be creative.

The Heritage Foundation's research indicates that the major underlying factors producing child poverty in the United States are welfare dependence and single parenthood. Race per se is not a factor in producing child poverty; race alone does not directly increase or decrease the probability that a child will be poor. When a black child is compared with a white child raised in identical circumstances, both children will have the same probability of living in poverty. Similarly, when whites with high levels of single parenthood and welfare dependence (matching those typical in the black community) are compared to blacks, the poverty rates for both groups are nearly identical.

In 1996 Congress created the Personal Responsibility and Work Opportunity Reconciliation Act, which President Clinton signed into law. Since 1996 studies show a direct link between setting time limits on welfare benefits and a reduction in welfare rolls and poverty rates.[72] In fact, in August 1996 12.2 million people were on the welfare rolls. By December 2006 the number was 4.1 million – a decline of 67%.[73] Another part of this legislation was a work-requirement in order to receive monthly benefits. However, in 2012 President Obama issued a directive giving the secretary of Health and Human Services the power to waive federal work-requirements.[74]

It is interesting to note that welfare reform alone does not account for the economic gains some states have made over the past several years. Taxes matter, too.

The ten states with the lowest tax burdens saw a 13.7% drop in poverty during the last decade, while the ten states with the highest tax burden saw poverty rates increase by 3%.[75]

It makes economic sense – in any war against poverty and welfare dependence – to not only offer negative incentives of time limits and lower aid allowances but also positive incentives of being allowed to keep more of ones earnings after they leave the welfare rolls.

Slavery and Poverty

> Every race has a soul, and the soul of that race finds expression in its institutions, and to kill those institutions is to kill the soul. No people can profit or be helped under institutions which are not the outcome of their own character.
>
> Edward Blyden (1903)

Undoubtedly you have heard or read about the recent debate concerning the causes of earnings differences between black and white Americans. This debate is poised to create one of; if not the most, controversial socio-economic battles our nation has seen in years. The issue of course is the role that institutionalized slavery might have played in exacerbating the problem of poverty for black Americans who are alive today.

For black and white Americans alike, this is an emotionally painful and philosophically charged issue.

On one side of the debate you have Americans – black and white – who argue that the existence of slavery helped build the country but that the slaves were not compensated for their efforts as a free individual would be. To proponents of reparations for slavery, the contention is that the descendents of slaves have also suffered from the legacy of slavery.

This legacy, it is argued, includes Jim Crow laws, poll taxes, systemic labor market and educational discrimination, and segregation as well as the separation of the races in buses, hotels, restaurants, and other facilities. The

CONCEPT CHECK

In Germany, 75% of all workers have participated in vocational training or apprenticeships rather than college — yet earn 92% of what the average American college graduate makes.[76] Could following Germany's lead reduce poverty in America?

© Oleg Golovnev/Shutterstock.com

legacy of slavery, therefore, has impacted the social, economic, and political lives of black Americans long after the Emancipation Proclamation was signed. Therefore, proponents argue, current black Americans should receive monetary compensation for the government's compliance in allowing slavery to exist until 1865 and quasi-slavery to exist from 1865 until the passage of the Civil Rights Act in 1964.[77]

On the other side of the fence, you have black and white Americans who share the view of Henry Hyde (R–Illinois) who once said, "The notion of collective guilt for what people did 200-plus years ago, that this generation should pay a debt for that generation, is an idea whose time has gone. I never owned a slave. I never oppressed anybody. I don't know that I should have to pay for someone who did own slaves generations before I was born."

Walter Williams and Thomas Sowell — two prominent African-American economists — have gone so far as to argue that today's black Americans are the indirect beneficiaries of their ancestors' enslavement. This argument is based on the fact that if we compare the economic well-being of blacks in Africa to the well-being of blacks in America, there is no question that black people in America are better off. In fact, as Dr. Williams points out, if black people in America were thought of as their own nation, the total income of the 35 million blacks that live in this nation would make black Americans the 17th largest (with a net $2.8 trillion in income).[78]

If slavery had never existed, they argue, the overall population of black people would be far lower and therefore the total income of black people in America would be less than it is today. In addition, Mr. Williams asks:

Are the millions of Europeans, Asians and Latin Americans who immigrated to the U.S. in the 20th century responsible for slavery, and should they be forced to cough up reparations money? What about descendants of Northern whites who fought and died in the name of freeing slaves? [79]

As you can see this is a thorny issue for economists to evaluate. Nonetheless, if cities like Chicago — that once passed a resolution by a vote of 46–1 to look into slave reparations — are going to continue to move on this issue, economics students should be well versed in the method-

ology one might use to link the existence of slavery to the current plight of impoverished black Americans.

THE HISTORY OF THE REPARATIONS MOVEMENT

Dutch traders brought the first slaves to America in 1619. From that time until 1865, millions of other Africans followed. With the abolition of slavery in 1865, came the first call for reparations. General Sherman of the Union forces set aside land along the Georgia and South Carolina coasts for black settlement. Each family was to receive 40 acres, and Sherman later offered the loan of Army mules. Within six months, 40,000 freed slaves had settled on hundreds of thousands of acres of land. Several months later, Congress passed a bill establishing the Freedman's Bureau to oversee the transition of blacks from slavery to freedom. However, shortly after that President Andrew Johnson began allowing former Confederates to reclaim their property — a trend that continued in succeeding decades.[80] In 1866 and 1867 Representative Thaddeus Stevens introduced reparations bills that did not pass. In 1915 Cornelius Jones sued the U.S. government, arguing that it had profited from slave labor through a federal tax on cotton. Since the slaves had never been paid, Jones calculated they were owed $68 million. Jones lost his suit.

In 1963 — after decades of lynching, riots, and anti-black laws and legislation, Martin Luther King wrote, "no amount of gold could ever provide adequate compensation for the exploitation of the Negro in America down through the centuries."

King did believe, however, that a price could be placed on unpaid wages. Around that same time, a Detroit activist named Ray Jenkins took up the fight for reparations. In 1963 he formed the Slave Labor Annuity organization. Jenkins' grandfather, a former slave who died in 1958, had been part of an environment where the average slave was sold for $778 ($14,428 in 2009 dollars). Jenkins' campaign did not lead to any monetary payment to the descendents of slaves.

In 1988, Congress apologized to Japanese Americans interned in camps during World War II and authorized payments of $20,000 each to roughly 60,000 survivors. By one estimate, the German government has paid $60 billion to settle claims from victims of Nazi persecution. Today, the National Coalition for Blacks for Reparations in America (N'COBRA) has over 25 chapters and is working on a reparations lawsuit.

REPARATIONS ESTIMATES

If at some point the U.S. government takes up the issue of reparations – and decides to pay reparations to African-Americans – the taxpayers will be very interested in the formula used to determine how much money should be paid.

Economist Larry Neal, adjusting for inflation, has calculated that unpaid net wages to blacks before emancipation amount to $1.4 trillion today. If we were to divide that figure by 46 million (the current population of black people in the U.S.) the per-person payout would equal $32,850. Should that be the settlement? Have current black Americans suffered to the tune of $32,850 per person?

Would Denzel Washington, Oprah Winfrey and other wealthy black Americans get a check? Would $1.4 trillion impact the government's ability to pay for social security, defense, education, and health care programs? Would black people who pay taxes get a bigger payout than those who do not? Would people with one black and one Hispanic or white parent get $16,400?

Would white Americans who can prove that their ancestors fought against slavery be exempt from paying taxes to the reparations fund? What about white people whose ancestors were not living in America during the time of slavery? Would they have to pay? Should American Indians get reparations next?

Would all programs that have helped black Americans procure greater employment opportunities (affirmative action and college set-aside programs) be eliminated in response to the payout? Would black people notice higher prices being charged of them now that every black person would be financially better off?

Would the incentives of black children to do well in school be diminished with the receipt of such a huge payment? These and other questions like them are not posed lightly. They are serious questions that must be answered before any money is allocated to the reparations issue.

It is doubtful that many black people believe that they have been harmed $32,850 worth. Surely most of us would agree that the more years that pass since the end of slavery, the less likely it is that black people are victimized by slavery. Remember that Mr. Neal calculated the lost wages to slaves before emancipation. There are no black people alive today who would fit into that category.

The assignment of an economic variable that would accurately account for current damages stemming from the institution of slavery would be a monumental undertaking and perhaps an impossible one. Guessing the amount would be even more politically unsettling. Perhaps we will never know what impact slavery has had on black people today.

ENDNOTES

1 To take a look at his home page or to email Mr. Anderson about his research, go to www.centre.edu/web/academic/faculty/anderson. html or see "The Cost of Crime" for a detailed look at the various categories in this study. Log onto www.economics.about.com/money/economics/library/weekly/aa041300.htm.

2 See "Bowling Shoes Are So Hot, People Rent them to Steal a Pair" by Shirley Leung, *The Wall Street Journal,* April, 2001.

3 See Gary Becker (1968). "Crime and Punishment: An Economic Approach". *The Journal of Political Economy* 76: pp. 169-217.

4 See *The Economics of Life* by Gary and Guity Nashat Becker, McGraw-Hill, 1997, pp. 135–144.

5 In the week following the September 11th attacks, crime in New York City fell by 34%. This was partially attributed to an increased police presence in the city and thus, a higher probability of capture. See "Crime Rate in New York Fell Sharply After Attack," *The Wall Street Journal,* September 19, 2001.

6 See "The Economics of Crime" by Ed Rubenstein, Imprimis, Hillsdale College, Hillsdale, Michigan, 1995.

7 See "Increase in Murders Sharpest in Decades" by Devlin Barrett, *The Wall Street Journal,* September 27, 2016.

8 See "The Nationwide Crime Wave is Building" by Heather MacDonald, *The Wall Street Journal,* May 24, 2016 and "The New Nationwide Crime Wave" by Heather MacDonald, *The Wall Street Journal,* May 30-31, 2015.

9 See "Is America Facing a Police Crisis?" by Edward P. Stringham, *The Wall Street Journal,* July 30-31, 2016.

10 See "Poking Holes in the Theory of 'Broken Windows'" by D.W. Miller, *The Chronicle of Higher Education,* February 9, 2001, pp. A14–A16; "On Crime As Science (A Neighbor at a Time)" by Dan Hurley, *The New York Times,* January 6, 2004, p. D1; and "The Hallmark of the Underclass" by Charles Murray, *The Wall Street Journal,* September 29, 2005.

11 See "Economists Demonstrate That Neighbors, Not Wardens, Hold Keys to Cutting Crime" by Amanda Bennett, *The Wall Street Journal,* 1994.

12 See "A Crime Theory Demolished" by Heather Mac Donald, *The Wall Street Journal*, January 5, 2010.

13 See "Best Crime Stopper: A Father at Home" by William S. Comanor and Llad Philips, *The Wall Street Journal*, May 10, 1998, and www.ncpa.org/pi/crime/aug98g.html.

14 See "Identity, love and security from parents" by Parris Baker, *The Orlando Sentinel*, August 3, 2007, pg. A19.

15 See "Both Sides in Gun War Are Armed With Numbers, But Who is Right?" by Ray Rivera, *The Salt Lake Tribune*, August 22, 1999; and "Watchful dad slays gunman" by Rich McKay, *The Orlando Sentinel*, March 20, 2002.

16 See "Gun foes to warn tourists on law" by Linda Kleindienst, *The Orlando Sentinel*, September 26, 2005.

17 See "Weapons-on-campus push gains steam" by Zinie Chen Sampson, *The Orlando Sentinel*, August 13, 2007.

18 See "Justices Broaden Gun Rights" by Jess Bravin, *The Wall Street Journal*, June 29, 2010.

19 See "In the New Economics, The Economy Has Little to Do With It" by Jon. R. Hilsenrath, *The Wall Street Journal*, April 27, 2001; *Freakonomics* by Steven D. Levitt and Stephen J. Dunbar, Harper Collins, 2005; and "The Impact of Legalized Abortion on Crime" by John Donohue and Steven Levitt, *Quarterly Journal of Economics*, 2000.

20 See http://www.census.gov/hhes/www/poverty/threshld/thresh07.html for the government's data on poverty and other poverty measures.

21 See "Why Decry the Wealth Gap?" by W. Michael Cox and Richard Alm, *The New York Times*, January 24, 2000.

22 See "Movin' On Up" *The Wall Street Journal*, November 13, 2007.

23 See "Economic Scene" by Virginia Postrel, *The New York Times*, August 10, 2000; and "Impossible American Dream?" by Robert Samuelson, *The Orlando Sentinel*, November 29, 2007.

24 See "Haiti has it all—poverty, crime and political fraud" by Tasha C. Joseph, *The Orlando Sentinel*, April 15, 2001; and "Concern grows that kids are on slave ship", *The Orlando Sentinel* (from the *Associated Press*), April 15, 2001, page A3.

25 See "Who Wins in the New Economy?" *The Wall Street Journal*, June 27, 2000, page B1; and "White men with degrees earn the most" by Genaro C. Armas, *The Orlando Sentinel*, March 28, 2005.

26 See *Basic Economics: A Citizen's Guide to the Economy* by Thomas Sowell, Basic Books, 2001.

27 See "Clandestine population perplexed economists" *The Orlando Sentinel* (from the Los Angeles Times) March 11, 2001.

28 See "The Poverty Cure: Get Married" by William A. Galston, *The Wall Street Journal*, October 28, 2015.

29 See "Black, Successful—and Typical" by Jason L. Riley, *The Wall Street Journal*, May 13, 2002.

30 Source: United States Census Bureau and the National Poverty Center.

31 See "Hillary Clinton's School Choice" *The Wall Street Journal*, August 12, 2016.

32 See Dept. of Labor: Public School Teachers Are Highest Paid State Workers; Compensation Doubles the Average in Private Industry - See more at: http://cnsnews.com/news/article/dept-labor-public-school-teachers-are-highest-paid-state-workers-compensation-doubles#sthash.iYEuzW8F.dpuf.

33 For an interesting look at this reality, see http://www.youtube.com/watch?v=2bpb9DymmoU.

34 See http://www.capenet.org/pdf/Outlook399.pdf and http://www.nheri.org/research/research-facts-on-homeschooling.html

35 See http://www.cbsnews.com/news/us-education-spending-tops-global-list-study-shows/

36 See http://rossieronline.usc.edu/u-s-education-versus-the-world-infographic/.

37 For complete survey results see http://www.nationalgeographic.com/geosurvey/download/RoperSurvey.pdf.

38 See "Obama: Schools must buckle down" by Peter Nicholas, *The Orlando Sentinel*, September 28, 2010.

39 See "What, me worry?" by Thomas Friedman, *The New York Times* (published in *The Orlando Sentinel*), April 30, 2005.

40 See "Parents take another hit in the culture wars" by Kathleen Parker, *The Orlando Sentinel*, November 6, 2005.

41 See "Teacher Sexual Misconduct Runs Rampant in U.S. Public Schools" by Karla Dial, *School Reform News*, December 2007; and

"Class of '08 Fails to Lift SAT Scores" by John Hechinger, *The Wall Street Journal*, August 27, 2008, pg. D1.

42 See "Teacher Can't Teach" by Chester E. Finn Jr., *The Wall Street Journal*, March 11, 2005; and *The Conspiracy of Ignorance: The Failure of American Public Schools* by Martin Gross, Harper Collins, 1999.

43 See "Teacher Training is Panned" by Stephanie Banchero, *The Wall Street Journal*, November 16, 2010.

44 In Finland, teachers are required to have a master's degree and six years of preparation in a specific subject area before they are allowed to teach. It should also be noted that Finland's students rank first in the world in math, reading and science. See "Should U.S. try imitating Finland?" by Robert G. Kaiser, *The Washington Post*, October 2, 2005 (date published in *The Orlando Sentinel*); and "Finland tops global school table," *BBC News*, September 10, 2008.

45 See "The Education Manifesto" by Michelle Rhee and Adrian Fenty, *The Wall Street Journal*, October 30-31, 2010.

46 See "The Greatest Mistake in American History: Letting Government Educate Our Children" by Harry Browne, (speech before The Foundation for Economic Education, December 2004).

47 See "The Culture Gap" by Brink Lindsey, *The Wall Street Journal*, July 9, 2007.

48 See "Protect Our Kids from Preschool" by Shikha Dalmia and Lisa Snell, *The Wall Street Journal*, August 22, 2008, pg. A15.

49 See "If Schools Were Like 'American Idol'," by Rupert Murdoch, *The Wall Street Journal*, October 8, 2010.

50 See "Home-Schooled Kids Defy Stereotypes, Ace SAT Test" by Daniel Golden, *The Wall Street Journal*, February 11, 2000.

51 For the data on home schooling, see www.uhea.org/stats.html. For data on private school productivity, see "New Publication Documents Benefits of Private Education" by Joe McTighe, *School Reform News* (The Heartland Institute) February 2005; and *Let's Put Parents Back in Charge* by Joseph Bast and Herbert Walberg, The Heartland Institute, 2005.

52 For a detailed examination of this fact, you should watch the DVD entitled, "Stupid in America," which aired on January 13, 2006 (ABC; John Stossel as host). Log on to www.jackchambless.com, click on SPEECHES and scroll down to Stupid in America to watch this program.

53 See "Students in Failing Public Schools Need Federal Education Reform" by Dan Proft, *School Reform News*, September 2008, pg. 17.

54 See "Innovative Catholic schools target low-income students" by Jay Mathews, *The Orlando Sentinel*, April 6, 2003, from the *Washington Post*.

55 See "Blacks Support for School Choice Increases in New Orleans, Nationwide" by Jim Waters, *School Reform News*, September 2008, pg. 13.

56 See "State Flunks 68 Schools" by Lori Horvitz, *The Orlando Sentinel*, June 13, 2002; "Poorest Schools get the most F's" by Leslie Postal and Lori Horvitz, *The Orlando Sentinel*, June 23, 2002; and "DC Vouchers Approved" by Robert Holland, *School Reform News* (The Heartland Institute), March 2004.

57 See "For some black students, school is best at home," *The Orlando Sentinel*, January 16, 2011.

58 See "War Against Vouchers" by Andrew J. Coulson, *The Wall Street Journal*, January 9, 2006.

59 See "Florida's Unheralded School Revolution" by Adam R. Schaeffer, *The Wall Street Journal*, April 30, 2010.

60 For extensive analysis of what is taking place within this movement, see "School Choice Legislation is all the Rage in 2005" by Lisa Snell, *School Reform News* (The Heartland Institute) May 2005; "Federal Court Upholds Arizona Tax Credits" by George A. Clowes, *School Reform News* (The Heartland Institute) May 2005; "2,000 March for School Choice in Florida" by Jenny Rothenberg, *School Reform News*, July 2005; "Ohio Creates Nation's Largest Voucher Program" by Kate McGreevy, *School Reform News*, September 2005; "Georgia Parents Sue for Vouchers" by George A. Clowes, *School Reform News*, March 2005.

61 See "Milwaukee's model: City Schools that work" by John Tierney, *The New York Times*, March 8, 2006 (date published in *The Orlando Sentinel*).

62 IBID.

63 See "Would a School thrive if teachers made $125,000?" by Elissa Gootman, *The New York Times*, March 9, 2008

64 See "Charter Schools and Student Performance" by Paul E. Peterson, *The Wall Street Journal*, March 16, 2010

65 See "The Education Manifesto" by Michelle Rhee and Adrian Fenty, *The Wall Street Journal*, October 30-31, 2010

66 See "School Choice and the Standpoint of African-American Mothers: Considering the Power of Positionality," by Camille Wilson Cooper, *Journal of Negro Education*, Spring 2005; and see "Opportunity Scholarships: Chance for a better life" by Ed Rodriquez and Julio Fuentes, *The Orlando Sentinel*, September 15, 2005. For a detailed analysis of the impact of school choice on educational quality, see *School Choice – the findings* by Herbert J. Walberg, The Cato Institute, 2007.

67 http://www.ontheissues.org/2016/Donald_Trump_Education.htm

68 See http://www.nheri.org/research/research-facts-on-homeschooling.html

69 Source: Florida Center of Political History and Governance, Tallahassee, Florida.

70 See "In war on poverty, early gains and a long stalemate" by Peter Grier and Patrik Jonsson, *The Christian Science Monitor*, January 9, 2004.

71 See "How the War on Poverty was Lost" by Robert Rector, *The Wall Street Journal,* January 8, 2014 page A15.

72 Source: The Annie E. Casey Foundation.

73 See www.upjohninst.org/publications/titles/ecwr.html.

74 See "The Return of Welfare as We Used to Know It" by Rick Santorum, *The Wall Street Journal,* August 28, 2012 page A13.

75 See *Welfare Reform After Ten Years* by Gary MacDougal, Kate Campaigne and Dane Wendall, The Heartland Institute, July 2008.

76 See "Germany Offers a Promising Jobs Model" by Edward P. Lazear & Simon Janssen, *The Wall Street Journal,* September 9, 2016 page A11.

77 See "Low-Tax States Cut Poverty Rates" by Jessa Haugebak, *Budget & Tax News* March 2007, pg. 3.

78 See https://abagond.wordpress.com/2010/11/22/if-black-america-were-a-country/

79 For more from Dr. Williams see http://www.youtube.com/watch?v=OUL152yGVGI

80 www.jewishworldreview.com/cols/williams.html

CHAPTER REVIEW

1. What are some of the major economic causes of crime?

2. List and explain four factors that contribute to poverty.

3. What role does school choice play in explaining earnings differences?

4. What could help explain the rate of poverty found on American Indian reservations?

The MARKET EQUILIBRIUM PROCESS

*T*each a parrot the terms, supply and demand,
and you've got an economist.

THOMAS CARLYLE

THE CONFUSION ABOUT MARKETS

Former British Prime Minister Winston Churchill once asked Lady Astor if she would have sex with him for 1 million pounds. When she said, "Yes," he asked her if she would have sex with him for 100 pounds. She said, "What do you think I am – a prostitute?" He replied, "We've already established that. Now we're just haggling over the price." Mr. Churchill understood markets.

On any given day, we all, directly or indirectly, participate in some market transaction. If you have a job, you are the supplier of a labor resource to an employer, who is the demander of that resource, for a price known as the wage rate. Outside of your job, you might be the demander in any number of markets from hockey skates to sushi.

We all have some fundamental understanding of the forces of supply and demand that shape our lives. However, there is also a great deal of misunderstanding about markets. Sometimes this misunderstanding leads to emotional reactions (think gasoline) to changes in economic policies. Sometimes misunderstanding the market leads to people dying unnecessarily. This chapter will clear up the confusion that surrounds the concepts of supply and demand.

WHAT IS A MARKET?

When studying something new – especially when preconceived ideas are abundant – it is always a good idea to start with the most basic questions. To some of you, the question, "What is a market?" might seem silly, but unless we start here, many of you are going to end up lost.

> ➤ **A market is an arrangement through which buyers and sellers meet or communicate for the purpose of exchanging goods and services at mutually agreed-upon prices.**

Let's think about the significance of this definition for a moment, starting with the phrase "buyers and sellers." A buyer is a person who is willing and able to purchase a good at a particular price at some moment in time. Some of you might be willing to buy a Land Rover, but you might not be able. Others of you might be able to buy a CD featuring MC Hammer's greatest hits, but you might not be willing. A market cannot exist unless there are people who can satisfy both criteria of being a buyer.

A seller is someone who is willing and able to sell some good, or service, at a particular price, at some moment in time. The "willing and able" standard prevails here, too. You can be quite certain that there are individuals out there who would be willing to sell pills that will turn water into gasoline. However, if the technology needed to deliver such a product does not exist, then no one will be able to sell us this cheaper source of fuel. There are individuals in our economy who are able to sell hypodermic needles that have been previously used by drug addicts. However, they are probably not willing to go through the trouble of opening up a used needle stand in your city.

Another point of clarification that is needed is why we say buyers *and* sellers. Can't we have a market with just one of the two? Well, no. We cannot. If there are people willing and able to purchase an apartment on the moon, but no one is currently supplying such services, then we do not yet have a market. There are probably many people from Aleppo, Syria who would be willing and able to rent out their homes to people who might want to live there. It does not matter what they are willing and able to supply. It takes willingness to supply – and someone's willingness to *buy* to have a market.

Next we have the words *meet* and *communicate*. In most markets, buyers and sellers meet somewhere to conduct business. Restaurants, gas stations, toll roads, and so forth are examples of markets where buyers and sellers conduct business at some physical location. For centuries, all markets were based on meetings between people willing and able to buy and sell. This is no longer the case.

HOW THE INTERNET HAS ALTERED THE MARKET

> The real price of everything is the toil and trouble of acquiring it.
>
> Adam Smith

What Mr. Smith means is that with every purchase there is a transaction cost.

> ➤ **Transaction costs are the direct and opportunity costs of engaging in market transactions.**

For many everyday items, your transaction costs would entail getting dressed, getting in your car, driving to the local bookstore, grocery store, or car dealer(s) and spending varying amounts of time finding the romance novel, cantaloupe, or car that you wanted. If you found the item, you then would have to decide if the price was right. If you concluded that it was, you would proceed to the register – or office of the salesperson – and arrange to pay for the item in question.

This song and dance might seem like a scene from a million years ago, now that the Internet has fundamentally and permanently changed the way many markets work. Now if you want a book, you can go to any number of websites, and quickly order your selection and pay for it, all without ever getting out of your pajamas or starting your car in the middle of a rainstorm. There are sites in some cities that allow you to access a menu of your local grocer, order your items, and have them delivered to your home. Cell phones now have apps that allow consumers to comparison shop while using global positioning systems to identify exactly where to buy the less expensive products that were found by the phone.[1] This reduction in transaction costs has put tremendous pressure on retailers to keep prices competitive.[2]

Car buying has also seen a power shift from the sellers to the buyers in many ways.

It used to be that you never really knew how much the dealer had paid for the vehicle you wanted. You never knew how much profit they were going to make, and you certainly did not know if there was a better deal in another city.

Now you can go online and find out exactly what the invoice cost is for many dealers. You can find out where the same vehicle might be in any number of cities and what each dealer is asking. This means you can arm yourself with information that dramatically lowers the transaction costs of buying a car.

Whom do you have to thank for this dramatic change in our shopping lives? The list is endless, but it is made up of people with unquestionably large IQs, and bank accounts, who several years ago developed an information superhighway that is now serving millions of people very well.

What this all means is that the phrase "or communicate" in the definition of a market has become increasingly more important. This has lowered the search costs associated with our purchases and freed us up to pursue more pleasurable pursuits.

This trend towards online buying has not escaped the attention of our government. First, there is the fact that many online sales (see eBay) go without applying state sales taxes. This is upsetting to the more than 9,000 different sales tax districts – and the politicians who oversee them – that exist in the United States. This is why there has been a growing push to implement sales taxes on all internet transactions.[3]

Second, there is the "problem" associated with the growing number of companies that offer services that do not seem to comply with the myriad of state and federal government regulations.

© Bart Everett/Shutterstock.com

CONCEPT CHECK

Some economists have suggested that toll road fees should rise during peak-use hours to reduce traffic congestion.[4] Others have argued that the Internet will help reduce traffic jams over time without raising toll road prices. What logic is the latter argument based on?

A classic example is a company called Airbnb — a web service that helps travelers book couches, beds, rooms, houses, boats and even castles - all over the world. Founded by two unemployed industrial designers, the $2.5 billion company with over 700 employees often allows people to book properties for periods of time that don't fit within some city or state guidelines. New York City, for example, does not allow people to rent an apartment for less than a month. Airbnb was investigated for not complying with state regulations and for not paying occupancy taxes.[5]

The Internet will also lead to significant changes in labor markets. Millions of Americans have a home office, and more jobs are moving into the realm of "distance production." This means that over time, as technology continues to improve, we can expect to see less need for workers to commute to an office. Imagine the impact on traffic congestion, the market for day care, the environment, and our geographic mobility as we become better equipped to do our jobs from the home. This trend is particularly helpful during a time when the U.S. economy is struggling to emerge from recession. During the 2007-2009 Recession, many Americans were unable to sell their homes and move to a place offering better jobs. As online employment becomes more common, it will not be as necessary to wait for a house to sell before you can take a new job.

WHY MARKETS EXIST

I am quite sure you have never thought about this question. It is pretty easy to take for granted that every day someone is putting milk on the shelf for consumers to buy. But it is important to understand that throughout much of world history we have not witnessed the "I, Pencil" miracles shaped by modern markets. For the bulk of human history we bipeds have been hunter-gatherers; have engaged in small scale agriculture or barter (trading goods) on a limited scale. The concept of suppliers and demanders exchanging goods and services for prices is relatively new.

Therefore, we should be familiar with why we moved out of the past and into our modern system based on prices. Three dominant reasons prevail — the principle of comparative advantage; self-interest and scarcity.

The principle of comparative advantage (repeated later in the international trade chapter) teaches us that people can gain goods and services by specializing in the production of goods and services that they can produce at a lower opportunity cost than their trading partners can. We have already examined the issue of scarcity and Adam Smith's lessons on self-interest so let's put these together to understand a pretty unusual, but lucrative market.

WHAT COLLEGE-AGE WOMEN KNOW ABOUT MARKETS

O.K., ladies. Pay close attention, because you might be able to make a lot of money, legally, without having to find a job at this point in time.

That is because compared to men — and compared to women who are infertile — many of you have something valuable inside your body that the free market is demanding. If you guessed your eggs, you are right on the money.

Over the past several years an explosion has taken place in the number of people who are willing and able to pay healthy, intelligent, young women for their eggs. Many cash-strapped college girls with high SAT scores and good looks are making up to $35,000 for their eggs.[6] That is enough money to pay for a lot of books and tuition.

Since many couples around the U.S. struggle to have children — and since our quasi-capitalistic economy places a high economic value on looks and intelligence — there has been a natural gravitation to college campuses to find women who can help people create "desirable" children.

The comparative advantage here is pretty easy to detect. *Compared* to women who are infertile, or to women who are older, or less attractive, or who flunked out of middle school, the women with the preferred traits have an economic *advantage*. It only stands to reason that if a woman has a property right over her body, then she might decide to part with part of her private property for the right price.

This is a beautiful part of the market process. We can rest comfortably knowing that even if we are hopeless in thousands of areas of production, if we specialize in one — and if the market wants what we have to offer it — we can earn enough money to give it away to those people who have specialized in the things we are not as good at.

The second major reason for the existence of markets is *self-interest*. Once we decide what our comparative advantage is, and where we are going to offer our services, we do so in order to provide for our needs and the needs of our families, first and foremost. Without the guiding hand of self-love, markets would not work very effectively.

Finally, there is the issue of *scarcity*. We all have imbalances that we want closed. Our local grocer, eBay, and millions of other business firms help consumers with their imbalances while we help businesspeople with their desire to earn more money.

SHOULD MARKETS BE FAIR?

Often I travel with my family – and a few other families – to Tennessee to enjoy a week of camping.

One year while I was cooking breakfast for everyone, a lady from one of the families (whom I like) began fussing about a little business venture I had started with my sons. The venture involves finding things that people have for sale – that are way undervalued based on market conditions – and reselling those items on eBay.

According to her, I was simply taking advantage of people by not paying them a fair price to begin with and then I was taking advantage of other people by selling the item for far more than I paid, rather than for a "fair" price.

This argument did not sit well with me, or my sons, whom I am trying to help understand how markets work. In fact, I was tempted to jokingly (sort of) tell her that the pancakes and bacon she was about to eat were paid for by the cook (me) and that she was being unfair not to offer me a "fair" price for her breakfast.

Of course, my lovely wife would have had a heart attack if I said this; so I simply smiled, nodded and wished our friend would realize how futile it is to clearly define what the word *fair* means.

Yet, it is true that human beings have an innate sense of "fair play" that tends to separate us from the rest of the animal world. Over the past few years, behavioral economists have found in experiments that humans repeatedly show a tendency to share, and they expect others to reciprocate.[7]

Reciprocity can have its benefits, too. Organizations like the Rainforest Alliance, Fair Trade USA, and UTZ Certified have experienced tremendous growth in recent years, certifying that cocoa and coffee is grown by sellers who support sustainable farming and "equitable" prices for poorer farmers worldwide.[8] The result of this trend has allowed certified sellers to earn about $150 a ton more for cocoa than non-certified supplies.

A recent study found that 72% of consumers said they would be more likely to patronize a company with fair prices and a good cause, than a company offering deep discounts but little in the way of charitable or environmental initiative.[9]

Behavioral economists suggest that there is a "civilizing effect" of the marketplace that leads perfect strangers to develop more giving tendencies.[10]

After all, how many times during the day do you deal with complete strangers in the market? Do you know who makes and transports the gasoline you buy? Are you on a first-name basis with your favorite chef or author? When is the last time you had dinner with your grocer or the local movie theater manager?

Dealing daily with strangers in the free market creates a critical level of trust between you and the seller of goods and services. If you drink Budweiser, you have an implicit contract with Anheuser-Busch that the "born on" date that is provided is not a lie and that the beer does not contain laundry soap. Anheuser-Busch trusts you to pay the full price for a six-pack, rather than to steal it off the beer truck. Over time, trust leads all of us to develop a sense of fairness that tells Anheuser-Busch, "If you make me feel good and treat me fairly, I'll make you feel good and treat you fairly." We still may not care about the person who manned the bottling station the day our Bud was born, but we still help him or her get paid by not stealing from their company.

All of this leads us back to the original issue of whether or not markets are fair. On one hand we have seen that there seems to be a level of fairness that maintains some quality controls and product reliability. There also seems to be a sense of fair play when it comes to prices.

Oftentimes when hurricanes hit, grocery stores that could easily raise prices do not. Is that because the law prohibits price-gouging, or is it because the grocer does not want to take advantage of people during an emergency?

After September 11th, there was an increased need for vaccines, and that led to severe shortages. The free market would suggest that higher prices were necessary, yet drug companies did not follow the free market and left prices unchanged, all while shipping vaccines to the areas immediately impacted by the terrorist attacks.

On the other hand, we also see examples of things that seem to be unfair. Is it fair that the free market pays Tom Cruise $25 million per movie? Is it fair that teachers and firemen earn less money than bench-warming baseball players? Is it fair that hotel room prices rise in

Do you care where this comes from?

Daytona Beach, Florida, during spring break? How about business travelers? Is it fair that they pay hundreds of dollars more per airplane ticket than vacationers? Is it fair that some people can afford a mansion, while others live in a box? This is not a new debate. As far back as 1805 people were complaining about prices. During that winter, while Lewis & Clark were living in Oregon's Fort Clatsop, they regularly traded with American Indians that lived near by. William Clark once complained in his journal that the Indians, "….never close a bargain except when they think they have the advantage" and that they charged, "immodest prices."[11] Was Clark right?

It depends on whom you ask. Surely, we can all see that fairness is in the eye of the beholder. What is fair to one person – $30 for a steak, for example – might be unfair to the bologna-eater. A fair wage to a Taco Bell cook might be $117 per hour – if you ask him – yet to the customer of Taco Bell, who would have to pay $39 for a chalupa, the $117 wage might seem excessive.

Some economists have tried to find the answer to this "fairness" issue, but the answer eludes us. The subjectivity of the word makes coming up with a definitive answer impossible.

WHO CONTROLS THE MARKET?

Many people are under the misconception that the market is controlled by consumers through our wants and needs. Others are willing to argue that it is the sellers of goods and services that control our lives. Both of these perceptions are far from reality.

For those of you who are convinced that it is consumer sovereignty that dictates market outcomes, I have a couple of little tests I would like you to perform. First, go down to a local car dealership that is featuring their line of new automobiles.

Tell the salesperson that, as a consumer, you are in control of the car market and that you insist that he sell you a new car for under $2,400. At that time you will be politely escorted out of the dealership and pointed in the direction of the nearest used car lot. When you get to the used car lot, and find a car for under $2,400, tell the salesperson that you insist that your used car be equipped with a device that helps you know if someone is texting while driving within 4 miles of your car anytime you are on the road. At this time the dealer will laugh you off the lot and tell you to stop watching so many science fiction shows.

The preceding exercise was designed to help you understand that, as a consumer, you are part of the market process, but not the process itself. Your demands are counterbalanced by the willingness and ability of multitudinous sellers to provide you with goods and services at prices from which they can earn profit. New cars for $2,400 may be purchased in your dreams, but not in reality. By the same token, asking for or demanding features that are not technologically feasible or cost-effective at this time will also leave you with no service from your fellow man.

On the other hand, if you believe that evil and greedy businesses are all conspiring to charge whatever price they want and produce whatever product they deem sufficient, you probably also believe in Santa Claus and the Easter Bunny. A wonderful example of the hysteria that markets can create can be found in the gasoline market of 2008.

You may recall that in July of 2008, gasoline prices topped $4 per gallon. This price caused some people to conclude that we are at the mercy of the oil companies and the Organization of Petroleum Exporting Countries (OPEC). After all, isn't gasoline an extreme necessity? Won't we have to pay any price that is charged by the big oil companies?

The answer is a resounding no! If it were true that the oil companies control our lives, why did the price of oil fall from $147 per barrel (when gas prices topped $4) to under $32 per barrel by February 2009, where gas prices fell to under $2 per gallon in much of the country?

Photo courtesy Jack Chambless

SUGGESTED CLASSROOM DEBATE

This photo was taken near Ely, Minnesota. The guy who sells the wood is never standing near his woodpile. Instead, he has a box (locked) near his wood, his price per bundle on the box, and people can simply pull over, pick up this wood, and put money in the box. Does this system elicit more or less honesty from people who buy firewood? Why?

Did the executives at BP, Chevron, and ExxonMobil decide to take it easy on us? Were they all economically illiterate during the spring of 2009?

Gas prices – just like any other good or service – change not because sellers decide they should, but because sellers and buyers interact to create a price that is mutually agreed upon. Our increasing consumption of oil – along with more consumption in India and China – lead to the dramatic increase in prices. When the world economy began to slow down in the latter part of 2008 through 2009, there were fewer buyers of oil and thus prices began to fall sharply. This will be clarified in much greater detail in the next chapter.

Suppose that, as you read this chapter, gas prices are $4.79 per gallon. Buying into the idea that the gas suppliers can operate with impunity begs the question of how much more we would pay for gas before their power was undermined.

Would you pay $5.79 per gallon? $8.79? $11.79? If you think about this situation from a sane and dispassionate point of view, you will quickly realize that there is a limit to how much of these price hikes we will stand by and take. At some point you would see a huge increase in the demand for small cars – just as we did in 2008. You would also see more people moving closer to work, commuting with their friends, taking the bus, or riding bicycles. The point is that the sellers may have a great deal of power over price, but they cannot charge whatever price they want. Consumers inevitably have a say in the matter.[12]

WHICH COMES FIRST, SUPPLY OR DEMAND?

Most students answer by saying, "Both" or "Demand." As it turns out, supply has to appear first. Did consumers line up outside the post offices of America protesting the slow pace of mail delivery – demanding, in essence, that someone ship boxes overnight? Did unhappy moms demand disposable diapers? Did children demonstrate in the streets for novels about wizards? No, no, and no.

Capitalism is the epic search for fixable problems. If you want to become rich, listen to what people are complaining about and fix it – or invent something that people never knew they wanted. Our markets are dependent on entrepreneurs who notice that something is missing or wrong in our economic system, then take the risks of fixing it. This means we have to wait for the supplier to appear first. Fred Smith, the founder of FedEx, got his idea for this company while in college. He turned in a paper proposing an overnight mail delivery business and received a poor grade and criticism by his professor. Oops. Then he turned his vision, into a service. There was *no market* for overnight mail delivery services. He had to turn his comparative advantage and his self-interest into a service, and then supply that service to whoever might be willing and able to purchase it. Only then did we find out whether, or not, there was a market. This is known as *Say's Law.*

> ➤ Say's Law – named after the French economist Jean Baptiste Say – states that supply creates demand.

According to Mr. Say, who was a follower of Adam Smith, the production of goods and services leads to income earned for the producer and the employees of the producer. This *income leads to a demand* for even more production and the production of new goods and services. Going back to chapter two for a moment, this means that for a free market to work, government must first encourage suppliers to "show up" by not taxing and regulating the market too heavily. If government tells suppliers that they can enter the market, make money and keep the bulk of their earnings, the suppliers of everything from dresses to dog food will appear, create jobs and those jobs will create the income that fuels demand in the long run.

We could argue that Fred Smith "knew" that there must be a demand for his product offering and therefore he was simply responding to the guaranteed demand. We can argue this, but we would be incorrect to do so. No supplier ever knows with 100% certainty that demand will be there, or that if demand is there, that demand will be large enough to create a profit.

Which brings us to Harry Potter, or more appropriately, J.K. Rowling – the creator of Harry Potter.

In 2010, Universal Studios Orlando opened the nearly $400 million Wizarding World of Harry Potter attraction.

CONCEPT CHECK

In 2016 1980 Olympic gold medalist, Jim Craig, decided to auction off his gold medal, jersey and all of his hockey gear from that year – for more than $1 million.[13] Is this a fair price? Was he in control of the final value for his gold medal? Would Adam Smith approve of this act? Why, or why not?

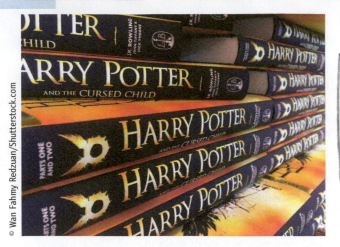

© Wan Fahmy Redzuan/Shutterstock.com

This attraction was the culmination of an incredible story born out of poverty and imagination – and is proof of Say's Law.

Consider this: when Ms. Rowling began writing her first Harry Potter book, she was living in poverty in England. In 2009, she ranked 709th on the list of the richest people in the world, with a net worth of $1 billion.

No one saw Harry Potter coming except for her. Until she put pen to paper, there were none of the thousands of jobs she helped create. Once she did, think about what happened next. All of the jobs she created or supported in the book publishing and marketing industry. The jobs she created in the movie industry. Then there are the hundreds of people who became employed in the construction of the Universal Studios attraction and the people who now work at the attraction or in hotels that are filling up because of this attraction.[14] Universal Orlando reported that 1 million more people visited this park in 2010 compared to 2009 and that over 1 million mugs of "butterbeer" were sold.[15]

In 2014 Universal Studios – in response to overwhelming attendance and profit – introduced a multi-million dollar expansion called 'Diagon Alley' – which features new rides, shops and a train linking the two parks in Orlando.[16] This addition also created hundreds of new jobs and income for residents of Central Florida.

Out of the mind of this entrepreneurial author came one of the greatest examples of the importance of the supplier – and why the most prosperous nations are the ones that attract more people like her.

THE DETERMINANTS OF SUPPLY

Now that we know that we have to wait for suppliers to appear first, let's look at what issues the supplier has to resolve before he or she can offer us goods and services. What follows is a list of the determinants of supply – the factors that influence the existence of suppliers and the amount of production once suppliers appear.

- Price
- Input costs
- Technology
- The number of sellers serving the market
- The price of other goods that can be produced with inputs that are used or owned by the seller
- Expectations concerning future prices

Price is the most important determinant of supply. The next time you are in a job interview, ask yourself what is the most important aspect of the job you have applied for. Is it the health care plan? The size of your office? The work hours? The morals of the company? All of these things might be important to you, in varying degrees, but chances are money is the main thing you are concerned about. After all, how many people do you know who would be willing to take a big office, a flexible schedule, and a position with a firm that donates money to the "Save the Weasels" campaign, all for the wage of $1.27 per hour? Not many would.

In the labor market, just as in the markets for hybrid cars, shaving cream, and day-old donuts, price is the most important factor in determining whether a person or business will supply a good or service.

Input costs are costs associated with the price of land, labor, capital, and entrepreneurship. Do not discount the importance of this determinant to millions of individual participants in our economy. In an era where global competition and the Internet have dramatically increased the competitive pressure faced by business firms, there has never been greater pressure to control the costs of production. Approximately *70%* of the cost of production in America is associated with labor! This includes wages, salaries, health care costs, pensions and other benefits, lawsuits, workman's compensation claims, and so forth.

Other costs can include rent, materials, debt obligations, and of course government-mandated licenses, taxes, insurance, litigation costs, and regulations. These last two items have become increasingly major factors in determining the ability of firms to stay in business.

In fact, when we look at some of the major forces that can disrupt the supply of goods and services in any country, at or near the top of the list are government regulations.[17] Regulations over wages, work hours and working conditions, and other well-meaning regulations can stifle the production process by raising costs to the point where suppliers question the rationality of being in business.

Technology is the knowledge of how to produce a good or service. Recently, Psychemedics Corporation did parents all over America a huge favor when the company introduced home drug test kits that allow parents to get

IMPORTANTE

a sample of their kids' hair to test whether their little one has been hitting the bong lately. Part of what makes Say's Law so powerful is this technology determinant. Without new technology, this product – and others like it – does not get supplied to begin with.

Another factor that determines the overall supply of a good or service is the **number of sellers** serving the market or, put another way, the level of competition. The market for beef cattle has over 1 million producers and is extremely competitive, to the point that no individual rancher has even a modicum of control over prices. The market for professional hockey games in Edmonton is not competitive. The Edmonton Oilers is a virtual monopolist in this market, thus the supply of games is much smaller than if the Oilers had four other teams selling hockey games in the area.

In 2016 an interesting thing happened in the market for beer. As the overall consumption of mainstream, "corporate" beers continued to fall, growers of hops (an ingredient in beer) found that more and more craft beer breweries were willing to pay very high prices for specialty hops.[18] Many hops farms - seeing rising prices for "aroma hops" and falling prices for alpha hops began to switch to the aroma hop production. They had the land to produce both varieties. This illustrate show the **price of other goods used or owned by the seller** is often a determinant of supply.

More recently, central Kentucky farmers have begun turning their tobacco farms into goat farms, as a result of the growing demand for goat meat and the declining demand for cigarettes. In each case, the supplier will allocate resources based on what market conditions call for.

The last determinant of supply is **expectations concerning future prices**. Often, as hurricanes approach the East Coast of the United States, generator and lumber dealers withhold the supply of their products. Do they do this to avoid shortages? Not exactly. They reduce the available supply in order to get a higher price *after* the storm.

They realize that if prices are going to rise due to the increase in demand for storm necessities, it would be profitable to wait until the storm is over and then offer up these items. Therefore, an expectation of higher prices in the future leads to a reduction in supply today. The opposite is true

when businesses expect prices to fall in the future. This is why you see sales on summer clothing before the summer is over. Retailers fear that if they do not make more items available at slightly discounted prices, they may have to practically give the clothes away when cooler weather arrives.

THE SUPPLY CURVE

We have seen that we can use diagrams to simplify complex economic models. Supply analysis is no different. When we illustrate the behavior of a supplier, we do so with the use of a supply curve.

> ➤ **A supply curve illustrates the relationship between the price of an item and the quantity supplied, ceteris paribus.**
> ➤ **Quantity supplied is the amount of an item sellers are willing and able to sell at a particular price.**

The difference between supply and quantity supplied is that supply measures the relationship between all possible prices and all possible quantities supplied at various prices. Quantity supplied, on the other hand, measures a specific amount that is offered up for sale at a particular price, at some particular moment in time.

Ceteris paribus is a Latin term that means "other things being equal." For our purposes, the supply curve will be drawn under the assumption that input costs, technology, the number of sellers, and the other determinants of supply do not change. While this is not a realistic assumption

© Heidi Brand/Shutterstock.com

CONCEPT CHECK

In 2011, the price of cotton rose to a 140-year high. In response, cotton farmers in China began hoarding cotton and refusing to sell their crop.[19] What supply determinant were Chinese cotton farmers reacting to? With thousands of cotton farmers worldwide, was this a good strategy? Why, or why not?

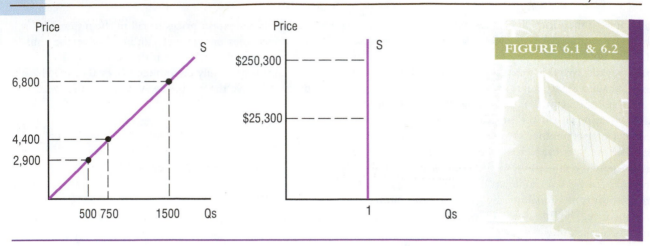

FIGURE 6.1 & 6.2

to make over a period of time, it is helpful in isolating the specific relationship between price and quantity supplied. Graphs 6.1 and 6.2 will help us understand what is on the mind of the supplier.

Have you ever wondered what it would be like if you could own a device that would record your dreams while you are asleep?

A device like this would almost certainly be a hit with consumers, but alas, Say's Law is in the way. We will have to wait for the technology to show up before the supplier shows up. Researchers in Japan have taken the first steps towards supplying us with such a device by training computers to recognize images in the mind of sleepers in the earliest stages of dreaming. Capturing REM dreams – with "complex imagery, high emotional content and bizarre jumble of logic, time and space – largely remain a mystery."[20] But for a moment, let's think about what the Acme Dream Recorder Company might do if it is ever possible to supply us with this remarkable item.

In graph 6.1 we see that, at a price of $2,900, Acme offers up 500 recorders per week. However, at a price of $4,400, the company is willing and able to sell 750 per week. Finally, if Acme can get $6,800, quantity supplied increases to 1,500 per week. Why does the company increase production as prices increase? Is this positive relationship between price and quantity supplied an anomaly, or do all suppliers act this way? Does graph 6.2 make more sense for Acme and other suppliers?

The answer is very simple. Graph 6.1 represents one of the most important of all economic laws. It is called the law of supply.

> ➤ **The law of supply states that, as prices increase, quantity supplied will increase, and as prices decrease, quantity supplied will decrease.**

Why is it a law, rather than a theory? Recall from the chapter on economic modeling that economists often find a cause-and-effect relationship between two variables. This is what has happened here. Ever since markets first appeared, people and businesses have responded to higher prices by increasing production. There are two basic reasons for this positive relationship. The first reason has to do with self-interest and the ability to earn more money at higher rates of output. The second reason has to do with the impact of rising output on total costs.

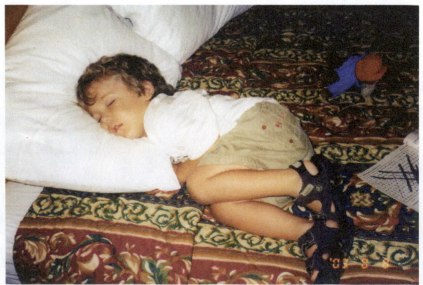

What if his dreams were on DVD?

> ➤ **The total revenue effect shows that, at higher prices, increased production is desirable because it leads to higher total revenue for the supplier.**

Think of it this way: At a price of $2,900, Acme decides to produce 500 dream recorders. Five hundred machines equals the amount the company is willing and able to provide given the costs of production, available technology, and so forth. If we simply multiply $2,900 by 500 machines, we get total revenue of $1.45 million.

At a price of $4,400, the company is willing to increase production to 750. That is because $4,400 × 750 = $3.3 million.

Finally, if the company could get $6,800 per machine, it would be willing to increase output to 1,500. $6,800 × 1,500 = $10.2 million.

At this point you might be wondering who would pay $6,800 – or even $2,900 – for one of these machines. It does not matter. When we are studying what motivates the supplier, we do not take into consideration whether there would be a demand for this machine or how much of a demand there would be. We are simply looking for what the supplier would do if it could get these prices.

A more realistic way of thinking about the supply curve is to consider what you would do if your fellow economics students offered to pay you for tutoring services. You tell them that you can offer one hour of tutoring for $10 per hour. Suppose the hour has concluded, and they start begging you to stay to help them. They pool their resources and offer you $75 to stay one more hour. What would you do? At the end of that hour, they are still in dire need of help and offer you $380 to stay one more hour. What would you do?

It should be fairly easy to see that, in the real world, few of your classmates would demand your services at $380 per hour. If they offered you $380 for that last hour, you – or someone like you – would agree to stay and prove the existence of the law of supply.

The second reason why there is a positive relationship between price and quantity supplied is because of the total cost effect.

> ➤ **The total cost effect shows that, at higher rates of production, the short-term costs of production tend to increase; therefore, higher prices are necessary to justify the increase in quantity supplied.**

When Acme increases the production of dream recorders, the company has to hire more workers and order more materials. This leads to higher production costs and the need to increase prices to help cover those costs.

The same is true for you in the tutoring example. Staying an extra hour comes at an increasing opportunity cost. Every hour you stay is an hour you cannot devote to the next-best thing you would like to do. At your job, every extra hour you work is more money you have to pay in taxes and perhaps more money spent on driving to work, cleaning your work clothes, tolls, and so forth. Therefore, your employer offers you your wage, plus a little extra, to entice you to hang around a few more hours.

Graph 6.2 represents a minor "exception" to the law of supply. This diagram illustrates a supply curve where – no matter what price is offered – production levels do not change. In 2006 a $20 bill was auctioned off for $25,300. The bill was not even old. What made it unique is the fact that it has a Del Monte sticker on it, with the serial number over the Del Monte sticker.[21] This means before the bill was finished printing, the sticker got on it, then it went on to the next step of the printing process. There is now exactly one of these bills on Earth. Therefore, if the next buyer offers $250,300 there would be no way to increase the quantity supplied from one to two.

Of course, the law of supply is not nullified by this fact. If the government could get a high enough price, it is possible to increase the quantity of dollars supplied that are precise duplicates of the original.

DEMAND

During the next few seconds, think of something you really want to have. A bigger apartment might be nice. How about tickets to the next Daytona 500? Would a year's supply of massage therapy do it? Now think of something you need. A new car? A do-it-yourself tattoo removal kit?

Earlier we looked at how the market serves our wants and needs, but as it turns out, the word "demand" is *not* the same as the words "want" or "need." The problem with wanting to see the next Daytona 500 or needing to remove an inappropriate tattoo is that we may not be able to purchase these things. Our wants and needs are largely irrelevant if we cannot afford to act on them. Therefore, in this section, we will focus on the factors that influence both our willingness and ability to demand certain goods and services.

> ➤ **Demand is the relationship between the price of an item and the quantity demanded, ceteris paribus.**
> ➤ **Quantity demanded is the amount of an item buyers are willing and able to buy, at a particular price, at a particular moment in time.**

Just like supply and quantity supplied, demand is a relationship between all prices and all possible quantities demanded, while quantity demanded is one amount of purchased goods or services at one particular price. If you spent $4.19 per gallon today on nine gallons of gasoline, the quantity demanded equaled nine at the price of $4.19.

THE DETERMINANTS OF DEMAND

Economists have uncovered over time that the following factors are of significant importance in establishing the demand for goods and services.

• Price
• Income
• Wealth
• Tastes and fashion
• The number of buyers in the market
• The price of substitutes
• The price of complements
• Expectations concerning future prices

Price is clearly the most important determinant of demand. It does not matter how much income or wealth you have, if the price is beyond your ability to pay, you have to move on.

Apartments in Boston can easily rent for over $3,000 per month. This is because of the greater level of **income** and **wealth** that exists in that city compared to other areas around the country. Income is important in all demand considerations. In fact, right after a prospective tenant in Boston learns the price of an apartment, the next step will be to figure out whether the individual brings home enough money to make the payments. Wealth – the accumulated value of our assets – is more important for big-ticket items like a new home, a car, or the purchase of an entire apartment building.

Few things change as fast as consumer **tastes and fashion**. One trip to a clothing store will bear this out. In the mid 1980s a typical college student probably wore Levi's 501 jeans, white canvas Nike shoes, an Izod shirt, and a Members Only jacket. In 2016 you could not find many young folks who would be caught dead in these items – but weathered looking t-shirts, baggy jeans and tattoos were abundant.

While it is very difficult, or even impossible, to measure why or when tastes and fashion change, one thing is very clear to businesses. Once male consumers in Japan decided they wanted to wear lipstick, Japanese retailers did not ask "Why?" Their next step was to react to those changes and serve the customers with lipstick – no matter how the buyers decided on what it is they wanted.[22]

India has a much larger population than the United States. Why then does the U.S. consume far more goods and services than India? The answer lies in the **number of buyers** in the respective markets. A buyer is someone who is willing and able to buy.

The U.S. has far more people with the income and wealth to purchase any number of goods and services; therefore, we have a greater demand than the Indians for almost everything. Within the U.S. this determinant can also be found. Just look at the number of Mercedes dealerships in Beverly Hills compared to Jackson, Mississippi. Jackson is a larger city, but it has a lower per capita income and thus, a lower demand for expensive cars.

The **price of substitutes and complements** also matters in many demand decisions.

If the price of milk skyrocketed next summer, you would see a decrease in the overall demand for cereal. Complements are goods and services that are jointly consumed, while substitutes are goods and services that are rivals in consumption. During the winter of 2005 the price of home heating oil shot up dramatically. This led to an increase in the demand for firewood in Maine and other New England states.[24] Firewood is a substitute for home heating oil. So, if the price of oil increases, people will be more inclined to switch to an alternative source of heat.

Finally, **expectations of future price changes** can also impact demand. If you saw a report on the news tonight that a major explosion at a gasoline refinery had taken place, you might conclude that the price of gasoline was going to increase in the next few days. That expectation would send you – and/or others like you – out looking for gasoline today before the price increase took place. The opposite is also true. If consumers believe prices will fall in the future, demand tends to decrease today.

CONCEPT CHECK

In 2013, Kid Rock spent his summer performing at concerts at a price of $20 per ticket – a much lower price, on average, than other singers.[22] What does this suggest about his view of the relationship between price and quantity demanded? How does a sluggish economy contribute to this pricing strategy?

THE DEMAND CURVE

As you might imagine, self-interested consumers respond very differently to price changes than suppliers do. In fact, our reaction to price changes is the exact opposite of the sellers.

> ➤ **A demand curve illustrates the relationship between the price of an item and the quantity demanded, ceteris paribus.**

Just like the supply curve, a demand curve is drawn under the assumption that all demand determinants – other than price – are held constant. Let's revisit the dream recorder example to see what this means. Figure 6.3 illustrates a typical consumer response to changes in prices.

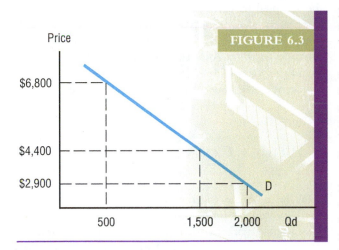

FIGURE 6.3

Notice that at a price of $2,900 the quantity of machines demanded is 2000 per week. If the price were to increase to $4,400, consumers would be willing and able to buy 1500 per week.

Raising prices to $6,800 and higher would continue the downward pressure on quantity demanded. This behavior is typical of how consumers in all markets act. In fact, it does not matter if we are discussing insulin for diabetics, tickets to Oklahoma City Thunder basketball games, or rhubarb pie in British Columbia – every market is ruled by the *law of demand*.

> ➤ **The Law of Demand states that, all things being equal, an increase in prices will lead to a decrease in quantity demanded, while a decrease in prices will lead to an increase in quantity demanded.**

Are there any cases where the law of demand can be challenged?

How many of you did not cut back on the consumption of gasoline as prices increased? If the price of toothpaste increased by $1 a tube, would you walk around with a dirty mouth? If the price of toilet paper increased would you – oh, never mind.

Figure 6.4 illustrates what some students believe to be a valid demand curve for some products that are absolute necessities to our lives. You might be willing to argue that no matter what the price, consumption of certain extreme necessities like electric power and water would never drop. You might make this claim, but you would be wrong to do so.

The more likely demand for electric power looks like figure 6.5, where changes in prices bring about negligible changes in consumption. This is also what the demand for college textbooks, shampoo, soap, car insurance, and other necessities looks like. Notice that, whether prices rise or fall, there is a small change in quantity demanded. This does not mean quantity demanded does not change at all – even for extreme necessities.

The law of demand tells us that consumption levels change as prices change. The law does not tell us *when* you will change your behavior. If gas prices increased to $9

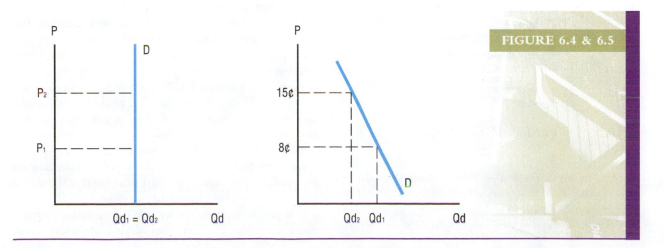

FIGURE 6.4 & 6.5

per gallon, you would alter your driving behavior. Higher electricity or water prices *eventually* would lead to a more uncomfortable house or a thirstier lifestyle. In some countries in Africa people die because of the law of demand. They cannot afford food. No matter what product or service we are talking about, there is a price where all of us would, at some point, change our behavior. It is just a question of when.

THE FOUR ROLES PRICES PLAY IN ANY ECONOMY

"....by directing that industry in such a manner as its produce may be of the greatest value, he intends only by his own gain, and he is in this, as in many other cases, led by an invisible hand to promote an end which was not part of his intention"

Adam Smith,
The Wealth of Nations page 423

Now that we understand the forces of supply and demand as separate motivations, let's consider what happens when these opposing forces are thrust together in the market. We will find that Adam Smith was a genius when he discussed the market process as a mechanism driven by "an invisible hand." This invisible hand is the process of establishing prices and output levels without the formal process of communication – i.e. letters, email, phone calls, riots, and so forth. The invisible hand is a hand guided by self-interested but interdependent parties who realize that each will go without service if a compromise is not sought out.

If the Acme Dream Recorder Company ever becomes a reality, it will face the same problem every company faces when it comes to prices. No one knows exactly what consumers will pay. Businesses have to rely on trial and error to find out what the market will support. Of course, Acme would like to charge $900,000 per machine. Potential customers would like to see a sign that reads "Free Dream Recorders." Neither price is realistic. The moment a price appears on the dream recorder, it will begin a process of creating a mutually agreed-upon price. That price will play at least *four important roles* in our economy.

PRICES HELP PREVENT BARTER

While running for a seat as Senator from Nevada, Sue Lowden suggested that "bartering is really good" and that people should "go ahead and barter with your doctor." In a television interview that sought clarification for these comments, she said, "You know, before we all started having health care, in the olden days, our grandparents, they would bring in a chicken to the doctor."[25]

Before coinage, and eventually currency, became widely used to buy goods and services, barter was a major part of the world's economy. *Barter* is the trading of goods and services to meet our wants and needs. The dilemma this poses is clear. Barter, for it to be successful, hinges on the *double coincidence of wants*. That means that you and the person you are trading with have to each want what the other is offering. If you offer your doctor 19 chickens in exchange for a physical, you are going to have a problem if the doctor is a vegetarian or is allergic to chicken feathers.

You should be glad that this is no longer the predominant system that prevails in the United States. You can imagine how long even the most basic transactions would take if every time you ventured into some market you had to bring along a variety of goods in the hope they would be accepted by the seller. By having a system that puts a monetary value on all goods and services, we can easily make a decision on whether or not we will supply or demand anything. After all, your doctor can easily understand your offer of $200 and does not have to inspect your chickens to see how many of them are healthy.

PRICES CONVEY INFORMATION

Let's bring Acme together with potential customers to see how valuable information can be. Figure 6.6 illustrates the possible market conditions that exist for this product.

Notice that, at a price of $2,900, the quantity of recorders supplied by Acme equals 500 per week. Acme isn't saying that this is the *fairest* price possible. Remember, fairness is a subjective evaluation. All we can say is that this is the price Acme wants for one recorder. In this example Acme has 2,000 people who are willing and able to pay $2,900. Since the quantity of recorders demanded is greater than the quantity supplied, a *shortage* of recorders exists. Does the shortage exist because Acme did not provide enough recorders? No. The shortage exists because the *price is too low*.

This is the first, and often the most difficult, lesson students must learn about markets. When a shortage exists, it means the buyers are telling the seller – through our nonverbal behavior – that the seller could have charged a higher price. We send this information out in an informal manner. Few, if any, of you have ever faced a shortage and explicitly asked the seller to charge you more. Instead, it is the mere fact that there are more people searching for the product than there is product available that signals the seller that they could have charged more.

If people email Acme and ask the company to make more recorders, they are not paying attention to an

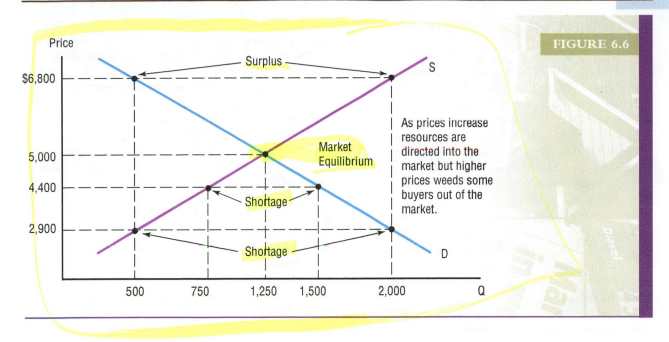

FIGURE 6.6

As prices increase resources are directed into the market but higher prices weeds some buyers out of the market.

important lesson from Adam Smith: He reminds us that we do not speak to people about our necessities, but rather about their self-love.[26] If we say, "I need you to make more recorders," Acme can say, "I need you to offer more money to convince me to make more."

What should Acme do now? The company has *three choices*. The first option is to lower prices. This would make no sense whatsoever for Acme's potential customers or for Acme. Lowering prices would decrease the quantity of recorders supplied, because at lower prices Acme has less incentive to build more. At the same time, lower prices would entice some people who were not willing or able to pay $2,900 per machine to come into this market to look for a dream recorder. As a result the shortage would be even worse! In this case Acme would be worse off, and the customers would be worse off because of the lower probability of getting a recorder.

The second option is to keep prices at $2,900. This is also foolish and inefficient, because leaving the price alone will cause Acme to manufacture more recorders (remember the Law of Supply?) and will not change the number of competing customers.

The only sensible option if Acme wants to be better off while *helping* the customers is to raise prices. Some of you might react by saying, "How is Acme serving people by ripping them off with higher prices!?!" If you think about this option from a rational perspective, you should quickly realize that by raising the price to, say, $4,400, two things would happen. First the resource-directing role of prices will come into effect, and second, the rationing role of prices will appear.

PRICES DIRECT RESOURCES TO THEIR MOST VALUED USE

Let's not romanticize this. Players don't play for little Johnny in the fourth row. A lot of guys who tell you they love this game, wouldn't love it if you didn't pay them $8 million per year.

John Amechi, former NBA Basketball Player

What Mr. Amechi can help Acme with is the fact that prices tell us where to put our talents and our resources. You recall that resources are land, labor, capital, and entrepreneurship. As prices increase from $2,900 to $4,400, Acme will be able to cover the costs of producing more machines. This will lead to Acme directing steel, computer chips, and other resources away from less profitable pursuits and into dream recorder production. As a result, the quantity of recorders supplied will increase. In figure 6.6 the output level increases to 750.

It is interesting to note that Acme does not need to know why people would pay $4,400 for a dream recorder. As a *self-interested* company it is instinctively guided to offer more recorders for more money with no other information necessary, just as NBA players are guided to play more years for more money and car manufacturers are persuaded to produce more small cars when gas prices shoot past $4 per gallon.

PRICES RATION SCARCE GOODS

To the average person who tends to be carried through life by emotion, the last role of prices in our free-market economy is the one that is the most upsetting. Figure 6.6 illustrates why. Notice that, as the price of a recorder increased to $4,400, the quantity of recorders demanded fell from 2,000 to 1,500. Five hundred people decided, for whatever reason, that they were not willing and/or not able to pay an extra $1,500 for a dream recorder.

This is the heart of the fairness versus efficiency debate. If you argue that this system is unfair, you are right. It is a totally subjective evaluation that you use to judge unfairness. Those who can afford the dream recorder – or who can't and don't allow emotion to cloud their reasoning – could argue that this change in price is fair. They would be right, too.

What is unquestionable is the fact that this increase in prices is very *efficient*. As prices increase, only those people who are most willing and able to buy will get a dream recorder. Everyone else is weeded out of the market. This is efficient because it has induced Acme to produce more recorders. At the same time, higher prices have also lessened the degree of competition that potential buyers face. This process has thus made the shortage a smaller one and increased the chances of people being served.

What if Acme gets carried away and raises prices to $6,800 per machine? Maybe Acme sees that there is a shortage at $4,400 and miscalculates how much more people would be willing and able to pay for a recorder. At $6,800 the quantity of recorders supplied skyrockets to 2,000 per week. However, the quantity of recorders demanded falls to 500 per week. At this price the quantity supplied exceeds quantity demanded; therefore, a surplus exists. When a *surplus* exists, the information being conveyed by the buyers, is that the price of the product is *too high*.

Once again Acme faces three choices. Raise prices, keep prices where they are, or lower prices. Raising prices would make the surplus even bigger and Acme's profit smaller. Leaving prices alone would guarantee that the surplus continues. Acme will notice the dust gathering on the recorders in the stores and pursue the third option, which is to lower prices. Acme is not lowering prices out of love for its customers, Acme is doing it because of self-love, yet the customers ultimately benefit.

Notice that when the price falls to $5,000 Acme cuts back on production. However, more people come back to look for a recorder. At this price, notice that the quantity of recorders demanded just equals the quantity of recorders supplied. This is known as *market equilibrium*.

> ➤ **Market equilibrium is established when the economic forces of supply and demand have balanced to the point where the quantity buyers are willing and able to buy just equals the quantity sellers are willing and able to sell, at a mutually agreed-upon price.**

At this point there are no angry customers waiting for a chance to record their dreams because of a shortage. Furthermore, at this price, retailers are not standing around with nothing to do while people with dreams to record wait for a sale. For Acme – and the customers left in the market – everyone is satisfied with the result.

APPLICATIONS OF THE INVISIBLE HAND

Now that we have a sound conceptual understanding of how markets work, we can branch out and examine more unusual and analytically challenging examples. So if you are ready to put your mind to work, we will begin.

CONCEPT CHECK

Professional football players in the United States make for more money than teachers or police officers. How does the information role of prices and the invisible hand explain these earnings differences?

CONCEPT CHECK

It could be argued that the free market practices a form of "discrimination" – but not the type of discrimination we are used to reading about. What does this mean in the Nova Scotia lobster trap market?

Photo courtesy Jack Chambless

WHEN IS A SALE NOT A SALE?

The Wall Street Journal once ran an article that examined the practice of discounting products like washing machines and cameras by offering a mail-in rebate.[27] "The whole point behind rebates is to entice purchases and hope (consumers) don't remember to submit" their claims, according to Charles Weil, president of Young America Inc., whose company mails out about 30 million rebate checks a year on behalf of various companies.

With a redemption rate of "only 5–10%," it is obvious how compelling it must be for companies to choose this format to eliminate surpluses. If prices are above equilibrium, and a television company knows that prices will have to fall in order to move the merchandise, why not put the responsibility on the consumer to work for the discount? The consumer sees the ad stating that the set is $150 off the regular price and reacts to that price cut, as the law of demand would predict.

However, when the consumer gets the television home, the hassle of mailing in the rebate form – along with the receipts, UPC symbols, and other items that must accompany the form – makes mailing it in an uneconomic endeavor.

A similar situation exists with coupons that appear in your Sunday paper. How many of you take the time to cut out coupons to save money on deodorant and cat food? If the opportunity cost of cutting out coupons is measured by the value of doing nothing – and doing nothing is more valuable – you will pay full price for cat food, but will at least be well rested when you do.

What was Ms. Swarr talking about? As it turns out, she was complaining about the fact that the University of Minnesota was expected to collect more than $300 million in royalties from its patent on Ziagen, an AIDS drug, sold by GlaxoSmithKline.

The protestors, like the ones at Yale, who were successful in getting Bristol-Myers Squibb Co. to relinquish patent rights for an AIDS drug in South Africa, were up in arms over profit being earned in the Africa market for AIDS medication.

Over 23.5 million people in Africa[28] – by far more than in any other continent – suffer from AIDS. Making matters worse is the fact that new drug-resistant strains of HIV have been spreading throughout the world, lowering the odds of helping as many people as society would like to see helped.[29]

In response to mounting international pressure, many of the drug companies have lowered the price of AIDS medication – in some cases below the actual cost of manufacturing the drugs.[30] As figure 6.7 illustrates, the price cuts may not be enough to satisfy the AIDS patients or the student activists.

PROFITS OVER PEOPLE IN AFRICA?

We are furious at the university's complicity in the denial of access to life-saving medication to poor people across the world. We are disgusted.

Amanda Swarr,
University of Minnesota graduate student

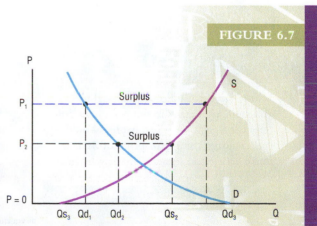

FIGURE 6.7

Even with lower prices, the overall quantity demanded has not increased very much, because the income of the average African with AIDS is so low that – even at an average price of $1 per day for some medication – there is still going to be a surplus of unsold treatments.

For the student protestors, only a price of zero would satisfy them. However, we can use market equilibrium analysis to see that, at a price of zero, the quantity demanded would increase, but the incentives to provide medication in Africa would fall dramatically. Maybe some donations would occur to foster goodwill, but the cost of production would far exceed the total revenue ($0), and therefore a massive shortage of medicine would break out. Ultimately, the shortage of medicine would hurt far more Africans then the market price would.

WHAT IS A NEW BABY WORTH?

> I've got championship Rottweilers. I sell them by supply and demand. I raise thoroughbred racehorses. I sell them by supply and demand. I'm not going to let people sell children by supply and demand. What's the difference between that and slavery?
>
> Reverend Ken Hutcherson

What is the reverend talking about? Well, he is talking about the fact that there is a market for children, and the market price is a function of race. Yes, that's right: Children of different races are "worth" different amounts of money in the adoption business.

Reverend Hutcherson is fighting to change the laws of supply and demand from his Redmond, Washington, church. He is upset because in the market for adopted babies, white children routinely "sell" for $35,000. Latino babies go for $10,000, and black babies are sold for $4,000 to their new parents.

The reverend argues that, besides putting a price on children, the practice discriminates against white babies and people who seek to adopt them by charging them more. "I know about discrimination," said Hutcherson, who is black. "Tell me if it was black babies that cost $50,000 and white babies that cost $4,000, people would be screaming their heads off."

THE ECONOMICS OF RECYCLING

If you are like many Americans, you want to leave the Earth as clean as you can for your children and grandchildren. This is a noble goal that I share with you, but the economics of recycling does not add up as nicely as we would like for it to.

According to *BioCycle* magazine's annual survey, the United States has over 7,200 curbside recycling programs serving 108 million people. Furthermore, every state in the union has some type of program aimed at recycling. The programs range from diverting large amounts of plastics, aluminum, paper, and cardboard from landfills to sorting facilities, which send them on their way to be reused in manufacture, to simply having state governments buy products containing recycled materials. "It's become a way of life," says Donald Berman, director of solid waste management for Allegheny County, Pennsylvania, which includes Pittsburgh.

But is it a way of life that makes economic and environmental sense? Recently a number of economists and policy analysts have questioned whether the benefits of recycling outweigh the cost of disposing of waste materials in landfills. Critics say that what seems at first to make a great deal of sense doesn't always stand up to a close examination. For instance, some critics argue that collection costs make recycling a bad bargain for many

CONCEPT CHECK

Using three separate diagrams, illustrate and then explain why the prices are different for each group of babies. Would a law creating a uniform price of $10,000 make economic sense? Why or why not?

localities because the costs often exceed the prices that the recyclables bring on the open market. They also charge that operating additional trucks to pick up recyclables increases toxic diesel emissions, offsetting any environmental gains.[31]

As figure 6.8 illustrates, in many cities, the government doesn't even pay for paper, cans, and bottles. The recycler – the good citizen – has to pay the government to take the stuff away. This means supply and demand intersect at a *negative* price! Not many markets are characterized by the seller paying the buyer. It appears that in order to keep Earth clean, we have to.

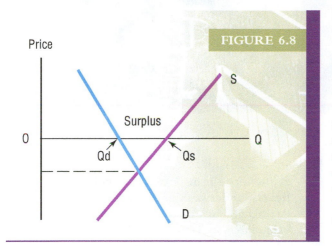

FIGURE 6.8

WHEN FAIRNESS IS AN UNFAIR THING

The following photo is of the Snappy Lunch – a restaurant so famous for its fried pork chop sandwiches that Oprah Winfrey regularly flies all the way to Mt. Airy, North Carolina, to eat here. Why is there a waiting line at this place?

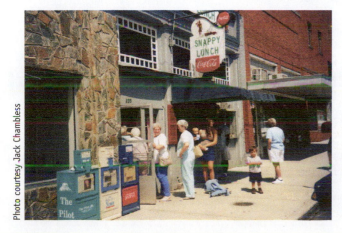

Photo courtesy Jack Chambless

Look at the little boy waiting in the July heat for a sandwich. Should he have to suffer because this restaurant does not comply with the laws of supply and demand? What if he fainted from hunger? The elderly folks in front of him don't seem to care that he is hungry. Of course, after waiting over an hour for a table, maybe they should tell him that part of life is learning to suffer.

However, we could argue that if the Snappy Lunch raised prices from less than $3 per sandwich to say, $5, then some people who were only marginally interested in a pork chop sandwich would not go in. This would ration the sandwiches to the parents of this little fellow, Oprah Winfrey, and anybody else who were willing and able to pay. The higher price in effect is arguably the fairest price since there would be less wasted time in lines, people who like pork chops – and who have $5 – would be served, and the Snappy Lunch would earn more money! Now we turn to the government's handling of park entrance fees.

It should not come as any great shock that the United States government has blown it when it comes to pricing a service. After all, since the government is a not-for-profit agency, what reason would it have to let market forces dictate entrance fees to our national parks? You might even agree that the government should not act like Disney World and charge over $90 per day. However, there is an untold part of the story that you need to know.

Traffic jams like the one depicted in the photograph on the following page have caused severe damage to Yellowstone National Park.[32]

With prices well below equilibrium, an artificially high number of cars enter this valuable park each year. This leads to a shortage of space for vacationers to enjoy the mountains, geysers, and wildlife, and – perhaps more troubling – a shortage of quiet, clean air and protection that the animals and the ecosystem need to survive.

Each year, the NPS reports that Yellowstone's infrastructure is crumbling due to too many cars. Each year, the NPS reports that not enough money is available to hire people to protect the animals and animal habitat. And each year, the NPS charges prices that are so far below the market equilibrium price that these problems only intensify.

What if the NPS charged $100 per car, per week? On one hand you could say, "Unfair! The parks belong to all of us, and $100 fees discriminate against the poor!" On the other hand you could argue that if the poor really care about the long-term health of the park, they will understand the need to raise prices. Then you could argue that, if the poor want to see the parks enough, they will save the extra money needed to visit. Finally, you could argue that there is no guarantee the poor will see Yellowstone at $25 if the NPS ever sets limits on the number of cars that can enter to ration the scarce space.[33]

It should be noted that the cost to drive through the Great Smoky Mountain National Park is $0. Consequently,

© Guoqiang Xue/Shutterstock.com

at popular attractions like Cades Cove, it can take two hours to travel just a few miles and this park has been hit by some of the highest levels of air pollution in the Eastern United States.[34]

WHAT TO DO IF A GUN RANGE OPENS NEAR YOUR HOME

Ronald Coase won the Nobel Prize for Economics in 1991. During his lifetime as an economist, he distinguished himself by a paper he published in 1960 that revolutionized the economics profession.[35]

It was in this paper that Mr. Coase argued that, as long as property rights are clearly defined and transaction costs are low, any two people facing a disagreement should be able to use the market system to reach a reasonable accord. Before we explore his views, let's take a brief look at four types of goods and the degree to which each is excludable (one where the supplier of the good can prevent people who refuse to pay from consuming it) or non-excludable (one where the supplier cannot prevent non-payers from using it).

> ➤ **Private goods are goods that are excludable and rival in consumption. Rival in consumption means that the same good cannot be consumed by more than one person**

at the same time. Examples include airline tickets, underwear, and contact lenses.

> ➤ **Artificially Scarce Goods: Goods that are excludable, but nonrival in consumption. This means that more than one person can consume the good at a time but some can be excluded. Examples include video games and pay-per-view movies.**
> ➤ **Common Property Resources: Goods that are non-excludable and rival in consumption. Fish from a lake, the air we breathe, and a forest trail come to mind.**
> ➤ **Public Goods: Goods that are non-excludable and nonrival in consumption. National defense is the classic example of a good that everyone gets to enjoy and no one can be turned away.**

The people in eastern Georgia could use Ronald Coase right now. In many rural areas, residents are awakening to an entrepreneurial endeavor that is a bit noisy – and at times that is somewhat inconvenient. What residents are upset about is the opening of a gun range near local farms.

The basic problem in this case is that farmers own their land (a private good, excludable in consumption) – as do the gun range owners – but no one owns the air surrounding the land. The air is *common property*, so the farmers face some difficulty in claiming that they should be guaranteed quiet. It would appear that they have no recourse, unless they understand the Coase Theorem.

> ➤ **The Coase Theorem states that if people can negotiate the purchase and sale of the right to perform activities that cause externalities, they can arrive at efficient solutions to the problems caused by externalities. An externality is any positive or negative spillover effect from the consumption of a good or service.**

In this case the *negative externality* is the noise generated by the rifle range. Suppose the value of quiet to a local farmer is $80 per hour after 5 a.m., while the value of running the rifle range is equal to $60 per hour after 5 p.m. At an official price of zero, the quantity of silence demanded exceeds the quantity of noise supplied. Notice that, at a price equal to zero, the farmer does not expect total silence, but he doesn't want the quantity being supplied either. Therefore, there is a shortage of quiet in his home.

If the *transactions cost* of negotiating with the rifle range equals zero – meaning he doesn't mind approaching the range owner with an offer, or working out an offer – he could consider letting the range owner know that he would be willing to pay $80 per hour – after 5 p.m. – for quiet. Of course, if the farmer is smart, he will attempt to pool the resources of the local farmers so he doesn't have to pay the entire cost.

If the range owner is smart, he will agree, since he was earning $60 per hour after 5 p.m. and the farmers are offering $80 to close down in the evening hours. The farmer could actually approach the range owner and say, "How much would you be willing to take to close down at 5 p.m.?" The range owner might say "$61," in which case both parties are still better off.

Through negotiation the parties have simply changed the air around them from common property to private property.

ENDNOTES

1 Authors note: This is the one area where I envy people with cell phones…

2 See "Phone-Wielding Shoppers Strike Fear into Retailers" by Miguel Bustillo and Ann Zimmerman, *The Wall Street Journal,* December 16, 2010.

3 See "The Internet Sales Tax Rush" *The Wall Street Journal,* April 21, 2013.

4 See "Keep it Moving" by Bruce Ingersoll, *The Wall Street Journal,* January 20, 1993.

5 See "The 'Sharing Economy' and its Enemies" by Andy Kessler, *The Wall Street Journal,* January 18-19, 2014 Page A11.

6 See "Egg-donor business booms on campuses" by Jim Hopkins, *The USA Today,* March 16, 2006; and "Women touting their bodies to sell dream of the perfect child" by James Bone, *The London Times,* March 20, 2006.

7 See "A fair debate: Do human beings possess a genetic drive for fairness?" by Faye Flam, *The Orlando Sentinel,* from Knight Ridder Newspapers, September 24, 2000; and "There's economic theory, and then there's reality" by Steven Pearlstein, *The Orlando Sentinel* from *The Washington Post,* February 10, 2002.

8 See "Selling Candy With a Conscience" by Leslie Josephs, *The Wall Street Journal,* December 24, 2010.

9 See "Charity, hope and consumer faith in both" by Beth Kassab, *The Orlando Sentinel,* December 24, 2010.

10 See "The Civilizing Effect of the Market" by David Wessel, *The Wall Street Journal,* January 24, 2002.

11 Source: Fort Stevens State Park, Oregon.

12 See "In Central Florida, gas prices pump up bike, scooter sales" by Sarah Hale Meitner, *The Orlando Sentinel,* June 8, 2004.

13 See "'80 Olympic Goalie Puts Collection Up for Sale" *The New York Times,* May 25, 2016.

14 See "Can Potter Lift Lagging Resort?" by Jason Garcia, *The Orlando Sentinel,* May 30, 2010; and "Potter Works Magic for Hotels" by Sara W. Clarke, *The Orlando Sentinel,* January 21, 2011.

15 See "Universal Draws 46% more visitors" by Jason Garcia, *The Orlando Sentinel,* January 22, 2011.

16 See "Peek into Diagon Alley" by Dewayne Bevil, *The Orlando Sentinel,* January 24, 2014.

17 For example, new regulations on the way shrimp can be caught in the Gulf of Mexico has dramatically increased the cost of fishing for shrimp. This has led to the bankruptcy of many shrimpers in the Gulf Coast region and an opening for foreign shrimpers – who do not face the same regulations – to enter the market and take over for the Americans that are now unemployed. See "Sunset for Shrimpers?" by Mark Holan, *The Tampa Tribune,* April 4, 2004.

18 See "Small Breweries Hurt by Own Success" by Tripp Mickle, *The Wall Street Journal,* September 28, 2016.

19 See "Chinese Cotton to Hoarding" by Carolyn Cui, *The Wall Street Journal,* January 29-30, 2011.

20 See "Can computers decode dreams? Researchers take a first step" by Geoffrey Mohan, *The Los Angeles Times,* April 5, 2013.

21 See "The $25,300 Bill" by Christopher Boyd, *The Orlando Sentinel,* January 7, 2006.

22 See "Asia's Lipstick Lads" by Geoffrey A. Fowler, *The Wall Street Journal,* May 27, 2005.

23 See "With fuel costs up. Firewood prices, sales, soar" *The Orlando Sentinel,* January 2, 2005.

24 See "Kid Rock's Plan to Change the Economics of Touring" by John Jurgensen, *The Wall Street Journal,* June 7, 2013.

25 See "Chickens for check-ups and a cup of GOP tea" by Eugene Robinson, *The Orlando Sentinel,* May 2, 2010.

26 See *The Wealth of Nations* by Adam Smith, 1776 Book 1; pg. 14.

27 See "Rebates Secret Appeal to Manufacturers: Few Consumers Actually Redeem Them" by William M. Bulkeley, *The Wall Street Journal,* February 10, 1998.

28 Source: Avert.org.

29 See "Student Protestors Target Universities Profiting from AIDS Research" by Rachel Zimmerman, *The Wall Street Journal,* April 12, 2001.

30 See "Drug Resistant Strains of HIV Are Spreading" by Mark Schoops, *The Wall Street Journal,* February 8, 2001.

31 See www.ehpnet1.niehs.nih.gov/docs/1995/103-11/focus2.html.

32 Take a look at www.cnn.com/2000/NATURE/04/05/endangered.
parks/ as well as www.yellowstone.net/.

33 Only recently did the NPS raise prices from $20 per week to $25.
At the Smoky Mountain National Park – where there is no fee at
all – the air pollution that has been generated in places like Cades
Cove is among the worst in the entire United States. See "Entrance
fees to rise at some national parks" www.cnn.com, September 27,
2005; and "Visitors flock to Smoky Mountains valley, www.cnn.com,
September 13, 2005.

34 Source: nps.gov.

35 For more on Coase, see www.nobel.se/economics/laureates/1991/
coase-autobio.html. To read his paper, "The Problem of Social Cost,"
see 3 *Journal of Law & Economics* 1 (1960).

CHAPTER REVIEW

1. What is Say's Law? Does this law apply to medicine, food, and education? Why, or why not?

2. Why do demand curves and supply curves have the slope that they do?

3. The September 21–22, 2013 edition of *The Wall Street Journal* reported that wool jackets made from Vicuna can cost up to $21,000. What determinants of demand and supply might lead to this price?

4. What are the four key roles prices play in a market? Use the market for steak to explain.

5. Explain how the Coase Theorem could be used to clean up the Earth's oceans.

Chapter Seven

CHANGES *in* SUPPLY *and* DEMAND

© Cheryl Casey/Shutterstock.com

*I*t will not make a difference if Saudi Arabia ships an extra million or two million barrels of crude oil to the United States if you cannot refine it. It will not turn into gasoline, and it will not turn into lower prices.

ADEL AL-JUBEIR, FOREIGN POLICY ADVISOR TO
CROWN PRINCE ABDULLAH OF SAUDI ARABIA

147

FROM SNAPSHOT TO VIDEO

As your income and age increases, do you think you will eat out at nicer restaurants and wear different clothing than you do now? If you thought gasoline prices might increase tomorrow, what would you do today? Does it make sense that the technology associated with producing self-driving cars will change, or that the number of sellers in the videogame market will remain what it is today?

In the last chapter we focused solely on changes in prices and the way price changes impact quantity demanded and quantity supplied. In this chapter we will relax the assumption that the other determinants of demand and supply do not change. We will take an in-depth look at what happens when market equilibrium is disrupted by changes in supply and/or demand. This investigation will put you in a much better position to understand the changing world around us.

while egg prices dropped 40%![4] All across America, lower prices meant fewer people eating out in restaurants. Did the falling price of food in grocery stores cause a decrease in the demand for restaurant meals or a decrease in the quantity of restaurant meals demanded?

The answer is: demand. Why? Recall from chapter six that, if the price of a good or service changes, there will be a change only in the *quantity demanded* for that good or service.

If you went into a restaurant today and saw that the price of hamburgers had increased by 10% you and others like you would be inclined to order something else. This would mean a *decrease in the quantity of hamburgers demanded*. On figure 7.1 this is illustrated by a change in price from P1 to P2 and a drop in the quantity of restaurant hamburgers demanded from Q1 to Q2.

Notice that as the price changes, only quantity demanded changes. However, this is a *monumentally different* event compared to a change in demand.

CHANGES IN DEMAND VS. CHANGES IN QUANTITY DEMANDED

In the wake of rising gasoline prices in 2008, newspapers around the country reported on the drop in demand for large trucks and SUVs – and the increase in demand for small cars.[1] As the economy weakened during that time we also observed an increase in consumer spending at places like Wal-Mart and Costco, while Target and Kohl's suffered.[2] We also witnessed a huge drop in the demand for real estate agents as the housing market seemed to fall apart.[3]

You (or your parents) might have noticed that food prices in grocery stores dropped in 2016. From the summer of 2015 to 2016 milk prices fell by 11% nationwide

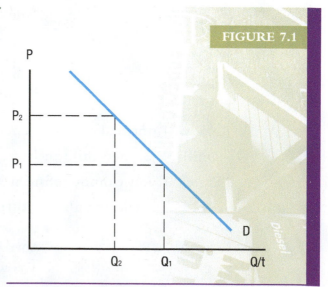

FIGURE 7.1

A change in demand occurs if, and only if, some demand determinant, *other than the price*, changes.

Let's review what those "other" determinants are:

• Income
• Wealth
• Tastes and fashion
• The number of buyers in the market
• The price of substitutes
• The price of complements
• Expectations concerning future prices

In figure 7.2 you can see what happens if the demand for a good or service changes. As the price of food in grocery stores dropped this meant that a *substitute* for restaurant meals was now more desirable. It also meant that *fewer buyers* existed in the restaurant meal market. Thus, the overall demand for restaurant meals shifted from D1 (in figure 7.2) to D2. This leftward shift in the entire demand curve means that at all prices, buyers were less willing and able to eat out. Remember, the only way there could be a decrease in quantity demanded is if the price increased. A change in non-price determinants shifts the entire demand curve.

It is also true that lower grocery prices led to an increase in the quantity demanded for grocery store food. If, however the U.S. economy saw an increase in consumer income next year it would mean an increase in the overall demand for grocery food. D3 in figure 7.2 reflects the fact than an increase in demand means that at all prices buyers are more willing and able to buy. That is why you see a rightward shift in the entire demand curve.

If any of you get stumped on the difference between changes in demand and changes in quantity demanded, your professor will accurately suggest that you practice the following analysis and simply keep in mind that a demand curve represents all possible prices and all possible quantities demanded at those prices. Therefore, *any time prices change, the only thing that can happen is a change in quantity demanded.*

CHANGES IN DEMAND AND THE IMPACT ON MARKET EQUILIBRIUM

In order to grasp the impact of a change in demand on a stable market condition, you must be able to work through the *chain of causation* that takes place. The term "chain of causation" means that as one event takes place it will cause the next event to take place. The causal links in demand analysis can be summarized in the following four questions that you must be able to answer:

• What demand determinant or determinants has/ have changed or will change, and in what direction?
• What was, or will be, the impact on the demand for the good or service?
• What was, or will be, the impact on the price of the good or service?
• What was, or will be, the impact on the quantity of the good or service supplied?

For most students, the most difficult step in this process of analysis is step one. You may have a hard time at first being able to single out which determinant or determinants are changing. Two helpful tools to man-

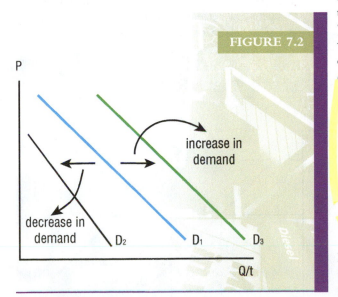

FIGURE 7.2

P

increase in demand

decrease in demand

D2   D1   D3

Q/t

CONCEPT CHECK

During the 2014 National Football League post-season, successful teams like the Green Bay Packers and Indianapolis Colts struggled to sell tickets to important playoff games. Many economists argue that the size and quality of television sets has negatively impacted NFL ticket sales.[5] Has the growth in high-definition television sales caused a decrease in the demand for NFL tickets, or is it a decrease in quantity demanded? Why?

age step one are to commit to memory the determinants of demand and to try to use logic to determine which determinant is changing. A good memory and sense of logic will help you here.

© photazz/Shutterstock.com

CASE STUDY #1: HAVE YOU HAD YOUR GRASS-FED BEEF TODAY?

As we all know, it seems like every other week someone is on television telling us about the latest and greatest food or supplement that we should eat more of in order to avoid dying before we are 50.

Dennis and Alicia Stoltzfoos operate Full Circle Farms near Mayo, Florida. Their farm specializes in beef from cattle that has grazed entirely on organically grown grasses. No hormones, steroids, or corn-based feed ever enters the bodies of their cattle. They had a nice business going until the movie *Food, Inc.* came out. Now they are so busy fielding emails, phone calls, and processing new orders that they normally put in dawn to dusk work hours.[6]

This movie depicted the very difficult lives that cattle, chickens, pigs, and other animals we eat go through in large, commercial operations. Once people got to see how their food is treated, it led to a huge increase in the demand for humanely raised animal products.

As you can clearly see in figure 7.3, we are depicting an increase in the demand for grass-fed beef. If we refer back to the four questions in the chain of causation, we can see what has occurred in this market.

1. As people have become more health-conscious, there has been an increase in the *number of buyers* in the market for grass-fed beef. There was also an increase in *consumer tastes* for this product.

2. With more buyers in the market – along with an increase in consumer tastes – the *demand* for grass-fed beef has *increased*. In figure 7.3 this is represented by a rightward shift in the entire demand curve.

3. What would have happened if demand had increased, but grass-fed beef suppliers had kept prices constant at P1? At this price you can take one look at where

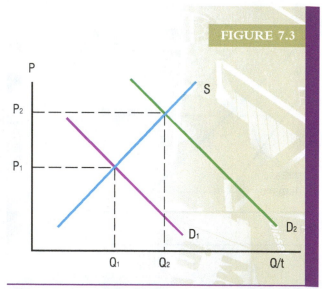

FIGURE 7.3

CONCEPT CHECK

In 2016 Samsung stopped producing the Galaxy Note 7 cell phone after several cases where the phone caught on fire. Use the chain of causation to illustrate what happened in the market for this phone.

quantity demanded would be on the new demand curve (D2), and you will see that a *shortage* of this product would have emerged. How does the market get rid of shortages? *Prices must increase.* On figure 7.3 you can see that the new price (P2) establishes a new equilibrium condition. This is precisely what has happened all over America as a 40% increase in the demand for grass-fed beef had led to a 30-80% increase in prices by the fall of 2016.[7]

4. What do you suppose beef suppliers did in response to higher prices? If you are guessing that they *increased quantity supplied,* then you are correct. The last step is simply verification of the law of supply. The more money you can make, the more incentives you have to offer grass-fed beef to consumers who are concerned about their health and the humane treatment of animals.

The Economics of Price-Gouging

A huge question for debate is whether or not higher prices during wars or natural disasters constitute a form of reprehensible "price-gouging" or a much-needed dose of free-market economics.

When natural disasters strike, hoarding becomes pervasive. Ask any resident of Florida what the plywood and generator market looked like as Hurricane Matthew approached in October 2016 and they will tell you that it resembled the earliest stages of a riot.

Impending storms creates panic buying that makes the average consumer buy a great deal more plywood, water, ice, etc. than he or she normally would. The demand determinant at work here is *expectations of future prices.* When people think that prices will rise in the future, demand increases significantly.

As demand increases, the natural progression of events suggests that prices will rise. Rising prices lead to a much-needed dose of market-correcting in many ways.

First, as prices rise, hoarding is dramatically reduced. The entire reason people buy enough bread to hold a picnic for some small countries is because the government prohibits grocery stores from raising prices to a level that would slow down the rate at which people stock their shopping carts. If prices are allowed to rise, more of these essential items would be available for more of our fellow shoppers. This is simply the *rationing role of prices* at work. Some would argue that higher prices would mean that poorer people would be shut out of the market. The problem with this argument is that poor people are no better off showing up only to find the shelves are bare. At least with higher prices the poor have a chance of finding a little of what they need.

A second benefit of price-gouging is that it speeds up the rate at which suppliers send products to areas affected by disasters. This is the *resource-directing role of prices.* If the quantity of plywood demanded exceeds the quantity supplied, but prices are not allowed to reflect that, what incentive does a lumber company have to incur the expense of rushing extra plywood into that area? Should the lumber companies operate under the mantra of promoting the moral good of the community? Is this why they are in business?

No. The companies are in business to make money. If, in the process of making a few extra bucks per foot of plywood, they are given the incentives to rush the wood to people who need it, this assures that more of us get plywood.

When my daughter was in the first grade, she came into my office to show me three "books" she had constructed. One was a book about a bat, one was about a cat, and the third one was about a dog. When she asked me if I would like to have one of the books,

How much should water cost when the wind is blowing 127 mph?

© Tkavsilimonov/Shutterstock.com

I jokingly asked, "How much money do you want?" She replied, "Zero dollars for one, $3 for two and $30 for three." When I queried her as to why she wanted such a high price for all three books, she said, "Because if you take all three, Sarah [my wife] and Gehrig [her brother] won't get any."

If a six-year old understands the importance of how prices ration scarce goods, then anyone should be able to.

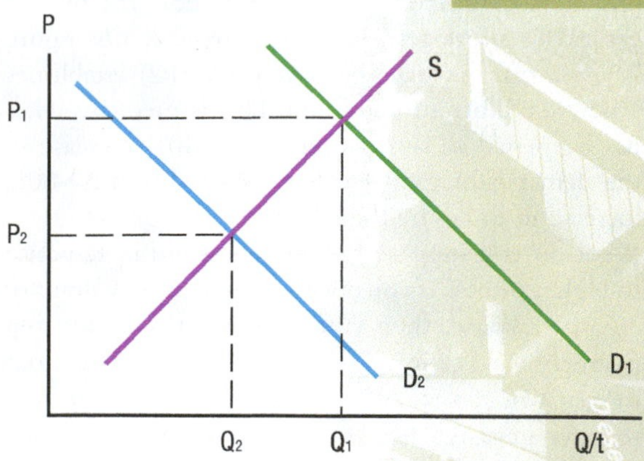

CASE STUDY #2: DO YOU MIND TELLING ME WHERE THOSE OYSTERS CAME FROM?

FIGURE 7.4

This is a question that hundreds of thousands of sea-food loving Americans may have found themselves asking over the past few years.

That is because people have this really funny aversion to eating oysters that are tainted with petroleum…

The BP oil spill constituted an unmitigated disaster for businesses that deal in wholesale and retail oysters. With the threat of contamination in one of the world's greatest oyster-producing regions, it was not long before dramatic changes took place in this market.

1. As a result of the oil spill in the Gulf of Mexico, *the number of buyers* and consumer *tastes* for Gulf oysters plummeted.[8]
2. As the number of buyers in the market fell, the over-all *demand* for Gulf oysters *fell*. Figure 7.4 illustrates a decrease in demand. A decrease in demand means that at all prices, buyers were less willing to buy Gulf oysters than they had been before.

3. As the demand for Gulf oysters fell, a surplus of oysters broke out at the old price (P1). This left many oyster dealers with no other option than to begin to offer lower-priced options, (P2), which is precisely what happened over time.
4. As prices fell, oyster sellers saw that selling Gulf oysters in many locations was not very profitable, so the overall *quantity supplied decreased* as the less profitable suppliers closed down. After all, why would they maintain the same output if fewer buyers existed?

WHY AMISH GROCERS ENJOY RECESSIONS

Normally, when the economy is strong the demand for most goods and services goes up.

Conversely, when unemployment is rising and people are earning less money, the demand for various products tends to fall. That is not the case when people consider some goods to be *inferior goods*.

SUGGESTED CLASSROOM DEBATE

In an early 2014 interview, President Obama indicated support for the growing number of states that have legalized the consumption of marijuana. Arguing that "it's important for it to go forward because it's important for society not to have a situation in which a large portion of people have at one time or another broken the law and only a select few get punished."[9] Would continued legalization lead to an increase, or decrease in the demand for marijuana? Why?

> ➤ **An inferior good is a good that people buy more of during bad economic times and less of during times where consumer income and wealth is increasing.**

A lot of college students drive used cars, eat low-quality fast food, and drink cheap beer. However, you might find that as your income goes up over time, your demand for these things will drop because you consider them inferior when compared to new cars, expensive meals, and imported beer.[10]

When the U.S. economy slid into a recession in 2007 an interesting thing happened in parts of the country where Amish retail shops exist – the demand for goods in these shops actually increased.[11]

With traditional grocery store prices rising, many Americans opted for inferior goods like pesto sauce that was five months past the "best if used by" date; boxes of corn taco shells that had water damage – and were taped up and other expired, dented or questionable items.

CHANGES IN SUPPLY

Now that we know what happens when consumers change their mind about a product – for better or worse – we now turn our attention to how changes in supply determinants (other than price) can impact the market. Recall that, other than price, our supply determinants are:

- Input Costs
- Technology
- The number of sellers serving the market
- The price of other goods that can be produced with inputs used or owned by the seller
- Expectations concerning future prices

If any of these determinants change, there will be a change in the supply of the good or service in question. This is different than a change in quantity supplied. If the price of snowmobiles increases in New Hampshire, the quantity of snowmobiles supplied will increase and vice versa. If the input costs of making snowmobiles change, there will be a new supply curve in the snowmobile market. This is because changes in input costs, technology, or any other determinant of supply alters the willingness and ability of the supplier to provide the good or service. The following questions must be answered in analyzing a change in supply.

- What determinant or determinants of supply has/have changed or will change, and in what direction?
- What was, or will be, the impact on the supply of the good or service?
- What was, or will be, the impact on the price of the good or service?
- What was, or will be, the impact on the quantity of the good or service demanded?

CASE STUDY # 3: ANYONE FOR AN LCD TELEVISION?

Over the past several years the pace of technological change has been staggering. While this can be scary for some, there is no question that our lives have been positively impacted by the emergence of things like computers, cell phones, remote control, DVD players, and satellite dishes.[12] Can you imagine what your life would be like if you had to rely on typewriters, pay phones, and record players?

Not only have we been exposed to an array of new technological goodies to consider buying, the prices of all of these items continues to fall and the products have become better and better at serving us. Is this magic? Yes. It is the magic of the free market. In figure 7.5 and 7.6 we examine the LCD (liquid crystal display) television market to find the explanation for why all of the high-tech items we crave have become more powerful and less expensive.

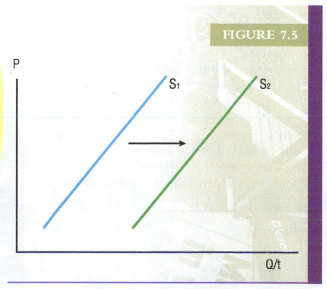

FIGURE 7.5

1. Over the past few years, the *technology* associated with making LCD televisions *has increased* dramatically as manufacturers have learned more and more about how to improve the efficiency of their production processes.

As technology has increased, the *input costs* of producing LCD televisions have *fallen*. This is because better technology in the production of liquid-crystal display panels led to economies of scale – cost savings associated with large-scale production. As the input costs of production have fallen, this has led to *more sellers* entering the market for LCD televisions.

2. With more sellers and lower costs of production, the result has been (and will continue to be) an *increase in the supply* (S2) of LCD televisions. An increase in supply means that at all prices sellers are more willing and able to supply than before. If we superimpose figure 7.5 on 7.6 we see that an increase in supply – in the market – is a rightward shift in the entire supply schedule.

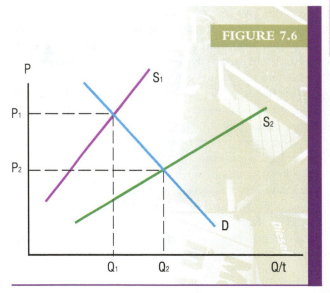

FIGURE 7.6

3. While LCD manufacturers would love to be able to continue charging the $8,990 price that was being fetched for 42-inch models in 2004, they can't. This is because, with heightened competition, an increase in supply with no corresponding cut in prices would lead to surpluses of LCD televisions. At some point one or more companies had to *lower prices* – and still make profit – due to falling costs of production. By 2016 many of these sets could be had for well under $300.

4. As prices have fallen, self-interested consumers have become more willing to buy an LCD television. As you recall from the law of demand, lower prices will lead to an *increase in the quantity demanded*. This has been precisely the case in all markets where technology is important, from laptop computers to DVD burners.[13]

CASE STUDY # 4: STELLA LIEBECK AND YOUR BIG MAC

> Coffee is supposed to be hot.
>
> Jerry Seinfeld

If you are like many other college students, good nutrition constitutes eating cheeseburgers – for breakfast. If you are like all consumers, the price you pay for everything from cheeseburgers to movie theater tickets is impacted greatly by lawsuits and government regulation.

Several years ago, Stella Liebeck – aged 81 years at the time, entered the drive-through window at a McDonald's near her home and ordered a cup of coffee. While removing the lid to add cream and sugar, she spilled the coffee, causing third-degree burns of the groin, inner thighs, and buttocks. Her lawyers argued that the coffee was too hot and therefore defective, and a New Mexico jury awarded her $2.9 million in damages.

More recently, two class-action lawsuits were filed against McDonald's and others charging that the restaurants are responsible for customers becoming obese. The

Photo courtesy Jack Chambless

CONCEPT CHECK

In the wake of Hurricane Katrina, a surplus of unskilled labor emerged in places like Houston, Texas,[14] while in southern Mississippi many fast-food restaurants had to put up signs like the one seen above. On two graphs, illustrate the labor supply changes that took place in Houston and in Biloxi, Mississippi.

most recent class-action lawsuit was on behalf of some of New York's homeless children, claiming that fast foods were causing a national epidemic of obese children. These lawsuits are causing many people to wonder where the responsibility for obesity lies – in the hands of those who eat the food or those who make it.[15]

Before you jump up and down in celebration over lawsuits that punish "evil" corporations, please bear in mind that lawsuits like these, along with the threat of lawsuits and overt government regulation of businesses, all have one thing in common: They lead to higher prices for all of us. Figure 7.7 illustrates this fact.

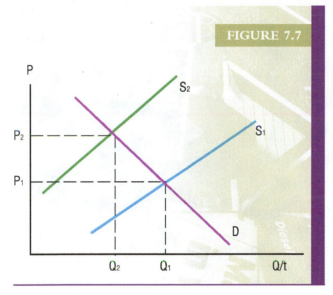

FIGURE 7.7

1. As you can clearly see, when a jury awards staggering damages to the "victims" of "careless" companies, this translates into *higher costs of production* for the company in question. The higher costs may come in the form of the damages paid out, but more likely in the form of rising insurance costs to cover potential lawsuits over fatty hamburgers and hot coffee!

2. As the input costs of production increase, this means sellers are less willing and able to supply their products at the previous price level. The result? *A decrease in the supply of the good or service* (S2). The decrease in supply

does not necessarily mean less coffee will be served. It simply means that McDonald's will be less willing and able to supply coffee for the price we used to pay.

3. As supply decreases, *upward pressure is put on prices* (P2) to help recover the higher costs of production.

4. As the prices of these products increase, the *quantity demanded will fall* – forcing consumers who do not spill hot coffee to help pay the price for those who do.

Ms. Liebeck is not alone. In 2005 Roy Pearson took a pair of pants to his drycleaner for a $10.50 alteration. Apparently, the pants were misplaced and Mr. Pearson sued the business for between $54 million and $67 million – plus $2 million for "pain and suffering."[16] This mentality has also led to lawsuits claiming that smokers are the victims of tobacco companies. Tobacco companies recently agreed to pay damages of over $200 billion to settle the suit with states seeking money to pay for the health care needs of smokers. A growing number of metropolitan areas have begun suing the makers of guns, claiming that the gun industry victimizes people by selling guns in an irresponsible manner.[17]

For you readers who enjoy surfing in Florida, you may have noticed a change that has taken place in the surfboard industry. This change has some of you reaching a bit deeper into your wallets, in order to catch a nice wave.

From 1961 to 2005, Gordon Clark ran the Clark Foam company – a business that produced about 80% of the polyurethane foam "blanks" used to produce surf boards.

All of a sudden, Mr. Clark decided he was leaving the business. The reason for his sudden departure was pretty straightforward. He got tired of getting pushed around by people who don't surf.

The lawsuits were not coming from surfers who kept getting hurt. In this case, the lawsuits kept coming from government regulators who were constantly bothering Clark Foam about the environmental implications of the company's production process.

The production of blanks relies on the use of a chemical called Toluene diisocyanate, or TDI, which manufacturers say made Clark's foam core light and sturdy.[18] The government apparently did not care about light or sturdy

CONCEPT CHECK

In the wake of the fears stirred up by "Mad Cow Disease," the German government now requires that German pig farmers follow new regulations. The regulations include a rule that a pig should get one square meter of stall space and a straw or soft rubber mat for napping. When it's time to play, the pigs must have chains or chewy toys on hand. Each pig must get at least eight hours of daylight. During the darker, shorter days of winter, farmers must compensate with lamps. Finally, there is the declaration that a farmer or farmhand must spend at least 20 seconds looking at each pig each day – and back up the loving care with paperwork showing he has enough pig-hands to provide quality time.[19] What, do you suppose, this has meant for pork *consumers* in Germany? Why?

as much as the effects of this chemical spilling during the production process. Thus, after years of hassling with regulators, Mr. Clark abruptly left the business.

The impact of his departure was felt immediately. With a major supplier gone, the remaining sellers in the market increased their prices substantially. Then, the surf shops, facing higher input costs, increased prices as well.[20]

By the second half of the last decade prices had fallen slightly – as suppliers from China and other foreign sources stepped in[21] – but for thousands of surfers around the country, a painful lesson in the cost of overzealous regulation and litigation made their sport a bit less enjoyable than before. For the workers at Clark Foam that lost their jobs, the pain was even more pronounced.

In 2013 Canada's Fraser Institute reported that America's economic freedom ranking had fallen steadily since 2000 in part because of a legal system that increasingly fails to protect people from government; has more corruption; reduced fundamental rights and falling access to civil justice. The U.S. ranked behind every former British colony except Botswana.[22]

WHAT YOU SHOULD KNOW SO FAR...

The following table represents a summary of the analysis we have undertaken thus far. Keep in mind that this table should serve as a guide to working out any problems you may have with the chain of causation. You would be wise not to simply memorize the contents of the table but to practice the concept checks and make up your own examples as you go along. Any economics professor will concur that by setting up multiple diagrams and problems, you can pick up the skills necessary to master this rather difficult material. Or you can ignore us and fail the upcoming exam.

IF	AND	THEN
Demand increases	Price increases	Quantity supplied increases
Demand decreases	Price decreases	Quantity supplied decreases
Supply increases	Price decreases	Quantity demanded increases
Supply decreases	Price increases	Quantity demanded decreases

SIMULTANEOUS CHANGES IN DEMAND AND SUPPLY

O.K., so we have seen how markets can change over time as demand or supply changes. But what happens if supply and demand changes at the same time? Is that even possible? Given the complexity of the graphs you are about to interpret you will probably wish it was unrealistic for buyers and sellers to alter their behavior simultaneously, but alas, they often do.

CASE STUDY # 5: IT'S GREAT TO BE A CORN FARMER – BUT FOR HOW LONG?

© Jorge Moro/Shutterstock.com

Sometimes it really pays well to work hard every day and wait for your government to do something colossally stupid. In this case, the hard workers are corn farmers who probably get up early and work late on many days out of the year. Now their long work days are translating into huge paychecks thanks to the U.S. Congress and President Bush decision that one-third of the nation's corn crop should be shoved into our gas tanks every time we fill up.

In 2007 President Bush signed legislation that mandated increased usage of biofuels for all American drivers of gasoline-powered cars. The law also required refiners to replace 36 billion gallons of gasoline with biofuel by 2022.[23]

In Brazil, biofuels come from processed sugar cane – which is nearly eight times more energy efficient to use than biofuels from corn and creates between 55 to 90% less air pollution when burned.[24] So why don't we just import this highly efficient and planet-friendlier source of fuel from Brazil?

Because the agricultural lobby in the United States was successful in pressing our government to use an American crop instead.

Since Mr. Bush signed this legislation, the demand for corn has skyrocketed. The initial pressure on the demand

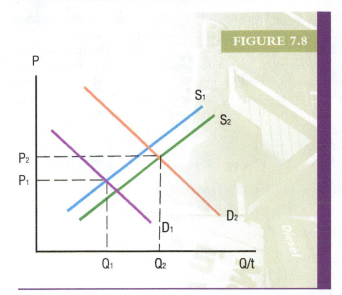

FIGURE 7.8

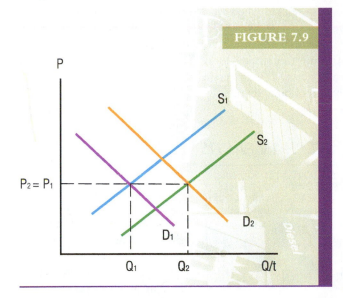

FIGURE 7.9

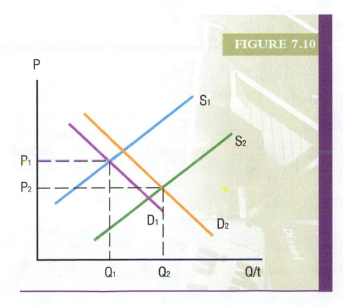

FIGURE 7.10

for corn meant that shortages broke out and prices increased accordingly.

However, as prices increased not only did we see the normal reaction on the part of existing corn farmers (more corn planted and an increase in quantity supplied), but we ended up with billions of extra bushels of corn being grown from farmers who previously grew wheat, soybeans and other crops.

Figures 7.8-7.10 illustrate the short- and long-run adjustments that are under way in this market. In each market, both the demand for, and supply of corn is increasing. The difference in each case is the *magnitude* of the change in supply and demand.

In figure 7.8 you can see what it would mean to the corn industry if the demand for corn increases by a larger amount than supply increases. If demand increases to D2, but supply increases to S2 (due to the lure of higher profits), the long-run impact will be higher prices (P2) and a higher output level. In this case, prices would increase in the long run – even though supply increased – because demand increased by a larger amount than supply.

For much of 2007–2011, this is what was occurring in much of the country as oil refineries were forced to buy corn. Even with an increase in the number of corn farmers – and an increase in corn supplies to 12.3 billion bushels, it was estimated in 2008 that it would take another 10 *million* acres of harvested corn to meet the expected demand for corn over time.[25]

In figure 7.9 we see that *demand and supply have increased by the same amount.* If this occurs, the equilibrium output level will increase – due to the greater demand and greater supply – but prices in the long run will fall back to where they were. In this case, farmers had better enjoy their good fortune while they can, because higher prices will direct more growers into the market, and increased competition will drive down prices and profits in the long run.

Figure 7.10 presents the worst-case scenario for farmers and the best-case scenario for consumers. In this instance, the increase in demand – driven by expectations of higher prices and more buyers in the market – has led to a flood of new sellers entering the market. With no ability to foresee what demand growth will exist into the future, there is no way to keep some farmers from taking a chance that they will be successful. *If supply increases by a larger amount than demand increases,* the overall impact will be higher equilibrium output levels, but lower prices!

Figure 7.10 represents what did take place in the corn market from 2013-2016. As enormous plantings of corn took place all over the Midwest, the overall supply of corn increased faster than demand leading to a drastic drop in prices.[26]

It would be an irresponsible omission to fail to mention the impact ethanol legislation has had on food prices in the United States and around the world.

If you recall from chapter one, economists sometimes try to warn policy makers that laws tend to create *unintended consequences*. In this case the consequences have been seen in grocery stores and food markets all over the world.

With the dramatic movement by farmers toward corn production – and away from other crops – we have seen higher corn prices stemming from greater demand and rising soybean, wheat and other crop prices resulting from a falling supply. As farmers moved away from wheat and soybeans the price of these crops increased. The increase was more than 70%.[27]

Higher corn prices led to an increase in the price of corn syrup, corn-based cereals and the price of feed for animals. Of course, since the price of food increased, ranchers and processors of pork, chicken and other animals had to raise their prices to cover rising input costs, while bread companies and firms that produce soybean products did the same.

The result was the largest increase in food prices since the 1970s – along with rising gas prices as the price of corn shot up.

As food shortages mounted around the globe riots began to break out in the Caribbean, Mexico, Africa and Europe, prompting European officials to formally announce plans to mandate less use of biofuels in order to free up crops for human consumption instead.[28]

Compounding the problem created by irrational government policies, a massive drought in 2010 and 2012 (the worst drought in 50 years)[29] led to spiraling wheat, soybean, and corn prices. In the absence of our ethanol laws, the price hikes would have been less severe.[30]

CASE STUDY # 6: THE ECONOMICS OF DONALD TRUMP'S DEPORTATION PLAN

While he was running for president of the United States, Donald Trump gained enormous support from Americans who agreed with his plan to round up and deport the estimated 11 million undocumented immigrants in this country.

Figures 7.11–7.13 provide valuable insight into the economic ramifications of this idea. As you will see, as is most often the case, the ideas of politicians don't line up very well with economic reality. In short, this plan is an economic disaster.

Before we plow into the supply and demand implications of his idea we need to examine a few facts concerning deportation.

Economists who study the economic impact of illegal immigration have found that these immigrants pay over $11 billion in state and local taxes each year and nearly $2 billion in property taxes.[31] Illegal immigrants create fewer crimes than native-born Americans[32] and do not take jobs away from Americans, but rather take jobs that U.S. employers have found that Americans refuse to take. For example, after a 2014 crackdown on illegal immigration, American farmers found that even at average wage offerings of $17 per hour they still could not get Americans to work long days – or any days – in agricultural fields.[33]

Despite the large body of evidence that supports the argument that illegal immigrants create more benefits for the

PEARLS BEFORE SWINE   **BY STEPHAN PASTIS**

American economy than costs, Mr. Trump – and his legion of supporters – maintained the call for a border wall and deportation.

A study by economists at the American Action Forum found that this plan would have cost $400 billion in new federal spending and reduced America's GDP by over $1 trillion.[34] Trump's plan would have overwhelmed the 34,000 beds in our 250 detention centers and would have required the use of 84 buses and 47 chartered flights per day, every day, for two years.

Now to the supply and demand implications.

Let's look at one industry – the housing market – to illustrate the economics of Trump's vision.

In figure 7.11 we see the impact of removing 11.3 million consumers of goods and services – including homes in our economy. With 11.3 million *fewer buyers,* the demand for homes (and other goods and services) shifts to D2. But that is not the end of the story. Deporting 11.3 million workers – nearly 6.4% of the American labor force would mean *fewer sellers of labor and higher input costs* for home builders. Imagine what American home builders would have to pay U.S. citizens to work as roofers, carpenters and drywall installers. These occupations, especially in America's border states, are often largely filled by undocumented workers. If they are deported it would mean higher labor costs.

If the impact of fewer workers and higher input costs is *greater than* the impact of fewer buyers in the market we would see a large drop in the supply of new homes and a relatively small decline in demand. In the final equilibrium the price of a new home would increase (P2) and quantity would fall (Q2).

In figure 7.12 we see the effects of a simultaneous change in supply and demand *of the same magnitude.* If Trump's plan is carried out, a drop in the supply of new homes of the same proportion at the drop in demand would lead to a large drop in the equilibrium quantity of homes but no change in prices. That is because the upward pressure on housing prices (from the drop in supply) is offset by the downward pressure on prices (from the drop in demand). The final result here is a contraction in the housing market - and part of that $1 trillion drop in GDP alluded to earlier.

Finally, we look at what would happen if the overall supply of new homes falls by a smaller amount than the demand decreases. In figure 7.13 we see that a relatively modest decline in supply, coupled with a large drop in demand would lead to a decrease in prices (P2) and a decrease in equilibrium quantity (Q2).

Given the relatively modest earnings of most undocumented workers figure 7.13 is the least realistic outcome of a mass deportation plan. The most likely scenario would be in 7.11 where housing prices would rise sharply from the drastic loss in employees.

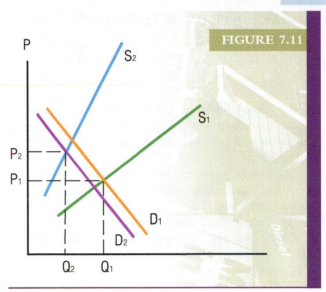

FIGURE 7.11

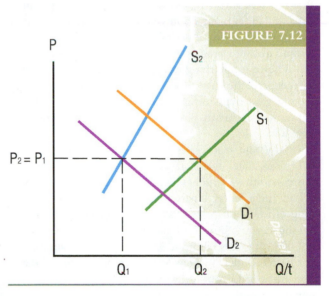

FIGURE 7.12

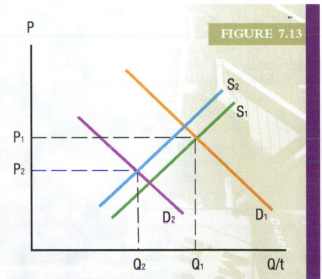

FIGURE 7.13

Case Study #7: Why Going to the Gas Station was less painful in 2016

In the last edition of this book it took four pages to explain to students why gas prices increased from 94 cents per gallon to $4.08 per gallon between December 2001 and July 2008.

As I write this section of your book, gasoline costs about $2.09 per gallon, but was less than $2 per gallon in the earliest stages of 2016.

It is important to point out these figures because one of the greatest areas of hysteria and economic illiteracy takes place when discussing your trips to the gas station. Everyone – which means virtually no one – is an "expert" when it comes to the fluctuations in gas prices. When prices started to shoot past $3 and $4 per gallon in 2007 and 2008 many doomsayers began predicting a new energy crisis. In July 2008 oil prices hit $147 per barrel – leading many to predict that $200 was not far off.

Then a funny thing happened on the way to another flawed prediction. With oil approaching $150 per barrel and gas prices rising to previously unheard of levels, consumers began to show that the law of demand was alive and well.

SUV and truck sales began to plummet, small and hybrid car sales took off and people became generally more sensitive to higher prices. Demand even began to fall in India and China as well. This led to the beginning of lower oil prices and a new "surplus psychology" among commodities dealers. From July through March of 2009 oil prices fell from $147 per barrel to almost $30 per barrel. Traders in New York became convinced that a slowing world economy would put downward pressure on the global demand for oil.

Thus, they began receiving orders to sell their contracts for the best price possible. As more traders were attempting to sell, the buyers began expecting prices to fall even more. This forced the sellers to continually lower their prices in order to find someone willing to take their futures contracts.[35] All of a sudden, the millions of Americans who kept saying that the oil companies were ripping us off and that we were helpless in our struggles against corporate greed were left – mouths agape – wondering why those "mean old oil companies" were suddenly cutting prices by more than $110 per barrel.

It is because the oil companies never did control our lives to begin with.

The historically high oil and gas prices of the latter part of the first decade led to a great global hunt for more oil reserves. You will recall in chapter six that prices direct resources to their most valued use. In Alberta, Canada, the U.S. Department of Energy estimates that 174 billion barrels of oil can be found in the tar sands of this region.[36] With $80 billion worth of development projects underway, Canada stands to move into second place, behind Saudi Arabia, in total oil supplied to the world. And Canada does not have a track record of aiding terrorists....

Even better news from the supply side of the equation comes from the United States – specifically in North Dakota.

Due to a new technology called "fracking" which allows oil companies to extract oil from previously hard to access shale, North Dakota has been the home of a major expansion in crude oil supplies. With oil prices still over $90 per barrel early in 2014, this high-cost form of energy exploration remained profitable. As a result, according to the International Energy Agency, by the year 2020 the United States will replace OPEC's Saudi Arabia as the world's largest producer of crude oil with over 11 million barrels per day.[37]

The Organization of Petroleum Exporting Countries found itself in a unique position in 2016. With oil supplies increasing sharply from The United States, the OPEC cartel was unable to exert the same power over oil supplies that it had enjoyed since the 1970s. But it has never had as much power as people think. In the 1970s gas prices increased tremendously in response to the Arab Oil Embargo of 1973, strikes in the Iranian oil fields, and the

Do we owe North Dakota a thank you note?

Iranian revolution of 1979. At that time OPEC thought that it could get away with "practically anything with respect to price."[38] Soon, high prices acted as a magnet that drew in production from the North Sea and Alaska, which caused an increase in supply, lower prices, and the collapse of oil markets in 1986.

Not only do we still see the temptation to cheat showing up, but we also have the fact that high oil prices has allowed OPEC to invest in new exploration techniques. This expansion in exploration has taken Saudi Arabia alone from 88 billion barrels of proven oil reserves to almost 264 billion barrels.[39]

Now to the demand side of the equation.

In January 2016 crude oil prices fell below $27 per barrel and gasoline prices in much of America approached $1.50 per gallon.

While much (most) of this price collapse was based on the record surge in global supply, there were some demand factors that played in as well.

It might come as a surprise to you, but 2016 saw the overall global demand for oil fall considerably because of weak economic growth in China, the United States and other major oil-consuming nations.[40] In addition to a slowdown in global growth, the significant increase in energy efficient cars, power plants and industrial manufacturing processes helped push down the overall demand for oil.

Figures 7.14-7.16 illustrate the combined effects of an *increase in supply and a decrease in demand.*

First, in figure 7.14 we see the *impact of a large drop in demand and smaller increase in supply.* Suppose over the next few years we see this trend play out. What would be the impact on global prices and the equilibrium quantity of oil and gasoline?

Notice that if demand falls by a larger amount than supply increases (D2 & S2), the downward pressure on prices will take place from both of these events. However, a relatively large decrease in demand, which leads to lower prices and a decrease in quantity supplied, would offset the increase in quantity demanded that comes from the supply increase. In the final equilibrium we would see lower prices and a decline in the world's equilibrium output. For people who are concerned about climate change, this would be a favorable outcome. Yet, for oil field workers around the globe it would be a disaster.

Figure 7.15 illustrates a *decrease in demand and increase in supply of the same magnitude.* In this case we see that both changes force prices down, but the amount of oil produced and consumed does not change over time.

Finally, in figure 7.16 we examine what happened in the world in 2016. There was a somewhat *small decrease in demand but a much larger increase in supply.* This reality led to a collapse in prices in early 2016 and a global glut (oversupply) of oil for much of the year. Any

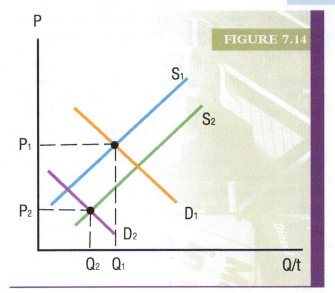

FIGURE 7.14

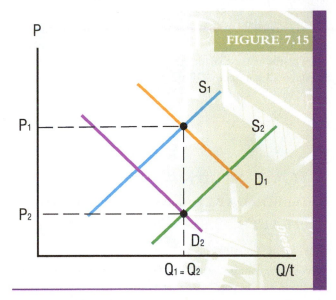

FIGURE 7.15

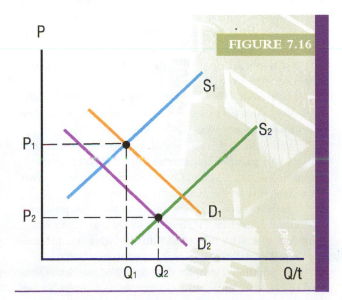

FIGURE 7.16

time supply increases by more than demand decreases you will get a larger equilibrium quantity and lower prices at the same time.

It is important to point out that by the fall of 2016 gasoline prices had risen from nearly $1.50 per gallon in January to over $2 per gallon. A few factors contributed to this increase. First, the historically lower prices caused many independent oil producers to go out of business when they could not afford to pump oil at less than $30 per barrel. This meant that supply decreased somewhat during the latter half of 2016. Also, in October of that year OPEC announced plans to cut production which caused investors in oil contracts to expect higher future prices and therefore reluctant to trade contracts at lower prices.

Hurricane Matthew also led to a sharp increase in demand for gas in Florida and much of the Eastern Seaboard.

By the time you are reading this chapter gasoline could be back to $1.50 per gallon – or closer to the $4 we saw in 2008. No matter what the price, know this…

It is always supply and demand – not a grand conspiracy theory – that drives gas prices. After all, if there is some oil company/OPEC conspiracy they are doing a lousy job of keeping prices high.

CASE STUDY # 8: HOW THE AFFORDABLE CARE ACT MADE HEALTH CARE UNAFFORDABLE

If you are young – and healthy – you better pay close attention to this particular part of this chapter. When you are done reading this case study I would suggest that you flip to the chapter on the economics of health care to learn more. Why? Because in 2009 a law was passed that may end up costing you a fortune.

In a nutshell, before 2009 the market for health insurance worked this way:

If you were 116 years old – and did not have health insurance – buying a policy would have meant paying higher prices than someone who was 36 years old.

If you were 36 years old – and weighed 511 pounds and smoked four packs of cigarettes per day and had a sexually-transmitted disease – attempting to buy a policy would have meant rejection by the health insurance industry.

President Obama thought that these situations presented an unfair marketplace for America so for this – and many, many other reasons, he signed into law what has become known as The Affordable Care Act, or ObamaCare.

The health care chapter provides all of the details you need to know about this law. For purposes of brevity we are going to look at two particular aspects of it and the impact on health insurance markets in the United States.

The 2009 law make it illegal for insurance companies to charge prices based on age and also prohibits health insurance companies from denying coverage for people with pre-existing conditions.

This might sound like a "fair" thing to do – that is until you look at the unintended consequences of these provisions.

During the 2016 presidential campaign, former president Bill Clinton called ObamaCare "crazy". There is a reason for this.

In the wake of the passage of this law insurance companies found out the hard way that the law of demand is called a law for a reason. With no barriers to health insurance – and no ability to charge disparate prices based on age and risk, a tremendous surge of new policy holders among the aged and sick took place. The problem, of course, is that unlike younger, healthier people who pay health insurance premiums each month and rarely use their policies, sicker Americans who got coverage tended to use that coverage right away. That meant that insurance companies were paying out more in coverage than they were receiving in premiums and the losses began to mount. For example, Blue Cross Blue Shield of Texas lost $416 million in 2014 and $592 million in 2015.[41]

Facing this historic increase in the demand for insurance policies and no legal ability to maintain profits, 2016 was a watershed year in America's health insurance market. Simply put, in that year a trend began taking place that may

A Bigger Bite

Middle-class families' spend on health care has increased 25% since 2007. Other basic needs, such as clothing and food, have decreased.

Percent change in middle-income households' spending on basic needs (2007 to 2014)

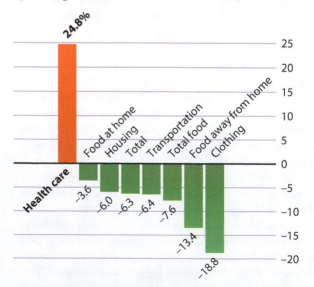

Sources: Brookings Institution analysis of Consumer Expenditure Survey, Labor Department

have ramifications for years to come as health insurance companies began leaving many of the most expensive states to do business in.

Figures 7.17-7.19 illustrates what came next.

In figure 7.17 we examine the impact of a *large decrease in supply and smaller increase in demand*. The decrease in supply comes from the number of sellers in the insurance market decreasing while the increase in demand stems from the new patients signing up for insurance. As you can see, if demand increases to D2 and supply decreases to S2, the overall effect is a large increase in health insurance prices and fewer total policies being written.

In figure 7.18 we have a *decrease in supply and increase in demand of the same magnitude*. In this case there is still an increase in prices but the final equilibrium quantity of policies remains unchanged.

Finally, in 7.19 the situation is reflected by a *large increase in demand and smaller drop in supply*. Here, we end up with an increase in prices but also an increase in the number of policies written as the impact of the demand change offsets the impact of the supply change.

Notice that in *all three cases* prices have to go up! This is exactly what happened in 2016. In state after state insurance premiums jumped by the largest amounts ever recorded in the U.S. with premiums rising by 18-23% on average.[42]

As the accompanying chart illustrates, the share of household budgets allocated to health care has increased dramatically since the passage of The Affordable Care Act. The Kaiser Family Foundation found that deductibles for individual workers increased 67% from 2010 to 2016 while patient cost-sharing rose by 77% during that time.[43]

Now comes the important part. You might have read this section thinking, "Why didn't people just refuse to buy insurance?"

In case you have been paying no attention to this powerful law, you missed a significant provision that made it illegal to not have insurance. That's right. For the first time since 1776 the U.S. government decided that it wanted to force you to engage in commerce whether you like it or not.

If you refuse, the Internal Revenue Service levied a penalty of $695 or 2.5% of your income.

In 2016 16% of Americans from the age of 25 to 34 had opted to pay the fine rather than get insurance.[44] This is one reason for the spike in health insurance premiums. President Obama was counting on young – and healthy – Americans to sign up in large enough numbers to generate sufficient income for the health insurance companies. Without the young and healthy paying every month the revenue is not there to pay for the older and/or sicker people.

President Trump promised to repeal and replace ObamaCare during his run to the White House. In the health care chapter we will examine his proposal to change to health savings accounts and what that would (does) mean for Americans.

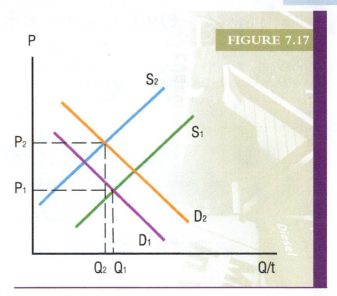

FIGURE 7.17

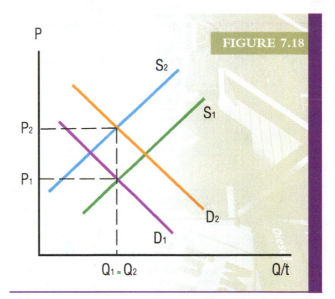

FIGURE 7.18

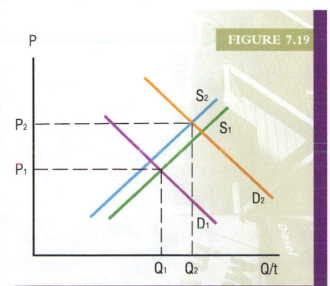

FIGURE 7.19

SUMMARY – SIMULTANEOUS CHANGES IN DEMAND AND SUPPLY

The table that follows summarizes all the possible combinations of simultaneous changes in supply and demand and the effect on the market equilibrium price and output level. It is again important to remind you to practice by creating your own examples from the news or newspaper. This is the most efficient way of learning this material.

IF	AND	THEN
Demand increases	Supply increases by less than demand increases	Equilibrium output will increase and price will increase
Demand increases	Supply increases by an equal amount	Equilibrium output will increase and price will not change
Demand increases	Supply increases by more than demand increases	Equilibrium output will increase and price will decrease
Demand decreases	Supply decreases by less than demand	Equilibrium output will decrease and price will decrease
Demand decreases	Supply decreases by the same/ equal amount than demand	Equilibrium output will decrease and price will not change
Demand decreases	Supply decreases by more than demand	Equilibrium output will decrease and price will increase
Demand decreases	Supply increases by more than demand	Equilibrium output will increase and price will decrease
Demand decreases	Supply increases by the same/ equal amount than demand	Equilibrium output will not change and price will decrease
Demand decreases	Supply increases by less than demand	Equilibrium output will decrease and price will decrease
Demand increases	Supply decreases by more than demand	Equilibrium output will decrease and price will increase
Demand increases	Supply decreases by the same/ equal amount than demand	Equilibrium output will not change and price will increase
Demand increases	Supply decreases by less than demand	Equilibrium output will increase and price will increase

ENDNOTES

1 See "Car lots suffering fuel sadly" by Andy Vuong, *The Denver Post*, June 12, 2008; "Local car buyers dream small" by John Gillie, *The News Tribune* (Tacoma, WA), July 13, 2008; and "Used small cars net big bucks" by Tom Krisher, *The Orlando Sentinel*, May 23, 2008.

2 See "A Retail Mixed Bag" by Jackie Crosby, *The Star Tribune* (Minneapolis, MN), August 8, 2008.

3 See "Drop in Home Prices Accelerates to 14.1%" by Sudeep Reddy, *The Wall Street Journal*, May 28, 2008.

4 See http://www.wsj.com/articles/food-price-deflation-cheers-consumers-hurts-farmers-grocers-and-restaurants-1472490823.

5 See "Football Fans Forgo Tickets, Prefer View from the Couch" by Kevin Clark & Jonathan Clegg, *The Wall Street Journal*, January 4-5, 2014.

6 Source: December 2010 interview with Dennis Stoltzfoos.

7 See "Grass-Fed Beef Is on a Roll" by Ellen Byron and Sarah Nassauer, The Wall Street Journal, September 21, 2016.

8 See "Oysters, a New Orleans Staple, Are Latest Victim" by Perry Stein, *The Wall Street Journal*, June 19-20, 2010.

9 See http://www.washingtonpost.com/blogs/plum-line/wp/2014/01/20/obama-nudges-the-ball-forward-on-marijuana/

10 See "Sorry, We're Booked: The Restaurant Slump Ends" by Katy McLauglin, *The Wall Street Journal*, March 30, 2004, p. D1.

11 See "Strapped shoppers try Amish Salvage" by Meghan Barr, *The Orlando Sentinel*, May 24, 2008, pg. A17.

12 In fact, by the time you are reading this, you may have already purchased the first $100 laptop. See "$100 Laptop Moves Closer to Reality" by Steve Stecklow, *The Wall Street Journal*, November 14, 2005.

13 See "Cordless Computers Get Affordable" by Nick Wingfield, *The Wall Street Journal*, June 26, 2002, p. D1; and "Is It Time to Get a DVD Burner?" by Anna Wilde Mathews, *The Wall Street Journal*, December 18, 2002, p. D1.

14 See "Job Outpouring For Evacuees Sparks Backlash" by Ilan Brat and Janet Adamy, *The Wall Street Journal*, September 13, 2005, page B1; and "Louisiana Frets About Job Poaching" by Jeff D. Opdyke and Dionne Searcey, *The Wall Street Journal*, September 12, 2005.

15 See "How a Jury Decided That a Coffee Spill is Worth $2.9 million" by Andrea Gerlin, *The Wall Street Journal*, September 1, 1994.

16 See "$67 Million Pants," *The Wall Street Journal*, June 26, 2007.

17 See "When All Else Fails, The American Way is to File a Lawsuit" *The Wall Street Journal*, November 14, 2000; and "Is Food the Next Tobacco?" by Shelly Branch, *The Wall Street Journal*, June 13, 2002.

18 See "Wipeout for Key Player in Surfboard Industry" by Peter Sanders and Stephanie Kang, *The Wall Street Journal*, December 8, 2005.

19 See "After Mad-Cow Scare, German Pigs, Farmers 'Enjoy' More Quality Time" by Vanessa Furhmans, *The Wall Street Journal*, March 6, 2002.

20 See "To Central Florida surfers, factory closing's a wipeout" by Harry Wessel, *The Orlando Sentinel*, December 8, 2005.

21 See "Surfboard Costs Subside" *The Orlando Sentinel*, February 4, 2006.

22 See "How America Lost Its Way" by Niall Ferguson, *The Wall Street Journal*, June 8-9, 2013 page C1.

23 See "Increase ethanol production?" by Lynn Edward Weaver, *The Orlando Sentinel*, June 24, 2007.

24 See "Green Dreams" by Joel K. Bourne Jr., *National Geographic*, October 2007.

25 See "Corn pops back, may be 2nd largest crop" by Sue Kirchhoff, *USA Today*, August 13, 2008, pg. 13.

26 See http://www.wsj.com/articles/as-crop-prices-fall-farmers-focus-on-seeds-1476669901.

27 See "Historic Surge in Grain Prices Roils Markets" by Scott Kilman, *The Wall Street Journal*, September 28, 2007.

28 See "Europeans backpedal on switch to biofuels" by James Kanter, *The Oregonian*, July 8, 2008.

29 See "Ethanol vs. the World" *The Wall Street Journal*, August 11-12, 2012 page A16.

30 See "Wheat Prices Surge to a Two-Year High" by Tom Polansek, *The Wall Street Journal*, December 29, 2010, p. C10; and "Prices Soar on South America Drought" by Liam Pleven and Matt Moffett, *The Wall Street Journal*, December 30, 2010.

31 See "Let's have an honest debate about immigration in the U.S." by Bonnie Ross, *The Orlando Sentinel*, September 1, 2015.

32 See "The Mythical Connection Between Immigrants and Crime" by Jason L. Riley, *The Wall Street Journal*, July 14, 2015.

33 See "Even at $17 an Hour, Farms Can't Fill Jobs" by Ilan Brat, *The Wall Street Journal*, August 13, 2015.

34 See "The Costs of Mass Deportation" *The Wall Street Journal*, March 19-20, 2016.

35 See "Another bubble – commodities - may have burst" by Stevenson Jacobs, *The Star Tribune* (Minneapolis, MN), August 9, 2008, pg. D1.

36 See "A Black-Gold Rush in Alberta" by Tamsin Carlisle, *The Wall Street Journal*, September 15, 2005; and "Tides turn for companies that seek new energy sources" by Paul Luke, *The Edmonton Journal*, July 26, 2008.

37 See "U.S. Redraws World Oil Map" by Benoit Faucon & Keith Johnson, *The Wall Street Journal*, November 13, 2012.

38 See *The Prize: The Epic Quest for Oil, Money and Power* by Daniel Yergin, Simon & Schuster, New York, 1992.

39 See "Some Wonder if the Surging Oil Market is Ignoring Supply and Demand" by Simon Romero, *The New York Times*, March 15, 2005; and "The Oil Bubble" *The Wall Street Journal*, October 8-9, 2005.

40 See http://www.wsj.com/articles/global-demand-growth-for-oil-may-fall-by-a-third-in-2016-1445430195.

41 See "More Insurers looking to raise Obamacare rates" by Ricardo Alonso-Zaldivar, *The Orlando Sentinel*, June 2, 2016.

42 See "ObamaCare Sticker Shock" *The Wall Street Journal*, August 13-14, 2016 and "Insurers Seek Big Premium Boosts" by Louise Radnofsky, The Wall Street Journal, May 26, 2016.

43 See "Health Burden Moves to the Middle" by Anna Louie Sussman, *The Wall Street Journal*, August 26, 2016.

44 See "A Millennial's ObamaCare Lament" By David Barnes, *The Wall Street Journal*, September 26, 2016.

CHAPTER REVIEW

1. The May 5, 2016 *Wall Street Journal* reported that consumer tastes for chickens that grow more slowly and are treated humanely has increased sharply. Graphically illustrate and explain what this would mean for this market-place over time.

2. On April 27, 2013 the *Savannah Morning News* reported that growing demand for baby food in China had caused shortages of baby food in Europe. On two graphs, illustrate and explain what was happening in China and Europe.

3. The June 3, 2014 *Tulsa World* reported that greater EPA rules and regulations threaten to increase the input costs of supplying electric power. Graphically illustrate and explain what this would mean for electric power consumers.

4. Suppose the number of buyers in the market for camping tents increases next year while the input costs associated with making tents decreases. If the impact of falling input costs is greater than the impact of more buyers in the market, what will be the effect on tent prices and the final equilibrium quantity?

Chapter Eight

GOVERNMENT INTERFERENCE *in the* MARKET

Photo courtesy Jack Chambless

*G*overnment's view of the economy could be summed up this way. If it moves, tax it. If it keeps moving, regulate it. If it stops moving, subsidize it.

RONALD REAGAN

THE VISIBLE FOOT

In much of America it is legal to consume cigarettes, but not marijuana. You can visit a strip club, but not a prostitute. You may abort an unborn child, but you cannot kill yourself with the aid of a doctor. You can drink whiskey all day long, but you cannot bet on National Football League games. You can get tattoos placed all over your body, but you cannot drive a motorcycle without a helmet. You can sell your house for an unlimited amount of profit, but you cannot sell a ticket to a sporting event for more than $1 above face value. You can buy books on satanic cults, visit a body-piercing establishment, and watch graphic horror movies but you cannot buy wine on Sunday in many cities.

A major question that every market-based economy must answer is, to what extent certain market activities should be regulated, taxed, or banned outright. This is a very difficult issue because it delves into the rights of the individual and our property, versus the rights of the public to go unharmed by negative externalities.

> ➤ **A negative externality exists when the transaction between two parties impacts a third party who was not part of the transaction.**

Who determines the definition of the word "harm"? How much of a negative externality is acceptable? How should negative externalities be dealt with? Consider the following:

THE ECONOMICS OF BILLBOARDS

In 1999 I was traveling on the Florida Turnpike with my daughter, who was six at the time. When we were approximately an hour south of Gainesville, she looked up and saw a billboard advertising an adult entertainment club.

Having learned to read months earlier, she said, "Daddy, what does 'We bare all' mean?"

Naturally, this question caused me to come close to wrapping my car around a tree, but I quickly recovered from the trauma of my little girl's exposure to the "real world." I attempted to explain to her that there are certain things that are difficult for her to understand and that when she is a little older, I would try to clear up the meaning of this billboard.

I have no idea what an expert in child psychology would say about my approach to this sticky situation, but I wonder if I should be allowed to ask what in the world a billboard like that is doing near a public road? After all, isn't it one thing to allow someone the right to visit a strip club, but an entirely different matter to have the advertisement for the strip club imposed upon unwilling drivers who are offended by this industry? The line isn't very clear. First, the billboard was sitting on private property, and the U.S. Constitution is very clear on the rights of the individual to use their property in a manner that does not violate the rights of others. Second, the billboard does not depict naked women.

Nonetheless, if I was (am) offended, do I have the right to argue that the rights of the property owner and the strip club have violated my rights to not be harmed by such a display? Should I find a new route to travel in Florida? Should the billboard be able to show naked women? Should we remove religious billboards that offend atheists? What about billboards featuring fast-food restaurants? Are they offensive to vegetarians and people with weight problems?

What then, is the proper role of government in our economic system? When should our freedom be reined in for the betterment of society? To the extent that freedom has shown to be a valuable tool for helping human beings, most economists suggest that government exercise a great deal of caution when considering what markets to interfere with.

Of course, we have to realize that what makes good economic sense may not get politicians elected! This means that often politicians feel compelled to alter the final market outcome in the name of the public good or some normative definition of fairness. When the government decides to interfere with the natural workings of the free market, it usually takes the form of:

- Forcing prices downward through price ceilings and laws against unfair pricing
- Forcing prices upward through artificial price supports and minimum wages
- Banning the good or service
- Regulating the manner in which the good or service is sold
- Creating regulations or subsidies to impact prices and output

As the following examples will illustrate, when political pressures rather than economic principles determine public policy, some very bizarre, inefficient, and even deadly outcomes can, and do, emerge.

WAL-MART AND THE GERMAN GOVERNMENT

Decades ago, Sam Walton envisioned a time when consumers in small and mid-size towns could have access to the same goods and services as citizens in large towns, without having to pay relatively high prices. His vision led to the creation of today's retail giant known as Wal-Mart. With low prices and large shopping selections, Wal-Mart has put intense competitive pressure on other retail establishments.

This seems to be a good thing for budget-conscious Americans. Just don't tell that to German bureaucrats in that nation's cartel office that ordered Wal-Mart and retailers Aldi Nord and Lidl Stiftung & Company to raise prices on items like milk, sugar, and flour or face fines up to $443,900.[1] Why?

As it turns out, Wal-Mart is just too good at discounting prices. According to the German government, Wal-Mart deliberately discounted prices in Germany in order to hurt smaller competing retail companies. The government felt that, while this practice helped consumers in the short term, it would hurt small and medium-sized rivals that "can't match the lower prices."

Wal-Mart's entry into Germany created 88 superstores[2] and had, according to The Wall Street Journal, "forced rivals to remodel stores, realign prices, and change procurement policies to cut costs." German consumers like Claudia Haemel seemed to like this change. "I have nothing against these prices if it makes basic foods cheaper for the consumer," she says.

The German government seems to believe it knows best what Claudia should pay for food. It doesn't matter much now, because in 2006 Wal-Mart announced that it was closing all of its stores in Germany.

ABORTION? LEGAL. SELLING A KIDNEY? FIVE YEARS IN PRISON...

On Oct. 5, 1983, Al Gore – at the time a representative from Tennessee – sponsored a Senate bill that became the 1984 National Organ Transplant Act. He worked vigorously to get this bill passed. But were his efforts misguided?

If you, a friend or loved one aren't waiting for an organ, you probably aren't familiar with Title III of this law, which makes the selling of any organ a federal crime, an act penalized at a maximum of $50,000 or five years in prison – or both.

The legislation doesn't note that the person selling the organ could benefit because of the monies received, nor is there any mention of how the potential recipient, who may die if a kidney isn't recovered, could benefit from this voluntary transaction. Most importantly, there's no mention that this transaction takes place between two emancipated humans and doesn't deny anyone else the right to life, liberty and the pursuit of happiness.

A nationwide shortage has created a bleak outlook for those who are waiting for a new lease on life. In January 2016, The United Network for Organ Sharing reported that 119,939 individuals were waiting for organs.[3] One could easily conclude that there aren't enough organs to go around, but this is far from the truth.

SUGGESTED CLASSROOM DEBATE

A few years ago a mother from Maine sued the U.S. Justice Department in an attempt to legalize the buying and selling of bone marrow.[4] All three of her daughters had a disease known as Fanconi anemia – a genetic disorder that causes marrow failure. Should people be allowed to sell their marrow to other people who are willing and able to pay? Why or why not?

The National Organ Transplant Act has helped create this shortage by ignoring the fundamentals of the law of supply and instead relying on a system known as non-price rationing.

> ➤ **Non-price rationing is the practice of rationing a good or service through a waiting line, waiting list, or lottery.**

The first consequence of non-price rationing is the *opportunity cost of wasted time*. In essence, without a free market with equilibrium prices, thousands of people are required to wait in their homes, near a hospital, hoping and praying that an organ will become available. If the market were allowed to work, those same people would be able to find an organ much faster and would not have to spend so much time inefficiently.

The second problem with non-price rationing is that the *seller* (or prospective seller in this case) *fails to maximize revenue*. Many people who donate organs would rather earn some money for their valuable resources. Others who refuse to donate, would do so if they could earn cash for themselves or their family. At a price of $0, we are not given the proper incentives, nor receive the maximum reward for supplying these "products."

The final inefficient outcome is that the *buyer who places the highest value on the good or service, does not necessarily get the good or service*. This means that someone who might be on the list who is willing and able to pay $20,000 for a new kidney, might get one ahead of someone who would have paid $200,000 for one. The person who is lucky enough to be next in line might be 71 years old in declining health, while a 33-year-old mother of four young children is in an unlucky spot in the line. In this case, the younger person might have been willing to sell their home or borrow the money to stay around for their children, while the older person might not decide (in a market system where the price is set by supply and demand) that a new organ is worth the cost.

More and more economists are now lobbying the federal government to change this system by allowing willing buyers and sellers to meet in a formal marketplace and make private exchanges for money or other property.[5] Meanwhile, people wait and suffer.

WHY ECONOMISTS LOVE AUCTIONS

I have never been to Cuba or North Korea. Like most Americans, I can normally find everything I need when I go shopping. However, sometimes I wish more suppliers would use the tools of economics to help me live a less stressful life.

One supplier that comes to mind is the Minnesota Department of Natural Resources. It is this government agency that uses a well-meaning approach to rationing camping spaces that almost gave me a heart attack.

A few years ago I was driving down highway 61 along Minnesota's famous Lake Superior shoreline with the intention of camping in the famous Split Rock Lighthouse state park.

When we arrived at the park office to register for a campsite, we were told that almost all the sites were full and that we would have to be added to a waiting list. The ranger also mentioned that four sites would be opening up at 9 a.m. My name was number five on the list.

Rather than leaving, I hung around just in case any of the four people ahead of me did not show up at 9 a.m. when the rangers planned on registering the lucky few.

The next hour dragged on forever. Every time someone walked into the office I panicked, thinking they were one of my competitors.

At 9 a.m. there were four of us waiting for the names to be called. I was tempted to lock the door just in case one of the people in front of me on the list was about to come in.

Fortunately, the other person ahead of me on the list did not show up, we got a spot for the next few nights and had a great time.

Why did it have to come to this? Why couldn't the state of Minnesota

Photo courtesy Jack Chambless

What is sleeping on this shoreline worth?

opt for a system that would take less time, create less stress, and raise added funds to help count moose and wolves?

The perfect system to ration something that is in short supply is an *auction*. With an auction there could have been 5 or 500 people in the office that day. It would not have mattered. I could have relaxed, had a cup of coffee, and returned at 8:59:59 a.m. At 9 a.m., the ranger could have said, "What am I bid for campsite number ..."

Each of the four sites would have been auctioned off to the highest bidder. Instead of getting $17 per night, the state of Minnesota could have earned $50 a night. For sites closer to Lake Superior, someone might have bid $100 per night.

The bottom line is that an auction could help the market equilibrium appear within seconds; help people who really, really want to sleep in Minnesota's woods get the site they are willing and able to pay for; encourage those who lose out in the bidding to either work harder or save more money for the next time there is an auction and help Minnesota earn more money from its scarce resources.

THE ECONOMICS OF WORLD SERIES (AND OTHER) TICKETS

In an era where we can go online and find concert and sporting event tickets at the click of a mouse, it is somewhat amazing that in many states, it is still illegal to buy and sell tickets for more than face value.

In October 2016 the Chicago Cubs faced off against the Cleveland Indians in Major League Baseball's World Series. The Indians had not won the World Series since 1948. Not to be outdone, the Cubs had not won it all since 1908! This combined record of over 170 years of futility created such a huge demand for World Series tickets that the face value of a few hundred dollars for games in Chicago did not matter. The average ticket to a game at the Cubs home park was over $10,500!

This brings us to the question of whether ticket scalping – the practice of charging more than face value – *should* be illegal. If you think carefully about the full magnitude of this type of transaction, you would be hard-pressed to defend the government's intrusion into

our entertainment life.[6] Where is the harm? The seller offers a product for a price. The buyer decides that price is what they are willing to pay. The buyer gives the seller money, and neither party has inflicted any measurable damage on a third party.

If we argue that the seller is the owner of the ticket, shouldn't sellers be allowed to do whatever they want with *their* property? If you argue that scalping takes advantage of customers, the question is how?

The customer can walk away, if the price is too high. Attending a concert is not one of life's necessities – nor is there a Constitutional guarantee to cheap tickets. Maybe you think that ticket scalping robs the National Football League of money it could have earned. Maybe the NFL should charge the equilibrium price to begin with and there would be no scalping at all.[7]

Notice in the following photo something quite funny. Depicted here are ticket scalpers outside of Florida State University's football stadium. On this day, it was still illegal in Florida to do this. However, the owner of the parking lot they are standing in – who normally lets people park their cars free of charge – is charging $20 per car and no police officers chased him around the block.

It is also somewhat ironic that, if scalpers are forced to charge prices that *are below face value* (a common occurrence for events that do not sell out), there is no law against that.

In August of 2005 I was driving into Chicago with plans to take my family to a Chicago Cubs baseball game. My youngest son, a huge Cubs fan, was so excited he could barely contain himself. I kept telling him there was one potential problem. We did not have any tickets.

Should they be arrested?

Photo courtesy Jack Chambless

The Cubs were playing their arch rivals, the St. Louis Cardinals, which normally means a sell-out and huge profits for scalpers. However, that day it was raining when the game started. I put on a rain jacket and staked out near the main entrance waiting for the scalpers to panic.

After a one-hour delay I finally got what I wanted. One scalper, convinced the game would be rained out, sold me tickets only 15 rows from the field for $8.50 each. The face value of the tickets was $46. Had it not been raining, the tickets would have cost over $100 and my son would have had to watch on television.

Why is it that I am assumed to be smart enough to know when I am getting a good deal, but not smart enough to know when I am getting ripped off?

The final argument by the government is that tickets sold on the black market are not taxed. That is easily fixed, too. Legalize ticket scalping and require tickets to be sold from a legitimate brokerage business. The government can then apply sales tax laws to the product and collect whatever money they deem necessary. Or the government could just let the market fix itself.[8]

This is already happening to an extent. In 2008 the NFL's New York Jets announced that the best seats to their new stadium would be auctioned off on eBay.[9] Eager to get in on profits being earned in the secondary market, other professional sports teams have finally wised up and have begun creating websites where season ticket holders can resell tickets they cannot use. By 2016 many more teams had realized the profitability of the secondary market for tickets. The NHL's Los Angeles Kings announced a policy where brokers could buy tickets and use a website created by the Kings to resell tickets to games where demand is higher than predicted.[10] Of course, the teams get a percentage of any transaction, but at least everyone wins in this situation. Someone who might get a chance of being close to the action once in a season fills the seat. The season ticket holder gets some extra money, as does the team. Should this be illegal, too?

The bottom line is that, from the economic perspective, it seems to be a colossal waste of taxpayer money to have the police arresting people for interjecting the lessons of Adam Smith into a market sorely in need of the invisible hand.

THE ECONOMICS OF PRICE CEILINGS

So far, we have seen how the government tries to force prices down by making certain discounts illegal and by outlawing private property exchange. In the case of price ceilings, the government actually enters the market and picks the price for the buyer and seller!

Consider the market for apartments in Santa Monica for a moment. For 20 years, this beautiful city in southern California was home to more than just surfers and sushi bars. It was also home to a great deal of economic illiteracy in the form of rent-controlled apartments. Figure 8.1 illustrates this fact.

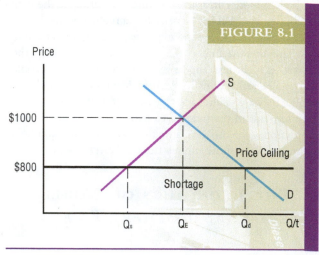

FIGURE 8.1

Back in the 1970s, the Santa Monica government decided that many people — mostly the poor and young — simply could not afford to rent an apartment in this increasingly affluent city. In order to make this market more equitable, the government voted to impose a price ceiling on apartments in this city.

> ➤ **A price ceiling is an artificial limit on what a business can charge for a good or service. Usually, the price ceiling is set below the market equilibrium price.**

Suppose that, at the time of this ruling, the average equilibrium price of an apartment was $1,000 per month. A price ceiling of $800 per month would, in theory, lead to greater assistance for the targeted groups. In reality, rent control in Santa Monica and other cities that jumped on this bandwagon of good intentions led to an increase in the quantity of apartments demanded, but also a decrease in the quantity of apartments supplied.

Many landlords simply vacated their buildings or turned them into condominiums. In New York City, rent control programs that were started in 1947 prompted some building owners to burn their buildings down to collect insurance, rather than rent them out at unprofitable prices. The result has been major shortage of apartments and no significant help for the very people that the law was intended to assist. Approximately 70% of New York's apart-

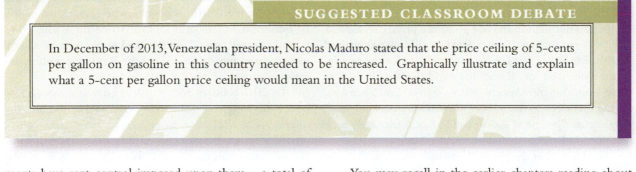

In December of 2013, Venezuelan president, Nicolas Maduro stated that the price ceiling of 5-cents per gallon on gasoline in this country needed to be increased. Graphically illustrate and explain what a 5-cent per gallon price ceiling would mean in the United States.

ments have rent control imposed upon them – a total of over 1.32 million units. Fully 35% of the people who live in these apartments have incomes of over $50,000 per year and 87,358 of these "apartments for the poor" have tenants who earn more than $100,000 per year.[11]

It is interesting to note that rent control was eventually lifted in Santa Monica. As expected, rents initially shot up to well over $1,000 per month. At these prices, *The Wall Street Journal* reported that surpluses broke out. Over time, prices began to come back down toward a market equilibrium condition.[12]

HOW PRICE CEILINGS HELPED DESTROY THE SOVIET UNION

The dustbin of history is littered with the remains of those countries which relied on diplomacy to secure their freedom. We must never forget in the final analysis that it is our military, industrial and economic strength that offers the best guarantee of peace for America in times of danger.

Ronald Reagan, address as Governor of California, 1974

1980 was a terrible year in American history. The overall level of unemployment was on the rise, inflation hit a one-year record of 13.5%, and the economy was in a recession. Making matters worse was an ongoing increase in crude oil prices and a hostage crisis in Iran that paralyzed the nation and the presidency of Jimmy Carter.

In the meantime, the Soviet Union was not standing still in its attempts to push the doctrine of communism on the rest of the world. Tremendous inroads were made in Asia, Africa, and Latin America, while the Soviet Union's stranglehold in Eastern Europe and influence in the Middle East remained strong. In 1980 the Soviet Union invaded Afghanistan in a move that stunned the world. On the surface, the Soviet Union looked invincible. But deep inside the economic corridors of the USSR, the foundation of communism was crumbling under the weight of massive shortages.

You may recall in the earlier chapters reading about the implementation of production quotas and price ceilings by Josef Stalin. Under this centrally planned system, the Soviet government hoped to simultaneously prevent the pursuit of profit and hold down prices for consumers. Figure 8.2 illustrates the problems this system created.

You might find yourself wondering whether the shortages were a big deal to the Soviet people. After all, for decades they had accepted the long lines and empty shelves.

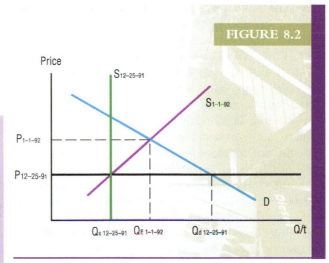

FIGURE 8.2

The Soviet people accepted this condition because to complain about it openly could lead to execution or slave labor camps. It was not until 1981 that the Soviet leadership began to worry about where shortages might lead them.

In 1980, Ronald Reagan easily won the presidency over Jimmy Carter and subsequently pushed for a massive buildup in America's military power. Hundreds of billions of dollars later, the United States was in an accelerated arms race with our Cold War rivals.

Mikhail Gorbachev, the last Soviet leader Reagan would deal with, faced a big problem in trying to keep up with the military spending that was taking place in America. While the United States was enjoying record prosperity during the 1980s, the Soviet Union was floundering.

This came to pass because, in the U.S., the military and the private sector are essentially separate entities. The Reagan administration did not go to the private sector and take away resources to be redirected to military production. The private sector was left alone to provide for the people. In the Soviet Union, the military and private production came from the same source – the government. Therefore, during the 1980s, as the military demanded more and more resources, the people of Russia had to face increasingly long lines for food, clothing, and other necessities.

Realizing that the people were suffering and that dissent was mounting, Gorbachev embarked on a campaign known as *perestroika* (restructuring) and *glasnost* (openness). Under these two reforms, Gorbachev sought to allow more private control over the means of production and the profit that might result from it. In addition, he allowed people to be more openly critical of the government – hoping that these changes would ease some of the pressure that was building behind the Iron Curtain. It was too late. As the Soviet Union lost the economic and political ability to maintain power throughout Eastern Europe, one by one those nations that had lived under the shadow of tyranny broke away and pushed for democratic reforms.

In September of 1991, a military coup in the Soviet Union led to the ousting of Gorbachev and the ascension of Boris Yeltsin as the eventual president of Russia.[13]

It is stunning that Gorbachev was not thrown out for violating the basic tenants of communism. He was thrown out because, once people gained a taste of political and economic freedom, there was no amount of moral or military force that could contain their demands to accelerate the march toward democracy and free markets.

On Christmas day of 1991, with the Soviet Union bankrupt, Gorbachev officially dissolved this once-feared and seemingly invincible nation and allowed the individual republics to operate on their own. Six days later, Mr. Yeltsin removed most of the price ceilings and production controls in Russia. The result was mass chaos, as prices increased by *300%* for the most basic goods and services! However, shoppers immediately noticed more of everything in Russian stores. As can be seen in figure 8.2, lifting the ceilings and the production controls meant that Russian suppliers were given the proper incentives to increase production.

Today, Russia is on a journey toward freer markets. It has not been easy. The Russian mafia is a significant problem. Tax collections are sporadic. Abuses of private property and widespread hunger are omnipresent, and the Communists are wrestling to regain power, as Vladimir Putin's invasion of Ukraine illustrated. Some economists have expressed concern that Russia has backtracked on protection of private property and wealth accumulation. The arrest of Mikhail Khodorkovsky, the head of the Yukos oil company, is one example of why some are worried about Russia's future.[14]

If Russia makes the final painful turn and beats back the calls for the return of government control, we will all be better off. Russia had seemed to be on a path committed to freer trade, flat taxes, and more sound financial management, which has helped the Russian economy see some economic growth.[15]

By 2016 Russia's economy was once again staggering under the weight of falling oil prices (a key export) and international reluctance to engage in business or tourist activities in an increasingly hostile environment. Thus, Russia's transition to a market-based economy is at best, incomplete.

This painful transition could have been avoided. In 1917, Russia had a choice between two economists – Adam Smith or Karl Marx. They simply picked the wrong one.

WAS RONALD REAGAN SIMPLY IN THE RIGHT PLACE AT THE RIGHT TIME?

The following quotes are from economists prior to the collapse of the Soviet Union.

> The Soviet economy has made great national progress in recent years.
>
> John Kenneth Galbraith, Harvard University

> It is a vulgar mistake to think that most people in Eastern Europe are miserable.
>
> Paul Samuelson, Nobel Laureate

> Can economic command significantly compress and accelerate the growth process? The remarkable performance of the Soviet Union suggests that it can. In 1920 Russia was but a minor figure in the economic councils of the world. Today it is a country whose economic achievements bear comparison with those of the United States.
>
> Lester Thurow, Massachusetts Institute of Technology

Why were the prominent economists wrong? How could Reagan have seen the demise of Marxism nine years before the Soviet Union collapsed? In the early '60s many political and economic experts believed that the United States and the Soviet Union were destined to go to war. The prevailing "wisdom" was that the only way war could be averted was to engage in commerce with the Soviet Union, contain communism where we could, and not engage in acts that were seen by the USSR as provocative. Reagan did not share this view. In 1963 Reagan argued:

If we relieve the strain on the shaken Russian economy by aiding their enslaved satellites (Eastern Europe and Cuba), thus reducing the danger of uprising and revolution, and if we continue granting concessions which reduce our military strength giving Russia time to improve hers as well as shore up her limping industrial complex – aren't we perhaps adding to the communist belief that their system will through evolution catch up and pass ours?

If we truly believe that our way of life is best aren't the Russians more likely to recognize that fact and modify their stand if we let their economy come unhinged so that contrast is apparent? Inhuman though it may sound, shouldn't we throw the whole burden of feeding the satellites on their slave masters who are having trouble feeding themselves?[16]

Eighteen years later, as president of the United States, Ronald Reagan fully implemented the incredible vision he singularly held in 1963. By halting trade in the area of military equipment and petroleum technologies Reagan ravaged the Russian economy and forced a deep recession in the Soviet Union.

By building up the U.S. military – and simultaneously cutting taxes and deregulating the private sector – Reagan helped launch an economic boom in the United States that created $400 billion in extra revenue for the government.

The Soviet Union tried to keep up, but the centrally planned economy was doomed to failure. It simply could not adapt fast enough. It could not offer its people the proper incentives to produce. It could not offer the average Soviet citizen any reason to believe that working for the government was better than working for one's own self-interest.

In June of 1982, in an address to the British Parliament, Ronald Reagan said,

In an ironic sense, Karl Marx was right. We are witnessing today a great revolutionary crisis – a crisis where the demands of the economic order are colliding directly with those of the political order. But the crisis is happening not in the free, non-Marxist west, but in the home of Marxism-Leninism, the Soviet Union. What we see here is a political structure that no longer corresponds to its economic base, a society where productive forces are hampered by political ones.

Economists are very bright people. Sometimes we make predictions that are accurate. In the great battle of ideas that pitted the free-market vision of Ronald Reagan against the iron fist of communism, Reagan seemed to see what no one else could see.

The world is indeed fortunate that he had the opportunity to put his vision for our nation – and the world – to a test. That test lasted from 1981 to 1989. In just eight short years, Mr. Reagan managed to undo almost 75 years of Marxist ideology. The people of Eastern Europe and the former Soviet Union have more freedom than at any time in recent history. Estonia has even passed the United States in the rankings of economic freedom.[17]

To say that Reagan was simply in the right place at the right time is not an intellectually honest assessment of his presidency. If the Soviet Union would have eventually failed anyway – as Reagan's critics are quick to argue – the question that must be asked is, how – and due to what forces – would the collapse have taken place? There was no sign that the USSR was ready to collapse until it was *forced* to the brink of bankruptcy.

It should also be noted that the Cold War of 1947-1991 was ended without any Americans dying on Soviet soil. It was ended with zero missiles being fired from the Soviet arsenal of 45,000 nuclear weapons.

In an era when the U.S. is concerned about other nations having weapons of mass destruction, it is all the more impressive that our arch-enemy – an enemy that considered starting WWIII as its economy spiraled downward – never attacked us. The U.S. won the Cold War by destroying an ideology from within the borders of the enemy. We won because of the moral superiority of liberty over tyranny. For this, it could be argued, all of us owe Ronald Reagan a great deal of gratitude.

THE ECONOMICS OF PRICE FLOORS

In the 1930s, American farmers were ravaged by falling prices for a number of agricultural products. The Great Depression caused a staggering decline in household income, which translated into stagnant demand for food and into bankruptcy for many family farms. In response to this collapse in prices, farmers across the nation appealed to Franklin Roosevelt to do something to save farmers.

CONCEPT CHECK

A humanities professor at Valencia College once argued that, "No American should be allowed to earn over $250,000 per year." Graphically illustrate and explain what would happen in U.S. labor markets if his wish became a reality.

The resulting aid – which is still in place today – took the form of *agricultural price supports* as depicted in figure 8.3.

Suppose the price of milk is $2.75 per gallon in its equilibrium state. You might wonder where you could get milk for such a good deal. Don't spend too much time shopping around, because it will be an exercise in futility. Dairy producers in this country have tapped into one of the most lucrative forms of welfare that has ever been conjured up by Washington, D.C.

In this case, dairy farmers (and producers of a number of other commodities) do not have to worry about the price of milk falling to a level that will jeopardize their profits. That is because the government has imposed, on their behalf, a price floor well above the market equilibrium price of milk.

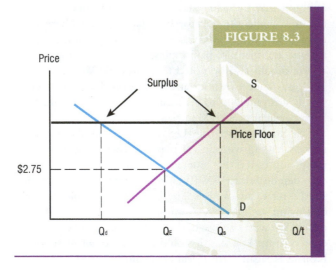

> ➤ **A price floor is an artificial limit on how far prices can fall in a particular market. Usually, a price floor is set above the market equilibrium price.**

The price floor tells the dairy producer to take his milk to the market and charge whatever he thinks he can get. If consumers do not purchase the milk that is offered up, the federal government will step in and buy the milk from the producer – at the floor price!

The result is straightforward and predictable. The quantity of milk demanded comes down due to the higher price. However, the quantity of milk supplied increases. After all, if the government is going to buy up any milk that is not purchased in the open market, wouldn't the dairy farmer be crazy to not increase production? For taxpayers, the result has been less than ideal.[18] Even if prices in the free market are low, some farmers do quite well. Consider this:

- From 2007 to 2008 total farm income increased by 56% to $92.3 billion.
- From 2009 to 2010 farmland values rose 10% while the residential and commercial real estate values plummeted.[19]
- The average farmer in America had an annual income of $121,600 in 2015.
- 75% of all price support payments are given to the wealthiest 10% of the farmers.
- The average farmer in America has an income that is 30% higher than the average for all other workers.
- The average net worth for an American farmer is over $830,000.[20]

As a result of price floors in agricultural markets, enormous surpluses have sprung up from time to time. Some of the surplus food rots. Some is given away in federal food relief programs overseas. Some is given to poor people in this country. In the past, the government has tried everything from paying farmers to kill their excess cows to paying them not to produce milk![21]

The surpluses end up being paid for by consumers in several ways. First, you pay artificially higher prices at the grocery store, because the

Guilty of plunder?

farmers send the food to market at prices near the floor level. In 2013 alone, Americans paid $14 billion more for groceries as a result of price supports. Farmers don't care if you buy their products at these inflated prices because whatever you don't buy, the government gets out of your other pocket – using your tax dollars to relieve the plight of corporate farms.

By the way, those milk ads that you sometimes see with celebrities posing with milk mustaches? You helped pay for those, too! Years ago, the dairy industry convinced Congress that they needed help slowing down the decline in milk consumption in the United States. $169 million dollars later, you helped develop – unbeknownst to you – these ads.[22]

It should be comforting for you to know that, after the milk ad campaign began, the consumption *fell* by over 4%. Don't expect to see the ads cancelled, though. According to the milk industry, they need to keep spending your money on the ads, or demand might fall even faster. Only in Washington, D.C., is an ad campaign that fails to boost sales seen as a successful ad campaign.

Perhaps we taxpayers should create our own billboard ad campaign in Washington that shows a perplexed milk consumer asking "Got common sense?"

Does it matter to Uncle Sam that most farmers who receive the subsidies have net incomes of over $100,000 per year? No, not really. After all, it is not the politician's money that is being transferred to farmer Bob. It is your money. In fact, the top 1% of farmers – 24,111 recipients – "raked in $13.5 billion over five years, an average of $558,698 per farmer."[23]

Ted Turner – yes the same billionaire who founded CNN – got some free money, as did at least 20 Fortune 500 companies and 1,200 universities.[24] Other "farmers" getting your money included ExxonMobil, Chevron, International Paper and Caterpillar.

It should also be pointed out that many critics of our farm subsidy programs cite the implicitly racist outcomes that many agricultural price supports create.[25] The peanut program, for example, provides generous subsidies for southern peanut farmers. In order to prevent rampant surpluses from emerging, the government assigned quotas to various peanut farms during the 1930s that limited how much each farm could produce.

These quotas were handed out during a time when most of the farms were white-owned. Black farmers today are often not allowed to participate in the peanut program since they were not farming peanuts when the quota was established. It is a bit ironic that it was a black man – George Washington Carver who was almost solely responsible for discovering all of the various uses for peanuts.

MINIMUM WAGE LAWS

We continue to look at initiatives and how we work to offset any impacts of future wage inflation through technology initiatives, whether that's customer self-order kiosks, whether that's automating more in the back of the house in the restaurant. And you'll see a lot more coming on that front later this year from us.[26]

Todd Penegor, CFO, Wendy's

A final, but no less controversial, example of the impact price floors have can be found in many inner cities and impoverished rural areas around our country.

Franklin Roosevelt was on a roll in the 1930s when it came to propping up sellers in America. At about the same time the farmers were lining up for their taxpayer-funded aid program, Mr. Roosevelt signed into law the first federal minimum wage. The well-intended law was designed to increase the hourly earnings of poor Americans who were suffering from the Depression.

While the Depression ended in the 1930s, the minimum wage lives on. What few people realize is that the people who were supposed to be helped by this price floor in unskilled labor markets have often fallen victim to government's attempt to repeal the law of demand.

CONCEPT CHECK

U.S peanut farmers receive federal subsidies of $125,000 per year. Because of these subsidies, large peanut surpluses have emerged. The U.S. governments' response to this surplus has been to give away the peanuts (for free) to Haiti.[27] Haiti has 150,000 peanut farmers. Graphically illustrate and explain the impact of dumping American peanuts in Haiti.

Figures 8.4 and 8.5 illustrate the disparate impact the minimum wage has on entry-level workers.

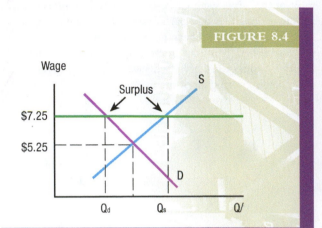

FIGURE 8.4

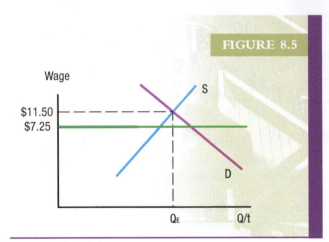

FIGURE 8.5

Suppose the equilibrium wage rate for fast-food workers is $5.25 per hour in Yuma, Arizona. Yuma had an unemployment rate of over 20% in 2016. Suppose employees in Bismarck, North Dakota – where unemployment was about 2.2% – can command $11.50 per hour.[28] With the federal government providing a price floor of $7.25 per hour, notice that the overall quantity of labor demanded in Yuma decreases.

This is because many small business owners, who operate on very thin profit margins, are often unable to absorb forced increases in wage rates. If fast-food restaurants were left alone in Yuma, wages would fall to $5.25. That would mean more teenagers and unskilled workers finding employment. At the mandated wage of $7.25 the quantity of labor supplied is greater than the quantity demanded. This leads to a surplus of labor services. That is another way of saying unemployment. The empirical evidence also links increases in the minimum wage to higher levels of crime, higher drop-out rates, and poverty.[29]

However, in places like Bismarck, San Antonio, Minneapolis-St. Paul, Oklahoma City, and other growing metropolitan areas, the equilibrium wage rate has been pushed up – by the invisible hand – to a level well above the minimum wage.

This means that where the price floor is below equilibrium, the minimum wage had no effect on the unemployment rate. Unfortunately, in other cities, the guarantee of at least $7.25 – or more – per hour has led to a guarantee of zero dollars per hour as the benevolence of the United States Congress destroys jobs.

The most recent increase in the minimum wage could not have come at a worse time for teenagers. In the middle of the 2007-2009 Recession, the unemployment rate for teenagers rose to 27.6%. For black teenagers the numbers were even worse. As employers struggled to cover their costs, the increase in the wage floor led to a 52.2% unemployment rate.[30]

This did not stop thousands of fast-food workers in over 60 cities from walking off the job in August of 2013 demanding an increase in the minimum wage to $15 per hour.[31] It also did not deter President Obama, who despite residing over an economy with persistently high unemployment rates for teens and the unskilled[32] from

SUGGESTED CLASSROOM DEBATE

Economist Philip Verleger once argued that the federal government should impose a price floor of $4 per gallon of gasoline. If prices ever fell below $4, government would impose a gas tax to force prices for the consumer back to $4. If prices rose above $4, the market would be left alone.[33] What benefits, if any, would this create for the U.S.? What would be the costs?

proposing an increase in the minimum wage to $10.10 per hour during his 2014 State of the Union address.

Not to be outdone, in 2016 Bernie Sanders and Hillary Clinton (eventually) pushed for an increase in the federal minimum wage to $15 per hour. This figure had already been legislated in Seattle, Washington where 1,100 food service jobs were eliminated following the first hike from $9.47 to $11 per hour.[34] In San Francisco, an increase in the minimum wage in 2016 from $10.74 to $12.25 per hour led to the loss of 2,500 restaurant positions.

Throughout the United States, another effect in states that increased the minimum wage above the federal minimum (and above where supply and demand intersect) was an increase in prices. Facing higher input costs of production from mandated pay raises, businesses all over America sought to charge people more in order to offset higher costs. The higher prices naturally fell disproportionately on the backs of poorer Americans who spend a greater percentage of their income to live than other Americans do.[35]

Meanwhile, restaurants all over the nation have begun using machines, rather than people to take customer orders. This makes sense to Bill Gates, who in an interview on MSNBC warned that hikes in the minimum wage would create an incentive for businesses to "buy machines and automate things."[36]

Perhaps Congress and President Obama – when it comes to regulating the terms in which emancipated human beings can interact with one another – should at least consider the words of Chief Justice John Marshall who in the case of *Ogden v. Saunders* stated:

> Individuals do not derive from government their right to contract, but bring that right with them into society every man retains [the right] to dispose of [his] property according to his own judgment.

DO GOVERNMENT BANS WORK?

What happens when the government tells people they can no longer demand or supply a good or service? The good or service goes away, right? No, it doesn't. That does not mean that government should never try this strategy. Sometimes banning a good or service is precisely what the economy needs to preserve liberty.

In the United States it is illegal to own slaves, burn down businesses for money and hire yourself out as a hitman. This is a good thing. If we legalized hit men, we would see person A – the person who wants someone rubbed out – hire person B (the hit man) in order to kill person C. The problem is that person C not only did not voluntarily consent to be part of this transaction, but person C's rights are violated when he or she is shot while mowing the yard one day.

Another example of where attempting to ban something can promote liberty is in the area of child pornography. A recent estimate put the number of children who are trafficked as sex slaves at between 30,000 and 50,000.[37] This horrifying reality definitely fits into the negative externality category since children are not consenting adults.[38]

Clearly, the government can and should play a role in trying to fight the laws of supply and demand where life, liberty, and property rights are in jeopardy. However, the legal system can also seek to ban things that a lot of people want and where it is unclear that measurable negative externalities exist.

THE DRUG WAR

Have you ever used illegal drugs? Perhaps you should not answer out loud. Some of, maybe most of, your classmates have at least experimented with marijuana at some point in their lives. If you know someone who has smoked marijuana, did they engage in violent acts while they were stoned, or did they munch on a bucket of chicken wings while watching *SouthPark* reruns?

Either way, the federal government does not care. By 2016 the following unintended consequences had come to fruition as a result of America's decades-long war on drugs:

- America has spent at least $1 trillion on the drug war. It cost U.S. taxpayers at least $31 billion in federal taxes in 2016 alone.
- The number of people behind bars for drug law violations rose from 50,000 in 1980 to 1.56 million in 2015, according to the Bureau of Prisons.
- Drug arrests have more than tripled in the last 25 years, totaling more than 1.49 million arrests in 2015.
- From 2001 to 2010 8.2 million people were arrested for marijuana violations. Of those 88 percent were for possession.
- Despite an increase in spending and arrests by 2016 the demand for cocaine had increased by half while the demand for heroin and other opiates had tripled, helping the international drug industry create $300 billion in world-wide sales.[39]

The unintended consequences of the drug war are no laughing matter. In addition to the bloated prison population, we have young people in the inner cities dying in gun battles as drug sellers compete with one another. Drug prices are artificially high, so more people engage in crime to pay for their habits. Police officers are often corrupted by the allure of drug money. The government earns no tax money from the sale of drugs, while the individual rights of people to use drugs – the same as they can cigarettes, alcohol, and Internet pornography – are taken away. In Mexico, the drug war had claimed over 60,000 lives by 2014[40] and had turned the northern part of that country into one of the most dangerous places on Earth.[41]

Nearly 100 years ago, Austrian economist Ludwig Von Mises said, "Once the principle is admitted that it is the duty of government to protect the individual against his own foolishness, no serious objections can be advanced against further encroachments. As soon as we surrender the principle that the state should not interfere in any questions touching on the individual's mode of life, we end by regulating and restricting the latter down to the smallest detail."[42]

HOW THE U.S. HELPED AFGHANISTAN'S OPIUM DEALERS BECOME MORE PROSPEROUS

You may recall that we learned how the principle of comparative advantage is an important function in determining success in the marketplace. This principle applies not only to the individual trying to decide what to produce, but also to an entire nation trying to decide what to produce. In Afghanistan, the land is perfectly suited to grow the poppy flower. Poppy flowers are perfectly suited to produce the powerful drug known as opium.

The problem for poppy farmers was that the Taliban did not like the idea of allowing people to buy and sell drugs. That led to a ban on opium poppies for the brief time that the Taliban was in power. Just like women who are happy to shed their burkhas, poppy farmers in Afghanistan are somewhat thankful that the United States has helped them earn a living once again.[43]

Now that the Taliban is weakened, farmers like Gul Haidar are back in business. In Mr. Haidar's case, he has sown 250 acres of poppies, which will yield about 650 pounds of opium. Mr. Haidar – and farmers like him – produced 75% of the world's supply of opium (3,611 tons) before the Taliban came into power. Production fell to 204 tons by the year 2000.

With the increase in the number of farmers re-entering the market, the overall supply of opium increased from 185 tons to 8,200 tons from 2001 to 2007. Predictably, the increase in the supply of opium has led to lower prices and an increase in quantity demanded. This prompted the Bush Administration to step up its efforts to fight opium production in Afghanistan.

SUGGESTED CLASSROOM DEBATE

If the U.S. legalized drugs, would quantity demanded increase by a large amount or by a small amount? Why? Does the drug war harm young black men in America's cities – as some critics charge – more than young white men?[44] Why, or why not? Should the National Football League and Major League Baseball encourage or discourage steroid use among professional football and baseball players?[45] Why or why not?

As it turns out, Afghanistan is not the only worry for drug enforcement officials. In 2005 the U.S. put pressure on the Canadian government to arrest Marc Emery – a man accused of being one of the biggest marijuana suppliers to the U.S.[46] Apparently, so many border patrol officers were diverted into the war effort following September 11th that drug dealers from Latin America and Canada found it less risky and less costly to smuggle cocaine and marijuana into the U.S. As the supply of these drugs increased by 25% in Florida alone, the United States found that the laws of supply and demand undermined the war on drugs as the war on terrorism became the priority.[47]

President Obama's approach to the war on drugs changed American policy from one of "supply reduction" to "demand reduction" when he pushed for greater funding for rehabilitation and research. His 2017 budget called for $15.8 billion in federal spending geared towards reducing the number of buyers in the market and changing consumer tastes.[48]

In 2016 the state of California joined with others to legalize recreational marijuana. President Trump supported slow steps towards de-criminalizing marijuana during the 2016 campaign but was less clear on whether the war on drugs should be escalated or scaled back.

MARKET FAILURES

> There are all kinds of reasons why liberal economists say that markets are inefficient and that we must replace the invisible hand with a visible hand.
>
> Jagdish Bhagwati, economics professor,
> Columbia University

From the days of Adam Smith, economists have debated the degree to which free and unfettered markets work efficiently. While no economist – other than a few Marxist holdouts – ever argues that markets fail to produce efficient prices and outputs, we do sometimes disagree over how often markets fail to accomplish efficiency.

After all, we did see massive bank failures in 2008. Toyota got in a lot of trouble a few years ago when they had to spend $2 billion on a recall of cars with faulty brakes and acceleration issues that led to multiple deaths.[49] From time to time we read about tainted food – from profit-seeking businesses – making it into the food supply and of course,

who among us has never felt "ripped off" by a company that refused to honor a warranty or who sold us a product that was, to put it bluntly, "a piece of junk"?

All of this means that economists sometimes wonder if *market failures* are possible.

> ➤ **A market failure takes place when the free market fails to produce an efficient price or market equilibrium outcome, or when one side of the market violates the rights of the other.**

In 2001, three economists – Joseph Stiglitz, George Akerlof, and Michael Spence –shared the $1 million Nobel prize in economics for their work in the area of market failures.[50] Up until these gentlemen won the most prestigious award in economics, the award had routinely been awarded to economists from the University of Chicago, where Adam Smith and the free market are held as sacrosanct. Mr. Stiglitz and his colleagues have spent their careers looking into instances where market failures arise.

What causes market failures? According to the Nobel laureates, market failures typically occur when the problem of asymmetric information or externalities appears.

> ➤ **Asymmetric information occurs when one party in a transaction has perfect information about the price, quality or availability of a good or service and the other party does not.**

Consider for a moment the market for used cars. If you have ever been involved in this market as a seller or a buyer, you know how frustrating – if not downright scary – this process can be. How does the seller of a used car that has been beautifully maintained get skeptical potential buyers to believe that they will not be ripped off? In this case, imperfect information might cause the seller to have to settle for less money than the car might actually be worth, because the buyer has no way of verifying the true

© wannapong/Shutterstock.com

history of the car. For buyers, how do you know whether the car you are looking at has been taken care of?

If you are in the market for a used car, and the one you settle on for what appears to be a great price was once under water in Iowa, how do you find this information out? Again, the problem of asymmetric information leads to your paying either more than you should have or paying for a total piece of junk.

Stiglitz pointed to the breakdown in security at airports on September 11th as an example of a market failure. "There are certain activities like airport security that should not be in the private sphere. That market is not self-adjusting," he argued.

What he means by the term "self-adjusting," is that the market, in his opinion, does not respond quickly enough or does not have the proper incentives or information necessary to keep us safe when we get on a plane. The pre-September 11th market for flying demanded a quick, relatively unobstructed, process of getting on our airplanes. The free market told private companies that people were more interested in getting checked in and boarding in the least amount of time possible – even if it meant that not everyone got checked who needed to be checked.

Stiglitz and other economists, who do not have as much faith in the efficiency of the market, would suggest that the market failed to recognize that security is actually more valuable than a speedy check-in process, and that the terrorist hijackings of four jets indicate that the market did not know best what consumers really need.

What then, do Stiglitz and others in his camp suggest we do when the market fails to operate efficiently? They believe that where markets fail, government intervention is necessary. In the used car market, they would argue that disclosure laws with respect to odometer readings, previous wrecks, and so forth be strictly enforced with vigorous government oversight of the used car industry, and they would advocate tough penalties for violators of the law.

In the case of airport security, Stiglitz argued strongly in favor of turning over security to the government, with the theory that government – being nonprofit – will not have to worry as much about consumer demands and cost controls. Government uses taxes to provide security, and therefore, has access to a deep pool of money from which to launch increases in security that the private sector might find too costly.

In the case of Toyota and the recent financial crisis, critics of capitalism seemingly had truckloads of ammunition to fire away at the followers of Adam Smith and largely unregulated markets. As *The Wall Street Journal* uncovered, executives at Toyota may have known about braking and acceleration issues with many Toyota cars, long before it became a nationally-discussed issue.[51] Meanwhile, banking executives all over the world, in the face of mounting evidence that

the housing bubble was about to burst, kept betting on ever higher prices – only to run for taxpayer aid when the bets did not pay off.

When it comes to the issue of prices, many economists argue that markets sometimes fail to accurately reflect the full cost of certain goods and services. Consider gasoline as an example.

Whatever you paid today for gasoline is not enough, many argue, when you take into account the *marginal social cost* of gasoline.

> ➤ **The marginal social cost is the total cost to society as a whole for producing one further unit, or taking one further action, in an economy. This total cost of producing one extra unit of something is not simply the direct cost borne by the producer, but also must include the costs to the external environment and other stakeholders.**

In the market for gasoline many costs are taken into account – the price of crude oil, marketing, transportation, refining, and so forth. What is not taken into account is the net damage to the environment from creating and burning gasoline, and the net cost to society from the thousands of people who have died in wars to protect the supply of oil, and thus, the relatively low price of fuel.

If we took into account the marginal social cost of the fuel we buy, the total cost would be higher. With higher input costs would come a decrease in supply and higher prices would follow. Higher prices would reduce quantity demanded and thus, reduce not only pollution but the pressure to go to war to secure low gas prices.

Figure 8.6 illustrates this idea of the negative externalities created by oil. Left alone, the November 2016 price of gasoline equaled $2.09 per gallon. This price reflects the supply and demand conditions that do not take into account the pollution generated by the burning of fossil

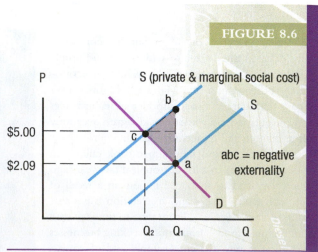

FIGURE 8.6

fuels or the more than $2 trillion that was spent on the war in Iraq. While economists do not contend that the entire war in Iraq was "about oil", it is a fact that the United States government has a vested interest in oil-rich regions of the world.

Critics of "the invisible hand" argue that the Adam Smith view of markets does not accurately reflect, for example, the nearly 500,000 Iraqi's and over 4,800 coalition forces that saw their lives end prematurely as a result of the war. Nor does $2.09 – they argue – reflect the hidden cost of climate change, for example.

Therefore, if we take into account the marginal social cost of gasoline the supply curve would actually be S (private + marginal social cost). This would push the price of gasoline to say, $5 per gallon and would reduce consumption as well. Notice the triangular region marked 'abc'. This is the total negative externality created, according to critics, by not having a policy – such as higher gas taxes – that would reduce consumption and therefore reduce the negative externality created.

It is also worth noting that many economists point out another 'market failure' caused by *positive externalities*.

> ➤ **A positive externality is created when buyers and sellers create benefits that are externalized, or captured, by some third party that was not directly involved in the original transaction.**

A classic example of this can be found every spring across America. When the weather warms up, many families purchase new flowers, shrubs and other plants to beautify their property. The homeowner is better off. The store selling the flowers is better off. But the neighbor who spends nothing on their yard is also better off when everyone around them has a nicer yard – and therefore potentially higher property values.

In this case, you might find yourself thinking, "O.K., so what is the problem here?" Well, to many economists,

Should tax dollars support this scene?

when positive externalities exist it means that left alone, the free market *fails to produce enough of the desired good or service.*

Historically, the government has used this argument to justify spending taxpayer dollars on libraries, national parks, road beautification projects and public schools.

DO MARKETS FAIL DURING WAR?

We have looked at the argument in favor of government intervention when markets fail to provide good information or don't work as well as capitalists argue they should. We now turn to a defense of government-created shortages through the use of non-price rationing. The idea that shortages, long waits, and mass inconvenience could ever be a good thing might seem odd, but had you been alive during World War II, you might have been happy that the invisible hand was replaced with the government hand.

In 1940, the United States government spent (in today's dollars) just over $17 billion for national defense. That same year Germany spent over $250 billion.[52] Of course, Germany was already one year into World War II, and America was still avoiding military intervention in Europe and Asia.

All that changed with the bombing of Pearl Harbor. Almost overnight, the U.S. economy shifted into high gear to prepare America for entry into WW II in 1942. The problem was that, for much of the 1930s and early 1940s, the U.S. economy had either been in the depths of the Great Depression or attempting to get out of the worst downturn in our history. This meant that there was no vibrant economy from which to draw the necessary resources. That meant that the government had to turn to private citizens and ask them to – voluntarily in some cases and through force in other cases – submit to massive rationing of almost all goods and services.

For example, during WW II, there were drives to preserve rubber, scrap metal, rags, paper, and grease.[53] People were asked to plant "victory gardens" and adhere to "meatless" days to stretch the nation's food supply.

Shortages and rationing of various goods became commonplace during the war. Rationing boards were established in every county, with the power to regulate the sale of 90% of all civilian goods. Every man, woman, and child received a ration book, limiting what could be purchased.[54]

In early 1942, rubber became the first item to be rationed by the Federal Government's Office of Price Administration (OPA). Gasoline soon followed, with mandatory rationing becoming effective on December 1, 1942. Citizens were issued A, B, or C stickers, allowing them a specific number of gallons per week, depending on their occupation. Those unfortunates with 'A' stickers were authorized only four gallons per week, a paltry total

RATIONING MEANS A FAIR SHARE FOR ALL OF US

WITHOUT RATIONING

WITH RATIONING

Were shortages necessary to win the war?
Source: Minnesota Historical Society

that was actually decreased to three gallons later in the war. In 1943, gasoline rationing became even more severe, with all forms of "pleasure driving" becoming illegal.

The rationing of food had a great impact on the lives of average Americans. As with gas, the government issued ration books authorizing the purchase of only a certain amount of various products per week. Beginning in April of 1942, sugar was rationed, followed by coffee, meats, butter, canned goods, dried peas and beans, and a variety of other products. In addition to food, consumer products like shoes and clothing were rationed or restricted. Alcohol was not rationed, but it remained in critically short supply and black markets sprung up all over the nation.

In one instance a warehouse in Sugarland, Texas had 22,000,000 pounds of sugar that the refinery refused to offer up to the marketplace. The general manager, M.G. Thompson, cited the inability to earn any profit as the reason for keeping the sugar warehoused.[55]

An underlying force behind the explosion of government-planning was Franklin Roosevelt's general mistrust of businesses and lack of economic expertise in how a free market economy – even during a war, can function. During the war, industry leaders like Bill Knudson were appointed to head up war-time production but found that the federal government's anti-profit stance was often a major obstacle. For much of the war, Knudson and other heads of industry battled the Roosevelt Administration over the idea that victory over Germany and Japan would be more likely if, as one businessman put it, "I don't think of the hope of reward as selfishness. Work is the prime mover of our economy, and the fuel that makes people work is profit."

By the end of the war, even Roosevelt was routinely stunned by the massive production gains by companies that were allowed to charge free market prices. The B-29 plane, with more than 40,000 separate parts, was but one of the success stories where the government saw workers turning out far more output per day under a market-reward system than when government planning boards – under the assumption that market failures and greed would hurt the war effort – were in the way.[56]

THE ECONOMICS OF FLORIDA WATER—MARKET FAILURE OR GOVERNMENT FAILURE?

We close this chapter with a blended look at the importance of the market, and the role government can play in cleaning up the problem of asymmetric information, with a detailed examination of a brewing crisis of epic proportions. We are speaking of Florida's growing shortage of water.

Some of you – especially those of you not from Florida – might find yourself saying, "That's absurd. There is water under the ground. We have tons of lakes, the Atlantic Ocean, and just about every afternoon in the summer it rains so hard, I am tempted to build an ark!" Others might say, "Hey, buddy, water is common property. We deserve it. It falls from the sky for free, and it ought to be free when we use it!" Sound familiar? After all, if gasoline and Budweiser fell out of the sky to the tune of 150 billion gallons per year (the annual quantity of Florida rainfall), we might expect to drive and drink free of charge, too.

Let's start with science before we do economics. First, of the 150 billion gallons that drench us, 110 billion gallons evaporate in the sweltering heat.[57] That constitutes 38 out of the 53 inches of annual rainfall. Another 8 inches runs off into lakes, rivers, wetlands, and eventually the ocean, where salt water remains at the bottom of the list of desired beverages. Only 7 of the 53 inches drip down into the aquifer (the underground supply of water that we rely on).

Now to the economics. The overall demand for water has grown exponentially in Florida for several years. The state's population now tops 19.9 million residents, who consume 2.7 billion gallons of water every day. Florida's agricultural industry is the biggest user at 3.2 billion gallons per day. Daily use by industry, power generators, and recreational entities amounts to 1.6 billion gallons. This includes Walt Disney World, which consumes more water in one day than the nation of Somalia (10.2 million people) consumes in a day.[58]

The problem is that the demand for water is growing at a faster rate than nature or God (depending on your view) is supplying it. By now, you have learned enough about economics to knock out a diagram in just a few seconds, showing that if demand increases a lot and supply is increasing only a little, a shortage will persist at the prevailing price, and therefore, prices will have to rise to re-equilibrate the market. Problem solved.

Not so fast. That would be true if economics and the free market dictated the price of water. In Florida, politics and the government dictate the price of water. Do you remember the common property problem? In chapter one, we saw that if something is considered to be "owned by all," there is not much of an incentive for any one individual to be conservative in using that product. Water is considered by many to be common property.

As Joseph Stiglitz would say, the market has failed to accurately deliver good information about the amount of water available and the real price of water. As free-market economists would say, the market has not been allowed to convey information about the scarcity of water or the real price of water, because the government has disrupted the invisible hand.

You are probably aware of the fact that Pepsi owns the Aquafina brand of bottled water and Coca-Cola produces Dasani. Pepsi and Coke do not run Florida's water supply. No private company does.[59] Municipal governments control municipal water supplies, and prices are generally established on a monthly basis by those governments.

Since the officials in charge of setting water rates are elected and the public (a) does not know how acute the shortage is and (b) believes abundant, cheap water is our birthright, we end up with (c) prices well below market equilibrium and the virtual guarantee of ongoing shortages.

The government's response to the water shortage in many places like Central Florida has been to resort to Soviet-style rationing, where residents are told they cannot water their lawns during certain days or times of the day. Residents facing such watering restrictions largely ignore the government edicts. Why? Because there is an imbalance between how pretty and green we want our lawns to be and how pretty and green they would be if we listened to the government. Ignoring the government is also the rational thing to do. As long as the expected benefits (pretty green lawn) exceed the expected costs (the chance of getting caught and punished, plus the slight increase in their water bill), the residents will take their chances and water their lawns.

The price of water is set so low by government that about half of all water that goes to homes is used on lawns, and half of that is wasted on inefficient sprinkler systems. How many of you have ever driven down the road and seen badly aimed sprinklers watering the road or sidewalk rather than the grass? How many of you have seen sprinklers running during a rainstorm? Have you ever seen people turn on a garden hose to spray their driveway?

Consider this. A six-pack of Fat Tire Amber Ale (a really good beer) costs about $9. Six beers at 12 ounces each amounts to 72 ounces. One gallon equals 128 ounces. That means that Fat Tire – which is 92% water – costs $14.22 cents per ounce or $18.20 per gallon. On January 23, 2017, a gallon of regular unleaded gasoline averaged $2.27 in Winter Garden, Florida – a suburb of Orlando. That same day, the city of Winter Garden charged residential customers $1.03 per 1,000 gallons of water,[60] up to 10,000 gallons. From 10,000-15,000 gallons, the price increased to over $1.273 per thousand gallons. Over 15,000 gallons equals a price of $1.5339 per gallon.

The average Floridian consumes between 147 and 180 gallons of water per day. If we conservatively put Winter Garden usage at 147 gallons per person per day, that would be 4,410 gallons per month. Since the city of Winter Garden does not round up to calculate the water bill of its residents, 4,410 gallons would be a bill of $45.43 plus a surcharge of $6.18, for a total of $51.60. 4,410 gallons of Fat Tire would cost $80,262! We have plenty of beer, because the price is set by supply and demand. We are running out of water because our system is modeled after the same planning and rationing that bankrupted the Soviet Union.

What if water cost the same amount as gasoline?

SOME FINAL THOUGHTS

Do you remember the movie *Jurassic Park*? In that film, the mathematician tried to explain to the owner of the park that it would be impossible to keep his dinosaurs from breeding because "life finds a way."

The same could be said about the interaction of supply and demand in the face of market failures. In essence we can say, "Markets find a way."

I am sure some of you read the section on used cars and thought, "Hold on a second. Didn't the free market, rather than government, give us Carfax?" Well, yes. Carfax is the online service that allows you to submit the vehicle identification number of the car you are considering purchasing. For a fee, Carfax will give you a detailed vehicle history report that dramatically reduces the asymmetric information problem.

Some of your classmates, while reading about September 11th and the "market failure" surrounding security were saying, "Wait a minute! Before September 11th, the average consumer wanted to get on the airplane as fast as they could with minimal hassles. Therefore the market did not fail on September 11th at all. It was simply bound

to happen that if consumers wanted few hassles, some consumers would hijack airplanes." This is a strong argument, too. After all, the government set the standards for screening passengers before the hijackers boarded the planes. Why is it that the market failed when government was ultimately in charge of our safety? Why, after 15-plus years of government control over airport security, do we still see TSA officials failing its own tests of airport security?[62]

Moreover, any astute observer of our housing market and financial industry would note that it was the government-chartered Fannie Mae and Freddie Mac, along with Bush-era rules that forced taxpayer dollars into the subprime market that helped fuel the overheated market.[63] One could also accurately point out that Toyota – even if it intentionally covered up any wrong doing – was ultimately held accountable by the millions of customers that it stood to lose to Honda, Ford, and other companies. That threat alone forced Toyota to respond faster than government does, when it fails to inspect our food, bridges, schools, medicines, and other products properly.[63]

This leaves us with an unresolved debate. Do markets ever fail? If they do, is the government or the invisible hand the most efficient correction tool? That is for you to decide over time.

ENDNOTES

1 See "Stores Told to Lift Prices in Germany" by Ernest Beck, *The Wall Street Journal,* September 11, 2000.

2 See http://walmartstores.com/GlobalWMStoresWeb/navigate.do?catg=376&contId=5382 for more on Wal-Mart in Germany.

3 Source: www.unos.org.

4 See "Pay Bone-Marrow Donors, Save Lives" by Jeff Rowes and Bob McNamara, *The Wall Street Journal,* August 24, 2016.

5 See "Cash for Kidneys" by Gary S. Becker & Julio J. Elias, *The Wall Street Journal,* January 18-19, 2014 page C1 & "The Moral Case for Legalizing Organ Sales" by Jack A. Chambless, *The Orlando Sentinel,* September 29, 2013.

6 In one case police arrested a man in Jacksonville, Florida, for selling $34.72 tickets to a Jacksonville Jaguars football game for $35! See "State tosses scalping case over six cents," *The Orlando Sentinel,* November 26, 1998.

7 Apparently, rock stars now realize the error of their ways because ticket prices to many shows have increased significantly over the past few years. See "The show must go on, but at higher prices" by Kati Schardl, *The Tallahassee Democrat,* March 13, 2004.

8 As it has in many cases with websites like www.stubhub.com. See "Need a ticket?" by Kathy Bergen, *The Orlando Sentinel,* September 11, 2005; and "Wait Till Next Year, but Lock in the Ticket Price Now" by Alan B. Krueger, *The New York Times,* February 2, 2006.

9 See "Jets to Auction Seats on eBay" by Matthew Futterman, *The Wall Street Journal,* September 17, 2008.

10 See "Sports Teams Try New Game: Scalping Tickets" by Hannah Karp, *The Wall Street Journal,* June 15, 2106.

11 See "Rent Control is the Real New York Scandal" by Eileen Norcross, *The Wall Street Journal,* September 13-14, 2008, pg. A11.

12 "In Santa Monica, Rent Decontrol Brings Surprises" by Stacy Kravetz, *The Wall Street Journal* 1999.

13 See "End of an Empire," *Newsweek,* September 9, 1991.

14 See "Crime and Punishment for Capitalists" by Leon Aron, *The New York Times,* October 30, 2003; and "In Russia, Apathy Dims Democracy" by Steven Lee Myers, *The New York Times,* November 9, 2003.

15 See "Russian economy perks up" by Michael Wines, *The Orlando Sentinel*, November 18, 2001, p. A19.

16 See *Reagan's War,* by Peter Schweizer, Doubleday books, New York, 2002, pp. 35-36.

17 Log on to www.heritage.org/research/features/index/downloads.cfm.

18 In 2002 as part of an election-year campaign, Congress passed a $73.5 billion subsidy bill that added chickpeas, peanuts, and other "second-tier" commodities, to go along with the money that continues to flow to corn, wheat, cotton, and rice. See "Farm Subsidies Blossom Anew, Fertilized by Election Politics" by David Rogers and Jill Carroll, *The Wall Street Journal,* April 2, 2002.

19 See "The Farm Belt Boom," *The Wall Street Journal,* December 9, 2010, p. A22.

20 See "Farming for Dollars," *The Wall Street Journal,* July 6, 2007, pg. A8; and "The No Farmer Left Behind Act," *The Wall Street Journal,* November 14, 2007, pg. A16.

21 See *The Farm Fiasco* by James Bovard, ICS Press, San Francisco, 1991.

22 See the December 2, 1998, edition of NBC Nightly News titled "The Fleecing of America."

23 See "Prairie Plutocrats," *The Wall Street Journal,* February 1, 2002, p. A18.

24 See "America's Sugar Daddies," *The New York Times,* November 29, 2003, p. A32; and "…and too many lumps" *The Orlando Sentinel,* April 7, 2002.

25 See "Why Did FDR's New Deal Harm Blacks?" by Jim Powell, *The Cato Institute,* December 3, 2003; and "Black Farmers down to a precious few" by E.G. Vallianatos, *The Seattle-Post Intelligencer,* February 22, 2005.

26 See "Another Minimum Wage Backfire" *The Wall Street Journal,* August 11, 2015.

27 See "A Subsidy as Shameful as They Come" by James Bovard, *The Wall Street Journal,* May 26, 2016.

28 See "Fast-food strike doesn't impact Bismarck" by Jessica Holdman, *The Bismarck Tribune,* September 4, 2013.

29 See "Minimum Wage vs. Supply and Demand," *The Wall Street Journal,* April 24, 1996; "Minimum Wage Hikes Help Politicians, Not the Poor" by Bruce Bartlett, *The Wall Street Journal,* May 27, 1999; "The Minimum Wage Law and Youth Crimes: Time–Series Evidence," by Masanori Hashimoto, *The Journal of Law and Economics,* October, 1987; "Higher Minimum Wage, Higher Dropout Rate" by Robert J. Barro, *The Wall Street Journal,* January 11, 1996; and "Job Slayers," *The Wall Street Journal,* August 29, 2005.

30 See "The Lost Wages of Youth," *The Wall Street Journal,* March 5, 2010, p. A20.

31 See "Fast-food employees' protests fan out in U.S." by Tiffany Hsu and Alana Semuels, *The Orlando Sentinel,* August 30, 2103.

32 See "Minimum wage well-intentioned but it upsets market's balance" by Daniel Tyrrell, *The Orlando Sentinel,* December 14, 2013.

33 See "Set floor of $4 a gallon" by Thomas Friedman, *The Orlando Sentinel,* May 31, 2008

34 See "A Post – Labor Day, Minimum Wage Hangover" by Andy Puzder, *The Wall Street Journal,* September 8, 2015 pg. A 13 and "Minimum Wage, Maximum Politics, by Andy Puzder, *The Wall Street Journal,* October 6, 2014.

35 See "The Minimum-Wage Stealth Tax on the Poor" by Thomas MaCurdy, *The Wall Street Journal,* February 23, 2015.

36 See "The Employee of the Month Has a Battery" by Michael Saltsman, *The Wall Street Journal,* January 30, 2014 page A13.

37 See "The Girls Next Door" by Peter Landesman, *The New York Times Magazine,* January 25, 2004.

38 On April 16, 2002, the U.S. Supreme Court seemingly weakened the laws against "virtual child-pornography" by ruling that the 1996 Child Pornography Prevention Act violated the first amendment by outlawing computer-generated child pornography. See "High Court strikes down child-pornography law" by David Stout, *The Orlando Sentinel,* April 17, 2002.

39 See "If Economists Wages the Drug War" by Tom Wainwright, *The Wall Street Journal,* February 20-21, 2016 pg. C3.

40 See http://www.cnn.com/2013/09/02/world/americas/mexico-drug-war-fast-facts/

41 See "Acapulco staggers under drug war" by Ken Ellingwood, *The Orlando Sentinel,* January 16, 2011.

42 See "Mises Explains the Drug War" by Laurence M. Vance *The Free Market,* Vol. 31, No. 9 September 2013.

43 See "War on opium flawed, group says" by Stephen Graham, *The Orlando Sentinel,* February 1, 2005.

44 See "How the War on Drugs is Destroying Black America" by John McWhorter, *Cato's Letter,* Winter 2011, Volume 9, Number 1.

45 For more on the ephedra ban and the issue of steroid use, see "Fans of Ephedra rush to stock up" by Paul McLeod, Melinda Fulmer and David Wharton, *The Los Angeles Times* (appearing in *The Orlando Sentinel*), January 4, 2004; and "In Pursuit of Doped Excellence" by Michael Sokolove, *The New York Times Magazine,* January 18, 2004.

46 See "Uncle Sam orchestrates Vancouver pot busts" by Brad Badelt and Amy O'Brian, *The Vancouver Sun,* July 30, 2005.

47 See "Smuggling Drugs? Let Us Count the Ways" by Mary Anastasia O'Grady, *The Wall Street Journal,* August 26, 2005, p. A13.

48 See "The Radical way Obama wants to change the Drug War" by Christopher Ingraham, *The Washington Post,* February 10, 2016.

49 See "A Crisis Made in Japan" by Jeff Kingston, *The Wall Street Journal,* February 5, 2010.

50 See "Three Americans Win Nobel for Economics" by Jon E. Hilsenrath, *The Wall Street Journal,* October 11, 2001.

51 See "Secretive Culture Led Toyota Astray" by Kate Linebaugh, Dionne Searcey and Noriiko Shirouzu, *The Wall Street Journal,* February 10, 2010.

52 Source: The National D-Day Museum, New Orleans, Louisiana.

53 Source: The Museum of Florida History and the Florida Department of Veterans' Affairs, Tallahassee, Florida.

54 Source: "Keeping the Home Fires Burning: Florida's WWII Experience" by David J. Coles and the Museum of Florida History, Tallahassee, Florida.

55 Source: *The Oregonian,* June 23, 1942.

56 See *Freedom's Forge* by Arthur Herman, Random House, New York, 2012.

57 See "A Drying Oasis" by Debbie Salamone, *The Orlando Sentinel,* March 3, 2002.

58 See "The Human Thirst" by Debbie Salamone, *The Orlando Sentinel,* April 7, 2002.

59 In places where private companies do own the water supply, shortages do not exist and poor people have ample water supplies. See "Water Works" by Luis Alberto Moreno, *The Wall Street Journal,* March 10, 2006.

60 Source: City of Winter Garden, FL.

61 See "Black Market for Salt at Ind. School Cafeteria" by Kenneth Artz, *Health Care News,* August 2015

62 See http://www.msnbc.msn.com/id/11863165/ns/nightly_news-nbc_news_investigates/

63 See "Market Failure or Government Failure?" by Allan H. Meltzer, *The Wall Street Journal,* March 19, 2010, p. A19.

64 See www.freemanonline.org.

CHAPTER REVIEW

1. What is non-price rationing and what are all of the reasons this type of rationing is considered to be inefficient by economists?

2. Fully explain what the market for parking spots would look like at your college if an auction were held each semester.

3. What is the difference between a price ceiling and price floor?

4. Do rap and/or country music cause negative externalities? If so, what would have to happen to the price of concert tickets to reflect the marginal social cost of these events?

Chapter Nine

HEALTH CARE ECONOMICS

*T*he truth is, in order to get things like universal health care and a
revamped education system, then someone is going to have to give up a
piece of their pie so that someone else can have more.

MICHELLE OBAMA

THE DEFINING ECONOMIC "CRISIS" OR NOT?

In 1787 delegates met in sweltering heat in Philadelphia to craft the Constitution of the United States of America. When the subject of "commerce" came up, the Founders added Clause 3 to Article One, Section 8 of this document. This Clause gave Congress the authority to "regulate commerce with foreign nations, and among the several states, and with the Indian Tribes." The word commerce, to the Founders – and Adam Smith – and to those engaged in it meant the act of buying and selling goods and services. By definition, commerce does not take place until a willing buyer and willing seller come to a voluntary agreement over prices and the terms of trade.

225 years later, the United States Supreme Court gave Congress the authority to impose taxes on Americans who refused to engage in commerce. For the first time in our nation's history, the simple act of being unwilling to purchase something could mean a fine and/or imprisonment.[1]

As you are reading this chapter, the economics of health care is still evolving. From 1776 to World War II the market was largely based on "the invisible hand". From World War II until 2017 the market was a mix of voluntary exchange and government planning and control. As you are reading this paragraph the health care industry is once again going through transition. You will discover what led President Obama towards the idea of what we know as "ObamaCare" and what led President Trump to work towards dismantling Mr. Obama's signature piece of legislation.

In 2017 the U.S. health care system comprised roughly 18% of the gross domestic product ($3.2 trillion) of the United States.[2] Moreover, for the past several years, the cost of health care has increased faster than the core rate of inflation.

In 2017, health insurance premiums increased by 18–23%.[3] In 2013, the year before the Affordable Care Act's major provisions kicked in, insurers all over America raised rates an average of 7.5%, with California, New York, Florida, Ohio and others that saw rates in some cases go up by well over 30%.[4] As costs have accelerated, more and more Americans have come face to face with a key problem associated with scarce financial resources. It is for this reason that President Obama signed the Patient Protection and Affordable Care Act on March 23, 2010. He made the argument that the financial strain that rising health care costs imposed on millions of American families would be relieved by this law. The irony is that the major reason why health care is so expensive, is that in many cases it is partially to totally free.

In early January 2000, I flew with my family to Boston to present a paper at an economics conference. On the one day I had off, I traveled to the Cranmore Resort in North Conway, New Hampshire, for a day of snow skiing. My wife, a native Floridian, had never seen snow, much less traveled 50 miles per hour on it, and was very excited to partake in this winter sport. On the way, I convinced her that she did not need a skiing lesson and that she would be fine swooshing down the slopes. Sure enough, on her last run of the day, she wiped out, and ended up with a concussion from the fall. When the first-aid team got her to the bottom of the mountain, she had quite a headache, but was aware of where she was, who I was, and what had happened.

Since I knew I was in bad trouble for talking her out of taking skiing lessons – and because I am a wonderful husband – I took her to the local hospital where she was admitted into the emergency room (cost: $254). The attending physician told us that she had a slight concussion and that she needed to rest for several days. When we told him that we had to fly from Boston back to Orlando the next day, he ordered an MRI and CT-Scan just to make sure nothing more serious might be wrong with her (cost: $1,162). Fortunately, the wonders of medical technology revealed that she was safe to travel, and the next day we were on our way, having completed a very expensive skiing trip.

Many of you probably see this bill of $1,416 as an outrageous example of a health care system that gouges people in their most critical time of need. After all, how would I have looked if I had queried the doctor as to the cost of such procedures upon hearing the recommendation for further testing? I would have come across as an uncaring husband who was concerned only with money – even though it was my wife's fault for listening to me when I told her to skip the skiing lessons. What you will learn is that the $1,416 bill is simply the *effect* of a health care system plagued with unusual problems. The *cause* of that effect is what you need to be concerned with.

COST-SHIFTING

Suppose, on the very day my wife bonked her noggin on the slopes, several other people who did not have any insurance or any ability to pay for their care, had been admitted to the emergency room. If this were a grocery or hardware store, the lack of ability to pay would mean a quick exit out the door, with no service provided.

However, in the health care industry it is *illegal* for public hospitals to turn away emergency-room patients for lack of money. This means in many, many cases that people with little or no economic resources get "free" health care. The hospital simply has to absorb the cost of providing care to those who cannot pay. Moreover, there are also many individuals who are on the taxpayer-funded Medicaid or Medicare programs. Typically, Medicaid and Medicare reimburse hospitals for about half the cost of delivering a service.[5]

This leaves U.S. hospitals with literally millions of dollars in unpaid or partially paid health care bills each year. The solution? Obviously, the hospitals are not going to stand by and go bankrupt providing charity. Instead, the hospitals play an economic game of *cost-shifting*.

> ➤ **Cost-shifting is the practice of shifting the cost of those patients who can only partially pay their health care bills – or pay nothing at all – to those people who are fully insured by a health care provider.**

This means exactly what you think it means. When we walked through the door, before we were even asked what the problem was, we were asked for our insurance card. When I pulled it out, the hospital, in essence, shifted the cost of much of that "free" health care to my bill.

Is this legal? It most certainly is. Did I freak out over this huge bill? Absolutely not. The reason? Because I am part of the problem of cost-shifting as well.

When the doctor, who I guessed had about 25 years of medical experience, recommended an MRI and CT-Scan, I knew that my insurance would pick up a very large portion of the tab. Knowing that a *third party* would help offset the full cost of my wife's health care needs, I did not feel pressured to make a tough financial decision.

Suppose I did not have insurance at that time and the hospital asked me to write a check for over $1,000 for these tests. I may have very well turned to my wife and said, "Honey, you look like you are recovering nicely. Let's walk gently back to the car, go back home, and rest awhile."

When we are asked to be fully responsible for the cost of our decisions, it is amazing how much more judicious we are with our money. But as long as a third party is paying, why not order up more from the health care menu?

The cost shifting does not end with my shifting her bill to my insurance carrier. When my carrier gets the inflated bill for the services rendered, along with inflated

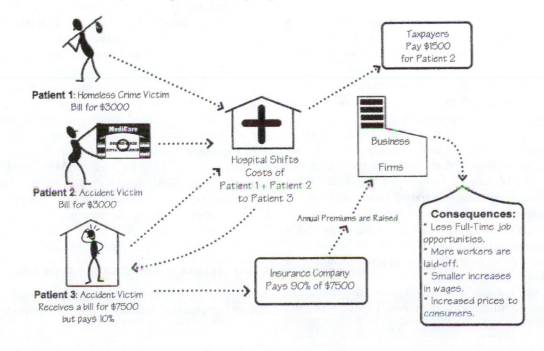

CONCEPT CHECK

A study in Oregon found that when Medicaid coverage increased for residents of this state, it led to a 40% increase in emergency room visits.[6] Where does the law of demand enter in to this finding? Does this bode well for taxpayers that Medicaid is now being offered to millions more people? Why, or why not?

bills from other policy holders, the company simply shifts the burden to all policyholders – typically our employers – in the form of *rising annual premiums.*

What do employers do as their premiums rise? You guessed it! They also participate in the cost-shifting dance by spreading the pain out to consumers in the form of *rising prices* and to employees in the form of *smaller salary gains* and *fewer full-time job opportunities.*[7]

In addition, more and more companies have opted to hire people on a part-time or temporary basis in order to avoid paying for health care benefits. Of course, we blame the employers, but the real culprit is the "welfare mentality" people have as they overuse the services of our health care industry. The preceding diagram summarizes the problem of cost-shifting.

THE REST OF THE STORY

Cost-shifting is just one reason for ballooning health care costs. There are many other culprits that must be exposed as well.

THE AGING POPULATION

As a direct result of advances in medical technology and greater awareness about the risk factors that can lead to an early demise, life expectancies in the U.S. are increasing annually. In addition, there are approximately 76 million Americans known as the "baby boomers," whom have now begun retiring from the labor force and will continue to do so for the next 15-plus years.

Our aging population is putting mounting pressure on the demand for health care. This situation will only get worse in the future. Many of the baby boomers will flood into the tax-funded Medicare system. In 2015, the federal government allocated $646.2 billion to Medicare (14% of the federal budget). When we add the more than $1 trillion allocated to prescription drug benefits for senior citizens and the guarantee of Social Security, the total national debt created by these programs will be over $100 trillion.

To cover the cost of these programs, the tax burden of the average American – who now pays 33% of their income in combined taxes, would have to rise by 81% – translating into an average tax burden of almost 60% of our income.[8]

Moreover, the existence of Medicare has been shown to dramatically increase the demand for the services of specialists, even when they are not medically necessary.[9] The cumulative effect of this natural increase in the demand for health care – plus the artificial increase stemming from the perception that care is free – will be upward pressure on prices for all of us. In fact, as much as *40% of our lifetime health care bill will come in the last month* of our lives, which adds significantly to the cost-shifting problem.[10]

TECHNOLOGY

When my wife and I went back to Cranmore in February 2003, I got a chance to shift my irresponsible behavior to you. That's right, I got hurt at the same resort she did. I tried to jump over a snow-packed ramp to "catch some air" late in the day and missed the ramp. I hit a wall of ice and snow that allowed me to catch some air and also catch a cracked rib, bruised lungs, and a bruised ego. Total cost? Over $1,500. This is not only because I am a big baby and thought I was dying, but because I wanted Mercedes-Benz quality care while I was in pain.

In this respect I am no different than any of the millions of Americans who expect the highest quality health care when we are beset by illness or injury. The problem – if we wish to call it a problem – is that Mercedes-Benz quality care comes at Mercedes-Benz prices. This is largely due to a medical arms race that pits competing hospitals against one another for paying patients.

By the very nature of the business, life-saving (or enhancing) equipment, drugs, and procedures are very expensive. For example, a Computed Tomography Scanner can cost $3.5 million. An MRI machine can cost over $3 million. This equipment must be paid for. Therefore, when we demand its use, part of our bill reflects the enormity of the expense in acquiring the machine to begin with.

COMPETITION – AND THE LACK OF IT...

Unlike any other industry, competition in health care can lead to higher rather than lower prices. Suppose you need

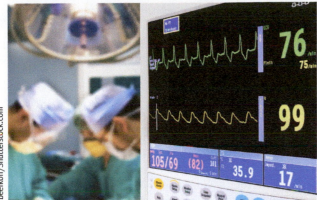

What should this cost?

a heart bypass operation some day. You have plenty of time to shop around for the hospital you feel most comfortable with, so you visit all of them in your area that offer this service.

During the search process, you discover that all of the hospitals, with one exception, have equipment that is two years old. The exception has brand-new equipment. Who are you most likely to go with? If you are like most patients with insurance, you will seek the services of the hospital with the most up-to-date technology. This is not because two-year-old equipment would be obsolete, but rather because you think "the newer the better." Since a third party will pick up part of the tab, choosing the newest equipment makes economic sense.

This reality is not lost on hospitals around the country. Administrators realize that if it does not have the latest and greatest equipment the hospital will lose paying customers to their next-best competitor. In essence, hospitals rarely have a chance for any of their equipment to generate economies of scale that might bring down the cost of health care.

If the equipment were used for say, five or six years, over that time it would pay for itself, and the hospital would realize lower costs of providing heart by-pass surgery. Lower costs could conceivably lead to lower prices. Instead of cost savings, hospitals face pressure to constantly update whether it is technically necessary or not. This means that hospitals make new equipment purchases on a more frequent basis, so duplication of technology across hospitals takes place, which leads to rising, — rather than falling — health care bills for all of us.

Unfortunately, there is also a situation that has contributed to rising health care costs that has to do with the lack of competition.

If you are a resident of Maine and hear about lower health insurance rates in Kansas, you might be inclined to call a few providers in Kansas to see if you can get a good price. The only problem is that under the McCarran-Ferguson Act (1945), it is against the law to shop across state lines for health insurance.[11]

Unlike virtually every other market where you are free to search the nation for the best deal, when it comes to health insurance, the state you live in determines where you shop. A brief look back at chapter 7 on what happens when supply is reduced will help you understand that this law has artificially suppressed supply and driven up prices.

MERGERS

In 1890 Congress passed the Sherman Antitrust Act. Section 2 of this Act states:

> Every person who shall monopolize, or attempt to monopolize, or combine or conspire with any other person or persons to monopolize any part of trade or commerce among the several states, or with foreign nations, shall be guilty of a misdemeanor.

The law has been applied to every industry from oil to computer software.[12] The intent of the law is to promote competition, increase quality, and lower prices. However, the law has actually contributed to increasing, rather than decreasing, health care costs.

Several years ago, three hospitals in Rockford, Illinois, attempted to merge and gain efficiencies by sharing equipment. The U.S. Department of Justice blocked that merger, claiming it would monopolize the local market.[13] Since the hospitals were forced to compete, the pressure to buy more and more equipment went unabated, and prices continued to rise in Rockford, just as they have in other markets around the country.

This perceived flaw in the antitrust laws led to a philosophical change in courts during the Clinton administration. The courts — over the objections of the Clinton Justice Department — began allowing more mergers — more than 700 in all from 1996 to 2000.

In cities like Houston, Texas; Richmond, Virginia; and Cleveland, Ohio, mergers have led to an explosion in health care costs. This greater concentration of market power has given HCA and other companies greater control over the prices charged to commercial insurance companies.

Hospitals argue that consolidation has been economically necessary for many reasons. Among them has been the increase in Medicare claims as the population gets older. Hospitals nationwide have lost over *$76 billion* in reimbursements that did not meet the full cost of providing care.

The hospitals contend that these mergers will eventually lead to increased cost-savings and lower prices for consumers, and that the market simply has not yet generated those cost-savings. So far, the courts agree, having ruled in more than one case that mergers will not lead to long-run anti-competitive behavior since hospitals tend to compete over a wider geographic area than the government has claimed they do. For now though, consumers are feeling the pinch of the rise of oligopoly power.

ASYMMETRIC INFORMATION

Would you ever buy a new car or house without first asking the price? Maybe if you won the lottery, but in any other case you expect information about prices, services, etc. to flow evenly, or symmetrically, from the seller to the buyer. This is how virtually every other market, other than health care, functions.

Suppose you were attacked by a wolverine while hiking in Alaska. When you got to the emergency room, do you suppose you would ask about the price of emergency room care before it was served? Does anybody ask? Probably very few would. Perhaps it is because it is considered to be bad form to ask those who are saving our lives what the bill will be. Maybe we don't ask because we don't want to upset the doctor before she sews our arm back on.

Of course, the third-party payment system might make us reluctant to ask. Finally, there is the fact that even if we did ask, and found out that repairing injuries sustained from a brawl with a wolverine will run into the thousands of dollars, we would probably not ask to be transported to another hospital that might offer a better deal. All these factors lead to asymmetric information – the hospitals know what will be charged, but we don't.

Ask yourself what you might adopt as a pricing policy if customers came to you as spur-of-the-moment shoppers and did not ask about the price before you served them. Would you charge more than if they did ask and did shop around?

Ironically, the managed-care system that was supposed to help contain costs has actually exacerbated the problem of asymmetric information and has contributed to higher health care costs.[14] When health maintenance organizations (HMOs) entered the health care arena, employees were thrilled with the idea of co-payments as low as $5–10 for office visits and drugs.

As anyone familiar with the law of unintended consequences could have predicted, these artificially low prices not only encouraged more office visits for minor ailments, but consumers were not encouraged to shop around for the best prices for drugs or to choose generic drugs over the more expensive name-brand products.

Naturally, this led to a distortion in the flow of information from the health care system to the consumer. People thought drugs were cheap, since the co-payments were cheap. When people see something as inexpensive, they will not be judicious in their purchases. The result has been an increase in the demand for medical treatment and name-brand drugs and an increase in health costs for employers.

Employers are now combating this problem by trying to bring about more symmetrical information between health care providers and customers. This has come in the form of increased co-payments and "tier-pricing," where generic drugs come at the lowest price (tier one), common name-brand drugs are a little more expensive (tier two), more expensive name-brand drugs are even more expensive (tier three), and "lifestyle" drugs like anti-baldness drugs, or rare or experimental drugs (fourth tier) require the highest co-payment of all.[15]

CRIME

Hardly a day goes by without a news report about a drive-by shooting, a drug overdose, an assault, or some other type of violent crime. When crime victims are taken to emergency rooms, how many of them do you suppose have insurance? Most victims of violent crimes are relatively poor. Many of them are uninsured.

It is also highly unlikely that criminals are covered by some insurance plan when they are shot or stabbed during the course of carrying out their occupational requirements. The last time I checked, the Crack Dealers Association of America did not offer group health care coverage in case one of its members encounters a bullet or knife blade.

As you can clearly surmise, with crime comes an intensification of the cost-shifting problem. Criminals and crime victims crowd inner-city emergency rooms, often requiring very expensive care. By one recent estimate, crime-related health care costs total $574 billion in the form of 72,000 deaths and 2.5 million injuries per year.[16] Who pays this astronomical bill for crime-related health care? All of us do – in the form of higher prices and taxes.

UNHEALTHY LIFESTYLES

If you are one of the millions of Americans who is overweight, smokes, drinks to excess, practices unsafe sex, or uses illegal drugs, you are part of a multi-billion-dollar problem that the rest of us who live pure and virtuous lives have to pay for. Consider these numbers:

Sixty-three percent of Americans are overweight or obese, adding $147 billion a year to our nation's health care bill in 2008 alone.[17] Since 1996 the number of men who are morbidly obese (100 pounds or more overweight) increased by 50%. The number of women in this category has increased by 67%. Researchers at Johns Hopkins recently projected that by 2015, 75% of Americans would be overweight or obese.[18]

In 2016 the CDC issued a report finding that obesity and diabetes – largely driven by America's growing sugar intake – imposed approximately $1 billion per day in health care costs in this country.[19]

Doctors are now even worried about children and heart disease. The number of kids who are overweight today has increased by 15% compared to 20 years ago.[20] Moreover, hospitals are facing increasing pressure to build facilities with extra-large rooms, expensive scales, extra-wide wheelchairs, and larger beds.[21] Finally, weight-based

This photograph is of a package of cigarettes purchased in Canada. The Canadian government requires such advertising of all companies that sell tobacco products. Would this type of advertising – if forced upon cigarettes sold in the U.S. – lower the cost of health care in the U.S.? Why, or why not?

Photo courtesy Jack Chambless

discrimination lawsuits continue to impose added costs on hospital finances.[22]

15% of Americans smoke, including 11% of teenagers who are increasingly using e-cigarettes.[23] By one estimate, smoking adds $100 billion per year to our health care costs.[24]

The National Institute on Drug Abuse reports that alcohol and drug abuse imposes a $366 billion cost on the economy.[25] This cost reflected treatment and prevention as well as health care costs.

© Monkey Business Images/Shutterstock.com

The American Social Health Association found that one out of every five people has had a sexually transmitted disease – adding $8 billion per year to U.S. health care costs. Many of these individuals – including the 65 million with viral STDs[26] – have no health insurance or are only partially covered by Medicare or Medicaid. When their vices lead to health problems for them, or people around them, the cost of delivering care is often shifted to taxpayers and insured patients. Even people with private insurance who get sick more often, due to smoking or drinking, add to the demand for care, and thus, the price that we all have to pay.

THE MEDICAL MONOPOLY

You recall that a monopoly is the single seller of some good or service that has few or no close substitutes. If a person or business or organization has monopoly power, this means they have some power over prices and output in that industry. Historically, monopolies have been vilified for providing poor service (cable television) and/or charging much higher prices than competitive institutions. This problem is pervasive in the health care industry.

For starters, there is the licensing process that people who practice medicine go through. You might find yourself thinking, "You better believe we should license doctors! I don't want some unemployed carpenter off the street telling people he is a neurosurgeon just because he is good with a saw!"

Before you get too carried away, you should know that this process – according to many economists who study health care markets – is not always done with your best interest in mind. Instead, the licensing process is a way for the medical establishment to *artificially control the supply* of caregivers and thus artificially hold up health care prices.[27]

In fact, the American Medical Association established, as a primary reason for licensure, the desire to restrict entry into the profession and thereby secure a more stable financial climate for physicians. As a result of the desire to maintain market power in health care, the AMA helped facilitate a decline in the number of medical schools from 160 at the turn of the nineteenth century to 76 by 1930.[28]

Today there are other ways the medical community restricts the supply of practitioners. One way is to have competitors' services ruled illegal. This has been a common practice to reduce the demand for midwives, who often practice alternative child delivery techniques, at an average savings of $3000 compared to the standard obstetrician fee.[29] Another mechanism is to restrict or limit substitute providers' services from payment by government health programs.

For example, Medicare regulations prohibit reimbursement to chiropractors for services they are licensed to perform in all 50 states.

To many economists, the fact that the AMA has been allowed to manipulate the market for health care in the name of "consumer protection" is a less-than-convincing claim. From restricting entry into medical schools for non-academic reasons to limiting the ability of competing practitioners to enter the market and succeed, the AMA has contributed billions of dollars to our health care bills for reasons unrelated to our health. It should be noted that these restrictions are allowed despite the fact that U.S. taxpayers pay over $10 billion a year in subsidies to help train the very doctors who operate in this restricted market.

Then, there are the lawyers...

THE LAWYER EFFECT

> No one has ever been healed by a frivolous lawsuit.
>
> President Bush, January 28, 2003

You have probably heard of cases where a doctor has made a mistake that led to the loss of a human life or some permanent injury. This is known as medical malpractice. Many of you may have been pleased when you heard about a jury awarding millions of dollars to the malpractice victim. After all, we do not go to the doctor expecting to end up worse off, or dead. Before you rejoice over the perception that justice is served by enormous damage awards, you should consider the following:

In 2009 the average ob/gyn in Dade County Florida paid $238,728 in medical malpractice premiums – the highest in the United States.[30] Across the states, it was not much better for those who deliver babies. Doctors in Utah paid $95,213 per year. In Nassau and Suffolk counties (New York), it was $194,935. In Los Angeles county, where malpractice lawsuits have a cap on the damage awards, it still cost $86,348 to carry insurance and $51,812 to practice general surgery.

What do you suppose such high premiums mean to our health care bills? Of course, it means we have to

When doctors face lawyers, why do you pay for it?

© Everett Collection/Shutterstock.com

pay more to receive care. If you were a doctor in Florida, would you charge just enough to cover your insurance bills?

Malpractice awards have led to higher prices, stemming from rising premiums, but also rising fees that result from doctors having to add larger and larger staffs of employees who do nothing more than move piles of paperwork that provide a detailed track record of the doctor's every move. These staff members have to have salaries, so you pay more for that, too. In addition, doctors often order up services that they may not believe are 100% medically necessary, but that are very much *legally necessary* in order to create a paper trail that, doctors hope, keeps the lawyers at bay.

All of these factors have led to dramatic increases in the input costs of providing care to all of us. Nationwide, 1 out of every 12 doctors gets sued each year. In Florida it is one out of six. Keep in mind that whenever a doctor is exposed to a massive lawsuit – whether he or she is guilty of malpractice or not – this leads to insurance companies raising malpractice insurance premiums. In addition to rising premiums, the extra paperwork, less time spent with patients, and the pressure to order up too much care just to be on the safe side, all lead to rising prices.

Compounding matters is the fact that in most cases there is no cap on the amount of money someone can win in a malpractice suit. It should not come as any great shock that doctors in many states have gone on strike, threatened to leave in large numbers, or stopped carrying insurance altogether.[31] With lawyers getting very large portions of such suits, it is no wonder that malpractice lawsuits have become so pervasive and expensive for doctors, patients, and taxpayers.[32]

THE FDA APPROVAL PROCESS

If you are like millions of Americans, you implicitly trust the government to use the money that is taken from you each year in a wise and judicious manner. How silly of you. A glaring example of your government at work is the process that the Food and Drug Administration uses to approve new drugs and medical equipment. Have you ever seen a snail crawl along the ground? The snail looks like Usain Bolt compared to the FDA.

Since its inception in 1938, the FDA's regulation of the medical device and drug industry has increased in scope, detail, and cost to the American people. You may be of the opinion that we need the FDA to make sure products and drugs do not harm or kill large (or even small) portions of the country. You should consider two things. First, at what cost should the people of this country be made safe from faulty medical equipment or drugs? As television reporter John Stossel has noted, when the FDA announces that it has finally approved a drug that will save 14,000 lives, that means the year before – when emancipated adult human beings were not allowed to buy the drug – 14,000 lives were *lost*.[33]

Second, could it be suggested that profit is enough of a motivator to keep drug and equipment companies from harming us? After all, if we haven't forgotten the lessons of Adam Smith, self-interested equipment and drug companies may not care about us at all, but they do care about money. Ask yourself how much money these companies would make if they sold us products that made us sicker or even dead. The last time I checked, killing people is not exactly an industry that is thriving in this country. This is not to suggest that private companies never make mistakes.

It does suggest that cost-benefit analysis and the concept of self-interest keeps us very safe from faulty drugs and equipment. With or without the FDA, profit-seeking companies would strive for this outcome.

Yet, we do have government oversight, so let's look at what the government is doing for us. The government has decided that herbal products – an industry that has seen its revenue climb dramatically over the past few years – are so dangerous that without FDA approval, herb makers cannot make claims that their products have specific medicinal value. The problem is that getting herbal remedies through the drug-approval process is unrealistic. Botanicals are naturally occurring and therefore cannot be patented.

Therefore, the companies that make herbal treatments have to ask themselves if it is worth even attempting to incur the average cost of *$400 million* and the average wait *of 15 years* to have a new drug approved by the government. Medical equipment manufacturers also face a daunting task. In the wake of the silicone breast implant and defective heart valve cases, the FDA has stepped up the amount of paperwork and regulatory hoops that firms must go through. This does not even take into account the number of drugs that are taken off the market because a fairly small portion of the population had a bad reaction to some pill.[34]

The result has been a dramatic slowdown in the number of devices that are approved and an increase in the number of Americans who are suffering or dying while waiting for life-saving or enhancing equipment to reach the market.[35] In the meantime, the new regulations have added millions of dollars to the budgets of health care companies and have led to companies raising prices[36] while some companies have moved overseas – where drugs are approved much faster to control regulatory costs.[37] For example, the only medicine known for treating the rare and fatal lung disease known as idiopathic pulmonary fibrosis, has been used in Japan since 2008 and was approved in Europe in 2010. It is illegal in the United States – even if the person with this disease is willing to take their chances with the medicine.[38]

Finally, consider this: In May 2007, a new treatment for prostate cancer was announced and rejected by the FDA. Three years later, the FDA approved the drug with the exact same clinical trial results that the company had submitted three years earlier. Eighty-thousand men died of prostate cancer during that time span.[39]

THE ORPHAN DRUG LAW

An orphan drug is a drug developed under the U.S. Orphan Drug Act (1983) to treat a disease that affects a relatively small number of people. The terms of the orphan drug law offer tax breaks and a seven-year monopoly on drug sales to induce companies to undertake development and manufacturing of such drugs, which otherwise might not be profitable. The cancer-fighting drug Taxol is an example of the type of drug that was covered by this law.

Critics of the law point out the fact that drugs developed and protected for seven years come at a very high price to consumers, and that often the government uses tax dollars to assist in the development of life-saving drugs and then gives the selling rights away. This leads to double-charging for these drugs – first in the form of taxes and second in the form of monopoly pricing.[40]

ADDING IT ALL UP

As you can clearly see, the issue of health care reform is not an easy one. There are simply too many variables working together to drive up costs and decrease access. That does not mean individual components of the prob-

lem could not be addressed. It also does not mean that we cannot improve the overall picture. What it does mean is that any attempt to "fix" health care in an economically pragmatic way, has to take into account the benefits and costs of every proposal.

OPTION ONE: "OBAMACARE"

Unless you have been hiding under a rock for the past several years, you know about legislation that was signed by President Obama in 2010. The legislation set off a firestorm of protests and celebrations over the perceived costs and benefits of this historic reach into the health care market.

Here are some of the key provisions that the law established:[41]

> ➤ **Starting in 2010, insurance companies were no longer allowed to place a lifetime dollar cap on how much coverage would be provided. Furthermore, health insurance providers are required to allow parents of dependent children to continue coverage for their offspring until the child was 26 years old.**
> ➤ **Starting in 2013, Medicare payroll taxes on couples earning more than $250,000 and individuals earning $200,000 were increased. The law also added a 3.8% tax to investment income.**
> ➤ **Starting in 2014, insurers were prohibited from denying or limiting coverage based on pre-existing conditions; Medicaid expanded to cover people up to 133% of the poverty line; citizens and legal residents had to have insurance or pay a fine.**
> ➤ **Starting in 2015, employers with 100 employees or more were required to offer health insurance to employees who work 30 hours per week or more, or pay a fine.**
> ➤ **Starting in 2016, employers with 50-99 employees or more were required to offer health insurance to employees who work 30 hours per week or more, or pay a fine.**

The first 10 years of this plan were projected to cost $2.7 trillion.[42] Aside from that price tag, many questions have been raised that will be addressed here. It should first be noted that in 2010, a federal judge in Virginia ruled that the requirement of all Americans to purchase insurance was a violation of Article One, Section

Eight, Clause Three of the United States Constitution.[43] In 2011, a judge in Florida ruled the *entire* legislation Unconstitutional.[44]

However, in June 2012 the United States Supreme Court, in a 5-4 vote ruled most provisions of the Patient Protection and Affordable Care Act constitutional. In writing for the majority, Chief Justice John Roberts argued that while the federal government did not have the constitutional authority to force people to buy health insurance, it did have the authority to lay and collect taxes. Justice Roberts declared that the penalty those of us who refuse to buy insurance would have to pay is a tax and since Congress has taxing authority it can impose taxes on us if we do not purchase health care insurance.[45] In his words,

> Congress may . . . 'lay and collect Taxes, Duties, Imposts and Excises, to pay the Debts and provide for the common Defense and general Welfare of the United States.' U. S. Const., Art. I, §8, cl. 1. Put simply, Congress may tax and spend. This grant gives the Federal Government considerable influence even in areas where it cannot directly regulate. The Federal Government may enact a tax on an activity that it cannot authorize, forbid, or otherwise control. . . . And in exercising its spending power, Congress may offer funds to the States, and may condition those offers on compliance with specified conditions. . . These offers may well induce the States to adopt policies that the Federal Government itself could not impose.
>
> We do not consider whether the Act embodies sound policies. That judgment is entrusted to the Nation's elected leaders.
>
> Members of this Court are vested with the authority to interpret the law; we possess neither the expertise nor the prerogative to make policy judgments. Those decisions are entrusted to our Nation's elected leaders, who can be thrown out of office if the people disagree with them. It is not our job to protect the people from the consequences of their political choices.

With the constitutionality of ObamaCare settled, the economic ramifications take center stage.

Starting with the 2010 provisions, the requirement that insurers cover dependent children until the age of 26 had the immediate impact of leading insurance companies to drop "child only" policies.[46] Before the law, many parents – especially during the "Great Recession" – opted to cover only their children while forgoing insurance for themselves.

When the legislation passed, Aetna, Cigna, Humana, and other companies told parents that if they wanted their children to be covered, they (the parents) would have to purchase insurance as well – 2.4 million children were potentially impacted by this business decision.[47] Furthermore, in 2010, with insurers now required to cover people well into adulthood, many companies began raising their insurance premiums. Compounding the rate hikes was the mandate that the companies could no longer place a lifetime maximum on how much health care they would provide.[48] Therefore, the benefit that many thought they were going to receive (more coverage over their life and expanded coverage for older kids) ended up coming with the cost of higher monthly premiums.

As for the 2013 tax increases, you will recall from chapter five that more often than not, tax increases on wealthier Americans leads to less revenue for government as people attempt to shield their private property from the IRS. When investment income taxes fell under Bill Clinton and George W. Bush, tax revenue increased markedly.[49] When income tax rates fell dramatically under John F. Kennedy; under Ronald Reagan, tax revenues shot up.[50] Many economists openly questioned the wisdom of attempting to extract health care revenue from people who not only already pay most of the nation's taxes, but who are needed to provide jobs in the wake of the historically severe recession.[51]

Speaking of 2013, this was a particularly troublesome year for millions of Americans – and the Obama Administration. The Affordable Care Act's threat of a tax for those without insurance meant that tens of millions of Americans – mostly young – were compelled to start shopping.

The legislation created something called "Health Care Exchanges" where residents in every state could go online, or on their phone, or in person to purchase various health care coverage plans. Under these exchanges we were told

Photo courtesy Sarah Chambless

SUGGESTED CLASSROOM DEBATE

Should 48-year-old men who play tackle football with no pads receive taxpayer-subsidized health care benefits? Why, or why not?

that we could select from Bronze, Silver or Gold coverage, at varying coverage options and, of course, varying prices.

Then the sign ups began. Or were supposed to begin....

As President Obama put it in late October of 2013, "There is no sugarcoating it. The website has been too slow. People have been getting stuck during the application process."

He could have also mentioned that people were having their information stolen by identity thieves; that people were sold policies they did not sign up for; that eligibility information was often wrong and that at one point one in five Americans were pushed into Medicaid when they were attempting to purchase private plans.[52]

Also somewhat disconcerting to economists were two major developments. First, as predicted by many, younger Americans were slow to sign up for health insurance under the exchanges. A major provision of ObamaCare is the rule that prevents health insurance companies from denying coverage to Americans with pre-existing conditions.

Before the law if you were a person who had lung cancer from 30 years of smoking, for example, if you applied for private health insurance you would have most likely been denied coverage. That is because of the simple fact that the person with cancer, shortly after paying his or her first premium, would have walked into a hospital seeking care that could cost hundreds of thousands of dollars. Logic would suggest that it would be irrational for a health insurance provider to give $400,000 in covered treatment to someone who has paid $400 in monthly premiums. This would force the insurer to raise premiums to all of the other customers in order to remain economically viable.

Therefore, getting the millions of young, healthy Americans to sign up was critical to generating enough revenue to offset the rising cost of covering unhealthy Americans. As the March 31, 2014 deadline for signing up – or face the "tax" approached, only 25% of those registered came from the vital 18-34 age range, fueling fears that health insurance rates would have to rise sharply in the future to cover the growing demands of our less healthy population.[53]

Furthermore, starting in January 2014, insurers were no longer allowed to set premiums for "small-group plans" – which apply to employers with fewer than 50 or 100 employees based on a firm's industry or health or gender of its staff. This meant that companies with younger, healthier workers faced large premium increases to balance out the costs of covering companies with older or less healthy profiles.[54]

According to President Obama, the problem of cost-shifting could be efficiently reduced if every American were required to purchase health care. Economically, this argument would seem to have some merit. After all, if you are not insured and go to the hospital following a car wreck, either the taxpayers have to pick up the tab (Medicaid or Medicare) or people with insurance have to pay more once your bill is passed on to some other person with insurance. If everyone without insurance is forced into the pool of paying customers (see car insurance), the amount of dollars available to treat people goes up, while the average cost per person treated goes down.

However, part of the Affordable Care Act appeared to go against his argument. Starting in 2013, Americans living at least 33% above the poverty line were added to the Medicaid roles. The poverty line for a family of four was $23,550 in 2013. That means as of 2013 a family with an annual income of $31,321.50 would qualify for taxpayer dollars in their health care needs. Millions of Americans were added under this provision, making health care appear to be "free" to those who used to have to pay for it. One quick review of the law of demand would suggest that we would (and did) see a vast increase in the quantity of health care demanded by this group, which would exacerbate the cost-shifting problem.

Also, by forcing people to pay for insurance or face an IRS-levied fine, the government created more economic hardship for people who are healthy and needed the money to pay for housing, food, college expenses, and other necessities. Moreover is the issue of allowing government to force us to engage in commerce. If you do not drive a car, you do not have to buy car insurance. The federal government, before 2010, never passed a law saying to all of us, "We have selected a business that we are going to force you to purchase something from." One might ask the question, if government can force us to buy insurance, does this mean that a precedent has been set that allows government to force us to buy other things that might "be good for us"?

By making it illegal for businesses with 50 or more workers to not offer insurance, government increased the risk of raising the cost of doing business at a time when economic growth was sluggish. The government unwittingly caused businesses to pick between paying a fine instead of providing health insurance.

President Obama said many times in 2010, that if we liked our insurance we could keep it. However, he did not tell us what to do if we liked our insurance but our businesses did not. By telling American companies to provide health insurance or pay a fine, he immediately set in motion a huge cost-benefit calculation that had led many companies to forecast that it would be cheaper to pay the fine than to continue to pay for increasingly expensive health insurance.[55]

Employers are not the only ones making cost-benefit calculations. A February 2014 *Wall Street Journal* article found that:

The new health law is projected to reduce the total number of hours Americans work by the equivalent of 2.3 million full-time jobs in 2021, a bigger impact on the workforce than previously expected, according to a nonpartisan congressional report.

The analysis, by the Congressional Budget Office, says a key factor is people scaling back how much they work and instead getting health coverage through the Affordable Care Act. The agency had earlier forecast the labor-force impact would be the equivalent of 800,000 workers in 2021.[56]

The CBO forecast was based on a provision of the law that limits the annual earnings that a person or household can take in and still qualify for taxpayer-support of their health care needs. It is a straight-forward question for many Americans. If earning an extra few thousand dollars at a job would cost a family several more thousand dollars in lost taxpayer support, it would be rational for many families to cut back on their hours at work and depend on other workers – and their tax dollars – for health care.

Another issue that came up in 2013 – which caught almost 5 million Americans by surprise – was the fact that millions of us who had health insurance policies before the Affordable Care Act was passed received cancellation notices from private health insurers that year because the plan was not legally recognized by the new law. Simply put, for 4.8 million Americans the new health care law had regulations addressing coverage, deductibles and other aspects of health insurance that had to be complied with. In most instances, when these Americans were cancelled and attempted to re-apply for a legally-recognized plan, the new plan was 30% more expensive than their old coverage.[57]

Then, there is the question of what to do with the estimated 31 million people – illegal immigrants and people who pay the fine rather than buy health insurance.[58] If we go from 50 million people to 31 million without insurance – at a cost of $2.7 trillion in just 10 years, is that enough of a benefit to justify the cost?

In January of 2014 I received an email from the president of a company in Florida which read;

After 25 years of continuous governmental "poaching" of my income, I find it harder and harder to have any desire to continue to risk my personal earnings for business expansion. Next year the Affordable Care Act alone will strip over $100,000 from our profits. With only 190 employees you probably can figure out that $100K is painful and damaging to our long term financial stability.

I feel for my children currently entering college as they have the entrepreneurial spirit, yet they see the continuous erosion of rewards for risk and hard work.

This man was not alone. By 2017, countless articles had appeared in newspapers all over America chronicling the explosion in health care costs. The Kaiser Foundation found that since 2010 health care deductibles had increased by 67% to 256% across the country and health care spending per family had increased from 5.8% of the average household budget to 8%.[59]

Because of mounting losses incurred by insurance companies associated with covering far more people with pre-existing conditions, insurance premiums for healthy Americans rose substantially. Blue Cross Blue Shield of Texas, for example, lost $592 million in 2015 and $416 million in 2014, prompting the company to seek premium increases of 57.3 to 59.4%.[60]

Meanwhile, younger, healthier Americans continued to face the difficult cost-benefit calculation associated with buying insurance versus paying the federal penalty. As of 2016 16% of people between 25-34 years of age opted to forgo insurance as more than 40 insurers raised rates to cover the growing cost of ObamaCare. The IRS penalty of $695 (or 2.5% of income) was not enough to encourage young Americans to sign up for health insurance. With the lack of young, healthy paying customers, rates were expected to continue to rise through 2017.[61]

HEALTH CARE REFORM AND THE CONSTITUTION

During the 2008 presidential campaign, Barack Obama called health care a "right." In 2004 George W. Bush signed into law the biggest single expansion of health care benefits in U.S. history.

Recall that Article One, Section Eight, Clause One reads:

The Congress shall have the power to lay and collect taxes, duties, imposts and excises, to pay the debts and provide for the common defense and general welfare of the United States; but all duties, imposts and excises shall be uniform throughout the United States.

If you were to take a close look at this rulebook for public officials, you would not find one reference to the government's role in providing for free health care. You may recall from chapter three that the founder's view of the enumerated clauses were clear, but the Supreme Court sided with Alexander Hamilton as to the true interpretation of the words, general welfare. Whom would you side with regarding the question over health care and this clause? Before you answer, consider this:

In February 2009, I severely sprained my left ankle while playing football in my back yard. In August 2010, I sprained the right one while portaging a canoe in Northern Minnesota. Between the multiple sets of X-Rays, MRIs, walking boots (two different types), and rehabilitation, I probably rang up several thousand dollars in doctor bills. If I did not have insurance, should you be forced to help my ankles get better? Should I be asked to help you if you smoke too much or don't eat right?

Well before the Patient Protection and Affordable Care Act was passed, legal and economic scholars were questioning whether the law would ultimately prevail.[62] When the 2,700 page health care legislation was passed, then Speaker of the House, Nancy Pelosi was asked about the bill's constitutionality. "Are you serious?" was her reply.[63]

The Cost of "Free" Health Care

For many, the health care system is so fundamentally flawed that the argument of turning over the entire system to the government is appealing.[64] For those folks, the health care legislation signed by President Obama did not go far enough in dealing with our health care situation.

Turning over the entire health care system to elected officials and a system of socialistic rationing may sound appealing, but ask yourself why so many foreigners come to the U.S. when serious health concerns must be addressed. Why is there now a *waiting list to get on the waiting list* for health care in Great Britain – a nation where dirty hospitals and botched care are not uncommon?[65] Why has the life expectancy of Canadian women actually fallen over the years? Is there a rational reason why Canadians face an average wait of 17.7 weeks to see a general practitioner, or 18.2 weeks for surgery?[66] Why do half of all Canadians want a different health care model?[67] Why has cervical cancer doubled in Cuba, at the same time patients are now required to bring their own syringes, towels, and bed sheets to hospitals where doctors make $25 per month?[68]

It is because in those nations – and others where the government runs health care – the people have traded in the freedom to navigate through health care markets for the security of having taxpayers pick up the tab. In these nations, taxpayers pay for the care of everyone. Government then sets a budget for hospitals and fixes prices below the equilibrium level on doctors' fees, drugs, medicine, and other forms of care. The low fees are designed to keep people from being "exploited" by higher prices.

However, since the prices are set artificially low, the governments that use taxpayer money to provide care must set budgets; otherwise, people would try to use much more care than they need. This may sound good, but the result has been very

hard on the very people who traded in their economic liberty.

A few years ago, citizens of Ottawa faced the following situation in the market for surgeries:

Delays in getting treatment associated with government cost controls, having hospitals that run out of money and close their doors, elective surgeries postponed for months (if not years), and the tax burdens to pay for it all make national health care a highly questionable objective by any measure. That might be why many doctors in Canada continue to lobby for privatization of the Canadian health care system – while others illegally operate for-profit health clinics.[69]

Furthermore, while Americans have become enticed by the prospect of finding cheaper drugs in Canada, the Canadian pharmaceutical industry has come under fire for lax safety standards and inefficient production processes.[70]

And if you are a healthy person in Canada – and other countries with socialized medicine – you arguably get the worst deal of all – because you pay for a service you don't use.

The United States is not immune to this problem. Since the 1960s, the federal government has run a form of socialized medicine in this country known as Medicaid and Medicare. Medicaid is a taxpayer-financed health program for poor people. Medicare is the taxpayer-financed health care system for older Americans – including the 76 million Americans who are about to become old…

States all over the U.S. are increasingly faced with the age-old problem of opportunity cost in the face of scarce resources. The scarce resources in this case involve tax dollars. After all, there is only so much money governments can squeeze out of people to pay for anything. The dilemma that we face is that as the demand for "free" health care grows each year, the supply of money to match this demand is not keeping pace.[71]

This means that officials at the state and federal level are facing budget crisis after budget crisis associated with

STILL WAITING?
Wait times for common surgical procedures in Ontario, Canada
Source: Canadian Ministry of Health & Long-Term Care

65 Days – Cardiac Bypass
68 Days – All Cancers (avg)
73 Days – CT Scan
96 Days – Prostate Cancer
126 Days – MRI
141 Days – Cataract Surgery
168 Days – Breast Cancer (to MRI)
210 Days – Hip Replacement
291 Days – Knee Replacement

paying for health care – often at the expense of roads, education, and other items the voters expect to see funded.[72]

COULD THE FREE MARKET SOLVE THE "PROBLEM"?

If we apply a free-market approach to rising health care costs and declining access, we would conclude that the most efficacious policy would be to allow market forces to correct as much of the problem as possible.

In the past 50 years, death from cardiac arrest in the U.S. has fallen by 67%. The Nobel Prizes in medicine and physiology have been awarded to more Americans than to researchers in all other countries *combined*. Eight of the top ten selling drugs in the world come from the U.S., while we rank first or second in the world in kidney transplants, liver transplants, heart transplants, total knee replacements, coronary artery bypass, and percutaneous coronary interventions – all while having the shortest wait time for surgeries in the world.[73]

The best cars in the world cost a lot of money. So does the best food and the best World Series tickets. Can everyone afford a Rolls Royce, lobster, and box seats at Fenway Park?

We have seen numerous cases where the free market has acted to control the growth of health care costs. Look at HMOs and health clinics that you find inside malls and other shopping centers.

What about generic drugs and nontraditional medical approaches? Doesn't the free market cause these examples of cost-containment?

In 2017, 29 million people were still without health insurance – even with the prospect of paying a fine looming.

One question that could be asked – from a free market perspective – is how many of these people could afford health care *but decided to spend their money on something else?* Isn't that part of our market-based economy – the rational choice to spend our income on what we value?

One free-market response to rising health care costs has been the new trend of consumers negotiating health care prices with doctors and hospitals.[74] What would have seemed like an absurd notion not so long ago is gaining momentum. The key to negotiation seems to be driven by consumers who are willing to pay their bill up front in exchange for a discounted price and employers who have changed their health insurance policies to a "lump sum" plan, where workers are given a certain amount of money to spend on health care each year. With a budget constraint now in place, workers have an incentive to negotiate lower prices.

With cost-shifting leading to so many unpaid bills, doctors and hospitals are increasingly willing to take less money in exchange for the guarantee that the bill will be paid at the time services are rendered.

The free market has also led to more and more consumers buying drugs from India (where drugs are less expensive) or switching from brand-name drugs to generics in order to save money.[75] The movement toward generics has not only led to a significant drop in the profits of major drug companies, but has forced the drug companies to resort to greater advertising to try to regain market share.

The Internet has begun to play a role in dealing with the problem of asymmetric information. If you ever need surgery, you may want to log onto to the Internet to see if your state has a system where a person can find comparisons of hospitals for prices, length of stay, and many other facts that previously you could not ascertain.[76] The Leapfrog Group has even gone so far as to rate hospitals on the issue of safety.[77]

Finally, the free market has revealed some rather creative ways to fight health care inflation in some obvious – and not so obvious places.

Wal-Mart and other stores have begun opening health care clinics that typically charge between $25 – 60 per visit. This price is far below what many poorer people would have to pay to visit a doctor elsewhere.[78]

More and more companies are now adopting policies that ban smoking and discourage unhealthy people from applying for jobs in order to lower health care costs. This type of reaction to rising health care premiums is a natural one – and one that could bring about more rational decisions by prospective employees as it pertains to drugs, sex, and alcohol.[79]

Insurance companies have also discovered the same thing the automobile industry did years ago. That is the fact that poor people can be profitable customers, too.

Increasingly, many of the uninsured are gaining some access to insurance plans that are targeted at college students, retirees and others that are often turned off by the high deductibles that traditional insurance requires.[80] This was threatened by one provision of the 2010 health care law that caps how much insurers can spend on expenses and take for profits. In response, many insurers had called into question the economic rationality of offering these riskier policies.[81]

Finally, there is a more traditional way the free market has lowered costs. Over the last several years as the technology associated with LASIK eye surgery has increased, the costs of such surgery has fallen and thus, prices have come down considerably. What used to cost thousands of dollars now costs hundreds in some cases, as the free market has acted the same way it does in HDTVs, cell phones, and other areas of our lives.

OTHER "SOLUTIONS"

If solving what ails us in the health care market seems like an exercise in futility, there might be some alternatives for the U.S. to consider that in the long run could at least help to slow the rate of health care inflation and increase the number of people who have access to health care services.

Among the solutions that have been offered are health savings accounts, tax credits for living wills, higher taxes on products that create health care problems, Medicare and Medicaid reform, the legalization of euthanasia, privatization of the FDA, malpractice litigation reform, and modification of the antitrust laws. Let's look at some of these ideas.

HEALTH SAVINGS ACCOUNTS

The concept of health savings accounts is gaining popularity as a quasi-free-market approach to increasing access to health care.[82] During his State of the Union address in 2006, President Bush made this idea a centerpiece of his health care reform proposal.[83] The idea is that a person would be allowed to put a certain amount of money into an interest-bearing account, much like a savings account in a bank that would be tax-deductible and available to them only for medical purposes.

The appeal of this idea is straightforward. Rather than have Americans buy insurance or run the risk of going without insurance, the government would create an economic incentive for people to save money (the tax deduction) while at the same time reducing the number of Americans who have no money available to pay for health care needs.

Of course, the unanswered question is whether Americans would respond to the incentive by saving. We Americans are already notoriously lousy savers for our retirement and our children's educational needs, so saving for the possibility of a health problem might not be at the top of our list of priorities. The incentive might have to be quite large to induce the behavioral response needed.

However, we do see companies like Whole Foods and Safeway offering HSAs with a great deal of success. These companies have insurance plans with high deductibles.[84]

You might have to pay for the first $1,000 of your care before insurance kicks in. However, the company gives you money – in the case of Whole Foods, about $1,500 per year – to put into an account. If you do not use the money, it rolls over to the next year so that a worker can actually build up cash over time, to pay for their health care needs.

The result has been more price-conscientiousness by the workers, lower costs for Whole Foods, and a lessening of the third-party payer problem.[85]

THE LIVING WILL TAX CREDIT

The average American will spend almost half of his or her lifetime expenditure on health care in the last month of life. This is a staggering statistic born out of our innate desire to prolong life as long as possible. The problem for many elderly Americans is that when the end is near, they are incapable of making this decision.

Such a painful dilemma often leads the relatives of the dying to ignore the medical experts and opt for any and all technology that can give their loved one a few more chances. This reality leads to an incredible increase in the cost of providing health care and adds billions to the collective bill each year. As baby boomers age, this dilemma will get even worse.[86]

A living will gives a person the opportunity – while alive and coherent – to legally put into place the parameters for extending or saving his or her own life.[87]

These parameters could include "do not resuscitate" provisions or statements that remove the life-ending decision from family members. The problem is, that living wills cost money to create, and few of us are willing to take on this responsibility. If a tax credit (my suggestion) were made available for this expense, it would lower the cost of obtaining such a will. For just a few hundred dollars of tax relief, the government could save millions, if not billions, of dollars over time in Medicare costs from patients who have no chance to live, but have no incentive to say "enough" when someone else will see the bill.

SUGGESTED CLASSROOM DEBATE

Should physician-assisted suicide be legalized as part of any plan designed to reduce health care costs? Why or why not?

SIN TAX INCREASES

Currently, the federal government taxes cigarettes and alcohol in order to deal with the negative externalities and raise revenue. Should these taxes be even higher?

One proposal that Congress briefly considered called for the government to create a progressive tax on the saturated fat content of food, in order to raise revenue to fight heart disease brought on by bad diets.[88] Based on the current price elasticity of demand for high-fat foods, it was estimated that such a tax would generate just over $20 billion annually.

MEDICARE AND MEDICAID REFORM

Medicaid and Medicare are taxpayer-funded health care programs that cost hundreds of billions of dollars per year. The problem is that many of those billions of dollars are fraudulently spent. Here are some examples from Justice Department records: The supplier who went door-to-door, promising beneficiaries' free milk, and then billed Medicare for expensive nutritional supplements.

Then there was the lab that encouraged physicians to order free tests, as part of a testing panel, and then billed Medicare separately for these unnecessary tests. The durable medical equipment supplier who billed Medicare for canes, wheelchairs, and other items allegedly supplied from his offices on the sixth floor of a five-story building. The guy down in Florida who was billing Medicare for oxygen and supplies for a number of beneficiaries, and when the staff got to his office for a site visit, they found lots of neat souvenirs, like stuffed alligators.[89] By some estimates, Medicare fraud alone costs taxpayers $100 billion per year.[90]

This means any discussion of reducing health care costs must look at these and other examples of wasted taxpayer money.

ELIMINATION OF THE FDA

As we have seen, the FDA approval process has added years and millions of dollars to the development of new drugs. This has prompted some economists to call for the elimination of the FDA.[91] Would the free market do a better job of regulating new drugs and medical equipment?

If the FDA disappeared tomorrow, and if no one were in control of determining the safeness and effectiveness of drugs and medical technology, would it be disconcerting to most Americans? Of course it would be. Disconcerted consumers are seen as potential customers of entrepreneurs. Shortly after the dissolution of the FDA, one or more private companies would jump into the market – as the argument goes – specializing in examining drugs and equipment to determine if they are safe and effective. Just like Underwriters Laboratories has made a reputation for assuring homebuilders that wiring is safe, these new entrepreneurs would know that they would have to gain the trust of the American consumer.

If the new companies put their "seal of approval" on a new drug and people end up dead, or worse off, from taking the drug, how long will it take for that company to go out of business? If the FDA does the same thing, will it go out of business? As long as the FDA is funded with your tax dollars, if it makes a mistake, no matter how bad the mistake is, you will still have to see your taxes go to the FDA. The private business does not work that way. It knows that you can voluntarily refuse to buy anything with its name on it, so in order to make profit the private business has to be diligent, resourceful, and effective in delivering the service.

This also means that the private business would have to be efficient with your money. Long delays would push up costs and prices, and would therefore lower the amount of the drugs or equipment consumed. The private research company would be faster than the FDA but would not be able to simply rush drugs through for fear of making a mistake that could cost lives and profits.

If you recall the concept of self-interest and what self-interest tends to accomplish, it makes a great deal of sense to speculate that drug prices would be lower and drugs and equipment would get to people faster if the FDA did not exist.

MALPRACTICE LITIGATION REFORM

We have seen that lawsuits cause health care costs to rise for several reasons. Lawsuits cost money. Higher insurance premiums and unnecessary tests stemming from fear of lawyers, all drive health care costs up. Some solutions to this problem could be caps on damage awards, the "loser pays" scenario that is common in Great Britain, and more economic analysis of what damages were caused by the doctor, as opposed to hysterical damage awards driven by emotional juries.

Capping damage awards means just that. For a lost leg, death, or whatever, there would be a limit as to how much someone could get in an award. *Forensic economics* – the use of economics to determine the value of life and body parts – could be used to set the awards. For example, if a right-handed economics professor and a left-handed major league baseball player each had rotator cuff surgery on their left shoulders, and the surgeon blew the operation, resulting in the amputation of each man's arm, a forensic economist would measure the total projected earnings lost by each person and conclude that the pitcher should get a far larger award.

Currently, we have economists do this type of analysis and testimony, but juries often disregard statistics in favor of some normative evaluation of damages. A stricter criterion based on forensic modeling could reduce jury awards to a more rational level and help bring down health care costs.

SOME FINAL THOUGHTS

At the beginning of this book, you learned how the perpetual problem of scarcity forces all of us to make decisions using cost-benefit analysis. Depending on your perspective, the lack of cost-benefit analysis utilized in the health care market is a good thing or a bad thing.

For you, it might be a good thing that the government provides some basic level of health care. Even groups that have seen health care costs explode and understand the problem of cost-shifting still feel that any government reforms of the system should come with some guarantee of basic health care for all.[92] Yet, without some basic level of care, would people die in the streets, or would families and charities provide the needed assistance? It is hard to imagine that we as a society would let our fellow citizens suffer without any aid.

On the other hand, it is easy to understand why so many of you might be furious with your experiences with the health care system. Like many of you, I have waited hours outside of an emergency room wondering how many people ahead of me in line were there for reasons associated with texting while driving, drugs, alcohol, or other bad choices (not skiing or backyard football…), or were there without any real emergency at all.

You might say, "I think people should pay their bills, and if they can't, make them work it off!" Maybe that is not such a bad idea. What if they are too ill to work? Who pays for the administrative and monitoring costs to make sure they do the work? It is not as simple as it sounds.

Nonetheless, one salient fact emerges from this health care mess. That is that no one really seems to know how to fix a system that began unraveling after World War II.

Before the war, if you got sick, you paid your bill and left. During the war, it was illegal for businesses to offer higher wages to entice workers to move from job to job, so businesses instead began offering health insurance as a non-monetary form of compensation.[93]

FDR had instituted wage and price controls to prevent businesses from earning "too much" profit. Excess profits were taxed at very high rates. Frozen wages were taxed at the prevailing income tax rates. But the government decided to exempt health benefits from taxation. So corporations took their wartime profits and began offering generous health care benefits. In 1953 the IRS tried to overturn this exemption. Congress overruled the IRS.[94]

Once the third party entered the picture, all incentives on everybody's part – patients, doctors, hospitals, insurance companies, lawyers, the government, and so forth – flew right out the window. More than 70 years later, we are on the verge of an epic budgetary meltdown when the children born right after World War II begin demanding their medical entitlement. When that happens, all bets are off as to what the health care market – and the proposed "fixes" for the market – will look like.

As Donald Trump moved into the White House in January 2017 he did so promising to "repeal and replace" ObamaCare. As this paragraph is being written, 20 million Americans have access to health care that was created by the 2010 law.   Repealing the law that provides this access posed troubling questions for Congress – chief among them, what to replace ObamaCare with.

Undoubtedly, this repeal push is (was) controversial since throughout our nation's history our government has discovered that taking away social welfare benefits can be as difficult as it is to create the benefit to begin with.

ENDNOTES

1 See "Court Backs Obama on Health Law" by Jess Bravin & Louise Radnofsky, *The Wall Street Journal*, June 29, 2012.

2 Source: The Worldbank.

3 See "ObamaCare Sticker Shock" *The Wall Street Journal*, August 13-14, 2016.

4 See "Health Insurers Raise some Rates by Double-Digits" by Reed Abelson, *The New York Times*, January 5, 2013.

5 See "Do Some Pay Too Little for Health Care?" by David E. Rosenbaum, *The New York Times*, October 26, 2003.

6 See "In Oregon study, upping Medicaid access results in more ER visits" by Mone Morin, *The Orlando Sentinel,* January 5, 2014 page A14.

7 See "Shifting Burden Helps Employers Cut Health Costs" by Vanessa Fuhrmans, *The Wall Street Journal*, December 8, 2003, p. B1.

8 See: "The 81% Tax Increase" by Bruce Bartlett, *Forbes*, May 15, 2009.

9 See "Patients in Florida Lining Up For All That Medicare Covers" by Gina Kolata, *The New York Times*, September 13, 2003.

10 See www.pbs.org/wnet/bid/sb-howmuch.html.

11 See http://www.ncsl.org/research/health/out-of-state-health-insurance-purchases.aspx

12 For more on the Sherman Antitrust Act, see *The Economics of Antitrust* by Don E. Waldman, Little Brown, 1986, or *Antitrust Law and Economics in a Nutshell* by Ernest Gellhorn, West Publishing Co., 1990.

13 See The Brokaw Report: America's Health Care: Going Broke in Style, *NBC*, December 30, 1992.

14 See "Uncertainty Inside Emergency Rooms" by Michelle Andrews, *The New York Times*, September 21, 2003.

15 See "Workers swallow bitter pill" by Greg Groeller, *The Orlando Sentinel,* April 28, 2002.

16 See www.economics.about.com/money/economics/library/weekly/aa041300.html.

17 Source: WebMD and "Our Big Problem" by Theodore Dalrymple, *The Wall Street Journal*, May 1-2, 2010.

18 Source: Reuters July19, 2007.

19 See "Is Sugar Killing Us" by Gary Taubes, *The Wall Street Journal*, December 10–11, 2016.

20 See "Heart Disease Hits the Preschool Set" by Ron Winslow, *The Wall Street Journal*, March 18, 2003.

21 See "As Obesity Rises, So Do Indignities in Health Care" by Richard Perez-Pena and Grant Glickson, *The New York Times*, November 29, 2003.

22 See "Obesity's Hidden Costs" by Rhonda L. Rundle, *The Wall Street Journal*, May 1, 2002.

23 See https://www.cdc.gov/media/releases/2016/p0609-yrbs.html.

24 Source: Science Progress and the Congressional Budget Office.

25 The U.S. Department of Justice.

26 Source: The Guttmacher Institute.

27 See "The Politics of Health Legislation: An Economic Perspective" by Paul J. Feldstein, (Ann Arbor: Health Administration Press, 1988), p. 81; and "Birth Choices, the Law, and Medicine: Balancing Individual Freedoms and Protection of the Public's Health" by Chris Hafner-Eaton and Laurie Pearce, *Journal of Health Politics, Policy and Law* 19 (Winter 1994): 815.

28 See the Final Report on the Commission on Medical Education (New York: Association of American Medical Colleges, 1932), pp. 151–153, by A. Lawrence Lowell.

29 See "Federal Acute Back Pain Guideline Recommends Medication, Spinal Manipulation, and Exercise: Most Patients Can Safely Defer Specialized Diagnostic Testing," by Mark L. Schoene, *Back Letter* 10 (January 1995) 1.

30 Source: mymedicalmalpracticeinsurance.com.

31 See "So Sue Me: Doctors Without Insurance" by Rachel Emma Silverman, *The Wall Street Journal*, January 28, 2004, p. D1.

32 For more on the nationwide malpractice crisis, see "Legal Malpractice" by Philip K. Howard, *The Wall Street Journal*, January 27, 2003, p. A16; "Health care remains critical" by Ronald Brownstein, *The Orlando Sentinel*, January 5, 2003; "Insurers Missteps Helped Provoke Malpractice 'Crisis'" by Rachel Zimmerman and Christopher Oster, *The Wall Street Journal*, June 24, 2002; and "Flaws riddle state's trauma system" by Greg Groeller and Stephanie Erickson, *The Orlando Sentinel*, March 30, 2003.

33 See *Give me a Break* by John Stossel, Harper Collins, 2004, pp.43-47.

34 See "Paternalism Costs Lives" by Henry I. Miller, *The Wall Street Journal*, March 2, 2006.

35 Policy Analysis No. 235, August 7, 1995, "Wrecking Ball: FDA Regulation of Medical Devices" by Robert Higgs, The Cato Institute.

36 See "High U.S. Drug Prices May Give Pharmaceutical Makers a Migraine" by Laurie McGinley and Rachel Zimmerman, *The Wall Street Journal*, July 21, 2000.

37 For more on how the free market works faster–and creates lower prices–than the FDA, see "Drug makers feel squeeze" by Don Lee and Ronald D. White, *The Orlando Sentinel*, August 18, 2002; and "Rush to Fill Void in Menopause-Drug Market" by Gina Kolata, *The New York Times*, September 1, 2002.

38 See "The FDA is Evading the Law" by Scott Gottlieb, *The Wall Street Journal*, December 23, 2010.

39 See "The FDA vs. Bone Cancer Patients" by Mark Thornton, *The Wall Street Journal*, May 7, 2010.

40 See the April 13, 1998, segment of *NBC Nightly News* titled, "The Fleecing of America."

41 Sources: The Kaiser Family Foundation, House Energy Subcommittee, AP and Tribune Newspapers reporting.

42 See "The Real Impact of the New Health Care Law" by Michael D. Tanner, *Cato's Letter*, Fall 2010, Volume 8, Number 4.

43 See "Ruling likely puts health law into extended legal morass" by Noam N. Levey and David G. Savage, *The Orlando Sentinel*, December 14, 2010.

44 See "Judge Rejects Health Law" by Janet Adamy, *The Wall Street Journal*, February 1, 2011.

45 See "Chief Justice Roberts Taxes Credibility" by William McGurn, *The Wall Street Journal*, July 3, 2012.

46 See "Kids 0, Insurance 0," *The Wall Street Journal*, September 25-26, 2010.

47 See "No thanks to Obama's deal on health care" by Austin White, *The Orlando Sentinel*, November 27, 2010.

48 See "Health Insurers Plan Hikes" by Janet Adamy, *The Wall Street Journal*, September 8, 2010.

49 See "ObamaCare's Worst Tax Hike" *The Wall Street Journal*, March 17, 2010, p. A20.

50 See "The Rich Can't Pay for ObamaCare" by Alan Reynolds, *The Wall Street Journal*, March 30, 2010.

51 See "The $31 Billion Revenue Fantasy," *The Wall Street Journal*, August 28-29, 2010.

52 See "Errors Continue to Plague Health Site" by Christopher Weaver, *The Wall Street Journal*, December 14-15, 2013 & "Obama Admits Health Website Flaws" by Louise Radnofsky, Amy Schatz & Christopher Weaver, *The Wall Street Journal*, October 22, 2013.

53 See "Health Sign-Ups Skew Older, Raising Fears of Higher Costs" by Louise Radnofsky & Christopher Weaver, *The Wall Street Journal*, January 14, 2014 and "Insurance Costs Set for a Jolt" by Louise Radnofsky, *The Wall Street Journal*, July 1, 2013.

54 See "Young, Healthy Employees? You Will Pay More" by Sarah E. Needleman, *The Wall Street Journal*, June 7, 2013 page B1.

55 See "Documents reveal AT&T, Verizon, others, thought about dropping employer-sponsored benefits" by Shawn Tully, *CNNMoney.com*, May 6, 2010; and "Goodbye, Employer-Sponsored Insurance" by John C. Goodman, *The Wall Street Journal*, May 21, 2010.

56 See "Health Law to Cut into Labor Force" by Louise Radnofsky & Damien Paletta, *The Wall Street Journal*, February 4, 2014.

57 See "ObamaCare's Troubles are Only Beginning" by Michael J. Boskin, *The Wall Street Journal*, December 16, 2013 page A15.

58 See "Obamacare: Reality versus the rhetoric" by David Moreland, *The Orlando Sentinel*, July 3, 2010.

59 See "Health Burden Moves to the Middle" by Anna Louie Sussman, *The Wall Street Journal*, August 26, 2016.

60 See "More Insurers looking to raise Obamacare rates" by Ricardo Alonso-Zaldivar, *The Orlando Sentinel*, June 2, 2016.

61 See "A Millennial's ObamaCare Lament" by David Barnes, *The Wall Street Journal*, September 26, 2016.

62 See "ObamaCare and the General Welfare Clause" by Randy E. Barnett and David G. Oedel, *The Wall Street Journal*, December 27, 2010; and "Why the ObamaCare Tax Penalty is Unconstitutional" by J. Kenneth Blackwell and Kenneth A. Klukowski, *The Wall Street Journal*, July 22, 2010.

63 See Congress's Montrous Legacy" by Kimberly A. Strassel, *The Wall Street Journal*, December 24, 2010.

64 In 2004 the National Academy of Sciences recommended that the government find a way to provide coverage for all Americans. See "Panel urges health coverage for all" by Rob Stein, *The Washington Post*, January 15, 2004.

65 See "Britain's Prescription for Health Care: Take a Seat" by Sarah Lyall, *The New York Times*, April 18, 1999; and "The Health care Wars Are Only Beginning" by Fred Barnes, *The Wall Street Journal*, March 18, 2010.

66 See "Waits for Canadian Health Care Shorten a Bit" *The Wall Street Journal*, October 19, 2005; and *Waiting Your Turn: Wait Times for Health Care in Canada* by Mark Rovere.

67 See "Woe, Canada," *The Wall Street Journal*, September 8, 2002, p. A20; and "Why not buy American health care?" by Anthony Westell, *The Globe and Mail*, August 2, 2005, p. A13.

68 See "Dr. Berwick and That Fabulous Cuban Health Care" by Bret Stephens, *The Wall Street Journal*, July 13, 2010.

69 See "Doctors to argue for private health system" by Gloria Galloway, *The Globe and Mail*, July 27, 2005; and "Sick in America: Whose Body is it, Anyway" John Stossel reporting, *ABC News* 2007.

70 See "Canadian Pharmacies Flunk Inspections" by Conrad F. Meier, *Health Care News* (The Heartland Institute), Volume 4, Number 5, May 2004.

71 See "Governors Chop Spending" by Conor Dougherty and Amy Merrick, *The Wall Street Journal*, February 7, 2011.

72 See "Surging Costs for Medicaid Ravage State, Federal Budgets" by Sarah Lueck, *The Wall Street Journal*, February 7, 2005; "How to Ride the Medicaid Tidal Wave" by James Frogue, *Budget & Tax News* (The Heartland Institute) February 2005; and "Maine's State-Run Health Plan Faltering" by Tarren Bragdon, *Health Care News* (The Heartland Institute), January 2006.

73 See "The Failure of RomneyCare" by Grace-Marie Turner, *The Wall Street Journal*, March 17, 2010.

74 See "Where U.S. Health Care Ranks Number One" by Mark B. Constantian, *The Wall Street Journal*, January 7, 2010.

75 See "Can We Talk Price?" *The Wall Street Journal*, February 8, 2002.

76 See "For Drug Makers, Good Times Yield to a New Profit Crunch" by Gardiner Harris, *The Wall Street Journal,* April 18, 2002; "How Drug Makers Use Pharmacies to Push Pricey Pills" by Ann Zimmerman and David Armstrong, *The Wall Street Journal,* May 1, 2002; and "Generic Drugs From India Prompting Turf Battles" by Saritha Rai, *The New York Times,* December 26, 2003.

77 See "New Ratings Let Patients Shop for Hospitals" by Bernard Wysocki Jr. *The Wall Street Journal,* May 1, 2002.

78 See "Report Card to Rank Hospitals on Safety" by Laura Landro, *The Wall Street Journal,* April 22, 2004, p. D1.

79 See "Getting Your Health Care at Wal-Mart" by Jane Spencer, *The Wall Street Journal,* October 5, 2005.

80 See "Can Employers Alter Hiring Policies to Cut Health Costs?" by Ann Zimmerman, Robert Guy Matthews, and Kris Hudson, *The Wall Street Journal,* October 27, 2005.

81 See "Health Insurer's New Target" by Vanessa Fuhrmans, *The Wall Street Journal,* May 31, 2005.

82 See "No, You Can't Keep Your Health Plan" by Scott Gottlieb, *The Wall Street Journal,* May 18, 2010.

83 For more on health savings accounts, see www.americanhealthvalue.com/

84 See "President Proposes 'Impressive' Health Reforms in State of Union Address" by Susan Konig, *Health Care News* (The Heartland Institute), March 2006.

85 See "How Safeway is Cutting Health Care Costs" by Stephen A. Burd, *The Wall Street Journal,* June 12, 2009.

86 "Sick in America: Whose Body is it, Anyway," John Stossel reporting, *ABC News* 2007.

87 Increasingly, hospitals are attempting to save money by simultaneously denying care that does not raise the chances of living, while providing special palliative-care units that seek to provide comfort for dying patients. See "Unlikely Way to Cut Hospital Costs: Comfort the Dying" by Gautam Naik, *The Wall Street Journal,* March 10, 2004.

88 See "Demand for living wills surges on fears of agony" by Sandra Pedicini, *The Orlando Sentinel,* March 24, 2005.

89 See "Eating with Impunity" by Jack A. Chambless and Sarah C. McAlister, *The Orlando Sentinel,* December 22, 1996.

90 See www.hcfa.gov/medicare/fraud/transcr7.htm

91 See http://www.cbsnews.com/stories/2009/10/23/60minutes/main5414390.shtml

92 See www.aei.org/cs/cs5581.htm

93 See "Health Debate Emerges As Costs Rise Again" by Ron Winslow, *The Wall Street Journal,* December 17, 2001.

94 See "A Way Out of Soviet-Style Health Care" by Milton Friedman, *The Wall Street Journal,* March 20, 2010.

CHAPTER REVIEW

1. Fully explain how a car accident involving a person with no health insurance, can lead all the way to higher prices for your next cup of coffee.

2. What are four of the major reasons for rising health care costs in America? Explain each in detail.

3. What did the legislation signed by President Obama say about how health care markets would work in the future? Give specifics.

4. What is the difference between the Affordable Care Act and what goes on in Canada?

Chapter Ten

GDP, UNEMPLOYMENT, *and* INFLATION

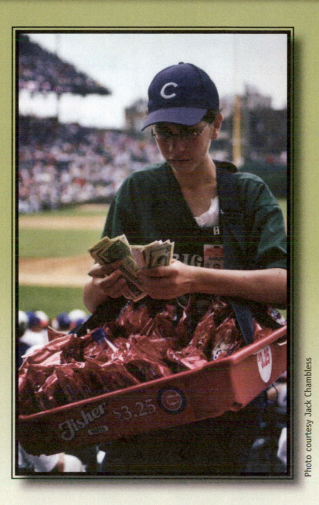

*I*f you can't pay your bills or your mortgage, it's still a recession. No matter what the economists say, it's not a real recovery until people can feel it in their own lives.

PRESIDENT BARACK OBAMA

THE BIG PICTURE

Now that you have a firm grasp on the forces that shape individual, consumer, and business decisions, we turn to the aggregate (total) economic picture. In macroeconomics, rather than studying changes in gasoline prices, we study the causes and consequences of price changes for *all* goods and services. Instead of examining layoffs in specific industries we study the reasons why the economy sometimes loses jobs across the *entire* nation. Finally, rather than focusing on the reasons why the demand for, and supply of, houses has changed, we address the implications of changes in the demand for and supply of *all* goods and services. In short, *macroeconomics is the study of the economy as a whole.*

MEASURING AGGREGATE ECONOMIC OUTPUT

What if, on the next test you took in your economics class, your professor – rather than assigning a letter or numerical grade on your test – simply wrote, "Better luck next time" or "You must be joking." Would this concern you? Of course, it would. The reason you would be concerned is that you would have no idea what these statements mean. You would have no measuring tool with which to gauge your performance.

This is precisely the problem that plagued the U.S. government in the early 1930s. Everyone knew the economy was in terrible shape as a result of the onset of the Great Depression, but no one knew exactly how bad things were. For years preceding the Depression, there had been no official measurement tool to add up the value of all goods and services produced in the economy. The problem with not having a gauge of the macroeconomic health of our nation was that, when the economy began to enter the worst collapse in our history, few people really knew what to do about an unmeasured crisis.

It was during this time that Simon Kuznets, an eventual Nobel laureate, developed a system for measuring the economic output of our nation. This system, known as the National Income and Product Accounts (NIPA) became the methodology for calculating the total dollar value of all final goods and services produced in the economy each year. This value became known as the Gross National Product (GNP). While the U.S. currently uses a measuring tool known as the Gross Domestic Product (GDP), there is only a slight variation in the way GDP and GNP are calculated.

CALCULATING THE GROSS DOMESTIC PRODUCT (GDP)

> ➤ **Gross Domestic Product is the value of all final goods and services produced each year.**

Until 1991, the United States measured the nation's output by looking at the total dollar value of all goods and services produced by U.S. firms in America and abroad. Over time, this created a very inaccurate picture of our economic well-being. By counting the value of toys produced by Disney in China as part of America's GNP, we were ignoring the fact that China counted the toys in *their* GDP. This led to double counting of toys that were basically Chinese products. In the meantime, the U.S. totally ignored the value of Japanese cars – and other items produced by foreign companies – in our GNP.

As the world economy became more integrated, refusing to acknowledge production on our soil by any other country became an ongoing miscalculation of our wealth. Therefore, in December 1991, the U.S. Department of Commerce began using GDP as our official measure of output. We no longer count American production abroad but do count all production in the U.S. by any country.

GDP is broken up into two parts – *income* and *expenditures*. Expenditure means spending by some individual or institution for a good or service. Of course, income – in the form of wages, salaries, business profits, rents, return on investments, and so forth – would naturally be part of the macroeconomic picture because any expenditure (spending) will end up as income for some individual or business firm. Expenditure data is what you hear most about on the news and read about in the newspaper. The formula for the expenditure side of GDP is:

> **GDP = C + I + G +/- NE**

CONSUMPTION

C is household consumption of durable and nondurable goods and services. Consumption makes up almost 70% of America's approximately $19 trillion GDP. *Durable goods* include items like washers and dryers, refrigerators, lawn-mowers, and furniture. *Nondurable goods* would include theater tickets, food, gasoline, and other items that are consumed immediately. In the years leading up to the "Great Recession" of 2007-2009 the largest source of America's economic growth was based on consumer spending, fueled largely by home refinancing and credit cards.

It is important to note that while consumer spending is an important – and necessary part of the GDP – economists became increasingly concerned about the mounting debt burden of Americans in the early part of the last decade. In 2007, household debt (including mortgages) totaled $14.4 trillion, which was 139% of the average American's personal income. In 2000 the figures were $7.4 trillion in debt and 103% of our income.[1]

By 2014 total household debt had fallen to $11.36 trillion[2] (from $13.5 trillion in 2010). 2010 represented the first annual drop in private debt since 1945 – as millions of Americans were forced to cut spending in the wake of the economic downturn and others cut spending in order to maintain more responsible household budgets.[3]

By 2016 household debt was $12.25 trillion and was beginning to increase once again as consumers gained confidence that the American economy was mending at a slightly higher pace.

INVESTMENT

I stands for *Gross Domestic Private Investment*. This is the amount of money spent by business firms for new plants and equipment, and investments made in residential and nonresidential construction. Investment spending by business firms makes up about 15% of the expenditure component of GDP.

Investment spending is, of course, critical to the economic vitality of any nation. In 2013 half of the largest 40 publically-traded companies in America were in the midst of dramatically lowering investment spending (for the first time since 2009) in the wake of tax increases, the uncertainty surrounding the total cost of the Affordable Care Act and ongoing federal budget controversies.[4]

By 2017 investors were beginning to feel a bit more optimistic. President Trump's proposal to dramatically lower both personal and capital gains taxes (taxes paid on the profit from investments) contributed to a sharp increase in stock prices as investors became more optimistic that the returns to investment (profit) would increase under the new administration.

GOVERNMENT

G equals *government spending* for domestic goods and services. Making up approximately 25% of GDP, this type of spending is for bombs, health care, computers, accounting services, and millions of other goods and services. Transfer payments (social welfare checks) do not count in this category.

For much of the 20th century, government made up about 20% of the GDP. Under the administrations of George W. Bush and Barack Obama, government spending recently reached one-fourth of all economic activity. The wars in Iraq and Afghanistan, bailouts of financial and other industries, along with stimulus spending and exploding levels of social welfare payments designed to stimulate economic activity, were the prime reasons for the surge in government outlays.

NET EXPORTS

NE equals *net exports*. This is simply the difference between the total dollar value of goods and services exported from the U.S. to other countries and the total dollar value of goods and services we import from foreign nations. This value can be positive or negative, depending on whether exports exceed imports, or vice versa. For the past several years there has been a trade deficit – meaning more imports, in total dollar value, than exports in the U.S.

While many Americans get very upset when they hear that we perpetually run trade deficits with China and other nations, economists don't always worry about this trend.

First, we have a trade deficit because we are the richest nation in the world. Simply put, we have the ability to buy a whole lot more goods and services from the rest of the world than the world can afford to buy from us.

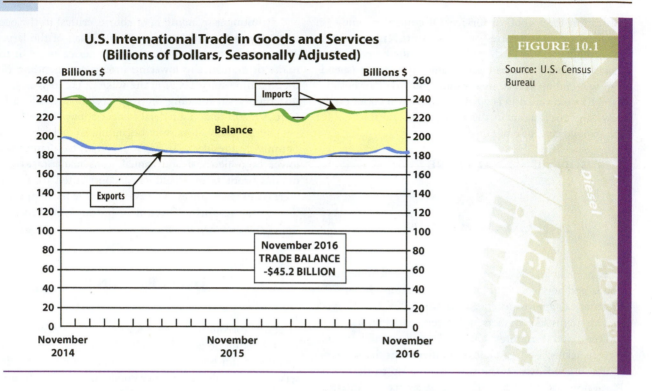

**U.S. International Trade in Goods and Services
(Billions of Dollars, Seasonally Adjusted)**

FIGURE 10.1

Source: U.S. Census Bureau

November 2016
TRADE BALANCE
-$45.2 BILLION

Second, when Sony builds a DVD player in Asia and exports it to the United States, the dockworker that unloads the DVD player in Seattle gets paid in dollars. The truck driver that takes the DVD player to Cincinnati is paid in dollars, as is the sales clerk in the electronics store, the repair technician that fixes the machine when it breaks, and the garbage collector who hauls it away when it breaks for good.

The bottom line is that there are millions of jobs that are directly created or indirectly supported by the existence of foreign goods on our soil.

Finally, as we will see later on, Sony and other companies invest and save billions of dollars in the U.S. from their profits. This saving helps offset the meager savings of American citizens and helps keep interest rates lower than they otherwise would be. The more money that foreign companies pour into U.S. banks (to invest and make payroll obligations) the greater the overall supply of money is. A larger money supply allows interest rates to stabilize at lower rates.[5]

WHAT IS NOT COUNTED IN THE GDP

Not all of the economic activity in America shows up in GDP calculations. In fact, hundreds of billions of dollars of

transactions are excluded. The following is a list of those items that economists leave out of NIPA calculations.

1. The *value of stocks and bonds.* Stocks and bonds are not counted because they represent a paper transfer of wealth, rather than the actual production of a good or service. The money paid to a broker would be counted in GDP; the value of the stock the broker sold would not be.

2. The *cost of environmental damage.* When Houston or Los Angeles residents suffer from high levels of smog that might make them ill or less productive, how is this reflected in the GDP? There may be a drop in output stemming from a destroyed lake or dirty air, but measurement problems abound in attempting to quantify this problem. Since it is very hard to measure the damage from pollution, we do not subtract any dollar amount from the GDP to reflect the costs of pollution. However, we do count the value of pollution abatement equipment, the value of doctors' services and other final goods and services that might be related to the creation of, prevention of, or treatment stemming from pollution.[6]

3. *Existing assets that change in value.* Suppose your parents bought a house in 1977 and sell it in 2021. Would this transaction be counted? The answer is no. If the house was built and bought in 1977, it was counted in GDP only in 1977 and will never be counted again. Counting this house in 2021 would

CONCEPT CHECK

When a new hotel is built in Las Vegas, what gets counted in the GDP – the price to stay in the hotel, or the construction costs *plus* the price to stay in the hotel?

Photo courtesy Jack Chambless

lead to the double-counting problem that economists seek to avoid. Of course, if the house bought in 1977 goes through a renovation in 2021, and the people doing the renovating buy new goods and services from a local home-improvement store, then this would be counted.

4. The *underground economy*. Every year, billions, if not tens of billions, of dollars change hands in the market for illegal drugs, gambling, weapons, and prostitution.[7] One study placed the underground economy at over $1.25 trillion.[8] Moreover, many people work "off the books" for cash only.

   These transactions are not counted in GDP, partly because they are so hard to measure, and partly because it might be political suicide for the politician that argues that we should count income earned by prostitutes, drug dealers and illegal arms sales in our GDP.

5. *Nonmarket production*. If you mow your own lawn or have your spouse cut your hair, you are engaging in nonmarket production – production that was not purchased in a market. Since these services were not purchased, they are not counted in GDP.

6. *Intermediate goods*. The paper used in this book is an example of an intermediate good – a good used to produce some final product. Intermediate goods are not counted in the GDP because it would lead to the same double-counting problem addressed earlier.

7. The *value of leisure time*. When someone in Hawaii goes windsurfing, does this get counted in the GDP? It depends on what we are counting. If purchased new, the wetsuit, the board, and the soft drink enjoyed afterward would be counted. However, the value of windsurfing to the Hawaiian resident is not counted in GDP due to obvious measurement problems. Since he probably did not pay someone for the right to windsurf, a transaction did not take place, and therefore it is too difficult to ascertain precisely what value windsurfing would add to the GDP.

WHY AMERICANS SPEND MORE THAN EUROPEANS DO

If you think of the American marketplace as a gigantic store, consumers buy roughly $13 trillion worth of goods and services from that store. That figure is not only larger than any other nation, but it is larger than the *sum* of consumption, investment spending, government and net exports of any other nation, including China.

Of course, one of the major reasons consumption is so much higher in America is that our economy has fewer restrictions and lower income taxes than you will find in much of Europe. With much tougher regulations and higher taxes on industry and individuals, the prices of most goods and services are higher, and disposable income is lower than in the U.S. This combination naturally puts downward pressure on consumer spending.

Our debt-driven economy is also culturally different than what you find in Europe, where people tend to place a higher value on saving for the future. Then again, with Europe's *high value-added taxes*, a high rate of savings is almost a necessity.

COUNTRY	VAT RATE	COUNTRY	VAT RATE
Denmark	25%	Greece	23%
Iceland	25.5	Netherlands	21
Norway	25	U.K.	20
Finland	24	Portugal	23
Belgium	21	Spain	21
Ireland	21	Germany	19
Austria	20	Luxembourg	15
Italy	22	Turkey	18
Sweden	25	Cyprus	19
France	20	Switzerland	8
		U.S.	0

The preceding table illustrates a little-known secret about the reasons for high savings rates in Europe and other nations. A value-added tax is a tax on every stage of the production process. This means that when BMW builds a car in Germany, the steel is taxed at 19%, as are the tires, wiring, glass, leather, batteries, and so forth.

The more socialistic mindset we examined in detail in chapter three has led to much higher prices, and thus far, less consumption in these nations. With less consumption, there is a greater likelihood that people in these nations will allocate what is left of their disposable income to save for retirement. At the same time, however, the VAT has led to less economic prosperity for the people to enjoy *before* retirement.

REAL VS. NOMINAL GDP

When calculating GDP, it is important to distinguish between real and nominal GDP. *Real GDP* is GDP based on our country's level of production without factoring in changes in prices. *Nominal GDP* is GDP based on current-year prices. The following example should help clear up this concept.

Suppose in 2017 there were only two goods produced in America: pizza and blue jeans. Further suppose that in 2017, 10 million pairs of jeans were sold at a price of $30, while 50 million pizzas were produced and sold for $7 each. What would be the GDP of America in 2017?

10 million jeans × $30 + 50 million pizzas x $7 = $650 million

While we are supposing, suppose that in the year 2027, the production of jeans and pizzas doubled to 20 million and 100 million, respectively. If the price of jeans is $60 and the price of pizza is $14 in 2027, the nominal GDP of America would be:

20 million jeans × $60 + 100 million pizzas x $14 = $2.60 billion

Do you see anything misleading about our results – other than the fact that we produce more than just jeans and pizza? The problem with the calculation above is the fact that, when we want to know how much better or worse off our country is, we need to focus only on how production levels have changed.

Changes in output indicate whether GDP is growing and at what rate. Changes in prices do not indicate that we are better off. What we want to be able to do is isolate changes in output by factoring out changes in prices. The way we do that is to look at changes in production levels multiplied by some *constant price level*.

Suppose we use 2017 as our base year, or reference year, and look for changes in real GDP from that point. Doing so means we still have $650 million for the 2017 GDP, since that is the reference year, but the 2027 real GDP would be different than the 2027 nominal GDP.

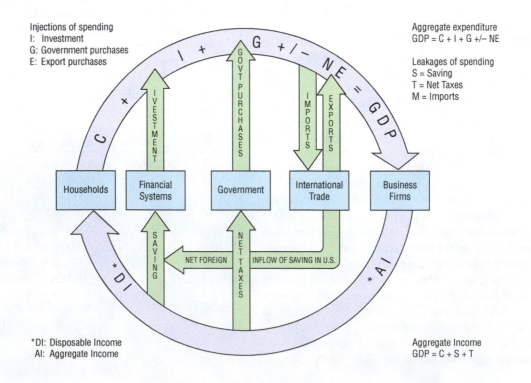

Real GDP = 20 million jeans x $30 (the 2017 price) + 100 million pizzas $\times$ $7 = $1.3 billion

Notice that with the price increases factored out, GDP increased from $650 million to $1.3 billion. This is a doubling of GDP. This is precisely what happened to the number of jeans and pizzas produced! Therefore, by factoring out $1.3 billion in price increases, we have a much more accurate picture of our economic progress.

The Circular Flow of Expenditures and Income

Since the GDP calculations entail both expenditures and income, economists often rely on a diagram depicting a "pipeline of money" to illustrate the basic functions of the macroeconomy. Every decision an individual or business makes, impacts this pipeline. Thus, this pipeline contains the major economic components that make up the GDP, as well as the leakages and injections of money that take place in our economy. The following diagram illustrates this concept.

On the top part of the diagram we see the *expenditure* side of the economy (C + I + G +/- NE). On the bottom half we see the *income* side of the economy, where all expenditures end up. You will also notice that there are places where money either leaks out of, or is injected into, the economy. These *leakages* and *injections* will be the focus of this section.

First, on the upper left side of the chart you can see that households, through consumer spending push money into the pipeline. Business firms also spend money on investments that come in part from the profit earned from consumer spending and part from an injection of money from the lower half of the circular flow pipeline. This injection comes from the banking system in the form of loans to business firms. The second injection comes from

the government in the form of purchases of final goods and services. The government gets the money for this injection by either borrowing the money or through taxes paid by individuals and businesses.

As we move along, you will notice a leakage that has taken place in the form of imports. As Americans purchase goods and services from foreign nations, this leads to money leaving the U.S. and flowing to foreign firms.

Notice, however, that some of this money that leaks out of the economic pipeline is injected back into America's banking system in the form of *net foreign inflows of savings* by foreign firms. This is a very critical part of our economy. It is both interesting and ironic to note that, as a result of this saving by foreign firms the overall pool of money flowing into our banks is larger than it would otherwise be if only saving by Americans made up total savings in banks.

As aforementioned, by increasing the overall savings rate, foreign firms cause the supply of money in our banks to increase. This puts downward pressure on interest rates and makes it possible for consumers and businesses to enjoy more goods and services. Indirectly, we receive a *foreign-subsidized* low-interest loan every time we buy on credit.

Continuing along the diagram, we see export earnings comprising an injection of money back into our country. All of this money leads to aggregate income paid out by business firms.

On the bottom half of the diagram, we see that some of this income is taxed (leading to government spending). Whatever is not taxed, or eventually saved (leading to investments), is called disposable income. This is the income used by households to start the spending process all over again.

Photo courtesy Jack Chambless

CONCEPT CHECK

When tourists in northern Oregon buy honey from lavender plants, where does this appear in America's circular flow model? How do you know? If the lavender farm is bought up by an investor from Norway, is this a leakage or an injection for the U.S.?

THE BUSINESS CYCLE

One of the first things you learn as an economist is to avoid acting like Joe Namath. Mr. Namath was a Hall of Fame quarterback for the New York Jets back in the 1960s and 1970s. He became famous on the eve of Super Bowl III in 1969, when he "guaranteed" his Jets would upset the heavily favored Baltimore Colts. The Jets won the game, and since then, athletes routinely emulate Mr. Namath with their own guarantees of victory.

Good for Joe Namath, and good for the athletes who understand that they have at least a 50/50 chance of being right. In the world of economics, there are no such guarantees, and therefore economists are taught early on to avoid the pitfalls that come with making definitive claims about changes in the GDP.

Nevertheless, one of the major objectives of economists is to *predict* changes in the gross domestic product. This is an important objective for several reasons. By understanding the forces that can cause fluctuations in the GDP, economists can craft policy recommendations that might contribute to milder economic downturns – or prevent a downturn altogether.

The problem we face in accomplishing this goal is nothing short of overwhelming. There are literally thousands of factors that can cause changes in economic conditions – many of which (wars, drought, housing bubbles, supply disruptions, etc.) we cannot predict with any certainty.

There were economists in the early part of 2000 who were suggesting that America might go on for years without seeing a recession. Two years later we had not only had a recession, but the events of September 11th made it much more difficult to accurately gauge future economic conditions. By 2008 many people were wondering if the U.S. economy was going to go through the worst turn in the business cycle since 1929. By February 2017 the "Great Recession" had been over for over seven years, yet the economy was growing at the slowest post-recession rates since World War II. By the time you are reading this paragraph we might be in another recession or the economy could be roaring!

What we are left with is the simple reality that the economy is *cyclical* in nature. That means that sometimes the GDP increases and sometimes it falls. It means that there have been times in our nation's history where real estate bubbles and banking crises have occurred – and will occur again. Yet, we have always come out of any downturns in the economy. Changes in GDP over time are referred to as the *business cycle*.

These changes can be broken up into the following categories:

CONTRACTION

According to the Commerce Department, a contraction is *one quarterly drop in real GDP*. The term "quarterly drop" refers to the manner in which the United States Commerce Department measures the GDP. This department divides the calendar year into four quarters for this purpose. The first quarter is January–March, the second quarter is April–June, and so on.

The Commerce Department gathers data on the GDP for the first three months. Then on or around April 28th of each year, the department announces the first-quarter totals for GDP. The announcement shows not only how much GDP was produced and what the projection is for the year, but also shows by what percentage GDP increased compared to the previous year. If the Commerce Department announced that GDP had actually dropped (meaning less output was produced), this initial drop would be called a contraction. The contraction is depicted as the movement from point A to B on figure 10.2.

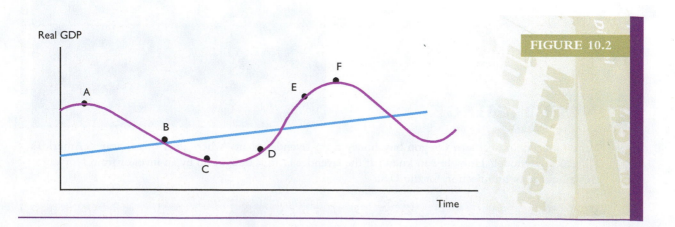

FIGURE 10.2

RECESSION

A recession is *two or more consecutive quarterly drops in real GDP*. The recession is the movement from point A to C on the diagram. Normally, recessions do not last more than one year, but even if GDP fell for 20 years, there is no official definition of a depression. It simply got that name because of the magnitude of the drop in GDP and the length of time GDP fell during the 1930s.

THE NBER

The nonprofit National Bureau of Economic Research (NBER) is widely considered to be the organization that is most accurate in measuring changes in the GDP. With data sets that now date back to 1854, the NBER's official record of the GDP is even recognized as the official record by the Commerce Department's Bureau of Economic Analysis.[10]

The NBER measures recessions differently than the Commerce Department. According to the NBER, "A recession is a significant decline in activity spread across the economy, lasting more than a few months, visible in industrial production, employment, real income, and wholesale-retail sales."[11]

In October of 2008, all of the signs were there – a rising unemployment rate, falling consumer confidence, declining factory orders, a slumping stock market, and even collapsing energy prices to suggest that the United States was in our first recession since 2001. However, the data had not yet confirmed what the American people seemed to sense was taking place. According to the Commerce Department, the economy grew in the first, second, and third quarters of 2008. The NBER and other forecasting firms projected during this time that there was a 50% chance of a recession but had not, by the fall of that year, announced that we were indeed in a recession.[11]

By the summer of 2010, the NBER had officially marked the 18-month long recession as having begun in December 2007 and lasting until June 2009.[12] As the data on the following table clearly illustrates, it was, by any measure, one of the longest and deepest downturns in our nation's history – the causes of which will be examined in the next chapter.

EXHIBIT 11.14 A Historical Record of U.S. Recessions, 1920–2009		
Peak	**Trough**	**Length of Recession (months)**
January 1920	July 1921	18
May 1923	July 1924	14
October 1926	November 1927	13
August 1929	March 1933	43
May 1937	June 1938	13
February 1945	October 1945	8
November 1948	October 1949	11
July 1953	May 1954	10
August 1957	April 1958	8
April 1960	February 1961	10
December 1969	November 1970	11
November 1973	March 1975	16
January 1980	July 1980	6
July 1981	November 1982	16
July 1990	March 1991	8
March 2001	November 2001	8
December 2007	—	—

SOURCES: National Bureau of Economic Research, Inc., *Business Cycle Expansions and Contractions*, U.S. Department of Commerce. Washington, D.C., December 1, 2008. Available at http://www.nber.org/cycles.html (accessed March 18, 2010).

WHAT GOES DOWN DOES COME UP

All recessions come to an end. So far, that is the truth. If the world ever ends, GDP will go to zero and we will have a permanent recession. Until then, economists can tell you, with great confidence, that any downturn will be followed by an upturn. The phases of the upturn are generally described as follows:

EXPANSION

An expansion is the *initial increase* in real GDP following a contraction or recession. Point C to D on the previous diagram would represent an expansion. Bear in mind that most economists refer to the initial increase in GDP as an expansion. Some economists refer to this phase as the recovery phase.

RECOVERY

A recovery is a *period of continual increases in real GDP,* typically lasting from one to two years, following a contraction or recession. Point C to E represents a recovery.

During a typical "U-shaped" recovery, the GDP increases at a very slow pace initially, as business firms begin to expand output and hire new workers at a moderate pace. Sometimes a "V-shaped" recovery takes place (1983–84) where the initial increases in GDP are quite large, making the business cycle look more like a "V" than a "U." Figure 10.3 illustrates this possibility.

ECONOMIC GROWTH

Economic growth is a period of continual increases in real GDP, historically lasting three to five years, following a contraction or recession. Point C to F on figure 10.2 represents the growth phase. The terms "expansion," "recovery," and "growth" are very often used interchangeably among economists. You should also take a look at the preceding table to see that when we say, "historically lasting three to five years," we mean dating back to World War II. In the more recent past, we have seen much longer periods of economic growth and much shorter recessions.

From World War II to 1982 we averaged 2.5–4.0% GDP growth. If you are wondering what the big deal is when we talk of 2.5–4.0% growth, think of it this way: The U.S. economy produces around $19,000,000,000,000 in output. A 4% increase in GDP would be an increase of $760 billion. That is a very large increase in output.

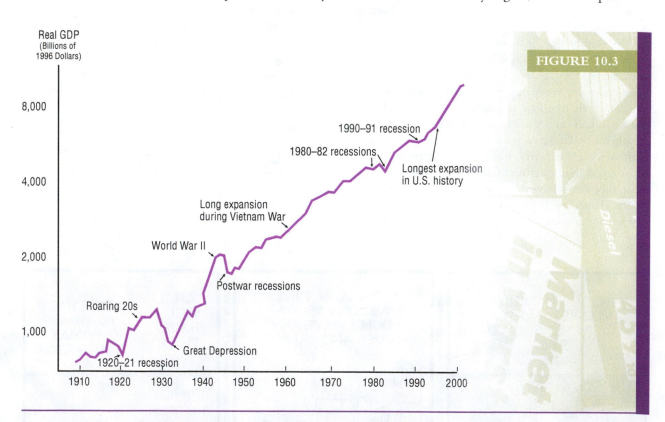

FIGURE 10.3

Real GDP (Billions of 1996 Dollars)

Why was the post "Great Recession" Recovery so slow and small?

For millions of Americans, the time period since the end of the 2007-2009 recession has been one of great frustration. As the following graphs illustrate, the Great Recession was the longest since the 1930s. Compounding matters was the fact that the recovery period was painfully slow and did not generate new jobs at anywhere near the rate at which past recoveries had.

The January 10, 2014 *Wall Street Journal* ran a headline that read: "Factory Output Flat; Construction Falls: Weaker-Than-Expected Data Suggest Economic Recovery May Have Slowed."

Two weeks later the headline read: "U.S. Markets Tumble as Fear Spreads."

Each of these headlines came *four and a half years* after the recession ended. During that 55-month time span there was very little in the way of good news for the American economy. In much of the country the housing market struggled to regain the values lost over the past several years. A record increase in the number of Americans receiving food stamps (a 39% increase from 2009 to 2013) and other social welfare benefits took place. And perhaps the worst news of all came in the form of an enormous decrease in the number of Americans working full-time or seeking full-time work.

In 2006, 63.4% of the working-age population was employed. By 2013 it was down to a near-historic low of 58.6%.[13]

In 2013, President Obama increased income tax rates on the top-earners and raised payroll taxes on every working American. Since 2014, millions of Americans faced large increases in their health insurance premiums, and therefore a reduction in their disposable income for other goods and services, in order to comply with new health care legislation.

A major impediment to faster economic growth – if you believe the men and women who run businesses in America – was the massive amount of uncertainty surrounding President Obama's economic priorities.

Economists from Stanford and The University of Chicago found that on average, U.S. economic policy uncertainty had been 50% higher in the 2011–2012 time period than it had been since 1985. This means that the men and women who run our businesses – and create our jobs – felt that it was more difficult to make economic plans with respect to expansion, hiring and other decisions because of the ongoing threat of greater government intrusion into the marketplace in the form of higher taxes and the cost of new EPA, health care, banking, student loan, automotive and other regulations.

It was estimated that "since 2011 the rise in overall policy uncertainty had created a $261 billion cumulative drag on the economy (the equivalent of more than $800 per person in the country). Without this uncertainty tax, real U.S. GDP could have grown an average 3% per year since 2011, instead of the recorded 2% average in fiscal years 2011-12. In addition, the U.S. labor market would have added roughly 45,000 more jobs per month over the 2011–2012 time period. That adds up to more than one million jobs that we could have had by now, but don't."[14]

All of this combined to create the last thing businesses want – an economic environment lacking in transparency. With the uncertainty surrounding their ability to pursue profits, most American firms sat on any profits earned and refused to take the risks associated with adding more employees.[15]

The election of Donald Trump did not dramatically change the level of uncertainty facing our business leaders. On the one hand, vowing to lower taxes and reduce regulations was a cause for celebration for our companies. On the other hand, Mr. Trump's promise to deport

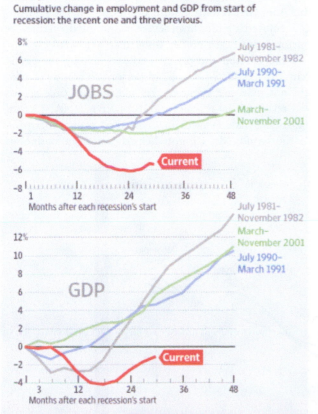

Deeper Recession, Slower Recovery
Cumulative change in employment and GDP from start of recession: the recent one and three previous.

Sources: Labor Department; Commerce Department; National Bureau of Economic Research

millions of undocumented workers; impose tariffs on Mexico and China and increase America's debt load with trillions in new government spending did not ease the economic pressure or give businesses a clear picture of what the future might hold.

CAN WE GO BACK TO THE 1980S AND 1990S?

Most of you reading this book have just recently felt the effects of a significant macroeconomic crisis for the first time in your life. Most of you were not even on the planet when America's great economic boom began in late 1982. Since that time, Americans have lived through some of, if not the best times in our history.[16] Even when taking into account the "Great Recession," the U.S. economy remains fundamentally strong – with a per capita income of over $52,400 in 2016 – compared to other times in our history and in comparison to other developed nations.[17]

As you are reading this, the economy might be growing steadily again. Once the recovery is complete, can we see 8, 10 or even 20 years of growth before the next downturn occurs?

The two longest peacetime growth periods in our history were from November 1982 to July 1990 (92 months) and the period of growth from March 1991 through March of 2001. During that time, many economists were wondering if the United States had entered a new period of cyclical changes in the GDP that would be markedly different from what the past yielded. This "new economy" theory gained steam among old and

young economists alike, whom contended that, because of fundamental changes in the global economy, we might never again see the frequent upturns and downturns that we used to experience. Figure 10.4 illustrates what took place from November 1982 to December 2007.

The long periods of growth in the last part of the 20th century centered largely on a handful of factors:

> ➤ **Changes in technology**
> ➤ **The collapse of communism**
> ➤ **Expansions in world trade and investment**
> ➤ **Historically low taxes**
> ➤ **Deregulation efforts of the 1980s**

Technology – Computers, wireless communication technology, and the Internet dramatically improved the productivity of workers over this time period; while making markets more competitive around the world. In the old days, consumers and businesses incurred substantial search costs associated with procuring needed goods and services.

The collapse of communism helped our economy grow at unprecedented rates. Before 1989, the United States had a limited range of trading partners from which jobs could be created within our borders. China, Russia and India alone account for 40% of the world's population – a population that is now engaging in more capitalism and thus, more trade. With Eastern Europe also in the fold, the U.S. enjoyed a buffer from severe economic downturns as our options to earn money from trade expanded.

Bill Clinton also played a role in helping the economy expand. While his record personal income tax hike did not help the economy, his *international trade policies* and relative fiscal restraint did. By ratifying NAFTA and expanding trade in Vietnam, China, and many other parts of the world, Mr. Clinton helped American businesses

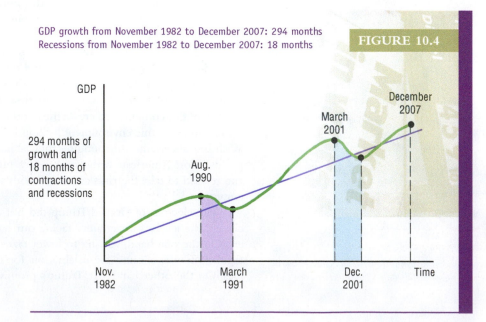

GDP growth from November 1982 to December 2007: 294 months
Recessions from November 1982 to December 2007: 18 months

FIGURE 10.4

open up new markets that were relatively closed before. Greater trade helped create new competition to keep American businesses productive and helped fuel economic growth and job expansion as well.[18]

Mr. Clinton also spent an inordinate amount of time traveling around the world seeking ways to open up international markets to American investors. After all, money is our biggest asset in this country and our money is constantly looking for places to gain a high rate of return. By opening up emerging markets to direct American investment Mr. Clinton helped fuel part of the rise in the global economy during the 1990s. In the meantime, during his time in office, government spending grew at a slower rate than in the past — freeing up resources for businesses to prosper.[19]

The Reagan administration also helped matters in 1981 and again in 1986 with the largest *income tax cuts* in our nation's history. Remember that the top tax rate out of the 14 brackets we had in 1980 was 70%. By 1986, the top rate was 28%. Such a massive cut in taxes helped provide the necessary money for businesses and individuals to take the entrepreneurial risks associated with new technologies and businesses.[20] Had taxes not fallen, it would have made it much more difficult to create the type of growth that we enjoyed during the 1980s and 1990s.

Beginning with Jimmy Carter and carrying through the Reagan years, *deregulation* helped fuel much of our growth. Mr. Carter deregulated the airline and trucking industries. Mr. Reagan helped deregulate the telecommunications, banking, and energy sectors. Deregulation meant that more and more companies could enter these industries with fewer rules and less burdensome paperwork. As a result, millions of jobs were created, prices fell in all of these areas, and our GDP increased as a result.

What does this mean for today, and the future? Can we rationally expect to go back to an era of less regulation, expanded free trade, and lower taxes?

Someone once said, "An economist is someone who can explain to you tomorrow, why the predictions he made yesterday did not come true." From 2008-2014, at varying times, the stock market took a nose dive, gasoline prices remained at historically high levels, the value of the dollar fell, as did gold and silver prices, while the federal government dramatically increased its role in the private economy with partial takeovers of the automobile, banking and health care industries. Meanwhile, foreclosures increased, housing values dropped, and millions of Americans were left wondering how much longer they would be gainfully employed.

Not many economists would have predicted such an epic collapse of the investment banking industry. Fewer would have predicted that the government would reduce the role of free markets throughout the country, reshape health care along socialist lines, and spend trillions of dollars on stimulus programs.

If what took place in the past few years becomes a trend and if this trend toward more government interference in the market becomes our new economic system, then the new economy theory might be relegated to the dustbin of economic theories.[21]

In the next section you will learn how economists make predictions concerning changes in the business cycle.

THE INDEX OF LEADING INDICATORS

While all reputable economists (there might be some disreputable ones out there) agree that predicting changes in the business cycle is an overwhelming task, there is at least one very important tool that we use to make a sound intellectual attempt at measuring future changes in the nation's output.

Experts who try to forecast changes in real GDP, keep a close watch on various sectors of the economy and use the Index of Leading Indicators to do it.

> ➤ **Leading economic indicators are economic variables whose values are normally expected to decline prior to a decline in real GDP and rise prior to a rise in real GDP.**

Among the leading economic indicators watched in the United States are:

1. Average workweek of production in manufacturing
2. Average weekly initial claims for unemployment insurance
3. New orders for manufacturing, consumer goods and materials
4. A measure of vendors reporting slower deliveries
5. Plant and equipment contracts and orders
6. Building permits for new residential construction
7. Changes in manufacturers' unfilled orders for durable goods
8. Changes in the prices of certain materials used in production
9. Common stock prices (an index of 500 stock prices)
10. Checking deposits, currency in circulation, and certain liquid assets
11. An index of consumer expectations about the future

If you watch the news on any given night, chances are you will see the network anchor give some reference to one or more of these important variables. Certainly, every day you can hear how the stock market fared, but economists also pay close attention to consumer confidence reports, new unemployment claims, and the rest of the factors on this list.

It is not a guarantee that, if the numbers are changing in a way that appears to suggest a downturn, then a downturn in real GDP will take place. Other variables like the weather, terrorist attacks, political upheaval, and so forth can impact the GDP as well. If another major hurricane hits New Orleans in 2023, while at the same time interest rates increase and the price of copper skyrockets, those events might bring down new building permits and stock prices. Does that mean we would face a recession in 2023? Not necessarily.

Sustained bad news on a monthly basis is a more accurate gauge of whether the total economic picture is changing for the worse. In 1974 and 1982 the index of leading indicators declined sharply in advance of recessions. In 1984 the index fell, yet 1984 was a year of tremendous economic growth. It is important to keep in mind that forecasting is an imprecise science. However, at the same time, we have to ask, what if we had no forecasting tools? Without the index of leading indicators, recessions could come upon us in such a sudden manner that it would make it more difficult for policymakers to fight the downturn.

UNEMPLOYMENT

Of all of the problems that recessions create, unemployment is by far the biggest and most troublesome. When general unemployment levels rise, politicians begin to worry. Voters tend to look at the number of people who are unemployed then look to see who occupies Congress and the White House. The more people who are out of work, the more likely it is that politicians will join them.

> ➤ **The unemployment rate is the percentage of the labor force that is not working but is actively seeking work.**

The *labor force* is the number of Americans 16 years of age or older, who are either working, or are actively seeking work. In 2017 there were approximately 160 million people in the labor force.[22]

CONCEPT CHECK

Economists grow worried when the price of corrugated boxes begins to fall consistently. Why? Economists also worry when there is a decrease in the number of vendors reporting slow deliveries. Why?

For much of the late 1990s and 2000, the U.S. unemployment rate was below 5%. In April 2000 it hit a 30-year low of 3.9%! By October 2009, the unemployment rate was 10.2% – the highest level since 1982 – and was still 9.8% as of November 2010.[23] In particular, men were hit hard by the recession. Jobs in construction, manufacturing, finance, and other industries that traditionally employ men suffered greater job losses than education and health care services, where more women are employed. Thus, for the first time in U.S. history, there were more women working full-time than men during this downturn.[24]

PERSONS NOT COUNTED IN THE LABOR FORCE

Not everyone in our population of over 320 million gets counted in the labor force. For purposes of calculating the unemployment rate, the Bureau of Labor Statistics does not count the following people:

FULL-TIME STUDENTS

Students who are over the age of 16 but are not working or actively seeking work due to school responsibilities are excluded from the labor force data.

HOMEMAKERS

Men and women who are at home taking care of the household and/or children or other individuals, are not counted in the labor force if they are not actively seeking work. A person could actually be a homemaker and be counted if he or she were seeking work to do from the home.

© Dmitry Kalinovsky/Shutterstock.com

PRISONERS AND OTHER INSTITUTIONALIZED INDIVIDUALS

Even though convicts might like to be out looking for work, if a person is in prison or any other institution that prevents that person from voluntarily leaving, he or she is not counted in the labor force.

RETIREES

People who are no longer working because they have retired are not counted in the labor force. There is no minimum age at which a person is not counted.

DISCOURAGED WORKERS

A discouraged worker is not someone who hates his or her current job. A discouraged worker is a person, who after a period of unsuccessfully searching for a job, for at least one year, gives up and leaves the labor force. Because of these types of individuals, the unemployment rate tends to underestimate the true picture of the number of able-bodied Americans who do not have jobs.[25]

It is actually a gross understatement to say, "tends to underestimate." During the 2007-2009 Recession, a startling statistic emerged that magnified the fact that the unemployment data does not always fully capture the extent to which people are suffering.

As the calendar turned to 2017, the nation's unemployment rate was only 4.8%. However, when counting the number of people working part-time who were looking for a full-time job and the number of discouraged workers in the U.S., the *"underemployment rate"* was nearly 14%. As one might imagine, if the government added in the number of people working full-time in jobs that did not match their set of skills – like executives working as janitors – the numbers would be much worse.[26]

Finally, the government reports on unemployment fail to calculate another fact. That is that as people go back to work for lower wages than they were earning before, there is a wage compression that forces down the long run distribution of earnings for people in that and similar fields. This leads to lower earnings in the long run for new workers and a lower standard of living over time.

One study found that for a typical worker who graduated in 1982, when unemployment was 10.8%, his pay was 23% less his first year out of college and 6.6% less 18 years later, than one who graduated in May 1981 when unemployment was 7.5%. For a typical worker, that meant $100,000 less money over that time period.[27]

What will that mean for people who graduated during the last major recession and subsequent slow recovery?

TYPES OF UNEMPLOYMENT

Not all unemployed people are unemployed for the same reasons. The unemployment rate is actually divided up into three types of unemployment.

> ➢ *Structural unemployment* is unemployment associated with changes in technology and permanent decreases in the demand for certain goods and services.

The accompanying photo may not appear to say much about unemployment in America, but for young boys who used to earn money hauling hay for ranchers, this is a dying scene in the United States.

Before the introduction of new technology that made baling hay in large round bales cost-effective, scenes like this one in southeastern Idaho were very common. Small square bales of hay provided jobs for kids who would walk alongside of trucks, tossing hay into them during the summer (I used to get paid 8 cents per bail as a teenager in Oklahoma….). When round bales came along, the demand for this type of labor all but vanished throughout

Photo courtesy Jack Chambless

the United States. This caused a form of structural unemployment in this market.

The 2007-2009 Recession contributed to a rise in structural unemployment as well. Industries that were hit the hardest by the downturn were forced to find ways to adapt to the new economic environment. For many, it meant hiring fewer workers, using more technology, or making their operations smaller.[28] When legislation was passed in 2010 that imposed massive new health care costs on businesses, many firms like the restaurant chain, Chili's, opted for new equipment – that does not need health care – to replace new workers.[29] All of these changes meant more structural unemployment going forward.

> ➤ *Frictional unemployment* **is unemployment associated with people who have left jobs that did not work out, people who are entering the labor force for the first time, and people who are re-entering the labor force.**

At the end of World War II, hundreds of thousands of veterans returned from the war ready to resume their domestic lives. As they flooded into labor markets looking for work, the frictional rate of unemployment increased markedly.

Ironically, as the economy begins to grow, more discouraged workers begin to re-enter the labor force. This often causes the unemployment rate to increase at the beginning of an upturn in the business cycle."

> ➤ *Cyclical unemployment* **is unemployment associated with contractions and recessions, and is typically temporary in nature.**

The increase in the unemployment rate to over 10% in 2010 was due to layoffs stemming from the stumbling economy.

People who were laid off during this time could take some comfort in the fact that as the recession eventually ended, they – or people like them with similar skills – would be called back to work.

Frictional and structural unemployment make up what economists call the *natural rate of unemployment.* This means that there are certain types of unemployment that are natural to the economy and cannot be eliminated. This should make perfect sense. On the frictional side of the equation, how many of you have ever quit a job because you hated the job or thought your boss was the devil? The period of time in between quitting your job and finding another job was a natural part of the economy's unemployment rate.

Is it natural that there are people who will enter the labor force for the first time? As long as Americans continue to procreate, people will turn 16, desire more money than they get for doing the dishes at home, and will enter a business looking for a job. It is also true that it is natural for many Americans to have a job or career, leave the labor force, and then return. Many women leave their jobs to take care of children, only to return when the kids go off to school or start to drive mom crazy with 17 hours of mayhem each day.

As for structural unemployment, will changes in technology always be with us? Will we always see certain products decline in desirability, rendering jobs in those markets obsolete? Absolutely. Ask film developers, bank tellers, and phone operators about their job prospects now that digital cameras, ATMs, and automated phone-answering devices abound. This permanent destruction of jobs is what economist Joseph Schumpeter called "creative destruction." When jobs are destroyed in the horse shoe, VCR or payphone manufacturing industries, resources are freed up to invent – and create far more jobs – in the automobile, DVR and cell phone industries. This helps fuel creative energy that can be redirected toward more productive industries over time.[30]

That is, if the government doesn't interfere…

As you will see in the international trade chapter, often government steps in and uses protective tariffs and quotas to support dying, or struggling, American industries. We also saw how crony capitalism, subsidies, bailouts,

Photo courtesy Jack Chambless

SUGGESTED CLASSROOM DEBATE

How many weeks of unemployment benefits should be paid to telecommunications workers who lost their jobs to cell phones?

and so forth can artificially insulate businesses – and their workers – from the process of ending certain jobs so new ones can emerge.

One more way the government impedes the process of self-improvement is by providing unemployment benefits week, after week, after… 99 weeks?

In 2010, Vice President Joe Biden credited unemployment benefits as a way to stimulate the economy.[31] Even dumb economists had to laugh at this remark. Sarcastic economists (no one I know) pointed out that if giving people checks for being unemployed is a way to stimulate the economy, the government could get us out of any recession in one day, by simply giving everyone in America a check to stay home.

For much of the last couple of decades, depending on the state you lived in, if you lost your job you could expect to receive unemployment compensation for 13-26 weeks. By 2010 the federal government had extended aid to 99 weeks. That means you could be out of work for almost two years while living off of taxpayer aid.

Countless empirical studies show that the longer government provides this type of aid, the worse the economy does[32] and the longer people stay unemployed.[33] Moreover, prolonged aid tends to undermine the technical skills of those who opt for longer periods of relief. Amazingly, economists have found that if you are at home, you are less likely to increase your stock of human capital.

On December 31, 2013 the eleventh in a series of extensions in unemployment benefits came to an end. This meant that for 1.3 million Americans, taxpayer assistance for their period of unemployment came to an end.

This reality prompted President Obama to push for a $6.89 billion twelfth extension in this program. In defending this initiative, the president stated, "The long-term unemployed are not lazy. I can't name a time when I met an American who would rather have an unemployment check than the price of having a job."[34]

Based on what we economists know, the President should have left the White House more often to walk around a few neighborhoods....

WHAT IS THE IDEAL UNEMPLOYMENT RATE?

What may come as a surprise to you is the belief of economists that not only is there a natural component of the unemployment rate that will never let the unemployment rate equal zero percent, but that some unemployment is actually *good* for the economy. This statement is one reason why many people would like to see all economists sent off

to a deserted island with only a few days of food available, but it is also a true statement for several reasons.

First, having people leave jobs for better ones is a good thing. This prevents people from feeling "job-locked" and allows for greater geographic mobility and maximization of one's lifetime earnings. Second, many people who re-enter the labor force after retirement or temporary career disruptions are much more productive than some of the people who have just entered the labor force. These individuals, who often have a tremendous work ethic and valuable experience, help boost productivity.

Third, with changes in technology come increased jobs and increased income over time. Should cars have been banned to save the horse and buggy industry? Should computers have been avoided to save the typewriter market? Finally, as we will see in the next chapter, if the unemployment rate equaled zero percent, the ensuing inflation this situation would create would wreck the economy.

The type of unemployment economists do worry about a lot is cyclical unemployment. This is because recessions are bad news for the country. Cyclical unemployment is the type of unemployment that we try to help design policies to prevent.

So, what is the natural rate of unemployment?

Before the recession of 2007-2009, many economists believed the nation's "natural" rate of unemployment was 5%. By 2012, the nonpartisan Congressional Budget Office said it was 6% as did a survey of economists by the Federal Reserve Bank of Philadelphia.

The increase can be attributed "to America's more than five million long-term unemployed, those jobless for 27 weeks or more, who may struggle for years to find positions as their skills and attractiveness to employers erode. The recession also heightened a mismatch between employers' needs and job seekers' skills, which is considered a 'structural,' or longer-term, problem rather than a 'cyclical' one. In addition, more-generous unemployment insurance means people can take longer to look for positions."[35]

Today, estimates ranging from 4.5 to 5.5% seem to be the agreed upon range for the natural rate of unemployment. By the end of 2016, with unemployment falling below 5% the Federal Reserve Bank began slightly increasing interest rates in order to prevent unemployment from falling to levels deemed to be "too low."

INFLATION

One day – when I was about eight years old – I was watching *The Flintstones,* when a news brief came on with the announcement that the government was reporting that the dollar was now worth 25 cents. At this time in my life, I had probably stashed away about three or four bucks in savings. When I heard this news, I burst into tears and ran into the kitchen to tell my mom that someone called "the government" was turning all dollars into quarters.

Trying to contain her laughter, my mother gently informed me what the reporter had meant that the amount of things a kid could buy in the "old days" for a quarter would take a dollar to buy in 1974. I was not sure what that meant, but I left the room relatively unhappy – just as I am as a grown man when I hear that inflation might be on the horizon.

MEASURING INFLATION

Friedrich Hayek once called inflation the worst of all economic evils. To a large extent, he was right. As you will see in the chapters that follow, higher rates of inflation – like much of the planet experienced in 2011[36] – leads to an erosion in our purchasing power and a deterioration in our standard of living.

> ➤ **Inflation is the rate of upward movement in the price level for an aggregate of goods and services.**

When the economy experiences inflation it means that overall, the price of goods and services purchased by a typical urban consumer are increasing. This is not to say that all prices must increase for inflation to occur. For example, the price of health care insurance and tuition have increased over the past few years, while the price of television sets and cell phone plans have fallen.

The data on inflation takes into account all of these changes to indicate the general movement in prices. To calculate the rate of inflation we use the following formula:

$$\left[\frac{\text{CPI (current year)} - \text{CPI (previous year)}}{\text{CPI (previous year)}} \right] \times 100$$

In order to help you better understand how inflation is calculated, the following information from the Bureau of Labor Statistics is provided. It is the most complete description of the basic determination of inflation you can find anywhere.

1. WHAT IS THE CPI?

The Consumer Price Index (CPI) is a measure of the average change over time in the prices paid by urban consumers for a market basket of consumer goods and services.

2. WHOSE BUYING HABITS DOES THE CPI REFLECT?

The CPI reflects spending patterns for each of two population groups: all urban consumers (CPI-U) and urban wage-earners and clerical workers (CPI-W). The CPI-U represents about 87% of the total U.S. population. It is based on the expenditures of almost all residents of urban or metropolitan areas, including professionals, the self-employed, the poor, the unemployed, and retired persons, as well as urban wage-earners and clerical workers. Not included in the CPI are the spending patterns of persons living in rural non-metropolitan areas, farm families, persons in the Armed Forces, and those in institutions, such as prisons and mental hospitals.

The CPI-W is based on the expenditures of households that are included in the CPI-U definition that also meet two requirements: More than one-half of the household's income must come from clerical or wage occupations, and at least one of the household's earners must have been employed for at least 37 weeks during the previous 12 months. The CPI-W's population represents about 32% of the total U.S. population and is a subset, or part, of the CPI-U's population.

3. DOES THE CPI MEASURE MY EXPERIENCE WITH PRICE CHANGE?

Not necessarily. It is important to understand that BLS bases the market baskets and pricing procedures for the CPI-U and CPI-W on the experience of the relevant average household, not on any specific family or individual. It is unlikely that your experience will correspond precisely with either the national indexes or those for specific cities or regions.

4. HOW IS THE CPI MARKET BASKET DETERMINED?

The CPI market basket is developed from detailed expenditure information provided by families and individuals on what they actually bought. More than 5,000 families from around the country provided information on their spending habits in a series of quarterly interviews. To collect information on frequently purchased items such as food and personal-care products, another 5,000 families in each of the three years kept diaries detailing everything they bought during a two-week period.

Altogether, more than 30,000 individuals and families provided expenditure information for use in determining the importance, or weight, of the more than 2000 categories in the CPI index structure.

5. WHAT GOODS AND SERVICES DOES THE CPI COVER?

The CPI represents all goods and services purchased for consumption by the reference population (CPI-U or CPI-W). BLS has classified all expenditure items into more than 200 categories, arranged into eight major groups. Major groups and examples of categories in each are as follow:

- Food and beverages (breakfast cereal, milk, coffee, chicken, wine, full-service meals, and snacks);
- Housing (rent of primary residence, owners' equivalent rent, fuel oil, bedroom furniture);
- Apparel (men's shirts and sweaters, women's dresses, jewelry);
- Transportation (new vehicles, airline fares, gasoline, motor vehicle insurance);
- Medical care (prescription drugs and medical supplies, physicians' services, eyeglasses and eye care, hospital services);
- Recreation (televisions, cable television, pets and pet products, sports equipment, admissions);
- Education and communication (college tuition, postage, telephone services, computer software and accessories);
- Other goods and services (tobacco and smoking products, haircuts and other personal services, funeral expenses).

Also included within these major groups are various government-charged user fees, such as water and sewage charges, auto registration fees, and vehicle tolls. The CPI also includes taxes (such as sales and excise taxes) that are directly associated with the prices of specific goods and services. However, the CPI excludes taxes (such as income and Social Security taxes) not directly associated with the purchase of consumer goods and services.

6. HOW ARE CPI PRICES COLLECTED AND REVIEWED?

Each month, BLS data collectors called economic assistants visit or call thousands of retail stores, service establishments, rental units, and doctors' offices, all over the United States to obtain price information on thousands of items used to track and measure price change in the CPI. These economic assistants record the prices of about 80,000 items each month. These 80,000 prices represent a scientifically selected sample of the prices paid by consumers for the goods and services purchased.

During each call or visit, the economic assistant collects price data on a specific good or service that was precisely defined during an earlier visit. If the selected item is available, the economic assistant records its price. If the selected item is no longer available, or if there have been changes in the quality or quantity (for example, eggs sold in packages of eight when previously they had been sold by the dozen) of the good or service since the last time prices had been collected, the economic assistant selects a new item or records the quality change in the current item.

The recorded information is sent to the national office of BLS where commodity specialists, who have detailed knowledge about the particular goods or services priced, review the data. These specialists check the data for accuracy and consistency and make any necessary corrections or adjustments. These can range from an adjustment for a change in the size or quantity of a packaged item to more complex adjustments based upon statistical analysis of the value of an item's features or quality. Thus, the commodity specialists strive to prevent changes in the quality of items from affecting the CPI's measurement of price change.

7. HOW IS THE CPI CALCULATED?

The CPI is a product of a series of interrelated samples. First, using data from the Census of Population, BLS selects the urban areas from which prices are to be collected and the housing units within each area that are eligible for use in the shelter component of the CPI. The Census of Population also provides data on the number of consumers represented by each area selected as a CPI

© RAGMA IMAGES/Shutterstock.com

CONCEPT CHECK

Suppose over the next year the price of fresh fish from Seattle's Pike Place Market increases by 8.23%. Is fresh fish counted in the market basket of goods and services? Would increases in the price of fresh fish, combined with falling prices for diesel fuel, lead to a change in the CPI? Why, or why not?

price-collection area. Next, another sample (of about 16,800 families each year) serves as the basis for a point-of-purchase survey that identifies the places where households purchase various types of goods and services.

8. How do I read or interpret an index?

An index is a tool that simplifies the measurement of movements in a numerical series. Most of the specific CPI indexes have a 1982-84 reference base. That is, BLS sets the average index level (representing the average price level) for the 36-month period covering the years 1982, 1983 and 1984 – equal to 100. The Bureau measures changes in relation to that figure. An index of 110, for example, means there has been a 10% increase in price since the reference period; similarly an index of 90 means a 10% decrease.

In December 2016 the CPI was equal to 241.432 (1982-84 = 100). Remember, this figure of 241.432 does not mean that the average price of a market basket of goods and services equaled $241.43. Nor does it mean that we spent $241.43 on average that month. The number 241.432 is simply a number to be used in direct comparison to the previous month's CPI, so that we can gauge how prices, on average, changed for that market basket.

Movements of the index from one date to another can be expressed as changes in index points (simply, the difference between index levels), but it is more useful to express the movements as percentage changes. This is because index points are affected by the level of the index in relation to its base period, while percentage changes are not. Historically, BLS has updated its reference periods every ten years or so.

The Consequences of Inflation

Now that you are an expert on how inflation is calculated, we turn to the consequences of higher prices. The biggest single problem that inflation creates is an *erosion of the purchasing power* of your money. Think of it this way.

If the rate of inflation is 6% next year and you get a pay raise of 2.5%, this actually means you took a *pay cut* of 3.5% in real terms. Of course, not everyone loses from inflation. If you have a loan payment with a fixed interest rate, you will welcome inflation, because as prices increase and your interest rate does not, in real terms that amount of money you are paying the bank for your house or car is falling! People with certificates of deposit and other interest sensitive investments also don't mind inflation because

as prices increase, interest rates tend to rise, and thus, the banks pay more for these types of investments.

Overall, however, inflation imposes deleterious impacts on workers and, if left unchecked, can cause an economic downturn as we respond to the devaluation of our money with less and less spending.

This is precisely the problem the U.S. and other nations faced in early 2011. After enjoying low rates of inflation (the lowest in 44 years) in 2010,[37] fueled largely by rising prices for commodities like oil, grains, copper, and other raw materials used in manufacturing, 2011 saw the threat of some of the largest increases in prices in recent memory.[38]

In particular, the price of food – driven up largely by increases in global demand, rising oil prices that impacted fertilizer and transportation costs, and supply disruptions caused by crops being diverted for biofuel production – began to rise by a larger amount than most other products.

It is important to mention food and energy because the Federal Reserve Bank, in determining whether to increase or lower interest rates, examines the overall rate of change in the price level. However, the Fed looks only at the "core rate of inflation," which does not include food and energy costs, which can be more volatile. Therefore, when the Federal Reserve Bank reports that inflation seems to be under control, that could come at a time when food and gas prices are rising sharply! This policy of looking only at the core rate of inflation has led many economists to criticize the Fed for being out of touch with the day to day prices most Americans face.[39]

Hyperinflation

From time to time government does silly things. This fact is as salient as the sun coming up in the morning. When government action with respect to the printing of money, gets out of control, the consequences can be catastrophic.

When Germany signed the Treaty of Versailles to end World War I, this European nation was required to pay billions of dollars in war reparations debt to the nations that had been invaded. To help pay the war debts, the German government of the early 1920s began printing currency at an alarming rate. In 1922 alone, the Weimar Republic increased the production of money by *30% per month*.[40] By the end of 1922, the rate of inflation in Germany was 5,000%.

Prices increased so fast that grocery stores and other shops would raise prices by the hour. Prices were not even printed on restaurant menus because, between the time a person sat down for dinner and the time the bill came, the prices would have risen. In 1918 a pound of butter cost 3 marks. In 1922 a pound of butter cost Germans (bring your wheel barrows) 6,000,000,000,000 (six trillion) marks!

Postwar Germany is not alone. As recently as the mid-1990s in the former Yugoslavia and 1989 in Argentina, nations have found that the quickest way to economic ruin is by treating the nation's financial printing press like a machine that produces monopoly money. More recently, the war with Iraq caused severe shortages that led to astronomical price increases.[41]

In Zimbabwe, the government has attempted to deal with the massive economic struggles created by President Robert Mugabe by printing so much money that inflation hit 40,000,000% in 2008. Mugabe has succeeded in ruining his country by taking away private property rights and allowing government corruption to destroy the incentives of the citizenry to produce goods and services.[42]

Therefore, the next time someone says, "We should just print $20 trillion and pay off the national debt!" you should remind them of how many wagonloads of cash a candy bar would cost.

© Steve Allen/Shutterstock.com

ENDNOTES

1 See "Shopping spree, rest in peace" by Robert Samuelson, *The Orlando Sentinel*, April 28, 2008.

2 See http://www.nerdwallet.com/blog/credit-card-data/average-credit-card-debt-household

3 See "Americans Pare Down Debt" by Mark Whitehouse, *The Wall Street Journal*, March 12, 2010.

4 See "Investment Falls Off a Cliff" by Sudeep Reddy and Scott Thurm, *The Wall Street Journal,* November 19, 2012.

5 See "Counting on a Miracle With U.S. Debt" by David Wessel, *The Wall Street Journal*, September 29, 2005.

6 For more on the difficulty of adding up this cost, see "For People and Planet" by Al Gore and David Blood, *The Wall Street Journal,* March 28, 2006.

7 In Thailand, prostitution accounts for as much as 14% of the GDP. For a detailed look at the move to add this service to Thailand's GDP, see www.hartford-hwp.com/archives/26/119.html.

8 See "Look Underground, and Unemployment is Low" by Daniel Akst, *The New York Times, September 7, 2003.*

9 To examine the data that the NBER publishes, log on to http://www.nber.org/.

10 See www.nber.org/cycles/recessions.html.

11 See "Recession is Inevitable" by David Roche, *The Wall Street Journal*, March 14, 2008.

12 See "Revisions Show Slower Recovery, Deeper Recession" by Sara Murray, *The Wall Street Journal*, July 31-August 1, 2010.

13 See "The Hidden Jobless Disaster" by Edward P. Lazear, *The Wall Street Journal*, June 6, 2013.

14 See "Uncertainty is the Enemy of Recovery" by Bill McNabb, *The Wall Street Journal,* April 28, 2013.

15 See "Uncertainty and the Slow Recovery" by Gary S. Becker, Steven J. Davis and Kevin M. Murphy, *The Wall Street Journal*, January 4, 2010; "The 2010 Recovery," *The Wall Street Journal*, April 3-4, 2010; "The 1.6% Recovery," *The Wall Street Journal*, August 28-29, 2010; "Tale of Two Recoveries," *The Wall Street Journal,* September 21, 2010; and "Corporate Profits Rise to Record Annual Rate" by Luca Di Leo and Jeffrey Sparshott, *The Wall Street Journal*, November 24, 2010.

16 See "The Best Economy Ever" by David Hale, *The Wall Street Journal*, July 31, 2007, pg. A15.

17 See "Bush Has a Good Economic Record" by Keith Marsden, *The Wall Street Journal*, September 3, 2008, pg. A23.

18 See "The New Inflation Equation" by Richard W. Fisher and W. Michael Cox, *The Wall Street Journal*, April 6, 2007, pg. A11.

19 See "Reaganomics: What We Learned" by Arthur Laffer, *The Wall Street Journal*, February 10, 2011.

20 IBID.

21 See "Our Uncertain Economy" by Edmund S. Phelps, *The Wall Street Journal*, March 14, 2008.

22 Source: CIA World Fact Book.

23 See "Unemployment rate creeps higher" by Don Lee, *The Orlando Sentinel*, December 4, 2010.

24 See "Meet the Unemployable Man" by David Wessel, *The Wall Street Journal*, May 6, 2010.

25 See "Jobless Numbers are Worse Than you Think" by Paul Godek, *The Wall Street Journal*, July 23, 2010.

26 See "From Executive to Janitor: Some Statistics" by Catherine Rampell, *The New York Times*, March 4, 2009.

27 See "The Curse of the Class of '09: Low Wages for Years to Come" by Sara Murray, *The Wall Street Journal*, May 9-10, 2009.

28 See "Fed Chief: Expect jobs to be long gone" by Don Lee and Walter Hamilton, *The Orlando Sentinel*, July 22, 2010; and "Joblessness will linger for years" by Jim Stratton, *The Orlando Sentinel*, January 16, 2011.

29 See "Chili's Feels Heat to Pare Costs" by Julie Jargon, *The Wall Street Journal*, January 28, 2011.

30 See "Creative Jobs Destruction," *The Wall Street Journal*, January 6, 2004.

31 See "Stimulating Unemployment," *The Wall Street Journal*, July 20, 2010.

32 One study found that if the benefits had not been extended to 99 weeks, the unemployment rate in the summer of 2010 would have been 6.8% rather than 9.5%. See "The Folly of Subsidizing Unemployment" by Robert Barro, *The Wall Street Journal*, August 30, 2010, p. A15.

33 See "Unemployment Benefits Aren't Stimulus" by Arthur B. Laffer, *The Wall Street Journal*, July 8, 2010.

34 See "Jobless benefits bill clears initial hurdle" by Lisa Mascaro and Christi Parsons, *The Orlando Sentinel*, January 8, 2014 page A3.

35 See "Decoding Natural Rate of Unemployment" by Neil Shah, *The Wall Street Journal,* September 7, 2012.

36 See "Global Price Fears Mount" by Brian Blackstone and Marcus Walker, *The Wall Street Journal*, January 24, 2011.

37 See "Inflation at 44-Year Low" by Mark Whitehouse and Alex Frangos, *The Wall Street Journal*, May 20, 2010.

38 See "The Latest American Export: Inflation" by Ronald McKinnon, *The Wall Street Journal*, January 18, 2011.

39 See "Inflation May Be Worse Than We Think" by David Ranson, *The Wall Street Journal*, February 27, 2008.

40 See *Economics* by David N. Hyman, 4th edition, Irwin, p. 529.

41 See www.afsc.org/iraq/guide/worldalso.shtm for more on hyperinflation in Iraq.

42 See "Think U.S. inflation is bad? Zimbabwe's is 40,000,000%" by Celia W. Duggar, *The Orlando Sentinel*, October 3, 2008, pg. A25; and "Freedom for Zimbabwe" by Morgan Tsvangirai, *The Wall Street Journal*, March 21, 2008.

CHAPTER REVIEW

1. What are the key components of the GDP? Which one is the most important to the long-run health of an economy? Why?

2. What is the business cycle? Why do we have to have recessions? What is the new economy theory? Is that theory effective today? Why or why not?

3. What are the three types of unemployment? Which one concerns economists the most? The least? Why?

4. With respect to the Circular Flow Model, what would be the impact – in the U.S. – of major new tariffs on goods from China?

5. What is so bad about inflation? Does inflation create any good news for anybody? Why?

Chapter Eleven

AGGREGATE DEMAND *and* AGGREGATE SUPPLY ANALYSIS

© Andresr/Shutterstock.com

*W*hen times are good, be happy; but when times are bad, consider this: God has made the one as well as the other. Therefore, no one can discover anything about their future.

ECCLESIASTES 7:14 NEW INTERNATIONAL VERSION

DID THE FINANCIAL WORLD ALMOST COME TO AN END?

In 2008 most of you who are reading this chapter were around 10 years old. That, as it turns out, is a positive thing. Because if you had been an adult you would have been looking for signs of locusts, plagues and dust storms sweeping across the United States. Consider some of these headlines from *The Wall Street Journal:*

"Crisis on Wall Street as Lehman Totters, Merrill is Sold, AIG Seeks to Raise Cash" September 15, 2008

"AIG, Lehman Shock Hits World Markets" September 16, 2008

"U.S. to Take Over AIG in $85 Billion Bailout; Central Banks Inject Cash as Credit Dries Up" September 17, 2008

"Mounting Fears Shake World Markets as Banking Giants Rush to Raise Capital" September 18, 2008

"U.S. Drafts Sweeping Plan to Fight Crisis as Turmoil Worsens in Credit Markets" September 19, 2008

"WaMu is Seized, Sold Off to J.P. Morgan, In Largest Failure in U.S. Banking History" September 26, 2008

"Bailout Plan Rejected, Markets Plunge, Forcing New Scramble to Solve Crisis" September 30, 2008

"Markets Fall on Doubts Rescue Will Succeed" October 7, 2008

With headlines like these, it was little wonder that everyone from bank executives to presidential candidates

to religious scholars, were wondering if perhaps our darkest days were ahead of us.

In this chapter we will seek to add a little bit of rational economic logic to what defied all logic during this time. By the end of the chapter you will know what causes recessions, inflation, stagflation, and non-inflationary economic growth. You will learn, along the way, that even in the worst economic times, good news can be found – just as you will discover that there are reasons to complain even when good news predominates.

A MACROECONOMIC APPROACH TO SUPPLY AND DEMAND

In a nation where more people watch zombie movies than read *The Wall Street Journal*, it should not come as a great shock that many Americans blamed President Bush for the worst recession since the 1930s and President Obama for the meager recovery in 2009-2016. To economists, it is somewhat disconcerting that so many people who work in the private sector each day, actually believe that the economic health of the nation rises and falls based on the decisions of a person who has to get permission from Congress to do almost anything.

In this chapter, we turn our attention to the forces that cause changes in real GDP, unemployment, and inflation. Not surprisingly, aggregate output and prices change as a result of changes in the aggregate demand for, and aggregate supply of, final goods and services.

AGGREGATE DEMAND

Aggregate demand is the relationship between the nation's price level (CPI) and the quantity of final goods and services demanded each year (real GDP). The nation's aggregate demand curve is simply the summation of all

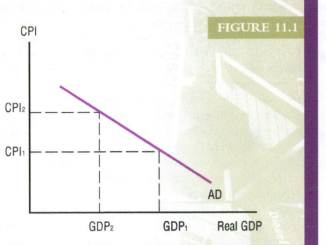

FIGURE 11.1

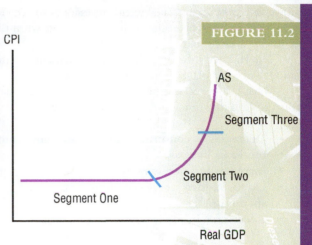

FIGURE 11.2

individual demand curves in the United States. Figure 11.1 illustrates a typical aggregate demand curve.

Notice that the aggregate demand curve has the same slope as the demand curves we studied earlier. This is because there is a *negative relationship between the nation's price level and real GDP.* As inflation increases, the overall level of consumption, investment, and net exports tends to fall. This leads to a lower level of GDP. Government spending, not surprisingly, tends to be insensitive to changes in the price level.

AGGREGATE SUPPLY

Aggregate supply is the relationship between the nation's price level and the quantity of final goods and services supplied each year. Just like aggregate demand, aggregate supply is the summation of all individual supply curves around the country. However, the aggregate supply curve has three theoretical segments. *Segment one,* sometimes known as the *"Keynesian segment"* was widely argued to exist during the Great Depression (to be explored later in the text). The *second segment* illustrates the traditional upward-sloping supply curve you are accustomed to studying. The vertical or *"Classical segment" (segment three)* comes from the work of economists like Ludwig von Mises who, as we will later see, argued that in the long-run the aggregate supply curve is vertical based on free-market responses to changes in aggregate demand. All three of these segments will be carefully examined.

THE CAUSES OF RECESSIONS

Recall that a recession occurs when real GDP falls for a significant period of time. A recession is caused by a decrease

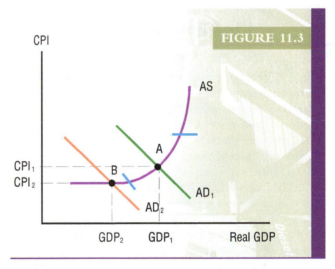

FIGURE 11.3

in the nation's aggregate demand curve into segment one of the aggregate supply curve. When a recession occurs, the nation's GDP falls below the real GDP that corresponds to "full employment." *Full employment* occurs at the point where the actual unemployment rate equals the natural rate of unemployment. A recession means an increase in the cyclical rate of unemployment as businesses lay off workers. Figure 11.3 illustrates this problem.

Notice that when aggregate demand decreases into segment one, this also leads to a lower level of inflation (CPI2). This is because businesses accumulate a great deal of unsold inventory as demand falls. To get rid of this surplus inventory, prices must fall. This is why *recessions create good news and bad news.* The good news is that products like new homes and cars become less expensive. Some economists refer to this reality as the "vulture economy." When the economy is in terrible condition people start selling their personal assets in order to raise money.[1] Suppliers of any number of goods and services become desperate and start slashing prices on their products. For people who have secure jobs, good credit, ample savings or accumulated wealth, recessions can become wonderful buying opportunities that do not exist when the economy is strong and prices are rising.

The bad news is that cyclical unemployment and the amount of idled plants and equipment increases.

What causes recessions? Not surprisingly, several factors can lead to a downturn in the business cycle.

- **Decreases in consumer and business confidence**
- **Increases in taxes**
- **Increases in interest rates**
- **Large, sudden decreases in government spending**
- **Recessions in foreign nations**

THE LONGEST RECESSION OF YOUR LIFETIME (SO FAR...)

In 1938 economist Melchior Palyi warned that the government should not encourage universal home ownership, because to do so would "make the population fixed to the ground" and prevent worker mobility during recessions. He also warned that too much credit always turns into a giant debt as borrowers become overwhelmed with escalating interest payments.[2]

In December of 2007, the U.S. economy began what was to be the longest recession since 1933. For 18 months we watched as millions lost their jobs, businesses closed, and people were forced to leave their homes under the threat of foreclosure. To better understand what happened during this time period, we need to go back to 1999.

During Bill Clinton's second term in office, he signed into law the Financial Services Modernization Act of 1999. This act did away with many of the regulations that had prohibited the integration of commercial and investment banks. These regulations – put in place by the Glass-Steagall Act of 1933 – had prevented investment banks from engaging in financial transactions with commercial banks (the type of bank where we put our savings).

With the restrictions lifted, commercial banks were free to sell investments to large banks like Bear Stearns and Lehman Brothers. Of course, as the book examined several chapters ago, some of the investment vehicles that were sold to large banks on Wall Street came in the form of bundled subprime mortgages, that Lehman and others thought would rise in value as the demand for real estate and homes increased.[3]

When housing prices started to fall, delinquent mortgage payments hit an 11-year high and foreclosures mounted. The five largest investment banks on Wall Street began losing billions of dollars.[4] By October of 2008, every one of these investment banks were gone – either bought by other banks, converted to commercial banks, or seized by the federal government.[5]

As the federal government rushed to provide a $700 billion bailout for the banking industry the U.S., European and Asian stock markets dropped dramatically.[6] In one month almost $2 trillion of losses came out of this epic collapse in the demand for stocks.[7]

The ways in which events like these can cause a recession are pretty straightforward. Foreclosures lead to a large drop in the overall income for banks and businesses that sell goods to homeowners. Even the threat of foreclosure can erode consumer confidence and drive down spending. When the worst banking crisis since the 1930's hit, businesses began reducing expenditures for new plants and equipment, consumers pulled back even more, and banks became reluctant to extend credit to the private sector, for fear of exposing dwindling assets to risky customers.[8] When you throw in a $2 trillion loss in the stock market which deteriorates the net wealth of the entire nation, you get a recipe for a large drop in aggregate demand.[9]

Another piece of the recession puzzle was the increase in crude oil prices that contributed to much higher gasoline and food prices. As consumers saw food and gasoline prices rise faster than at any time in almost 20 years, cutbacks in spending for vacations and other conspicuous consumption fell sharply.

With aggregate demand falling, the American people were wondering what would happen to end the free fall. By 2010, the specter of *deflation* (falling wages and prices throughout the economy) had reared its ugly head. Deflation makes it harder for people and businesses to pay off debts. With falling incomes, but fixed debt obligations on homes, equipment, and more, our country's recovery was hampered by the general price declines that we saw.[10] Many economists pointed out that America faced a real chance of a "double-dip recession" – an event characterized by a recession, followed by a brief period in which the economy begins to recover, only to slip back into another recession.[11] This concern was even greater in 2011 as unrest in the Middle East and a nuclear scare in Japan created rising oil prices and faltering demand from one of the largest economies in the world.

SUGGESTED CLASSROOM DEBATE

The February 4, 2014 *Wall Street Journal* ran a front-page article that examined how record-cold weather, sluggish holiday sales and low factory orders had combined to send stocks plummeting.[12] How could many Americans find this to be *good news*?

OTHER FACTORS THAT CAN CAUSE A RECESSION

While declining confidence on the part of consumers and businesses is important, there are many other factors that can cause aggregate demand to fall.

A LARGE, SUDDEN DROP IN GOVERNMENT SPENDING

In 1948, with World War II over, there was no longer a need for large government expenditures for military goods and services. After the war, government spending dropped significantly, leading to layoffs around the country and reductions in income for individuals and businesses whose jobs the previous five years had hinged on government contracts. With the reduction in spending came a decrease in aggregate demand.

This is not to suggest that cuts in government spending are always bad. You will see in the next chapter that reductions in government spending can actually help lower interest rates and fuel economic growth. However, with government spending accounting for 25% of economic activity, enormous or sudden cuts in spending would cause economic problems in the short run.

RECESSIONS IN FOREIGN NATIONS

During the banking crisis that plagued the United States in 2008, many other nations that had invested in the housing boom of the first decade found that America's troubles can easily become global troubles. In Europe, Asia and Russia, the inability of American banks to provide credit during this time, combined with the uncertainty about America's ability to buy foreign goods in the future, led to equally sharp drops in the overall level of economic activity among our trading partners.[13]

When our foreign trading partners fall on hard times, demand for our goods and services falls. As a result, our net exports to other nations decrease. If the drop in exports is severe enough our aggregate demand can fall, and a recession can follow, or intensify.

This was precisely the case when Herbert Hoover signed the Smoot-Hawley Tariff Act on June 17, 1930. What began as a movement to help shield farmers from international competition, lead to multitudinous members of Congress clamoring for protection for everything from animal hides to shoes.[14]

One thousand economists signed a petition against the bill but to no avail. As we will see in more detail in the following chapter, this anti-trade bill helped propel the world into the Great Depression and magnified our own economic struggles.

This is precisely why economists have been so concerned with President Trump's stance on trade. One study from 2016 found that if Mr. Trump was successful in carrying out all of his tariff threats it would send the United States into a recession and destroy 5 million U.S. jobs.[15]

AN INCREASE IN TAXES

On August 2, 1990, Iraq invaded Kuwait, triggering a massive effort on the part of the United States and other nations to save world oil supplies from falling dramatically. American consumers remembered the last time an oil crisis had hit the country. In 1979 the Iranian revolution sparked an embargo of oil to the United States, leading to huge increases in gas prices and a severe recession. Wary of a repeat of 1979, millions of consumers feared that the Iraqi invasion would trigger an economic downturn. With consumer confidence plummeting, consumption decreased, and the very thing consumers feared – our first contraction since 1982 – actually occurred in the fall of 1990.

Some economists believe that the downturn that occurred in 1990-1991 was magnified by the then-record $150 billion increase in income taxes that occurred with the passage of the 1990 Omnibus Budget Reconciliation Act. This act, designed to reduce America's burgeoning budget deficit, came at a terrible time.

With a contraction already under way, the tax increase further eroded business and consumer confidence, leading to an accelerated decline in aggregate demand and a recession that cost George Bush Sr. his job in 1992. Although the recession ended in March 1991 – over a year and a half before the election – the tax hike contributed to very sluggish economic growth during 1991 and much of 1992. In the summer of 1992 the unemployment rate was still well over 7%. This allowed Bill Clinton to seize the opportunity to place blame for the sluggish economy on the Bush administration and capture the presidency.

There is an old saying in baseball that goes, "It isn't always how you pitch, but when you pitch." This is also true in politics. It isn't always what economic policy you pursue, but when you pursue it. In 1993, Bill Clinton passed the largest tax increase in the history of the world, yet the economy did not fall into another slump.

This is because by 1993, the economy was very strong and growing stronger as a result of continual cuts in interest rates by the Federal Reserve Bank and the technology boom. In this sense Mr. Clinton was very fortunate. While his tax increase did slow down the rate of growth for a time, the economy kept creating more income at a faster rate than his tax increase was able to bring it down. Had he increased taxes during a time of economic sluggishness, he would have been a one-term president.

AN INCREASE IN INTEREST RATES

In 1982 the Federal Reserve Bank embarked on a campaign to rid the U.S. of inflation once and for all. The strategy involved increasing interest rates to record levels. For a time, the prime rate of interest – the interest rate banks charge their biggest customers – hovered around 21%! With rates rising well into double digits,

American households stopped buying homes, and businesses scrapped investment plans. The combined impact on consumption and investment led to a drop in the nation's aggregate demand and our last severe recession. This may have seemed like a particularly cruel policy for the Fed to pursue, but it was very effective. Since the early 1980s, there has been virtually no sign of the high levels of inflation that existed in the 1970s.

WHAT RECOVERIES LOOK LIKE

Since there are five events that can lead to a decrease in aggregate demand, the opposite of any of those events – increased confidence, lower taxes, lower interest rates, growth in foreign nations, and increased government spending – can lead to an increase in aggregate demand and the end of a recession over time.

Most often, the first policy prescription is *expansionary monetary policy*, which is the lowering of interest rates through the stimulation of the money supply. This is the first choice because it doesn't take long to implement. In this scenario, as interest rates come down, consumers and businesses choose to spend and invest more money. This hopefully leads to an increase in aggregate demand to AD3. From 2008 into 2014, through a program called quantitative-easing, the Federal Reserve Bank lowered interest rates in an attempt to stave off a recession, yet aggregate demand did not grow much. The problem, of course, is that if people are worried about losing their jobs – or have lost them – lower interest rates tend not to encourage people to spend money that they do not have.

Notice that when aggregate demand increases, real GDP rises back to GDP$_3$, but the price level does not change. When we studied supply curves earlier, we found that when output rises, prices rise, but here they do not. Why?

John Maynard Keynes – one of the most influential economists of all time – argued in his research concerning unemployment, inflation, and economic growth, that during the initial stages of an economic recovery (points B-C on Figure 11.4), national output can increase without causing inflation because business firms simply

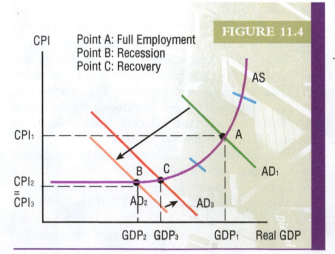

FIGURE 11.4

CPI — Point A: Full Employment
Point B: Recession
Point C: Recovery

AS

CPI$_1$ — A

B   C — AD$_1$

CPI$_2$
CPI$_3$ — AD$_2$ AD$_3$

GDP$_2$ GDP$_3$ GDP$_1$ Real GDP

re-employ previously unemployed labor and capital.

When workers are recalled, after perhaps several months of unemployment, do you suppose they demand higher wages upon their return? Business firms know that with a surplus of cyclically unemployed labor, employees can be recalled at the same, if not a lower, wage rate than before. Workers who balk at the offered wage rate will simply be passed over, and someone who is all too grateful just to have a job will jump at the chance to earn an income once again.

As the recession ended in the summer of 2009 and the slow recovery began, many workers discovered that the supply and demand conditions they were facing, were far less favorable to them than just a few years earlier. Workers being recalled to work, or who took new jobs during the initial stages of the recovery, saw their pay

What can fill this place up?

rates equal a level that was up to 40% less than what they had earned before.[16]

A similar story unfolds with respect to the use of capital. During an economic recovery, companies can simply use the equipment and floor space that had been sitting idle during the downturn. By using existing capital, these firms do not incur much, if any, increase in their costs of production. Therefore, with wages and other input costs remaining flat, companies can afford to increase production and thus, the GDP without raising prices. Hence, Keynes argued inflation remains under control while the unemployment rate decreases.

This is precisely what we saw in the beginning stages of the 2009-2011 economic recovery. Led largely by lower interest rates, cost-cutting measures taken by business firms to boost profits, and a small tax cut by President Obama, the economy began to show signs of strength but inflation remained largely under control into the early months of 2011.

In addition to lowering interest rates, the other policy tools that can be used include cuts in taxes, increases in government spending, expanded trade agreements or lowering of tariffs and policy proposals that boost consumer and business confidence. However, one policy that does not work well is the issuance of tax rebate checks.

During the spring and summer of 2008, you and/ or your parents got a check in the mail from the U.S. treasury. Depending on your tax filing status, you got as little as $300 or perhaps more than $1,000, in the form of a tax rebate.

President Bush and Congress passed the rebate plan in early 2008 in an effort to keep aggregate demand growing.

However, historically rebate checks have very little, if any, impact on aggregate demand – especially in the long run. Workers tend to alter their behavior on expectations of somewhat permanent changes in their economic well-being, rather than in temporary changes. If *income tax rates* are cut – creating some permanency in what people have to pay year in and year out, this can bring about changes in work hours, productivity, and ultimately, the overall level of consumer spending required to create real increases in aggregate demand. Rebate checks tend to be fun to get, but fleeting and marginal in their effectiveness.[17]

When it comes to *increases in government spending,* we will see in the next chapter that there are many reasons to doubt the long-run effectiveness of taxpayer dollars put toward "make-work" projects. In 2009 the American Recovery and Reinvestment Act – an $862 billion bill – was passed by President Obama to drive aggregate demand out of segment one of the aggregate supply curve and restore full employment. By early 2014 – almost five full years after the passage of this bill – the U.S. economy was still slogging through a historically slow recovery with unemployment well above the rate we normally see.[18] Moreover, median household income was $54,916 in December 2007 (when the recession began).

More than three years after this act was passed, median income was down to $50,964. In 2014 alone the number of men in their prime earning years (ages 25 to 54) who were unemployed was one in six, or total of 10.4 million.[19] Among younger men and women the prospects were even dimmer. Over four years after the "stimulus" bill was passed the unemployment rate for people under 25 was 15.6%.[20] By contrast, during the 1981-1986 economic recovery, median income increased by 7.7% and unemployment fell to below 5%.[21]

This is not to say that government spending never benefits any person or business. During World War II, increases in government spending did lead to more people being employed to build bombs and airplanes. The creation of the interstate highway led to more money for asphalt companies. The approximately $145 billion (current dollars) spent to send men to the moon in the 1960s, along with the hundreds of billions spent on the 1980s military build-up and today's expenditures on "green" technology and other programs certainly led to some people and businesses benefitting who otherwise may not have.

However, it is important to note that unlike the Kennedy and Reagan tax cuts, for example, that allowed the American people to spend, save or invest their own earnings, government spending – every dollar of it – starts with a taking of income away from some person. If the federal government spends $100 billion next year to refurbish bridges and highways it means that $100 billion must first be confiscated from a current or future taxpayer to pay for these repairs. In pure accounting terms we start with a *negative $100 billion* (taxes paid) then expend $100 billion. The sum of that "transaction" is zero – unless the government is particularly gifted at spending our money in a more efficacious manner than we are.

Lowering tariffs and negotiating expanded trade agreements can also help increase aggregate demand. As you will see in the international trade chapter, agreements like NAFTA that seek to impose lower taxes on our trading partners that have some comparative advantages leads to lower prices for Americans and expanded job opportunities for the U.S. in areas we specialize in and can offer to our trading partners. 2008-2010 actually saw an increase in our net exports as a result of a more favorable trading environment and a declining price of our dollar. It was

this sector, more than any other part of the GDP formula that kept aggregate demand growing during a time when consumers and businesses were cutting back on spending.

Finally, there is something to be said for policies that help restore *confidence* in the private sector. Regardless of the overall benefits of rebate checks, bank bailouts, promises to increase spending for alternative fuels or any number of other ideas, for many Americans the idea that policy makers are trying to do something can help spur on more economic activity.

When Ronald Reagan ran for office he had a series of commercials that were called the "Morning in America" commercials that kept telling the American people that better times were ahead of us. This ran in sharp contrast to Jimmy Carters' message that we were in the midst of an economic "malaise." The American people responded to Reagan's message with hope and optimism that translated into a slow and steady expansion in consumer and business spending, even before he took office.

INFLATION

How long can aggregate demand increase before trouble starts? On this point you will find a very vigorous debate among economists. For those of us who tend to focus on demand-side issues like consumer spending and business investments, there tends to be a great deal of collective hand-wringing over increases in aggregate demand. The theory – based, in part, on realities of the past – is that if aggregate demand increases too much, inflation will eventually become a problem.

Suppose that in October 2020, the economy is at point C on Figure 11.4 when the Federal Reserve Bank

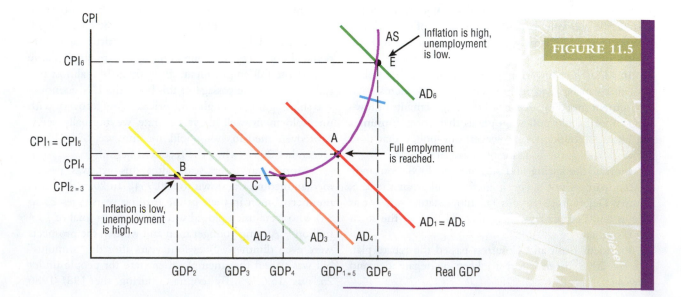

FIGURE 11.5

CONCEPT CHECK

During periods of tremendous economic growth, the quality of customer service tends to decline.[22] Why?

© wavebreakmedia/Shutterstock.com

announces a major interest rate cut designed to boost consumer spending. Where will that take us? Figure 11.5 shows us that initially the news would be good.

The interest rate cut would propel aggregate demand toward point D, where there is still a very small gap between real GDP and the ideal level of real GDP (the point where full employment is reestablished).

The increase in prices would stem from the fact that as aggregate demand increases, the demand for capital and labor increases. In some parts of the country where demand grows faster than the national average, there may even be capital and labor shortages.[23]

In 2010 as the American economy was in the recovery stages, equipment shortages began to appear. Having seen one of the largest drops in aggregate demand in over 70 years, many manufacturing plants not only used less equipment, but actually got rid of a large amount of machinery and other physical capital.[24] Therefore, as the economy grew, businesses were unable to gain the access to the equipment needed to meet the rising aggregate demand.[25]

As shortages begin to emerge, the input costs of production increase, which leads business firms to raise prices.[26] Inflation would not yet be an overwhelming concern, but it would bear careful watching. By 2014 the specter of inflation was less of a threat as aggregate demand began to grow more slowly.

Yet, by 2017 prices were once again increasing at a faster pace, prompting economists to argue that full employment (point A) was close to being achieved.

FULL EMPLOYMENT AND BEYOND

Suppose as you are reading this section of the book aggregate demand has increased from point D on figure 11.5 to point A (where we were in 2007). This would mean further reductions in cyclical unemployment. In short, we would be back to "full employment" and within the range of aggregate supply where prosperity is occurring for more people.

But what if the unemployment rate kept falling? Recall that the April 2000 unemployment rate was 3.9%.[27]

All economists agree that if, for any reason, aggregate demand increases to point E, the economy would be *overheated*. At this point, high levels of consumer spending, extremely low interest rates or runaway government spending could be taking place. We will see in the next chapter that this vertical segment of the aggregate supply curve, sometimes called the "Classical segment" gets its name from economists who argue that in the long run the economy adjusts to such increases in aggregate demand without government intervention.

But for now the question is, what would such a large increase in aggregate demand mean to the economy? It would mean that GDP is now barely increasing (as producers have less capacity to increase production) and accelerating rates of inflation.

As companies add more and more workers, they begin to dip so far down into the labor pool that the only workers left to hire are those with the least amount of skill and thus, the lowest productivity. The skilled workers have been hired long ago.[28]

As a matter of fact, during an overheated economy, especially in the construction industry, skilled workers often hop from one company to the next, being bid away by dramatic increases in wages. The relatively unskilled workers left over must be trained and often do not work as hard; therefore, the labor cost of production rises sharply. This event, coupled with suppliers raising prices and materials being in short supply, means that output barely increases, while inflation rates accelerate quickly.

President Trump has called for a $1 trillion infrastructure spending campaign. Based on where unemployment is today, does this make economic sense?

ADDING IT ALL UP

To summarize, we saw that a recession is brought on by a decrease in aggregate demand below the point of full employment, while inflation is caused by an increase in aggregate demand where we exceed full employment (the actual unemployment rate falls below the natural rate of unemployment).

During a *recession*, the *bad news* is that unemployment is increasing. The *good news* is that inflation is low.

During a period of *inflation*, the *bad news* is that prices are rising. The *good news* is that virtually everyone – even a good number of people who would normally be frictionally or structurally unemployed – is employed.

CHANGES IN AGGREGATE SUPPLY

Up until 1971, virtually the entire economics community embraced this good news/bad news perspective on macroeconomic equilibrium. Consumers and businesses alike were convinced that there would always be a tradeoff between unemployment and inflation. The Phillips Curve, named for A.W. Phillips, can illustrate this belief. Dr. Phillips empirically proved (for awhile) that there is (was) a negative

relationship between inflation and unemployment. Figure 11.6 illustrates this idea.

As you will see in much greater detail in chapter 12 and perhaps in the video series, *The Commanding Heights* (available on the course website), the early 1970s represented a dramatic change in the health of the American economy. For the first time, a new – and very bad – situation had appeared. Simply put, inflation and unemployment were increasing *simultaneously*.

How did this happen? In hindsight, the answer is pretty clear. From the Great Depression until the 1970s, governments around the world opted for macroeconomic

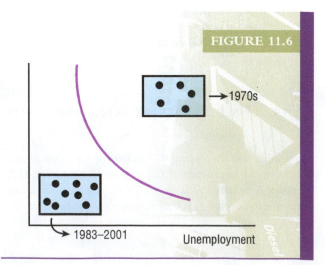

FIGURE 11.6

→1970s

1983–2001

Unemployment

policies that called for huge increases in government spending, tough regulations on businesses, and increased taxes. During this time labor unions gained significant power in the U.S. and Europe, that led to a decrease in the productivity of the economy in each continent.

Recall that the determinants of aggregate demand are consumer confidence, government spending, interest rates, taxes, and net exports. If any of those factors change, aggregate demand will change. What about aggregate supply? Aggregate supply will change as a result of changes in any of the following.

> **The input costs of production (taxes, regulations labor, raw materials, energy, interest rates, etc.)**
> **The quality of inputs – measured by changes in technology, worker productivity, and educational quality.**
> **The quantity of inputs – the actual amount of land, labor, capital, and entrepreneurs available to an economy.**

Therefore, with rising taxes and regulatory costs, and increased government spending to subsidize consumption and production, the overall productivity of the economy began to drop, while the input costs increased sharply. The economics community – and the Phillips Curve – was turned on its head when, for the first time, the world saw that the traditional tradeoff between prices and jobs does not always hold true. A new term, known as *stagflation*, became the most pressing problem of that time.

> **Stagflation occurs when aggregate supply decreases, causing a recession, combined with high rates of cyclical unemployment and inflation. It is the worst event that can happen to any economy.**

The stagflation that began to appear in 1971 was magnified by a geopolitical and economic crisis that hit the U.S. in October 1973. On the eve of the Jewish holiday, Yom Kippur, Syrian and Egyptian forces invaded Israel. The Israelis were caught off-guard and were in severe trouble when they appealed to President Nixon for help. The problem for the United States was that it wanted to see Israel emerge victorious, but at the same time not offend the members of OPEC, who controlled the bulk of the world's supply of oil.

The U.S. offered to airlift vital military equipment to Israel – but only under the cover of darkness – so that the Arabs would not discover this plan. The airlift got off to a later start than it was supposed to, and instead of landing in Tel Aviv under the cover of darkness, the U.S. cargo planes landed in bright daylight, in full view of Arab television cameras.

The members of OPEC were not pleased. Israel quickly turned the tide of battle around and won the war. In response to this event, OPEC delegates, meeting in Kuwait, decided to increase the price of crude oil and severely curtail shipments of oil to the U.S. This led to what became known as the *Arab Oil Embargo*. Virtually overnight gas prices increased by 40% in America.

Oil is a key input in the production of everything. Plastics, gasoline, fertilizer, and thousands of other goods are at least partially derived from crude oil. When oil prices shot up, the input costs of producing and transporting goods increased. As input costs increased, America's aggregate supply of goods and services decreased at a faster rate. Figure 11.7 illustrates the consequences of stagflation.

Notice that when aggregate supply decreases, the new macroeconomic equilibrium occurs at a much higher price level and at a point where real GDP is less than the ideal real GDP – indicating a recession. The term stagflation came to be known as a situation where the economy becomes *mired in a recession with high rates of inflation, due to a sudden drop in aggregate supply.*

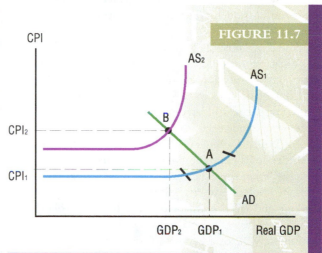

FIGURE 11.7

How common is stagflation in America? If you are a student of history, you know that strikes in the Iranian oil fields in 1979 that led to the second oil crisis of that decade caused an even larger jump in inflation and unemployment. By 1980 unemployment had risen to 7.1%, from 5.8% in 1979, and the rate of inflation was a whopping 13.5%!

Stagflation came to an end in America during the 1980s and has only occasionally appeared on the horizon since that time. Recent record-setting droughts,[30] along with ongoing struggles with K-12 education, long-term (and productivity-reducing) unemployment, and a rising tide of new (and input cost-impacting) regulations and taxes contributed to paltry 1.1% growth in productivity from 2011 to 2014, which is less than half the average gain in output we have seen since 1948.[31] For many economists the U.S. is not out of the woods when it comes to the possibility that stagflation will once again appear.

In January 2014 former Federal Reserve Chairman Ben Bernanke said, "It (low productivity) may be a result of the financial crisis, for example, if tight credit conditions have inhibited innovation, productivity-improving investments, and the formation of new firms. Another possibility is weak productivity growth reflects long-term trends largely unrelated to the recession. Obviously, the resolution of the productivity puzzle will be important in shaping our expectations for longer-term growth."

Yes, it will....

businesses cannot afford to open up and compete with the government's wages and pension plans, so businesses don't open. The lack of suppliers, aggregated across an economy, leads to higher inflation (stemming from the lack of competition) and high unemployment (from not having new businesses).

Thus, it was not a great shock to the economics community when mostly young, college graduates in this ancient land, took to the streets to demand the right to look for a job and have a future that would not be mired by stagflation.

EGYPT

For 18 days in January and February of 2011, the world watched as citizens of Egypt poured into the streets of Cairo demanding that their leader for 30 years step down immediately. For many viewers, it seemed as if the world was witness to something akin to the revolutions we have witnessed in former Communist Bloc nations 20 years earlier and in America, 200 years before that.

What many could not have known was that a large part of Egypt's eruption stemmed from chronic stagflation, born out of decades of political and economic corruption, rising taxes, a bloated public employee payroll, and burdensome regulations.

In 2011, Egypt ranked 96th in the world on the Index of Economic Freedom.[32] According to the Heritage Foundation, Egyptian citizens were shackled with low levels of property rights protection, limited labor freedom, and faced constant pressure to bribe politicians just to have the right to exist as a business. 92% of Egyptians had property in 2011 that had no legal title and thus, no protection from government coercion.[33]

Rising food prices and declining labor productivity had led to years of high unemployment and inflation.[34]

Finally, 35% of Egypt's labor force works for the government. In Turkey, a nation with far more economic growth, the figure is 13%. Many studies show that the higher the percentage of people working for the government, the poorer the nation can expect to be.[35] That is because government tends to pay workers more than what the free market pays. Private

NON-INFLATIONARY ECONOMIC GROWTH

When George Bush took office on January 20, 2001, he inherited an economy that was in the midst of the greatest run of economic growth in the history of our nation. The economic growth that had been experienced not only led to an increased GDP, but unemployment rates fell below 4%, and we had the first budget surplus since 1969.

All of this had been accomplished with very small increases in the rate of inflation. Table 11.1 illustrates the fact that GDP and labor productivity can increase as inflation rates fall.

As the table clearly illustrates, for the decades of the 1980s and 1990s, there was no tradeoff between unemployment and inflation. Notice that we experienced significant gains in GDP and productivity, all while inflation fell or remained at relatively low levels. There are many factors that led to this wonderful run of economic growth,

YEAR	PRODUCTIVITY	% CHANGE IN REAL GDP	RATE OF INFLATION	YEAR	PRODUCTIVITY	% CHANGE IN REAL GDP	RATE OF INFLATION
1959	51.3	7.3	0.7	1981	83.0	2.5	10.3
1960	51.9	2.5	1.7	1982	82.5	−2.0	6.2
1961	53.7	2.3	1.0	1983	86.3	4.3	3.2
1962	56.1	6.0	1.0	1984	88.1	7.3	4.3
1963	58.1	4.3	1.3	1985	89.3	3.8	3.6
1964	60.6	5.8	1.3	1986	92.0	3.4	1.9
1965	62.4	6.4	1.6	1987	92.3	3.4	3.6
1966	64.6	6.6	2.9	1988	93.5	4.2	4.1
1967	65.8	2.5	3.1	1989	94.2	3.5	4.8
1968	67.8	4.8	4.2	1990	95.3	1.8	5.4
1969	67/9	3/0	5.5	1991	96.4	−0.5	4.2
1970	68/9	0/2	5.7	1992	100.0	3.0	3.0
1971	71.8	3.3	4.4	1993	100.5	2.7	3.0
1972	74.1	5.4	3.2	1994	101.8	4.0	2.6
1973	76.6	5.8	6.2	1995	102.8	2.7	2.8
1974	75.3	−0.6	11.0	1996	105.4	3.6	3.0
1975	77.4	−0.4	9.1	1997	107.5	4.4	2.3
1976	80.3	5.6	5.8	1998	110.3	4.3	1.6
1977	81.5	4.6	6.5	1999	112.9	4.1	2.2
1978	82.6	5.5	7.6	2000	116.6	4.1	3.4
1979	82.2	3.2	11.3	2001	118.9	−1.3	2.8
1980	82.0	−0.2	13.5				

TABLE 11.1

Changes in Real GDP, The Rate of Inflation, and Worker Productivity* from 1959–2001
*Productivity equals real GDP per hour per worker

but the primary reason was a major increase in aggregate supply.

The computer and Internet revolution led to such a large increase in the productivity of American workers and businesses, that the input cost of production fell for many companies — especially those that rely more on technology than energy — to supply goods and services. Relatively low interest rates, expanded world trade, income tax cuts from the Reagan era, capital gains tax cuts signed into law by Bill Clinton, and increased productivity overall, has led to this increase in the aggregate supply. This means that up until December 2007, we were able to enjoy lower rates of inflation, lower rates of unemployment, and an increase in real GDP.

Figure 11.8 depicts an economy that is experiencing *non-inflationary economic growth* — increases in output that stem from an increase in aggregate supply. Notice that while aggregate demand has increased, aggregate supply has increased even more. This is what we experienced for much of the 1980s, 1990s, and the first few years of this century.

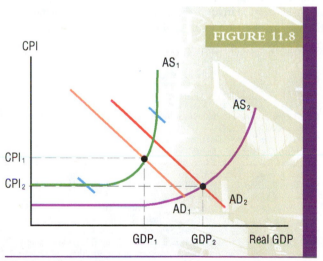

FIGURE 11.8

SUGGESTED CLASSROOM DEBATE

In her classic book, *Capitalism, The Unknown Ideal,* Ayn Rand argued that public education mirrors Communism in many respects and that in order for a nation to be free and prosperous, the entire education system should be supplied by the private sector. If we followed her advice, what would be the long run implications for aggregate supply in America? Why?

SOME FINAL THOUGHTS

We close the chapter with a serious look at the prospects for America's long-run growth in aggregate supply. You will recall that aggregate supply can be impacted by changes in productivity. Productivity, of course, is impacted by the overall quantity and quality of education the labor force has. What if, over time, America continues to fall behind other nations in terms of educational quality, while those same nations that have superior education systems continue to move toward freer markets?

You will recall from chapter five, that America ranks very low internationally in the overall quality of education. If this trend continues – and if China, India, Brazil, and other nations continue to combine better schools with a push toward capitalism, the United States could very well find itself steeped in long-run bouts of stagflation. The ramifications of that end result should not be lost on anyone.

ENDNOTES

1 See "Many cashing out their attics" by Anne D'Innocenzio, *The Orlando Sentinel,* May 4, 2008.

2 See "The Man Who Called the Financial Crisis – 70 Years Early" by Jason Zweig, *The Wall Street Journal,* November 6-7, 2010.

3 See "The Roots of the Mortgage Crisis" by Alan Greenspan, *The Wall Street Journal,* December 12, 2007, pg. A19.

4 See "Fear, Rumors Touched Off Fatal Run on Bear Stearns" by Kate Kelly, *The Wall Street Journal,* May 28, 2008.

5 See "Goldman, Morgan Scrap Wall Street Model, Become Banks in Bid to Ride Out Crisis" by Jon Hilsenrath, Damian Paletta and Aaron Lucchetti, *The Wall Street Journal,* September 22, 2008.

6 See "Dow Falls 777.68 Points on Bailout's Delay" by E.S. Browning and Tom Lauricella, *The Wall Street Journal,* September 30, 2008.

7 See "Turmoil Prolongs Misery" by Jeannine Aversa, *The Orlando Sentinel,* October 8, 2008.

8 See "Worst Crisis Since '30s With No End in Sight" by Jon Hilsenrath, Serena Ng and Damian Paletta, *The Wall Street Journal,* September 18, 2008.

9 See "Wave of Foreclosures Drives Prices Lower, Lures Buyers" by James R. Hagerty and Kris Hudson, *The Wall Street Journal,* March 25, 2008; and "Consumers Cut Health Spending as Economic Downturn Takes Toll" by Vanessa Fuhrmans, *The Wall Street Journal,* September 22, 2008.

10 See "Deflation Fears Stir in Developed Economies" by Jon Hilsenrath, *The Wall Street Journal,* June 11, 2010, p. A4.

11 See "Don't Rule Out a Double Dip Recession" by Christopher Wood, *The Wall Street Journal,* May 24, 2010; and "Waning Economic Recovery Fuels Global Uncertainty" by Mark Whitehouse, Marcus Walker and Joann S. Lublin, *The Wall Street Journal,* September 23, 2010.

12 See "Factory Weakness Hits Stocks" by Dan Strumph and Neil Shah, *The Wall Street Journal,* February 4, 2014.

13 See "Europe Races to Shore Up Banks as Crisis Spreads" by Marcus Walker, Sabrina Cohen, Dana Cimilluca and David Gauthier Villars, *The Wall Street Journal,* October 6, 2008; and "Turmoil Threatens Russia's Rise" by Gregory L. White, *The Wall Street Journal,* September 18, 2008, pg. A4.

14 See "How Protectionist Became an Insult" by Douglas A Irwin, *The Wall Street Journal,* June 18, 2010.

15 See https://www.wsj.com/articles/trump-trade-plan-could-push-u-s-into-recession-study-says-1474257662.

16 See inspiredeconomist.com and "Recession Strikes Deep Into Work Force" by Miriam Jordan, *The Wall Street Journal,* June 30, 2010 p. A2

17 See "Feel-Good Economics" by Bruce Bartlett, *The Wall Street Journal,* January 19-20, 2008 and "Bush's Stimulus Flop" by Alan Reynolds, *The Wall Street Journal,* January 22, 2008.

18 See "Slow-Motion U.S. Recovery Searches for Second Gear" by Brenda Cronin, *The Wall Street Journal,* June 24, 2013.

19 See "More Men in Their Prime Are Out of Work and at Home" by Mark Peters and David Wessel, *The Wall Street Journal,* February 6, 2014.

20 See "Help Wanted: Struggles of a Lost Generation" by Ben Casselman and Marcus Walker, *The Wall Street Journal,* September 14-15, 2013.

21 See "Reagan and Obama: A Tale of Two Recoveries" by Phil Gramm, *The Wall Street Journal,* August 30, 2012 page A15.

22 See "Win Back the Customer" by Mark Albright, *The St. Petersburg Times,* April 9, 2006.

23 For more on this phenomenon, see "0% Unemployment" by David Brooks, *The New York Times Magazine,* March 5, 2000; "Wanted: Construction workers" by Jack Snyder, *The Orlando Sentinel,* May 3, 1998; and "Survey finds 'Help wanted' signs out across country" by George Hager and Dina Temple-Raston, *USA Today,* May 4, 2000.

24 See "Manufacturing Capacity Going...." by Justin Lahart, *The Wall Street Journal,* May 17, 2010.

25 See "Machinery Shortages Put Businesses in a Bind" by Justin Lahart, *The Wall Street Journal,* May 27, 2010.

26 See "Firms Start to Raise Prices, Stirring Fear In Inflation Fighters" by Jacob Schlesinger and Yochi J. Dreazen, *The Wall Street Journal,* May 16, 2000; and "Firms Gain Power to Boost Prices in Some Sectors" by Jon E. Hilsenrath & Peter Sanders, *The Wall Street Journal,* November 12-13, 2005.

27 See "Jobless Rate Declines to 30-Year Low" by Yochi J. Dreazen, Carlos Tejada, and Partrick Barta, *The Wall Street Journal,* May 8, 2000.

28 See "People Who Need People" by G. Pascal Zachary, *The Wall Street Journal,* September 25, 2000, p. R8.

29 See "Unfreezing Arctic Assets" by Laurence C. Smith, *The Wall Street Journal,* September 18-19, 2010.

30 See "U.S. Suffers Widest Drought Since '50's" by Jim Suhr and Steve Karnowski, *The Star-Tribune,* July 17, 2012.

31 See "U.S. Productivity Growth Has Taken a Dive" by Edward C. Prescott and Lee E. Ohanian, *The Wall Street Journal,* February 4, 2014 page A11.

32 Source: The Heritage Foundation.

33 See "Egypt's Economic Apartheid" by Hernando de Soto, *The Wall Street Journal,* February 3, 2011.

34 See "Let's Start the Green Revolution" by Holman W. Jenkins, Jr., *The Wall Street Journal,* February 2, 2011, p. A15.

35 See "Is Egypt Hopeless?" *The Wall Street Journal,* February 10, 2011.

CHAPTER REVIEW

1. Under what conditions would a decrease in aggregate demand be good for the economy? Graphically illustrate and fully explain your answer.

2. Graphically illustrate and fully explain where aggregate demand and aggregate supply are most likely intersecting on the day you are reading this question. What economic forces have led to this reality?

3. What causes inflation? What causes stagflation? Which is worse for employees and employers? Why?

4. What are some of the policies a government can pursue to create non-inflationary economic growth? Does anything negative come from this result? Why, or why not?

5. The July 17, 2012 Minneapolis *Star Tribune* reported that in the Canadian province of Alberta, dramatic increases in the extraction of oil from 'tar sands' has helped create rising levels of economic growth in Canada. Is this a change in aggregate demand, aggregate supply, or both?

Chapter Twelve

HAYEK, KEYNES, *and the* MONETARISTS

© Luna Vandoorne/Shutterstock.com

The disposition to hunt down rich men as if they were noxious beasts, is a very attractive sport. But confidence is shaken and enterprise chilled, and the unemployed queue up at the soup kitchens or march out to the public works with every growing expense to the taxpayer and nothing more appetizing to take home to their families than the leg or wing of what was once a millionaire.

WINSTON CHURCHILL

THE ECONOMICS OF DISAGREEMENT

In the last chapter we examined the four major economic changes that can bring about shifts in the aggregate demand and supply curves and thus, bring about changes in the GDP, unemployment and inflation.

It is one thing to become an expert in the area of what causes inflation, unemployment, stagflation and economic growth. It is, arguably, far more important to recognize from a distance which policy proposals make the most economic sense to fight economic maladies and promote non-inflationary economic growth.

Several years ago economists from every conceivable philosophical vantage point were called upon to assess and help fix what was shaping up to be one of the most significant economic downturns since the Great Depression.[1] In one week alone in 2008 the stock market lost more of its value than in any other week in our nation's history;[2] General Motors indicated that bankruptcy was not out of the question and the Federal Reserve Bank announced that for the first time ever it would lend directly to businesses that were struggling to come up with enough cash to simply meet payroll obligations.[3]

The "Great Recession" of 2007-2009 wiped out 4.1% of America's Gross Domestic Product – the largest drop since the 1930s.[4] Historically high levels of federal debt, failed stimulus spending of nearly $1 trillion, potentially inflationary Federal Reserve Bank policies, all combined to make the dismal science the most important topic of the day.

Nearly a decade after the end of this recession economists were still arguing about what to do to increase America's anemic economic growth.

A new argument – from an old theory – emerged during this time. For some economists, America was suffering from *secular stagnation* – a problem that is caused by slowing population growth and insufficient technological progress. First offered up in 1938 by economist Alvin Hansen, this theory seeks to make the case that more government spending is needed to offset these two deficiencies.[5]

Over the next several decades, you will be asked by politicians to vote in a way that shapes your economic future. How you and others vote will help determine whether you will be prosperous or will struggle. Which macroeconomic theory is the ideal path to prosperity? The problem is that there is no one universally accepted theory, no panacea to solve a country's macroeconomic problems. Therefore, in this chapter, we will explore the four major schools of thought that have emerged since 1776 on how to create a healthy economy. From there, it will be up to you to decide which one carries the highest probability of success in this century.

THE CLASSICAL/AUSTRIAN SCHOOL OF THOUGHT

The Classical School has its roots in the works of Adam Smith, who, as you will recall believed in the power of largely uncontrolled markets to bring about desirable economic outcomes. Smith and the other Classical thinkers of the time argued that the proper role of government was to protect individual liberties and property rights and to provide goods and services, like national defense, that the private sector could not provide efficiently.

Other than that, the Classical economists believed that individuals make better decisions than governments do, and should be left alone to pursue their self-interest in a productive manner. The timing of Smith's famous book could not have been more fortuitous. It was, of course, in that same year that the United States declared its independence from Great Britain and embarked on the great experiment of political and economic freedom. From

1776 until 1932, the Classical ideology of limited government involvement in the economy was embraced as the proper model for the United States.

Friedrich Hayek was a Nobel-winning Austrian economist renowned for both his popular arguments against collectivism in *The Road to Serfdom*, and his scholarly work on the business cycle, the function of prices, and the nature of spontaneously emerging social orders. Hayek studied economics at the University of Vienna under Ludwig Von Mises and at the Institute for Business Cycle Research, which he helped Mises to found.[6]

Hayek's key insights included the recognition that, because knowledge is dispersed and depends on time, place, and context, no central authority could acquire all the knowledge required to plan an economy. For Hayek, market competition generates a particular kind of order – an order that is the product "of human action but not human design."

This "spontaneous order" means that individuals, not governments, are ideally suited to make rational, self-interested choices that, when combined with the choices of others, leads to the creation and distribution of goods and services in an orderly, efficient manner that no government planner could ever hope to achieve.

For Classical economists – later called Austrian economists – the best results for society as a whole come from minimal government intervention in the form of rules, regulations, bureaucratic red tape and taxation.

This argument came to the forefront during the banking crises of 2008.

Austrian economists opposed the $800 taxpayer bailout of the banking industry just as much as they opposed the government regulations that forced banks to lend money to risky loan applicants before the banking system collapsed.

Such regulations, dating back to 1977, in combination with poor decisions by bankers who participated in mortgage-backed investments, led to an artificial run up in housing prices and when everything collapsed, an artificial level of protection at the expense of American taxpayers.

Hayek and Smith would have argued for the elimination of banking regulations that call for "fairness" in lending practices but would have also argued that for banks that made bad investments in these bundled mortgages the answer to all bailout pleas should have been, "No." With no bailout, the banks that avoided investing in these incredibly risky instruments would have been stronger as their rival banks failed and ultimately the economy would have been stronger in the long run as homeowners, real estate speculators and the surviving financial institutions would have learned to use money wisely.

Ron Paul was the lone presidential candidate preaching the Classical line in 2008.[7] He routinely received about 3% of the popular vote – an indication of how popular the Classical view was at that time in history.[8] By 2010-2011, a growing number of economists were also openly advocating for Hayek's views to become macroeconomic policy in Washington, D.C.[9]

THE CLASSICAL SOLUTION FOR RECESSIONS

Suppose it is 2043 and you are asked to be the chief economic advisor for the president. The economy is in recession, and you are called upon to provide some course of action that the president can follow to lead the nation out of this slump. If you are a Classical economist, you advise the president to "do nothing," stating that the economy has a built-in *self-correcting mechanism*, capable of ending the recession without government intervention. What exactly is meant by the "self-correcting" mechanism? Figure 12.1 illustrates this concept.

Friedrich Hayek

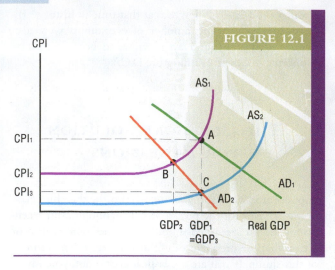

FIGURE 12.1

Smith, Hayek, and other Classical economists believed that if the economy goes into a recession, *eventually wages and other input costs of production will fall, leading to an increase in aggregate supply* (AS2 on graph 12.1). Aggregate supply will continue to increase until full employment is restored at much lower price levels (CPI3).

Before 1933 there were virtually no social welfare programs of any kind. If the economy went into a recession, workers faced the choice of losing their jobs or taking a pay cut. The same was true for suppliers. If the demand for their products or services dropped, they could not turn to the government for relief. They had to lower prices or lose business. When workers and suppliers lowered their wages and prices, it led to lower production costs for American businesses. Recall that production costs are a key determinant of aggregate supply. Once these costs come down, it is possible for full employment to be eventually restored.

This is precisely what occurred during the most recent historic downturn. Kenneth Couch, an economics professor at the University of Connecticut, found that on average, workers returning to work during the recovery were earning *40% less* than what they had earned before.[10] At the same time, housing prices fell dramatically[11] and companies all over America began shedding unproductive capital equipment, outdated technologies, and poor locations in order to lower the costs of production.[12]

In figure 12.1, notice that at the new price level, prices are much lower than they were in the initial equilibrium condition. Does this mean workers are better off? Not necessarily. Remember that wages have fallen, too. Workers are better off to the extent that they have their jobs back and that prices have fallen.

This means that if we were to draw a line connecting points A and C on figure 12.1 and continue that line down to the horizontal axis and up from point A we would notice that the *long-run aggregate supply curve is actually a vertical line.* Simply put, any change in economic

conditions brought on by a shift in aggregate demand will always lead to a shift in aggregate supply – naturally, and without government intervention – causing a new equilibrium condition – at full employment.

What would have been the harm of limited government involvement designed to speed up the recovery process? To a Classical economist, the major problem with government is the way decisions are made. Politicians often make decisions based more on political pressure than on sound economics. For example, in 2005 Congress appropriated $454 million to build a bridge to a community in Alaska that has *50 residents.* As you might have guessed at the time the Chairman of the House Transportation Subcommittee was from Alaska.[13]

Former West Virginia senator, Robert Byrd was hugely successful in getting federal tax dollars poured into his state. One year, out of the entire federal budget for new highways, he managed to get half the money for his state, with the other 49 states splitting the rest of the money.[14] By the time he died, West Virginia's economy was based more on government aid (51.3% of the entire state's economy) than any other state and West Virginia ranked 48th in family income and per capita income.[15]

To Hayek, short term spending on political projects leads to long term increases in taxes to pay for them.[16] Higher taxes – in the long run – erode economic liberty and make the economy stagnant. There is no guarantee that the government would ever or could ever target the areas of the economy that needed to be assisted and provide the assistance in an economically prudent way. Government spending, to Hayek, has a negative impact on the economy because the private sector, if allowed to keep the money that has been spent by government, would make more efficient decisions as to how to fix any recession[17]. Would the private sector spend that much money to build a bridge to 50 customers?

Moreover, government spending on things like banking bailouts, hurricane rebuilding, or crop disasters, tend to make perpetual victims of otherwise productive human beings. If individuals and businesses see the government as a sort of pig trough where free taxpayer dollars can be found, it encourages even more irresponsible and costly behavior in the long run. Hayek would argue that the real cost of the $800 billion bailout would be the even higher cost of the next bailout.

THE CLASSICAL SOLUTION FOR INFLATION

It is 2021, and the economy is roaring. People are enjoying prosperity of historic proportions and spending money like never before. As a result of this spending, aggregate demand has increased enough to create inflationary pressure in the U.S. economy. You are the chief economic advisor to the new President. What do you recommend? As a Classical economist, there is only one thing the government can do, and that is absolutely nothing.

For the Classical School, inflation is dealt with by the same self-correcting mechanism we addressed when a recession was under way. However, in this case, the opposite occurs in labor and capital markets. Figure 12.2 illustrates how.

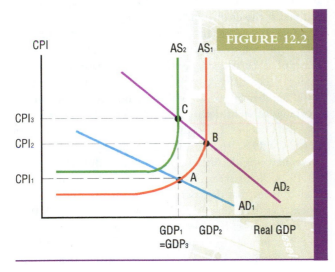

FIGURE 12.2

When aggregate demand increases enough to cause inflation, *eventually, wages and other input costs will begin to rise*. Wages and input costs increase, you will recall, because an acceleration of aggregate demand into segment three of the aggregate supply curve leads to labor and capital shortages. These shortages are corrected by increasing wages and prices paid to suppliers. Since input costs are now rising, aggregate supply will decrease (AS2), until full employment is restored at higher price levels (CPI3). Workers are not worse off, however, because wages have increased along with the cost of living.

THE CLASSICAL SOLUTION FOR STAGFLATION

In the early 1970s, Hayek and the Classical economists of the day vehemently opposed a government fix for the ravaging effects of high inflation and high unemployment. The Classical economists argued that the forces that led to this stagflationary period should be reversed in order to stimulate aggregate supply. Hayek contended that in America as well as Great Britain, suffocating government regulations of industry, wage, and price controls and high taxation had led to stagflation, so government needed to undo these policies in order to eliminate stagflation. As aggregate supply increased – they argued – full employment would be restored. Even when the oil embargo hit, the Classical economists suggested that in the long run new oil supplies would materialize if the government stayed away.

The Classical economists proved to be right on the money. Within a few years, millions of barrels of oil were flowing out of Alaska, the North Sea, and off the coast of Texas and Louisiana. Market forces had prevailed. Self-interested companies, driven by the pursuit of profit, had proven that new oil supplies could be demonstrated, developed, and delivered to consumers. By the mid-1980s, oil prices were lower, adjusted for inflation, than they were before the embargo!

Margaret Thatcher and Ronald Reagan also implemented much of the Classical School during the 1980s. Subsidies for businesses and individuals were cut dramatically in Britain and the U.S. Regulations were relaxed, taxes were slashed and many previously state-owned industries in Great Britain were privatized.[18] The result in both nations was nothing short of astounding as the GDP increased with lower rates of inflation and unemployment.

Many economists, and even some politicians, began worrying in 2008 that capitalism was going to get much of the blame for the financial crisis. The election of Barack Obama, who openly criticized the "excesses" of the free market, was the culmination of the financial panic that year. Blame has a way of leading to rules and regulations,[19]

CONCEPT CHECK

From 1348 to 1450, France's population fell dramatically as a result of a plague. The large drop in population caused stagflation in France. How? In order to combat stagflation, French scholar Jean Bodin advocated a policy of trying and executing midwives for practicing witchcraft.[22] Midwives during this time often helped women have abortions. Fully explain the logic behind Bodin's proposal. Does it make any economic sense? Could this proposal have lead to even more stagflation? Why or why not?

which have a way, in the long run, of leading to stagflation as more and more businesses struggle under the financial weight of bureaucracy.[23]

THE GREAT DEPRESSION

We in America today are nearer to the final triumph over poverty than ever before in the history of any land. The poorhouse is vanishing from among us.

These were the words of President Herbert Hoover in August 1928 – 15 months before the largest economic collapse in America's history.

For 156 years, the United States had operated under the teachings of the Classical economists. By 1930, Karl Marx and John Maynard Keynes had come to the forefront of economic thought. What happened?

Throughout the 1920s the U.S. enjoyed record levels of prosperity. With rising incomes and personal wealth came increased consumer goods like the automobile and radio. People were dancing the Charleston and watching Babe Ruth crush home runs in the newly built Yankee Stadium. The stock and real estate markets also enjoyed double-digit gains year after year, as billions of dollars of speculative investments flowed freely into these high-risk markets in the wake of massive income tax cuts. To some, the days of recession seemed to be over. But unforeseen – or perhaps ignored – warnings of trouble were omnipresent.

First, there was the crisis in agriculture that was ravaging farmers throughout the land. Overproduction in some instances and the "Dust Bowl" that had led to *the collapse of farming* in the Midwest had put many Americans into poverty.

In February 1928, stock prices began a steady climb that continued, with only a few interruptions, until September of 1929. During this period, stock prices climbed by over 40%. Trading on the New York Stock Exchange went from two to three million shares per day to ten to 12 million shares as more and more investors jumped at the chance of "easy money."

Compounding this "problem" was the fact that investors were required to put only 10% of the value of one share of stock to gain control of that share. This *margin buying* – especially in radio company stocks – led to a good number of people, who were not well-versed in the workings of securities investing, to enter the market.

By October 1929, the speculative bubble began to burst. On October 21, and again on October 24, there were alarming declines in stock prices. But on October 29, 1929, the market collapsed. A total of 16 million shares traded hands that day, as investors panicked and dumped stock at virtually any price they could get. By July 9, 1932 the stock market had lost 91% of its value.[24]

The problem, of course, was that as brokerage firms began to make margin calls – calls for investors to pay up the remaining 90% of the price of the stock purchased – many investors did not have the money. Those who did have the money often had it tied up in banks that had contributed to the overvalued real estate and stock markets by being all too eager to float loans to speculators.

When people realized that much of the money in America's banks had been loaned out in markets that were collapsing, and that zero percent of the deposits in any bank were insured, a series of *bank runs* began – massive withdrawals of money that inevitably caused widespread bank failures and the beginning of the depression.

Making matters worse was the *tight monetary policy* of the Federal Reserve Bank during the early 1930s.[25] In spite of the fact that banks were failing all over the United States, the Federal Reserve Bank, perhaps reluctant to encourage borrowing when few could repay loans, allowed the money supply to drop dramatically. The money supply fell 27% from 1929 to 1933, and real economic output fell 29% accordingly. The drop in the money supply kept interest rates at damagingly high levels and prevented consumption and investment from increasing enough to stimulate aggregate demand. The Federal Reserve Bank even *increased rates* in 1931 in an attempt to shore up the value of the dollar.

Another blow to the American economy came at the hands of Congress in 1930. In an attempt to protect

American businesses from foreign competition and promote consumption of domestic goods and services, Congress passed the *Smoot-Hawley Tariff Act*.

This Act increased tariffs by approximately 60% on the nation's trading partners. Many economists believe that it was this act, more than the stock market crash and the mistakes of the Federal Reserve Bank that caused the decade-long economic collapse. Some have even made the inferential leap of connecting the Smoot-Hawley Tariff Act to the rise of Adolf Hitler and the onslaught of World War II. The argument is that without this act, the entire world might have never seen the Great Depression and thus, the rise of fascism and, eventually, World War II.[26]

© Everett Historical/Shutterstock.com

Finally, under the political thinking of the day, the federal government decided it was morally prudent to pursue a balanced budget. As tax revenue was plummeting along with economic activity in the period from 1929 to 1932 taxes were increased to cover the rising federal budget deficit.

In 1932, Republican president Herbert Hoover, with the support of the newly elected Democratic majority in the House of Representatives, passed an enormous *tax increase*. Marginal income tax rates were raised from 1.5% to 4% at the low end and from 25% to 63% at the top of the scale.

The timing for this couldn't have been worse, because tax increases lead to decreases in aggregate demand for goods and services and reduces the incentive to work, save and invest.

THE EMERGENCE OF JOHN MAYNARD KEYNES

It was during this time that the American people lost faith in the free market's ability to bring about an end to economic crises. In fact, during the 1930s, the Communist party of the United States saw a surge in new members as many Americans believed Karl Marx had been proven right: Capitalism was a model doomed to failure.

Under Herbert Hoover, attempts to pull the country out of the Great Depression were limited.

In 1932 President Hoover signed the Emergency Relief and Construction Act. Under this law the states were given $300 million of taxpayer money to help feed needy Americans. While every American state was suffering from rising unemployment, some politicians were better at "feeding at the public trough" than others. Illinois received $55,443,721. Pennsylvania got over $34 million; New York and Michigan more than $20 million. Massachusetts, Connecticut, Vermont, Delaware, Nebraska and Wyoming received nothing.[27]

As mistrust of Herbert Hoover grew, more and more Americans began to demand that the government do something to ease their plight. Sharing this opinion was a British economist named John Maynard Keynes.

John Maynard Keynes was one of the preeminent economists of his time. At a very young age, he wrote a book, *Economic Consequences of Peace*. He claimed that the Treaty of Versailles, which ended WWI, would lead to instability in Europe, due in large part to the huge financial strain it placed on Germany. While this work was certainly prophetic, it was another book – *The General Theory of Employment, Interest and Money* – that brought him worldwide acclaim. Written during the Great Depression, it relied on very sophisticated mathematical models to tackle a problem that seemed to be above the heads of Classical economists. That problem was what to do about chronic unemployment and a stagnating economy.

By the time his work was done, he had not only influenced a massive change in economic policy in the United States, but also caught the attention of Adolf Hitler, who eventually resorted to Keynesian economics to build up Germany's military-industrial complex. Keynes had observed at close hand how Hjalmar Schacht,

John Maynard Keynes

Adolph Hitler's chief economic adviser, had applied Keynes' model to combat Germany's Depression. As economist John Kenneth Galbraith later wrote, Hitler "was the true protagonist of the Keynesian idea."[28]

Keynes was convinced that the drop in the GNP from $104 billion in 1929 to $76.4 billion in 1932, and an increase in the unemployment rate to 24.9% by 1933 was magnified by government's near refusal to come to the aid of the citizenry. Keynes conjectured that during the Great Depression, the Classical model was plagued by two enormous problems: *downward wage rigidity* and *socioeconomic problems* that prevented the self-correcting mechanism from working.

DOWNWARD-WAGE RIGIDITY

Recall that for the Classical model to work, as aggregate demand falls, wages must be flexible enough to drop by a large enough amount to increase aggregate supply. If wages are not flexible, the Classical model will not work very well. Although the influence of labor unions declined during the 1930s, they were still part of a labor market that did not take the demands for lower wages without some resistance.

During the Great Depression, wages simply did not respond to downward pressure by a large enough amount to restore full employment quickly. Without the artificial influence in labor markets by unions and legislation passed by the Roosevelt Administration that made it difficult to get labor costs down the Classical Model may have

worked as it had in all of the other prior recessions. Union membership rose to 25% in 1938 from 12% in 1934. Constant strikes led to an increase of 10% in wages and employment fell.[29]

Roosevelt's New Deal also made it extraordinarily difficult for prices to fall. One would think that with a declining aggregate demand, consumer prices would naturally fall to a new, lower equilibrium price level. This was not the case. In 1933 the National Industrial Recovery Act (NIRA) was passed. Under this law businesses were allowed to collude to raise prices. It also became illegal for any business to lower prices below the "standards" set by the largest businesses in any key industry.[30]

From 1933 until this Act was ruled unconstitutional in 1935, thousands of businesses were prosecuted for secret discounts, privately negotiated wages and even for allowing customers to pick their own chicken out of a chicken coop.

The law was intended to keep prices – and thus wages – high enough to combat "underconsumption." It inevitably made the Depression even worse as unemployed and struggling Americans, already dealing with declining incomes, had to bear the burden of government-created price hikes at the same time.

SOCIOECONOMIC PROBLEMS

During prolonged recessions, suicide, drug and alcohol abuse, divorce, malnutrition, and cases of depression all increase.[31] In the 2001 and 2007-2009 downturns, domestic abuse shelters around the country filled up at alarming rates.[32] In addition, more people drop out of school to meet immediate economic needs, when times are bad. These and other socioeconomic problems lead to a reduction in productivity and the inability of aggregate supply to increase. As a result of these two realities, when asked about the ability of the economy to self-correct in the long run, Keynes said, "Yes, but in the long run we are all dead!"

THE KEYNESIAN SOLUTION FOR RECESSIONS

According to Keynes, since the private sector is often unable to restore full employment at a desirable pace, it becomes necessary to introduce government into the economy.

The Keynesian model works this way: The government should first *announce its intention* to spend money on a massive *infrastructure building* campaign. Infrastructure is made up of the roads, bridges, dams, power lines, water systems, etc. that are the foundation of the productive capacity of the economy. Once the announcement is made, consumer confidence will increase, and as a result, *autonomous purchases* will rise. Autonomous purchases are purchases based on future expected income, rather than current disposable income. As autonomous purchases increase, aggregate demand will begin to slowly increase along segment one of the aggregate supply curve.

The next step in this process is for the federal government to engage in *deficit-spending*. This occurs when government prints money, borrows from the banking system or sells government securities such as Treasury bills, bonds or notes. It is necessary to borrow the money in this instance, because recessions erode the tax base, and any further tax increases to pay for infrastructure spending would be counterproductive.

It should be noted that while Keynes did not advocate tax hikes during the Great Depression, Franklin D. Roosevelt pursued this odd strategy anyway. During the 1930s not only did the top income tax rate rise to 79%, but excise taxes - taxes on tobacco, alcohol, radios, cameras, telegrams, cosmetics, bank checks, cars, movie tickets and more.

In 1929 total individual income tax revenue equaled $1.096 billion while excise tax revenue totaled $540 million. By 1935 income tax revenue had fallen to $527 million while excise taxes - assessed mostly on lower income Americans - had risen to $1.364 billion as a function of consumers not being as willing or able to reduce consumption on the targeted items.

THE MULTIPLIER EFFECT

Once the government begins spending, the *"multiplier effect"* will kick in. The Keynesian demand multiplier effect is the belief that for every increase in government spending by $1, real GDP will increase by more than $1. This is because once the government gives a company a contract to do work, the company and its workers spend this money. The places where they spend the money (the grocery store, car dealership, and so forth) will benefit and spend more as well on clothes, vacations, etc. As spending increases, businesses (in theory) will expand, new business firms will show up and of course new jobs will follow. All of this, according to Keynes, would take place much faster than waiting for the self-correcting mechanism to kick in.

The multiplier effect is given by the following formula:

1/1-MPC

MPC is the *marginal propensity to consume*, which means the fraction of every dollar earned that is devoted to the consumption of domestic goods and services.

For example, if out of $1, the average American spends 19 cents on imports, saves 4 cents, and pays 29 cents in taxes, then the marginal propensity to consume is .48 (1-. 19-. 04-. 29).

Therefore, if the MPC =. 48, the multiplier is **1/1-. 48 = 1/.52 = 1.92**

This means that if the government spends $1, *real GDP will increase by $1.92.*

As the multiplier effect propels aggregate demand toward full employment, some inflationary signs normally would appear. However, in this model, inflation is not a problem, because once the infrastructure is completed, the government has added to the productive capacity of the economy. Recall that expanded productivity causes aggregate supply to increase. The increase in aggregate supply, following the rise in aggregate demand, leads to non-inflationary economic growth in the long run.

Essentially, the Keynesian multiplier is the opposite theory of Say's Law. Recall in chapter six that Say's Law states that supply creates demand and thus, in order to have a vibrant economy, the government must first encourage new suppliers to show up. Keynesian economists argue that *demand creates supply* and therefore, the best way to create long run growth is to first stimulate spending by businesses and individuals.

This is why infrastructure, as opposed to just sending out checks in the mail, is the spending the Keynesians suggest in order to promote growth. When businesses are given access to better roads or more reliable phone and electric services, it improves productivity, lowers input costs, and increases the quantity of inputs available in the economy. All of this translates into an increase in aggregate supply and downward pressure on inflation.

CONCEPT CHECK

Suppose aggregate demand decreases in 2022 until we are in a recession. If full employment real GDP = $18.27 trillion, and after the decrease in aggregate demand real GDP = $17.94 trillion, the recessionary GDP gap is $330 billion. If the multiplier at that time equals 1.43, how much money, according to Keynes, would the government have to spend to restore full employment?[33]

In 1931, the Canadian government put hundreds of unemployed Canadian men to work building the Icefields Parkway through the heart of the Canadian Rockies. On what grounds would a Classical economist contend that the Canadian economy expanded by a *lower amount* than the government spent on this road?

Photo courtesy Jack Chambless

Finally, there is the issue of the deficit. Without raising taxes, the Keynesians believe the deficit will be paid off. This is because as economic growth increases the nation's income level, tax revenues will rise sufficiently to pay off the deficit. Once this occurs, according to the Keynesians, the government's work is done, and the spending should be reduced and that the government should run budget surpluses until the next recession.

FDR AND THE NEW DEAL

When Franklin D. Roosevelt took office in 1933 he was staring an economic disaster of historic dimensions in the face. Unemployment was almost 25% and there were no signs whatsoever that the economy was going to recover from the Great Depression.

In response, FDR continued the social welfare programs that were started under Hoover and expanded them. However, by 1935 he was having a change of heart.

> The lessons of history, confirmed by the evidence immediately before me, show conclusively that continued dependence upon relief induces a spiritual and moral disintegration fundamentally destructive to the national fiber. To dole out relief in this way is to administer a narcotic, a subtle destroyer of the human spirit. It is inimical to the dictates of sound policy.

To his credit, President Roosevelt seemed to understand the long-run threat to the nations' aggregate supply (in the form of declining productivity) if the U.S. maintained a policy of expanding welfare benefits.

He thus changed directions and embraced the economic arguments of John Maynard Keynes and embarked on a program called "The New Deal." Under the New Deal, the government created work programs such as the Works Progress Administration and the Civilian Conservation Corps and set out to build up America's infrastructure – like the Golden Gate Bridge in San Francisco and the Hoover Dam in Nevada. All together there were 8,000 parks, 40,000 public buildings, 72,000 schools and 80,000 bridges built during this time.

Under the CCC men between seventeen and twenty-five earned 35 dollars per month, of which 25 dollars was sent home to their families. They lived in military-style facilities and worked on national park lodging, the planting of trees in forests, construction of state parks and on soil erosion projects.[34]

One look at the list of spending initiatives above would suggest that FDR was a sort of economic savior at a time of national distress. The history books certainly tend to lean in that direction. However, a deeper look also shows that, for example, the government spent millions teaching children piano lessons; millions more to pay 7,000 men to write a guide book of America. Taxpayer dollars were also allocated to projects that amounted to no more than hiring men to move dirt from one side of roads to another or to employ people to drive around and add up the number of insects they could find. And, of course, there were untold millions in waste, fraud, bribery and questionable agencies.[35]

Economist Henry Hazlitt argued during the 1930s that the WPA destroyed as many jobs as it created.

> Every dollar of government spending must be raised through a dollar of taxation. If the WPA builds a $10 million bridge, for example, the bridge has to be paid for out of taxes. Therefore, for every public job created by the bridge project a private job has been destroyed somewhere else. We can see the men employed on the bridge. We can watch them work. The employment argument of the government spenders becomes vivid, and probably for most people convincing. But there are other things that we do not see, because, alas, they have never been permitted to come into existence. They are the jobs destroyed by the $10 million taken from the taxpayers. All that has happened, at best, is that there has been a diversion of jobs because of the project.[36]

and heavy industry – were doing so at the great risk of destroying their economy over time and turning over the economic decisions to political bodies who might not be efficient, or worse, evil.

According to the Classical economists, the following list represents the major flaws with the Keynesian doctrine:

> ➤ **The Crowding Out Effect**
> ➤ **Pork**
> ➤ **The Imaginary Multiplier Effect**
> ➤ **Lag Effects**
> ➤ **The Broken Window Fallacy**
> ➤ **Long Run Stagflation**

CLASSICAL CRITICISMS OF KEYNES

> It is necessary now to state the unpalatable truth that it is Germany whose fate we are in danger of repeating.
>
> Friedrich Hayek, as quoted in
> *The Road to Serfdom*

Hayek's lamentations on repeating the mistakes of Nazi Germany did not come after WW II, but rather *during* WW II. In 1944 Hayek argued that Germany's problem began before Adolf Hitler with the idea that the government should own the means of production and determine output, employment, and price levels.[37] For Hayek, nations that attempted to control the commanding heights of the economy – e.g. coal, steel, railroads,

THE CROWDING OUT EFFECT AND PORK

According to many Classical economists, when the government runs deficits to pay for infrastructure or any other spending, it causes an increase in the demand for credit.

As can be seen in Figure 12.3, an increase in the demand for credit above the level that would exist if only the private sector borrowed funds, causes a shortage of loanable funds. The shortage of money leads to an increase in interest rates, which in turn, "*crowds out*" private sector investment. In the diagram you can see the loss in private-sector investment spending as the difference between Ql and Qp.

Suppose, for arguments sake, the Keynesian multiplier is equal to 2.00. If the government borrows $100 billion to build new roads or provide Internet connections to

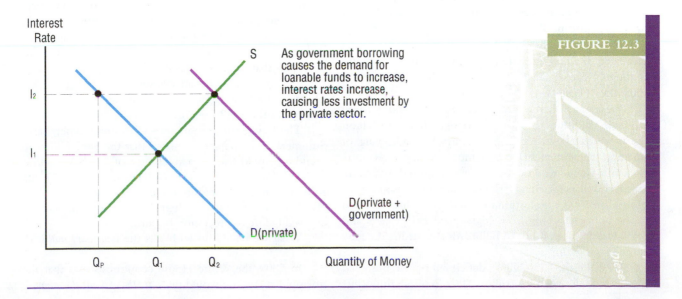

FIGURE 12.3

As government borrowing causes the demand for loanable funds to increase, interest rates increase, causing less investment by the private sector.

elementary schools around the country, real GDP, according to the Keynesians, will rise by $200 billion.

What if the private sector had been able to get that money? As Milton Friedman and other economists have proven, the private sector creates a much larger multiplier effect on the economy than the government,[38] simply because the private sector makes decisions based on the pursuit of profit rather than politics. When Disney built the Animal Kingdom theme park near Orlando, more than $1 billion was spent on construction. Do you suppose Disney's shareholders and executives would be happy with a net return of $1 billion on this park?

Unless the park generates far more than $1 billion, Disney executives will be forced to address the opportunity cost of this investment – that is, what other investment could have been made with this money that would have yielded a higher return? To the private sector, the bottom line is the bottom line. Investments that do not generate more income than the sum of the direct cost plus opportunity cost of that investment are deemed failures. A failed investment can lead to losses, declining stock prices, lower bond ratings, and even bankruptcy.

On the other hand, when the president or members of Congress decide how to "invest" your money, their first thought is what political need is being satisfied. In 2003, President Bush signed a bill that provided over $500 billion in taxpayer-financed prescription drugs for senior citizens.

For many, if not most economists, this plan did not make the most economic sense.[39] The net return to economic growth, GDP, the unemployment rate, technological advancement, and so on would be far greater if this money were returned to the businesses and individuals who sent it to Washington, D.C., to begin with. By spending $500 billion on prescription drugs for individuals who are no longer contributing much to the economic progress of the country, the government may have helped satisfy the most aggressive voting group in the nation, but it did little to create economic opportunities for those of us whose most productive years are ahead of us.

When President Bush left office he did so with an estimated $750 billion deficit for Mr. Obama. That figure is roughly 5% of the GDP – one of the largest deficits since the 1960s.[40]

President Obama proceeded to outspend George Bush. In addition to smaller proposals like $50 billion for new roads[41] and airport runways, a quadrupling of unemployment benefits, 116% more money for education, an 84% increase in housing spending, and 81% more taxpayer dollars for energy; the new president also passed a more than $800 billion stimulus bill in 2009 that showered money on everything from high-speed rail projects and teacher retirement funds to billboards advertising the new stimulus program.

By 2011, the $750 billion deficit left by Mr. Bush had grown to well over $1.4 trillion. Bear in mind, this is just one year where the government spent more money than was collected in taxes.

As a result of mounting deficits, interest payments on the federal debt now range into the hundreds of billions of dollars – dollars that you and I cannot borrow from a bank to start a business or invest in our future.

Much of the spending by our government is called *pork*. The money is designed to be spent in a specific jurisdiction, so the politician pushing for the pork can increase the probability of being re-elected. A politician would be irrational to turn away funds that will keep his or her voters happy – even if the money does not help the country as a whole.

Therefore, it should not come as much of a surprise that since 1982 the number of special pork projects earmarked in highway spending bills has increased from 10 projects to more than 6,300 in 2006.[42]

Suppose the *private-sector investment multiplier effect*, (the increased GDP that results from household and business investment spending), is equal to 3.00. Using the numbers from before, the $100 billion spent by the government would lead to a $200 billion increase in GDP, but would be offset by a $300 billion loss in GDP as a result of the crowding-out effect. The net effect is a reduction in real GDP by $100 billion and no multiplier effect from government spending at all!

$862,000,000,000

The figure above represents how much of our money (from the future) was taken in order for the federal government to stimulate the economy in 2009. The Obama Administration did not have the $862 billion on hand at the time, so the money was simply borrowed, to be repaid with interest, with taxes collected in the future.

The idea was that the future was not going to be so bright unless the economy was kick-started out of its doldrums that year. So, a historic bill was passed – under the prodding of Keynesian economists working for Mr. Obama – to create significant economic growth like we enjoyed in the 1982-2007 time span.

The Keynesian economists – Christina Romer, Larry Summers, and others – calculated that the $862 billion in spending would lead to a multiplier of 1.5.[43] Therefore, the $862 billion would cause GDP to increase by $1.221 trillion – enough to restore the economy to the low levels of unemployment and high levels of output that we enjoyed before the recession began.

What we ended up with was the *imaginary multiplier effect*.

In 2009, the White House economists said that the unemployment rate would peak at 9% *without the stimulus*

How much will it cost to rebuild this bridge in Minnesota? How much *should* it cost?

package and that with the stimulus, the rate would stay at 8% or below.[44] In November of 2010, the unemployment rate – 20 months after the $862 billion package was passed – was 9.8%. Therefore, if the economists argued in 2009 that if the government did nothing and let the readers of this book, and others, keep their future $862 billion, the unemployment rate would actually have been .8% less than it ended up being with the stimulus! In other words, the federal government spent $862 billion and the unemployment rate stayed near levels not seen for 27 years.

By the summer of 2010, real personal disposable income was still flat, capital goods orders by businesses had declined by 8%, new home sales were down 12.4%, and initial jobless claims had risen to 500,000. Meanwhile, the stock markets were lower than in 2009.[45]

When Christmas 2010 arrived and the two-year anniversary of the stimulus package approached, more than one study was published showing that the net effect of the mammoth spending bill was zero[46] on economic growth over that time period. Zero? How can $862 billion in spending lead to no impact on the GDP?

As it turns out, this is not a historically unique development. In recent times, Japan has suffered from chronic recessions and the Japanese government has responded with Keynesian vigor by spending its way into…more recessions.[47] In 2008, Sweden, France, Italy, Germany, Great Britain, Spain, the United States, and Japan all saw an increase in government spending to fight recessions in each nation. In every nation, the GDP fell more after the spending took place. Meanwhile, in nations like Australia, India, and China, where spending remained largely under control and government's share of the economy was lower than the aforementioned nations, the GDP increased.[48]

The same result was true for the United States during the Great Depression. Numerous empirical studies confirm that the Keynesian policies of the Hoover and Roosevelt Administrations actually prolonged the Great Depression.[49] Bear in mind, during the Great Depression, by his own admission, Mr. Roosevelt had feared that capitalism had simply failed. He then embarked on a campaign that dramatically increased corporate and personal income taxes; imposed innumerable new regulations on industry; created social welfare programs; and maintained a prolonged verbal assault against business leaders whom he called "economic royalists" and "malefactors of great wealth."[50]

Similarly, President Obama campaigned on the pledge to rein in banks and Wall Street; argued for higher taxes on businesses and workers; signed many new orders and legislation that increased regulations on student loans, health care, labor, banking, and the environment; and was a vocal critic of the same people Mr. Roosevelt held in contempt.

It should come as no great surprise that during the Great Depression and the more recent Great Recession, that business leaders were reluctant to hire new workers in an era of open hostility toward their profit motive. Hence, even as government spent taxpayer dollars to promote growth, it found out that the creators of growth – men and women who own businesses – do not have to add workers as the government is adding taxes, rules, and uncertainty to their business models.[51]

By 2014 – fully five years after the spending program began – the U.S. economy, as previously addressed, was nowhere near re-establishing full employment, or anything even remotely close to it.

It is worth noting that during the early part of Mr. Obama's first term – when the stimulus bill was being debated – economists Lawrence Summers, Tim Geithner and Jason Furman – all working for President Obama, continually argued that fellow economist Mark Zandi of Moody's Analytics was correct in his assessment that for every dollar the Obama Administration would be willing to spend on unemployment benefits the economy would grow by $1.64.

Furthermore, Zandi contended, every dollar allocated to food stamps would grow the economy by $1.73. Yet, according to his analysis, cuts in income taxes would yield *only 29 cents* in growth for every dollar we were allowed to keep in our wallets.[52]

LAG EFFECTS

Suppose the economy experiences a recession next year where real GDP falls by $125 billion. Even if a multiplier exists, there are significant lag effects that dilute the effectiveness of fiscal stimulus through government spending. First, there is the *recognition lag*.

This is the amount of time between the occurrence of a recession and the government's official recognition of the recession. Since the Commerce Department must spend months compiling data, the economy may be well into a recession before the depth of the downturn is fully understood.

The second – and most damaging to the Keynesian case – is the *administrative lag*. This is the period of time between the government's recognition of the recession and the administering of the solution for the recession. With the lengthy debates and hearings and formal process of creating spending packages filled with numerous pork projects, it can take months for Congress and the president to come to an agreement about what course of action is best.

This leads to the final lag, known as the *operational lag*. This is the amount of time it takes for an increase in government spending to manifest itself in the form of an increase in real GDP.

For example, in 2009 Congress allocated $5 billion to insulate homes from the weather as part of a stimulus/fight global warming initiative. Yet, when companies began applying for their fellow man's money to caulk and insulate homes, they found that they would have to adhere to several regulations over wages, advertising, historic preservation issues, and local labor standards. The result was that 18 months after the billions became "available," very little work had been done to make homes more energy efficient. In more than half the states, less than half the targeted homes had been worked on.[53]

THE BROKEN WINDOWS FALLACY

Suppose a shopkeeper in Chambles, France is sweeping his floor one day when a rock comes flying through his front window. He is told that to replace the window the bill will total $50. Should he, in the name of John Maynard Keynes, then say, "Merveilleux, cela signifie que l'économie de Chambles va croître de plus de 50 $!"[54]

Not if we look at Frederic Bastiat and his classic work on "The Broken Window Fallacy".

If one looked only at what is seen, one could understand, he said, the common reaction to a shopkeeper's window broken by vandals: "At least it creates work for the glazier." The shopkeeper's misfortune is quickly transformed into a benefit for the community because it makes money circulate and "creates" work.

SUGGESTED CLASSROOM DEBATE

University of Chicago economist, Harald Uhlig found that for every dollar government spends, the GDP goes down by $3.40.[55] Christina Romer – one of President Obama's top economic advisors – once published a paper that found that for every $1 cut in taxes, the GDP increases by $3. Why then, would politicians support more government spending over tax cuts?[56]

An opportunity to make the economy grow?

However, Bastiat argued, if the shopkeeper is forced to spend $50 to replace his windowpane that is $50 he can now no longer spend on the new cash register that he wanted. And he had a perfectly good window before it was broken. Far from the broken window creating a social benefit, it is, in fact, a tiny social calamity.

The $50 has been spent employing the glazier it is true, but only at a *net loss* to the community as a whole. Before, the shopkeeper had a window and $50. Now, he has exactly what he had before (a sound window), but not his $50, and so cannot buy his cash register. Both he and the community have been impoverished, not enriched.

Which brings us to September 11th, hurricanes, drought, war and other disasters.

From the previous example of the shopkeeper one can see the flaw in the argument that the new Freedom Tower in New York (that replaces the World Trade Center) led to a multiplier effect. Nearly $4 billion was spent on this 1,776 foot building. 43,600 windows were lost when the World Trade Center went down. If one is to take Keynes's argument literally, then we could say that not only were the attacks in New York City and at the Pentagon beneficial because of all the construction jobs that will be created, but that we should actually hope for another attack to take place during our next recession, so that our economy can grow even faster as all of the unemployed people rush in to rebuild the results of terrorist activity.[57]

KEYNES AND WORLD WAR II

It has been argued for decades that the triumph of government as a source of economic stimulus was World War II. Everyone knows that the war ended the Great Depression. Or did it?

CONCEPT CHECK

On May 6, 1939 Treasury Secretary Henry Morgenthau said, "We are spending more than we have ever spent before and it does not work... We have never made good on our promises...I say after eight years of this Administration we have just as much unemployment as when we started...And an enormous debt to boot!"[58] How is it possible that with all of the spending FDR authorized, the economy was still struggling?

World War II and the Triumph of Keynesianism

By Robert Higgs, *The Independent Institute, Freedom Daily 6,* March 1995, pp. 27–34

War, everybody says, is hell. But many Americans do not really believe this truism, especially when the war in question is World War II. Of course, for the men who had to endure the horrors of combat, the war was terrible – just how terrible, hundreds of thousands of them did not live to say. But the great majority of Americans never experienced the fighting directly. It was something that went on "overseas," and government censors kept reports of its brutal realities from the public.

For many Americans, at the time and since, World War II actually seemed to be a fine thing, mainly because, as the hackneyed expression has it, "the war got the economy out of the depression" in which it had wallowed for more than a decade.

During the Great Depression, many people had despaired over whether the economy would ever again operate satisfactorily. Then, the mobilization for war coincided with what appeared to be a great economic boom.

By 1944, all the usual indicators of economic well-being signaled that the economy was enjoying unprecedented prosperity. Most important, the official rate of unemployment had sunk to just 1.2% – the lowest rate ever achieved before or since. After years of turning away qualified job seekers, employers were beating the bushes in search of warm bodies. Official figures showed that the Gross National Product (GNP), adjusted for inflation, had risen some 70% since 1939 – later Commerce Department figures would revise the increase upward, making it more than 90%.

For the economists who had recently embraced the ideas of John Maynard Keynes, expressed in his *General Theory of Employment, Interest, and Money* (1936), the war seemed to validate their beliefs. In Keynes's theory, in contrast to the previously accepted view, an economic depression might continue indefinitely unless government spending, financed by a budget deficit, were increased sufficiently. The Keynesians believed that the federal deficits of the 1930s, never more than $3.5 billion per year, had been too small to lift the U.S. economy from its slough.

The huge wartime deficits, however, reaching as high as $55 billion in 1943, seemed to have accomplished precisely what Keynes had said they would.

Ever since, most economists, historians, and educated laymen have accepted the Keynesian conclusion. It seems obvious that the war got the economy out of the depression, that it created a condition commonly called wartime prosperity.

How could anyone argue otherwise? Certainly no one can deny that the wartime budget deficits were immense – in terms of today's dollars, they added some $2.2 trillion to the national debt.

Appearances, however, can be deceptive, and correlations can be spurious. Did American participation in the most destructive event of all time really have positive economic consequences? When something seems counterintuitive, it often helps to reexamine the terms in which the puzzle is expressed. This is certainly the case with the "wartime prosperity" of World War II. What did this condition consist of? Consider first the labor market. Although unemployment virtually disappeared, the disappearance owed nothing to Keynesian fiscal policy. In truth, it owed everything to massive conscription. Between 1940 and 1944, the number of unemployed persons fell by 4.62 million, while the armed forces increased by 10.87 million.

For the whole war period, more than 10 million men were drafted. The enormous forced withdrawal – the number of draftees was equivalent to nearly 20% of the prewar labor force – drastically reduced the number of potential workers and depleted the ranks of the unemployed, and would have done so with or without the government's budget deficit. The Keynesian correlation is spurious.

But what about the enormous increase of the economy's total output? This, it turns out, is nothing more than an artifact of the accounting system used by the government to keep the national product accounts. In the official system, spending for military goods and services gets counted as part of the dollar value of national output, as does spending for consumer goods and new capital goods. So every dollar the government paid for the services of military personnel or for the purchase of battleships, tanks, bombers, and other munitions during the war was included in the GNP. Hardly surprising, then, that GNP skyrocketed as the government created a command economy geared for "total war." But when we examine the rest of the GNP – the part consisting of spending for civilian consumer goods and new capital goods – we find that after 1941 (adjusted for actual as opposed to official inflation), it declined for two years; and even though it rose after 1943, it was still below its 1941 value when the war ended.

Thus, the war years witnessed a reduction of the total real output flowing to civilian consumers and investors – a far cry from "wartime prosperity."

My estimates of real personal consumption expenditures per capita show a similar pattern – down during the first two years of direct U.S. involvement in the war, up slightly during the next two years, but not up enough to erase the initial declines. Historians who have spoken of a "carnival of consumption" during the war are simply mistaken.

Many aspects of economic well-being deteriorated during the war. Military preemption of public transportation interfered with intercity travel by civilians, and rationing of tires and gasoline made commuting to work very difficult for many workers. More workers had to work at night. The rate of industrial accidents increased substantially as novices replaced experienced workers and labor turnover increased. The government forbade nearly all nonmilitary construction, and housing became extremely scarce and badly maintained in many places, especially where war production had been expanded the most. Price controls and rationing meant that consumers had to spend much time standing in lines or searching for sellers willing to sell goods at the controlled prices. The quality of many goods deteriorated, as sellers forbidden to raise prices adjusted to increased demands by selling lower quality goods at the controlled prices.

After the war ended in the late summer of 1945, a genuine economic miracle took place during the next two years. More than 10 million men were released from the armed forces. Industry, which had occupied itself largely in producing war goods from 1942 to 1945, switched back to the production of civilian goods.

The huge government budget deficit disappeared, and during the fiscal years 1947-1949, the federal budget actually had a small surplus. Yet, despite the fears and warnings of the Keynesian economists that such events would plunge the economy back into depression, civilian production boomed, increasing by nearly 27% from 1945 to 1946, and the rate of unemployment never exceeded 4% until the recession of 1949. Why the economy performed so successfully during the reconversion is an economic mystery that a few economists, including the present writer, have recently begun trying to understand better.

The mainstream economics profession, however, never faced the contradictions between its Keynesian theory and the events of the reconversion. According to this theory, the huge turnaround of the federal budget – from a deficit equal to 25% of GNP during 1943-1945 to a surplus during 1947-1949 – should have sent the economy into a tailspin.

It did not, which refutes the theory. Ignoring this embarrassing fact, the Keynesians continued to cite the war "boom" as a definitive demonstration of the correctness of their theory.

Reflecting the conventional wisdom, a leading textbook in U.S. economic history gave its chapter on World War II the title "War Prosperity: The Keynesian Message Illustrated."

The lesson was false but, for politicians and certain others, immensely useful. For decades, secretaries of defense helped to justify their gargantuan budget requests by claiming that high levels of defense spending would be "good for the economy" and that reduced defense spending would cause recession. So common did this argument become that Marxist critics gave it the apt name military Keynesianism. On both the left and the right, people believed that huge military spending propped up an economy that, lacking this support, would collapse into depression. Such thinking played an important part in the political process that directed into defense spending some $10 trillion dollars (in today's purchasing power) between 1948 and 1990.

Military Keynesianism was always an intellectually bankrupt theory. As I have shown above, it was not proven by the events of the war years; all that those events proved was that a command economy can, at least for a while, keep everyone busy building munitions and using them to demolish the nation's enemies. But the munitions production was far from free. It entailed huge opportunity costs, even though part of it could be accomplished simply by employing workers and capital that had been idle before the war.

During the Cold War, however, the nation had very few unemployed resources to call into defense production, and using lots of resources for this purpose meant that the civilian goods that those resources might otherwise have produced had to be sacrificed.

Keynesian economics rests on the presumption that government spending, whether for munitions or other goods, creates an addition to the economy's aggregate demand, which brings into employment labor and other resources that otherwise would remain idle. The economy gets not only the additional production occasioned by the use of those resources but still more output via a "multiplier effect." Hence the Keynesian claim that even government spending to hire people to dig holes in the ground and fill them up again has beneficial effects; even though the diggers create nothing of value, the multiplier effect is set in motion as they spend their newly acquired income for consumption goods newly produced by others.

Such theorizing never faced squarely the underlying reason for the initial idleness of labor and other resources.

If workers want to work but cannot find an employer willing to hire them, it is because they are not willing to work at a wage rate that makes their employment worthwhile for the employer. Unemployment results when the wage rate is too high to "clear the market." The Keynesians concocted bizarre reasons why the labor market was not clearing during the Great Depression and then continued to accept such reasoning long after the depression had faded into history.

But when labor markets have not cleared, either during the 1930s or at other times, the causes can usually be found in government policies – such as the National Industrial Recovery Act of 1933, the National Labor Relations Act of 1935, and the Fair Labor Standards Act of 1938, among many others – that obstruct the normal operation of the labor market.

So, government policies created sustained high unemployment, and Keynesians blamed the market. The Keynesians then credited the government's wartime deficits for pulling the economy out of the Great Depression and continued to credit defense spending for preventing another economic collapse. In this way, sound economics was replaced by economic ideas congenial to spendthrift politicians, defense contractors, labor unions, and left-liberal economists.

How much better it would have been if the wisdom of Ludwig von Mises had been taken to heart. In Nation, State, and Economy (1919), Mises said, "War prosperity is like the prosperity that an earthquake or a plague brings." The analogy was apt in World War I, in World War II, and during the Cold War. It is still apt today.

From Future of Freedom Foundation, *Freedom Daily 6*, March 1995, by Robert Higgs, Senior Fellow in Political Economy at the Independent Institute. Reprinted by permission.

THE KEYNESIAN SOLUTION FOR INFLATION

While much of his professional life was devoted to the problem of recessions, Keynes did have some strong thoughts on the problem inflation, caused by increases in aggregate demand. In a nutshell, Keynes believed that if aggregate demand increased to the point where inflation was a problem, the solution should be an *increase in taxes* levied on businesses and households.

Higher taxes, according to Keynes, would have two effects. First, greater taxation would mean less money to spend or invest, therefore, aggregate demand would be cooled off and full employment restored.

Second, Keynes was concerned that inflation was the result of people having too much money and time on their hands to spend money in a conspicuous manner. He argued that with rising income and wealth, people become less productive and more prone to engage in wasteful activities, rather than pursuits that create long-run economic growth.

Therefore, Keynes believed that higher taxes would keep people from making too much money, keeping them thrifty and hard-working.[59] This was a major justification for tax increases during World War II.

In late 1943, Treasury Secretary Henry Morgenthau asked Congress for another tax increase. He framed his appeal, in large part, as an anti-inflation effort. The new act, he argued, must help stop inflation. "Nothing in the economic field can interfere with the war effort as much as an uncontrolled rise in prices," he told the House Ways and Means Committee. "An inflationary price rise is a source of grave social injustice. It undermines morale and impedes war production. It strikes at random without consideration of equity or ability to bear the hardships, which it imposes. Once it has acquired momentum, inflation is extremely difficult to control, and leaves a heritage of post-war stresses and strains that will haunt us for decades."[60]

CONCEPT CHECK

In recent years the German economy recorded impressive economic growth, prompting workers in Germany to push for higher wages.[61] How could the Keynesian orthodoxy, with respect to "too much demand," lead to a recession in Germany if adhered to by politicians there?

© Giancarlo Liguori/Shutterstock.com

THE KEYNESIAN SOLUTION FOR STAGFLATION

While Keynes never had occasion to ponder a world where inflation and unemployment coexisted, the economists who followed in his footsteps – sometimes called the New Keynesians – were called upon to deal with this challenge in the 1970s. The problem for the Keynesians was not easy to tackle. If the government increased spending to deal with the recession part of stagflation, inflation would be even worse.

On the other hand, if taxes were increased to cool off inflation, the recession would intensify. So the Keynesians, in the tradition of a government-based solution for economic ills, opted to simply not let prices increase. Under the administration of Richard Nixon, who once exclaimed "We are all now Keynesians," the government embarked on a campaign of *wage and price controls,* designed to keep inflation in check. These price ceilings proved to be disastrous as shortages of gasoline, food, and a number of other goods broke out during this time.

This was not the first time wage and price controls had been used to "subdue" inflation. In the year 301 (yes, over 1,700 years ago...) The Roman Empire was experiencing escalating rates of inflation stemming from the debasement of coinage. Specifically, coins that had 40% silver content in 250 A.D. dropped to less than 4% by 270 A.D. (in an effort to expand the money supply). With Roman coins worth less and less, prices began to rise – because sellers demanded higher payments to make up for the loss of silver in Roman coinage.

Thus, in 301 A.D. the Emperor Diocletian imposed price ceilings across the empire and wage controls for a range of jobs from architects to stonemasons. The penalty for charging more than the legally-established prices was death.

Not surprisingly, sellers hoarded goods and production plummeted.

At the end of World War II the same situation plagued Germany. To control inflation in that ravaged nation the Allied authorities imposed wage and price controls only to see black markets – with cigarettes and cognac as currency – pop up everywhere. This prompted economist Ludwig Erhard to abolish the controls put in place by wartime planning boards. The results were nothing short of miraculous as virtually overnight the black markets vanished and goods and services that had been hoarded for years began showing up in markets all over Germany.

The lesson, of course, is that wage and price controls always fail to control inflationary pressures because the invisible hand of the marketplace is a more powerful influence than the laws written by man.

THE MONETARIST SCHOOL OF THOUGHT

During the latter part of the nineteenth century, the U.S. economy experienced major swings in domestic output. In fact, in 1893, the United States fell into a severe depression brought on by the bankruptcy of the Philadelphia and Reading Railroads. When the National Cordage Company failed two months later, the stock market crashed. Since many of the major New York banks were heavy investors in the market, a wave of bank failures ensued.

Within six months, more than 8,000 businesses, 156 railroads, and 400 banks failed. With 20% of the labor force unemployed, the economic quagmire of the 1890s lasted until 1898, precipitating a national call for congressional action.

In 1913, Congress finally acted when it created the Federal Reserve Act. This Act established the Federal Reserve System and the twelve regional Federal Reserve Banks.[62] More importantly, the Act signaled markets around the world that the U.S. was serious about smoothing out the wild fluctuations in the business cycle by establishing some semblance of stability in the banking industry.

HOW THE FEDERAL RESERVE IS ORGANIZED

The Federal Reserve is broken up into three major components: the Board of Governors, the regional Federal Reserve banks, and the Federal Open Market Committee (FOMC). Each is addressed below.

THE BOARD OF GOVERNORS

Located in Washington, D.C., this part of the "Fed" supervises the operation of the nation's banking system and acts as an authority to regulate the money supply. It consists of seven governors, each of whom is appointed by the president of the United States and approved by the Senate for a 14-year term. One of the governors serves as the Chairman of the Board. The chairman officiates for a term of four years. In 2014 Janet Yellen was confirmed as the new Chairperson of the Federal Reserve. Ms. Yellen replaced Ben Bernanke (who replaced Alan Greenspan) as arguably one of the most powerful people in the world.

She is a former head of the Council of Economic Advisors under President Clinton and served as the president of the San Francisco Federal Reserve Bank.

For Ms. Yellen 2014 posed a significant challenge. Under Ben Bernanke the Federal Reserve Bank had embarked on a program known as quantitative easing (more on that shortly) in order to keep the fragile economic recovery going. This program was responsible for historically-low interest rates and fears of a sharp decline in the value of the dollar. Balancing the need for growth and the economic desirability for a strong dollar (one that is holding its value in comparison to other currencies) was foremost on her mind as she took on this new job.[63]

It comes as a surprise to many Americans that the Board of Governors is an independent, self-supporting authority. It does not receive funds from Congress, and it does not take orders from the president or any other political official. In essence, Ms. Yellen and the other Board members are largely autonomous, making the Board of Governors one of the most powerful institutions on Earth.

THE REGIONAL FEDERAL RESERVE BANKS

These banks perform central banking functions for banks within each of 12 Federal Reserve Districts. There are regional banks located in San Francisco, Minneapolis, Kansas City, Dallas, Chicago, St. Louis, Atlanta, Cleveland, Richmond, Philadelphia, New York, and Boston.

Each of the regional Federal Reserve Banks is a corporation. These banks earn income that more than covers their expenses from assets they hold.[64] The banks are not government agencies. The primary function of these

FIGURE 12.4

banks is to issue currency and hold deposits from both commercial banks and thrift institutions.

FEDERAL OPEN MARKET COMMITTEE (FOMC)

The most important policymaking component of the Fed is the FOMC, located on the eighth floor of the New York Federal Reserve Bank. This body makes decisions that influence the amount of excess reserves available to banks. The FOMC's decisions and their implementation are a major determinant of interest rates and the availability of credit each day.

The FOMC is made up of the seven Governors of the Federal Reserve System, the president of the Federal Reserve Bank of New York, and presidents of four additional regional Federal Reserve Banks. The FOMC meets regularly to make critical decisions influencing the nation's money supply.

THE MONEY SUPPLY

Money has been used as a medium of exchange and a store of value (a way to store purchasing power) for centuries.

Throughout history, many items have been used as money. Beaver pelts were considered to be one of the greatest sources of money in Canada and America during

© Alexander Kirch/Shutterstock.com

the 1800s.[65] In post World War II Germany, cigarettes and cognac were used instead of the worthless German paper currency. In California's prisons, cans of mackerel — yes the fish — are used for currency.[66]

Of course, gold has long been recognized as a source of money and for years the U.S. money supply was supported by the stock of gold held by the government. Today we no longer have a "gold standard." We have coins and currency that make up the money supply, supported by the perceived value of our dollar around the world.

The Federal Reserve System has developed several measures of the nation's money supply. The narrowest measure includes only items that serve as a medium of exchange. This part of the money supply is known as M1.

> ➤ **M1 is a measure of the money supply that includes only currency and account balances commonly used to pay for goods and services; the sum of currency, traveler's checks, and checkable deposits.**

In 2016, the M1 part of the money supply was approximately $3.354 trillion.

The Federal Reserve also measures what economists call *near monies.* Near monies are assets that can be easily converted to money because they can be liquidated at low cost and little risk of loss. Because near monies can be easily converted into money, some economists prefer to include them in the measure of the nation's money supply.[67] The Federal Reserve System measures the sum of M1 and certain near monies like money market deposit accounts at banks, money market mutual fund accounts, savings accounts, and small-denomination certificates of deposit to create M2. M2 equaled approximately $13.247 trillion in 2016.

Finally, we have M3, which is the sum of M2 plus large-denomination ($100,000 or more) certificates of deposit and other large-denomination liquid assets.

For our purposes, when we talk about Federal Reserve Bank actions to impact the money supply, we will reference M1. Since M2 and M3 represent assets that cannot be easily liquidated (turned into cash), it is most accurate to use M1 as a guide to understanding Fed policies.

SUGGESTED CLASSROOM DEBATE

Go online and conduct research on a new form of currency called the 'Bitcoin'.[68] Do you think this currency could someday replace the dollar as the dominant form of currency? Do you think it should be legal for people to engage in commerce with Bitcoins? Why, or why not?

THE MONETARIST CRITICISMS OF THE CLASSICS AND KEYNESIANS

A monetarist economist is one who believes that macro-economic policy is most efficient when it largely depends on the manipulation of the money supply and interest rates. It should be noted that Milton Friedman and other prominent Monetarists are basically Classical economists, who believe that the self-correcting mechanism can work, but that it needs the assistance of monetary policy.

With respect to the Keynesians, the Monetarists agree completely with the Classical economists that the crowding-out effect and lag effects make government spending a relatively useless policy tool. As a matter of fact, Alan Greenspan testified, on occasion, before Congress on the dangers of government spending.[69]

THE MONETARIST SOLUTION FOR RECESSIONS

When the economy entered into recession, the Federal Reserve Bank lowered interest rates several times to some of the lowest levels in decades. To the casual observer, the Fed simply announced that rates were lower and that was it. It is not that simple. When the economy suffers a recession, there are actually three ways the Fed can engage in *expansionary monetary policy.*

First, the Fed has the authority to *lower the discount rate.* This is the interest rate the Federal Reserve charges its member banks. The Fed rarely lowers the discount rate for fear of encouraging irresponsible behavior on the part of banks. The Fed is often called "the lender of last

resort." The second way the Fed can lower interest rates is to *lower the required reserve ratio.* This is the percentage of excess reserves banks are required to hold and not loan out. By lowering this ratio, the Fed can increase the supply of excess reserves, and lower interest rates. This is also a rarely used policy. The Fed wants to make sure banks are always solvent. Lowering this ratio exposes the banking system to heightened risks.

The third way the Fed can pursue expansionary monetary policy is to *engage in the buying of government securities.* Government securities are interest-bearing debts of the federal government. These securities take the form of treasury bills, treasury bonds, and treasury notes. The Fed has the ability to buy and sell these securities when engaging in monetary policy, and prefers this mechanism to the others. Figures 12.5–12.7 illustrate this popular tool of monetary policy.

Suppose that American households and businesses were holding $200 billion in treasury bonds when the economy slumps into the next recession. Treasury bonds have a face value of $10,000 and a maturity of 30 years.

When the economy enters a recession, the Fed wants to encourage businesses to invest and households to spend. It does this by discouraging the holding of government securities.[70]

When the economy goes into a recession, the Board of Governors authorizes the FOMC to *buy government securities.* When securities dealers put in buy orders, this causes the demand for government bonds to increase (D2). As demand increases, the price of bonds, which in this case had started out at $9,500,[71] begins to rise. As the price of bonds increases, individuals around the country release their bonds to the FOMC in order to make a profit on their sale.

When the bonds are transferred to the FOMC, the FOMC, using the *FedWire* — a wire transaction service — sends money to the accounts of individuals and busi-

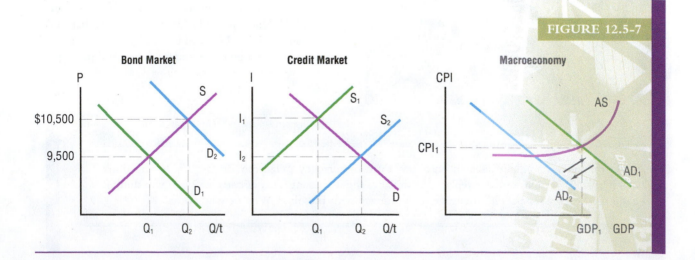

FIGURE 12.5-7

nesses around the country. This leads to an increase in the amount of excess reserves available in the banking system and thus, an *increase in the money supply.* As the supply of money increases, *interest rates fall,* and the quantity of money demanded by the private sector increases. Once businesses and households take on new loans for homes, cars, new technologies, etc., *aggregate demand begins to rise.* The Fed will continue on this course of expansionary monetary policy until full employment is restored.

Bear in mind that during this process, the Fed will be ever-mindful of the dangers of causing inflation through monetary policy. When the Fed cuts interest rates, it is usually in very small increments and relatively infrequently. The Fed wants to engineer what economists refer to as a "soft landing" – a slow increase in aggregate demand back into segment two of the aggregate supply curve.

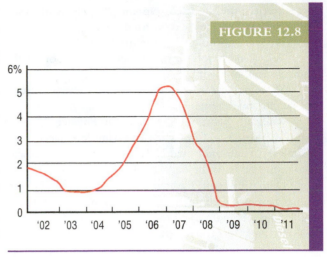

FIGURE 12.8

CLASSICAL CRITICISMS OF MONETARY POLICY

For many economists, the housing bubble and inevitable collapse of the financial system can be traced back to the year 2000, when Alan Greenspan and the Federal Reserve Bank pushed for reductions in interest rates to stem the losses that were mounting from the dot-com stock collapse. This stock market bubble led to a slowdown in the economy that was magnified by the events of September 11, 2001.

By keeping interest rates near historically low levels for much of the first decade, the fuel to light the housing market was readily available. During this time the federal funds rate (the interest rate banks charge one another for overnight loans) was actually *negative* when adjusting for inflation. Figure 12.8 illustrates this reality. In 2004, for example, the rate of inflation was 3.3%. So if a bank borrowed $50 million at 1% interest, the repayment of this loan would be eroded by an inflation rate of 3.3%. The net interest rate, therefore, would be negative 2.3%. This encouraged banks to be willing participants in the exponential rise in demand for houses and real estate.

Critics charge that if the Federal Reserve Bank had not been willing to add to the money supply and lower interest rates during a time the economy was overheating, we would have seen a slowdown in housing and housing-related purchases, and perhaps avoided such a large collapse in this market in 2007 and 2008.[72]

Hayek argued that inflation was one of the worst evils that humans could endure. Having lived in Austria where he witnessed how inflation destroyed the savings of the German people and fueled the rise of the Nazi Party, Hayek argued that keeping the government from turning

on the printing presses to prime the borrowing pump, would help preserve economic liberty.

By 2011, we began to see what he was worried about.

For the years 2007–2010, the problem of inflation was really not on many people's radar. However, as the federal government continued to increase its borrowing, the value of the dollar began to fall. Compounding matters was ongoing expansionary monetary policy by the Federal Reserve that culminated with a – shocking to many – $4 trillion round of 'quantitative easing' that took place into 2014. This policy, known as QE1 and QE2 involved Fed purchases of bonds, including mortgage bonds. In nearly the first 100 years of the existence of the Federal Reserve Bank it had never bought one mortgage. Then it bought over $1.2 trillion worth of these risky bonds. The Federal Reserve hoped that by taking these bonds "off the books" of America's banks that it would free the banks to use the $4 cash infusion to make new loans and spur aggregate demand towards a quick economic recovery.

As of early 2014 this had not happened even though bond purchases averaged $85 billion per month. By some estimates, the Fed may have added only .25% to the GDP over the few years of aggressive bond purchases while the banking industry largely sat on the new cash and was reluctant to lend the money.[73]

In January 2013 I attended an economics conference where officials of the Federal Reserve carefully explained the purpose of quantitative easing and how it was supposed to eventually pull aggregate demand to the right. At one point a participant in the conference asked, "So, if all of this extra cash eventually causes high rates of inflation, what is the Fed prepared to do?"

The Federal Reserve official proceeded to tell us that since quantitative easing of this nature had never been tried before, the Fed only had computer models of what the responses could be. We were then told that we could be sure than the modeled responses "would work" even though they had "never been tried".

We were not told what the models were.

You could have heard a feather hit the floor for the next several moments…

Many nations around the world were sharply critical of quantitative easing.

Wolfgang Schauble, the German Finance Minister said, "It doesn't add up when the Americans accuse the Chinese of currency manipulation and then artificially lower the value of the dollar."

Dilma Rousseff, President of Brazil stated, "The last time there was a competitive devaluation of currencies, it ended up where it did, in the Second World War."

It might seem a bit odd to worry about inflation when the unemployment rate is around 10%, but history is a very solid guide for the ramifications of expansive easing of the money supply.

It should be noted that in December 2016 the Federal Reserve Bank finally backed off of its "easy money" policy and increased interest rates slightly. In January 2017 the Fed kept interest rates constant but indicated that 2017 might see higher rates if the economy picked up steam.

KEYNESIAN CRITICISMS OF MONETARY POLICY

John Maynard Keynes was sharply critical of the inaction of the Federal Reserve Bank during the Great Depression, but he also pointed out that even if the Fed had loosened the money supply, it would, in all likelihood, not have rescued the country. According to Keynes, expansionary monetary policy not only suffers from some of the same lag effects as expansionary fiscal policy, but also from the following problems:

DURING SEVERE RECESSIONS, INDIVIDUALS AND BUSINESSES MAY BE RELUCTANT TO BORROW MONEY

This criticism is well founded. After all, in the middle of a downturn in the business cycle, many unemployed workers, along with employed but fearful workers and struggling businesses, might not believe that they can afford to take on new debt. If you don't have a job, an interest rate of zero percent may not encourage more spending. This was a major problem during the 2001 and 2007-2009 downturns.

The Fed continued to lower interest rates, while the country "sat on the fence" and did not respond for months.[74] In 2001 it wasn't until people were able to shed other debt burdens, and until interest rates fell to levels not seen since the early 1960s that aggregate demand began to rise, as a result of the expansion of credit. Of course, some felt that even with the rate cuts, the Fed did not move fast enough or cut rates by an amount that was perceived to be big enough by investors, businesses, and consumers.[75]

In 2008 people were even more reluctant to borrow for new homes or business expansions. In early October the Federal Reserve Bank lowered interest rates to 1.5%.[76] In September of 2007 the federal funds rate – the interest rate banks charge one another for overnight loans was 5.25%. However with almost daily reports of economic stress not seen in 70 years, it became increasingly rational for consumers and businesses to avoid taking on new debt.

Shutterstock © Kalim, 2011.

From 2010 into 2014 the Federal Funds rate was nearly zero percent, yet the economy barely broke the 7% unemployment barrier. Home mortgages fell to their lowest levels in 50 years. Yet, there was little movement in the demand for homes or in the amount of new investment spending by businesses.

It was not until 2015-16 that we began to see a significant increase in the demand for homes and higher housing prices. As unemployment finally fell below 5% the economy had enough momentum to give the Federal Reserve some relief from years of expansionary monetary policy.

DURING SEVERE RECESSIONS, BANKS MAY BE RELUCTANT TO LEND MONEY

Very simply, if banks are concerned about the prospects for repayment of loans, lendable funds may be hard to come by, even at lower rates. These two problems create what Keynes referred to as the *liquidity trap* – a situation where the economy gets stuck in segment one of the aggregate supply curve as a result of insufficient business and consumer activity. As a result of this problem, Keynes argued that monetary policy is largely ineffective during a recession. Of course, the Monetarist response to this concern is that eventually, expansionary monetary policy creates an elastic response to falling interest rates; therefore, the government should stay out of the economy until this occurs.

The Keynesians appeared to be extremely accurate in 2007-2010. As the subprime mortgage market led to the banking crisis, even with lower interest rates banks were extremely hesitant to extend financial capital to millions of individuals and businesses who otherwise would be deemed to be acceptable risks. This "credit crunch" played a huge role in the dramatic economic slowdown and forced the Federal Reserve Bank to undertake dramatic steps such as directly lending money to businesses for the first time since the Great Depression.[77]

MONETARY "NEUTRALITY"

For the monetarist economist, once expansionary monetary policy has restored full employment, there is no reason to continue to lower interest rates, nor a very compelling reason to raise them.[78] When the economy has reached full employment, oftentimes the Federal Reserve Bank will adopt a "neutral" policy with respect to the money supply and interest rates. This means that as long as the economy does not appear to be heading for segment three of the aggregate supply curve or slipping back into segment one, interest rates will not be raised or lowered for the foreseeable future.

THE MONETARIST CURE FOR INFLATION

As aforementioned, in December 2016 the Federal Reserve Bank increased interest rates by .25%. This move was an attempt to slow down the rate at which aggregate demand was increasing. This move was not in response to significant increases in inflation but rather a preemptive move to keep inflation from accelerating in 2017. This policy is known as *contractionary monetary policy*, and it is carried out by the FOMC. Figures 12.9-12.11 illustrate how.

When aggregate demand increases enough to cause inflationary pressure, the Fed authorizes the FOMC to *sell government securities*. When the FOMC puts in sell orders, this causes the supply of government securities to increase. As the supply of government securities increases, the price of securities falls. When prices fall, the quantity of securities demanded increases.

As more and more households and businesses buy up these discounted securities, they send money to the FOMC, leading to a decrease in the overall pool of excess reserves.

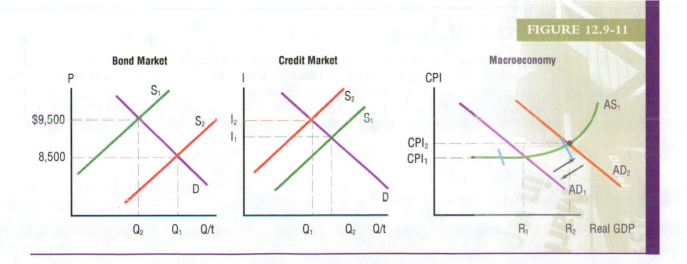

FIGURE 12.9-11

As excess reserves diminish, the *supply of money decreases*, leading to an *increase in interest rates* and a decrease in the quantity of money demanded. As the quantity of money demanded falls, consumption and investment decrease and *aggregate demand is slowly pulled back down* toward the point where real GDP equals potential real GDP.

However, the Fed is very careful not to raise rates too much or too fast. Doing so could propel the economy into a contraction or recession.

THE MONETARIST SOLUTION FOR STAGFLATION – USUALLY...

During the stagflation of the 1970s, President Jimmy Carter appointed Paul Volcker as Chairman of the Federal Reserve Bank. By the time stagflation hit its peak in 1980, Mr. Volcker had seen enough. Early in the first term of Ronald Reagan, Mr. Volcker attacked stagflation by killing off the inflation part of the problem. He did this by driving interest rates up to a level not previously seen in America's modern history.[79]

This policy worked. Inflation was vanquished and the economy, aided by tax cuts and deregulation, soon began its longest period of economic growth in history.

Ironically, Ben Bernanke came into office during a time when stagflationary concerns were beginning to grow once again.

Ironically, Mr. Bernanke pursued the exact opposite monetary policies during this time of a shrinking aggregate supply. Mr. Bernanke opted to fight the recessionary problems that accompany stagflation and kept interest rates low. As aforementioned, many charge that low interest rates and a massive decline in the value of the dollar that stemmed from supplying more and more money into the economic system only made the inflation part of this stagflationary period even worse.[80]

FINAL THOUGHTS

We have seen in this chapter a tremendous debate between economists who have widely divergent views on what to do about recessions, inflation and stagflation. The Classical economists have significant faith in the free market's ability to self-correct without the "clumsy hand of government intervention." Of course that solution requires time and patience and tremendous personal responsibility on the part of businesses and individuals.

John Maynard Keynes once said, "To dig holes in the ground will increase, not only employment, but the real national dividend of useful goods and services when once we understand the influences upon which effective demand depends."[81] Keynes' demand-side approach required tremendous faith in the government's ability to use taxpayer dollars more efficiently than private citizens could if they were allowed to keep their own money. This faith requires evidence that government tends to work well and create jobs. The evidence, no matter where you look, is spurious at best.

Finally, led by economists like Milton Friedman, the monetarists offer a sort of "Classical-leaning middle ground" where government-chartered banks like the Federal Reserve are given the power to manipulate the money supply in an effort to change the cost of borrowing and thus the level of aggregate demand. Controversy abounds with this approach as well.

So which approach do you agree with so far? Why?

CONCEPT CHECK

Suppose the price of oil rises to $170 per barrel in 2026, causing gasoline prices to surge past $4.50 per gallon. Would it then make sense for the Federal Reserve Bank to lower interest rates in order to help people buy new, more energy efficient homes and cars? Why, or why not?

ENDNOTES

1 See "Investors Succumb to Fears of Recession" by E.S. Browning and Ianthe Jeanne Dugan, *The Wall Street Journal*, October 7, 2008.

2 See "Market's 7-Day Rout Leaves U.S. Reeling" by E.S. Browning and Annelena Lobb, *The Wall Street Journal*, October 10, 2008.

3 See "Wild Day Caps Worst Week Ever for Stocks" by E.S. Browning, Diya Gullapalli and Craig Karmin, *The Wall Street Journal*, October 11-12, 2008; "GM Had Talks with Chrysler" by Jeffrey McCracken and John D. Stoll, *The Wall Street Journal*, October 11-12, 2008; and "U.S., Britain Up Ante in Fight to Stop Crisis" by Jon Hilsenrath, Diya Gullapalli and Randall Smith, *The Wall Street Journal*, October 8, 2008.

4 See "Slump Over, Pain Persists" by Sara Murray, *The Wall Street Journal*, September 21, 2010.

5 See "Economists Split on Growth Recipe" by Victoria McGrane and Jon Hilsenrath, *The Wall Street Journal*, January 6, 2014.

6 For more on Hayek, see *Friedrich Hayek* by Alan Ebenstein, St. Martins Press, 2001.

7 See "Ideas on economy start to add up" by Don Lee, *The Orlando Sentinel*, January 10, 2010.

8 See "The Gospel of Paul" by Kimberly Strassel, *The Wall Street Journal*, November 4, 2007.

9 See "Why Friedrich Hayek is Making a Comeback" by Russ Roberts, *The Wall Street Journal*, June 28, 2010; and "Spreading Hayek, Spurning Keynes" by Kelly Evans, *The Wall Street Journal*, August 28-29, 2010.

10 See "Returning Workers Face Steep Pay Cuts" by Ianthe Jeanne Dugan, *The Wall Street Journal*, November 12, 2009.

11 See "Home Prices Sink Further" by Nick Timiraos, *The Wall Street Journal*, January 31, 2011.

12 See "As Global Economy Shifts, Companies Rethink, Retool" by Bob Davis, *The Wall Street Journal*, November 7, 2010.

13 See "A Moronic Proposal," *The Wall Street Journal*, September 14, 2005.

14 See "King of Pork – and Proud of It" by Fred Barnes, *The Wall Street Journal*, June 29, 2010.

15 See "Robert Byrd's Highways to Nowhere" by Brian Bolduc, *The Wall Street Journal*, July 10-11, 2010.

16 See "The Real Cost of Bailing Out Bear Stearns" by James B. Stewart, *The Wall Street Journal*, March 26, 2008.

17 See "The Government is Contributing to the Panic" by Jonathan Macey, *The Wall Street Journal*, October 11-12, 2008, pg. A13.

20 See "Inflation Worries Spread" by Bob Davis and Aaron Back, *The Wall Street Journal*, February 9, 2011.

21 See "Commodity Prices Surge" by Liam Pleven, Carolyn Cui and Scott Kilman, *The Wall Street Journal*, November 10, 2010 and "Price of Silver Soaring" by Carolyn Cui and Robert Guy Matthews, *The Wall Street Journal*, December 27, 2010.

22 See "Inflation and Witchcraft: The Case of Jean Bodin Reconsidered" by Gunnar Heinsohn & Otto Steiger, University of Bremen, March 1, 1996.

18 For more on this, log onto www.jackchambless.com Click on SPEECHES and scroll down to The Economics of Privatization.

19 See "Political Pendulum Swings Toward Stricter Regulation" by Elizabeth Williamson, *The Wall Street Journal*, March 24, 2008.

23 See "Feeney: Restrictions risk a new Great Depression" by Tom Feeney, *The Orlando Sentinel*, April 17, 2008.

24 See "What History Tells Us About the Market" by Jason Zweig, *The Wall Street Journal*, October 11-12, 2008, pg. W1.

25 For an in-depth look at this problem, see *FDR's Folly* by Jim Powell, Three Rivers Press, 2003.

26 For more on this theory, see www.escape.com/~paulg53/politics/great_depression.shtml.

27 See *New Deal or Raw Deal: How FDR's Economic Legacy Has Damaged America* by Burton Folsom, Threshold Editions, New York, 2008 pp. 78-81.

28 See www.ncpa.org/edo/bb/2001/bb100101.html for more on the Hitler-Keynes connection.

29 See "FDR and the Lessons of the Depression" by Thomas F. Cooley and Lee E. Ohanian, *The Wall Street Journal*, August 27, 2010, p. A17.

30 See *New Deal or Raw Deal?* By Burton Folsom, Jr., Simon and Schuster 2008 pp. 43-59

31 See "Divorce Makes a Comeback" by Jeffrey Zaslow, *The Wall Street Journal*, January 14, 2003.

32 See "Tense times bring new stresses home" by Willoughby Mariano, *The Orlando Sentinel*, November 4, 2001; and "Child abuse, neglect are a consequence of slowing economy" by David A. Bundy, *The Orlando Sentinel*, March 24, 2008.

33 For more on Keynes and this theory of the multiplier effect, see www.bizednet.bris.ac.uk/virtual/economy/library/economists/keynes.htm.

34 Source: Florida's Civilian Conservation Corps Museum, Highland Hammonds State Park, Sebring, Florida.

35 *New Deal or Raw Deal?* Pp. 84-92.

36 See *Economics in One Lesson* by Henry Hazlitt, (New Rochelle, New York: Arlington House, 1979 [1946], pp. 32-33.

37 See *Friedrich Hayek*, by Alan Ebenstein, St. Martin's Press, 2001, p. 115.

38 See "Obama's Investment Charade" by Stephen Moore, *The Wall Street Journal*, January 27, 2011; and "Government Spending is No Free Lunch" by Robert J. Barro, *The Wall Street Journal*, January 22, 2009.

39 See "President Signs Budget-Busting Medicare Reform" by John Skorburg, *Budget & Tax News* (The Heartland Institute), January 2004.

40 See "Ignoring Reality Has a Price" by David Leonhardt, *The New York Times*, October 8, 2008.

41 See "Obama seeks funds for roads" by Kathleen Hennessey and Don Lee, *The Orlando Sentinel*, September 7, 2010.

42 See *Getting America Right* by Edwin J. Feulner and Doug Wilson, Crown Forum, 2006; and "Welcome to the GOP's New New Deal" by Stephen Moore, *The Wall Street Journal*, September 19, 2005.

43 See "The Obama Economy," *The Wall Street Journal*, September 7, 2010, p. A22.

44 See "Three Million Imaginary Jobs," *The Wall Street Journal*, July 15, 2010, p. A16.

45 See "Summer of Discontent" by Michael Boskin, *The Wall Street Journal*, September 2, 2010.

46 See "The Obama Stimulus Impact? Zero" by John F. Cogan and John B. Taylor, *The Wall Street Journal*, December 9, 2010; "The Stimulus Didn't Work" by John F. Cogan, John B. Taylor and Volker Wieland, *The Wall Street Journal*, September 17, 2009; and "Why Obamanomics Has Failed" by Allan H. Meltzer, *The Wall Street Journal*, June 30, 2010.

47 See "Barack Obama-san," *The Wall Street Journal*, December 16, 2008.

48 See "How Government Prolonged the Depression" by Harold L. Cole and Lee E. Ohanian, *The Wall Street Journal*, February 2, 2009.

49 See "Big Government, Big Recession" by Alan Reynolds, *The Wall Street Journal*, August 21, 2009; *The Forgotten Man* by Amity Shlaes, Harper Collins 2007; and *New Deal or Raw Deal?* by Burton Folsom, New York: Threshold Editions, 2008.

50 See "Echoes of the Great Depression" by Phil Gramm, *The Wall Street Journal*, October 1, 2010.

51 See "FDR, Obama and Confidence" by Amity Shlaes, *The Wall Street Journal*, July 13, 2010; and "Employers on Strike," *The Wall Street Journal*, June 5-6, 2010.

52 See "The U.S. Needs More i-Side Economics" by Andy Kessler, *The Wall Street Journal*, September 18, 2012.

53 See "A Stimulus Project Gets All Caulked Up" by Louise Radnofsky, *The Wall Street Journal*, September 21, 2010.

54 Translation: "Wonderful, this means the economy of Chambles will grow by more than $50."

55 See "Obama's Economic Fish Stories" by Michael J. Boskin, *The Wall Street Journal*, July 21, 2010, p. A17.

56 See "Why the Spending Stimulus Failed" by Michael J. Boskin, *The Wall Street Journal*, December 1, 2010.

57 After four hurricanes hit Florida in 2004, one economist argued that the storms would be good for the economy. See "Rebuilding will provide boom" by Jerry W. Jackson, *The Orlando Sentinel*, August 18, 2004.

58 See "Three Myths of the Great Depression" by Burton Folsom, Jr. – from a speech delivered at The Foundation for Economic Education, July 2004 – *Notes from FEE*, September 2004.

59 For a modern-day look at this problem, see "The New Consumerism" by Juliet Schor, *The Orlando Sentinel*, May 17, 1998. For an examination of how Great Britain adopted this strategy in increasing the top tax rate to 98%, see www.polyconomics.com/searchbase/07-20-01.html.

60 See www.tax.org/THP/Articles/wartaxes.htm.

61 See "Germany Recovery Spurs Push for Higher Pay" by Brian Blackstone, *The Wall Street Journal*, September 9, 2010.

62 See *The Federal Reserve System: Purposes and Functions*, Board of Governors of the Federal Reserve System, Washington, D.C., 1984.

63 See "Yellen Stands by Fed Strategy" by Jon Hilsenrath and Victoria McGrane, *The Wall Street Journal,* November 15, 2013 A2.

64 See *Economics*, by David N. Hyman, Irwin 1989, pp. 748–751.

65 Source: The Royal Alberta Museum, Edmonton, Alberta, Canada and the National Mississippi River Museum and Aquarium, Dubuque, Iowa.

66 See "Mackerel Economics in Prison Leads to Appreciation for Oily Fillets" by Justin Scheck, *The Wall Street Journal*, October 2, 2008.

67 See *Economics* by David N. Hyman, Richard D. Irwin 1997, pp. 634–636.

68 See "Bitcoin: A new – and strange – way to pay" by Jim Stratton, *The Orlando Sentinel,* February 3, 2014 page D1.

69 For some of Greenspan's thoughts on economic policy, see www.bog.frb.fed.us/BOARDDOCS/SPEECHES/19970905.htm.

70 It should be noted that in October 2001, the United States Treasury Department announced it would no longer sell any new 30-year bonds. These bonds carried a higher interest rate payment to the possessor and thus, caused the government to pay higher interest on our national debt obligations. The Treasury Department hoped to not only lower interest rates for the government but to encourage more people to buy Treasury bills and Treasury notes, which have a shorter time period for the payout and a lower interest rate. By encouraging purchase of these securities, the Treasury Department aided the Federal Reserve Bank's attempts to lower interest rates and spur economic growth in 2001. See "Goodbye to the 30-Year Treasury Bond" by Gregory Zuckerman and Michael Schroeder, *The Wall Street Journal*, November 1, 2001.

71 The government often discounts the price of securities off their face value to encourage people to buy them.

72 For much more on this argument, see "The Song of Bernanke," *The Wall Street Journal*, August 31, 2007; "Behind the Food-Price Riots" by Vincent Reinhart, *The Wall Street Journal*, April 18, 2008; "Loose Money and the Roots of the Crisis" by Judy Shelton, *The Wall Street Journal*, September 30, 2008, pg. A19; "Adam Smith Growls," *The Wall Street Journal*, November 9, 2007, pg. A18; and "The Dollar and the Credit Crunch" by Ronald McKinnon, *The Wall Street Journal*, March 31, 2008, pg. A19.

73 See "Confessions of a Quantitative Easer" by Andrew Huszar, *The Wall Street Journal,* November 11, 2013.

74 See "As Fed Cuts Rates Yet Again, Its Powers Seem to Be Limited" by Greg Ip and Greg White, *The Wall Street Journal,* October 3, 2001. For information on a similar problem in Japan, see "A Puzzle for Japan: Rock-Bottom Rates, But Few Borrowers" by Phred Dvorak, *The Wall Street Journal*, October 25, 2001.

75 See "Cut Rates Fast" by Marc Miles, *The Wall Street Journal,* January 4, 2001; "Rate-Cut Disappointment Sparks a Late Selloff" by Gregory Zuckerman, *The Wall Street Journal*, March 21, 2001; and "The Stock Market vs. The 'Real Economy'" by Steven Pearlstein, *The Washington Post* (published in *The Orlando Sentinel*), April 1, 2001.

76 See "Central Banks Launch Coordinated Attack" by Jon Hilsenrath, Joellen Perry and Sudeep Reddy, *The Wall Street Journal*, October 9, 2008.

77 See "U.S., Britain Up Ante in Fight to Stop Crisis" by Jon Hilsenrath, Diya Gullapalli and Randall Smith, *The Wall Street Journal*, October 8, 2008.

78 See "Fed Keeps Rates Flat as GDP Increases," *The Wall Street Journal*, January 31, 2002.

79 See "Washington is Quietly Repudiating Its Debts" by Gerald P. O'Driscoll Jr., *The Wall Street Journal*, August 22, 2008, pg. A15.

80 See "Enough With the Interest Rate Cuts" by Martin Feldstein, *The Wall Street Journal*, April 15, 2008.

81 See "Someday we'll pay for all this easy money" by Jason Lewis, *The Start Tribune*, July 22, 2013 page OP3.

CHAPTER REVIEW

1. What is the Classical solution for long recessions? What criticisms can be offered up toward this model? What would be the Classical response to such criticism?

2. What caused the Great Depression? What could the Federal Reserve Bank have done during this time to ease the effects of the Depression?

3. What is the Keynesian multiplier effect? What are three major criticisms of this theory?

4. What does each School of Thought say about the problem of stagflation? Which one makes the least amount of economic sense? Why?

5. What is contractionary monetary policy? When is it used? What is the Keynesian solution to inflation?

Chapter Thirteen

SUPPLY-SIDE ECONOMICS

Photo courtesy Jack Chambless

*L*ittle else is requisite to carry a state to the highest degree of opulence from the lowest barbarism but peace, easy taxes, and a tolerable administration of justice: all the rest being brought about by the natural course of things.

ADAM SMITH

A DIFFERENT APPROACH TO MACROECONOMIC DISTORTIONS

The natural progress of things is for government to gain ground and liberty to yield.

Thomas Jefferson, 1788

This sentiment – echoed by economic thinkers like Adam Smith, Frederic Bastiat, and Friedrich Hayek – was largely responsible for a fairly small and limited federal government for much of America's long history. For over 150 years, it was an accepted argument that individuals make better decisions than government – even when the government's intentions were good.

After all, it was not long before Jefferson's quote that America had broken away from British rule, ostensibly to extricate us from an environment of high taxes and exorbitant limitations on our personal and economic freedom.

By the twentieth century, the government began to do exactly as Jefferson had predicted. With each advance into the market – in the name of the public good – came less and less efficient decisions and more intrusions into the lives of Americans. These intrusions, in the form of increased taxes and regulations, were well-meaning, but the result was a cloak of bureaucracy that stifled innovation, incentives, and helped contribute to the economic stagnation of millions of American families during the 1970s.

1933–1981

With the election of Franklin Roosevelt as president in 1932, came a complete shift in America's way of looking at economic policy and the role of government. During severe economic crises, oftentimes people are willing to listen to social, political, and economic theories that might have been

heresy a few years earlier.[1] How do you explain the rise of fascism in the world? Would Hitler have come to power in a strong, vibrant economy? Would Americans have accepted the socialist underpinnings of social security, welfare, the minimum wage, farm supports, and government work projects during an economic expansion? It is highly unlikely. Would President Obama have argued for "spreading the wealth" during a period of rapid economic growth?

Once the federal government intervened and created the appearance that politicians, rather than markets, leads to prosperity, people became willing to accept more and more programs and higher taxes to pay for them. World War II saw an epic jobs program created to employ Americans to defeat the Axis powers. It also saw the government imposing price controls and rationing of rubber, food, metals, and electric power. The American people – to their credit – were willing to go along with such intrusions in the name of a greater cause.

No self-interested American wanted to risk doing anything that would jeopardize the freedom of the nation in the long run. The end of World War II saw the government spending millions of dollars of taxpayer money to fund the G.I. Bill – a law that provided funding for veterans to pursue higher education.

As soldiers came home and went off to college, they became engineers, architects, and educators who helped fuel an amazing economic recovery from the Great Depression. Part of the wealth from this recovery was used to finance spending for the Cold War – the arms race with the Soviet Union – as well as the interstate highway system and the space program. All the while the tax burdens of the American people grew. By the early 1960s, the top tax rate was a staggering 91%, and government spending had increased from $42.6 billion in 1950 to $106.8 billion the year John F. Kennedy called for tax cuts.[2]

Kennedy was not immune from the temptation to allow increased government involvement in our lives. The use of tax dollars to finance the extremely expensive and miserably failed war effort in Vietnam is one example. His vision for a social welfare state to pull people out of poverty was another.

After President Kennedy died, Lyndon Johnson oversaw one of the largest and most expensive government social programs in our history, with the programs like Aid to Families with Dependent Children, food stamps, school lunch programs, government housing, subsidies for heating and electric bills, Medicare and Medicaid, and dozens of other welfare programs have cost the country almost $21 trillion since 1964. All the while, very little evidence has been produced that poverty has been eradicated or even dealt a serious blow as a direct result of government benevolence with your tax dollars.

In the meantime, laws covering affirmative action, product liability, energy conservation, environmental protection, worker safety, family leave, disability and age discrimination, and many others have added thousands upon thousands of pages to the federal docket of expensive government regulations.

In the 1970s, people began to blame the government for the sorry state of the economy. With runaway inflation and unemployment, the Keynesian way of looking at the economy was losing its popularity. For many, it was a time for a new way of promoting economic prosperity.

THE EMERGENCE OF SUPPLY-SIDE ECONOMICS

By 1979, a new group of economists, called "supply-side" or neo-classical economists, had begun to step to the front of the stage in the economics community. The term "neo" means *new*. Supply-side economists are basically economists who recognize that the massive scale of government is here to stay and therefore, concentrate their analysis on getting the government out of the economy as much as possible.

With marginal tax rates topping out at 70% and massive government regulations imposed upon the economy, the United States had entered a period of economic stagnation during the 1970s that had not been seen since the Great Depression. This new group of economists argued that the government was the source of, rather than the solution for, economic misery.

To the supply-siders, the only way the economy would ever be strong again would be to unshackle free enterprise from the grip of government and allow individuals and businesses to operate in a less-intrusive and lower-taxed environment. Recall that the major focus of the 1933-1981 economic policies revolved around changes in aggregate demand. Yet whenever aggregate demand changes, there is always a tradeoff between unemployment and inflation.

By 1979, a growing number of economists became convinced that policymakers should forget about aggregate demand and concentrate on ways to *stimulate aggregate supply*. One of those economists was a young professor at the University of Southern California named Arthur Laffer.

Laffer believed that the stagflationary periods of the 1970s had as much, if not more, to do with excessive government regulation and high taxes than high oil prices had. Laffer's argument was straightforward: The more money the government takes from people's paychecks, the less incentive people have to work and maximize the productivity of their capital or labor. He argued that less taxation and less-burdensome regulation would lead to an increase in the productivity of workers and businesses alike. They would now reap the rewards of extra education, training, or investments in new technology or capital equipment.[3]

If workers and businesses were permitted to keep the bulk of the fruits of their labor, Laffer insisted, economic output would increase, and as a result, the government would *get more tax revenue from less taxation*. On what might be the most famous cocktail napkin in history, Mr. Laffer drew his basic theory (Figure 13.1) over lunch with friends one day.

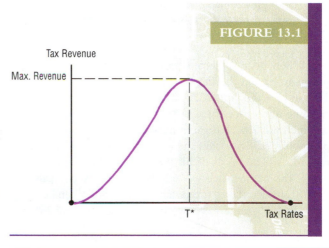

FIGURE 13.1

In 1980, the Republican candidate for president, Ronald Reagan, shared Laffer's opinion. Reagan had long embraced the concept of lower taxes leading to better productivity. In his autobiography, *An American Life*, Mr. Reagan stated:

At the peak of my career at Warner Bros., I was in the ninety-four percent tax bracket; that meant that after a certain point, I received only six cents of each dollar I earned and the government got the rest. The IRS took such a big chunk of my earnings that after a while I began asking myself whether it was worth it to keep on taking work. Something was wrong with a system like that. When you have to give up such a large percentage of your income in taxes incentive to work goes down. When government confiscates half or more of a corporation's profit, the motivation to maximize profits goes down, and owners and managers make decisions based disproportionately on a desire to avoid taxes, they begin looking for tax shelters and loopholes that contribute nothing to the growth of our economy. Their companies don't grow as fast, they invest less in new plants and equipment, and they hire fewer people.

According to Reagan:

Any system that penalizes success and accomplishment is wrong. Any system that discourages work, discourages productivity, discourages economic progress is wrong. If on the other hand, you reduce taxes and allow people to spend or save more of what they earn, they'll be more industrious; they'll have more incentive to work hard, and money they earn will add fuel to the great economic machine that energizes our national progress. The result is more prosperity for all – and more revenue for government. A few economists call this principle supply-side economics. I just call it common sense.

When he was elected president in 1980, the unemployment rate in the U.S. was over 7%. Inflation was over 13% and for the year, GDP fell by 0.3%. Recall that when he came into office, there were 14 tax brackets, the highest of which was 70%. Reagan immediately began to act on his philosophy of lower taxes and less regulation of business and individuals. The result of his push to get the government out of the marketplace was a $750 billion tax cut, passed in 1981, followed by another tax cut in 1986. When he left office in 1989, there were two tax brackets – 15 and 28%.[4]

WHAT DID THE REAGAN TAX CUTS DO?

I think Ronald Reagan changed the trajectory of America in a way that, you know, Richard Nixon did not and in a way that Bill Clinton did not. He tapped into what people were already feeling, which is, We want clarity, we want optimism.

President Obama

For nearly the past three decades, economists have wrestled with one of the most argued-about topics in recent economic history. The debate centers on the extent to which Reagan's tax cutting caused, contributed to, or had nothing to do with the boom of the 1980s and 1990s. On one end of the fence, you have economists like Laura D'Andrea Tyson, who once stated,

In direct contradiction to 12 years of Republican ideology, there is no relationship between the taxes a nation pays and its economic performance.

On the other hand are economists who claim that much, if not most, of the credit for our unprecedented economic prosperity stems from the technology gains created by the "new" economy and the greater level of economic freedom from confiscatory taxes that took place under Reagan's watch.[5] During the eight years he was in office, the unemployment rate in America fell from 7.6% in 1981 to 5.3% in 1989. The Gross Domestic Product increased on average, 4.3% per year during this time frame.[6]

The rate of inflation was 10.3% in 1981 (13.5% in 1980). In every year he was in office, inflation rates fell – eventually to 4.8% in 1989. Productivity of American workers fell by 0.3% in 1980, but increased throughout the rest of the 1980s.

Even Laffer's prediction of increased federal revenue came true. The government collected just over $599 billion from taxpayers in 1981. By 1989 the amount was over $990 billion. This was not an uncommon result. When marginal rates were cut in the 1920s from a top rate of 73% to 25%, government revenue grew from $719 million to $1.1 billion, and the economy expanded by 59%.[7]

Due, in large part, to the massive tax cuts and a move to continue the deregulation of industry that began during the Carter administration, the U.S. experienced unprecedented growth during the 1980s. Reagan's plan was aided significantly by the collapse of oil prices in 1986 and the emergence of new technologies, but the bottom line was indisputable: Greater economic freedom from burdensome tax rates created much of the good fortune we enjoyed for more than twenty five years. This occurred as a result of expanded productivity, greater labor force participation rates – especially for women[8] – and less tax avoidance.

JOHN F. KENNEDY AND BILL CLINTON – SUPPLY-SIDE DEMOCRATS?

While he was president, Democrats sharply criticized George W. Bush for his relatively small cuts in income taxes. In every debate with John McCain, Barack Obama vilified Bush for cutting taxes for "the rich" even though

Bush cut tax rates from 15% to 10% on the poorest workers and reduced marginal tax rates for the middle class as well. Under his tax cuts federal tax revenues increased as well. In 2003 federal tax revenues totaled $1.782 trillion. By 2007 the figure was $2.568 trillion.[9] Ironically, the Democrats' chief arguments – that tax cuts unfairly favor the wealthy while creating ballooning deficits – was not shared by the icon of the Democratic Party.

Speaking before the Economics Club in New York in December 1962, John F. Kennedy said:

> Our true choice is not between tax reduction, on the one hand, and the avoidance of large federal deficits on the other. It is increasingly clear that… an economy hampered by restrictive tax rates will never produce enough revenues to balance our budget just as it will never produce enough jobs or enough profits. Surely the lesson of the last decade is that budget deficits are not caused by wild-eyed spenders but by slow economic growth and periodic recessions and any new recession would break all deficit records. In short, it is a paradoxical truth that tax rates are too high today and tax revenues are too low and the soundest way to raise the revenues in the long run is to cut the rates now.

These turned out to be very prophetic words of wisdom. In 1963, the top tax rate was 91%. It was cut to 70% by 1965 – two years after the assassination of one of the first supply-side presidents. Mr. Kennedy also administered the first investment tax credit – tax breaks to companies that invest in new plants and equipment.[10] Tax revenues *increased* by 33% as the economy expanded by 42%. Not surprisingly, the 1960s was one of four greatest periods of economic growth in America's twentieth century.

Now to President Clinton. If you were paying close attention earlier in the text you will recall reading that Mr. Clinton pushed for, and got, the largest tax increase in the history of the United States. Therefore, it would seem that any paragraph or so devoted to the question of Clinton as a supply-sider would be foolish. However, Mr. Clinton seemed to slide in this

direction in his second term in office. It was during that time that he supported broad tax cuts for capital gains (profit from the sale of stock, real estate, and so forth) as well as tax cuts for savings and retirement plans. When he took office the capital gains tax rate was 28%. He cut the rate to 20% in 1997.

As a result, tax revenue from the sale of investments skyrocketed and economic growth increased.[11] Moreover, under Mr. Clinton, millions of homeowners were granted the opportunity to sell their home for a profit and face a capital gains tax of *zero percent* for the first time in decades.

Therefore, while it is a fact that Supply-Side economics is often connected – and appropriately so – to the Reagan years, there were at least two presidents from the opposite side of the political spectrum – and many current Democrat governors[12] – who realized the benefits of lower taxes as well.

Which brings us back to Barack Obama. In his September 26, 2008 debate with Senator McCain, Mr. Obama said, "We have to grow the economy from the bottom up." He said this following his assertion that the economic struggles America was facing, was due in large part to an economic philosophy of letting rich people enjoy large tax breaks, while hoping that it would "trickle down" to the people who are not as rich.[13] His running mate, Joe Biden stated that paying higher taxes is "patriotic."[14]

What Messrs. Obama and Biden were unwilling to acknowledge is that tax cuts always stimulates growth and that economic growth is created top-down, not bottom-up. From 1983 to 2005 – a time period where marginal

Should tax cuts start with this guy?

© Stephen McSweeny/Shutterstock.com

tax rates on the wealthy fell to historically low levels, the poorest households in America saw their standard of living increase by roughly 25%.[15] In 1981, the top 1% of all income earners paid 17.58% of all federal income taxes. By 2005 – despite massive tax cuts for "rich" people – the top 1% was paying 39.38% of all income taxes. This seemingly illogical result is actually very logical.

When highly successful people are allowed to keep more of the money they create, they react by seeking ways to make even more money. This requires starting new businesses or expanding existing businesses, investing in new technologies and products, and spending more on research and development. All of this leads to more jobs for people all up and down the income scale and more money for every group.[16] The bottom income earners, through this job creation, see more prosperity; the rich earn more money, and even at the lower tax rates, the higher earnings lead to more money being paid in taxes by the very people Mr. Obama castigated for being "unfairly" better off.[17]

If this sounds a lot like Say's Law from chapter six, it is. It does not matter, according to the supply-siders, how much we "demand" from those who would serve us. Without the proper incentives to supply us with goods and services there will be no supply. Low taxes are a key to providing the incentives that suppliers need to supply us with the things we want.[18]

It is also important to recognize that not everyone would prefer an economic system where poor people must wait for rich people to provide jobs. Many – if you recall the concept of normative analysis – would prefer a society where government intervenes on behalf of the poor with revenue extracted from corporations and rich individuals. Yet, here we see the fallacy of taxing the rich to help the poor play out as well.

In 2007, the Exxon Corporation paid *$30 billion* in income taxes. That was as much revenue as the total amount collected from the states of North Dakota, South Dakota, Maine, Vermont, Montana, and Wyoming *combined*.[19] How much more revenue could the federal government have gained if Exxon was forced to pay less in taxes? For people who want government revenue to be used to help the poor, wouldn't more revenue be desirable to help more poor people?

Hauser's Law gives us some insight into the revenue effects of income taxation and thus, the ideal policy to pursue if the desire is more money for the less fortunate.

> ➢ **Hauser's Law states that tax revenues as a share of GDP will average just under 19%, regardless of the average tax rate paid by citizens of our economy.**[20]

How can this be? Think of it this way: If the top income tax rate was over 90% like it was for much of the 1940s and all of the 1950s, the incentives to produce, invest, expand, and grow the economy would be truncated and overall economic activity would be reduced. Therefore, a high tax rate reduces the GDP. The evidence shows that at high tax rates and a lower economic output, the government collects around 19% of a smaller economic pie.

If the top tax rate equaled 28% like it did in 1987, or 7% as was the case in 1914, the overall rate of economic growth would be much greater, as would government revenue. Therefore, the government collects more cash from a larger pie, yet the percentage – 19% of the total pie – remains the same, as if the tax rate was much higher.

This begs the question – if you are going to take a slice of pie, and you can only have 19% of the pie – would you rather have 19% of a pie the size of a small table or 19% of a pie the size of the palm of your hand?

OTHER SUPPLY-SIDE PROPOSALS

While the primary focus of the supply-side school of thought is on the net income you take in from every dollar you earn, there are other issues that have raised the ire of this group of economists. The following represent some of the other ideas that have been put forth since the early 1980s.

CONCEPT CHECK

When Calvin Coolidge became President of the United States during the 1920s the federal government was experiencing a budget deficit and the top marginal tax rate was 56%. When he left office in 1929 the top tax rate was 25% and the government was running budget surpluses.[21] Are these two economic realities related? Why or why not?

CONCEPT CHECK

Over the past few years, Sweden, the Czech Republic, Estonia, Ireland, Kuwait, Spain, Bulgaria, Russia, and other nations have either gone to a flat income tax or have reduced personal income and/or corporate income taxes.[22] Ireland, for example, has a 12.5% corporate income tax compared to America's world-leading 39.5% tax.[23] If these and other nations continue to move in this direction, while at the same time the U.S. continues to maintain a progressive income tax and an expanding social welfare system,[24] what will be the long run impact on America's aggregate demand and supply curves? For assistance, see the footnotes to this concept check and read the articles referenced.

ABOLISH THE ESTATE TAX

> I think it's irritating that once I die, 55% of my money goes to the United States government... You know why that's irritating? Because you would have already paid nearly 50%...When you leave a house or money to people, then they're taxed 55%, so you've got to leave them enough so that once they're taxed, they still have some money.[25]
>
> Oprah Winfrey, August 4, 1997

What Ms. Winfrey is talking about is that there are only two things that are certain in life: death and taxes. But when death occurs, you might be taxed for that! The current estate tax at the federal level starts at 40% for estates valued at more than $5.34 million. This was the tax rate as of 2014. In 2010 the estate tax was 0%.

According to *Forbes Magazine*, in 2014 Ms. Winfrey was one of only 13 female billionaires in the world, with a net worth of $2.9 billion. If she passed away with this much wealth, her beneficiaries would receive a $5.34 million exemption and then pay 40% tax on $2.8946 billion. This would be a total tax bill of over $1.1 billion!

The government's primary rationale for the mere existence of an estate tax, is that it keeps the nation's wealth becoming concentrated in only a handful of families. The government believes that by taking a large portion of the money that a person might inherit, the distribution of income will become more even over time. This notion is flawed – according to supply-siders – for the following reasons.

First, the confiscation of such a large portion of valuable estates encourages the wealthy to shelter as much of their estate from taxation as possible. Second, the estate tax – by forcing the pursuit of shelters – has pulled a great deal of the wealth of the country out of productive uses and into tax-avoidance measures. This, by one estimate, costs the country 200,000 jobs per year.[26]

A third and more philosophical argument is that if you are fortunate to earn a great deal of money over your lifetime, and you want to preserve a great deal of it for your family or alma mater or religious or charitable foundation, you should be the one to determine where your money goes, not the government. Finally, many inherited small farms and businesses have been forced to close when children receive the tax bill from their parents' estates. To supply-siders, the government is basically taking the opportunity to steal your money when you are unable to do anything about it.

One more bizarre example of what the estate tax can do to families came in 2012 when Ileana Sonnabend left her heirs a $1 billion estate made up of rare art. Her

$29.2 million in taxes for this?

beneficiaries sold some $600 million of the art to pay a $471 million estate tax bill. But one piece of art – valued by the IRS at $65 million ($29.2 million in taxes for that) created quite a head-scratching moment.

The art called "Canyon" by Robert Rauschenberg is a large-scale collage that includes photos, pieces of wood, a mirror, a pillow and a stuffed bald eagle.

When the heirs of Ms. Sonnabend got the $29.2 million bill from the IRS they attempted to sell "Canyon" but were informed by the U.S. Fish and Wildlife Service that it is illegal to sell stuffed bald eagles.

Since the government did not allow the art to be sold, one might deduce that the IRS would then say, "Oh, since it has no legal value you don't owe us any estate tax on this item."

Nope. Instead the heirs were levied an additional $11.2 million – plus interest – to the tax bill as an "undervaluation penalty".[27]

As you are reading this, significant changes may have taken place to the estate tax. In the 2016 political season, Donald Trump – and other Republicans – called for the abolition of the estate tax.

ELIMINATE THE CAPITAL GAINS TAX

The appropriate capital gains tax rate is zero. The net effect of reducing the capital gains tax, as it impacts total revenue – corporate income taxes, individual taxes, and such – could very well be a positive. I view the capital gains tax as a poor means of raising revenue… and I certainly do not think it effectively functions for any other purpose.

Alan Greenspan, January 1997, in testimony
before the Senate Budget Committee

The argument for getting rid of this tax or lowering it, is an intellectually simple one. If taxes on investments are too high, this lowers the amount of investment that will take place. One of the major reasons for the struggles of the American economy during the 1970s, was centered on the capital gains tax of 50% of all profit from savings and investments.[28] With lower investment comes slower growth in technology, job creation, and productivity. This translates into less growth in aggregate supply and lower levels of non-inflationary economic growth.[29] In America's inner cities, where rampant poverty exists and businesses are reluctant to venture due to a shortage of skilled workers, high insurance costs, and crime, lower or non-existent capital gains taxes could play a huge part in lowering the cost of serving America's poor families.

In 1963, in a speech before Congress, John F. Kennedy said, "The tax on capital gains directly affects investment decisions, the mobility and flow of risk capital from static to more dynamic situations, the ease or difficulty experienced in new ventures in obtaining capital, and thereby the strength and potential for growth in the economy."

Mr. Kennedy – just as in the case of income taxes – seemed to have a very firm grasp of the appropriateness of rewarding risk-taking from those who are needed in the supply equation.

John Maynard Keynes was not convinced. During World War II, Keynes recommended large tax increases on the profits from investments to pay for the war. Great Britain responded by imposing a 90% tax on capital income.

When another British economist, John Hicks, wrote to Keynes arguing that high capital gains taxes would erode growth, Mr. Keynes wrote back saying, "I doubt if people are often as actuarily minded as your calculation makes them."[30]

From 1940 to 1960 Great Britain's economy grew, on average, less than 1% per year. Apparently, the British people were very actuarily minded…

In 2008 Barack Obama told reporter Charles Gibson that we would not rule out raising the capital gains tax back to 28% in order to, "make sure that our tax system is fair and that we are able to finance health care for Americans who currently don't have it and that we're able to invest in infrastructure and invest in our schools."

Given the evidence from Great Britain – and from the Clinton years where capital gains revenue increased following his tax cut – Mr. Obama would have been wise to rethink his belief that school children and sick people

SUGGESTED CLASSROOM DEBATE

Paul Kagame, the President of Rwanda, has pushed his nation toward an environment that receives less foreign aid, lower taxes, and less regulation over businesses. In September 2009, the World Bank named Rwanda its "top reformer of business regulation."[31] Log on to the Heritage Foundation website that ranks nations based on economic freedom. What else does Rwanda need to do in order to increase aggregate supply?

would have been better off by taking more money from those who made astute investments.

Under the American Taxpayer Relief Act of 2012, the top capital gain tax rate was permanently increased to 20% (up from 15%) for single filers with incomes above $400,000 and married couples filing jointly with incomes exceeding $450,000. In addition, a new 3.8% Medicare surtax was imposed on net investment income, which includes capital gains. This means that for higher-income taxpayers the capital gains tax rate was 23.8% in 2014 – a 58% increase from 2012 tax rates.

Hillary Clinton – who apparently did not pay attention to the success of her husband's reduction in capital gains taxes – pushed for an increase in this tax to 47.4% on investments held less than two years. She also called for several different brackets of capital gains tax rates with the lowest equaling 27.8% on investments held more than six years.[32]

Not to be outdone, Bernie Sanders wanted a capital gains tax rate of 54.2% in high-income Americans.[33]

On the other hand, President Trump advocated eliminating the capital gains tax on Americans at the lower rungs of the income ladder while setting a maximum of 20% on the richest Americans.

ELIMINATE TAXES ON SAVINGS

Another feature of supply-side policies is the belief that increased savings leads to the funds that are necessary for increased investment. To this end, President Clinton received high marks from supply-side economists for going along with increased tax deductions for Individual Retirement Accounts, and the creation of the Roth IRA. As taxes on this activity fell, not only did more Americans invest in their future, but also more businesses had access to the funds necessary for capital improvement.

PROMOTE IMMIGRATION

This part of the equation may come as a surprise to many of you, but the economic evidence is pretty dramatic that immigration, both currently and historically, is of tremendous net value to the United States.[34] Even when you consider the fact that some immigrants end up using our social welfare system and contribute to school overcrowding, crime, and the loss of some American jobs,[35] there is also a great deal of evidence that immigrants are a boon to our economy.

Many studies find that immigrants actually lead to more jobs available in America, not less.[36] One researcher found that, "Immigrants expand total output and the demand for labor, offsetting the negative effects that a greater labor supply might have. Immigrants tend to be highly productive and promote capital formation through high savings rates."[37]

Other studies have found that, despite complaints made by anti-immigrant forces, immigration has created more total revenue than it has cost our country.[38]

How do they keep your grocery bill down?

© mikeledray/Shutterstock.com

Immigrants also have lower crime rates than native-born Americans.[39] Immigrants, through very high levels of savings, human capital, and entrepreneurial spirit, also promote an increase in the GDP through increases in consumption of homes and investment in businesses from Silicon Valley to Harlem.[40]

From 1995-2005, 52.4% of the new high-tech jobs created in California's Silicon Valley were from immigrant business owners. Many critics of America's immigration policies point out that we allow far too few scientists and engineers to enter the country and fill shortages in those areas. As a result, American technological progress is slower than it could be, while bright people from around the planet now stay home and create competing businesses in other nations.[41]

Recent research on the impact of skilled immigrants has found that from 1990-2010 foreign scientists and engineers brought into the U.S. under the H-1B visa program contributed 10-20% of the yearly productivity growth in the U.S. This allowed the GDP per capita to be 4% higher than it would have been without them – an aggregate boost to the economy of $615 billion.[42]

It has also been estimated that by the year 2020 1.5 million jobs will go unfilled in the United States because of the ongoing shortage of skilled workers. This shortage was projected in part because in 2013 the government planned to raise the cost of an H-1B visa application from $2,000 to between $4,000 and $10,000 depending on the number of applications a business firm applied for.[43]

Moreover, even when immigrants – legal and illegal – send money back to their homelands, the U.S. economy benefits from this. According to the World Bank, these "remittances" average about $100 billion per year.[44] Not only did this help keep illegal immigration from growing even more, but many of the people who received the money used it to buy American products and even start businesses that sold goods to American consumers.[45]

While the influx of immigrants does cause an expansion in the labor supply and some downward pressure on wages – particularly for American high school dropouts – this was also somewhat beneficial to the economy. Downward pressure on wages translates into more overall jobs (as the quantity of labor demanded increases) and lower input costs of production. As input costs fall, the price of everything from cell phones to computers begins

to decline. In the long run, the lower prices help offset the impact on wages.[46]

Which brings us to President Trump. As all of you are aware, when he took office in 2017 he immediately signed an executive order to begin the process of building a wall between the United States and Mexico. He also called for the mass deportation of the 11.3 million immigrants who were in the United States illegally.

The American Action Forum – a free-market think tank led by economist Doug Holtz-Eakin – estimated that these plans would increase federal spending by $400 billion and would reduce the GDP by nearly $1 trillion.[47] In 2016, eight million undocumented immigrants were employed in the United States. Removing them would reduce the labor force by 6.4% and drag the GDP down by 5.7% - a figure near the same amount we saw during the 2008 recession.

It is important to be reminded of the difference between normative and positive analysis (see chapter one).

Millions of Trump supporters argued that we "should" build a wall and throw people out of the country in order to preserve jobs, reduce crime and "make America great again."

Yet the evidence – compiled by professional economists – clearly shows that in every measurable category, the United States has always derived far greater benefits from all forms of immigration than we have incurred costs. Therefore, it does not matter how emotional the pleas are to build walls and deport. The pleas do not reflect sound economic policy.

PROMOTE FREE TRADE

Supply-side economists argue that free trade among nations leads to more benefits than costs for those nations. Expanding markets, increasing competition and choice, increasing the quality of products, promoting job creation, and taking advantage of the natural comparative advantages nations possess accomplish this.

In a nutshell, as we will see in the last chapter, free trade leads to more wealth and prosperity for the nations that engage in it, and more economic freedom for the citizens of those nations.[48]

CONCEPT CHECK

Would a Supply-Side economist favor school choice? Why, or why not? What would be the impact on aggregate supply from greater competition in K-12 education?

PROMOTE "SOUND MONEY"

When the U.S. economy was going through the worst years since the Great Depression, Federal Reserve Bank Chairman, Paul Volcker approached Ronald Reagan with the grim news that the money supply would have to contract sharply and interest rates would have to rise dramatically, in order to once and for all rid the country of runaway inflation.

President Reagan offered his full support of Volcker's policy recommendations even though the prime interest rate – the rate banks charge Microsoft, General Motors, and other major borrowers – rose to 21.5%! Stagflation turned into a severe recession with falling prices through-out the economy and Reagan's popularity plummeted.

It was not until November of 1982, that the combi-nation of contractionary monetary policy and supply-side tax policies began to create non-inflationary economic growth that persisted for more than two decades.

The idea of "sound money" therefore, can be best described as monetary policy that does not allow the economy to overheat from too much demand, while not keeping rates so high that the economy perpetually strug-gles. For many supply-side economists, the post-Volcker years saw too much "easy money," which contributed to the artificially inflated housing market and the correction that commenced in 2008.

DON'T OVER-REGULATE THE ECONOMY

As we saw in chapter three of the text, this could be called "The Era of Regulation" for the American economy. Throughout our 50 states and in Washington, D.C., work-ers in industries like cat grooming, tree trimming, tattoos, flower arranging, and hair shampooing are joining the thousands of other occupations that must hold a license and comply with a dizzying array of paperwork in order to simply serve their fellow human being, that adds $116 billion per year to the cost of services.[49]

Supply-side economists do not believe that businesses should be allowed to operate with no regulations. After all, given the nature of human beings, some businesses would, in the absence of law, be tempted to cheat employees, customers and other businesses. Adam Smith and every free-market economist since him understand the case for *rational* applications of the rule of law to profit-seekers.

The problem stems from regulations that defy cost-benefit analysis. Sometimes the law is used to completely take over businesses and industries in order to regulate the supply of a good or service in the way government believes will serve the greater good.

During the Great Depression, Franklin Roosevelt effectively nationalized the supply of electricity in order to have government provide power to areas that previ-ously did not have access to it. Even though private suppliers were in the process of running lines to rural residents all over the United States, FDR made it a crime – and had arrested – business owners who were trying to supply electricity during this time. The result was that it took even longer for power to reach the homes that the private sector was on the verge of serving.[50] FDR also nationalized the railroads and the coal industry during his tenure.

During the Korean War, the government imposed controls of raw materials, production, shipping, credit, wages, and prices. When the wage-price controls created a collective-bargaining impasse in the steel industry, threaten-ing a nationwide strike, President Harry S. Truman ordered the Secretary of Commerce on April 8, 1952, to seize and operate most of the country's steel mills for the ostensible purpose of maintaining production of critical munitions.[51]

In Great Britain, government forced suppliers of steel, railroad services and coal to sell their businesses to the government. By 1974, every one of these industries was in

© wantando/Shutterstock.com

Margaret Thatcher

decline and struggling under the weight of unproductive and heavily subsidized management systems.[52] As a consequence, Britain became one of the poorest nations in all of Europe within 30 years of the end of World War II.[53]

If the word, *nationalize*, sounds familiar to you, it should. In 2008 the U.S. government effectively nationalized both the investment bank and commercial banking industries. This took place as the government began bailing out large lending institutions. Part of the $700 billion bailout included $250 billion for large commercial banks in the form of government purchases of bank stock.[54] The Bush Administration forced banks to agree to use the money to help homeowners and continue lending as a part of the guarantee that taxpayer dollars would shore up these institutions.[55]

Supply-side economists worry a great deal about the impact of such nationalization efforts. The argument against government-run industries or government supported industries is straightforward.

The more involved government becomes in the day-to-day operations of previously privatized industries, the more government tends to impose layers of rules, standards, compliance measures, paperwork, legal reviews and bureaucratic manipulation of supply decisions. Historically, this effect leads to a dramatic slowdown in risk-taking, innovation and new product development. Thus, the long-run effect of nationalization or quasi-nationalization is stagnant growth of aggregate supply at best, or a reduction in aggregate supply in the worse case scenario.[56]

CRITICISMS OF SUPPLY-SIDE ECONOMICS

> Cutting taxes doesn't benefit the middle class, it doesn't create jobs or growth, and it doesn't give Americans the country they want.[57]
>
> Paul Krugman

Despite the overwhelming evidence that less taxation and regulation leads to expanded economic opportunities, critics of supply-side economics argue that during the 1980s and 1990s, two major problems emerged as a direct consequence of less taxation and regulation.

CRITICISM #1: THE RICH GOT RICHER WHILE THE POOR GOT POORER

While it is true that during the last two decades of the twentieth century, "the rich" gained at a faster rate than other income groups, there are at least three major flaws in this logic. First, the tax cuts of the 1980s removed millions

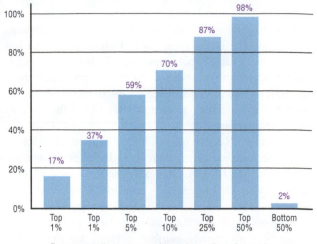

Percentage Shares of Income Tax Paid

Represents all tax returns with positive adjusted gross income

of poor people from the tax rolls altogether. By 2005 the income tax cuts had led to 58 million Americans paying no income taxes at all.[58] What happened during this time is that the rich simply got richer *at a faster rate* than every other group.

This is to be expected when taxes are cut by an equal percentage. When Mr. Reagan cut taxes by 30% across all tax brackets, which group was mathematically in a better position to gain income at a faster rate? Thirty percent off $1 million is more than 30% off $30,000 in annual income. In 2012, according to the latest IRS income-tax data, the top 1% of American taxpayers earned 20% of all income and paid 36% of all taxes. The top 5% (those earning roughly $160,000 or more) earned 36% of all income and paid 58% of all income taxes.[59] As the accompanying table illustrates, even when we go back to the time of the Great Recession we see that rich people pay a disproportionate share of all income taxes. Notice that the top one-tenth of 1% of all taxpayers paid a whopping 17% of the more than $2 trillion collected in taxes in 2009 while the bottom half of the country (a large portion of middle-income and all lower-income Americans) paid only 2% of the cost of running the federal government.

It is also true that the share of income taxes paid by the bottom half of income-earners has fallen over the past several years.[60] In 1979 the bottom 20% of workers paid 2.1% of all income taxes. By 2012 it was .3%. For middle-class Americans the share paid in income taxes has fallen from 13.6% to 9.4% over the past three decades. If you are measuring fairness by the extent to which we collect from the more successful citizens of our country, then you should be dancing in the streets over the fact that "the rich" are paying their fair share.

The third point about the castigation of the rich is the fact that if we look at who it is that creates most of the businesses and new inventions in a free-market economy we find that it is rich folks. If you cut the taxes of an economics professor by 10%, perhaps he or she will buy a new car or big-screen television. If you cut Mark Zuckerberg's taxes by 10%, because he is self-interested like the rest of us, he will want to use that money to make more money. As a result of his self-interest, the entire economy ends up growing. Maybe not every person, but every segment of society ends up better off than when we practice "Robin Hood" economics.

CRITICISM #2: THE TAX CUTS CAUSED HUGE DEFICITS

Once again, the critics miss the mark. It is true that the national debt increased by trillions of dollars during the 1980s. The source of the national debt was not falling tax revenue. Tax collections increased throughout the 1980s. The source of the spiraling national debt was dramatic increases in government spending during this time.

From 1981 to 1989, tax revenue increased from $599.3 billion to $990.7 billion. However, government spending increased during this same time from $678.2 billion to $1.143 trillion. Much of the increase in government spending came from expanded social welfare spending that Reagan was unsuccessful at cutting. Another prominent source of the increase in federal outlays was the enormous military buildup that occurred.

It would be irresponsible to repeat the oft-stated argument that swollen Pentagon budgets created our national debt. Upon further reflection we can see that the increase in military spending helped bankrupt the Soviet Union. The Soviets were unable to keep up with Reagan's acceleration of defense spending, and in 1991 the entire country collapsed, along with the rest of the Communist Bloc in Eastern Europe.

With the Cold War won, the United States has been able to significantly reduce military spending throughout the 1990s, which helped Bill Clinton preside over the first budget surpluses since 1969. Moreover, the end of the Cold War has propelled the former Soviet Union and other nations that used to be under the tyrannical rule of Moscow headlong into the experiment tax cutting.

As a matter of fact, the Russians seemed to have learned a great deal from Ronald Reagan and Art Laffer.[61] As the editors of *The Wall Street Journal* recently noted:

The Russian reforms began in earnest at the start of 2001, when Mr. Putin introduced a 13% flat tax on individual income, replacing a convoluted system that had a marginal rate of 30%.

Then came a cut in the tax on corporate profits by nearly one-third to 24%, the closing of a large number of tax loopholes for companies, and the simplification and reduction in social security levies. Tax revenues immediately began heading north, as citizens decided it was easier to pay taxes than go to the trouble of avoiding them.

What Mr. Putin does not seem to have figured out is that if a nation cuts taxes and creates greater economic incentives while at the same time it buys into the archaic economic theory that taking over the land of other nations leads to wealth, in the long run it exposes itself to economic sanctions, declining demand for its goods and services and a poorer economy.

It just is not smart policy to reward risk-taking with the tax code while damaging your economy with "zero-sum" actions that have never produced economic growth.

CRITICISM #3: ECONOMIC GROWTH WAS STIMULATED MORE BY AGGREGATE DEMAND THAN AGGREGATE SUPPLY

Some Keynesian economists argued that the Reagan tax cuts did more to stimulate aggregate demand than aggregate supply. There is a pretty simple test to see if this is true. If aggregate demand increased more than aggregate supply, the rate of inflation would have risen during the 1980s. Going back to the data you observed earlier, it is clear that as the GDP increased, inflation rates fell during this time.

Photo courtesy Jack Chambless

SUGGESTED CLASSROOM DEBATE

During the next Presidential debates, there will be one or more candidates who will advocate raising taxes in order to help pay for programs that aid the poor. Should the marginal utility of money theory – or the U.S. Constitution win out in this debate? Why or why not?

© MikLav/Shutterstock.com

The 1980s were called "the decade of greed" by many people because of the ostentatious spending that took place. While consumer demand did increase sharply during this time, the long-run effect of lower taxes did much more to stimulate technology, job creation, and productivity than it did to stimulate conspicuous consumption.

DO RICH PEOPLE HAVE A LOWER MARGINAL UTILITY OF MONEY?

One of the more interesting criticisms of supply-side, or trickle-down, economics is the belief that rich people should not pay lower taxes because they simply do not need the money as much as poorer people do.

In 2011, Dilbert creator (and former economics major), Scott Adams took the pages of *The Wall Street Journal* arguing that his fellow rich Americans are rich enough to afford higher taxes. He claimed that he – and other rich people – would not even mind paying more, in exchange for things like being allowed to drive in car pool lanes even when he is alone, being sent "Thank you"

notes from poor people, or giving rich people two votes in elections for every one vote a non-rich person gets.[62]

Economists often talk about *utility* as a measure of the satisfaction people get from each additional unit of some activity or outcome. For example, if you are very thirsty, the first glass of ice water you consume will carry a very high *marginal utility*, or usefulness, to you. However, as you consume the second and third glass of water, while there may be some level of utility from those glasses, the *marginal utility* will be lower with each sip.

When we think of tax policy we can see the points made by critics of tax relief. If someone who makes $1 million per year gets an extra $1 from a tax cut, how much will that $1 mean to the rich person? What will be the marginal utility of that extra dollar?

On the other hand, critics contend, if instead of letting the rich person keep the extra dollar of earnings, we could take that dollar and distribute it to people who are in the lower income brackets. That extra $1 would mean more to a person making $10,000 than it will for the rich person, so tax cuts for rich people end up creating a lower total utility for society.

TAX POLICY FOR 2017 AND BEYOND...

Jobs are created when the economy grows; the economy grows when Americans have more money to spend and invest; and the best, fairest way to make sure Americans have the money, is not to tax it away in the first place.

President Bush during his January 28, 2003,
State of the Union Address

In 2001, many Americans received checks (which were basically advances on their 2001 tax obligations) as high as $600 as part of a plan to jump-start the sluggish economy. These rebate checks, as it turned out, had no significant impact on the economy. The reason is simple. It is called the "permanent-income hypothesis."

➢ **The permanent-income hypothesis is the proposition that people make decisions on spending, saving, and investment based on expectations of long-run, permanent changes to their income, rather than short-term fluctuations in income.**

One survey found that only 18.8% of refund recipients planned to spend the money sent to them by the government. Around a third (33.6%) of respondents said they planned to save the money, and 47.6% planned to pay down their debt.[63] Naturally, paying down debt can be a good thing, but when the economy is in a recession, the government needs you to buy a new car or go out to dinner more often, not pay down your VISA bills.

In 2003, President Bush gave his State of the Union address that called for a $726 billion tax cut. The Democrats in the audience sat totally silent. This is a bit curious. Did silence mean that the Democrats believed that the economy grows when Americans have less money and that the fairest way for all Americans to have less money, is to tax it away in the first place?

By some estimates, the Bush tax cut promoted the creation of 5.3 million new jobs, productivity gains, and hundreds of billions of dollars in added tax revenue from 2003-2006;[64] but the president and others recognized that because the tax cuts were not perceived as permanent by the average citizen, the impact on aggregate supply and aggregate demand was smaller than desired.[65]

President Obama extended the Bush tax cuts for 2011 and 2012. But late in 2012 he signed legislation that increased taxes on income and investments. By 2014 the income tax code resembled the one that the country had in the early years of Bill Clinton's presidency.

Things seemed to be moving back towards the Kennedy and Reagan mindset in 2017.

Donald Trump argued for a reduction in the number of tax brackets to three (12, 25 and 33%) and lower tax rates than the U.S. had seen since Ronald Reagan.

However, many economists were concerned about two possible negative effects of this proposal. First, would the tax cut be so large as to push the overall tax rate *to the left of the peak of the Laffer Curve*? If this occurs, total revenue would decline.

Falling revenue is not necessarily damaging to the economy if (and it is a big if) the federal government simultaneously reduces spending. However, if government spending rises – and Trump showed every inclination in this direction – then falling revenue, combined with more spending would lead to larger budget deficits.

DO DEFICITS REALLY MATTER?

In November of 2002, Alan Greenspan, in speaking about calls to repeal the 2001 Bush tax cut said, "It would probably be unwise to unwind the long-term tax cut, because it is already built into the system."[66]

This was seemingly good news for Mr. Bush as he unveiled his plans to accelerate the long-term tax cut. Yet,

in the spring of 2003, Mr. Greenspan came out against accelerating the tax cut for fear that the more significant drop in tax rates would push up the deficit and create the crowding-out effect discussed in the last chapter.

While this setback did not stop Mr. Bush from supporting Alan Greenspan for another term, it must have made Mr. Bush and his supply-side economists pretty upset. After all, Mr. Greenspan did not say that he feared deficits as a result of falling tax revenue or from rising revenue that Congress would blow through. He just basically said that tax cuts equal deficits, and deficits are bad.

This brings us to our final topic: Do deficits really harm the economy as some economists suggest? Recall that the crowding-out theory suggests that rising levels of government borrowing pushes the private sector out of the market for credit and causes interest rates to rise to damaging high levels.[67]

There is a competing theory known as Ricardian Equivalence that argues that in the long run, deficits don't really matter that much at all.

> ➤ **Ricardian Equivalence is the theory that rational human beings, seeing rising deficits, will reach the conclusion that deficits will have to be paid for with higher taxes. As a result, these individuals increase their level of saving to be prepared for inevitable tax increases. In the long run, greater savings leads to an increase in the money supply, downward pressure on interest rates, and a counterbalancing effect on the crowding-out effect.**

During the Clinton years, the government ran surpluses for the first time since 1969, and interest rates rose. After Mr. Clinton left office the federal deficit began to rise once again but interest rates actually decreased.

Of course, by 2008-2016, the deficits of the early Bush years seemed like pocket change compared to the trillion-dollar plus shortfalls observed in the first five years of the Obama Administration. Yet, for much of that time period as well, home mortgage interest rates and other borrowing costs fell.

For economists there is general agreement that world economic history shows that in the long run, government deficits do indeed matter. From the fall of the Roman Empire through modern times, governments that perpetually print and borrow money ultimately cause the value of the currency in use to fall and inflation rates to rise. In the short run there may not be much crowding-out pressure and the defenders of Ricardian Equivalence would have a reasonable answer for why. However, in the long-run we do see more evidence that human beings do not have perfect foresight and therefore government debt tends not to be offset by rational savers.

Therefore, when Steve Bannon – President Trump's chief advisor – called for huge increases in government spending and promised that it would be "as exciting at the 1930s"[68] many economists wondered if Mr. Bannon was aware that in the 1930s government spending exploded, deficits increased the Great Depression went on and on and on....

ENDNOTES

1 See "Crisis Stirs Critics of Free Markets" by Jason Dean, Marcus Walker and Evan Ramstad, *The Wall Street Journal*, September 25, 2008, pg. A3.

2 See "Taxes are a Real Drag" by Burton G. Malkiel, *The Wall Street Journal*, March 6, 2001.

3 For a more recent look at Laffer's work, see "The Tax Threat to Prosperity" by Arthur Laffer, *The Wall Street Journal*, January 25, 2008; and "New Evidence on Taxes and Income" by Arthur Laffer and Stephen Moore, *The Wall Street Journal*, September 15, 2008, pg. A23.

4 See *The Seven Fat Years* by Robert L. Bartley, Free Press, 1995.

5 See "Supply side wasn't 'voodoo' after all" by Stephen Moore, *The Orlando Sentinel*, October 5, 1998; "The Road to Dow 10,000" by Lawrence Kudlow, *The Wall Street Journal*, March 16, 1999; "The Rest of Him," *The Wall Street Journal*, November 10, 1994; "How Most Economists Missed the Boat" by Michael Mandel, *Business Week*, November 15, 1999; "How Clinton and Dole teamed up with supply-siders" by Louis Uchitelle, *The Orlando Sentinel*, September 8, 1996.

6 See "Obamanomics Meets Incentives" by Robert J. Barro, *The Wall Street Journal*, September 14, 2010.

7 See "Tax Cuts vs. Government Revenue" at www.mackinac.org/article.asp?ID=676.

8 See "A marginal error," *The Economist*, April 2, 1992, p. 68.

9 See "Dynamic Scoring," *The Wall Street Journal*, January 29, 2008; "Their Income Up, U.S. Rich Yield a Tax Windfall" by Deborah Soloman, *The Wall Street Journal*, May 20-21, 2006; and "McCain and Taxes," *The Wall Street Journal*, April 25, 2008.

10 See "The JFK Stimulus Plan" by Ernest S. Christian and Gary A. Robbins, *The Wall Street Journal*, January 12-13, 2008.

11 See "Gaining Capital," *The Wall Street Journal*, January 24, 2005.

12 See "Democrats for Tax Cuts," *The Wall Street Journal*, July 5, 2006.

13 See "The Left's Inequality Obsession" by Arthur C. Brooks, *The Wall Street Journal*, July 19, 2007, pg. A15.

14 See "God, Patriotism and Taxes," *The Wall Street Journal*, September 22, 2008.

15 "New Evidence on Taxes and Income" by Arthur Laffer and Stephen Moore, *The Wall Street Journal*, September 15, 2008, pg. A23.

16 See "Tax Cuts vs. 'Stimulus': The Evidence Is In" by Alberto Alesina, *The Wall Street Journal*, September 15, 2010.

17 See "You Can't Soak the Rich" by David Ranson, *The Wall Street Journal*, May 20, 2008.

18 See "Hillary and Say's Law," *The Wall Street Journal*, January 23, 2008.

19 See "Bring jobs to America – lower corporate tax" by David Moreland, *The Orlando Sentinel*, February 12, 2011.

20 See "There's No Escaping Hauser's Law" by W. Kurt Hauser, *The Wall Street Journal*, November 26, 2010; and "The Revenue Limits of Tax and Spend" by David Ranson, *The Wall Street Journal*, May 17, 2010.

21 See "The Coolidge Lesson on Taxes and Spending" by Amity Shlaes, *The Wall Street Journal*, February 19, 2013.

22 See "A Supply-Side World," *The Wall Street Journal*, January 7, 2008; "The Stockholm Curve," *The Wall Street Journal*, September 29, 2008; "Those April Blues" by Stephen Moore, *The Wall Street Journal*, April 13, 2007; and "The Supply-Side Solution" by Stephen Moore, *The Wall Street Journal*, November 9, 2007.

23 See "The Smarts of the Irish" by Kyle Wingfield, *The Wall Street Journal*, May 24, 2007; "Ireland Uses Incentives to Help Start-Ups Flourish" by James Flanigan, *The New York Times*; "We're Number One, Alas," *The Wall Street Journal*, July 13, 2007; and The Foundation for Economic Education.

24 See "The Coming Tax Bomb" by John F. Cogan and R. Glenn Hubbard, *The Wall Street Journal*, April 8, 2008, pg. A21; and "The Coming Tax Tsunami" by Pamela Villarreal and D. Sean Shurtleff, *Budget & Tax News*, February 2008, pg. 16.

25 At the time Ms. Winfrey made this comment, the estate tax rate was 55%. See "Death's Taxes," *The Wall Street Journal*, July 28, 1999, p. A22.

26 See "The True Cost of Dying" by William Beach, *The Wall Street Journal*, July 28, 1999, p. A22.

27 See "The Illegal Eagle and a Badly Grasping IRS" by Eric Gibson, *The Wall Street Journal*, December 2, 2012.

28 See "How We Beat the '70s" by Mark Bloomfield, *The Wall Street Journal*, March 13, 2008.

29 See "The Heart of the Economy" by John W. Snow, *The Wall Street Journal*, February 15, 2006.

30 See "The Bush Tax Cuts Never Went Far Enough" by Thomas F. Cooley and Lee E. Ohanian, *The Wall Street Journal*, December 8, 2010, p. A23.

31 See "A Supply-Sider in East Africa" by Anne Jolis, *The Wall Street Journal*, April 24-25, 2010.

32 See https://taxfoundation.org/details-and-analysis-hillary-clinton-s-tax-proposals/.

33 See https://taxfoundation.org/details-and-analysis-senator-bernie-sanders-s-tax-plan/.

34 Approximately 80% of immigrant earnings stay in the United States. See "What it Means for Your Wallet," *Time*, April 10, 2006, p.43.

35 See "At what price the open door?" by David LaGesse, *The Orlando Sentinel*, June 26, 1994.

36 See "Good Policies Can Save the Economy" by Lee E. Ohanian, *The Wall Street Journal*, October 8, 2008, pg. A17.

37 See "Immigration Doesn't Displace Natives" by Richard Vedder, *The Wall Street Journal*, March 28, 1994.

38 See "Immigration benefits U.S., study says," *The Orlando Sentinel*, May 18, 1997, p. A-6; and "Demagoging the Immigration Issue" by Albert R. Hunt, *The Wall Street Journal*, July 7, 1994, p. A13.

39 See "Immigrant-Bashing's Latest Falsehood" by John J. Miller, *The Wall Street Journal*, March 8, 1994.

40 See "Immigrants Lead a Recovery" by Joel Kotkin, *The Wall Street Journal*, April 22, 1994.

41 See "We Need an Einstein Immigration Policy" by Darrell M. West, *The Wall Street Journal*, July 16, 2010.

42 See "The Economic Windfall of Immigration Reform" by Giovanni Peri, *The Wall Street Journal*, February 13, 2013 page A15.

43 See "Immigration Reform and the Skills Gap" by Rosario Marin, *The Wall Street Journal*, June 7, 2013 page A15.

44 See http://www.nytimes.com/2013/04/28/us/politics/immigrants-find-it-cheaper-to-send-money-home.html?pagewanted=all&_r=0.

45 See "Cash sent home lets ideas boom" by Richard Boudreaux, *The Los Angeles Times*, April 16, 2006.

46 See "For a Few Dollars Less" by George J. Borjas, *The Wall Street Journal*, April 18, 2006.

47 See "The Costs of Mass Deportation" *The Wall Street Journal*, March 19-20, 2016.

48 See "The Trade and Tax Doomsday Clocks" by Donald L. Luskin, *The Wall Street Journal*, October 4, 2010, p. A 25.

49 For more on regulations, see "A License to Shampoo: Jobs Needing State Approval Rise" by Stephanie Simon, *The Wall Street Journal*, February 7, 2011.

50 See *The Forgotten Man: A New History of The Great Depression* by Amity Shlaes, Harper Collins, New York 2007.

51 See "Truman's Attempt to Seize the Steel Industry" by Robert Higgs, *The Freeman*, March 1, 2004.

52 See *The Commanding Heights* by Daniel Yergin and Joseph Stanislaw, Simon & Schuster, 1998, pp. 25-26.

53 See "The Living Was Not Easy" by William Anthony Hay, *The Wall Street Journal*, May 19, 2008, pg. A13; and *Austerity Britain* by David Kynaston, Walker, 2008.

54 See "U.S. to Buy Stakes in Nation's Largest Banks" by Deborah Soloman, Damian Paletta, Jon Hilsenrath and Aaron Lucchetti, *The Wall Street Journal*, October 14, 2008.

55 See "Devil is in Bailout's Details" by Deborah Soloman and David Enrich, *The Wall Street Journal*, October 15, 2008; and "Push for Tough Restrictions Gains Ground in Bailout Talks" by Greg Hitt, Deborah Soloman and Damian Paletta, *The Wall Street Journal*, September 25, 2008.

56 See "We're Not Headed for a Depression" by Gary S. Becker, *The Wall Street Journal*, October 7, 2008, pg. A27.

57 See "The Tax-Cut Con" by Paul Krugman, *The New York Times Magazine*, September 14, 2003.

58 Source: *Budget & Tax News* (The Heartland Institute) July 2004.

59 See "Targeting the Wealthy Kills Jobs" by T.J. Rodgers, *The Wall Street Journal,* August 19, 2013 page A17.

60 See "The Latest News on Tax Fairness" by Ari Fleischer, *The Wall Street Journal,* July 23, 2012 page A13.

61 So has Iraq. In September of 2003, the new Finance Minister for Iraq, Kamel al-Gailani, implemented a flat income tax of 15% for all Iraqis – which is a large drop from the 46% rate charged by Saddam Hussein. See "Baghdad's Laffer Curve," *The Wall Street Journal,* September 22, 2003.

62 See "How to Tax the Rich" by Scott Adams, *The Wall Street Journal*, January 29-30, 2011.

63 See the October 17, 2001, Tax Report of *The Wall Street Journal*.

64 See "Help (Very Much) Wanted," *The Wall Street Journal*, April 10,2006; "Nation's Productivity jumps," *The Orlando Sentinel*, December 7, 2005; and "Revenues Rising," *The Wall Street Journal*, May 23, 2005.

65 See "Bush Pushes for Permanent Tax Cuts" by William W. Beach, *Budget & Tax News* (The Heartland Institute), March 2004; and "Tax Cuts Aren't Forever: Four Strategies to Lower your Tab in the Years Ahead" by Jonathan Clements, *The Wall Street Journal*, April 14, 2004.

66 See "Fed Chief Says He Backs Bush on the Tax Cut" by Edmund L. Andrews, *The New York Times*, November 14, 2002.

67 Economists at the Federal Reserve Bank have estimated that for every $100 billion increase in the deficit, interest rates increase by 0.5 to 0.6%. The Bush economic advisors have "found" that every $100 billion increase in the deficit leads to a 0.015 increase in interest rates. See "Fed Economists Link Deficits to Interest Rates," *The Wall Street Journal*, April 25, 2003.

68 See https://www.washingtonpost.com/news/the-fix/wp/2016/11/18/this-quote-from-donald-trumps-top-strategist-will-frighten-republican-deficit-hawks/?utm_term=.80c8a0695486.

CHAPTER REVIEW

1. What is the economic basis for Supply-Side economics? Where does Say's Law fit into this concept?

2. What is the Laffer Curve? Does this curve suggest that all tax cuts are good and all tax hikes are bad? Why, or why not?

3. What did John F. Kennedy and Ronald Reagan do with respect to taxation? What was the result?

4. List and fully explain four other policies recommended by Supply-Side economists.

5. What is Ricardian Equivalence? Does the experience in post-World War I Germany support this theory? Why, or why not?

Chapter Fourteen

The ECONOMICS *of* INTERNATIONAL TRADE

Photo courtesy Jack Chambless

*I*f a foreign country can supply us with a commodity cheaper than we ourselves can make it, better buy it of them with some part of the produce of our own industry, employed in a way in which we have some advantage.

ADAM SMITH

WHAT IS ALL THE FUSS ABOUT?

> "NAFTA is the worst trade deal maybe ever signed anywhere, but certainly ever signed in this country."
>
> Donald Trump

Economists joke about how we don't agree on much. In fact, even when two economists are in agreement about some issue, one of them is bound to pretend to disagree just so a good argument can break out.

That is why it is so nice that there is at least one topic where you will get near-universal agreement among professionals in the dismal science. The agreement surrounds our view of the importance of international trade in furthering the progress and happiness of mankind.

You might find yourself wondering how there can be a near-consensus among economists that trade is a wonderful thing when every time there is an international trade conference rioters and protesters take to the streets claiming that trade is so horrible that it must be dramatically reduced in order to save workers and the planet. As it turns out, there is a good reason why the rioters feel this way.

When we consider the fact that an increasing number of Democrats and

Rising Anxiety

Q: Do you think free-trade agreements have helped or hurt the U.S.?

Source: WSJ/NBC News poll. Margin of error in Sept. 2010 poll is ±3.1 percentage points.

The Wall Street Journal
by Dow Jones & Co. Copyright © 2010. Reproduced with permission of Dow Jones & Company, Inc. in the format Textbook via Copyright Clearance Center.

Republicans (including Donald Trump) think that international trade is doing more harm to the U.S. than good,[1] well, somewhere the economics community has dropped the educational ball…

THE PRINCIPLE OF COMPARATIVE ADVANTAGE

Virtually every year I take my family on a camping vacation somewhere in North America. While we are away, I don't think about my job much, but I do apply at least one part of my profession to our trips in order to assure peace and harmony. That is the concept of comparative advantage.

> ➤ **The principle of comparative advantage states that a person, or business or nation can gain production and consumption possibilities by specializing in the production of goods and services that can be produced at a lower opportunity cost than the next best competitor can.**

How does this apply to my camping trips, or to your life, or to the trade policies of the United States? Here's how…

I absolutely hate putting up a tent. I made a 'D' in high school geometry, so I am not even sure I could manage to understand how all of the tent poles are supposed to cross in order to keep the tent from collapsing. Mrs. Chambless, on the other hand, is a geometric genius.

However, she does not really enjoy gathering firewood, cleaning fish, or cooking outdoors. I love to cut up dead trees, filet fish, and cook over a fire. Bingo!

Since she has a *comparative advantage* in putting up tents and I have a comparative advantage with axes and fire, we each specialize in what we are best at. This does not mean that if push came to shove I could not put up a tent. It also does not mean that she doesn't know how to cook or burn wood. If that were the case we would both have an *absolute advantage* over one another.

Photos courtesy Jack Chambless

What comparative advantage means is that while each of us could do everything that needs to be done, neither of us should focus on what the other is best at. This *trade* we have with one another leads to an optimum condition for both, without incurring the high opportunity cost of attempting something we are not really best suited for.

Oregon is one of the leading hops-producing states in the U.S. Hops is the plant used to give beer a spicy flavor. Louisiana is one of the largest oil-producing states in America.

What if residents of Oregon decided to boycott oil from Louisiana, and at the same time, brewers in Louisiana began refusing to buy hops from Oregon? Furthermore, suppose Oregon decided to become self-sufficient in oil production, while down on the bayou, an attempt was made to grow hops.

What would it take for each state to become self-sufficient? First, it would require that each state *ignore the concept of opportunity cost*. If Louisiana shifted into high gear on hops production, more and more of the state's resources would have to be allocated to growing hops.

The same is true for Oregon. Imagine all of the hops farms that would have to be destroyed as the state cleared the land to make room for petroleum exploration and drilling. More resources devoted to hops growing in Louisiana and oil exploration in Oregon would mean less resources in each state to produce the most efficiently supplied product.

Residents of Oregon would be very upset to read geological reports indicating that there is little, if any, oil in Oregon. People in Louisiana – where the temperatures are not conducive to producing hops – would be equally upset to find out that a beer shortage is imminent because the state can't produce enough – or any – hops.

In the long run, each state will come to realize that, through trade, Oregon will realize a steady flow of high-quality oil from Louisiana while residents of Louisiana will be able to enjoy what might be America's finest hops. This is in addition to the fact that Louisiana and Oregon will enjoy a net increase in total jobs available. This takes place because Louisiana will produce more oil than it needs and simply sell off the excess to states like Oregon, while Oregon will do the same with the hops. Trade, therefore, is a positive-sum game – not the zero-sum game that enriches one party at the expense of another.

TRADE BETWEEN NATIONS

As you might expect what is good economics for two people, or two states, is also good economics for two countries.

Since the beginning of human beings, trade has been a natural function of any economy. This is true at the individual level, state to state, and at the international level as well. For this reason, over the past several centuries people have looked outward to meet their wants and needs when their own economy lacked the resources to do so.[2] As far back as the time when people got around on foot, horseback, or small canoes, trading between tribes, villages, and nations has been viewed as the best way to avoid pervasive scarcity.

Today, most people are aware of the fact that it makes sense for Saudi Arabia to export oil and import computers. Honduras has no business trying to catch the United States in jet aircraft production, so Honduras buys jets from us and we buy bananas from Honduras. What is unclear to many students is why, for example, the United States would ever import cars from Japan when we have shown that we can effectively produce them here.

This question is not limited to cars. The mere mention of washers and dryers, televisions, VCRs, DVDs, stereo players, steel, bulldozers, clothing and assorted agricultural products will create an uproar among Americans who recall a time when America dominated the world market in the production of these and other goods and services. Over time, that dominance has faded to the point where you would be hard-pressed to find an American-made television or DVD player. How America lost these markets and why we are strong in so many new ones, like computer software, energy equipment, medical technology, and movie production is a critical lesson in comparative advantage. Let's look at it.

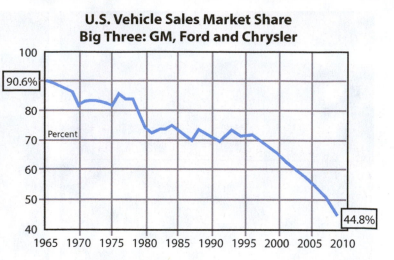

How America Lost the Automobile Market

While the automobile was not invented in America – the Germans actually beat us to it – the United States was the dominant nation in automobile production from the days of Henry Ford's Model T until the early 1970s. Mr. Ford got us off to such a great start by producing a high-quality affordable product on an assembly line that saved his company millions of dollars in production costs.

Over time, General Motors and Chrysler entered the arena – as did others with much less success – until by 1970 the world's automobile market was dominated by the "Big Three." Of course, Germany, Japan, Sweden, and Italy were also factors in the international marketplace, but the majority of cars sold in America were built in the U.S. by one of the three major companies.

In the early 1970s all of that changed. It started with the dramatic increase in oil prices that stemmed from the 1973 Arab Oil Embargo. With gas prices skyrocketing, all of a sudden the very large, gas-drinking cars of the U.S. were not as attractive. Americans had always had a love affair with speed and larger cars. Cheap gas helped fuel this market. However, with the days of inexpensive gas quickly disappearing, Americans began noticing the fact that Honda, Toyota, and other Japanese companies were producing much smaller, fuel-efficient cars.

As the demand for Japanese cars increased, the initial reaction in Detroit was one of indifference and some would say, arrogance. Former Ford and Chrysler Chairman Lee Iacocca even went so far as to say, "A true American will only buy an American-made car." What he and other American executives quickly learned is that a true American has a budget constraint to worry about and will be more loyal to her wallet than the origins of her car.

Eventually, the U.S. automakers woke up and realized that the Japanese were not going to go away. It was during the remaining years of the 1970s that the Americans responded with their own version of small cars. You may have heard of or seen such products as the Ford Pinto, the Chevy Vega, and the Gremlin. Not only were Americans not impressed with the rather hideous look of these cars, but the quality of these automobiles also left a great deal to be desired. As a result, the demand for American cars continued to fall.

Of course, the next response was predictable. With their market share eroding faster than they could fathom, the executives of the Big Three ran straight to Washington, D.C., and begged for protection from this "unfair" intrusion by the Japanese into our markets. It did not hurt that it was less than 40 years since the Japanese had bombed Pearl Harbor. The executives appealed to the consumers' sense of patriotism and residual resentment against our former enemy and Congress's sense of political savvy to help get very restrictive tariffs and quotas placed on the Japanese. At one point during the 1980s, things got so bad that Chrysler filed for bankruptcy.

Not only did the government use our tax dollars to bail out this firm that had been selected for extinction, but then the Reagan administration caved to the mounting pressure for protection and asked the Japanese to "voluntarily" reduce imports. The world "voluntary" actually meant "mandatory," lest the Japanese face even greater punitive measures.

It did not matter. The American consumers kept on buying the superior Japanese product. The Japanese, with

© OrchidFlower/Shutterstock.com

CONCEPT CHECK

Asia enjoys a tremendous comparative advantage in the shrimp business. Does this mean that Louisiana shrimpers should stop fishing? Should the U.S. government provide protection for American shrimpers? Why or why not?[3]

the use of "Kan-Ban" or "Just-in-Time" inventory management, continued to turn out better and better cars at terrific prices.

In 1986 oil prices collapsed. As a result, the demand for larger cars began to increase once again. The Japanese were years ahead of schedule in meeting this change in the market. Figuring that oil prices would not stay high forever and recognizing that Americans prefer bigger cars, the Japanese rolled out such products as the Toyota Camry, the Honda Prelude and Accord, and the Nissan Maxima.

These larger cars proved to be a huge hit with Americans and another blow to the American car-makers that were begging Americans to believe that quality problems were dissipating. The consumers were buying it.

By the late 1980s the American economy was roaring, and consumers had plenty of money to spend. It was then that the Japanese made the final monumental step in their march toward taking over the American car market. Automobiles called Acura, Lexus, and Infiniti appeared in showrooms around the country. These cars, produced by Honda, Toyota, and Nissan, respectively, did not bear the names of the Japanese producers. The Japanese did not want car shoppers to think that these new luxury models were simply slight alterations of the other Japanese cars. They wanted the consumer to perceive them as being like Mercedes-Benz or BMW.

Today, the Big Three, for the first time in history, sell less than 45% of the vehicles bought in America. In 2008, General Motors saw its stock fall to below $10 per share. Eventually the company filed for bankruptcy and received billions of dollars in taxpayer money to stay afloat.

Foreign automakers who build cars in the United States pay an average of $30 per hour in wages and benefits to non-union workers while U.S. companies pay over $70.[4]

Given what you learned in chapter seven about the impact input costs have on supply and prices, you might be inclined to believe that such a competitive disadvantage in labor costs would lead to higher prices for American cars relative to what Japanese producers charge. That is not the case. Japanese cars are actually around *$2,500 more* than comparable American cars and still the American consumer prefers the Japanese brand.[5]

American companies have scrambled to improve the quality of the cars built in this country. The minivan, the SUV, and divergent types of pickup trucks have helped companies like Ford survive – and at times prosper – in the world automobile market, but serious cost pressures and quality issues remain.[6]

While similar events in electronics, steel, and other industries have contributed to the emergence of other nations as world leaders in production, the primary reason why America is not self-sufficient is simple.

Whether it is red wine from France, DVD players from Japan, vodka from Russia, or sugar from Haiti, there are some countries (for reasons associated with climate, technology, years of experience, or perhaps national priority) that do a better job producing certain goods than we do. However, as the table that follows clearly illustrates, the United States has no reason to worry about being "taken over" by the rest of the world. The good news is that we enjoy a tremendous advantage over the rest of the world in most categories of production.[7]

THE ECONOMICS OF PROTECTIONISM

> The problem in a lot of our trade agreements is that the Administration tends to negotiate on behalf of multinational companies instead of on behalf of workers and communities.
>
> Barack Obama

Despite all of the evidence that trade creates a positive-sum game, there are still those who argue that the best use of public policy is to restrict trade – or even ban it under certain circumstances.[8] Where does this argument come from? Does it garner any support among economists? In this section, we will uncover the historical reasons for tariffs and quotas and whether or not trade restrictions make any economic sense.

> ➤ **A tariff is a tax on an imported good or service.**
> ➤ **A quota is an artificial limit placed on the amount of a good or service that can be legally imported each year**[9].

If you are wondering how the government decides which products are hit with tariffs and quotas and what formula is used to determine the amount of the tariff, it is very simple. The system used can be found in the invisible manual called *Twilight Zone Economics.* Consider this:

The United States allows Jamaica to sell only 950 gallons of ice cream to dessert-loving Americans each year. Mexico is allowed to export 35,292 bras per year to the U.S. Haiti – the world's most efficient producer of sugar – is allowed to sell only 7,730 tons to the U.S.[10]

Low-priced watch parts are hit with a tariff of 151.2%. Tobacco stem importers pay 458%. Shoe importers pay 67%. Pity the consumer whose watch breaks down the day he decides to take up smoking and cross-training.

If you eat food on occasion, keep in mind that the tariff on grapefruit juice is 41.3%. Carrot and dried prune importers pay 17.5%. Olives, dates, frozen chicken, cucumbers, watermelon, yogurt, garlic, and asparagus all are assessed tariffs of 20% or higher.[11]

Representative Richard Roe once proposed to reduce the 33% tariff on protective garments worn by firefighters. Even though no American companies make this garment, the American Textile Manufacturers Institute objected. ATMI argued that only if the tariff were kept high, would the price of these garments reach a level that *might* encourage some American firms to make this garment. The Bush administration followed the same logic when it imposed import quotas on Chinese brassieres to protect the totally nonexistent U.S. bra industry.[12]

In his second term, Mr. Bush approved billions of dollars in taxpayer-financed subsidies for American farmers. He indicated that unless India took steps to reduce assistance to Indian farmers, the U.S. would consider a tougher trade stance with India.[13]

In 1988, foreign ice cream makers "swamped" the U.S.; 576 gallons came from New Zealand and *12 gallons* from Denmark. With a whopping one-tenth of 1% of the domestic ice cream market dominated by foreigners, the United States government was outraged when Canada – banned from America's ice cream market altogether – imposed a quota on U.S. ice cream.

The first President Bush sent a letter to the U.S. International Trade Commission demanding an ice cream investigation, "telling the ITC to stop everything else and give ice cream imports their highest priority."[14] With over 30 people working on this project, a final report was submitted on August 28, 1989. The details of the report were never revealed for "national security" reasons.[15]

The U.S. recently complained about Australia's 12% tariff on almonds. The U.S. almond tariff is 14.8%. Also receiving criticism was Canada's 12.5% tariff on frozen peaches. The U.S. frozen peach tariff is 20%. We also do not like the 7% tariff Guatemala imposes on soybean oil. The Guatemalans are probably not thrilled with our 22% tariff on this product.[16]

A HEALTHY SHARE OF THE WORLD MARKET SHARES OF
GLOBAL CORPORATE PROFITS AND SALES

| | U.S. | | JAPAN | | EUROPE | |
| | PROFITS | SALES | PROFITS | SALES | PROFITS | SALES |
INDUSTRY	(%)	(%)	(%)	(%)	(%)	(%)
Energy equipment and services	99.6	92.7	0.8	1	★−0.4	6.3
Aerospace and military technology	81.6	75.8	0	0.4	18.4	23.8
Data processing and reproduction	65.1	73.2	10.7	22.2	24.2	4.6
Electronic components and instrument	65	61.8	30.5	35.8	4.5	2.4
Beverages and tobacco	63	63.4	3.6	16.4	33.4	20.2
Health and personal care	61.9	48.9	8.2	20.3	29.9	30.8
Leisure and tourism	60.3	45.7	7.4	16.3	32.3	38.1
Forest product and paper	59.7	51	7	17.4	33.3	31.6
Energy source	50.4	45.8	2.3	13.5	47	40.7
Metals–Nonferrous	45.7	30.2	11.9	30.8	42.4	39
Recreation and other consumer goods	44	33.2	46.4	60.7	9.7	6.1
Food and household products	42.6	32.6	7.8	21.7	49.6	45.7
Electrical and electronics	41.1	21.4	25.7	50.7	33.2	27.9
Chemicals	41	28.2	13.3	30.3	45.7	41.5
Industrial components	38.2	24.5	32.5	44.7	29.3	30.8
Automobiles	23.6	37	31	35.3	45.5	27.6
Machinery and engineering	19.2	18.9	34.3	46.3	46.3	34.9
Appliances and household durable	16.5	7.6	74.4	66.6	9.1	25.7
Metals–Steel	2.3	10.1	51.2	57	46.5	32.9
All industries	47.7	37.4	15.5	31.5	36.8	31.1

★Europe's businesses in the sector had a net loss.

Source: Morgan Stanley Capital International and Daniel Strickberger

Former U.S. Trade Representative Clayton Yeutter once noted, "The Florida Citrus Industry…believes that removal of Japan's unfair barriers could cut the price of oranges for Japanese consumers by one third." Interestingly enough, the price of orange juice would fall by an even larger amount in America if not for our *60%* tariff on Brazilian oranges.[17]

It is also interesting to note that Congress seems to have a great deal of concern for the plight of America's poor people. Mink furs are tariff-free. Polyester sweaters pay 34.6%. Lobster is duty-free. Baby food pays 17.2%. Orange juice pays 40%, so maybe a poor mom should give her baby Perrier water, which is taxed at 0.8%.

President Trump joined the tariff parade in 2016 when he campaigned on the desire to unilaterally impose 35% tariffs on products arriving from Mexico and 45%

tariffs on China. Precise reasoning for these figures were not provided by the new president.

THE HISTORICAL "JUSTIFICATION" FOR TARIFFS AND QUOTAS

No analysis of protectionism would be complete without some exploration into the reason tariffs and quotas are used against our trading partners. The defense of protectionism is vigorous. Therefore, each reason will be fully addressed, along with what economists know about the justifications offered.

TARIFFS AND QUOTAS PROTECT DOMESTIC JOBS

On July 7, 1999, President Clinton announced that the U.S. would impose stiff new tariffs on lamb imported from Australia and New Zealand. While New Zealand has a population of approximately four million people, the New Zealand sheep population totals sixty million. In contrast, the U.S. has a sheep population of about seven million.

With a tremendous comparative advantage in lamb and wool production, Australia and New Zealand have been able to sell lamb meat and wool to Americans at a much lower price than American producers can. Since the price of foreign lamb and wool is lower (and the quality arguably better), the demand for American-made lamb and wool is fairly low. This means that the derived demand for American workers in this industry is fairly low.

The way Mr. Clinton's tariff was designed to increase employment in this industry is straightforward. The imposition of a 40% tariff forced the Australians and New Zealanders to increase prices in America to cover the higher cost of selling their products. If prices increased enough, the average American consumer would opt to start buying American lamb and wool. As the demand for American lamb and wool increased, the demand for workers in these industries would follow, and voila! Jobs are saved in our country.

This has been the key argument for tariffs in almost every instance tariffs are considered. The only problem is with the research that suggests this argument is largely void of any economic merit.

> Every day we go without expanding trade is another day of missed opportunities to strengthen the economy.
>
> President Bush, April 27, 2002

Not long after these remarks, President Bush imposed a 30% tariff on foreign steel. Not only did the tariff lead to an increase in the price of goods made with steel (during a time when our economy was suffering the lingering effects of a recession), but the tariff led to a loss of $680 billion in national income and the elimination of 200,000 jobs in the *steel-using* industries![19] In California, 19,392 jobs were lost. Texas saw 15,553 more people lose employment, while Ohio, Michigan, and Illinois each lost nearly 10,000 jobs. The Consuming Industries Trade Action Coalition estimated that the steel tariff led to a loss of $4 billion in wages.

At least the tariff helped our steel industry, right? Well, no. It did not. While President Bush hoped that the higher tax on foreign steel would buy our steel industry time to improve efficiency and gain market share, the opposite actually occurred.

Steel prices shot up by a much larger amount than the administration had expected. The price for hot-rolled steel increased from $210 a ton to $350 a ton.

Since, in the short run, the demand for steel is fairly inelastic (meaning that it is a necessary good) the higher prices did not lead to a very large drop in quantity demanded around the globe. As a result, foreign steel producers like Brazil, Russia, and Japan increased their production of steel – in some cases by as much as 36%![20] Moreover, the higher prices did not help the U.S. steel industry that much.[21] Old and inefficient, the U.S. steel mills were unable to effectively increase output as much as our more efficient foreign rivals could. The end result

"...THE SINGLE WORST DECISION OF HIS PRESIDENCY."

That is what the conservative editorial board of *The Wall Street Journal* called Mr. Bush's 2002 decision to dramatically increase the tariff on imported steel.[18]

© Scott Richardson/Shutterstock.com

CONCEPT CHECK

The United States has a 60% tariff on cement from Mexico.[22] What would happen to the price of construction projects in the U.S. and unemployment in the U.S., if the tariff dropped to 6%? Why?

was a glut of steel coming in from foreign nations that, even with the tariff, were more cost-effective in their operations and in a better position to absorb the new tax.

Making matters even worse was a World Trade Organization ruling in November 2003 that found the Bush administration's steel tariff illegal under international trade law. The W.T.O. then gave Europe and other regions around the world the authority to impose up to $2 billion in sanctions on everything from U.S.-made orange juice to motor boats and sunglasses.[23]

The fact that our steel industry failed to expand is not surprising. Economists Robert Z. Lawrence and Robert E. Litan surveyed 16 major industries receiving protection from 1950 through 1986. They found that only one industry – bicycle making – expanded. How could this be true? It is very simple, as it turns out.

Suppose the Minnesota Twins baseball team – arguably one of the worst in recent history – struck an agreement with Major League Baseball that allowed the Twins to pitch to opposing teams from only 10 feet away instead of the normal 60 feet, 6 inches away. Would this encourage the Twins to try harder at improving their baseball skills, or would it give them a false sense of security, and erode their work ethic and the quality of their product? The answer is pretty obvious, and the applications to protectionism are clear.

Even with protection, industries like steel are in decline because consumers and businesses are not going to flock to the company that has been insolated from the free market. The market makes people and industries work hard or die. When the government protects inferior competitors, the incentive to improve is truncated, demand continues to fall, and jobs vanish. The U.S. steel industry is beginning to understand this reality. In Leipsic, Ohio, the 112-year-old U.S. Steel Corporation is now operating with a small, non-union workforce that earns $20 per hour on average.[24] The $400 million investment in a more efficient steel-producing process has great promise to help this company slowing regain market share and show other American producers how to compete in the new global marketplace.

Protecting sugar producers in Florida costs American taxpayers millions of dollars every year. This is because America does not possess a comparative advantage in sugar growing.[25] Consequently, many American candy makers have left America in order to be able to buy foreign sugar at lower prices. This move has led to thousands of Americans losing their jobs in the candy industry.[26]

Another issue that comes up with respect to the protection of domestic jobs is the cost of such protection. Import quotas on Japanese cars during the 1980s cost American car buyers about $4.3 billion. That's nearly *$160,000 per year for each job saved*. According to the Federal Trade Commission study, tariffs cost the American economy $81 for every $1 saved. This should not come as a great surprise.

If you were asked to use your money to help improve the productivity of two students – one who had a 3.93 GPA and studied 30 hours per week or one who had a GPA of 0.93 and smoked crack 30 hours per week – who do you think would be more expensive to help? If you said the crack smoker, go to the head of the class. The ratio of $81 per $1 saved is merely a function of whom we are attempting to help. Microsoft, Nike, and Rolex don't need much help – these companies are good at what they do.

In his first term, President Obama bought into the "save American jobs" argument when he decided to impose drastically higher tariffs on tires from China.

In 2010, roughly 51,600 people were employed by tire manufacturers, rising to 51,700 in 2011, according to the U.S. Bureau of Labor Statistics – a net gain of 100 jobs.

In 2009, 55,000 people were employed in the industry on average throughout that year, according to the BLS. However, 86,800 people made tires in America in 2000. Making tires overseas is simply less expensive for large companies, and they have been moving production overseas for several years.

As reported by *Forbes*: "The tariffs did ultimately lead to a 30% reduction in Made in China tire imports from 2009 to 2011, but that didn't mean 30% more tires were produced in the U.S. It just meant that 30% more tires were imported from Canada; 110% more from South Korea; 44% more from Japan; 152% more from Indonesia; 154% more from Thailand; 117% more from Mexico and 285% more from low volume provider Taiwan, according to the U.S. International Trade Commission."[27]

You may have noticed that in many cities, during this time, tire prices almost doubled.

Speaking of higher prices, in 2016 a study by the National Foundation for American Policy found that President Trump's plans to unilaterally increase tariffs on Mexico, Japan and China would cost a typical U.S. household $11,100 in higher costs of living.[28] Poor families, not surprisingly, were projected to pay upwards of 18% of their annual household income in higher prices if the tariff proposals passed.

ANOTHER LESSON FROM BASTIAT

You will recall from chapter three that we examined the views of the French economist, Frederic Bastiat in the area of government spending and taxation. Bastiat also held very strong views on the subject of economic liberty as it pertains to trade. What follows is one of his more famous works on the subject.

A PETITION From the Manufacturers of Candles, Tapers, Lanterns, Sticks, Street Lamps, Snuffers, and Extinguishers, and from Producers of Tallow, Oil, Resin, Alcohol, and Generally of Everything Connected with Lighting.

To the Honourable Members of the Chamber of Deputies.

Gentlemen:

You are on the right track. You reject abstract theories and little regard for abundance and low prices. You concern yourselves mainly with the fate of the producer. You wish to free him from foreign competition, that is, to reserve the *domestic market* for *domestic industry*.

We come to offer you a wonderful opportunity for your – what shall we call it? Your theory? No, nothing is more deceptive than theory. Your doctrine? Your system? Your principle? But you dislike doctrines, you have a horror of systems, as for principles, you deny that there are any in political economy; therefore we shall call it your practice -- your practice without theory and without principle.

We are suffering from the ruinous competition of a rival who apparently works under conditions so far superior to our own for the production of light that he is *flooding* the *domestic market* with it at an incredibly low price; for the moment he appears, our sales cease, all the consumers turn to him, and a branch of French industry whose ramifications are innumerable is all at once reduced to complete stagnation. This rival, which is none other than the sun, is waging war on us so mercilessly we suspect he is being stirred up against us by perfidious Albion (excellent diplomacy nowadays!), particularly because he has for that haughty island a respect that he does not show for us.

We ask you to be so good as to pass a law requiring the closing of all windows, dormers, skylights, inside and outside shutters, curtains, casements, bull's-eyes, deadlights, and blinds -- in short, all openings, holes, chinks, and fissures through which the light of the sun is wont to enter houses, to the detriment of the fair industries with which, we are proud to say, we have endowed the country, a country that cannot, without betraying ingratitude, abandon us today to so unequal a combat.

Be good enough, honourable deputies, to take our request seriously, and do not reject it without at least hearing the reasons that we have to advance in its support.

First, if you shut off as much as possible all access to natural light, and thereby create a need for artificial light, what industry in France will not ultimately be encouraged?

If France consumes more tallow, there will have to be more cattle and sheep, and, consequently, we shall see an increase in cleared fields, meat, wool, leather, and especially manure, the basis of all agricultural wealth.

If France consumes more oil, we shall see an expansion in the cultivation of the poppy, the olive, and rapeseed. These rich yet soil-exhausting plants will come at just the right time to enable us to put to profitable use the increased fertility that the breeding of cattle will impart to the land.

Our moors will be covered with resinous trees. Numerous swarms of bees will gather from our mountains the perfumed treasures that today waste their fragrance, like the flowers from which they emanate. Thus, there is not one branch of agriculture that would not undergo a great expansion. The same holds true of shipping. Thousands of vessels will engage in whaling, and in a short time we shall have a fleet capable of upholding the honour of France and of gratifying the patriotic aspirations of the undersigned petitioners, chandlers, etc.

But what shall we say of the *specialities* of *Parisian manufacture*? Henceforth you will behold gilding, bronze, and crystal in candlesticks, in lamps, in chandeliers, in candelabra sparkling in spacious emporia compared with which those of today are but stalls.

There is no needy resin-collector on the heights of his sand dunes, no poor miner in the depths of his black pit, who will not receive higher wages and enjoy increased prosperity.

It needs but a little reflection, gentlemen, to be convinced that there is perhaps not one Frenchman, from the wealthy stockholder of the Anzin Company to the humblest vendor of matches, whose condition would not be improved by the success of our petition.

We anticipate your objections, gentlemen; but there is not a single one of them that you have not picked up from the musty old books of the advocates of free trade. We defy you to utter a word against us that will not instantly rebound against yourselves and the principle behind all your policy.

Will you tell us that, though we may gain by this protection, France will not gain at all, because the consumer will bear the expense?

We have our answer ready:
You no longer have the right to invoke the interests of the consumer. You have sacrificed him whenever you have found his interests opposed to those of the producer. You have done so in order *to encourage industry and to increase employment.* For the same reason you ought to do so this time too.

Indeed, you yourselves have anticipated this objection. When told that the consumer has a stake in the free entry of iron, coal, sesame, wheat, and textiles, "Yes," you reply, "but the producer has a stake in their exclusion." Very well, surely if consumers have a stake in the admission of natural light, producers have a stake in its interdiction.

"But," you may still say, "the producer and the consumer are one and the same person. If the manufacturer profits by protection, he will make the farmer prosperous. Contrariwise, if agriculture is prosperous, it will open markets for manufactured goods." Very well, If you grant us a monopoly over the production of lighting during the day, first of all we shall buy large amounts of tallow, charcoal, oil, resin, wax, alcohol, silver, iron, bronze, and crystal, to supply our industry; and, moreover, we and our numerous suppliers, having become rich, will consume a great deal and spread prosperity into all areas of domestic industry.

Will you say that the light of the sun is a gratuitous gift of Nature, and that to reject such gifts would be to reject wealth itself under the pretext of encouraging the means of acquiring it?

But if you take this position, you strike a mortal blow at your own policy; remember that up to now you have always excluded foreign goods *because* and *in proportion* as they approximate gratuitous gifts. You have only *half* as good a reason for complying with the demands of other monopolists as you have for granting our petition, which is in *complete* accord with your established policy; and to reject our demands precisely because they are *better founded* than anyone else's would be tantamount to accepting the equation: + × + = -; in other words, it would be to heap *absurdity* upon *absurdity*.

Labour and Nature collaborate in varying proportions, depending upon the country and the climate, in the production of a commodity. The part that Nature contributes is always free of charge; it is the part contributed by human labour that constitutes value and is paid for.

If an orange from Lisbon sells for half the price of an orange from Paris, it is because the natural heat of the sun, which is, of course, free of charge, does for the former what the latter owes to artificial heating, which necessarily has to be paid for in the market.

Thus, when an orange reaches us from Portugal, one can say that it is given to us half free of charge, or, in other words, at *half price* as compared with those from Paris.

Now, it is precisely on the basis of its being *semi-gratuitous* (pardon the word) that you maintain it should be barred. You ask: "How can French labour withstand the competition of foreign labour when the former has to do all the work, whereas the latter has to do only half, the sun taking care of the rest?" But if the fact that a product is *half* free of charge leads you to exclude it from competition, how can its being *totally* free of charge induce you to admit it into competition? Either you are not consistent, or you should, after excluding what is half free of charge as harmful to our domestic industry, exclude what is totally gratuitous with all the more reason and with twice the zeal.

To take another example: When a product -- coal, iron, wheat, or textiles -- comes to us from abroad, and when we can acquire it for less labour than if we produced it ourselves, the difference is a *gratuitous gift* that is conferred up on us. The size of this gift is proportionate to the extent of this difference. It is a quarter, a half, or three-quarters of the value of the product if the foreigner asks of us only three-quarters, one-half, or one-quarter as high a price. It is as complete as it can be when the donor, like the sun in providing us with light, asks nothing from us. The question, and we pose it formally, is whether what you desire for France is the benefit of consumption free of charge or the alleged advantages of onerous production. Make your choice, but be logical; for as long as you ban, as you do, foreign coal, iron, wheat, and textiles, *in proportion* as their price approaches zero, how inconsistent it would be to admit the light of the sun, whose price is zero all day long!

JOBS AND NAFTA

This might come as a huge shock to many of you, but one of the first major economic decisions Bill Clinton made was associated with not telling the whole truth. Fortunately for America, his less-than-honest approach to trade helped America's economy tremendously during the 1990s.

When Mr. Clinton was running for president in 1992, he told union workers and environmental groups that he would not ratify the North American Free Trade Agreement with Mexico and Canada unless there were protections for union workers and adherence to environmental laws.

When he won the election he came into office and ratified NAFTA without any special protections for either group.[29]

Mr. Clinton also did not buy into the argument launched by Ross Perot and others, that NAFTA would kill jobs in America. Their argument was based on the simplistic theory that, since Mexican workers make so much less money than their American counterparts, once tariffs were lifted or even reduced, American companies would no longer be able to compete with the low wages paid to Mexican workers. Perot argued that the next event would be "a giant sucking sound of jobs leaving for Mexico."

When NAFTA was eventually ratified in 1993, America's unemployment rate was 7.5%. By May of 2000, the unemployment rate was 3.9%. While this is not all due to NAFTA, some interesting data has emerged about NAFTA's impact on the American economy.

On July 1, 1997, Congress issued a detailed "report card" covering the first three years of implementation of NAFTA. The data indicated that NAFTA had led to an increase in exports and imports by all three countries involved (U.S. exports to Mexico grew by 37%, to Canada by 33%) and the linkage of 2.3 million jobs in America to this agreement.[30]

By 2010, the data was even better. Trade between the U.S. and Mexico had increased from $40 billion in 1992 to $148 billion, while contributing to a 14.4% *increase* in the earnings of U.S. factory workers.[31]

Why did the dire predictions of net job losses to Mexico go unrealized? As it turns out, Perot is not totally off-base. Free trade has led to job losses for manufacturers of toys, food, and textiles, to name just a few. Where Mr. Perot was off-base was in his flawed assertion that low-wages is the predominant reason why companies relocate to other nations.

The accompanying chart showing the trend in U.S.-Mexico trade would seem to suggest that President Trump might be on to something when he claims that NAFTA has ultimately done more harm than good in the United

States. Yet, when we look closely at the NAFTA picture, even as Mr. Trump campaigned to change this agreement, the data still pointed to more benefits than costs.

First, the 2016 difference between our imports from Mexico and exports to our neighbor was approximately $40 billion – less than 1 percent of America's GDP.[32]

Second, NAFTA, with $1.2 trillion in total trade, had opened up opportunities for countries outside of North America to open factories to take advantage of low tariffs.[33] In auto parts alone, 264,800 jobs were created for U.S. workers as a result of $70 billion in new production plants in North America.[34] Moreover, the increase in exports to Mexico from $50 billion when NAFTA passed to well over $200 billion by 2016 meant that a wide-range of American industries were able to add jobs in order to support growing demand from Mexico.

It also meant that as Mexico became more affluent, there was downward pressure on Mexican citizens to engage in illegal immigration. In the late 1990s more than 500,000 illegal immigrants came in from Mexico every year. By 2015 the figure was down to approximately 100,000 per year as increased employment opportunities reduced the need for Mexican people to seek work in the United States.[35]

It is worth noting that one of the reasons America imports more from Mexico than the other way around is because the United States is a vastly richer country than Mexico. It stands to reason that if two nations engage in trade the wealthier one will automatically be poised to purchase more products than the poorer nation. This means greater product variety, lower prices and greater wealth for both nations as a result of expanding the marketplace.

But what about those low wages in Mexico (and other nations)? Does the fact that earnings differences between our nations mean anything in giving those countries an advantage in trade?

Uneven Trade

U.S. trade balace with Mexico since Nafta took effect

Source: U.S. Census Bureau

Revisiting the Low-Wage Fallacy

Suppose you were the owner of a company that produced the guiding systems for orbiting satellites. You have three choices of where you are going to build your next plant: the United States, Mexico, or Rwanda. Suppose the average salary of a guidance system programmer would be $120,000 per year in America, $48,000 in Mexico, and $19,000 in the impoverished African nation of Rwanda. There is no question: You are going to move to Rwanda, right?

Before you depart, please consider the following questions. Are you concerned about the overall level of skill, education, and training of the Rwandan labor force? Are you concerned about the stability of the government there? Does potential language or cultural problems worry you? What about the quality and reliability of the phone, computer, and electric power delivery systems?

How about the highway system you will use to transport your guidance systems? What about the availability and location of suppliers? Are you starting to see the problem? The reason why most companies in America that employ highly skilled, educated workers do not leave for low-wage nations is because you get what you pay for. Low wages often mean low skills. Low skill means low productivity, and low productivity means very high labor costs.

In reality, it is actually cheaper to build many products in the United States than in nations with very low wages, simply because of the vast differences in labor productivity.[36]

In July 2012 the *Star-Tribune* reported on an interesting trend taking place in Minnesota and all over America.

Over the past several years, as China's economy has grown, the demand for labor has increased significantly – leading to shortages of factory workers and an increase in hourly wages by 10 to 25% *per year*. With shipping costs at nearly $1,800 for a single cargo container leaving China, the overall cost of producing consumer goods like patio furniture has risen sharply. This trend has prompted many companies like Yard, Inc. to leave China and come back to the United States.[37]

WHY COMPANIES RELOCATE

Whether a company seeks to relocate to China, the U.S. or any other nation, it is usually done for one of the following reasons. One is to improve the *productivity-to-wage relationship*.

This means that in Malaysia, workers sitting at a sewing machine making bed sheets are performing a task that requires very little in the way of skill. Since this task can be done in a repetitive manner, the productivity of a 13-year-old girl in Malaysia would come close to that of an adult in a South Carolina textile mill. With the combination of high productivity and low wages, the average cost of the Malaysian worker makes them too cost-effective to keep the South Carolina plant open.

In this case – and others like it – people who oppose free trade have a point. Jobs will continue to be lost in American industries where foreigners have similar productivity but lower wages. This may seem horribly unfair, and certainly the person in South Carolina would have every reason to be angry, but let's consider the alternative.

Would you be willing to pay $15 for a cotton T-shirt made in America if it meant not being able to pay $7 for one from Malaysia? What about those Nike shoes you wear? How about a price of $200 rather than $75? You do have a choice.

If enough Americans decided to boycott all companies that use cheap foreign labor, the demand for their products would fall to the point that relocating back to America would be their only viable option. Once here, with the much higher wages being paid, we would then have to pay higher prices. Any takers?

A second reason U.S. companies relocate to foreign nations is to *reduce their regulatory costs*. It is a fact of life that American companies face much higher regulatory costs than many other nations impose. Regulations stemming from worker safety, environmental protection, health care, and other laws effectively increase the operating costs of doing business in the states. Moving to Indonesia and not having to worry about complying with thousands of pages of government rules and regulations can be enticing to many corporations.[38]

Increased regulations have also been the reason for many European companies leaving for the U.S. Laws that keep workers from working more than 40 hours (or even less) per week and mandating family leave and extended vacation time has made it very expensive for companies to survive in places like Spain and France.

© Dmitry Kalinovsky/Shutterstock.com

SUGGESTED CLASSROOM DEBATE

Do multi-national corporations exploit workers in poorer nations or are these workers better off as a result of these companies opening up factories?

Avoiding tariffs and quotas is another reason for the migration of U.S. and other nation's companies. If you drive a Japanese-brand car, chances are it was made in the United States.

According to the American International Automobile Dealers Association, over 50,000 American workers are employed in the building of cars like the Honda Accord (Marysville, Ohio) and Civic (East Liberty, Ohio); the Nissan Sentra (Smyrna, Tennessee); the Toyota Camry (Georgetown, Kentucky) and Corolla (Fremont, California); and the M-Class Mercedes-Benz (Vance, Alabama).[39]

A major reason for this proliferation of "foreign" auto production in America, is based on the protectionist legislation that raises the costs of building a car in Japan or Germany, then shipping it to the U.S. as well as the strong productivity of U.S. workers.

Reducing transportation costs and *opening new markets* are also valid justifications for plant location in foreign markets. When PepsiCo built a bottling plant in Vietnam, a big part of the decision to do this was to bring down the costs of shipping Pepsi products to this market and to open up this market that was impenetrable before Bill Clinton lifted the embargo against our former enemy.

Finally, as Donald Trump accurately pointed out during his bid for the White House, many American companies have left our shores over the past several years in order to *reduce their corporate tax burden*. As this chapter was being written, the United States had a corporate income tax rate of 35% - one of the highest in the developed world. From 2004-2013 47 U.S. companies purchased foreign companies and then changed their U.S. address to the foreign address in a practice known as tax inversion.[40] One popular landing spot has been Ireland, where American companies, once headquartered there pay only 12.5% corporate income tax.

As he took office in 2017 President Trump was advocating reducing the corporate income tax rate to 15% to encourage American companies to stay or even return.

PUNISHING RIVAL NATIONS FOR CLOSED MARKETS

In more recent times, this argument has been widely used by administrations when imposing tariffs and quotas.

The Clinton Administration once threatened to impose a tariff of 100% on the Japanese in retaliation for not opening up their markets to more American cars and car parts.[41] Japan has also been a target in cases involving cellular phones, citrus, and semiconductors. The U.S. has threatened Canada with tariffs and quotas for perceived unfairness in our market penetration with respect to beer, lumber, and wheat.

This argument for tariffs and quotas is not without merit. For economists the test is very simple. *If* the United States has a comparative advantage in the production of beer, economic reasoning would indicate that Canadians should be allowed to drink our product without having restrictions on the supply or without having to pay artificially high prices. Therefore, if we were to tell the Canadians that we would not import hockey sticks from them until more Calgary residents can drink Bud Light, this would promote efficiency in both markets. The problem is that the United States has often been guilty of world-class hypocrisy when it comes to this argument.

The U.S. once charged Japan with not allowing Motorola to sell as many cellular phones as Motorola argued it should be able to. The only problem was that, at the time, Motorola was trying to sell the Japanese phones that were made for America's frequencies and were useless in Japan!

The first President Bush flew to Japan in the early 1990s to try to open up the Japanese car market to American cars. The Japanese drive cars with the steering column on the right side of the car. The American carmakers kept trying to sell them cars with the steering column on the *left-hand side*. In one of the most egregious examples of corporate arrogance ever, the U.S. carmakers informed the Japanese that building cars with the steering column on the right-hand side would impose higher costs of production on the Americans.

The Japanese were therefore told that when they had purchased enough left-side steering column cars, the Big Three would use that revenue to finance the production of the models with the steering column on the right-hand side...

HOW NOT TO MAKE FRIENDS IN FOREIGN LANDS

In 2001, Congress approved huge increases in agricultural subsidies for U.S. farmers. The average cotton farmer, for example, now earns half his income from government subsidies, rather than from the actual sale of cotton. Moreover, the approximately 19,000 cotton farmers in the U.S. have an average net worth of $800,000. What's the point?

Armed with roughly $3.4 billion in subsidy checks, the U.S. cotton industry produced 6.47 billion pounds in 2015.[42] This level of production has led to a huge increase in the global supply of cotton, which in turn suppresses cotton prices for vastly poorer cotton farmers in Africa, Asia, and other parts of the world.

Many of the farmers in Mali, and other countries where subsidies do not exist, ended up going out of business because of America's arbitrarily anti-free-market welfare program for wealthy cotton farmers. The U.S. response to the increase in poverty for these farmers is not surprising. To offset the $30 million in losses for Mali farmers, the U.S. government sent them $40 million in foreign aid — paid for by the same taxpayers who were called upon to subsidize U.S. cotton farmers.

The 2002, $118 billion farm subsidy bill — which assured cotton farmers about 70 cents per pound — did not call for U.S. cotton farmers to leave any land idle, like past agreements had. The result was an even bigger surplus of cotton, even lower global prices, and more poverty for people in those nations.

Cotton is but one example of America's hypocritical stance on trade. From our recent steps to seek punitive damages against nations engaging in "unfair trade"[43] to rules that allowed the Export-Import bank to take U.S. taxpayer money and give it to wealthy corporations to promote trade,[44] America is often looked upon as a nation that believes in trade as long as the rules favor those with power and influence, rather than benefiting those that have a comparative advantage to begin with.

PUNISHING COMPETING NATIONS FOR PREDATORY PRICING, A.K.A. "DUMPING"

In 1997, the United States accused Chile of dumping salmon on American markets. This does not mean that the Chileans were piling up dead fish on our docks. It means we were piling up a rather smelly case against the Chileans for doing a great job of selling fish.

Predatory pricing occurs when a company or industry drops the price of some product below the costs of producing that product in an attempt to run its rival out of business.

In the short run, predatory pricing exacts an economic toll on the predator as prices fall to levels where losses are incurred. In the long run, after the predator's rivals are gone — unable to stay in business due to below-cost prices — the predator will dominate the market.

This allows the predator to raise prices to a level that not only helps them recover their losses from the predatory act, but also confers upon them the ability to take advantage of monopoly power and charge very profitable prices indefinitely.

With constant mild ocean temperatures, lower labor rates, and freedom from burdensome regulations, the Chileans have a comparative advantage in the harvesting of Atlantic salmon, which farmers grow in pens sunk along bays in the ocean.[45] From 1994 to 1997, exports of Chilean salmon increased from $46.5 million to more than $111 million, and Chile captured about 45% of the American market at prices that were up to 25% lower than American companies were charging.

If you are a lover of salmon, you might say "Great, now I can eat more of the product I enjoy." Not so fast. In America, this price advantage was not left unchallenged by fishermen hurt by the law of demand.

Led by international trade lawyer Michael Coursey, the U.S. charged that Chile had charged prices that were 42% below cost in America and the rest of the world. The solution? A 42% tariff on Chilean salmon.

For economists, this is a curious claim. Let's put on our critical thinking hats for a moment and reflect on what must take place for an industry to pull off a successful predatory pricing scheme.

First, the Chileans would have to *identify their rivals' cost of production*. In salmon fishing or farming, this might be easy to do, but this decision still carries two types of costs. The Chileans would have to willingly spend money to find out what it costs to harvest salmon in America. Without this information, they would not know by how much to lower prices. Spending this money raises their costs of production and therefore, causes profit levels to fall.

A threat to our prosperity?

The Chileans would also incur an *opportunity cost* from this decision. Spending money on industrial espionage is money that could have been spent on the next-best alternative, like better harvesting techniques, new nets, better marketing campaigns, and so forth.

Let's assume the Chileans are willing to fork over the money for this research. We come to step two. Once your rival's costs of production are identified, you must *lower your prices below their cost of production and keep the price there until they are out of business.* This is a sticky issue. Lowering prices to the point where your rival is gone may take a long time. In the meantime, your rival might merge with another company or be bought outright by a deep-pocketed investor.

The even greater problem is the issue of the Chileans' own profits falling from lowering prices to damagingly low levels. How smart can this strategy be when you have to inflict low profits or losses on your own firm in order to hopefully have long-run success?

Nevertheless, let's just assume the Chileans are willing to incur losses or that they have large profit reserves to support this venture. Step three takes place once your rival is gone. *When your rival is gone, you must increase prices to a level that recovers your losses from the predatory act and ensures monopoly profit in the long run.*

How likely is monopoly profit in the long run? Monopoly means the single seller of some good or service with no close substitutes. To earn monopoly profit in the long run, you would have to make sure no one ever entered the industry to challenge your economically enviable position. Is that possible? Could the Chileans patent their salmon? Can they create a cartel like the Colombian drug lords and execute any fisherman who ever ventures out looking for competing salmon? Can they make sure no salmon ever swim anywhere away from Chile?

If the Chileans can identify all the costs of production in America, and *if* they can afford to lower their prices, and *if* they can run all of the U.S. fishermen out of the market, there is no way they can keep one or more new firms from entering once they are raking in the profits from being the only country producing salmon. Profits act as a magnet to attract new competitors. This is always the case. This means that *in order to be a successful predator, you have to be willing to be a predator forever.*

It is not surprising that a growing number of economists not only question the merits of predatory pricing

Should Canadian beef compete with Longhorns from Texas?

claims, but now argue that what appears to be predatory pricing is just good, old-fashioned competition that leads to lower prices for consumers and the rewards for a comparative advantage to the nation accused of wrongdoing.[46]

That is why economists became so fatigued sorting through the dumping claims levied by the Bush Administration against Canada and China.

First, there was the accusation by the U.S. that "Mad Cow disease" was a threat from Canada. The U.S. government decided to temporarily create a quota of zero pounds per year in order to make sure now sick cows came in from Alberta and other provinces.[47]

Then we had the argument that the Canadians were dumping softwood lumber in our markets. With a red hot housing market already causing home prices to hit record levels, the 25% tariff on Canadian wood did not help consumers find much in the way of affordable housing in the last decade.[48]

China has not gotten off easy either. After years of protectionist tariffs and quotas on Chinese trousers, skirts, shirts and other clothing, China was finally allowed to export – with no quotas, various textile products. The lifting of the quota took place on January 1, 2005. In that year, exports from China increased by 60%.[49] Not surprisingly, the price of clothing in Wal-Mart and other stores fell as well.[50]

With such a huge increase in supply, many American textile manufacturers, already reeling from years of job losses and declining profit, lobbied the Bush Administration to stem the tide of low-priced imports from China.[51]

In the end, President Bush approved across the board increases in tariffs on Chinese textiles and the renewal of quotas as well. By some estimates the protection of

American textile makers effectively raised taxes by $55 billion on consumers in our country.[52]

In the meantime, China is not standing still. While U.S. companies continue to seek out ways to avoid direct competition with the world's largest emerging market, the Chinese government has embarked on a policy of seeking out alternative countries that might be willing to sign free trade agreements that the U.S. shies away from. In 2003 China had formal free trade pacts with *zero* nations. By 2005 China had agreements with 25 countries – proving that there is more than one way – and one place – to sell underwear.[53]

The three previous "justifications" represent the primary rationale for tariffs and quotas. The next few arguments are not used as much, but from time to time can be a thorn in the side of free traders.

TO PROMOTE HUMAN RIGHTS AND ENVIRONMENTAL PROTECTION

When demonstrators showed up in Miami and Seattle to riot over the issue of trade, a great number of them were there to show their support for human rights in China and other nations and to argue for greater environmental awareness. These are certainly noble and valuable goals.

© nui7711/Shutterstock.com

I cannot think of too many people who rejoice over the conditions in which many people in Asian factories work. Not too many people seem to be hoping for the eradication of the sea turtle and the pollution of the oceans, either.

Opponents of trade argue that the globalization of markets has led to companies exploiting workers in slave-like conditions around the world while ravaging the environment in nations that do very little, if anything, to stop them or even slow them down. Let's look at it.

Nike has been at the crux of the firestorm of criticism for employing thousands of Asians at pay rates that Americans would never accept in conditions that OSHA would squash in about 30 seconds. We now know why Nike is in Asia. This Portland-based company feels it is too expensive to make shoes in Oregon and still make profit. Since Nike is a private company, it can produce shoes wherever it can secure the property rights to do so. The question is what would the lives of the Asian workers be like if Nike did move back to Oregon?

Is Nike forcing anyone to work for them in Asia? Are they using slaves held at gunpoint? Do the workers in those factories have alternatives to Nike that pay more? The answer to all of these questions is obvious – and no. If Nike pulled out of Asia, the workers who lost their jobs would have to turn to their next-best choice. As you might imagine, their next best choice is worse than what Nike offers.

We cringe at the thought of working for pennies an hour, but all wages are relative. Recall that actor Ben Affleck cringed at the "low wages" paid to custodians at his alma mater, Harvard.[54] Bill Gates might cringe at the "low pay" Mr. Affleck takes in. Who are we to say that the Asians don't want Nike there? If Nike and other companies continue to set up shop in those developing nations, over time the demand for labor will rise, and so will wages. This has already been observed in China, where more and more factory bosses are lamenting the growing pay rates that workers can command as the Chinese economy continues to grow.[55] With pay rates rising by nearly 20% per year in some cases, companies like Ann

SUGGESTED CLASSROOM DEBATE

Before he left office in 2017, President Obama pushed for the passage of the Trans-Pacific Partnership – a trade agreement between the United States and 11 other nations.[56] Donald Trump and Hillary Clinton opposed the passage of TPP. Who was right? Why? You can read more about TPP at http://www.nytimes.com/2015/05/12/business/unpacking-the-trans-pacific-partnership-trade-deal.html?_r=0

Taylor Stores Corp., Guess Inc., and J.C. Penney have been leaving for Vietnam and Bangladesh.[57] Ironically, it was companies like these that helped create rising wages, higher standards of living and economic development that made China a more expensive place to do business. Thus, what some people call exploitation, is called opportunity by people in Asia.[58]

As for the issue of environmental protection, here is an interesting fact: The dirtiest nations in the world are the *poorest nations* in the world. In northern Bohemia in the Czech Republic, breathing the air is "like smoking 10 cigarettes a day" due to the smog created by antiquated coal-fired power plants.[59] In Mexico City, air pollution is so bad that cars are allotted specific times when they can be driven on the roads. In Africa, the chief source of energy creation is the burning of wood – one of the worst sources of air pollution. In the meantime, the quality of water in India and much of Africa, Asia, and South America would repulse the average American.

How can trade help these problems? It is true that with increased trade comes development, and development can damage the environment. However, studies show that as a nation develops, it gains the economic and political resources to emerge as a net protector, rather than damager of the environment.[5609]

The United States has cleaner air in many regions than ever before.[61] We have more trees than we did in 1900. Recycling programs flourish while we voluntarily buy environmentally safe products and insist on less pollution emanating from our cars and power plants. The Internet and other high-tech inventions continue to move us away from the old smokestack industries to industries that create virtually no pollution. All of this has been made possible by economic growth.

It is a paradoxical truth that if you want to see a nation stay dirty, keep them poor. Poor nations do not care about buying unbleached cotton t-shirts. Nor do they have the money to fund an Environmental Protection Agency or to assist in the fight against global warming. Poor nations are simply trying to survive. That means big trouble when the choice is burning a rainforest to create farmland versus protecting the rainforests so wealthy Americans can go on nice vacations in South America.[62]

PROMOTING NATIONAL SECURITY

> Without steel, we cannot guarantee our national security. Without steel, we cannot rebuild from our national tragedy.
>
> Senator John Rockefeller, D-West Virginia

Up until September 11th, one of the least-used argument in support of tariffs and quotas was the argument that trade jeopardizes the national security of our nation. After the attacks of that day a new anti-free trade argument began to emerge. This argument was that there are some industries (like oil and steel) that are so vital to the national security interest of the United States that tariff or quota protection makes sense.

Consider, for example, the oil industry. Suppose the domestic petroleum industry begins lobbying Congress to put more restrictive tariffs or quotas on our Middle-Eastern trading partners, in order to be less dependent on foreign oil, and protect America from being hurt by OPEC policies. After all, oil is of vital interest to our national security, so why not protect the domestic suppliers?

The problem with this argument is twofold. *First*, it is not as if we are at the mercy of OPEC. We have reserves in America (see North Dakota) and access to even more oil in non-OPEC nations like Canada and Mexico. Therefore, a cry for national security tariff protection is a bit spurious if our national security is not actually at stake. *Second*, if we confer this status on oil, what is next? Why can't farmers claim that we cannot afford to lose agriculture to foreign concerns? What about jets, computer software, and toothbrushes? Why can't Boeing, Microsoft, and Oral-B argue that we must protect America from foreign planes, software, and toothbrushes that are not made by people with American teeth?

It is hard for economists to accept the argument that there are industries in our country that are of vital national security and are simultaneously threatened with extinction at the hands of foreign competition.

ONCE AGAIN, STEEL...

> Ask anyone if we should have a steel industry in America, and they will say yes!–unless they're economists.
>
> Anonymous steel lobbyist

For years, the U.S. steel industry has sought protection from imported steel on the grounds that foreign steel makers were unfairly dumping cheap steel in America. From time to time, administrations from Reagan to Clinton bought this argument and provided relief in the form of tariffs and quotas. Yet the domestic steel industry never seemed to do any better in world markets. This led to some initial reluctance on the part of the Bush administration to offer even more protection for this floundering industry. That is, until the steel beams of the World Trade

What should this cost?

© Invisible/Shutterstock.com

Center melted and sent the icons of American capitalism crumbling into the streets of New York City.

Immediately after September 11th the steel industry junked its call for tariffs on the grounds of predatory pricing and adopted a new strategy for gaining artificial protection from competition. The new argument was simple. Steel is needed to build tanks, guns, and jets, and steel will be needed to rebuild the World Trade Center if that should occur.

If the steel industry in America dies, so say the steel unions and steel executives, terrorist organizations would eventually attempt to disrupt the supply of foreign steel coming to America and the U.S. would be at greater risk of losing the war on terrorism.[63] Thus began the lobbying efforts to impose tariffs on foreign rivals.

Not only that, but the steel industry sought a $12 billion bailout − specifically asking the Bush administration to use taxpayer dollars to take over the retiree pension and health insurance obligations of the major steel producers.[64]

President Bush finally caved into the political pressure to do something about the weakened steel industry. With steel-producing states being key battleground states in the 2002 Congressional elections and the 2004 presidential campaign, Mr. Bush felt the politically rational thing to do was capitulate to the calls for help. His help came in the form of the aforementioned 30% increase in the tariff on flat-rolled steel that is used to make cars and appliances. Steel rebar − used in construction and highways − got a 15% tariff, while other products like hot rolled steel, stainless wire, tool steel, stainless flanges, and slab got tariffs

ranging from 8% to 24%.[65] Do you remember the law of unintended consequences? This law came into effect about three seconds after the Bush announcement.

First, the European Union announced the possibility of increased tariffs on U.S. motorcycles, fruit juices, handguns, and textiles. Russia then banned the importation of all U.S. poultry − costing chicken producers over $600 million. Canada then imposed a 71% tariff on U.S. tomatoes. Canada also imposed a tariff on lumber from the U.S. that impacted our $6 billion market[66] and announced that a tariff on U.S. steel was being considered.[67]

Of course, well before President Bush imposed this tariff, steel-using companies and economists howled in protest. The Bureau of Labor Statistics pointed out that while approximately 160,000 people work in the steel industry, over *12 million* people work in steel-consuming jobs. This means companies like Whirlpool, Ford, John Deere and many other giants of industry would face much higher prices for steel. This would translate higher prices on consumers of washing machines, cars bulldozers, and so forth or a push to cut costs somewhere else − like labor hours, wages, benefits, or capital expenditures.[68]

Perhaps the greatest fear in the economics community was summed up by Gary Hufbauer of the Institute for International Economics, who said that the danger of the precedent-setting steel tariff was that, "the first big Faustian bargain on steel will be followed by a lot of mini-Fausts" in order to satisfy various constituencies.

For those of you who are unfamiliar with the famous story by Johann Wolfgang von Goethe, a "Faustian deal" is one where you give up a lot to gain a little. For President

Bush, his deal with steel could cause other struggling industries to line up and look for a hand-out instead of looking into ways they can be more competitive in the global arena. As we saw in the section on job losses, the steel tariff ultimately led to higher prices, less job creation, and a questionable use of taxpayer dollars just as the economy was struggling to rebound from the recession of 2001.

PROTECTING INFANT INDUSTRIES

An infant industry is one in its earliest stages of development. In some countries, this gives rise to the argument for government-induced insulation from competition. To economists, there is some merit to this type of protection under limited circumstances.

If Costa Rica – a nation rich in botanical wildlife – decided to create a biotechnology industry and protect it with tariffs and/or quotas on foreign pharmaceuticals, this would receive tepid support from a good number of economists if Costa Rica could rationally be expected to develop a comparative advantage in this relatively new industry. It would also be important to have some assurances that, once a comparative advantage was acquired and Costa Rican companies could compete head to head with U.S. and European drug companies, that the protectionist measures would be eliminated.

The fact that once support is given it may be lobbied for indefinitely is one reason why most economists would have trouble extending the hand of government to fledgling industries. Temporary support has a way of becoming permanent support very quickly.

TO PUNISH CHINA FOR "CURRENCY MANIPULATION"

A significant portion of this book has touched on China's rising economic power – and the factors that have precipitated this amazing occurrence.

What has not been broached is the question concerning the degree to which China has achieved some of this magnificent progress by artificial means. Specifically, many critics of China's economic policies point out the Chinese government places controls on the value of the Yuan – the Chinese currency.

The table following illustrates some of the various exchange rates when converting foreign currency into dollars, and vice versa. This data is from December 2, 2016, but will be useful for our purposes even if the data has changed by the time you are reading this section of the book.

Currency	1 U.S. dollar	in U.S. dollars
Euro	0.936611	1.067679
British Pound	0.788209	1.268699
Indian Rupee	68.020512	0.014701
Australian Dollar	1.341335	0.745526
Canadian Dollar	1.328904	0.752500
Singapore Dollar	1.420837	0.703810
Swiss Franc	1.009721	0.990373
Malaysian Ringgit	4.462449	0.224092
Japanese Yen	113.569957	0.008805
Chinese Yuan Renminbi	6.886330	0.145215

Suppose a citizen of China wanted to buy a GMC Yukon SUV that retailed for $38,000 in the United States. $38,000 × 6.886330 = 261,680.54 Yuan. By the same token, a new king-size bed sheet produced in China and sold for 444.71 Yuan, would mean a customer in a mall in Utah would pay $64.58 (444.71 × .145215).

The value of the dollar is determined by the same forces that create the value of anchovies and parachutes – the forces of supply and demand.

When people around the world are confident in the strength of the U.S economy and the economic policies of our government, the demand for our dollars typically rises. This causes the value of the dollar to rise. When the value of our dollar rises, our products become more expensive to folks in China and other nations; while Chinese, and other foreign goods, become cheaper in America.

In 2016, as the U.S. economic recovery gained steam the value of the dollar increased sharply. This helped Americans traveling abroad and buying foreign goods but hurt American exporters as our products became more expensive for other nations.

It is widely argued that if China allowed its currency to "float" with the forces of supply and demand, that the price of the Yuan would increase. Then each Yuan would be able to "purchase" fewer dollars. Let's say that a floating exchange rate would mean $1 (U.S) equals 4.24 Yuan. Therefore, each Yuan would now be worth $.235849. That GMC Yukon would now cost only 161,120 Yuan, while the bed sheet would cost $104.88 (444.71 × .235849).

The result, critics charge, would be greater exports of American goods to China, a falling trade deficit with this nation, and more economic growth for American industries that have a comparative advantage but are simply shut out of China's market.[69]

There are some problems with this argument that many economists have pointed out and can be discovered by you, if you are willing to take the time to do proper research.

For example, China has not officially pegged its currency to the dollar since 2005. During that time the value of China's currency has risen, but we continue to buy more from China than China buys from us. Among the many reasons for this reality is rising productivity in China; improvements in technological progress in China that has given it a growing share in world metals and equipment markets; a strong educational system that is turning out far more mathematicians, engineers, and scientists than America; and a continued move toward lower taxes and greater property rights.

It must also be pointed out that while the U.S. had a trade deficit of $334.1 billion with China in 2016, Chinese imports of American goods increased from $19.2 billion in 2001 to $169.2 billion by 2014.[70]

While it is certainly possible that China has engaged in "unofficial" limits on the Yuan-to-dollar ratio, our problems with China extend well beyond currency markets. Quite often political realities overcome economic ones, when facing economic realities would get politicians in trouble.

THE WINNERS AND LOSERS FROM TRADE

> We need to work together on tools like bipartisan trade promotion authority to protect our workers, protect our environment, and open new markets to new goods stamped "Made in the USA."
>
> President Barack Obama January 28, 2014

During his first five years in office, President Obama signed free trade agreements with Columbia, South Korea and Panama. He also sought greater authority to place on the "fast track" trade agreements known as the Trans-Pacific Partnership and the Transatlantic Trade and Investment Partnership.[71] His quote from the 2014 State of the Union address seemed to show that the President was a supporter of Thomas Jefferson's argument that "... all the world would gain by setting commerce at perfect liberty."[72]

Yet, the 2016 election seemed to suggest that the American electorate did not believe this to be true.

Bernie Sanders was opposed to greater trade. Hillary Clinton – who had been a supporter of NAFTA and TPP – changed her mind and became a vocal opponent of President Obama's position on the TPP. And, of course, Donald Trump was the loudest critic of all.

As the accompanying map illustrates, the darkest areas are counties where jobs have been most adversely impacted by international trade with China. President Trump was the overwhelming choice of voters in the vast majority of those counties.[73]

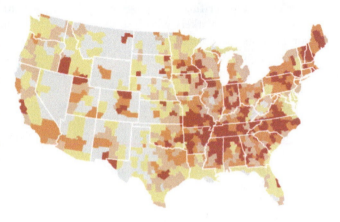

As trade has accelerated around the globe, winners and losers have emerged. Of course sometimes the lines are blurred and people can win and lose simultaneously from trade.

The winners in international trade, from the U.S. perspective, has been skilled workers in industries that possess a comparative advantage; consumers in the form of lower prices and governments in the area of tax collections from an expanding economy. Less visible, but no less important, has been the spread of economic freedom and prosperity internationally and the reduced threat of international conflict that trade helps create.

Many of the winners were small regional economies like Greenville, South Carolina, Waterloo, Iowa, and Kingsport, Tennessee, where the production of everything from turbines and forklifts to tractors and chemicals help propel much of the country forward while housing, banking, and other sectors faltered.

The losers from international trade have been relatively uneducated manufacturing workers in industries that do not possess a comparative advantage. While many of these workers have benefitted from lower prices on scores of household items, furniture and other products, it has often come at the expense of job losses or downward pressure on wages. For these Americans the benefits of trade are not as visible as the costs.

TRADE AND THE POLITICAL ECONOMY

In 2002, Congress voted to give President Bush five years of greater latitude to pursue expanded free trade opportunities. This agreement did not come without a potentially high price, however. In the narrowly passed legislation, U.S. union members stood to gain $1.2 billion from the newly created Trade Adjustment Assistance Program.

This taxpayer-financed program was designed to provide help to workers who lose their jobs to foreign competition. For example, people over 50 who lose jobs due to trade would qualify for $5,000 a year in "wage insurance" if they end up taking a job that is lower-paying than the one they had before trade eliminated their job.

Farmers also gained – at the expense of taxpayers – by authorizing subsidies of $100 billion over ten years. This particular feature was particularly galling to many of our foreign trading partners that have been trying to crack our agricultural markets for years. The subsidies give American farmers an advantage in global markets and thwart the progress toward more open markets.

During the 2004 presidential campaign, John Kerry moved away from the policy stance of Bill Clinton by advocating a much more interventionist role of government in international trade matters.[74] He advocated overhauling the U.S. tax code to raise taxes on corporations that outsource jobs and indicated that he would take a harder look at trade policies that did not provide more protection for labor union workers but did not advocate getting rid of agreements like NAFTA.[75]

In the 2008 campaign John McCain voiced support for free trade and said he would continue to work toward agreements with Columbia, South Korea, Panama and other nations. Barack Obama did not seem as enthusiastic about free trade – contending that he would renegotiate NAFTA and not pursue new trade agreements without more protections for union workers and the environment.[76] In the Ohio debate between Mr. Obama and Hillary Clinton, Mrs. Clinton repeatedly claimed that Ohio had suffered greatly because of free trade. When Tim Russert, the debate moderator, produced data showing that Ohio had seen more jobs created because of trade Mrs. Clinton struggled to defend her position that free trade was working to our detriment.[77]

Former Senator Robert Byrd from West Virginia was successful in getting legislation passed that has hurt the cause of freer trade. Under what is known as the Byrd Amendment, US companies that win anti-dumping and anti-subsidy cases against foreign rivals not only get higher US tariffs imposed on those competitors' goods but they also *receive the revenues* from those tariffs. This has led foreign governments to protest that the law unfairly punishes non-US suppliers not only with tariffs but also with subsidies for US rivals. In 2007 alone, companies received $264 million in compensation for not being an effective competitor.[78]

In this decade, we now face new challenges. As aforementioned, more and more Americans of all political persuasions and income brackets have come to believe that free trade is bad for our country.

In "The Fatal Conceit" (1988), Friedrich Hayek wrote that, "man's instincts were not made for the kinds of surroundings, and for the numbers, in which he now lives." According to Hayek and modern-day evolutionary psychologists, it is man's natural instincts to believe that the world is a zero-sum world with a fixed number of jobs and a static amount of wealth.[79] Hence, if you get more, I must get less, is the common view.

Recessions and 10% unemployment rates help magnify what may very well be our natural inclination to believe that one must lose if another person gains. The recent "Great Recession" therefore has quite possibly created a "Great Misunderstanding," that America can only regain her prosperity by closing off products from China and other nations.

Three final notes: First, the last time America bought into the wholesale notion that avoiding trade would rescue our economy, was in 1930 when we let our government pass the Smoot-Hawley Tariff Act. This Act led to enormous increases in the tariffs we required other nations to pay. Retaliation by those nations ensued, world trade collapsed, and the U.S. lurched even closer to entry into World War II.[80]

Second, as the United States continues its war against terrorism, it should be noted that there is a direct cause-and-effect link between open trade and economic wealth. The poorest nations – and the nations most plagued with terrorist activity – are the nations that are the most closed off from the rest of the world.[81]

Finally, it would be wise for President Trump to take another look at his campaign promises. According to the Peterson Institute, if President Trump succeeds in imposing 35 – 45% tariffs on China and Mexico it would lead to at least 1.3 million jobs lost in America, along with a recession within three years.[82]

ENDNOTES

1 See "Americans Sour on Trade" by Sara Murray and Douglas Belkin, *The Wall Street Journal*, October 4, 2010.

2 See "Aid is Good; Trade is Better" by Supachai Panitchpakdi, *The Wall Street Journal*, January 17, 2005; "Progenitor of the Paper Millionaires," *The Wall Street Journal*, July 19, 2000; and "We Want Trade, Not Aid" by Yoweri K. Museveni, *The Wall Street Journal*, November 6, 2003.

3 See "Shrimp Gets a Makeover, as Foreign Imports Rise" by Katy McLaughlin, *The Wall Street Journal*, August 19, 2004; and "Trade and Aid Clash over Shrimp Tariffs" by Greg Hitt, *The Wall Street Journal*, April 25, 2005.

4 See "The Decline of Detroit" by John Schnapp, *The Wall Street Journal*, July 14-15, 2007.

5 See "Detroit's automakers lose ground to imports" by Tom Krisher, *The Orlando Sentinel*, August 2, 2007.

6 See "Why Toyota Won" by James P. Womack, *The Wall Street Journal*, February 13, 2006; and "Behind GM's Slide: Bosses Misjudged New Urban Tastes" by Lee Hawkins Jr., *The Wall Street Journal*, March 8, 2006.

7 The last year such comprehensive data was available was 1992. However, individually, the numbers have not changed dramatically from 1992 through 2011.

8 This is not a new sentiment. During the time he was emperor of France, Napoleon implemented tariffs on farm products to aid French farmers. Source: Museum of Florida History, Tallahassee, Florida.

9 More than 8,000 products have tariffs attached to them when they arrive in the U.S.

10 See "'Fair Trade' is Unfair" by James Bovard, *Newsweek*, December 9, 1991, p.13.

11 See *The Fair Trade Fraud* by James Bovard, St. Martin's Press, 1991.

12 See "The Great Brassiere War," *The Wall Street Journal*, November 19, 2003; and "U.S. Moves to Limit Textile Imports from China" by Edmund L. Andrews, *The New York Times*, November 19, 2003.

13 See "Bush Seeks to Use Backlash on Jobs as Lever in India" by Michael Schroeder and Jay Soloman, *The Wall Street Journal*, March 8, 2004.

14 See "A U.S. History of Trade Hypocrisy" by James Bovard, *The Wall Street Journal*.

15 See "The Great Ice Cream War" by James Bovard, *The Wall Street Journal*, September 14, 1990.

16 See *The Fair Trade Fraud*, Bovard, p. 66.

17 See "U.S. panel order tariffs on Brazilian OJ" *The Orlando Sentinel*, August 18, 2005.

18 See "Steeling Our Wealth," *The Wall Street Journal*, September 23, 2003.

19 See "The Steel Tariffs' Costs," *The Wall Street Journal*, February 25, 2003; "Bush's Steel Opening," *The Wall Street Journal*, November 11, 2003; and "Lessons of Steel," *The Wall Street Journal*, December 2, 2003, p. A18.

20 See "So Far, Steel Tariffs Do Little of What President Envisioned" by Neil King Jr. and Robert Guy, *The Wall Street Journal*, September 13, 2002.

21 Arthur T. Denzau of St. Louis's Washington University found that restrictions on imported steel in the 1980s saved 17,000 jobs in the steel industry and among its suppliers. However, the higher prices that resulted led to the loss of 52,400 jobs in American steel-using industries. For every job saved, three were lost.

22 See "U.S. Tariffs on Steel are Illegal, World Trade Organization Says" by Elizabeth Becker, *The New York Times*, November 11, 2003; and "The White House Steel Trap" *The New York Times*, November 11, 2003.

23 See "U.S. Nears Mexican Cement Pact" by Jim Carlton, *The Wall Street Journal*, August 29, 2005.

24 See "U.S. Steel's New $20-an-Hour Worker" by John W. Miller, *The Wall Street Journal*, July 10, 2013.

25 See "Clinton's Sugar Daddy Games Now Threaten NAFTA's Future" by Mary Anastasia O'Grady, *The Wall Street Journal*, December 20, 2002.

26 See "A Saga of Politics and Candy Canes" by Sean Mussenden, *The Orlando Sentinel*, December 24, 2002.

27 See "Obama's Half-Truth on China Tire Tariffs" by Kenneth Rapoza, *Forbes*, January 25, 2012.

28 See http://www.ntu.org/governmentbytes/detail/study-trumps-tariffs-would-cost-average-american-family-11100.

29 See *The Commanding Heights* by Daniel Yergin and Joseph Stanislaw, Simon & Schuster, 1998.

30 See The Heritage Foundation's: NAFTA's *Three-Year Report Card: An "A" for North America's Economy* by John Sweeney.

31 See "The Triumph of NAFTA," *The Wall Street Journal*, January 12, 2004 p. A14; and "Free Trade Accord at Age 10: The Growing Pains are Clear" by Elizabeth Becker, Clifford Krauss, and Tiem Weiner, *The New York Times*, December 27, 2003.May 16, 1997.

32 See "Squaring Trumponomics with Reality" by Martin Feldstein, *The Wall Street Journal*, November 15, 2016.

33 See "How Trade made America Great" by Frederick W. Smith, *The Wall Street Journal*, March 26-27, 2016.

34 See "Trump's Nafta Mistakes Are Huge" by Mary Anastasia O'Grady, *The Wall Street Journal*, October 3, 2016 pg. A15.

35 See "Employer's Lament: Too Few Immigrants" by Miriam Jordan & Santiago Perez, *The Wall Street Journal*, November 25, 2016.

36 See "We're # 1 And It Hurts" by George C. Church, *Time*, October 24, 1994.

37 See "Made in America makes a Comeback" by Dee Depass, *The Star-Tribune*, July 15, 2012 page D1.

38 See "Is Free Trade Immoral?" *The Wall Street Journal*, February 26, 2004, p. A10.

39 Source: http://www.aiada.org/

40 For the list see http://www.bloomberg.com/graphics/infographics/tax-runaways-tracking-inversions.html.

41 Source: May 16, 1995, edition of the *CBS Evening News*.

42 See "Hanging by a Thread" by Roger Thurow and Scott Kilman, *The Wall Street Journal*, June 26, 2002.

43 See "Come on, America, Play By the Rules!" by Pascal Lamy, *The Wall Street Journal*, March 3, 2003; "Why Can't America Be More Like Us?" by Franz Fischler, *The Wall Street Journal*, February 19, 2004; and "Brave New World" by Supachai Panitchpakdi, *The Wall Street Journal*, February 26, 2004.

44 See "A Guardian of Jobs or a 'Reverse Robin Hood'" by Leslie Wayne, *The New York Times*, September 1, 2002.

45 See "The U.S. Builds a Fishy Case Against Chilean Salmon" by Greg Rushford, *The Wall Street Journal*, September 26, 1997.

46 See "Predation: The Changing View in the Economics and the Law" by James C. Miller III and Paul Paulter, *Journal of Law & Economics*, vol. XXVIII (May 1985); "Not So Fast: The Myth of Predatory Pricing–Exposed" by Rob Norton, *Fortune*, February 7, 2000, p. 49.

47 See "The errors in closing the border to our beef," *The Globe and Mail*, June 27, 2005.

48 See "It looks like it's time to play let's make a deal in the softwood dispute" by Barry McKenna, *The Globe and Mail*, July 26, 2005.

49 See "Deal expected on textile imports," *The Orlando Sentinel*, August 18, 2005.

50 See "Tension rises over textile exports" by Lorrie Grant, *USA Today*, June 1, 2005, p. 5B.

51 See "How the Textile Industry Alone Won Quotas on Chinese Imports" by Greg Hitt, *The Wall Street Journal*, November 10, 2005; and "Bush trade nominee talks tough on China" by Christopher Swann and Edward Alden, *Financial Times*, April 22, 2005.

52 See "Protect Us From Protectionists" by Richard W. Fisher, *The Wall Street Journal*, April 25, 2005.

53 See "China Irks U.S. as It Uses Trade to Embellish Newfound Clout" by Peter Wonacott and Neil King Jr., *The Wall Street Journal*, October 3, 2005.

54 See "Prime Numbers," *The Chronicle of Higher Education*, May 19, 2000, p. A14.

55 See "Rising Wages will Burst China's Bubble" by Peter Tasker, *Financial Times*, January 10, 2011.

56 See "Obama's Moment of Truth on Trade" by William Gaston, *The Wall Street Journal*, February 5, 2014.

57 See "U.S. Apparel Retailers Turn Their Gaze Beyond China" by Elizabeth Holmes, *The Wall Street Journal*, June 15, 2010.

58 See "The Left Should Love Globalization" by Francis Fukuyama, *The Wall Street Journal*, December 1, 1999; and "U.S. Trade Law Gives Africa Hope and Hard Jobs" by Marc Lacy, *The New York Times*, November 14, 2003.

59 See "Czech Republic's air pollution sickens and enrages citizens," *The Orlando Sentinel*, February 15, 1993.

60 See "Does Helping the Planet Hurt the Poor?" by Bjorn Lomborg, *The Wall Street Journal*, January 22-23, 2011, p. C1.

61 Source: The American Lung Association.

62 For more on this issue, see "NAFTA: Part of the Trade-Environment Solution" by Kathryn S. Fuller, *The Wall Street Journal*, July 16, 1993.

63 See "Steelmakers Say They Are a Key Component of Security" by Robert Guy Matthews, *The Wall Street Journal*, September 19, 2002, p. B4.

64 See "Big Steel Still Enjoys Outsized Clout on Trade" by David Wessel, *The Wall Street Journal*, December 6, 2001; and "Steel's Shakedown Attempt Will Test Bush's Resolve" by George Melloan, *The Wall Street Journal*, January 22, 2002.

65 See "Imposing Steel Tariffs, Bush Buys Some Time for Troubled Industry" by Robert Guy Matthews and Neil King Jr., *The Wall Street Journal*, March 6, 2002.

66 See "So Far, Bush's Gamble on Steel Tariffs Isn't Paying Off" by Neil King Jr. and Michael M. Phillips, *The Wall Street Journal*, March 27, 2002, p. A20.

67 See "Canada Weighs Imposing Tariffs on Steel," *The Wall Street Journal*, March 28, 2002, p. A2.

68 See "Bush's Steel Trap: Tariff to Aid Producers Anger Users" by Neil King Jr., *The Wall Street Journal*, February 11, 2002, p. A24.

69 See "China Trade and American Jobs" by Daniel Ikenson, *The Wall Street Journal*, April 2, 2010.

70 See "What the China Trade Warriors Get Wrong" by Alan Reynolds, *The Wall Street Journal*, October 27, 2016 page A15.

71 See "Obama's Moment of Truth on Trade" by William A. Galston, *The Wall Street Journal*, February 5, 2014 page A15.

72 See Jefferson to Adams, July 7, 1785 in *The Writings of Thomas Jefferson*, edited by Andrew Adgate Lipscomb and Ellery Bergh (Washington, D.C.: Thomas Jefferson Memorial Assocation, 1903-4), Vol. 5, p. 48.

73 See "Deep, Swift China Shock Drove Trump's Support" by Bob Davis & Jon Hilsenrath, *The Wall Street Journal*, August 12, 2016.

74 For more on the Clinton administration's trade policies, see "They Support Free Trade, Except in the Case of..." by David E. Rosenbaum, *The New York Times*, November 16, 2003, and *The Commanding Heights: The Battle between Government and the Marketplace that is Remaking the Modern World* by Daniel Yergin and Joseph Stanislaw, Simon & Schuster, 1998.

75 See "Kerry Targets Job Outsourcing With Corporate-Tax Overhaul" by Bob Davis and John Harwood, *The Wall Street Journal*, March 26, 2004; and "Free Trade becomes hot campaign issue" by Tom Raum, *The Associated Press* (appearing in *The Tallahassee Democrat*), February 22, 2004, p. 6A.

76 See "Trade: What Exactly is a Free Trader, Anyway?" *The Wall Street Journal*, August 25, 2008.

77 To see this exchange between Mr. Russert and Mrs. Clinton log on to: http://www.youtube.com/results?search_query=february+26+oh io+debate&search_type=&aq=f

78 See "An expensive Byrd," *The Wall Street Journal*, September 11, 2008, pg. A14.

79 See "The Protectionist Instinct" by Paul H. Rubin, *The Wall Street Journal*, October 7, 2010.

80 See "Goodbye, Free Trade?" by Douglas A Irwin, *The Wall Street Journal*, October 9-10, 2010.

81 See "The Map that Predicted the Terrorist Attacks" by Mark Skousen, *FEE Today*, 2002.

82 See "Study Sees Risk in Trump Trade Plan" by Bob Davis, *The Wall Street Journal*, September 20, 2016.

CHAPTER REVIEW

1. What is the principle of comparative advantage? How does this principle explain the benefits of open trade between states and nations?

2. Fully explain four of the major reasons given for tariff protection and what most economists think about the justification given.

3. What is predatory pricing? Does it work? Why, or why not?

4. Does free trade add to, or reduce the problem of, global warming? Why?

The United States Constitution

We the People of the United States, in Order to form a more perfect Union, establish Justice, insure domestic Tranquility, provide for the common defence, promote the general Welfare, and secure the Blessings of Liberty to ourselves and our Posterity, do ordain and establish this Constitution for the United States of America.

ARTICLE I

SECTION 1

All legislative Powers herein granted shall be vested in a Congress of the United States, which shall consist of a Senate and House of Representatives.

SECTION 2

CLAUSE 1: The House of Representatives shall be composed of Members chosen every second Year by the People of the several States, and the Electors in each State shall have the Qualifications requisite for Electors of the most numerous Branch of the State Legislature.

CLAUSE 2: No Person shall be a Representative who shall not have attained to the Age of twenty five Years, and been seven Years a Citizen of the United States, and who shall not, when elected, be an Inhabitant of that State in which he shall be chosen.

CLAUSE 3: Representatives and direct Taxes shall be apportioned among the several States which may be included within this Union, according to their respective Numbers, which shall be determined by adding to the whole Number of free Persons, including those bound to Service for a Term of Years, and excluding Indians not taxed, three fifths of all other Persons. The actual Enumeration shall be made within three Years after the first Meeting of the Congress of the United States, and within every subsequent Term of ten Years, in such Manner as they shall by Law direct. The Number of Representatives shall not exceed one for every thirty Thousand, but each State shall have at Least one Representative; and until such enumeration shall be made, the State of New Hampshire shall be entitled to choose three, Massachusetts eight, Rhode-Island and Providence Plantations one, Connecticut five, New-York six, New Jersey four, Pennsylvania eight, Delaware one, Maryland six, Virginia ten, North Carolina five, South Carolina five, and Georgia three.

CLAUSE 4: When vacancies happen in the Representation from any State, the Executive Authority thereof shall issue Writs of Election to fill such Vacancies.

CLAUSE 5: The House of Representatives shall chuse their Speaker and other Officers; and shall have the sole Power of Impeachment.

SECTION 3

CLAUSE 1: The Senate of the United States shall be composed of two Senators from each State, chosen by the Legislature thereoffor six Years; and each Senator shall have one Vote.

CLAUSE 2: Immediately after they shall be assembled in Consequence of the first Election, they shall be divided as equally as may be into three Classes. The Seats of the Senators of the first Class shall be vacated at the Expiration of the second Year, of the second Class at the Expiration of the fourth Year, and of the third Class at the Expiration of the sixth Year, so that one third may be chosen every second Year; and if Vacancies happen by Resignation, or otherwise, during the Recess of the Legislature of any State, the Executive thereof may make temporary Appointments until the next Meeting of the Legislature, which shall then fill such Vacancies.

CLAUSE 3: No Person shall be a Senator who shall not have attained to the Age of thirty Years, and been nine Years a Citizen of the United States, and who shall not, when elected, be an Inhabitant of that State for which he shall be chosen.

CLAUSE 4: The Vice President of the United States shall be President of the Senate, but shall have no Vote, unless they be equally divided.

CLAUSE 5: The Senate shall chuse their other Officers, and also a President pro tempore, in the Absence of the Vice President, or when he shall exercise the Office of President of the United States.

CLAUSE 6: The Senate shall have the sole Power to try all Impeachments. When sitting for that Purpose, they shall be on Oath or Affirmation. When the President of the United States is tried, the Chief Justice shall preside: And no Person shall be convicted without the Concurrence of two thirds of the Members present.

CLAUSE 7: Judgment in Cases of Impeachment shall not extend further than to removal from Office, and disqualification to hold and enjoy any Office of honor, Trust or Profit under the United States: but the Party convicted shall nevertheless be liable and subject to Indictment, Trial, Judgment and Punishment, according to Law.

SECTION 4

CLAUSE 1: The Times, Places and Manner of holding Elections for Senators and Representatives, shall be prescribed in each State by the Legislature thereof; but the Congress may at any time by Law make or alter such Regulations, except as to the Places of chusing Senators.

CLAUSE 2: The Congress shall assemble at least once in every Year, and such Meeting shall be on the first Monday in December, unless they shall by Law appoint a different Day.

SECTION 5

CLAUSE 1: Each House shall be the Judge of the Elections, Returns and Qualifications of its own Members, and a Majority of each shall constitute a Quorum to do Business; but a smaller Number may adjourn from day to day, and may be authorized to compel the Attendance of absent Members, in such Manner, and under such Penalties as each House may provide.

CLAUSE 2: Each House may determine the Rules of its Proceedings, punish its Members for disorderly Behaviour, and, with the Concurrence of two thirds, expel a Member.

CLAUSE 3: Each House shall keep a Journal of its Proceedings, and from time to time publish the same,

excepting such Parts as may in their Judgment require Secrecy; and the Yeas and Nays of the Members of either House on any question shall, at the Desire of one fifth of those Present, be entered on the Journal.

CLAUSE 4: Neither House, during the Session of Congress, shall, without the Consent of the other, adjourn for more than three days, nor to any other Place than that in which the two Houses shall be sitting.

SECTION 6

CLAUSE 1: The Senators and Representatives shall receive a Compensation for their Services, to be ascertained by Law, and paid out of the Treasury of the United States. They shall in all Cases, except Treason, Felony and Breach of the Peace, beprivileged from Arrest during their Attendance at the Session of their respective Houses, and in going to and returning from the same; and for any Speech or Debate in either House, they shall not be questioned in any other Place.

CLAUSE 2: No Senator or Representative shall, during the Time for which he was elected, be appointed to any civil Office under the Authority of the United States, which shall have been created, or the Emoluments whereof shall have been encreased during such time; and no Person holding any Office under the United States, shall be a Member of either House during his Continuance in Office.

SECTION 7

CLAUSE 1: All Bills for raising Revenue shall originate in the House of Representatives; but the Senate may propose or concur with Amendments as on other Bills.

CLAUSE 2: Every Bill which shall have passed the House of Representatives and the Senate, shall, before it become a Law, be presented to the President of the United States; If he approve he shall sign it, but if not he shall return it, with his Objections to that House in which it shall have originated, who shall enter the Objections at large on their Journal, and proceed to reconsider it. If after such Reconsideration two thirds of that House shall agree to pass the Bill, it shall be sent, together with the Objections, to the other House, by which it shall likewise be reconsidered, and if approved by two thirds of that House, it shall become a Law. But in all such Cases the Votes of both Houses shall be determined by yeas and Nays, and the Names of the Persons voting for and against the Bill shall be entered on the Journal of each House respectively. If any Bill shall not be returned by the President within ten Days (Sundays excepted) after it shall have been presented to him, the Same shall be a Law, in like Manner as if he had signed it, unless the Congress by their Adjournment prevent its Return, in which Case it shall not be a Law.

CLAUSE 3: Every Order, Resolution, or Vote to which the Concurrence of the Senate and House of Representatives may be necessary (except on a question of Adjournment) shall be presented to the President of the United States; and before the Same shall take Effect, shall be approved by him, or being disapproved by him, shall be repassed by two thirds of the Senate and House of Representatives, according to the Rules and Limitations prescribed in the Case of a Bill.

SECTION 8

CLAUSE 1: The Congress shall have Power To lay and collect Taxes, Duties, Imposts and Excises, to pay the Debts and provide for the common Defence and general Welfare of the United States; but all Duties, Imposts and Excises shall be uniform throughout the United States;

CLAUSE 2: To borrow Money on the credit of the United States;

CLAUSE 3: To regulate Commerce with foreign Nations, and among the several States, and with the Indian Tribes;

CLAUSE 4: To establish an uniform Rule of Naturalization, and uniform Laws on the subject of Bankruptcies throughout the United States;

CLAUSE 5: To coin Money, regulate the Value thereof, and of foreign Coin, and fix the Standard of Weights and Measures;

CLAUSE 6: To provide for the Punishment of counterfeiting the Securities and current Coin of the United States;

CLAUSE 7: To establish Post Offices and post Roads;

CLAUSE 8: To promote the Progress of Science and useful Arts, by securing for limited Times to Authors and Inventors the exclusive Right to their respective Writings and Discoveries;

CLAUSE 9: To constitute Tribunals inferior to the supreme Court;

CLAUSE 10: To define and punish Piracies and Felonies committed on the high Seas, and Offences against the Law of Nations;

CLAUSE 11: To declare War, grant Letters of Marque and Reprisal, and make Rules concerning Captures on Land and Water;

CLAUSE 12: To raise and support Armies, but no Appropriation of Money to that Use shall be for a longer Term than two Years;

CLAUSE 13: To provide and maintain a Navy;

CLAUSE 14: To make Rules for the Government and Regulation of the land and naval Forces;

CLAUSE 15: To provide for calling forth the Militia to execute the Laws of the Union, suppress Insurrections and repel Invasions;

CLAUSE 16: To provide for organizing, arming, and disciplining, the Militia, and for governing such Part of them as may be employed in the Service of the United States, reserving to the States respectively, the Appointment of the Officers, and the Authority of training the Militia according to the discipline prescribed by Congress;

CLAUSE 17: To exercise exclusive Legislation in all Cases whatsoever, over such District (not exceeding ten Miles square) as may, by Cession of particular States, and the Acceptance of Congress, become the Seat of the Government of the United States, and to exercise like Authority over all Places purchased by the Consent of the Legislature of the State in which the Same shall be, for the Erection of Forts, Magazines, Arsenals, dock-Yards, and other needful Buildings;—And

CLAUSE 18: To make all Laws which shall be necessary and proper for carrying into Execution the foregoing Powers, and all other Powers vested by this Constitution in the Government of the United States, or in any Department or Officer thereof.

SECTION 9

CLAUSE 1: The Migration or Importation of such Persons as any of the States now existing shall think proper to admit, shall not be prohibited by the Congress prior to the Year one thousand eight hundred and eight, but a Tax or duty may be imposed on such Importation, not exceeding ten dollars for each Person.

CLAUSE 2: The Privilege of the Writ of Habeas Corpus shall not be suspended, unless when in Cases of Rebellion or Invasion the public Safety may require it.

CLAUSE 3: No Bill of Attainder or ex post facto Law shall be passed.

CLAUSE 4: No Capitation, or other direct, Tax shall be laid, unless in Proportion to the Census or Enumeration herein before directed to be taken.

CLAUSE 5: No Tax or Duty shall be laid on Articles exported from any State.

CLAUSE 6: No Preference shall be given by any Regulation of Commerce or Revenue to the Ports of one State over those of another: nor shall Vessels bound to, or from, one State, be obliged to enter, clear, or pay Duties in another.

CLAUSE 7: No Money shall be drawn from the Treasury, but in Consequence of Appropriations made by Law; and a regular Statement and Account of the Receipts and Expenditures of all public Money shall be published from time to time.

CLAUSE 8: No Title of Nobility shall be granted by the United States: And no Person holding any Office of Profit or Trust under them, shall, without the Consent of the Congress, accept of any present, Emolument, Office, or Title, of any kind whatever, from any King, Prince, or foreign State.

SECTION 10

CLAUSE 1: No State shall enter into any Treaty, Alliance, or Confederation; grant Letters of Marque and Reprisal; coin Money; emit Bills of Credit; make any Thing but gold and silver Coin a Tender in Payment of Debts; pass any Bill of Attainder, ex post facto Law, or Law impairing the Obligation of Contracts, or grant any Title of Nobility.

CLAUSE 2: No State shall, without the Consent of the Congress, lay any Imposts or Duties on Imports or Exports, except what may be absolutely necessary for executing it's inspection Laws: and the net Produce of all Duties and Imposts, laid by any State on Imports or Exports, shall be for the Use of the Treasury of the United States; and all such Laws shall be subject to the Revision and Controul of the Congress.

CLAUSE 3: No State shall, without the Consent of Congress, lay any Duty of Tonnage, keep Troops, or Ships of War in time of Peace, enter into any Agreement or Compact with another State, or with a foreign Power, or engage in War, unless actually invaded, or in such imminent Danger as will not admit of delay.

ARTICLE II

SECTION 1

CLAUSE 1: The executive Power shall be vested in a President of the United States of America. He shall hold his Office during the Term of four Years, and, together with the Vice President, chosen for the same Term, be elected, as follows.

CLAUSE 2: Each State shall appoint, in such Manner as the Legislature thereof may direct, a Number of Electors, equal to the whole Number of Senators and Representatives to which the State may be entitled in the Congress: but no Senator or Representative, or Person holding an Office of Trust or Profit under the United States, shall be appointed an Elector.

CLAUSE 3: The Electors shall meet in their respective States, and vote by Ballot for two Persons, of whom one at least shall not be an Inhabitant of the same State with themselves. And they shall make a List of all the Persons voted for, and of the Number of Votes for each; which List they shall sign and certify, and transmit sealed to the Seat of the Government of the United States, directed to the President of the Senate. The President of the Senate shall, in the Presence of the Senate and House of Representatives, open all the Certificates, and the Votes shall then be counted. The Person having the greatest Number of Votes shall be the President, if such Number be a Majority of the whole Number of Electors appointed; and if there be more than one who have such Majority, and have an equal Number of Votes, then the House of Representatives shall immediately chuse by Ballot one of them for President; and if no Person have a Majority, then from the five highest on the List the said House shall in like Manner chuse the President. But in chusing the President, the Votes shall be taken by States, the Representation from each State having one Vote; A quorum for this Purpose shall consist of a Member or Members from two thirds of the States, and a Majority of all the States shall be necessary to a Choice. In every Case, after the Choice of the President, the Person having the greatest Number of Votes of the Electors shall be the Vice President. But if there should remain two or more who have equal Votes, the Senate shall chuse from them by Ballot the Vice President.

CLAUSE 4: The Congress may determine the Time of chusing the Electors, and the Day on which they shall give their Votes; which Day shall be the same throughout the United States.

CLAUSE 5: No Person except a natural born Citizen, or a Citizen of the United States, at the time of the Adoption of this Constitution, shall be eligible to the Office of President; neither shall any Person be eligible to that Office who shall not have attained to the Age of thirty five Years, and been fourteen Years a Resident within the United States.

CLAUSE 6: In Case of the Removal of the President from Office, or of his Death, Resignation, or Inability to discharge the Powers and Duties of the said Office, the Same shall devolve on the VicePresident, and the Congress may by Law provide for the Case of Removal, Death, Resignation or Inability, both of the President and Vice President, declaring what Officer shall then act as President, and such Officer shall act accordingly, until the Disability be removed, or a President shall be elected.

CLAUSE 7: The President shall, at stated Times, receive for his Services, a Compensation, which shall neither be encreased nor diminished during the Period for which he shall have been elected, and he shall not receive within that Period any other Emolument from the United States, or any of them.

CLAUSE 8: Before he enter on the Execution of his Office, he shall take the following Oath or Affirmation:—"I do solemnly swear (or affirm) that I will faithfully execute the Office of President of the United States, and will to the best of my Ability, preserve, protect and defend the Constitution of the United States."

SECTION 2

CLAUSE 1: The President shall be Commander in Chief of the Army and Navy of the United States, and of the Militia of the several States, when called into the actual Service of the United States; he may require the Opinion, in writing, of the principal Officer in each of the executive Departments, upon any Subject relating to the Duties of their respective Offices, and he shall have Power to grant Reprieves and Pardons for Offences against the United States, except in Cases of Impeachment.

CLAUSE 2: He shall have Power, by and with the Advice and Consent of the Senate, to make Treaties, provided two thirds of the Senators present concur; and he shall nominate, and by and with the Advice and Consent of the Senate, shall appoint Ambassadors, other public Ministers and Consuls, Judges of the supreme Court, and all other Officers of the United States, whose Appointments are not herein otherwise provided for, and which shall be established by Law: but the Congress may by Law vest the Appointment of such inferior Officers, as they think proper, in the President alone, in the Courts of Law, or in the Heads of Departments.

CLAUSE 3: The President shall have Power to fill up all Vacancies that may happen during the Recess of the Senate, by granting Commissions which shall expire at the End of their next Session.

SECTION 3

He shall from time to time give to the Congress Information of the State of the Union, and recommend to their Consideration such Measures as he shall judge necessary and expedient; he may, on extraordinary Occasions, convene both Houses, or either of them, and in Case of Disagreement between them, with Respect to the Time of Adjournment, he may adjourn them to such Time as he shall think proper; he shall receive Ambassadors and other public Ministers; he shall take Care that the Laws be faithfully executed, and shall Commission all the Officers of the United States.

SECTION 4

The President, Vice President and all civil Officers of the United States, shall be removed from Office on Impeachment for, and Conviction of, Treason, Bribery, or other high Crimes and Misdemeanors.

ARTICLE III

SECTION 1

The judicial Power of the United States, shall be vested in one supreme Court, and in such inferior Courts as the Congress may from time to time ordain and establish. The Judges, both of the supreme and inferior Courts, shall hold their Offices during good Behaviour, and shall, at stated Times, receive for their Services, a Compensation, which shall not be diminished during their Continuance in Office.

SECTION 2

CLAUSE 1: The judicial Power shall extend to all Cases, in Law and Equity, arising under this Constitution, the Laws of the United States, and Treaties made, or which shall be made, under their Authority;—to all Cases affecting Ambassadors, other public Ministers and Consuls;—to all Cases of admiralty and maritime Jurisdiction;—to Controversies to which the United States shall be a Party;—to Controversies between two or more States;—between a State and Citizens of another State; between Citizens of different States,—between Citizens of the same State claiming Lands under Grants of different States, and between a State, or the Citizens thereof, and foreign States, Citizens or Subjects.

CLAUSE 2: In all Cases affecting Ambassadors, other public Ministers and Consuls, and those in which a State shall be Party, the supreme Court shall have original Jurisdiction. In all the other Cases before mentioned, the supreme Court shall have appellate Jurisdiction, both as to Law and Fact, with such Exceptions, and under such Regulations as the Congress shall make.

CLAUSE 3: The Trial of all Crimes, except in Cases of Impeachment, shall be by Jury; and such Trial shall be held in the State where the said Crimes shall have been committed; but when not committed within any State, the Trial shall be at such Place or Places as the Congress may by Law have directed.

SECTION 3

CLAUSE 1: Treason against the United States, shall consist only in levying War against them, or in adhering to their Enemies, giving them Aid and Comfort. No Person shall be convicted of Treason unless on the Testimony of two Witnesses to the same overt Act, or on Confession in open Court.

CLAUSE 2: The Congress shall have Power to declare the Punishment of Treason, but no Attainder of Treason shall work Corruption of Blood, or Forfeiture except during the Life of the Person attainted.

CLAUSE 3: No Person held to Service or Labour in one State, under the Laws thereof, escaping into another, shall, in Consequence of any Law or Regulation therein, be discharged from such Service or Labour, but shall be delivered up on Claim of the Party to whom such Service or Labour may be due.

SECTION 3

CLAUSE 1: New States may be admitted by the Congress into this Union; but no new State shall be formed or erected within the Jurisdiction of any other State; nor any State be formed by the Junction of two or more States, or Parts of States, without the Consent of the Legislatures of the States concerned as well as of the Congress.

CLAUSE 2: The Congress shall have Power to dispose of and make all needful Rules and Regulations respecting the Territory or other Property belonging to the United States; and nothing in this Constitution shall be so construed as to Prejudice any Claims of the United States, or of any particular State.

SECTION 4

The United States shall guarantee to every State in this Union a Republican Form of Government, and shall protect each of them against Invasion; and on Application of the Legislature, or of the Executive (when the Legislature cannot be convened) against domestic Violence.

ARTICLE IV

SECTION 1

Full Faith and Credit shall be given in each State to the public Acts, Records, and judicial Proceedings of every other State. And the Congress may by general Laws prescribe the Manner in which such Acts, Records and Proceedings shall be proved, and the Effect thereof.

SECTION 2

CLAUSE 1: The Citizens of each State shall be entitled to all Privileges and Immunities of Citizens in the several States.

CLAUSE 2: A Person charged in any State with Treason, Felony, or other Crime, who shall flee from Justice, and be found in another State, shall on Demand of the executive Authority of the State from which he fled, be delivered up, to be removed to the State having Jurisdiction of the Crime.

ARTICLE V

The Congress, whenever two thirds of both Houses shall deem it necessary, shall propose Amendments to this Constitution, or, on the Application of the Legislatures of two thirds of the several States, shall call a Convention for proposing Amendments, which, in either Case, shall be valid to all Intents and Purposes, as Part of this Constitution, when ratified by the Legislatures of three fourths of the several States, or by Conventions in three fourths thereof, as the one or the other Mode of Ratification may be proposed by the Congress; Provided that no Amendment which may be made prior to the Year One thousand eight hundred and eight shall in any Manner affect the first and fourth Clauses in the Ninth Section of the first Article; and that no State, without its Consent, shall be deprived of its equal Suffrage in the Senate.

ARTICLE VI

CLAUSE 1: All Debts contracted and Engagements entered into, before the Adoption of this Constitution, shall be as valid against the United States under this Constitution, as under the Confederation.

CLAUSE 2: This Constitution, and the Laws of the United States which shall be made in Pursuance thereof; and all Treaties made, or which shall be made, under the Authority of the United States, shall be the supreme Law of the Land; and the Judges in every State shall be bound thereby, any Thing in the Constitution or Laws of any State to the Contrary notwithstanding.

CLAUSE 3: The Senators and Representatives before mentioned, and the Members of the several State Legislatures, and all executive and judicial Officers, both of the United States and of the several States, shall be bound by Oath or Affirmation, to support this Constitution; but no religious Test shall ever be required as a Qualification to any Office or public Trust under the United States.

ARTICLE VII

The Ratification of the Conventions of nine States, shall be sufficient for the Establishment of this Constitution between the States so ratifying the Same.

Amendments to the United States Constitution

AMENDMENT I

Congress shall make no law respecting an establishment of religion, or prohibiting the free exercise thereof; or abridging the freedom of speech, or of the press; or the right of the people peaceably to assemble, and to petition the government for a redress of grievances.

AMENDMENT II

A well regulated militia, being necessary to the security of a free state, the right of the people to keep and bear arms, shall not be infringed.

AMENDMENT III

No soldier shall, in time of peace be quartered in any house, without the consent of the owner, nor in time of war, but in a manner to be prescribed by law.

AMENDMENT IV

The right of the people to be secure in their persons, houses, papers, and effects, against unreasonable searches and seizures, shall not be violated, and no warrants shall issue, but upon probable cause, supported by oath or affirmation, and particularly describing the place to be searched, and the persons or things to be seized.

AMENDMENT V

No person shall be held to answer for a capital, or otherwise infamous crime, unless on a presentment or indictment of a grand jury, except in cases arising in the land or naval forces, or in the militia, when in actual service in time of war or public danger; nor shall any person be subject for the same offense to be twice put in jeopardy of life or limb; nor shall be compelled in any criminal case to be a witness against himself, nor be deprived of life, liberty, or property, without due process of law; nor shall private property be taken for public use, without just compensation.

AMENDMENT VI

In all criminal prosecutions, the accused shall enjoy the right to a speedy and public trial, by an impartial jury of the state and district wherein the crime shall have been committed, which district shall have been previously ascertained by law, and to be informed of the nature and cause of the accusation; to be confronted with the witnesses against him; to have compulsory process for obtaining witnesses in his favor, and to have the assistance of counsel for his defense.

AMENDMENT VII

In suits at common law, where the value in controversy shall exceed twenty dollars, the right of trial by jury shall be preserved, and no fact tried by a jury, shall be otherwise reexamined in any court of the United States, than according to the rules of the common law.

AMENDMENT VIII

Excessive bail shall not be required, nor excessive fines imposed, nor cruel and unusual punishments inflicted.

AMENDMENT IX

The enumeration in the Constitution, of certain rights, shall not be construed to deny or disparage others retained by the people.

AMENDMENT X

The powers not delegated to the United States by the Constitution, nor prohibited by it to the states, are reserved to the states respectively, or to the people.

AMENDMENT XI

The judicial power of the United States shall not be construed to extend to any suit in law or equity, commenced or prosecuted against one of the United States by citizens of another state, or by citizens or subjects of any foreign state.

AMENDMENT XII

The electors shall meet in their respective states and vote by ballot for President and Vice-President, one of whom, at least, shall not be an inhabitant of the same state with themselves; they shall name in their ballots the person voted for as President, and in distinct ballots the person voted for as Vice-President, and they shall make distinct lists of all persons voted for as President, and of all persons voted for as Vice-President, and of the number of votes for each, which lists they shall sign and certify, and transmit sealed to the seat of the government of the United States, directed to the President of the Senate;—The President of the Senate shall, in the presence of the Senate and House of Representatives, open all the certificates and the votes shall then be counted;—the person having the greatest number of votes for President, shall be the President, if such number be a majority of the whole number of electors appointed; and if no person have such majority, then from the persons having the highest numbers not exceeding three on the list of those voted for as President, the House of Representatives shall choose immediately, by ballot, the President. But in choosing the President, the votes shall be taken by states, the representation from each state having one vote; a quorum for this purpose shall consist of a member or members from two-thirds of the states, and a majority of all the states shall be necessary to a choice. And if the House of Representatives shall not choose a President whenever the right of choice shall devolve upon them, before the fourth day of March next following, then the Vice-President shall act as President, as in the case of the death or other constitutional disability of the President. The person having the greatest number of votes as Vice-President, shall be the Vice-President, if such number be a majority of the whole number of electors appointed, and if no person have a majority, then from the two highest numbers on the list, the Senate shall choose the Vice-President; a quorum for the purpose shall consist of two-thirds of the whole number of Senators, and a majority of the whole number shall be necessary to a choice. But no person constitutionally ineligible to the office of President shall be eligible to that of Vice-President of the United States.

AMENDMENT XIII

SECTION 1. Neither slavery nor involuntary servitude, except as a punishment for crime whereof the party shall have been duly convicted, shall exist within the United States, or any place subject to their jurisdiction.

SECTION 2. Congress shall have power to enforce this article by appropriate legislation.

AMENDMENT XIV

SECTION 1. All persons born or naturalized in the United States, and subject to the jurisdiction thereof, are citizens of the United States and of the state wherein they reside. No state shall make or enforce any law which shall abridge the privileges or immunities of citizens of the United States; nor shall any state deprive any person of life, liberty, or property, without due process of law; nor deny to any person within its jurisdiction the equal protection of the laws.

SECTION 2. Representatives shall be apportioned among the several states according to their respective numbers, counting the whole number of persons in each state, excluding Indians not taxed. But when the right to vote at any election for the choice of electors for President and Vice President of the United States, Representatives in Congress, the executive and judicial officers of a state, or the members of the legislature thereof, is denied to any of the male inhabitants of such state, being twenty-one years of age, and citizens of the United States, or in any way abridged, except for participation in rebellion, or other crime, the basis of representation therein shall be reduced in the proportion which the number of such male citizens shall bear to the whole number of male citizens twenty-one years of age in such state.

SECTION 3. No person shall be a Senator or Representative in Congress, or elector of President and Vice President, or hold any office, civil or military, under the United States, or

under any state, who, having previously taken an oath, as a member of Congress, or as an officer of the United States, or as a member of any state legislature, or as an executive or judicial officer of any state, to support the Constitution of the United States, shall have engaged in insurrection or rebellion against the same, or given aid or comfort to the enemies thereof. But Congress may by a vote of two-thirds of each House, remove such disability.

SECTION 4. The validity of the public debt of the United States, authorized by law, including debts incurred for payment of pensions and bounties for services in suppressing insurrection or rebellion, shall not be questioned. But neither the United States nor any state shall assume or pay any debt or obligation incurred in aid of insurrection or rebellion against the United States, or any claim for the loss or emancipation of any slave; but all such debts, obligations and claims shall be held illegal and void.

SECTION 5. The Congress shall have power to enforce, by appropriate legislation, the provisions of this article.

AMENDMENT XV

SECTION 1. The right of citizens of the United States to vote shall not be denied or abridged by the United States or by any state on account of race, color, or previous condition of servitude.

SECTION 2. The Congress shall have power to enforce this article by appropriate legislation.

I.R.

AMENDMENT XVI

The Congress shall have power to lay and collect taxes on incomes, from whatever source derived, without apportionment among the several states, and without regard to any census or enumeration.

AMENDMENT XVII

The Senate of the United States shall be composed of two Senators from each state, elected by the people thereof, for six years; and each Senator shall have one vote. The electors in each state shall have the qualifications requisite for electors of the most numerous branch of the state legislatures.

When vacancies happen in the representation of any state in the Senate, the executive authority of such state shall issue writs of election to fill such vacancies: Provided, that the legislature of any state may empower the executive thereof to make temporary appointments until the people fill the vacancies by election as the legislature may direct.

This amendment shall not be so construed as to affect the election or term of any Senator chosen before it becomes valid as part of the Constitution.

AMENDMENT XVIII

SECTION 1. After one year from the ratification of this article the manufacture, sale, or transportation of intoxicating liquors within, the importation thereof into, or the exportation thereof from the United States and all territory subject to the jurisdiction thereof for beverage purposes is hereby prohibited.

SECTION 2. The Congress and the several states shall have concurrent power to enforce this article by appropriate legislation.

SECTION 3. This article shall be inoperative unless it shall have been ratified as an amendment to the Constitution by the legislatures of the several states, as provided in the Constitution, within seven years from the date of the submission hereof to the states by the Congress.

AMENDMENT XIX

The right of citizens of the United States to vote shall not be denied or abridged by the United States or by any state on account of sex.

Congress shall have power to enforce this article by appropriate legislation.

AMENDMENT XX

SECTION 1. The terms of the President and Vice President shall end at noon on the 20th day of January, and the terms of Senators and Representatives at noon on the 3d day of January, of the years in which such terms would have ended if this article had not been ratified; and the terms of their successors shall then begin.

SECTION 2. The Congress shall assemble at least once in every year, and such meeting shall begin at noon on the 3d day of January, unless they shall by law appoint a different day.

SECTION 3. If, at the time fixed for the beginning of the term of the President, the President elect shall have died, the Vice President elect shall become President. If a President shall not have been chosen before the time fixed for the beginning of his term, or if the President elect shall have failed to qualify, then the Vice President elect shall act as President until a President shall have qualified; and the Congress may by law provide for the case wherein neither a President elect nor a Vice President elect shall have qualified, declaring who shall then act as President, or the manner in which one who is to act shall be selected, and such person shall act accordingly until a President or Vice President shall have qualified.

SECTION 4. The Congress may by law provide for the case of the death of any of the persons from whom the House of Representatives may choose a President whenever the right of choice shall have devolved upon them, and for the case of the death of any of the persons from whom the Senate may choose a Vice President whenever the right of choice shall have devolved upon them.

SECTION 5. Sections 1 and 2 shall take effect on the 15th day of October following the ratification of this article.

SECTION 6. This article shall be inoperative unless it shall have been ratified as an amendment to the Constitution by the legislatures of three-fourths of the several states within seven years from the date of its submission.

AMENDMENT XXI

SECTION 1. The eighteenth article of amendment to the Constitution of the United States is hereby repealed.

SECTION 2. The transportation or importation into any state, territory, or possession of the United States for delivery or use therein of intoxicating liquors, in violation of the laws thereof, is hereby prohibited.

SECTION 3. This article shall be inoperative unless it shall have been ratified as an amendment to the Constitution by conventions in the several states, as provided in the Constitution, within seven years from the date of the submission hereof to the states by the Congress.

AMENDMENT XXII

SECTION 1. No person shall be elected to the office of the President more than twice, and no person who has held the office of President, or acted as President, for more than two years of a term to which some other person was elected President shall be elected to the office of the President more than once. But this article shall not apply to any person holding the office of President when this article was proposed by the Congress, and shall not prevent any person who may be holding the office of President, or acting as President, during the term within which this article becomes operative from holding the office of President or acting as President during the remainder of such term.

SECTION 2. This article shall be inoperative unless it shall have been ratified as an amendment to the Constitution by the legislatures of three-fourths of the several states within seven years from the date of its submission to the states by the Congress.

AMENDMENT XXIII

SECTION 1. The District constituting the seat of government of the United States shall appoint in such manner as the Congress may direct:

A number of electors of President and Vice President equal to the whole number of Senators and Representatives in Congress to which the District would be entitled if it were a state, but in no event more than the least populous state; they shall be in addition to those appointed by the states, but they shall be considered, for the purposes of the election of President and Vice President, to be electors appointed by a state; and they shall meet in the District and perform such duties as provided by the twelfth article of amendment.

SECTION 2. The Congress shall have power to enforce this article by appropriate legislation.

AMENDMENT XXIV

SECTION 1. The right of citizens of the United States to vote in any primary or other election for President or Vice President, for electors for President or Vice President, or for Senator or Representative in Congress, shall not be denied or abridged by the United States or any state by reason of failure to pay any poll tax or other tax.

SECTION 2. The Congress shall have power to enforce this article by appropriate legislation.

AMENDMENT XXV

SECTION 1. In case of the removal of the President from office or of his death or resignation, the Vice President shall become President.

SECTION 2. Whenever there is a vacancy in the office of the Vice President, the President shall nominate a Vice President who shall take office upon confirmation by a majority vote of both Houses of Congress.

SECTION 3. Whenever the President transmits to the President pro tempore of the Senate and the Speaker of the House of Representatives his written declaration that he is unable to discharge the powers and duties of his office, and until he transmits to them a written declaration to the contrary, such powers and duties shall be discharged by the Vice President as Acting President.

SECTION 4. Whenever the Vice President and a majority of either the principal officers of the executive departments or of such other body as Congress may by law provide, transmit to the President pro tempore of the Senate and the Speaker of the House of Representatives their written declaration that the President is unable to discharge the powers and duties of his office, the Vice President shall immediately assume the powers and duties of the office as Acting President.

Thereafter, when the President transmits to the President pro tempore of the Senate and the Speaker of the House of Representatives his written declaration that no inability exists, he shall resume the powers and duties of his office unless the Vice President and a majority of either the principal officers of the executive department or of such other body as Congress may by law provide, transmit within four days to the President pro tempore of the Senate and the Speaker of the House of Representatives their written declaration that the President is unable to discharge the powers and duties of his office. Thereupon Congress shall decide the issue, assembling within forty-eight hours for that purpose if not in session. If the Congress, within twenty-one days after receipt of the latter written declaration, or, if Congress is not in session, within twenty-one days after Congress is required to assemble, determines by two-thirds vote of both Houses that the President is unable to discharge the powers and duties of his office, the Vice President shall continue to discharge the same as Acting President; otherwise, the President shall resume the powers and duties of his office.

AMENDMENT XXVI

SECTION 1. The right of citizens of the United States, who are 18 years of age or older, to vote, shall not be denied or abridged by the United States or any state on account of age.

SECTION 2. The Congress shall have the power to enforce this article by appropriate legislation.

AMENDMENT XXVII

No law, varying the compensation for the services of the Senators and Representatives, shall take effect, until an election of Representatives shall have intervened.

Index

Note: Page numbers in *italics* represent figures and tables.